Clinical Social Work Practice in Community Mental Health

ROBERTA G. SANDS
University of Pennsylvania

Merrill, an imprint of
Macmillan Publishing Company
New York

Collier Macmillan Canada, Inc.
Toronto

Maxwell Macmillan International Publishing Group
New York   Oxford   Singapore   Sydney

About the cover and part opening art: In February of 1989, I admitted myself to a publicly-funded psychiatric hospital. I had suffered from depression as far back as I can remember and obsessive compulsive disorder for 14 years. I was terrified at what to expect at the hospital, but even more frightened at the thought of not going. I had no choice. As it turned out the decision was one of the best of my life. Of the many therapies I was introduced to, traditional psychotherapy and art therapy proved the most useful. It was an intensely emotional experience to rediscover my love of drawing. I participated in the art therapy program for the length of my stay. Not surprisingly the artwork that I do contributes to a clearer understanding of myself. I may someday "repay" my debt, by choosing art therapy as my profession, but at this moment I'm getting joy solely out of making the art.

Amy Appelbaum
Artist

Editor: Linda James Scharp
Production Editor: Gloria Schneider Jasperse
Art Coordinator: Lorraine Woost
Photo Editor: Gail Meese
Text Designer: Debra A. Fargo
Cover Designer: Russ Maselli
Production Buyer: Pamela D. Bennett

This book was set in Clearface.

Macmillan Publishing Company
866 Third Avenue, New York, NY 10022

Collier Macmillan Canada, Inc.

Library of Congress Cataloging-in-Publication Data
Sands, Roberta G.
    Clinical social work practice in community mental health/Roberta
    G. Sands.
        p.   cm.
    Includes bibliographical references and index.
    ISBN 0-675-21232-4
    1. Psychiatric social work—United States.   2. Community mental
health services—United States.   3. Chronic diseases—Psychological
aspects.   I. Title.
    [DNLM: 1. Chronic Disease—therapy. 2. Community Mental Health
Services—United States. 3. Mental Disorders—therapy. 4. Social
Work, Psychiatric—United States. WM 30.5 S221c]
HV690.U6S26 1991
362.2'2'0973 —dc20
DNLM/DLC
for Library of Congress   90–13576
                                                                                       CIP
Printing: 1   2   3   4   5   6   7   8   9   Year: 1   2   3   4

In honor of my parents
Alan Nathan Goldsamt and
Alice Louise Goldsamt

Foreword

E very once in awhile a book appears on the scene that fills a vacuum so well that one
is left wondering why this wasn't done sooner. This is such a book. Finally, social
work has a quality text that goes to the heart of practice in community mental health.

The National Institute of Mental Health has adopted the search for a cure to mental
illness to be its centerpiece activity. While there is great excitement about the possibilities this suggests, we must remember that the psychiatric community has at other
times become excited about the potential of immediate cures. While the cures we desire
may yet be a long way off, the critical need for rehabilitation, treatment, and social care
is present now.

Because social workers, more than members of any other profession, serve as
directors of mental health centers, the importance of a book addressed to this audience
should be unquestioned. Further, almost a quarter of all MSW students specialize in
mental health. Expanding community support programs for people with severe mental
illness and community-based services for emotionally disturbed children and adolescents use a predominance of social work professionals. More social workers are direct-
ing research in community mental health than ever before.

Having a book where none previously existed is one matter; having a book of quality
is another. *Clinical Social Work Practice in Community Mental Health* is a book of
quality. It offers a number of features that promise to make it and subsequent editions
the dominant text in the field. For example, the author obviously respects the competence and intelligence of her readers. At the same time, she does not assume they
possess specific knowledge. She neither talks down to her readers nor speaks above their
heads. The book is well-organized and is a model of writing clarity. All technical terms
are defined and described. Dr. Sands never fails to recognize that for social workers,
knowledge always includes specific applications for practice. Case vignettes are brief, yet
they allow the material to come alive.

A careful look at a few chapters provides added insight into this excellent volume.
Much of contemporary mental health practice seems to be based on a generic imagery
whereby people are defined by their illness, deficit, pathology, or affliction and in which

standardized methodologies are employed. Yet mental health practice, at least as far back as the time of Freud, has suggested that help can only be provided when it is individualized. Dr. Sands never lets her readers homogenize the people they seek to help. The chapters on women and cultural issues serve as a "celebration of diversity." This content is usually omitted from most texts or given token attention; yet it is required content for all courses in Council on Social Work Education accredited programs. While describing gender and cultural patterns important to mental health practice, she avoids the trap of replacing one set of stereotypes with another by emphasizing that within-group differences are often greater than between-group differences. Furthermore, she pays attention to how this information can be used in practice.

Over the last decade, community mental health has rediscovered people with chronic mental disorders. This population is the first priority of the National Institute of Mental Health and most state mental health authorities, and it is rapidly assuming similar prominence within community programs. A new cadre of social workers, well-grounded in knowledge about this population and the skills needed to implement proven interventions on their behalf, is critical to this movement. In too many venues, community practice is "old wine in new bottles," despite the rapidly increasing body of credible research suggesting the efficacy of new approaches and the ineffectiveness and even toxicity of some older methods. The triology of chapters devoted to intervention with persons with chronic mental disorders is exceptional in its "practice informed by research" perspective. Each topic is based on the most recent research in the field and, as in all the chapters, each topic is grounded in actual social work practice.

This book is not only a scholarly achievement but also an eminently usable tool for social work education and practice. For those who have the good fortune to read it, the book will contribute to their professional knowledge and professional sensitivity. Most importantly, our clients will be the ultimate beneficiary.

Dr. Charles A. Rapp
University of Kansas
School of Social Welfare

Preface

The community mental health movement and the implementation of the policy of deinstitutionalization have opened the door to a large population of clients requesting and needing mental health services in their local communities. Some of these consumers have severe and persistent mental disorders which, in previous times, would have been treated in psychiatric hospitals. Others are persons with moderately debilitating impairments, such as anxiety and depression. With this influx of clients, there is a heightened need for up-to-date information on treatment.

Among community mental health practitioners, social workers are ubiquitous. They work with community mental health centers, emergency services, community residences, partial hospitalization programs, clubhouses, and vocational rehabilitation programs. Social workers provide clinical services to clients who have crises and to those who need ongoing supportive care and psychotherapy. Members of a profession that sees itself at the interface between the person and the environment, social workers offer a critical link between the client and the client's family or significant others, community services, and the mental health team.

This book is written for readers who wish to gain specialized knowledge of clinical social work practice in community mental health. One audience consists of social work graduate students who are taking courses or are specializing in mental health. Advanced undergraduate students who are interested in mental health are another audience. A third audience is made up of practitioners in mental health. Although clinicians and students of related mental health professions such as nursing may benefit from reading this text, this book is written from a social work perspective. Community mental practice is presented with respect to the history of what was once called "psychiatric social work," as well as the value base of the social work profession. This book assumes prior foundation knowledge of social work theory and practice, including the generalist perspective, microcounseling skills, and human behavior in the social environment, and some familiarity with the *Diagnostic and Statistical Manual of Mental Disorders (DSM-III-R)* (American Psychiatric Association, 1987).

In keeping with the needs of the clinical social worker, this book provides both a framework for practice and a description of diverse interventions. Guided by a conceptual framework that is biopsychosocial, it offers a way to understand clients holistically and to work in a milieu characterized by the "biological revolution," legal rights issues, and the *DSM-III-R*. Special features to be noted are that it:

- incorporates current biopsychosocial research findings
- provides extensive information about medication
- emphasizes empirically supported and research-informed practice
- describes and provides case examples of model treatment approaches
- includes chapters on women and minorities of color
- describes case management and other interventions with persons with chronic mental disabilities
- includes cases and questions at the conclusion of the chapters

The mental health practice described in this book applies primarily to noninstitutionalized adult clients, approximately 18 years and older, who live in the community. Particular attention is given to the treatment of populations with severe and moderate mental health difficulties, that is, persons with "chronic" psychiatric disabilities, dual diagnoses (substance abuse together with a mental disorder), depression, and anxiety. Although efforts have been made to be comprehensive, certain boundaries had to be drawn. This book does not discuss intervention with persons who simply have "problems in living" or difficulties which are principally environmental or existential. Moreover, it does not give specific attention to the treatment of persons with personality disorders and dementia, interventions with whom are discussed extensively in other textbooks. Children, adolescents, forensic, dual-diagnosed mentally retarded/developmentally disabled populations, and adults living in nursing homes or other institutions are also excluded.

The book begins with a prologue, which is presented as a personal statement. Next comes the introduction, designed to acquaint the reader with the leading concepts, themes, and issues that are addressed in the book. Community mental health, deinstitutionalization, and psychiatric epidemiology are discussed, and definitional issues surrounding mental health, normality, and mental illness are examined. The book then is divided into two parts. Part I, A Framework for Practice, contains seven chapters. The first, chapter 2, looks at the history of clinical social work practice in the context of mental health history in the United States. The next, the conceptual framework, describes the terms, theories, and perspectives utilized in this volume. An integrated biopsychosocial perspective that encompasses a number of theories is presented. Chapter 4 describes elements of a comprehensive biopsychosocial assessment that is in keeping with the conceptual framework. Here the mental status examination, a functional assessment, and the psychosocial summary are described. Chapter 5 is concerned with the legal and ethical dilemmas that have emerged while social workers try to practice within the framework of their professional values and the legal system. The next two chapters address the dimensions of gender and culture. Chapter 6 incorporates a feminist perspective and identifies mental health problems attributed to women. Chapter 7 discusses clinical practice with minorities of color, that is, African Americans, American Indians and Alaskan Natives, Asian Americans, and Hispanics.

Part II contains six chapters on intervention. Although the primary emphasis here is on research-informed psychosocial treatment modalities, information on psychotropic medication is included in several of these chapters. Because persons with chronic mental disorders constitute a population with a significant need for intervention in the community, three chapters are devoted to their treatment. Chapter 8 describes definitional issues and parameters, research findings, principles of intervention, and the philosophy of rehabilitation. The next chapter, on case management in a community context, examines several models of case management and describes a range of community resources appropriate for persons with severe and persistent psychiatric disorders. The third chapter on treatment with this population, chapter 10, focuses on medication, social skills training, and family psychoeducation. Chapter 11, which was written by Deborah K. Webb and Diana M. DiNitto, is on clinical practice with clients who abuse substances and have mental health problems. This chapter provides definitions of substance abuse and comorbidity, describes the continuum of educational and treatment programs, and addresses special treatment issues. Chapters 12 and 13 describe treatment approaches with persons suffering from depression and anxiety, respectively. Each of these chapters discusses and provides illustrations of therapeutic models that are strongly supported by empirical research. Here and elsewhere the criteria used to select model programs were that (a) social workers were instrumental in their conceptualization or design, (b) there is empirical support for their effectiveness, and (c) they are relevant to social work practice in community mental health. The book concludes with an epilogue.

I gratefully acknowledge the help of a number of individuals who made this book possible. First of all, I would like to thank the clients with whom I have worked over the years, who, in many ways, taught me how to help them. Some of their stories have been incorporated into this volume. Thanks go, too, to my family and friends, whose support and confidence sustained me through a period of intense isolation—in particular, my parents, whose support has been lifelong; my daughter, who took over the cooking when I was engrossed at the computer; and my son, who recognized that his mother, too, needed space. I would like to express my appreciation, also, to former colleagues at The Ohio State University, who read and made comments on drafts of some of the chapters—especially Beverly Toomey, Richard First, Kathleen Nuccio, and members of the postmodern feminist study group. Special thanks go to social work students, whose concerns are reflected in this text. Among them are Karin Gregory, Christopher Russell, Zelda Weaver, and Nella Garrett, who gave me permission to quote excerpts from their papers; Cathy Young, an outstanding graduate research assistant; and Laura Liss, whose excellent work as an indexer was vital to the completion of this book. The following individuals also made significant contributions to this text: Mary Linden-Salter from the Ohio Legal Rights Service, who was always responsive to questions about clients' rights; Daniel G. Hale, attorney, who reviewed the chapter on legal and ethical issues; and Charles Rapp of the University of Kansas, who field-tested the book. I am grateful, as well, to the reviewers whose comments and suggestions proved valuable to the development of the book: Maureen Maloney, of C-E-I Community Mental Health, Lansing,

Michigan; Kia J. Bentley, Virginia Commonwealth University; Mary E. Pharis, University of Texas at Austin; Amy Zaharlick, The Ohio State University; and Lowell Bishop, Ohio University. Finally, I thank all those at Merrill, an imprint of Macmillan Publishing, who worked to bring this book to print—in particular, Lorraine Woost and Gloria Jasperse for their work during the production phase; and Linda James Scharp, MSW, editor, for her support and encouragement throughout the project.

Contents

Prologue

According to the hospital report, 25-year-old Carla had lived an insufferable life. For 5 years prior to her hospital admission, she was the "old lady" of Rex, the leader of a motorcycle gang. Rex physically abused her himself and shared her with his friends. During her travels across the country with the gang, Carla was confined periodically in jails and mental hospitals. The state mental hospital which referred her to the local community mental health center gave her the diagnosis of "schizophrenia, chronic undifferentiated type."

Carla arrived at the community mental health center with her mother, a 50-year-old widow, with whom she was living. A clinical social worker conducted a screening interview with Carla alone and together with her mother. During the individual interview, Carla responded to questions, but she acted as though she could not remember much about her past association with the motorcycle gang. Her affect was neither flat nor animated; she appeared to be subdued. During the joint session, Carla maintained eye contact with the social worker, but avoided looking at her mother.

After the case was presented to the community mental health center's interdisciplinary treatment planning team, the staff recommended that Carla participate in the center's partial hospitalization program. The social worker would see Carla in individual therapy and intermittently would hold sessions that included Carla's mother.

A few weeks after Carla joined the program, she began to talk quietly with other clients and staff. Much to the satisfaction of the partial hospitalization staff, Carla became increasingly sociable over time. After 3 months, Carla mentioned that she was feeling "nervous" and wanted a change of medication. The social worker arranged for her to see the center's psychiatrist and advocated a change from an antipsychotic medication to some other drug. The psychiatrist changed her medication to an antidepressive agent. Before long, Carla became gregarious, flirtatious, and interested in evangelical religion. She reported sending monetary contributions to a number of television ministers.

Late one night the social worker was called at home by a counselor from the mental health center's 24-hour crisis line. The social worker was asked to contact the manager of a nearby motel who had told the crisis worker that Carla was lying naked with the curtains open in a motel room, where she could be seen partying with several men. The social worker responded immediately by calling the client and the manager. She urged Carla to close the curtains and send her friends home, and assured the manager that the situation would be resolved. A few weeks later Carla left town with a male client in the program—but not before asking the social worker for a referral to a mental health clinic in the city where she was headed.

"Carla" is a pseudonym for one of the first clients with severe psychiatric problems with whom I worked as a clinical social worker. At the time I was not much older than she. For a long time after this case was terminated, I was bewildered. Was Carla misdiagnosed? Was she on the appropriate medication? Did the treatment used by the mental health staff foster the radical change in her behavior? Did any of my interventions contribute to the negative outcome of this case? What kinds of interventions should have been used?

Years later, after I had more practice experience and had delved into the literature, I realized that Carla should have been given the diagnosis of bipolar (manic-depressive) disorder. Carla's increasing friendliness was symptomatic of a shift in her mood from a depressive to a manic state. Considering sociability a desirable outcome of the partial hospitalization program, the staff naively thought that she was making progress. When I reflected on this case later, I also recognized that the change in her medication probably fostered her manic reaction. At the time, neither I nor anyone else on the staff appeared to be aware of the tendency in the United States to give the diagnosis of schizophrenia when bipolar was in order. We accepted without question the diagnosis Carla was given in the hospital that referred her to us.

The community mental health center in which I was employed was created in response to federal legislation enacted in the 1960s, that appropriated funds to local communities developing systems of mental health care. At that time five kinds of services were required—inpatient care, partial hospitalization (day treatment), outpatient services, crisis intervention (emergency services), and consultation and education (C and E). My principal assignment at that time was with the partial hospitalization program, but in the course of my career I have worked in other areas of direct services.

I began working in this mental health center in the early 1970s, a period of social consciousness. I was still experiencing the fervor of the civil rights movement, the Vietnam War protest, and the women's liberation movement. Prior to taking this position, I had read Thomas Szasz's (1961) *The Myth of Mental Illness,* R. D. Laing's (1967) *The Politics of Experience,* and Seymour Halleck's (1971) *The Politics of Therapy,* as well as numerous other books that were coming out of the antipsychiatry movement (Cooper, 1970; Laing, 1971; Ruitenbeek, 1972). This body of writing questioned the nature of mental illness, particular treatment practices, and the inequality between clients and professionals. Families, social structure, and clinicians were implicated in the fabrication of mental illness and the "oppression" of psychiatric patients. Affected by these writings, I wondered to what extent culturally shared ideas about mental health and mental illness shaped perceptions of persons who were labeled mentally ill. Aware of the slogan of the women's movement—"the personal is political"—I asked myself whether the mental health problems presented by the "mentally ill" were manifestations of social injustices.

My personal struggles with the ideology of mental health derived from my social work values as well as my identification with the social movements of the 1960s. As a social worker, I believed in the dignity of the individual regardless of his or her social, economic, or mental condition. In keeping with my respect for the individual, I did not attach much significance to the *Diagnostic and Statistical Manual of Mental Disorders (DSM-II)* (American Psychiatric Association, 1968), which was used at that time. Furthermore, I recognized that individuals have rights such as self-determination and self-actualization and that social workers were responsible for promoting social justice and equality. In keeping with my values, I tried to create an atmosphere of openness, honesty, and mutual respect in my work with clients and colleagues. I did not want to be an "oppressor."

The major issues I grappled with in my years as a mental health practitioner were: labeling persons mentally ill; involuntary commitment of clients to mental hospitals; the client's right to treatment; and client rights versus professional responsibilities. The first two issues were reflective of social work values and ideas inherent in the civil rights movement. The last two issues were faced after I was able to accept that some individuals wanted, needed, and benefited from clinical treatment.

My resolution of these dilemmas was facilitated when I came to realize that community mental health is also a social movement and that it, like the social movements of the 1960s and 1970s, is driven by values that I espoused. In a community context it is possible to respect and advocate clients' rights, mobilize support from caring individuals, and prevent mental disability. The community mental health movement and its companion ideology, deinstitutionalization, have contributed to the policy of transferring treatment from remote hospitals to the community, where trained social workers, in tandem with other mental health professionals and local residents, promote clients' optimal psychosocial functioning in the community.

I now believe that one can help persons with serious mental health problems without oppressing them, and that in order to be as helpful as possible, one must be an informed practitioner. A clinical social worker practicing in a community mental health setting should be knowledgeable about biological concomitants of mental disorders, medication, epidemiological research findings, and research on effective psychosocial treatment modalities. I now recognize that my earlier belief that mental illness was a product of social politics interfered with my recognizing mental health disorders such as Carla's and how they can best be treated. Furthermore, I now see that before one advocates a change in a client's medication, one should be sensitive to possible diagnostic errors and knowledgeable about the risks associated with medications used to treat diverse disorders. Although I recognize that the antipsychiatry movement polarized the interests of helping professionals and clients, I continue to believe that social workers have a responsibility to protect clients' rights.

This volume is the outcome of my thinking about, practice in, and teaching of clinical social work in community mental health. It represents an integration of knowledge, experience, and values that I hope will be helpful to social work practitioners in the 1990s. Written at a time in which multiple theories guide practice, the biomedical model has gained prominence, and research-based practice is sought, this book argues for social work practice that is based on a thorough assessment of individual clients and their social milieux, knowledge of findings from biological and social science research, understanding and application of psychosocial theories, and a social work value orientation.

REFERENCES

American Psychiatric Association. (1968). *Diagnostic and statistical manual of mental disorders* (2nd ed.) Washington, DC: Author.

Cooper, D. (1970). *The death of the family.* New York: Vintage Books.

Halleck, S. L. (1971). *The politics of therapy.* New York: Science House.

Laing, R. D. (1967). *The politics of experience.* New York: Ballantine Books.

Laing, R. D. (1971). *The politics of the family and other essays.* New York: Pantheon Books.

Ruitenbeek, H. M. (Ed.). (1972). *Going crazy.* New York: Bantam Books.

Szasz, T. S. (1961). *The myth of mental illness.* New York: Delta.

1 | Introduction

C linical social workers are major providers of community mental health services. In 1986 social workers were the most numerous full-time professional staff working in freestanding outpatient psychiatric clinics, representing 47 percent of the professional patient care staff and 29 percent of all staff (National Institute of Mental Health, n.d.). They represented 28 percent of the community mental health staff in the state of Washington (Peterson & Cox, 1988). In a longitudinal study of 74 community mental health centers in 15 states, Larsen (1987) found that from 1976 to 1984 social workers were consistently prevalent among the clinical staff.

Mental health is the leading field of social work practice (Hopps & Pinderhughes, 1987). The predominance of mental health was revealed in a survey of members and a later salary study (National Association of Social Workers, 1983, 1987). Of the social work practitioners polled by the National Association of Social Workers for the salary study, direct-service social workers represented 67 percent of the respondents; 33 percent worked in the mental health practice area. These figures are thought to be representative of the membership (National Association of Social Workers, 1987). A survey of accredited social work programs found that in 1988 22 percent of the master's students were specializing in mental health or community mental health and 26 percent had field placement reflecting these areas (Spaulding, 1989).

The prominent role of social workers in the mental health field has not gone unnoticed by the media. An article in *The New York Times* (April 30, 1985) described a "quiet revolution" in psychotherapy. The medically trained psychiatrists are being displaced by psychologists, social workers, and other professionals.

> But the new shift is most pronounced in the comparison between psychiatrists and social workers. Ten years ago, for example, there were about as many psychiatrists as social workers offering psychotherapy, while today social workers outnumber psychiatrists two to one. ("Social Workers Vault into Leading Role in Psychiatry," 1985, C1)

Those social workers for whom psychotherapy represents a significant method of intervention are the clinicians. Like psychotherapists of related disciplines, clinical social workers use the face-to-face relationship to promote awareness, change, growth, and improved psychological functioning in individuals, families, and groups. Clinical social workers share with other therapists a body of knowledge about human behavior theory and therapeutic techniques and, like them, are capable of making assessments and providing treatment. Nevertheless, clinical social workers have a broader perspective on the client and the target for intervention than many of their colleagues in other disciplines. Clinical social workers view clients and their problems in relation to the multiple contexts in which problems occur and pursue interventions that focus on clients' social and political environments as well as the psychological and interpersonal domains. Clinical social workers are especially interested in enhancing clients' strengths and promoting connections between clients and the community that foster clients' functioning. Where interpersonal and institutional barriers interfere with clients, clinical social workers act to eliminate these obstacles and create resources that address identified needs. As professionals with a mission to promote human welfare and social justice, clinical social workers are particularly concerned with oppressed populations.

This description of clinical social work encompasses what is called "direct social work practice," a general term that describes the engagement of a client or client system in ameliorative activity. Direct practice applies to a wide range of fields of practice, populations, and problem areas and incorporates "a mosaic of methods and skills based upon many kinds of knowledge and guided by multiple theories" (Meyer, 1987, p. 409). The direct social work practitioner in most specialized fields utilizes multiple sources of knowledge, theories, and methods. The clinical social worker works directly with clients and systems to solve problems, change dysfunctional behaviors, resolve psychological issues, develop social networks, and utilize and benefit from community resources. Treatment is psychological and social.

In community mental health, the clinician's therapeutic and prevention roles predominate and are interconnected. Community mental health clinical social workers are principally psychotherapists and case managers. As therapists, they use their knowledge of human behavior theories, differential diagnosis, and treatment modalities, as well as research on practice effectiveness, to produce changes or promote the psychosocial functioning of clients and to remedy their situations. Siporin's (1983) conception of the "helping-therapeutic process" as "clinical social workers' actions that relieve clients' personal and social distress and that help clients to cope with difficulties in social functioning and social living" (p. 193) captures the process as it unfolds in an ecological context. An additional dimension of the therapeutic process, however, is the promotion of *empowerment*, enhanced feelings of competence resulting from self-directed activity on the part of clients.

Clinical social work in community mental health also includes case management. Work with the chronically mentally ill in particular necessitates that workers advocate on behalf of clients, link consumers with resources, monitor their treatment plans, and mediate solutions to problems. Clinical social workers functioning as case managers promote client utilization of sources of personal and institutional support in the community; in addition, social workers provide that support themselves. (See chapter 9 for a discussion of case management in relation to the chronic population.) Whether one functions as a case manager or as a therapist, or one integrates these roles, the social worker has extensive contacts with colleagues in related disciplines, employees of other human service agencies, landlords, physicians, lawyers, and others. Through these contacts clinical social workers connect clients with sources of support in the community and work to reduce institutional barriers to mental health services.

Clinical social workers also employ preventive strategies to remedy immediate problems and impede their recurrence. For example, intervention during a crisis followed by brief psychotherapy can reduce the likelihood of future mental health problems. Similarly the rehabilitation of severely mentally disabled clients and the education of clients and their families can provide the structure and knowledge that prevent the occurrence of mental health emergencies. Strategies of prevention that are used in community mental health practice are described in the following section.

COMMUNITY MENTAL HEALTH

Community mental health is a philosophy of treatment that developed from experience with a population that has been at different times described as mad, possessed, deviant, and sick. Although community treatment is not a new phenomenon (Caplan, 1969), its contemporary expression and contexts are unique. Furthermore, the role of social workers in the implementation of community treatment has become increasingly important. The historical development of community mental health and the role played by social work in this process are described in chapter 2.

Community mental health was conceived by Gerald Caplan (1961) as an approach to preventive psychiatry in which the community is seen as the target. Accordingly stress is viewed as a product of the culture or community. Intervention on a broad scale can help identify and reduce pathogenic patterns. Crisis intervention when individuals face threats to life goals can prevent the development of psychopathology.

Caplan (1964) incorporated a public health model into his conceptualization of community mental health. The goal was to reduce (1) the incidence (rate of new cases) of all kinds of mental illness, (2) the duration of many of the disorders that occur, and (3) the degree of impairment that results. In order to accomplish this, Caplan recommended that three levels of prevention be instituted.

Three Levels of Prevention

The first level of mental health prevention that is used is *primary prevention*, which refers to reducing the incidence of mental disorders by eradicating their causes. This level focuses primarily on the community (rather than the individual) and the conditions within that may be noxious. Caplan (1964) suggested that efforts at primary prevention be directed at the "provision of supplies" (p. 31). Individuals need physical (food, housing), psychosocial (cognitive and affective stimulation, interpersonal relationships), and sociocultural (cultural values, customs, and expectations) supports to develop and sustain mental health. The attitudes of others, such as racial prejudice, can block the flow of supplies (Caplan, 1964).

Primary prevention calls for the identification of causal factors (e.g., infectious agents, genetic factors, missing nutrients) so that they can be counteracted. Biogenetic and neurological research attempts to identify biological and physical causes of mental disorders. Psychiatric epidemiological research, which will be described later in this chapter, is a means to identify those environmental, demographic, and personality factors in populations and communities that contribute to mental illness. Often, however, the causes of psychiatric difficulties cannot be attributed to a single factor or agent; biological and psychosocial factors interact in a complex way (Langsley, 1985b). However complex the causes, research findings point to particular groups that are at risk of certain mental disorders. Some efforts at primary prevention, such as educational and counseling programs, are directed especially at community groups judged to be at risk (Borus, 1988).

The second level, *secondary prevention,* has the goals of reducing the prevalence of actual cases in the community and shortening the duration of time in which individuals experience mental health problems thus preventing identified problems from getting worse. Early identification (case finding), assessment, and intervention (crisis intervention and short-term therapy) are some ways in which this level of prevention is implemented. Prompt and effective individual, family, and group psychotherapy are also applicable on the secondary level.

Tertiary prevention refers to reducing the rate of mental disability in the community through efforts at rehabilitation. The goal is to restore individuals with serious psychiatric problems to as high a level of functioning as possible and to prevent complications (Langsley, 1985b). Tertiary prevention is directed at the community as well as at clients and their social networks (Caplan, 1964). Efforts are made to prevent or reduce stigma, ignorance, and other barriers to recovery through advocacy and community education. The lack of transitional facilities, outpatient services, and social programs can also interfere with the rehabilitation of persons with mental disabilities. When applied to the severely mentally disabled, tertiary prevention is rehabilitative, and the goal is to thwart rehospitalizations, decompensation, homicide, and suicide.

Table 1.1 illustrates how prevention applies to mental health practice. The goals and methods relevant to the three levels of prevention are outlined. These levels and their respective methods are implemented in accordance with a set of practice principles, which will be discussed next.

Principles of Community Mental Health Practice

The community mental health movement is guided by several principles (Langsley, 1985a). First of all, community mental health services should be *accessible to those who seek treatment,* that is, they should be near the residences and places of work of clients, rather than in remote hospitals. Accessibility also suggests that treatment facilities should be located near public transportation stops and that services should be available evenings and weekends. An additional aspect of accessibility pertains to the match between treatment provided and the population served. Community mental health services should be culturally and gender sensitive and tailored to clients' individual needs. Facilities should provide access to the physically handicapped, and provisions for communicating with the deaf should be available.

TABLE 1.1
Three Levels of Prevention of Mental Health Problems

Kind	Goal	Methods
Primary	1. Identify causal factors	Research
	2. Decrease incidence (new cases) of mental illness	Education (on broad scale or focusing on high-risk groups, e.g., sex education for junior high students)
	3. Eliminate causes of mental health problems	Counseling (e.g., premarital counseling)
		Experiential workshops (e.g., stress management)
		Crisis intervention following a stressful event but before the development of symptoms
Secondary	1. Decrease prevalence (total number of cases at any time)	Early intervention
	2. Decrease duration of existing mental health problems	Crisis intervention (following subjective distress)
		Short-term psychotherapy
	3. Deter an identified problem from getting worse	Individual, group, and family therapy
Tertiary	1. Reduce disabling effects of mental disabilities	Case management
	2. Restore functioning to the extent possible	Rehabilitation
		Psychoeducation
	3. Prevent decompensation	Community education
	4. Prevent self-injurious and aggressive behavior	Advocacy
	5. Prolong community tenure; prevent hospitalization or rehospitalization	

Community boards that govern mental health agencies have a responsibility not only to those who seek treatment, but also to those residents who are well or have hidden problems. Services that are delivered to local service units or *catchment areas* are driven by the second principle, *accountability to the entire community* (Langsley, 1985a). Community mental health boards are comprised of local citizens who view the needs of the catchment area corporately. In order to identify and meet the evolving needs of the locality, they arrange to have needs assessments performed and engage in planning efforts to meet identified needs (Langsley, 1985a). But accountability also suggests responsibility to the poor, ethnic minority groups, and consumers. These populations should have a voice in the governance of community mental health agencies.

Another principle is that services should be *comprehensive* (Langsley, 1985a). Community mental health services should include a range of services from outpatient clinics to day treatment centers to inpatient facilities. Within these programs, alternatives such as psychotherapies (individual, family, and group), social skill development, and vocational rehabilitation should be offered. At the same time, the community itself should have a diverse range of alternative residential settings in which clients may live (Bachrach, 1986). Community treatment should be responsive to all age groups (including children and older adults); available around the clock on an emergency basis; and address special problems, such as substance abuse. Furthermore, it should be flexible and adapted to the needs of the populations served. Services such as outreach programs, mobile treatment teams, and on-site consultation should be provided and needs such as transportation, housing, socialization, and leisure activities should be addressed (Bachrach, 1986).

A related principle is that *continuity of care* should be assured (Langsley, 1985a). The diverse services that are offered should be linked through cooperative relationships between providers or a consistent liaison between services, such as the case manager. Continuity of care is essential in the context of a complex, fragmented, bureaucratic social service delivery system. The chronically mentally ill in particular require continuous services that are longitudinal, psychological, and financial (Bachrach, 1986). First of all, this population needs services over a long period of time. Furthermore, they must feel comfortable, welcome, and encouraged to utilize services. In addition, services must be affordable or subsidized.

Another principle of community mental health is that treatment providers should constitute a *multidisciplinary team* (Langsley, 1985a). In order to provide comprehensive services that meet clients' psychiatric, social, and vocational needs, the expertise of professionals of different disciplines is needed. The knowledge, skills, and perspectives of diverse professionals contribute to a holistic understanding of the client and the provision of multidimensional treatment or rehabilitation. Psychiatrists, psychologists, community mental health nurses, social workers, recreation therapists, music therapists, counselors, and occupational therapists are among the professionals who participate in teams.

Finally, the ideology emphasizes *prevention,* which was discussed previously. Early casefinding and intervention, education, rehabilitation, and psychotherapy are ways of implementing this principle (Langsley, 1985a). However commendable these principles may be, they are not adhered to in their ideal form. In recent years, mental health centers have become less comprehensive (Larsen, 1987) and more specialized. The range of services needed for a comprehensive program of care is not available in many communities. Those services that are offered are not uniformly accessible to all geographic areas and populations. Accountability to minority groups, the poor, and other consumers or potential consumers is questionable. Not surprisingly, consumer groups have complained that the needs of the insured have predominated over those of the needy ("Mental Health Center Violations Alleged," 1990). Very often clinical social workers are called upon to fill in the gaps in the delivery system.

The Scope of Clinical Social Work
Practice in Community Mental Health

Social work practice in community mental health takes place in a number of different settings. Among these are community mental health centers, outpatient clinics (usually associated with general or psychiatric hospitals), partial hospitalization or day treatment programs, emergency or crisis intervention services, supervised apartments, transitional employment programs, and group homes. In addition, inpatient treatment in community hospitals (rather than remote public institutions) is also considered community mental health treatment. Nevertheless, some agencies that do not call themselves mental health organizations serve populations with mental health problems in the community. Among these are family service agencies, substance abuse programs (inpatient and outpatient), community shelters, employee assistance programs, and private practices.

In this volume community mental health will be viewed as a community-based treatment approach for clients (primary consumers) and their significant others (secondary consumers). The community and its constituent members and services will be viewed as potential resources for clients. Stress that derives from community living (Caplan, 1961) will also be recognized. The stress-diathesis model, which calls attention to the interaction between biological vulnerability and social experiences, will be used in the chapters on intervention with the severely mentally disabled (see chapters 8, 9, and 10). The potential contribution of the family to stress reduction will be particularly emphasized (see chapter 10). In addressing prevention, this book will concentrate principally on secondary and tertiary prevention, which have all but supplanted primary prevention in community mental health. The community treatment centers to which this volume applies are primarily outpatient mental health treatment facilities, emergency services, and residential and rehabilitation programs located in local communities. The client population will be adults with severely and moderately disabling mental health problems. For the more severely impaired persons, the concept of deinstitutionalization is relevant to their care.

DEINSTITUTIONALIZATION

Deinstitutionalization is a philosophy, process, and ideology (Bachrach, 1976; Mechanic, 1989) that began to unfold in the late 1950s and converged with the community mental health movement in the 1960s. The term refers to the shift in the principal locus of treatment from hospitals to the community. In 1955, the number of patients residing in state and county psychiatric hospitals peaked at 559,000. Thereafter these facilities were substantially (but not completely) depopulated. By 1986, the inpatient population was reduced 500 percent (see Figure 1.1). This process was facilitated by the discovery in 1953 of chlorpromazine. This antipsychotic medication controlled disturbing symptoms and behavior that had made hospitalization necessary. This medication and others that followed could be prescribed and ingested in the community.

The cumbersome term deinstitutionalization encompasses a philosophy about the appropriate use of hospitals. Under deinstitutionalization psychiatric hospitals continue to be utilized, but they are used differently. In the past, psychiatric institutions provided long-term custodial care for individuals judged chronic and incurable. Today clients with disabling psychiatric conditions can avoid hospitalization altogether if comparable treatment can be accomplished in the community. If hospitalization is needed, it is relatively brief and often is in a local community hospital. Individuals who are hospi-

FIGURE 1.1

Actual number of resident patients, end of year, in state and county mental hospitals; selected years 1950–1986. (*From National Institute of Mental Health, n.d.*)

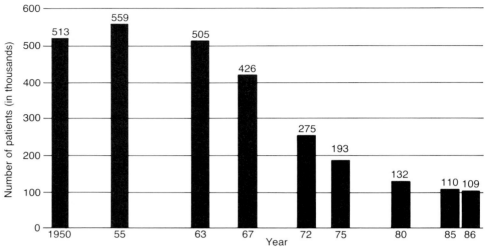

talized are retained only so long as institutionalization is necessary for their treatment, after which time they are released to community treatment services that match their needs.

Ideally deinstitutionalization involves two processes—(a) the avoidance of hospitalization and (b) the concurrent development of community services that serve as alternatives to institutionalization (Bachrach, 1976). The first process suggests that community treatment strategies should be considered before pursuing hospitalization. In order for community treatment to be possible, local communities are expected to develop and expand emergency services, group homes, family care homes, outpatient treatment centers, day hospitals, vocational rehabilitation centers, and other alternatives to hospitalization. The community offers a natural environment in which the same services offered in a total institution can be provided locally. Unfortunately many communities have not assumed responsibility for developing community alternatives and assuring their use. Many discharged patients have been "dumped" on city streets without a place to live, without outpatient care. The presence of deinstitutionalized mentally ill among the homeless is a reflection of the community's indifference toward a population that desperately needs services.

Another result of deinstitutionalization is the "revolving door syndrome." Clients who are admitted to hospitals for brief stays do not have sufficient time to recover or do not follow through with aftercare. As a result, they are readmitted frequently.

Deinstitutionalization evolved as a public policy during the 1960s, a period of heightened social consciousness and advocacy for the rights of marginalized populations. In the 1960s and 1970s practices such as involuntary commitment, custodial care without treatment, and coercive forms of intervention were challenged in courts on constitutional grounds. A series of judicial decisions supported the rights of hospital patients to be treated, to refuse treatment, and to live in the "least restrictive" environment. With the establishment of limits on the powers of institutions to restrict clients' rights, it became more difficult to admit and retain clients in hospitals.

Deinstitutionalization is an ideology that is historically associated with certain values (Mechanic, 1989). For one, institutionalization is considered undesirable. Even though some people have called for the elimination of hospitals, others have regarded them as necessary evils that should be used only if equivalent treatment could not be provided safely in the community. Another value is that it is desirable for persons with mental health difficulties to live as independently as possible, to assume responsibility for themselves, and to try to adapt to community life. The clients' right to treatment and their freedom of movement are also valued.

Clinical social workers who work with deinstitutionalized clients are also guided by some of the same principles as parallel workers in the fields of mental retardation and developmental disabilities. Two concepts developed by Wolfensberger et al. (1972)— *normalization* and *integration*—are applicable to the severely and persistently (chronically) mentally ill who live in the community. With normalization, one ought to utilize "means that are as culturally normative as possible, in order to establish and/or maintain personal characteristics which are as culturally (normative) as possible" (p. 28). This suggests that deinstitutionalized persons should live in the natural environment of the community, maintain standards of personal grooming, and participate in ordinary social activities. Integration suggests that the deinstitutionalized should have the opportunity and encouragement to enter as fully as possible into the fabric of the community. They should be able to go to the library, movies, concerts, parks, shops, and the polls without discrimination.

Community mental health social workers serve different populations of deinstitutionalized persons. One consists of individuals with severe mental disabilities who, after having spent years in hospitals, moved to local communities in the 1960s and 1970s. These individuals, who are middle aged and older adults now, had to make an adjustment from regimented institutional life to the vagaries of life in the community. In contrast, the "new generation of chronic psychiatric patients" (McCreath, 1984, p. 436) consists of young adults who have not been socialized by total institutions. These individuals' experiences include exposure to the drug culture in the community, dependence on parents, and indifference toward formal outpatient treatment. Special issues to be considered with respect to the younger population will be discussed in chapter 8. Strategies of intervention across age groups are described in chapters 9 and 10. The court cases, legislation, and value issues associated with deinstitutionalization and community mental health practice will be discussed in chapter 5.

EPIDEMIOLOGICAL RESEARCH

Clinical social work practice in community mental health is informed by psychiatric epidemiological research. *Epidemiology* is the study of the distribution of diseases in a population in an environmental context. A project of significance to public health, it looks at conditions that might point to the origin, cause, and distribution of pathology, such as the transmission of body fluids and AIDS. Epidemiological research involves the use of sophisticated methods of sampling and statistical methods of analysis.

Epidemiological research is predicated on the paradigm of "host/agent/environment" (Kellam, 1987). The host is the person with the disease; the agent is the causal factor. When epidemiology has been applied to psychopathology, research has rarely been able to identify a specific agent that causes a mental disorder. Unlike physical diseases, psychological disorders are not infectious. The causes are multiple and interactive. Epidemiological studies have found varying levels of association among a number of social, environmental, and demographic variables and the disorder. Segal and Baumohl (1981) suggest that in relation to community mental health, "contributors" be substituted for agents.

Two terms that are widely used in epidemiological research are *incidence* and *prevalence*. Incidence refers to the number of new cases of a particular disorder that occur in a given period of time (e.g., in a year). Prevalence refers to the total number of cases (new cases and existing cases) in a population. The term *point prevalence* refers to the prevalence at a particular point of time (e.g., 6-month-point prevalence) (Turns, n.d.).

Psychiatric epidemiological research has been conducted on two kinds of populations, each associated with methodological problems. One population consists of cases in treatment, aggregate data on which are obtained from public hospitals and community treatment centers. However comprehensive research on treated cases may be, this information is biased. Usage of treatment facilities is influenced by social and cultural factors (e.g., some groups find it easier than others to ask for help). Many individuals who have psychiatric problems for which they are not treated are not included in the statistics. Furthermore, data on cases in treatment usually do not include persons treated privately. The alternative approach is to conduct large surveys of communities. This strategy has been hampered by the collection of mental status data by lay interviewers, and by the difficulty of converting findings about symptoms into diagnoses. In the last 10 years, significant advances have been made in the development of instruments that yield diagnostic information, and which can be administered by nonprofessional interviewers (Weissman, Myers, & Ross, 1986). The Diagnostic Interview Schedule (DIS) has made it possible to engage in sophisticated epidemiological research (Freedman, 1984).

Since the 1950s, a number of epidemiological studies have been undertaken. Hollingshead and Redlich (1958), for example, conducted a study of the community and persons in treatment in the New Haven, Connecticut, area. They found a relationship between diagnosis and social class, that is, upper class persons were more likely to be given a diagnosis of neurosis; lower class, psychosis. Whereas the upper classes were treated primarily with psychotherapy, the lower classes received organic therapy and custodial care. Schizophrenia was disproportionately prevalent in the lower class.

The Midtown Manhattan Study was another significant epidemiological community study. Initially conducted by Srole and associates (1962) in 1954, the available original informants were revisited by a similar team 20 years later. During both time periods a large proportion (42 to 43 percent) of the population had mild symptoms and about 21 percent had moderate impairment. In 1954 14 percent were considered impaired, whereas in 1974 the proportion declined to less than 12 percent. Further analysis of the longitudinal data yielded surprising results. Although mental health declined with age in both time periods, when groups of the same age cohort but different study times (e.g., all who were in their 50s in 1954 and 1974) were compared, the 1974 group had a significantly lower rate of impairment. Similarly, women's rates of mental health impairment declined over 20 years. The authors concluded that historical trends are in a positive direction for cohorts of women and aging adults (Srole & Fischer, 1986).

A more recent community study of a catchment area in New Haven, Connecticut, was reported by Myers and Weissman (1986). This was a follow-up study of a sample that had first been studied in 1967. The authors found that close to 18 percent of the population surveyed had a psychiatric diagnosis. Consistent with previous research by Weissman and Klerman (1977), more women than men suffered from depression. Although lifetime rates of major and minor depression and grief were higher for women, there were no differences between men and women for the depressive personality.

New Haven was one of five sites in which the NIMH Epidemiological Catchment Area (ECA) Program was implemented in the late 1970s and early 1980s (Regier et al., 1984). The other sites were Baltimore, Maryland; Durham, North Carolina; St. Louis, Missouri; and Los Angeles, California. Both institutionalized and noninstitutionalized residents of these communities were surveyed once and then again a year later, thus providing comprehensive and longitudinal data (Freedman, 1984). These studies gathered information on the prevalence of specific psychiatric disorders, associated demographic factors, and patterns of usage of physical and mental health services for mental health problems. Table 1.2 describes the prevalence of psychiatric disorders among all the sites combined. Findings from these epidemiological studies are incorporated in the chapters comprising Part II of this volume.

Another focus of psychiatric epidemiological research has been the family. Some of these studies compare patterns of interaction in the family of origin of clinical cases with those of community cases. Others take a longitudinal look at the impact of family factors on the psychological outcome of the children ("developmental epidemiology," Kellam, 1987). One study of families of hospitalized adults (Hauser et al., 1987) found mother–adolescent conflict and nonreciprocal parent–parent interactions more prevalent in the clinical population than in the control group. A longitudinal study of a sample of children revealed that power assertive punishment techniques used by parents were associated with future problems for the children (Cohen & Brook, 1987).

A further avenue of epidemiological research has been on stress, vulnerability, and coping strategies. Some studies have looked at the relationship between stressful life events, such as widowhood and unemployment, and mental health problems. For the most part, this research has found that most people experiencing such events do not develop emotional disorders (Kessler, Price, & Wortman, 1985). Other studies look at vulnerability and resistance factors. Both psychological and physiological (biogenetic) factors are associated with vulnerability. Social relationships and emotional support can protect individuals from the impact of stress, although the mechanisms through which this occurs is not clear (Kessler, Price, & Wortman, 1985). Three coping strategies that are common to many of the studies are modifying the problem, changing how one views

TABLE 1.2

Comparison of Standardized 1-Month, 6-Month, and Lifetime Prevalence Rates of DIS/*DSM-III* Disorders per 100 Persons 18 Years and Older, All Sites Combined*

Disorders	Rate, % (SE)					
	1 mo		6 mo		Lifetime	
Any DIS disorder covered	15.4	(0.4)	19.1	(0.4)	32.2	(0.5)
Any DIS disorder except cognitive impairment, substance use disorder, and antisocial personality	11.2	(0.3)	13.1	(0.4)	19.6	(0.4)
Any DIS disorder except phobia	11.2	(0.3)	14.0	(0.4)	25.2	(0.5)
Any DIS disorder except substance use disorders	12.6	(0.3)	14.8	(0.4)	22.1	(0.4)
Any DIS disorder except substance use or phobia	8.3	(0.3)	9.4	(0.3)	13.8	(0.4)
Substance use disorders	3.8	(0.2)	6.0	(0.3)	16.4	(0.4)
Alcohol abuse/dependence	2.8	(0.2)	4.7	(0.2)	13.3	(0.4)
Drug abuse/dependence	1.3	(0.1)	2.0	(0.1)	5.9	(0.2)
Schizophrenic/schizophreniform disorders	0.7	(0.1)	0.9	(0.1)	1.5	(0.1)
Schizophrenia	0.6	(0.1)	0.8	(0.1)	1.3	(0.1)
Schizophreniform disorder	0.1	(0.0)	0.1	(0.0)	0.1	(0.0)
Affective disorders	5.1	(0.2)	5.8	(0.3)	8.3	(0.3)
Manic episode	0.4	(0.1)	0.5	(0.1)	0.8	(0.1)
Major depressive episode	2.2	(0.2)	3.0	(0.2)	5.8	(0.3)
Dysthymia†	3.3	(0.2)	3.3	(0.2)	3.3	(0.2)
Anxiety disorders	7.3	(0.3)	8.9	(0.3)	14.6	(0.4)
Phobia	6.2	(0.2)	7.7	(0.3)	12.5	(0.3)
Panic	0.5	(0.1)	0.8	(0.1)	1.6	(0.1)
Obsessive-compulsive	1.3	(0.1)	1.5	(0.1)	2.5	(0.2)
Somatization disorder	0.1	(0.0)	0.1	(0.0)	0.1	(0.0)
Personality disorder, antisocial personality	0.5	(0.1)	0.8	(0.1)	2.5	(0.2)
Cognitive impairment (severe)†	1.3	(0.1)	1.3	(0.1)	1.3	(0.1)

*The rates are standardized to the age, sex, and race distribution of the noninstitutionalized population of the United States aged 18 years and older. DIS indicates Diagnostic Interview Schedule.

†Dysthymia and cognitive impairment have no recency information; thus, the rates are the same for all three time periods.

Source: Regier, D. A., et al. (1988). Reprinted with permission from the *Diagnostic and Statistical Manual of Mental Disorders, Third Edition, Revised.* Copyright 1987 American Psychiatric Association.

the problem, and management of the emotional distress associated with the problem (Pearlin & Schooler, 1978).

Psychiatric epidemiological research is useful to the practitioner. For one, it gives one a picture of the distribution of psychopathology in the general population and among particular groups. As a result, one can identify high-risk groups for whom programs can be developed (e.g., depressed women, alcoholic men). When environmental factors are implicated (e.g., suicide as a peer group phenomenon), efforts can be made to address these factors. Overall, epidemiological research draws attention to the person–environment relationship, the stress that emanates from some of these transactions, and the potential inherent in social supports to remediate stress.

Epidemiological research is one of a number of kinds of research that informs community mental health practice. As indicated previously, needs assessments are conducted on a community or catchment area level to guide planners, administrators, and mental health boards in making decisions about needed programs. Programs that are implemented are assessed through program evaluation methods. Another approach to research that is germane to this book is research on practice.

RESEARCH-INFORMED PRACTICE

During the past two decades, social workers have participated in a lively debate about practice effectiveness. Several social work scholars reviewed controlled research studies conducted by social workers. Initially reports concluded that casework was not helping clients (Fischer, 1973). Later studies presented more optimistic findings (Reid & Hanrahan, 1982; Thomlison, 1984; Rubin, 1985). Evidence persists that social work interventions that are structured, specific, time-limited, and goal-directed are effective. Findings from a metaanalysis of studies of social work practice in mental health support environmental, action-oriented interventions with persons with chronic mental health problems, and structured, time-limited approaches with a more general outpatient population (Videka-Sherman, 1988).

During the 1980s, the discussion centered on concepts of science that guide researchers and thinkers in the field. Heineman (1981) was critical of the logical empiricism that provided criteria for the practice effectiveness debate. The series of letters and articles that followed Heineman's publication revealed dissension between researchers employing quantitative methods and those employing qualitative methods.

Regardless of one's concept of science and the research method one utilizes, empirical research (that is, research based on practice experience) is valuable. Practitioners have a responsibility to clients to be informed about and apply interventions that are informed by research findings. A further consideration is that agencies and their funding sources hold social workers accountable to perform effectively and efficiently. The use of theoretical knowledge and research findings distinguishes the professional social worker from the layperson.

A number of attempts have been made to identify those research studies that are particularly relevant to clinical practice in mental health (Rubin, 1984, 1985; Videka-Sherman, 1988). Findings from these and other studies will be presented in the following chapters where relevant. In this volume research that informs practice (e.g., the vulnerability of certain populations to stress) as well as research that supports the effectiveness of specific modes of intervention (e.g., the effectiveness of in vivo exposure in the treatment of persons with phobias) will be cited. The evolving research on mental health populations and practices provides guidance to the clinical social worker on how to intervene with persons with specific psychiatric conditions.

Furthermore, it is recommended that practitioners evaluate their own effectiveness. This can be done through the implementation of single case studies in which assessment instruments are used intermittently; through the use of case recordings reflecting on the content and quality of client–worker interactions over time; or through a periodic evaluation of the accomplishment of tasks and goals that the client and the worker negotiate.

DEFINITIONS

Many of the terms used in mental health practice today are problematic. There is little consensus about what is meant by *normality* and *mental health. Mental illness* has been regarded as both a "myth" and a "metaphor" (Szasz, 1961). Many terms, such as *psychopathology,* derive from the field of psychiatry. Other terms, such as *adaptation* and *problems in living,* are particularly compatible with the orientation of social workers.

Normality, Mental Health, and Mental Illness

The terms mental health, normality, and mental illness are value-laden concepts that invoke diverse images. Mental health and normality suggest positive psychological functioning, whereas mental illness suggests dysfunctioning. Mental health and mental illness suggest a medical model, whereas normality implies a statistical one. Mental health is frequently used as a euphemism for mental illness—as illustrated by the plethora of "mental health" centers that remediate "mental illness." Moreover, diagnoses of "mental illness" have been applied to transient situational problems and other conditions for which there is no scientific evidence of illness.

Normality.   The terms mental health and normality have similar meanings but different connotations. On the surface, normality suggests a statistical criterion (Offer & Sabshin, 1966)—the average or mean; the most common behavior, the mode; or two standard deviations from the mean. Studies employing statistical measures, however, have produced surprising results. Psychiatric epidemiological studies of normal community samples have found that a substantial proportion of the population had symptoms of psychological problems. In both the Midtown Manhattan Study of an urban area, described earlier (Srole et al., 1962), and a study of a rural community in Nova Scotia (Leighton et al., 1963), only about 20 percent of the subjects were rated "well." Other research has indicated that family violence, marital infidelity, and sexual deviance are pervasive in American society (e.g., Straus, 1977). Clearly, the range of behavior associated with normality is wider than what was previously thought.

The term normality also suggests adaptation to the social context (Offer & Sabshin, 1966). Normal persons accommodate to the demands of society, meet legal and social obligations, and generally fit in with the contours of society. Although such persons are not troublesome, they are not necessarily creative or self-actualized. Persons who merely adapt to situational demands generally do not have the "peak experiences" of insight, self-awareness, or integration described by Maslow (1968). Furthermore, they do not necessarily have integrity, independence, or courage. Indeed they may acquiesce to injustices, exploitation, and persecution.

Jackson (1977) described difficulties in defining normality in a penetrating paper, "The Myth of Normality." "There is no standard of psychological 'normality' or 'good health,' " he said (p. 157). The dichotomy between the normal and abnormal is false and based on the assumption that psychopathology is fixed and tangible. In fact, individuals, as well as families, vary in their potentialities, emotional expression, and behavior:

> . . . there is no such animal as the normal person. Instead there is a wide variance in adaptive patterns and behavioral repertoires. How a person acts varies with the culture, the subculture, the ethnic group, and the family group in which he lives. (p. 162)

In order to offset cultural biases that occur in evaluating a person in relation to conventional ideas about normality, Jackson recommended the assessment of individuals in terms of their functioning in a number of contexts and activities.

Regardless of how one defines normality, one must recognize the relation of prevailing concepts to the expectations of the culture. Cultures vary in their expression of and response to anguish, pain, and deviance. Judgments about what is good, desirable, and acceptable are culturally relative.

Mental health. On the simplest level, mental health is characterized by the *absence of mental illness* (Jahoda, 1958). Accordingly, mentally healthy individuals do not have psychiatric disorders, such as those described in the *Diagnostic and Statistical Manual of Mental Disorders, III-R* (American Psychiatric Association, 1987). Gross psychopathology (e.g., delusions, hallucinations) is not present or observed. Such persons do not communicate feelings of distress or present evidence of mental illness. Ordinarily they are not receiving mental health treatment.

The problem with this definition is that there is a sociocultural process that intervenes between the presence of symptoms and diagnosis. Many individuals have signs of psychiatric disorders that neither they nor others consider indicators of mental disorder. Individuals comprising the person's intimate network may view the person's behavior as a personal idiosyncrasy, a sign of divine powers, or a developmental stage. The group's ideas about what is normal may contrast with what mental health professionals consider mental illness. In order for diagnosis to take place, someone or some system will have to establish that what was previously considered normal is abnormal (Scheff, 1984).

Mental health also can be viewed as *an aspect of health.* The World Health Organization (1948) defined health as "the state of complete physical, mental and social well being and not merely the absence of disease or infirmity." Although this definition leaves open the nature of "well-being," it does suggest that health encompasses a few areas of functioning and that all are essential. Furthermore, it links mind, body, and social life.

Mental health also represents an *optimal or ideal state*. Jahoda's (1958) concept of "positive mental health" includes attitudes toward oneself; growth, development, or self-actualization; personality integration; autonomy; environmental mastery; and perception of reality. This definition emphasizes high levels of functioning, which go beyond well-being or the absence of disease. Accordingly, individuals may seek psychotherapy to promote their growth, self-acceptance, or confidence. The qualities selected, however, reflect what this culture values—the autonomous, striving, differentiated individual. For other cultures, humility or community responsibility characterize the ideal.

Another criterion for mental health is *subjective* (Scott, 1970). Accordingly, the mentally healthy individual feels happy, satisfied, or self-confident. This criterion has been measured in research studies with happiness and life satisfaction scales. Subjective perceptions are, however, problematic as a standard for mental health. Persons under the influence of substances may have artificially produced feelings of satisfaction or happiness. Similarly, individuals with bipolar (manic-depressive) disorder are likely to rate themselves as extremely happy when they are manic. Furthermore, happiness and unhappiness are, to some extent, related to one's environment. Under some environmental conditions, one cannot be happy (Jahoda, 1958).

When political conditions are oppressive, mental health takes on a cast that may differ from what looks like mental health under freedom. During the time of slavery, for example, acts of defiance and subterfuge may have been signs of mental health. Similarly members of the underground in Nazi Germany and dissidents under other repressive regimes can be viewed as healthy. Among those who are oppressed by political systems, some individuals are able to transcend their situations by discovering meaning in suffering (Frankl, 1984). Meaning can be realized through defiance, contemplation, or acceptance.

In this volume mental health will be considered a state of psychosocial functioning that ranges from dysfunctional (mental illness) to functional to optimal. Optimal captures qualities of positive mental health as defined by the individual's own culture. Functional refers to the ability to take care of oneself and participate in community life purposefully and constructively. Dysfunctional describes impairment in the capacity to take care of oneself and participate in the community and includes patterns that are destructive of oneself and others.

Mental health is described as a continuum in Figure 1.2. According to this model, an individual is more or less functional with respect to different activities. A person may function at a relatively high level in some areas (manages own apartment, uses transportation), but at the dysfunctional level in others (interpersonal relationships, employment). The goal of intervention is to help the person maintain, restore, or improve psychosocial functioning.

Mental health is a phenomenon of the individual, family, group, community, culture, and nation. What affects one of these systems affects others. On the individual level, mental health encompasses the expression and management of emotions, cogni-

FIGURE 1.2

Description of mental health functioning

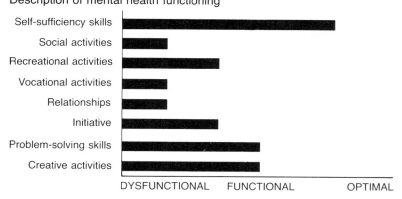

tions, behavior, and values as well as the social, occupational, and management skills needed for survival. Physical, psychological, and social dimensions are connected.

Mental Illness. During the early 1960s, Thomas Szasz (1960, 1961) launched an attack on the usage of the concept of mental illness. To Szasz the term applies appropriately to brain (organic) or neurological diseases but does not describe discrepant beliefs, values, behaviors, social relationships, and the like, which are commonly viewed as symptoms of mental disease. Many persons adjudged mentally ill hold unusual beliefs (e.g., "I am Napoleon") or violate legal norms (the criminally insane), but they do not have objective bodily illnesses. Although these individuals may be troubled, Szasz said, undoubtedly they are experiencing "problems in living," not mental illness. The practice of psychiatry is closely connected with ethics and values. Diagnoses of mental illness are performed in a social context in which the client's communications are viewed in relation to existing norms. "Much of psychotherapy may revolve around nothing other than the elucidation and weighing of goals and values—many of which may be mutually contradictory—and the means whereby they might best be harmonized, realized, or relinquished" (Szasz, 1965, p. 23).

Because the term mental illness is applied where there is no evidence of medical pathology, Szasz said, mental illness is a "myth." It is not like physical diseases—you cannot catch it, you do not have it, you cannot transmit it to others (Szasz, 1965). A successor to religious myths and witchcraft, the myth of mental illness provides a camouflage for human struggles to find meaning and make moral choices. Because mental illness is so loosely defined, some people have been falsely attributing their human struggles to mental illness while other persons adopt the sick role in order to avoid responsibility. Mental illness is more accurately a metaphor for psychic pain than a term that denotes a disease entity. The observed symptoms represent strategies to communicate (Szasz, 1961).

Szasz was not alone in his criticism of concepts of mental illness and related social practices. Scheff (1984) was interested in the social process that intervenes between the presentation of deviant behavior and the labeling of mental illness. Because of the human need for predictability, behaviors that disconfirm expectations arouse emotions such as anger, embarrassment, and fear. Nevertheless, these behaviors are frequently ignored. When intermediaries, such as social workers, define behavior as problematic, the behavior is reinforced and channeled into a deviant social role (mental patient). In crisis situations, when clients are suggestible, and in cultures that provide few alternative roles, the client accepts the patient role.

The concept of mental illness was also criticized by behaviorists and existentialists. Behaviorists objected to the medical vocabulary, labeling, and assumption that there was an inner cause of psychological problems. They preferred to look at environmental contingencies that support the presentation of maladaptive behavior. Existential-phenomenologists were critical of the use of the scientific method in the study of mental illness. According to their thinking (see, e.g., Esterson, 1970), it was not possible to be objective in assessing mental illness because such determinations are made in the course of interacting with a client. In addition, many social factors (family, environment) surrounding the client contribute to what is socially defined as mental illness.

Some of the criticism was in response to inappropriate labeling of mental illness. During the 1960s, for example, some young political activists who went south to register Black voters were incarcerated in mental hospitals for alleged paranoia (Coles, 1970). Historically, lifestyles or practices that differed from those valued by mainstream society (e.g., homosexuality, substance abuse, illegal acts) have been regarded as symptoms of mental illness instead of expressions of life choices.

The authors of the *Diagnostic and Statistical Manual of Mental Disorders, III* and *III-R* (also known as the *DSM-III* and the *DSM-III-R;* American Psychiatric Association, 1980, 1987) have attempted to address some of the definitional problems that have plagued the field of mental health over the years. For one, they assigned specific criteria to each psychiatric diagnosis. This should prevent the labeling of political activists and other inappropriate use of psychiatric diagnoses. Second, they ran extensive field tests on an early version of the manual in an attempt to arrive at reliable diagnoses. Although the results of the reliability studies were exaggerated (Kutchins & Kirk, 1986), the attempt at being more responsible than their predecessors is noteworthy. Finally, the authors of the two manuals came up with their own definition of *mental disorder,* a term that they used in place of mental illness:

> In DSM-III-R each of the mental disorders is conceptualized as a clinically significant behavioral or psychological syndrome or pattern that occurs in a person and that is associated with present distress (a painful symptom) or disability (impairment in one or more areas of functioning) or with a significantly increased risk of suffering death, pain, disability, or an important loss of freedom. In addition, this syndrome or pattern must not be merely an expectable response to a particular event, e.g., the death of a loved one. Whatever its original cause, it must currently be considered a manifestation of a behavioral, psychological, or biological dysfunction in the person. Neither deviant behavior, e.g., political, religious, or sexual, nor conflicts that are primarily between the individual and society are mental disorders unless the deviance or conflict is a symptom of a dysfunction in the person, as described above. (American Psychiatric Association, 1987, p. xxii)

This definition clearly places the disorder *inside the person,* and not in social interactions. It excludes individual reactions to painful life events (e.g., bereavement) unless these events are accompanied by an inordinate degree of distress. Furthermore, it discounts unhappiness, which often prompts people to seek psychotherapy. Although the definition draws a distinction between mental disorders and moral deviance, the *DSM-III-R* does not require that mental illnesses represent organic disorders. Behavioral, affective, and cognitive evidence of distress and impairment in psychosocial functioning are usually assessed through a clinical interview, not biological tests. Clinicians make judgments about whether certain behaviors, emotions, and beliefs are to be viewed as symptoms of mental disorders. Inevitably these judgments are made by referring to a vague normative model.

Another term used to describe mental illness is *psychopathology.* This medical term refers to the scientific study of diseases of the mind and refers to their etiology (origin or cause), their nature, and the course the diseases take. This term is used in the literature interchangeably with mental disorder, mental disease, mental illness, and abnormality.

Because of some of the definitional problems associated with the term mental illness, as well as research findings on brain pathology that apply only to certain psychiatric disorders, in this volume, the term *mental disorder* is preferred. Where the other terms are employed, they are used interchangeably with mental disorder. Moreover, the following criteria will be used as guidelines for identifying mental disorders:

1. *Subjective distress.* The individual must report emotional pain, somatic distress, discomfort, lack of control, or volitions that contradict personal values.
2. *Ineffective psychosocial functioning.* The individual is unable to take care of personal needs (bathing, dressing, grooming, eating) or cannot fulfill ordinary social functions (working, going to school, household management, caring for dependents, reciprocating in interpersonal relationships), or is oriented toward destructive or self-destructive activity. Other expressions of ineffective psychosocial functioning include indirect strategies of problem-solving (e.g., time-consuming rituals, approach-avoidance patterns, and passive-aggressive behavior).
3. *Bizarre behavior.* The individual initiates actions which have no instrumental purpose and which substantially deviate from behavior that is functional within the individual's subculture (e.g., smearing the walls with feces in mainstream American society).
4. *Sensory dysfunctioning.* The individual's sensory mechanisms are deficient, that is, the senses of vision, hearing, taste, touch, or smell do not correspond with stimuli emanating from the shared social environment.
5. *Disturbed thinking.* The individual has cognitions that are false, unrealistic, intrusive, or incongruent with those that are shared by the individual's subculture.

The most severely impaired clients will meet all of these criteria. Others will meet only a few. Clients who present concerns, symptoms, or behaviors that are not encompassed by two or more of the preceding disorders probably have "problems in living" or display socially deviant behavior.

Adaptive and Maladaptive Responses or Behaviors

Adaptive and *maladaptive* are adjectives that are frequently used in the field of mental health to describe functional and dysfunctional behavior, respectively. These terms appear less medical than "healthy" and "sick," and thus are more acceptable to mental health professionals with psychosocial perspectives. A key concept of ego psychology, adaptation refers to the process of developing a harmonious relationship between the person and the environment—one in which the demands are consistent with the individual's ability to respond effectively (Hartmann, 1958).

The concept of adaptation was incorporated into the life model of social work practice (Germain & Gitterman, 1980), which looks at the reciprocal relationship between the person and the environment. Adaptive behavior rises from a good fit between the person and a situation. For example, looking for a job after being laid off is an adaptive response. In contrast, maladaptive behavior is not compatible with the requirements of the situation. Getting drunk or getting into a fight are not compatible with being unemployed.

According to behavioral theory, adaptive and maladaptive behaviors are learned. They are reinforced in social relationships and through the provision of rewards or responses. Just as they can be learned, they can be unlearned. Behavioral theory provides a basis for changing maladaptive behavior to adaptive behavior (see chapter 3).

CONTEMPORARY ISSUES

During the last 10 years, many changes have occurred in thinking and practice in community mental health. Among these changes are a renewed focus on the biological factors as primary in the etiology of mental illness; the introduction of and controversies surrounding the *DSM-III* and the *DSM-III-R* (American Psychiatric Association, 1980, 1987); a recognition that the severely mentally disabled (chronically mentally ill) who live in the community are in great need of services (Schulberg & Killilea, 1982); and the emergence of new client and consumer groups. These contemporary issues affect clinical social work practice in community mental health.

The Biomedical Model

The definition of emotional difficulties as illness is not new. The organic perspective on mental illness has roots in the writings of Greek philosophers and developed with the unfolding of scientific knowledge. During the last two centuries this perspective has alternated with an environmental view (see chapter 2). In the last half of the twentieth century, the biomedical model has dominated the field of mental health.

In the 1950s, scientific breakthroughs in the development of psychopharmacotherapy facilitated the deinstitutionalization of state hospitals and the movement of the locus of treatment into the community. First, medication to treat schizophrenia was discovered. Later, results of successful treatment of persons with bipolar disorder with lithium were publicized in the United States. In recent years, drugs for depression, panic disorder, obsessive-compulsive disorder, and many other mental health difficulties have come into use.

Evidence that certain mental health disorders have a genetic or structural basis is increasing. Scientific studies of family pedigrees in which specific disorders are prevalent have lent support to a genetic explanation of certain disorders. Other studies using sophisticated brain imaging techniques identify structural impairments in the brains of persons with schizophrenia, providing strong support to the idea that schizophrenia is a brain disease. As these investigations have proceeded, theories suggesting that major mental disorders are caused by dysfunctional family patterns have been questioned. (The biological perspective and findings will be discussed in chapter 3.)

Scientific discoveries support a biomedical model, which places the cause of the illness and the locus of treatment within the individual, who is viewed as having an organic, biochemical, or genetic disease. Like other medical diseases, mental disorders are diagnosed, treated, and provided with a prognosis. Medical interventions such as pharmacotherapy and hospitalization are emphasized. Stages of illness such as "premorbid" (preexisting), "acute phase" (active), "chronic" (persistent), or "residual" (aftereffects) are utilized.

However significant the medical breakthroughs may be, the biomedical model does not account for interactions between individuals (e.g., in the family) and between the person and the environment that contribute to and ameliorate stress. Furthermore, the medical model represents a linear-causal approach that does not recognize the multidimensional contexts of individuals' lives. Social work practice theory of the 1980s has recognized the limitations of linearity in the ecological perspective and life model of practice (Germain & Gitterman, 1980).

The biomedical model has been subjected to criticism from scholars in the social sciences. Mishler et al. (1981) emphasize the imbeddedness of definitions of health, illness, and patient status in the culture and the situation. Diagnoses are negotiated in conversations between doctors and patients, a process that suggests that psychiatric illnesses are "social constructions." These authors cite epidemiological studies, analyses of the relationship between economic factors and psychiatric hospitalization, and studies of the utilization of medical facilities to show that there are many conditions extrinsic to biological factors that influence patienthood.

Bader (1989), a psychologist, is worried about the pendulum swing from family dynamics to "biological reductionism." He states that for some time, psychiatrists have been losing ground to related professions; that emphasis on psychopharmacology and neurobiology fosters the dominance of psychiatrists. Furthermore, Bader finds the biological arguments inconclusive. That there is a "general correspondence" between the biological and psychological states does not prove that the biological causes the psychological. Similarly, the partial genetic correspondence that is found in schizophrenia does not prove "that biology is the primary cause of schizophrenia, that social or interpersonal conditions might not be the more important factor" (p. 46).

In this book, biological and social explanations are not viewed as competing paradigms; instead they are seen as inseparable and integrally related. Although professional segmentation of areas of knowledge has fostered the belief that mental phenomena are either biologically, psychologically, or socially based, persons are complex biopsychosocial wholes embedded in the natural, social, and material world. Exclusive attention to biological, psychological, or social phenomena belies human experience. The integrative biopsychosocial conceptual framework that is used in this book is described in chapter 3.

Diagnostic and Statistical Manuals

The third edition of the *Diagnostic and Statistical Manual of Mental Disorders,* the *DSM-III,* and its revision, the *DSM-III-R* (American Psychiatric Association, 1980, 1987) have also presented a challenge to social workers. Although some social workers hailed the arrival of a system that incorporates multiple axes (e.g., Williams, 1981), others were concerned that it would foster the labeling of clients (Sands, 1983). A survey of clinical social workers, 75 percent of whom were employed in mental health/psychiatric settings, revealed that the major reasons social workers use the manual are administrative—to obtain third-party payments and because their agencies require that it be used—rather than clinical (Kutchins & Kirk, 1988). The social workers who participated in this survey did not look to the diagnosis for guidance about treatment.

The preceding study also raised issues of professional integrity among social workers. Kirk and Kutchins (1988) found that social workers deliberately underdiagnose and overdiagnose clients. Underdiagnosis seems to be an outcome of protecting clients from psychiatric labels that can be damaging to them. In contrast, social workers overdiagnose clients because some diagnoses, such as V-codes (for conditions such as an occupational problem that are not attributable to a mental disorder but are the focus of treatment), are not accepted by third parties for payment. Furthermore, social workers often use the individually oriented diagnoses in the *DSM-III-R* when the problems appear to be interactional (e.g., family dynamics); and overlook physical illnesses that should be considered before a psychiatric disorder is indicated (Kutchins & Kirk, 1987). Social workers have been forewarned about their legal liability when they use such methods, even if they believe that they are doing so in the interest of clients (Kutchins & Kirk, 1987; Kirk & Kutchins, 1988).

The *DSM-III-R* also poses problems for women and members of minority groups. Certain disorders seem to be diagnosed more frequently in women (depression, agoraphobia, histrionic personality disorder), whereas others seem to be more characteristic of men (substance abuse, antisocial personality disorder, impulse control disorder). The diagnostic labeling system that is used seems to reflect "masculine-biased assumptions about what behaviors are healthy and what behaviors are crazy" (Kaplan, 1983, p. 786). Blacks and Hispanics are frequently given the diagnosis of schizophrenia when bipolar disorder is appropriate (Kaplan & Sadock, 1988). Furthermore, "black rage" toward a racist society may be misinterpreted as a mental disorder (Grier & Cobbs, 1980). Mental health issues of significance to women and cultural minority groups will be developed in chapters 6 and 7, respectively.

In the face of all these issues, clinical social workers employed in mental health settings remain responsible for competence in the use of the current diagnostic manual. The *DSM-III-R* is taught in many graduate schools of social work (Raffoul & Holmes,

1986) and is widely used in practice settings (Kutchins & Kirk, 1988). Although it is essentially a medical system (Kutchins & Kirk, 1987), it is used by a variety of non-medical mental health professionals. Many state licenses recognize the social workers' ability to diagnose and treat persons with emotional problems.

Clinical social workers in community mental health seem to be in an untenable position. Guided by social work values that uphold individuality and human dignity, they are at the same time required by their agencies to use diagnoses that give clients stigmatizing labels. Avoidance of labeling by underdiagnosis and promotion of eligibility for services by overdiagnosis are dishonest and unethical. To refuse to use the diagnostic system is to say that clinical social workers do not have the knowledge and capabilities of other mental health professionals who perform parallel psychotherapeutic roles in the public and private sectors. This dilemma will be discussed further in chapter 5, which covers legal and ethical issues.

Severely Mentally Disabled

The focus on the chronically mentally ill or severely and persistently mentally disabled in community mental health has come to the fore only recently, despite the fact that deinstitutionalization began in the late 1950s. In the early years of community mental health, many practitioners were working primarily with distraught but healthy individuals and families. Many of these were Caucasian and of the middle class. Work with these target populations was supported by educational programs at that time, which adapted theories and techniques oriented toward verbal, English-speaking, middle-class Americans. Mental health practitioners functioned as psychotherapists whose goal was to promote insight, modify behavior, and induce change. In the last 10 years, there has been a greater recognition that the severely mentally disabled have been neglected. Some writers are critical of the mental health system and workers for allowing their preferences for working with more rewarding populations to supersede the commitment to serve those who need help the most (Stern & Minkoff, 1979; Minkoff, 1987).

Toward the end of former President Carter's term, legislation targeting the chronically mentally ill, the poor, and other vulnerable groups was passed. This resulted in the development of thinking and programs supporting the retention of the severely mentally disabled in the community. Communities were encouraged to develop psychosocial rehabilitative programs, alternative living arrangements, and a comprehensive system of care. Demonstration Community Support Programs (CSPs) that were instituted showed that supportive networks and other rehabilitative services had the potential to help this population remain in the community.

Since the implementation of the block grant program through former President Reagan's Omnibus Budget Reconciliation Act, decreased federal support has been available for community mental health. This legislation established that federal monies would be allocated to the states, which would determine how mental health dollars would be spent. Some states have used block grants to support programs for the indigent severely mentally disabled. Nevertheless, public support of mental health programs for the chronically mentally ill is insufficient to meet client needs. Local communities are experiencing the fallout of inadequate funding with the increasing population of persons with severe mental disorders who are homeless.

Meanwhile methods of intervention with the chronically mentally disabled and their families have been developed and refined. Evaluations of research programs demonstrate that pharmacotherapeutic and psychosocial interventions used concurrently can reduce the recurrence of schizophrenic episodes (see chapter 9). Model programs of intervention with persistently mentally ill and difficult to reach clients have also demonstrated effectiveness. Methods used will be described in chapters 9 and 10.

New Client and Consumer Groups

Additional changes have occurred in the populations who are clients, client advocates, and consumer groups. Clinical social workers in mental health settings are now serving persons with mental disorders who also abuse chemical substances, that is, persons with *dual diagnoses*. Treating persons with simultaneous conditions requires expertise in assessing and treating chemical dependence and psychopathology. This population challenges the skills of practitioners and the willingness of community treatment facilities to accommodate clients with complex needs. The assessment and treatment of persons with dual diagnoses are discussed in chapter 11.

Although persons with depression and anxiety have sought treatment by mental health professionals for years, new consumer groups are presenting these symptoms. Some of these clients are depressed because they or a loved one is dying of AIDS; or anxious that they are vulnerable to this disease. Parents who have lost children from sudden infant death syndrome (SIDS) or suicide are an additional population that is asking for help from clinicians in community mental health agencies. Another group of clients who are presenting themselves for treatment are veterans of the Vietnam War and survivors of rape or childhood incest. Some of these clients suffer from the anxiety disorder "posttraumatic stress disorder." Because depression and anxiety are pervasive among clinical and community populations, expertise in treating these symptoms is needed. Clinical treatment of persons with depression and anxiety is discussed in chapters 12 and 13, respectively.

Another phenomenon that has emerged in the mental health field is self-help and consumer advocacy groups. These groups provide everyday life support to clients and an ideology that helps them avoid self-rejection. The National Alliance of Mental Patients and the National Mental Health Consumers' Organization are consumer groups that provide mutual support and promote the rights of mental patients. Recovery, Inc., holds self-help group meetings throughout the country. The National Alliance for the Mentally Ill (NAMI), comprised primarily of families and loved ones of persons with mental disabilities, works actively through local affiliates that provide information, outreach, and advocacy on behalf of their family member. The National Depressive and Manic Depressive Association is another consumer group.

These organizations, and many other national and local groups, constitute a network of support, care, advocacy, and education that parallels the functions of the formal mental health delivery system. Furthermore, they promote the empowerment of clients and their families, who previously were not provided with sufficient information, did not know what their rights were, and therefore did not have the wherewithal to make informed decisions. The empowerment of consumers and their families has brought vitality to the community mental health movement and consumer accountability to the mental health delivery system.

Postmodernism

The current era, in which technology, information systems, and the mass media are so influential, has been described as postmodern. During this time, one experiences cross-currents of ideas from other disciplines that affect social work practice theory, research, and methods of intervention. At the same time, social work is maintaining its traditional place as a provider of mental health services. Although medical and positivistic ideas about science predominate and bureaucratic pressures prevail, alternative perspectives that derive from naturalistic research, feminism, cross-cultural studies, and other sources also exert an influence.

Currently social work values are being challenged by demands of the field. The contradictions between values and practices among social workers discussed by Kutchins and Kirk (1987, 1988) exemplify the situationally driven behavior that arises at this time. Social work is faced with a postmodern challenge to reaffirm and act on its values at the same time as it responds constructively and effectively to the demands of the field.

REFERENCES

American Psychiatric Association. (1980). *Diagnostic and statistical manual of mental disorders (DSM-III)* (3rd ed.). Washington, DC: Author.

American Psychiatric Association. (1987). *Diagnostic and statistical manual of mental disorders (DSM-III-R)* (3rd ed., rev.). Washington, DC: Author.

Bachrach, L. L. (1976). *Deinstitutionalization: An analytical review and sociological perspective* (DHEW Publication No. ADM 76-351). Washington, DC: U.S. Government Printing Office.

Bachrach, L. L. (1986). The challenge of service planning for chronic mental patients. *Community Mental Health Journal, 22,* 170–174.

Bader, M. J. (1989). Is psychiatry going out of its mind? *Tikkun, 4*(4), 43–48.

Borus, J. F. (1988). Community psychiatry. In A. M. Nicholi (Ed.), *The new Harvard guide to psychiatry* (pp. 780–796). Cambridge, MA: Belknap Press of Harvard University Press.

Caplan, G. (1961). *An approach to community mental health.* New York: Grune & Stratton.

Caplan, G. (1964). *Principles of preventive psychiatry.* New York: Basic Books.

Caplan, R. B., in collaboration with Caplan, G. (1969). *Psychiatry and the community in nineteenth-century America.* New York: Basic Books.

Cohen, P., & Brook, J. (1987). Family factors related to the persistence of psychopathology in childhood and adolescence. *Psychiatry, 50,* 332–345.

Coles, R. (1970, November). A fashionable kind of slander. *The Atlantic,* 53–55.

Esterson, A. (1970). *The leaves of spring.* Middlesex, UK: Penguin Books.

Fischer, J. (1973). Is casework effective? *Social Work, 18,* 5–20.

Frankl, V. E. (1984). *Man's search for meaning* (rev. & updated). New York: Washington Square Press.

Freedman, D. X. (1984). Psychiatric epidemiology counts. *Archives of General Psychiatry, 41,* 931–933.

Germain, C., & Gitterman, A. (1980). *The life model of social work practice.* New York: Columbia University Press.

Goleman, D. (1985, April 30). Social workers vault into a leading role in psychotherapy. *The New York Times,* p. C1. (Copyright 1985 by The New York Times Company. Reprinted by permission.)

Gottlieb, B. H. (1985). Assessing and strengthening social support on mental health. *Social Work, 30,* 293–300.

Grier, W. H., & Cobbs, P. M. (1980). *Black rage.* New York: Basic Books.

Hartmann, H. (1958). *Ego psychology and the problem of adaptation.* New York: International Universities Press.

Hauser, S. T., Houlihan, J., Powers, I., Jacobson, A. M., Noam, G., Weiss-Perry, B., & Follansbee, D. (1987). Interaction sequences in families of psychiatrically hospitalized and nonpatient adolescents. *Psychiatry, 50,* 308–319.

Heineman, M. B. (1981). The obsolete scientific imperative in social work research. *Social Service Review, 55,* 371–397.

Hollingshead, A. B., & Redlich, F. L. (1958). *Social class and mental illness.* New York: Wiley.

Hopps, J. G., & Pinderhughes, E. B. (1987). Profession of social work: Contemporary characteristics. In A. Minahan (Ed.), *Encyclopedia of social work* (18th ed., vol. 2, pp. 351–366). Silver Spring, MD: National Association of Social Workers.

Jackson, D. (1977). The myth of normality. In P. Watzlawick & J. H. Weakland (Eds.), *The interactional view* (pp. 157–163). New York: Norton.

Jahoda, M. (1958). *Current concepts of positive mental health.* New York: Basic Books.

Kaplan, H. I., & Sadock, B. J. (1988). *Synopsis of psychiatry* (5th ed.). Baltimore, MD: Williams & Wilkins.

Kaplan, M. (1983). A woman's view of the DSM-III. *American Psychologist, 38,* 786–792.

Kellam, S. G. (1987). Families and mental illness: Current interpersonal and biological approaches (Part 1). *Psychiatry, 50,* 303–307.

Kessler, R. C., Price, R. H., & Wortman, C. B. (1985). Social factors in psychopathology: Stress, social support, and coping processes. *Annual Review of Psychology, 36,* 531–572.

Kirk, S. A., & Kutchins, H. (1988). Deliberate misdiagnosis in mental health practice. *Social Service Review, 62,* 225–237.

Kutchins, H., & Kirk, S. A. (1987). DSM-III and social work malpractice. *Social Work, 32,* 205–211.

Kutchins, H., & Kirk, S. A. (1988). The business of diagnosis: DSM-III and clinical social work. *Social Work, 33,* 215–220.

Langsley, D. G. (1985a). Community psychiatry. In H. I. Kaplan & B. J. Sadock (Eds.), *Comprehensive textbook of psychiatry/IV* (4th ed., pp. 1878–1884). Baltimore, MD: Williams & Wilkins.

Langsley, D. G. (1985b). Prevention in psychiatry: Primary, secondary, and tertiary. In H. I. Kaplan & B. J. Sadock (Eds.), *Comprehensive textbook of psychiatry/IV* (4th ed., pp. 1885–1888). Baltimore, MD: Williams & Wilkins.

Larsen, J. K. (1987). Community mental health services in transition. *Community Mental Health Journal, 23,* 250–259.

Leighton, D. C., Harding, J. S., Macklin, D. B., et al. (1963). *The character of danger: Stirling County study no. 3.* New York: Basic Books.

Maslow, A. H. (1968). *Toward a psychology of being.* New York: Von Nostrand Reinhold.

McCreath, J. (1984). The new generation of chronic psychiatric patients. *Social Work, 29,* 436–441.

Mechanic, D. (1989). *Mental health and social policy* (3rd ed.). Englewood Cliffs, NJ: Prentice-Hall.

"Mental health center violations alleged." (1990, May). *NASW News, 35*(5), 16.

Meyer, C. (1987). Direct practice in social work: Overview. In A. Minahan (Ed.), *Encyclopedia of social work* (18th ed., Vol. 1, pp. 409–422). Silver Spring, MD: National Association of Social Workers.

Minkoff, K. (1987). Resistance of mental health professionals to working with the chronically mentally ill. In A. T. Meyerson (Ed.), *Barriers to treating the chronic mentally ill* (pp. 3–19). San Francisco: Jossey-Bass.

Mishler, E. G., Amarasingham, L. R., Hauser, S. T., Liem, R., Osherson, S. D., & Waxler, N. (1981). *Social contexts of health, illness, and patient care.* Cambridge, UK: Cambridge University Press.

Myers, J. K., & Weissman, M. M. (1986). Psychiatric disorders in a U.S. urban community: The New Haven study. In M. M. Weissman, J. K. Myers, & C. E. Ross (Eds.), *Community surveys of psychiatric disorders* (pp. 155–175). New Brunswick, NJ: Rutgers University Press.

National Association of Social Workers. (1983, November). Membership survey shows practice shifts. *NASW News,* 6–7.

National Association of Social Workers. (1987). *Salaries in social work: A summary report on the salaries of NASW members July 1986–June 1987.* Silver Spring, MD: Author.

National Institute of Mental Health. (n.d.). Table 13. Number of scheduled staff persons by employment status, staff discipline and organization type: United States, June 1986. 6. Freestanding psychiatric outpatient clinics. (Mimeo, p. 6).

Offer, D., & Sabshin, M. (1966). *Normality: Theoretical and clinical concepts of mental health.* New York: Basic Books.

Pearlin, L. I., & Schooler, C. (1978). The structure of coping. *Journal of Health and Social Behavior, 19,* 2–21.

Peterson, P. D., & Cox, G. B. (1988). Community mental health staff utilization in Washington State: Characteristics and target groups. *Community Mental Health Journal, 24,* 65–82.

Raffoul, P. R., & Holmes, K. A. (1986). DSM-III content in social work curricula: Results of a national survey. *Journal of Social Work Education, 22,* 24–31.

Regier, D. A., Boyd, J. H., Burke, J. D., Rae, D. S., et al. (1988). One month prevalence of mental disorders in the United States: Based on five epidemiologic catchment area sites. *Archives of General Psychiatry, 45,* 977–986.

Regier, D. A., Myers, J. K., Kramer, M., Robins, L. N., et al. (1984). The NIMH Epidemiologic Catchment Area Program: Historical context, major objectives, and study population characteristics. *Archives of General Psychiatry, 41,* 934–941.

Reid, W., & Hanrahan, P. (1982). Recent evaluations of social work: Grounds for optimism. *Social Work, 27,* 328–340.

Rubin, A. (1984). Community-based care of the mentally ill: A research review. *Health and Social Work, 9,* 165–177.

Rubin, A. (1985). Practice effectiveness: More grounds for optimism. *Social Work, 30,* 469–476.

Sands, R. G. (1983). The DSM-III and psychiatric nosology: A critique from the labeling perspective. *California Sociologist, 6,* 77–87.

Scheff, T. (1984). *Being mentally ill* (2nd ed.). New York: Aldine.

Schulberg, H. C., & Killilea, M. (1982). Community mental health in transition. In H. C. Schulberg & M. Killilea (Eds.), *The modern practice of community mental health.* San Francisco: Jossey-Bass.

Scott, W. A. (1970). Research definitions of mental health. In H. Wechsler, L. Solomon, & B. M. Kramer (Eds.), *Social psychology and mental health* (pp. 13–27). New York: Holt, Rinehart and Winston.

Segal, S. P., & Baumohl, J. (1981). Social work practice in community mental health. *Social Work, 26,* 16–24.

Siporin, M. (1983). The therapeutic process in clinical social work. *Social Work, 28,* 193–198.

"Social workers vault into leading role in psychotherapy." (1985, April 30). *The New York Times,* p. C1.

Spaulding, E. C. (1989). *Statistics on social work education in the United States: 1988.* Washington, DC: Council on Social Work Education.

Srole, L., & Fischer, A. K. (1986). The midtown Manhattan longitudinal study: Aging, generations, and genders. In M. M. Weissman, J. K. Myers, & C. E. Ross (Eds.), *Community surveys of psychiatric disorders* (pp. 77–107). New Brunswick, NJ: Rutgers University Press.

Srole, L., Langer, T. S., Michael, S. T., Kirkpatrick, P., & Rennie, T. A. C. (1962). *Mental health in the metropolis: The midtown Manhattan study.* New York: McGraw-Hill.

Stern, R., & Minkoff, K. (1979). Paradoxes in programming for chronic patients in a community clinic. *Hospital and Community Psychiatry, 30,* 613–617.

Straus, M. (1977). *Normative and behavioral aspects of violence between spouses: Preliminary data on a nationally representative USA sample.* Unpublished manuscript.

Szasz, T. S. (1960). The myth of mental illness. *The American Psychologist, 15,* 113–118.

Szasz, T. S. (1961). *The myth of mental illness.* New York: Delta.

Szasz, T. (1965). *The myth of mental illness.* In O. Milton (Ed.), *Behavior disorders: Perspectives and trends* (pp. 15–25). New York: Lippincott.

Thomlison, R. J. (1984). Something works: Evidence from practice effectiveness studies. *Social Work, 29,* 51–56.

Turns, D. (n.d.). Lecture notes on epidemiology.

Videka-Sherman, L. (1988). Metaanalysis of research on social work practice in mental health. *Social Work, 33,* 325–338.

Weissman, M. M., & Klerman, G. (1977). Sex differences and the epidemiology of depression. *Archives of General Psychiatry, 35,* 98–111.

Weissman, M. M., Myers, J. K., & Ross, C. E. (1986). Community studies in psychiatric epidemiology: An introduction. In M. M. Weissman, J. K. Myers, & C. E. Ross (Eds.), *Community surveys of psychiatric disorders* (pp. 1–19). New Brunswick, NJ: Rutgers University Press.

Williams, J. B. (1981). DSM-III: A comprehensive approach to diagnosis. *Social Work, 26,* 101–106.

Wolfensberger, W., Nirje, B., Olshansky, S., Perske, R., & Roos, P. (1972). *The principle of normalization in human services.* Toronto, Ont.: National Institute on Mental Retardation.

World Health Organization. (1948). Constitution and basic documents. Geneva, Switzerland: Author.

I | A Framework for Practice

2 Historical Context

"One of the most unsettling facts that I encountered while reading about current trends and the rise of the social work profession in mental health was that I have lived through these progressions. It is not just a matter of reading the history of the community mental health movement, it is remembering how the institutions were run, remembering the mistreatment that I and many others endured, remembering the promise of better days from President Kennedy and remembering the disappointment at the slow pace of change. None of this can be captured on the pages of a textbook, but between the lines lie a hundred million stories of individuals who were both the victims and the beneficiaries of these changing times."

—Nella Garrett, a student

In the last three centuries, enormous changes have taken place in mental health practice in America. In colonial times, public policies addressing the needs of persons with mental health difficulties were virtually nonexistent. During the nineteenth century and the first half of the twentieth century, the emphasis was on institutionalization. At first the states and later the federal government assumed responsibility for the mental health care of their citizens. Since the late 1950s, deinstitutionalization has become public policy. Today the federal government is assuming a lesser role, whereas the states and the private sector are doing more. Although hospitals continue to operate at some cost, they are but one component of a system that focuses on community mental health.

The social work profession developed within a changing historical context. Prototypes of social workers participated in reform movements of the nineteenth century. With the emergence of the social work profession early in the twentieth century, pioneer mental health social workers carved out a niche for themselves. Later two world wars, the establishment of the National Institute of Mental Health, President Kennedy's "bold new approach," as well as President Reagan's Omnibus Budget Reconciliation Act affected the climate and way in which social work has been practiced. This chapter will describe the evolution of clinical social work in community mental health in relation to broader historical events in mental health history. The historical development of clinical social work will be weaved into the narrative on the changing concepts of mental illness and ways to help persons with mental health problems. The context will be set with a brief review of the European backdrop, but this chapter will concentrate on the American experience. Themes, issues, and alternatives that have appeared, disappeared, and resurfaced over time will be identified.

EUROPEAN BACKDROP

Moral Treatment

During the eighteenth century period of the Enlightenment, a philosophy of "moral treatment" of the mentally ill emerged in several parts of Europe. By this time, the medieval belief that mental illness represented the working of supernatural powers had declined; instead problems of the mind were attributed to biological causes. Nevertheless, the treatment of persons with mental disorders in the eighteenth century was unsophisticated. The idea espoused by the Greek physician Hippocrates (460–377 B.C.) that mental illness represented an imbalance of the "humors" (body fluids) was translated into the uses of bloodletting, enemas, and emetics to restore harmony. These "therapeutic" techniques, as well as restraints such as chains and straitjackets, were still used in European mental asylums (Katz, 1985).

In response to these punitive practices, "moral treatment" was introduced by Philippe Pinel in France, William Tuke in England, and Vicenzo Chiarugi in Italy during the late eighteenth and early nineteenth centuries (Mora, 1985). In 1792, while serving as superintendent of La Bicêtre, a hospital in Paris for mentally ill men, Pinel (1745–1826) freed the patients from their chains. A year later, he freed the women patients at the asylum La Salpêtrière. Pinel developed a form of treatment which combined physician control over the patient's will with kindness. Soon thereafter Tuke (1732–1819), a layman, together with Quaker Friends, opened a Retreat in York, England (1796), for about 30 patients. The Friends' philosophy was to provide a wholesome environment that included manual work, exercise, conversation, and reading. They avoided mechanical restraints and the influence of physicians. Chiarugi (1747–1792) headed a hospital in Florence in which the patient was afforded respect and was not restrained (Mora, 1985).

"Moral treatment" was essentially a humane therapeutic program that incorporated kindness, activity, and concern for patients' physical, emotional, and spiritual well-being. The individual was respected as a human being. With this approach, the use of restraints was avoided. Optimism about providing a cure prevailed (Dain, 1964).

Community Mental Health in Europe

In some parts of Europe, the mentally ill were integrated into local communities. A stunning example is the community of Geel in Belgium. This early "therapeutic community" grew around the shrine of St. Dympna, where persons with mental illness came to be cured as early as the thirteenth century. Dympna was a legendary princess who, together with her confessor, Father Gerebernus, fled from her widowed father, an Irish king, who had incestuous desires for her. The king followed them to Geel, where he killed the priest. Rather than submitting to her father's wishes, Dympna allowed herself to be beheaded. Through Dympna's heroic act, she conquered what was perceived as her father's madness. Subsequently a church and shrine were built to honor Dympna, who had been conferred with sainthood (Roosens, 1979).

The church in Geel attracted large numbers of pilgrims. While they waited their turn to participate in a healing ritual at the church, they stayed with families in Geel. The residents of Geel began to provide boarding care for the mentally ill who decided to remain. The community absorbed the "boarders" and had them work on farms or perform chores. With the support of a nearby public psychiatric hospital, the community continues to function in this capacity today. The open, tolerant atmosphere is exemplary:

> To the outsider it is striking that the patients are not stared at in the streets or watched in any special manner. The average Geelian accepts without question the patient who gesticulates, who dresses in an old-fashioned or extravagant way, who sits down on the sidewalk, or who talks to himself. Boarders have become so familiar that they are part of the landscape. In public there is no suggestion given to the patients that they belong to a special category of people. They are allowed to go everywhere like anybody else (Roosens, 1979, p. 96).

THE AMERICAN EXPERIENCE

Mental health practice in America incorporated ideas of moral treatment as well as practices from earlier times. These ideas were adapted to conditions in this country as it became transformed from an agrarian to an industrial nation. The history of mental health social work is connected with larger events in American history and in the field of mental health.

Colonial Period

During the American colonial period, persons with serious mental difficulties were handled in a number of ways (Leiby, 1978). One alternative was to place them in private madhouses run by physicians in their homes. These arrangements, however, had a price and therefore were open only to those whose relatives could pay. Another solution was for families to keep the individual at home. Home care, however, often meant that the relative was confined in an attic or cellar, restrained behind bars, or put in chains. A third alternative remained for those who did not have a family that was willing to be responsible. These individuals fell under the aegis of the poor laws and their treatment depended on circumstances. Some were farmed out to families who gave them various degrees of freedom. Others lived in the woods. Vagrants and individuals who were violent were likely to be put in jail (Leiby, 1978).

There were, however, a few early institutions. The Quaker-run Pennsylvania Hospital was the first to accept the mentally ill (1756). Another in Williamsburg, Virginia, (founded 1773) was the first public institution for this population.

The Beginnings of American Psychiatry

The American physician credited with fathering American psychiatry was *Benjamin Rush* (1745–1813), a signer of the Declaration of Independence. Considered a proponent of moral treatment, Rush believed that although insanity was physiological, intense intellectual activity or emotional shock ("moral" influences) could damage the brain (Caplan, 1969). The brain was considered "malleable," and thus experiences that promote health can alter the brain:

> The essence of moral treatment was the belief that, because of this great malleability of the brain surface, because of its susceptibility to environmental stimuli, pathological conditions could be erased or modified by corrective experience. Therefore, insanity, whether the result of direct or indirect injury or disease, or of overwrought emotions or strained intellectual faculties, would be cured in almost every case (Caplan, 1969, p. 9).

This interpretation of moral treatment recognized the impact of the environment on psychological experiences.

Rush's ideas and practices contained many contradictions. A medical practitioner who believed that mental diseases were physiological, he did not adequately explain the linkage between environmental and organic factors (Dain, 1964). On the one hand he believed in kindness and humane care. On the other, he used techniques such as bleeding, purges, restraining devices, and shock (Caplan, 1969). Rush's political ideas and practices contained similar contradictions. A slave owner, he was active in the abolition movement. Although he thought women should have educational opportunities, he believed that they should be subordinate (Alexander, 1986).

Nineteenth Century

Moral Treatment.   During the early part of the nineteenth century, a number of other influential American physicians of the mind (called *alienists* at that time) embraced "moral treatment." Eschewing many of the physical methods inherited from medieval times and used by Rush, these physicians created in both private and public hospitals an environment that was intimate, caring, and beneficent. The Quaker model of moral treatment was adopted by four of the eight American asylums built prior to 1824 (Dain, 1964).

Moral treatment was administered personally by the medical superintendents, who lived on the hospital grounds and shared meals and activities with residents. Desirable behavior was conveyed through example. Patients were encouraged to work, play, read, and, if interested, attend religious services. Hospitals that were guided by a philosophy of moral treatment

> . . . resembled what is now advocated by community psychiatry. Environmental factors in the causation of mental disorder were recognized and were counter-acted by manipulation of the physical and social milieu of the asylum. This was done in large measure by mobilizing staff and patients into small groups to support and control the individual strictly but without undue coercion. . . . There were attempts to involve other care-giving groups, such as teachers and clergymen, in the treatment of the insane. And, in spite of geographic isolation, violent dislocation of the patient from the community was avoided because the undesirability of long-term institutionalization was recognized and because the entire therapeutic program was designed to inculcate normative cultural values and modalities so that the individual could return to society better able to cope with its demands (Caplan, 1969, pp. 37–38).

Moreover, physicians established relationships with nearby communities by educating the public about insanity, inviting the community residents to events at the hospital, and sending patients to live or work in these communities (Caplan, 1969). Clearly many of the ideas and practices of community mental health of today have roots in moral treatment as it was interpreted in nineteenth-century America.

Although some persons with psychiatric problems were treated in benign hospitals that provided moral treatment, there were few such facilities and many were private. Other institutions that took in deviant populations did not distinguish between the mentally ill and other populations, such as the mentally retarded, epileptics, criminals, and the homeless. Consequently many of the poor mentally disabled were confined in almshouses and prisons (Rothman, 1971).

It was in this context that *Dorothea Lynde Dix* (1802–1887) began her campaign. Dix was a schoolteacher who retired when she was in her thirties, following an emotional and physical collapse (Kreisler & Lieberman, 1986; Marshall, 1937). After returning home from a trip to Europe, where she had gone to recover her strength, she was uncertain about what to do with her life. In 1841 she was asked to teach a Sunday school class in a jail in East Cambridge, Massachusetts. Upon assuming this volunteer work, she found poor women who seemed to be suffering from mental disorders imprisoned together with criminals.

> She was shocked to see them among hardened criminals, and entirely devoid of medical and moral treatment. Upon inquiry she learned that their only crime against society was their affliction. She inspected their quarters and to her horror found them bare, cold, and unheated. She asked the jailer why there was no stove or other heat in the part of the jail reserved for the insane, and why nothing was done to make their living as comfortable as that furnished for persons who had committed actual crimes against society. The jailer tried to dismiss the matter by saying that "lunatics" did not feel the cold as others, and that a fire would be very unsafe (Marshall, 1937, p. 61).

Subsequently Dix visited other prisons, almshouses, and other places in which persons with mental disabilities were confined in Massachusetts and reported her findings of widespread inhumane care and neglect in a "memorial" to the state legislature. For 30 years Dix traveled from state to state, investigating conditions of the poor mentally ill and advocating for more humane care in public institutions. She traveled 60,000 miles by train, stagecoach, and riverboat, paying personal visits to over 9,000 individuals (Marshall, 1937). Dix is credited with the expansion or creation of 32 mental hospitals (Katz, 1985). In contrast with later community mental health advocates, however, Dix worked for the creation of more or expanded state hospitals rather than for their reduction.

One of Dix's goals was that the federal government assume some responsibility for the care of the mentally ill. As a result of vigorous lobbying activities, Dix got Congress to introduce a bill that would have had the federal government appropriate land to the states for the benefit of the indigent mentally ill. In 1854 the bill was passed by both houses of Congress but was vetoed by President Franklin Pierce, who said that the federal government would be overstepping its powers if it were to provide for the poor in the states. An attempt to override the veto failed (Marshall, 1937). Nevertheless, Dix served as a model for future social workers to emulate.

Decline of Moral Treatment.   Despite the work of Dix, the practice of moral treatment declined. Success stories told by early advocates of moral treatment were not borne out by later experience (Caplan, 1969). In the latter half of the nineteenth century, the population of public asylums grew and changed in complexion. It now included large numbers of alcoholics, violent persons, and immigrants, who reportedly did not adapt to the benign regime of moral treatment. With overcrowded conditions and a population that was difficult to manage, methods of restraint from previous eras were resurrected, and programs that primarily provided custodial care became the norm (Caplan, 1969; Rothman, 1971). Consequently, the institutions became warehouses for poor social rejects.

During this period, the ideas of Darwin and the organic viewpoint in medicine dominated thinking. The mentally ill were considered genetically defective inferior beings, who were unfit for survival. In view of their alleged deficiencies, treatment was deemed irrelevant (Williams, Bellis, & Wellington, 1980). Although some medication was dispensed, medical attention was largely given to conducting pathological research on the brains of deceased patients (Caplan, 1969).

Still some community treatment took place during the nineteenth century. Early in the century the Eastern Lunatic Asylum in Williamsburg, Virginia, sent some patients to live with families and others to work (Caplan, 1969). According to the *Social Work Year Book 1935*, family care was in use in the state of Massachusetts as early as 1885 (Pollock, 1935). The same year an outpatient mental hygiene clinic was established at the Pennsylvania Hospital and two years later a similar clinic opened at the Boston Dispensary (French, 1940).

Reform Begins Again.   During the last few decades of the nineteenth century, a movement for reform developed. One issue that provoked interest was the false commitment of individuals to mental asylums. Some of the victims of this practice were women, the most well-known being *Elizabeth (E.P.W.) Packard* (1816–1897). Packard's husband was able to commit her to the state mental hospital in Jacksonville, Illinois, against her will because the law at that time did not protect the rights of married women. After Packard was successful in suing her husband and the superintendent of the hospital in which she had been confined, she led a national movement to promote legislation protecting individuals from commitment without a jury trial and to assure that those who are hospitalized receive humane treatment. Some states responded by authorizing committees of visitors who could investigate conditions in mental hospitals. Others gave patients the right to send uncensored letters outside the hospital (Grob, 1983; Wrench, 1985).

Another manifestation of reform was the establishment of the National Association for the Protection of the Insane and the Prevention of Insanity, which advocated for better treatment and protection of the rights of patients in public asylums. A forerunner of the mental hygiene movement that was to follow early in the twentieth century, this organization was founded simultaneously with the annual meeting of the National Conference of Charities and Corrections that convened in Cleveland in 1880 and was initiated largely by social workers, psychiatrists, neurologists, and lay reformers. Unfortunately this organization died after only four years of existence (Deutsch, 1949; Grob, 1983).

Another organization that was critical of the prevailing practices in mental institutions ("asylums") was the New York Society of Neurology. This group had concerns about the medical qualifications of physicians as well as the supervision, treatment, and rights of patients. Nevertheless, neither the lay reformers nor the members of the National Conference of Charities and Corrections nor the Society of Neurology was able to overcome the power of the Association of Medical Superintendents of American Institutions of the Insane, members of which ran the principal psychiatric establishments and which functioned as a self-contained "guild" that did not listen to criticism from outside its ranks (Caplan, 1969). Their control over psychiatric institutions continued until they were challenged by stronger forces in the twentieth century.

The Reform Movement in the Twentieth Century

The years between the turn of the century and 1920 encompass what is known as the Progressive Era in U.S. history. This was a period of reaction to the consequences of unregulated free enterprise and industrialism—poverty, arduous working conditions, and politics corrupted by business interests. During this era of reform, the evils of child labor, sweatshops, prisons, and mental hospitals were publicized through the printed media. The responsibility of the federal government to the people and of people to each other was reconsidered.

During the Progressive Era, environmental and psychological perspectives on the cause and nature of mental illness were dominant (Rothman, 1979). The social sciences looked at the impact of social class and economic conditions on individual well-being. The social work scholars Sophonisba Breckinridge and Edith Abbott (1912) incorporated a social environmental perspective in their influential book, *The Delinquent Child and the Home*. Meanwhile new psychological theories were also introduced. Pioneer social workers and reformers whose thinking was consonant with the emerging social work profession assimilated these ideas.

Mental Hygiene Movement.   An individual who, like Elizabeth Packard, became a social reformer following his institutionalization was *Clifford W. Beers* (1876–1943), a graduate of Yale University. Following three years of confinement in public and private mental asylums, Beers recovered and published in 1908 *A Mind That Found Itself,* an autobiographical account of his experiences (1907/1923). Beers described his suicide attempt, delusions, depression, and mania in vivid detail and reported being constrained in a straitjacket, confined in a violent ward, and treated sadistically by physicians and aides. This book was praised by leading figures in psychology and psychiatry of that time and was widely read. The same year that the book came out, Beers founded the Connecticut Society of Mental Hygiene and in 1909 he started the National Committee for Mental Hygiene, which later became the National Mental Health Association. Thus began the mental hygiene movement, which "has generally been seen as a turning point in psychiatric history" (Caplan, 1969, p. 179).

The mental hygiene movement, in which lay citizens and professionals participated, laid the groundwork for the later community mental health movement. Although Beers' original goal was the reform of conditions in psychiatric institutions, prevention became the mental hygiene movement's primary mission. The National Committee on Mental Hygiene collected data, studied legislation, conducted surveys of institutions, encouraged research and publications, and educated the public (Bassett, 1933). These are the kinds of activities social work planners perform.

One of the early supporters of the mental hygiene movement was the neurologist and psychiatrist, *Adolf Meyer* (1866–1950). An immigrant from Switzerland, Meyer held positions in several state hospitals before becoming director of the Phipps Psychiatric Clinic at Johns Hopkins University in Baltimore, Maryland, in 1909. Meyer's conception of mental health was holistic, encompassing the mind, the body, and the environment. He viewed individuals as social beings whose life situations influence their psychological reactions. Accordingly, Meyer required that his staff of physicians collect data on the patient's life history, family, economic circumstances, and neighborhood—a process that required visits to the patient's home, work, and community (Deutsch, 1949). Meyer envisioned the development of a comprehensive mental hygiene system in the community with psychiatric centers that are linked to state hospitals (Lubove, 1965). His ideas are compatible with the person–environment perspective in social work as well as the integrated systems perspective of the community mental health movement. Not surprisingly, his ideas were attractive to pioneer mental health social workers.

Early Social Workers in Mental Health.   *Julia Lathrop* was a social work reformer who worked with Dr. Meyer when both were employed at the state hospital in Kankakee, Illinois. A resident of the settlement house Hull House in its early years, she was a strong advocate for the mentally ill (Costin, 1986). Upon reading the proof of Beers' *A Mind That Found Itself,* Lathrop wrote the following statement of endorsement of the author's proposed national organization:

> I have felt for some time that a national society for the study of insanity and its treatment, from the social as well as the merely medical standpoint, should be formed. I am glad to follow in the line you have indicated and to have my name appear as one of the honorary trustees. I have talked with Miss Addams and she has agreed to the use of her name and will so inform you soon by letter (Beers, 1907/1923, p. 271).

Lathrop became a founder of the National Committee for Mental Hygiene. She later served as Chief of the United States Children's Bureau.

During the first decade of the twentieth century, several social workers held positions in hospitals for the psychiatrically impaired. Adolf Meyer's wife, *Mary Potter Brooks Meyer,* appears to have been the first such worker. A volunteer recruited by her husband, she visited psychiatric patients in the wards of Manhattan State Hospital and in their homes (Deutsch, 1949; Lubove, 1965). Mary Meyer assumed this responsibility in 1904, after a need for special personnel who would make linkages with the community was recognized (Deutsch, 1949).

Elsewhere other social workers were employed in similar capacities. *Edith N. Burleigh,* who began working in the Neurological Clinic of Massachusetts General Hospital in 1905, was responsible for conducting social investigations and treatment (Southard & Jarrett, 1922). In 1906 a social worker was assigned to the psychiatric wards of Bellevue Hospital in New York City (Southard & Jarrett, 1922). The same year, the New York State Charities Aid Association hired *E. H. Horton,* a trained social worker, as an aftercare agent, who helped patients find housing, employment, and other resources in the community. Her employment was a significant moment for the aftercare movement that had been promoting assistance to discharged psychiatric patients since the 1890s (Deutsch, 1949). In 1911 Charities Aid convinced the State of New York to have Manhattan State Hospital hire an aftercare worker. Within a few years, other states (Massachusetts, Illinois, Pennsylvania, New Jersey) appointed social workers in inpatient psychiatric facilities.

The social worker who, together with Dr. E. E. Southard, coined the term *psychiatric social work* and pioneered the field's development was *Mary C. Jarrett.* Jarrett was a caseworker who in 1913 became Chief of Social Service of the Boston Psychopathic Hospital, of which Southard was medical director. This formal psychiatric social work department was designed to be an integral part of the hospital. Southard and Jarrett described the social work function in their classic book, *The Kingdom of Evils* (1922). They stated therein that the social worker's primary responsibility was social investigation—gathering facts regarding the patient's medical and social history from the patient and others in the community—a function that was viewed as extremely helpful to the diagnostic process in certain cases. Another important social work responsibility was individual casework, through which patients and families were helped "to secure the largest measure of social well being possible" (Southard & Jarrett, 1922, p. 526). Social workers also mediated relationships among doctors, social workers outside the hospital, patients, families, and friends. The social service department assumed responsibility for research and the training of social work students. Southard and Jarrett's description of the functions of the psychiatric social worker and the social work department provided a model for others to follow.

World War I and Its Aftermath

World War I created conditions that promoted the development of social work practice in mental health. During the war, the American Red Cross organized a Home Service Bureau that looked after the families of soldiers and sailors. Trained Charity Organization Society workers, working for this bureau and providing psychosocial services to military families, departed from their earlier focus on the poor; similarly, middle-class families who did not have previous exposure to social workers became recipients of a new kind of service (Briar & Miller, 1971; Robinson, 1930).

Meanwhile many soldiers were experiencing "shell shock" or "war neurosis." In response to the emergency needs of soldiers in army hospitals and those who would be returning, Boston Psychopathic Hospital, together with the National Committee for Mental Hygiene, and Smith College, developed the first training program for psychiatric social workers at Smith College in 1918. Mary Jarrett, who was responsible for the curriculum of this eight-week summer program, later became associate director of Smith College Training School for Social Work (Clark, 1966; Deutsch, 1949). Around the same time other schools of social work—The New York School, Chicago School of Civics and Philanthropy, and Pennsylvania School of Social and Health Work—began to include psychiatric studies in their educational programs (Fink, Anderson, & Conover, 1968).

Although interest in the psychological aspects of human functioning was growing, social work of the first two decades of the twentieth century adhered primarily to economic and sociological perspectives (Robinson, 1930). The settlement house movement drew attention to the effects of poverty and environmental deprivation on human lives while the charity organization movement tried to remedy poverty through discretionary giving of alms and friendly visiting.

A key social work publication of this period was Mary Richmond's *Social Diagnosis* (1917), which outlined for emerging professional social workers a way in which to collect social data from a variety of sources and examine evidence before coming to conclusions. Richmond contributed to the development of a professional (i.e., scientific) approach to casework. Although she believed that she was interested in personality, she focused primarily on the person in relation to the environment (Clarke, 1947).

Emergence of the Psychological Perspective.   The 1919 National Conference of Social Work was the scene of a turning point in the history of clinical social work in mental health. Mary Jarrett presented a paper, "The Psychiatric Thread Running Through All Social Case Work," in which she argued that the psychiatric thread "constitutes the entire *warp* of the fabric of case work" (Jarrett, 1919, p. 587). In this significant presentation, Jarrett noted that half the cases cited by Mary Richmond in *Social Diagnosis* were characterized by psychiatric problems. Jarrett urged that the mastery of psychiatric knowledge be required of all social workers, not only those who specialize in psychiatric social work. Other speakers at this historic conference (Jessie Taft, Dr. Southard, Dr. Glueck) echoed Jarrett's promotion of the psychiatric perspective. In keeping with the change in the climate of ideas, Richmond's later book, *What Is Social Case Work?*, emphasized the psychological dimension more than her previous work did (Deutsch, 1949).

The state of knowledge of the mind, meanwhile, was expanding. In 1909 Freud came to the United States to give a series of lectures on psychoanalysis at Clark University in Worcester, Massachusetts. Freud was interested in neuroses, which could be treated in the community through intensive analysis of the individual. Although his views about childhood sexuality were shocking to some, his ideas about the impact of early life experiences on adult personality and his "talking cure" were stimulating.

By the 1920s psychoanalysis acquired a following among intellectuals and medical professionals (Lubove, 1965). It appealed to social workers for a number of reasons. Despite Richmond's "scientific" casework, many clients were not responding to the approach she outlined. Psychoanalysis recognized that unconscious, irrational, intra-psychic dynamics comprise forces that resist treatment. "The client had to be enlisted in the struggle against his difficulties—caseworker and client were to be allies against the enemy within" (Briar & Miller, 1971, p. 13). Freudian theory provided both a framework for understanding the personality and a means to intervene. Social workers who underwent psychoanalysis themselves recognized the benefits of understanding oneself.

In the third decade of the twentieth century, however, psychoanalysis was only one of a number of theories that were under discussion. Behavioral psychology was developed in this country by Watson. An American psychiatrist, William Healy (1869–1963), was concerned with the psychological problems related to juvenile delinquency. Although he acknowledged the influences of genetics, the family, and environmental conditions, Healy was interested primarily in the psychology of the individual. His focus on "mental imagery" anticipates cognitive theory:

> . . . whatever influences the individual towards offense must influence first the mind of the individual. It is only because the bad companion puts dynamically significant pictures into the mind, or because the physical activity becomes a sensation with representation in psychic life, or the environmental conditions produce low mental perceptions of one's duty toward others, that there is any inclination at all toward delinquency (Healy, 1915/1924, p. 28).

With the impetus provided by the mental hygiene movement, interest in prevention abounded during the 1920s. Not surprisingly, children—especially delinquents—became the population of concern. The Commonwealth Fund supported the establishment of seven child guidance clinics throughout the country, ushering in the child guidance movement. The focus on children appears to have some relation to the emphasis in Freudian psychology on the formative role of the early years of life. Moreover, the writings of Healy, which were read by social workers, emphasized early intervention.

Robinson (1930) considered the 1920s a period in which the psychological perspective became important to social work. Two schools of thought—psychiatric interpretation and behavioristic psychology—were dominant. The former was based on the psychoanalytic ideas of Freud; the latter on social behaviorism. Psychiatric interpretation at that time looked at symptoms as responses to inner needs and encouraged a search for cause–effect relationships. In contrast, behavioristic psychology looked at external factors and emphasized "habit training, conditioning and reconditioning in treatment" and saw "the interview as a stimulus–response situation where the behavior of the interviewer sets the response of the interviewee" (Robinson, 1930, pp. 83–84). Robinson's review of case records reflected a contemporary interest in interactive patterns rather than a history of social facts. The importance of the relationship between worker and client was recognized (Robinson, 1930).

According to Grinker et al. (1961), the psychiatric knowledge that practicing psychiatric social workers of that time had was primarily of the diagnostic categories developed by the psychiatrist Emil Kraepelin. Still social workers employed in psychiatric settings began to think of themselves as specialists. In 1926 they formed the American Association of Psychiatric Social Workers (French, 1940).

The trend toward specialization within social work aroused some concern that the profession would become splintered. The Milford Conference of Social Work Professionals attempted to reconcile differences in its 1929 report, *Social Case Work: Generic and Specific* (1929/1974). This document outlined common features of all fields of social work and unique features of special fields. The psychiatric social worker was said to be able to function in hospitals and agencies that give special consideration to personality deviations. Psychiatric social casework included participation in diagnostic work and individual therapy.

The extent to which social workers employed in psychiatric settings actually did participate in diagnosis and treatment in the 1920s is not entirely clear. Grinker et al. (1961) identified three functions of inpatient psychiatric social workers—history taking, providing information about resources to psychiatrists and patients, making visits to homes, schools, and employers, and taking patients on special trips. In these capacities, the social worker functioned as a "handmaiden" to the psychiatrist, carrying out medical recommendations "without developing an independent relationship with patients" (Grinker et al., 1961, p. 118). In the next two decades, however, changes in the economy and in the field of social work paved the way for more professional autonomy.

The 1930s and 1940s

During the 1930s the country was plagued by the Great Depression and the government became sponsor of an array of services to relieve mass poverty and unemployment. Meanwhile psychiatric hospitals were becoming overcrowded (Deutsch, 1949), challenging inpatient facilities to come up with alternative ways to take care of residents. "To relieve the situation and to obviate the necessity of building new institutions, it is proposed to place patients in family care to a greater extent than has previously been attempted in this country" (Pollock, 1935, p. 274). Social workers were to arrange and supervise these community placements.

The 1930s and 1940s saw the expansion of outpatient services in public agencies and private offices, with mental health teams consisting of a psychiatrist, a psychologist, and a social worker providing the professional personpower. The *Social Work Year Book of 1935* reported that child guidance clinics had long waiting lists (Stevenson, 1935).

Meanwhile a schism between two schools of thought within the social work profession was brewing. The Diagnostic School, based in New York, was influenced by Freud's psychoanalytic theory. This school emphasized internal unconscious processes, which were diagnosed and treated through social casework. The Functional or Rankian School, represented by Virginia Robinson and Jessie Taft in Pennsylvania, espoused a theory that focused on time, conscious action, the agency's function, and client responsibility. The social work programs based in these cities offered different theoretical perspectives and modes of practice to their students.

By the late 1930s psychiatric social workers had established themselves in Red Cross and Veterans' Administration services, public and private hospitals, child guidance clinics, mental hygiene clinics (some of these "traveling clinics"), general hospital clinics, educational institutions, mental hygiene societies and state departments of mental hygiene, public health nursing organizations, family welfare agencies, and private practice (French, 1940). Functions varied by setting. Psychiatric social workers employed by hospitals gathered social histories, worked with inpatients and their families from the time of admission to the completion of parole (period of supervision following discharge), promoted adjustment and environmental changes, and participated in programs of community education. Outpatient social workers working with adults performed similar functions, whereas child guidance social workers were principally psychotherapists. Social workers employed by mental hygiene societies engaged in community organization, program planning, and data gathering. For social workers in outpatient clinics, knowledge of the community was important:

> . . . social workers in all mental hygiene or psychiatric clinics need to know the problems of the whole community, to understand the aims and needs of the community agencies, and to develop cooperative relationships. Such community contacts are coming to be fully as important as the case work with clinic clientele (French, 1940, p. 63).

The ability to penetrate the community's system of services was a distinguishing feature of the social worker employed in mental health settings. Nevertheless, psychiatric social workers were not principally psychotherapists.

World War II and Its Aftermath

Experiences related to World War II raised the consciousness of the nation about mental health problems and the need for expanded services. The high rate of rejection of prospective soldiers by the Selective Service system highlighted the prevalence of mental health problems among civilians. The psychiatric difficulties experienced by inducted soldiers who had passed the psychological screening examinations demonstrated that mental health difficulties could be experienced by healthy individuals who are exposed to stress (Klerman, 1986).

During the war, psychiatric social work services became part of the complex of military medical services—hospitals, mental health clinics, convalescent centers, and the like. The introduction of psychiatric services into the Veterans Administration facilities stimulated the growth of mental health social work (Knee & Lamson, 1971).

In 1946 The National Mental Health Act was passed, ushering in a period of federal responsibility for mental health. This significant piece of legislation authorized federal funds for training mental health professionals (including social workers), research, and the development of community-based psychiatric services. Three years later the National Institute of Mental Health (NIMH) of the Public Health Service of the Department of Health, Education, and Welfare was established, and Dr. Robert Felix became its first director. The function of NIMH was to administer programs outlined in the 1946 act and to promote mental health education and prevention.

During the 1940s and 1950s social workers in mental health settings expanded their roles. The social data that they gathered on clients' families and home environments were used to help establish the diagnosis. Social workers had increased contacts with the community because of the placement of discharged patients on "parole" or "convalescent care" with their own or foster families (Fink, Anderson, & Conover, 1968). Furthermore, the shortage of psychiatrists at this time necessitated the use of social workers as psychotherapists (Nacman, 1977).

Meanwhile, the knowledge base of social work was changing. Following the publication of Anna Freud's *The Ego and the Mechanisms of Defense* in 1946 in the United States, psychoanalysis was revised by a group of American psychiatrists. The "ego psychology" that emerged was more palatable to social workers because it was less deterministic than Freud's psychoanalysis and more emphasis was placed on reality and conscious processes. Ego psychology was absorbed by the Diagnostic School, which began to emphasize reality relationships, adaptation, coping, and mastery. Still the University of Pennsylvania continued to embrace the functional approach. Meanwhile new developments in the field of mental health, as well as national and international events, paved the way social workers would be practicing community mental health.

Changing Approaches to Mental Health Treatment

The second half of the twentieth century saw dramatic changes in mental health treatment, which had long-range implications for social work practice in mental health. In 1953 the therapeutic effects of the drug chlorpromazine on psychotic and agitated patients were reported. The symptom control produced by the medication made it possible for hospitals to discharge some of their residents. Around the same time reports from England about a therapeutic community (Jones, 1953) stimulated thought about community alternatives to hospitalization.

During the 1950s an ideology centered around community mental health was coalescing. In Boston Erich Lindemann and Gerald Caplan developed preventive strategies such as strengthening social networks, providing mental health education, and restructuring communities (Klerman, 1986). Lindemann developed theory and practice approaches about grief as he worked with survivors of the Coconut Grove nightclub fire. Both men developed the theoretical base for crisis intervention, which has been used extensively by social workers employed in community mental health agencies.

During World War II and the Korean War effective strategies to treat "shell shock" and related reactions were developed in the military. Wartime experience revealed that psychiatric disability related to combat could be reduced by adhering to the principles of *immediacy, proximity, centrality, expectancy,* and *simplicity* (Ursano & Holloway, 1985). Soldiers who were seen soon after they were affected and in close proximity to the combat zone had a better chance of recovering and returning to their units than those who were sent to remote hospitals. A central coordinating system (called *triage*) was used to identify those individuals with emotional problems and to give priority to those with the most urgent needs. Treatment was simple and was accompanied by a high expectation that the soldier would recover. These principles are compatible with crisis intervention theory.

In 1955 Congress passed and President Eisenhower signed the Mental Health Study Act, which authorized a national study of mental health treatment. The need for a study grew out of concern about the high numbers of patients residing in public psychiatric hospitals and the high cost of their care (Klerman, 1986). The Joint Commission on Mental Illness and Mental Health that was subsequently established undertook a comprehensive study of the domain of mental health practice, the results of which were reported in *Action for Mental Health* (Joint Commission on Mental Illness and Mental Health, 1961). The commission's report recommended comprehensive mental health services in local communities, the continuation of state hospitals, and increased federal funding.

On February 5, 1963, President John F. Kennedy delivered an address to the 88th Congress on the issues of mental illness and mental retardation. This was a momentous occasion—the first time an American president gave a special speech on these issues. Kennedy recommended a "bold new approach"—community care:

> This approach is designed, in large measure, to use Federal resources to stimulate State, local, and private action. When carried out, reliance on the cold mercy of custodial isolation will be supplanted by the open warmth of community concern and capability. Emphasis on prevention, treatment, and rehabilitation will be substituted for a desultory interest in confining patients in an institution to wither away (Kennedy, 1963, p. 3).

In October of 1963 Kennedy signed the Mental Retardation Facilities and Community Mental Health Center Construction Act.

Between 1965 and 1980 a series of federal mental health bills fostering the implementation of community mental health systems was passed (see Table 2.1). In 1965 funds were allocated for the construction and staffing of community mental health centers. The federal government outlined the kinds of services that should be included in a community mental health system—inpatient, outpatient, community education, partial hospitalization, and emergency services. Later acts identified specific services (e.g., alcohol and drugs) to be offered and populations (children, older adults) that should be served. Medicare and Medicaid, as well as Supplemental Security Income (SSI), provided sources of financial support for the mentally disabled. In 1977 the National Institute of Mental Health initiated the pilot Community Support Program (CSP) in order to stimulate states to develop support systems to sustain the chronically mentally ill who were living in the community. The last progressive federal mental health act was the Mental Health Systems Act of 1980, which focused on the chronically mentally ill and other underserved populations.

Although the original intent of the report, *Action for Mental Health* (Joint Commission, 1961), was to provide community support for persons with severe mental disabilities, the programs that were implemented in the 1960s and 1970s were for a wide spectrum of populations, many of whom had less serious difficulties (Klerman, 1986). Nevertheless, deinstitutionalization—the movement of severely mentally disabled patients from the hospital to the community—had a momentum of its own. The ideology underlying this policy holds that community treatment is preferable to hospitalization. Accordingly, unnecessary admissions to hospitals are avoided and, where implemented, they are as brief as possible. Discharge is to the "least restrictive environment" that is

TABLE 2.1
Major Mental Health Legislation: 1946–1981

Year	Act
1946	National Mental Health Act (P.L. 79–487): authorized the establishment of the National Institute on Mental Health
1955	National Mental Health Study Act (P.L. 84–182): authorized the establishment of the Joint Commission on Mental Illness and Mental Health
1963	Mental Retardation Facilities and Community Mental Health Center Construction Act (P.L. 88–164): outlined five community mental health services and authorized expenditures for construction only
1965	Community Mental Health Centers Construction Amendments (P.L. 89–105): construction and staffing
	Medicare Act (P.L. 89–97)
	Medicaid established in Title XIX of the Social Security Act
1967	Amendment to the community mental health center law, providing an extension of the staffing and construction funding (P.L. 90–31)
1968	Alcohol and Narcotic Addict Rehabilitation Amendments (P.L. 90–574): funding for facilities providing treatment of drug and alcohol addiction
1970	Reauthorization of community mental health center program (P.L. 91–211): continuing staffing grants, providing for services for children and adolescents, supporting services in poverty areas, and including consultation and education
1972	Supplemental Security Income (SSI) program established (P.L. 92–603)
1975	Amendments to community mental health center program (P.L. 94–63), expanding number of required services, including drug and alcohol rehabilitation and prevention and services for the severely mentally disabled
1977	Reauthorization of the community mental health center program for 1 year (P.L. 95–83)
1978	Reauthorization of the community mental health center program (P.L. 95–622) for two years
1980	Mental Health Systems Act (P.L. 96–398): gave priority to services for vulnerable populations such as persons with severe mental disabilities; increased emphasis on advocacy; authorized for four years
1981	Omnibus Budget Reconciliation Act (P.L. 97–35): established block grants to states for drug and alcohol and mental health services

compatible with individual needs. Community agencies were to provide treatment of discharged hospital patients and, through early intervention and emergency services, prevent hospitalizations. The shift in philosophy from an emphasis on institutionalization to community treatment created a need for social workers who were knowledgeable about community resources and strategies of prevention.

Deinstitutionalization was supported by a series of judicial decisions that, in effect, established mental health policy. Wyatt v. Stickney (1971/1972), a case in Alabama, concluded that patients who had been involuntarily committed had a right to treatment and that adequate standards of treatment should be defined. The decision stipulated that the institution should have sufficient, qualified staff and that each patient should have an individualized treatment plan. Several cases (Lake v. Cameron, 1966; Covington v. Harris, 1969; Dixon v. Weinberger, 1975; Welsch v. Likins, 1974) affirmed that treatment should take place in the least restrictive environment that was compatible with a client's needs. These cases gave recognition to the individual's capacity for autonomy and promoted discharge planning for community alternatives to hospitalization, such as halfway houses, nursing homes, and family care homes. In the case of O'Connor v. Donaldson (1975), the Supreme Court ruled that unless an individual was dangerous (to self or others), a state hospital could not retain the person involuntarily (Budson, 1978; Levine, 1981; Perlin, 1986).

The preceding court cases supported the rights of clients. They are reflective of a shift in the national climate from an ideology of "state as parent" that looks after human needs, which was characteristic of the Progressive Era, to a civil rights orientation (Rothman, 1978). The earlier perspective was paternalistic; yet it promoted care. The reformist politics of the 1960s and 1970s, however, challenged the integrity of the parent. No longer viewed as benevolent, the state was held responsible for coercive practices and social control (Rothman, 1978). (For a discussion of legal and value issues, see chapter 5.)

While mental health policy was debated in the courts, social workers and colleagues in related disciplines questioned standard theories and practices. This discussion moved the profession away from a psychological perspective to a social environmental one.

One line of criticism was directed at the welfare system. Activists affirmed that welfare recipients have the right to public aid and to know the particular welfare regulations. Some social workers helped welfare recipients organize welfare rights organizations that enabled recipients to challenge unjust application of the rules and advocate for higher payments. Another focus of criticism was the sexist biases in the profession. Sexism within psychoanalytic theory (still adhered to by many social workers) was identified (e.g., anatomical inferiority of women; vaginal orgasms) (Chesler, 1972; Lydon, 1970; Weisstein, 1970). Public welfare was described as "one of our society's attempts to preserve the traditional role of woman as childbearer, socializer, and homemaker" (Glassman, 1970, p. 102), and social work was seen as a profession that extends women's stereotypical role as nurturer from the home to the community (Adams, 1971). (For a fuller discussion of women's issues in mental health, see chapter 6.)

In the field of mental health, the practices of involuntary commitment, cruel or nonexistent treatment, and inhumane methods of control were criticized (Cooper, 1967; Laing, 1967; Scheff, 1966; Szasz, 1970). Kesey (1962) dramatized the concerns of an emerging "antipsychiatry movement" in *One Flew Over the Cuckoo's Nest,* a play in which a spirited hospital patient is subjugated by the staff. Participants in the antipsychiatry movement, which included some social workers, were critical of the use of shock treatment, lobotomies, and restraints, as well as the authority of psychiatrists.

Many sought the liberation of psychiatric patients from the oppressive mental health system. This movement was concurrent with the Vietnam War, during which time some conscientious objectors performed alternative service as aides in psychiatric hospitals.

Social work responded to the social movements of this era by exploring theories that are alternatives to psychoanalysis (Turner, 1974). The systems approach, which facilitates the identification of problems in the social environment, emerged as a perspective that could be adapted to social work practice (Pincus & Minahan, 1973; Siporin, 1975). With increased recognition that problems do not reside exclusively within the individual, attention was given to family and group processes. Social workers employed in mental health settings became aware of systemic impediments to the realization of the rights of clients to treatment and discharge, and advocated on behalf of mental health clients.

At the same time as social workers were broadening their understanding of social functioning and modes of intervention, graduate-level social workers who worked directly and therapeutically with clients began to call themselves "clinical social workers." In 1971 the National Federation of Societies for Clinical Social Work was founded. The National Association of Social Workers and the Clinical Association worked vigorously to help pass licensing laws in the states and advocated for insurance coverage for the services of social workers. Licensure and vendorship made it possible for many social workers to engage in private practice.

President Carter conveyed concern about mental health issues by establishing the President's Commission on Mental Health in 1977. Subsequently (1980) the Mental Health Systems Act, which recognized the needs of the chronically mentally ill and other vulnerable populations, passed. In 1981, however, under the Reagan administration, the Omnibus Budget Reconciliation Act passed. This legislation established block grants to states, which would determine how these funds would be used. This act replaced the progressive Mental Health Systems Act and promoted a shift of responsibility from the federal government to the states. The implementation of the Omnibus Budget Reconciliation Act during the 1980s was accompanied by a decline in federal funding. During this administration, too, many psychiatric clients were threatened with the loss of their Supplemental Security Income when stricter criteria for disability were applied. Many of these cases were appealed successfully.

Although federal leadership in mental health faltered during the Reagan years, a couple of developments during this administration aroused attention to mental health needs. During Reagan's first term, John Hinckley attempted to kill the President and seriously injured one of his associates. Hinckley was diagnosed as a paranoid type of schizophrenic who was not receiving proper mental health treatment. Since Hinckley's apprehension and hospitalization, his parents have been strong advocates of mental health treatment. Another development during the Reagan administration was Nancy Reagan's "just say no to drugs" campaign. Mrs. Reagan provided a strong stimulus to primary prevention of substance abuse among youth.

In the late 1980s community mental health systems faced financial constraints and increasing demands to serve the indigent chronically mentally ill and other vulnerable populations. Advocacy groups such as the National Mental Health Association, the National Mental Health Alliance, and the National Depressive and Manic Depressive

Association, as well as local self-help groups, became a significant force in community mental health. Revenues for community treatment came from private insurance, medical assistance programs, and block grants. Although many states have been assuming increased responsibility for community mental health care of the chronically mentally ill (James, 1987), funding is insufficient to meet client needs.

Indeed, history has been repeating itself. Today some of the homeless mentally ill sleep in community shelters, reminiscent of the old almshouses, while others are jailed for such reasons as assault, disorderly conduct, theft, and trespassing (Belcher, 1988). Outrage about inappropriate care of the indigent mentally ill, earlier expressed by Dorothea Dix, is still in order.

Meanwhile social workers through their professional associations continue to advocate for persons with mental health problems as well as for funding for programs of rehabilitation and therapy and for continued research. Increasing numbers of social workers are employed as psychotherapists or case managers in community mental health organizations. The Council on Social Work Education has produced several publications on social work with the chronically mentally ill (e.g., Bowker, 1988). In January, 1989, the National Institute of Mental Health forged a national task force of leading social work researchers to assess the status of research in social work education and practice and come up with a strategic plan for directions in social work research in mental health. According to Dr. Lewis L. Judd, Director of the National Institute of Mental Health, "We expect this document to have a major impact on the development of the profession in general, and ultimately on trends in mental health research" (Announcement, 1989).

SUMMARY

The history of treatment of persons with mental health problems in the United States shows the impact of the European experience, as well as home-grown reform movements. Curiously, what one generation regarded as reform (building hospitals) became a bone of contention for the next generation. Nevertheless, twentieth-century reforms, such as community treatment, have roots in the past.

What came to be called "psychiatric social work" arose in the context of changing ideas about the sources of mental health problems (biological, environmental, psychological) and modes of treatment (hospital, community). Furthermore, historical events—in particular wars—contributed to the development of social work as a profession. Mental health developed as a field of practice for social workers during the Progressive Era. During the past 85 years, it has grappled with theories that are prevalent in the broader mental health field, sometimes finding it difficult to reconcile them with the reformist orientation and progressive values that characterize the profession.

Despite internal debates, the profession has trained and maintained a large coterie of clinical practitioners in mental health. At first these social workers were called social investigators or aftercare agents; later they were known as psychiatric social workers; today they are called clinical social workers. Although the profession has made shifts in emphasis over time between a focus on individual psychology and the environment, social work practice in mental health has required an integration of both perspectives.

DISCUSSION QUESTIONS

1. Discuss changes over time in the role of the federal government in relation to mental health treatment. What has contributed to these changes?
2. How have changing concepts and ideas about the role of biology and the environment affected treatment of mental illness?
3. To what extent have charismatic individuals influenced the course of mental health history in the United States?
4. On the basis of the history presented in this chapter, what progress has been made in the treatment of persons with serious mental health problems?
5. Which populations have been the primary beneficiaries of the community mental health movement?
6. Discuss the relationship of wars to the evolution of clinical social work practice in mental health.
7. How have changing philosophies of treatment affected the development of social work practice in mental health?

REFERENCES

Adams, M. (1971). The compassion trap. In V. Gornick & B. K. Moran (Eds.), *Woman in sexist society: Studies in power and powerlessness* (pp. 555–575). New York: Signet.

Alexander, J. K. (1986). Rush, Benjamin. In W. I. Trattner (Ed.), *Biographical dictionary of social welfare in America* (pp. 644–646). New York: Greenwood Press.

Announcement. (1989, January). Blue ribbon panel to set new directions for social work research, under NIMH sponsorship. National Association of Social Workers.

Bassett, C. (1933). Mental hygiene. In F. S. Hall (Ed.), *Social work year book 1933* (pp. 297–301). New York: Russell Sage Foundation.

Beers, C. W. (1907/1923). *A mind that found itself: An autobiography*. Garden City, NY: Doubleday, Page.

Belcher, J. (1988). Are jails replacing the mental health system for the homeless mentally ill? *Community Mental Health Journal, 24,* 185–195.

Bowker, J. P. (Ed.). (1988). *Services for the chronically mentally ill: New approaches for mental health professionals* (Vols. 1 & 2). Washington, DC: Council on Social Work Education.

Breckinridge, S. P., & Abbott, E. (1912). *The delinquent child and the home*. New York: Charities Publication Committee.

Briar, S., & Miller, H. (1971). *Problems and issues in social casework*. New York: Columbia University Press.

Budson, R. D. (1978). In J. Goldmeir, F. V. Mannino, & M. F. Shore (Eds.), *New directions in mental health care* (chap. 1). (DHEW Publication No. ADM 78–685). Adelphi, MD: National Institute of Mental Health.

Caplan, R. B., in collaboration with Caplan, G. (1969). *Psychiatry and the community in nineteenth-century America*. New York: Basic Books.

Chesler, P. (1972). *Women and madness*. Garden City, NY: Doubleday.

Clark, E. (1966). The development of psychiatric social work. *Bulletin of the Menninger Foundation, 30,* 161–173.

Clarke, H. I. (1947). *Principles and practice of social work*. New York: Appleton-Century.

Cooper, D. (1967). *Psychiatry and antipsychiatry*. London: Tavistock.

Costin, L. (1986). Lathrop, Julia Clifford. In W. I. Trattner (Ed.), *Biographical dictionary of social welfare in America* (pp. 478–481). New York: Greenwood Press.

Covington v. Harris, 419 F. 2d 617 (D.C. Cir. 1969).

Dain, N. (1964). *Concepts of insanity in the United States, 1789–1865*. New Brunswick, NJ: Rutgers University Press.

Deutsch, A. (1949). *The mentally ill in America*. New York: Columbia University Press.

Dixon v. Weinberger, 405 F. Supp. 974 (D.D.C. 1975).

Fink, A. E., Anderson, C. W., & Conover, M. B. (1968). *The field of social work*. New York: Holt, Rinehart and Winston.

French, L. M. (1940). *Psychiatric social work*. New York: Commonwealth Fund.

Freud, A. (1946). *The ego and the mechanisms of defense*. Trans. by C. Baines. New York: International Universities Press.

Glassman, C. (1970). Women and the welfare system. In R. Morgan (Ed.), *Sisterhood is powerful* (pp. 102–115). New York: Vintage Books.

Grinker, R. R., et al. (1961). The early years of psychiatric social work. *Social Service Review, 35*, 111–126.

Grob, G. (1983). *Mental illness and American society, 1875–1940*. Princeton, NJ: Princeton University Press.

Healy, W. (1915/1924). *The individual delinquent*. Boston: Little, Brown.

James, J. F. (1987). Does the community mental health movement have the momentum needed to survive? *American Journal of Orthopsychiatry, 57*, 447–451.

Jarrett, M. C. (1919). The psychiatric thread running through all social casework. *Proceedings of the National Conference of Social Work*, Atlantic City, NJ.

Joint Commission on Mental Illness and Mental Health (1961). *Action for mental health*. New York: Basic Books.

Jones, M. (1953). *The therapeutic community*. New York: Basic Books.

Katz, S. E. (1985). Psychiatric hospitalization. In H. I. Kaplan & B. J. Sadock (Eds.), *Comprehensive textbook of psychiatry/IV* (pp. 1576–1582). Baltimore, MD: Williams & Wilkins.

Kennedy, J. F. (1963). Message from the President of the United States relative to mental illness and mental retardation. (88th Congress, House of Representatives Document No. 58, pp. 1–14).

Kesey, K. (1962). *One flew over the cuckoo's nest: A novel*. New York: Viking Press.

Klerman, G. L. (1986). The scope of social and community psychiatry. In G. L. Klerman, M. M. Weissman, P. S. Appelbaum, & L. H. Roth (Eds.), *Social, epidemiologic, and legal psychiatry* (pp. 1–14). New York: Basic Books.

Knee, R. I., & Lamson, W. C. (1971). Mental health services. In R. Morris (Ed.), *Encyclopedia of social work* (16th ed., Vol. 1, pp. 802–813). New York: National Association of Social Workers.

Kreisler, J. D., & Lieberman, A. A. (1986). Dorothea Lynde Dix. In W. I. Trattner (Ed.), *Biographical dictionary of social welfare in America* (pp. 241–244). New York: Greenwood Press.

Laing, R. D. (1967). *The politics of experience*. New York: Ballantine.

Lake v. Cameron, 364 F. 2d (D.C. Cir. 1966).

Leiby, J. (1978). *A history of social welfare and social work in the United States*. New York: Columbia University Press.

Levine, M. (1981). *The history and politics of community mental health*. New York: Oxford University Press.

Lubove, R. (1965). *The professional altruist: The emergence of social work as a career 1880–1930*. Cambridge, MA: Harvard University Press.

Lydon, S. (1970). The politics of orgasm. In R. Morgan (Ed.), *Sisterhood is powerful* (pp. 197–205). New York: Vintage Books.

Marshall, H. (1937). *Dorothea Dix: Forgotten samaritan*. Chapel Hill, NC: University of North Carolina Press.

Mora, G. (1985). History of psychiatry. In H. I. Kaplan & B. J. Sadock (Eds.), *Comprehensive textbook of psychiatry/IV* (4th ed., pp. 2034–2054). Baltimore, MD: Williams & Wilkins.

Nacman, M. (1977). Mental health services: Social workers. In *Encyclopedia of social work* (17th ed., Vol. 2). Washington, DC: National Association of Social Workers.

O'Connor v. Donaldson, 422 U.S. 563 (1975), 1 MDLR 336.

Perlin, M. L. (1986). Patients' rights. In G. L. Klerman, M. M. Weissman, P. S. Appelbaum, & L. H. Roth (Eds.), *Social, epidemiologic, and legal psychiatry* (pp. 401–422). New York: Basic Books.

Pincus, A., & Minahan, A. (1973). *Social work practice: Model and method*. Itasca, IL: R. E. Peacock.

Pollock, H. M. (1935). Mental diseases. In F. S. Hall (Ed.), *Social work year book 1935* (pp. 273–277). New York: Russell Sage Foundation.

Richmond, M. (1917). *Social diagnosis*. New York: Russell Sage Foundation.

Robinson, V. P. (1930). *A changing psychology of social case work*. Chapel Hill, NC: University of North Carolina Press.

Roosens, E. (1979). *Mental patients in town life: Geel, Europe's first therapeutic community*. Beverly Hills, CA: Sage Publications.

Rothman, D. J. (1971). *The discovery of the asylum. Social order and disorder in the new republic*. Boston: Little, Brown.

Rothman, D. J. (1978). The state as parent: Social policy in the progressive era. In W. Gaylin, I. Glasser, S. Marcus, & D. Rothman (Eds.), *Doing good: The limits of benevolence*. New York: Pantheon Books.

Rothman, D. J. (1979). *Incarceration and its alternatives in 20th century America*. Washington, DC: U.S. Department of Justice.

Scheff, T. (1966). *Being mentally ill*. Chicago: Aldine Atherton.

Siporin, M. (1975). *Introduction to social work practice*. New York: Macmillan.

Social case work: Generic and specific (1929). A Report of the Milford Conference. New York: American Association of Social Workers. Reprinted 1974 by the National Association of Social Workers, Washington, D.C.

Southard, E. E., & Jarrett, M. C. (1922). *The kingdom of evils*. New York: Macmillan.

Stevenson, G. S. (1935). Psychiatric clinics for children. In F. S. Hall (Ed.), *Social work year book 1935* (pp. 350–353). New York: Russell Sage Foundation.

Szasz, T. (1970). *Ideology and insanity*. Garden City, NY: Anchor Books.

Turner, F. J. (Ed.). (1974). *Social work treatment: Interlocking theoretical approaches*. New York: Free Press.

Ursano, R. J., & Holloway, H. C. (1985). Military psychiatry. In H. I. Kaplan & B. J. Sadock (Eds.). *Comprehensive textbook of psychiatry/IV* (4th ed., pp. 1900–1909). Baltimore, MD: Williams & Wilkins.

Weisstein, N. (1970). "Kinder, küche, kirche" as scientific law: Psychology constructs the female. In R. Morgan (Ed.), *Sisterhood is powerful* (pp. 205–220). New York: Vintage Books.

Welsch v. Likins, 373 F. Supp. 487 (D. Minn. 1974).

Williams, D. H., Bellis, E. C., & Wellington, S. W. (1980). Deinstitutionalization and social policy: Historical perspectives and present dilemmas. *American Journal of Orthopsychiatry, 50*, 54–64.

Wrench, S. B. (1985). Packard, Elizabeth Parsons Ware. In A. Whitman (Ed.), *American Reformers* (pp. 627–628). New York: H. W. Wilson.

Wyatt v. Stickney, 325 F. Supp. 781, *aff'd*, 334 F. Supp. 1341 (M.D. Ala. 1971) and 344 F. Supp. 373 (M.D. Ala. 1972), *aff'd sub nom*.

3 | Conceptual Framework

C linical social work in community mental health is based on multiple theoretical perspectives and diverse sources of knowledge. The practitioner uses an integrative understanding of biology, psychological and social theories, as well as the social environmental context to guide the assessment of the client and client system and the selection of the most appropriate practice modalities and techniques. The clinician is further informed by research findings on effective intervention strategies.

This chapter begins with a description of the biopsychosocial conceptual framework. Next biological knowledge, psychological theories, and social environmental perspectives will be introduced. Later chapters on intervention will demonstrate how practitioners utilize multiple perspectives and sources of knowledge together.

A BIOPSYCHOSOCIAL CONCEPTUAL FRAMEWORK

Clinical social work practice in community mental health is guided by a biopsychosocial framework. As practice moves into the 1990s, knowledge from the biological sciences is increasing and theories about human dynamics, therapeutic change, and the social environment have been refined. Although social workers have generated only a portion of this knowledge, they are significant participants in its implementation in the field.

The biopsychosocial perspective is illustrated in Figure 3.1. The triangle shows that biological, psychological, and social phenomena operate in the same field. On the surface, emotions and cognitions appear to be psychological (intrapsychic) and behaviors, social. Nevertheless biological factors affect behavior, cognition, and emotions; interactive (social) experiences affect thought, behavior, and emotions; both psychological and social experiences (e.g., stressors) can affect the body (biological).

This perspective is predicated on an integrative model of health, illness, and disease (Weiner, 1984; Weiner & Fawzy, 1989). Accordingly, health refers to adaptive biopsychosocial functioning, that is, functioning that promotes, assists, and fosters the ability to live fruitfully in the social environment. Health is a positive goal that depends on

FIGURE 3.1
Biopsychosocial perspective

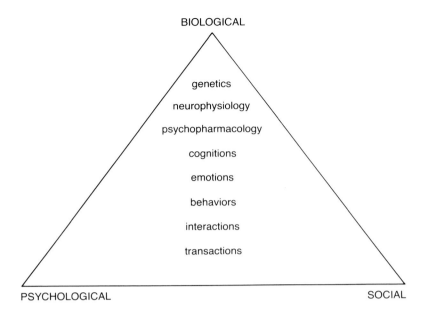

biogenetic, psychological, and social factors and is maintained by proper nutrition, good sanitation, stable political conditions, and an adequate standard of living (Weiner & Fawzy, 1989). Health can change as the person matures and acquires social experience over time. Disease is associated with biochemical, immunological, structural, functional, or genetic impairment, whereas illness is a psychosocial state characterized by malaise, dissatisfaction, or pain (Weiner, 1984).

In contrast with the western biomedical model, the integrative model views illness and disease as multifaceted and complex rather than as well-defined entities that have a single physical cause (Weiner, 1984). Diseases are heterogeneous (varied) and have diverse, multiple, and complex causes and manifestations. This model is not deterministic, that is, no assumption of linear cause–effect influences is being made (Zimmerman, 1989). Thus disease and illness are not necessarily related causally or sequentially. One can feel ill without having a disease, and one can have a disease without feeling ill (Weiner & Fawzy, 1989). Social supports can protect a person with a genetic predisposition from developing a disease, whereas poverty and other stressors can foster an outbreak or exacerbation of a disease (Weiner, 1984). Regardless of whether one is ill or has a disease, or both, one has a natural proclivity toward healing (Weiner, 1984) (see Table 3.1).

This model applies to mental as well as physical health. Accordingly, psychopathology is viewed as a disturbance in biopsychosocial integration and is manifested by difficulties in adapting to the demands of the environment. The person with psychopathology will have difficulty with cognition (or cognitive processing), performing adaptive behavior, emotional expression, or perceiving the demands of the environment. The person may experience or have symptoms of distress (illness) or manifest through laboratory examinations signs of structural or genetic impairment (disease).

TABLE 3.1

Characteristics of an Integrative
Biopsychosocial Perspective

Differentiation between health, disease, and illness
Multiplicity of influences and effects
Complex expression
Heterogeneity/diversity
Nonlinear causality
Health and growth as positive developments
Strength perspective
Proclivity toward healing
Client empowerment
Meaning-making

Take the case of a 26-year-old man named Daniel, who is a client at a state hospital aftercare unit. This man, who has been given the diagnosis of schizophrenia, undifferentiated type, chronic, has been hospitalized six times and has lived with his parents and in three group homes. Recently he moved into an efficiency apartment where he lives alone. Daniel has no overt symptoms of psychosis, but he has flat affect, responds slowly, and appears apathetic—symptoms that are viewed as "residual" or "negative." During a recent home visit by his case manager, Daniel appeared depressed and reported that he was not eating regularly and was sleeping a great deal. The case manager took him out for coffee at which time Daniel expressed his distress at having reached his goal of being independent while he remained lonely.

Daniel has the disease of schizophrenia. As the discussion on neurophysiology in the following section indicates, evidence of structural damage to the brain can be found in persons with schizophrenia in CAT scans and other neurophysiological tests. Furthermore, Daniel feels ill (depressed) not only because he has schizophrenia, but because he is alone and is wary about his future. Daniel's disease has residual effects that interfere with his social functioning. The biological, psychological, and social aspects of his disease are interrelated.

The evidence of a disease process is stronger for some mental disorders than for others. It is most convincing for schizophrenia and bipolar disorder. As for anxiety disorders and depressive disorders, evidence of a genetic or structural component is less clear, although these disorders are characterized by somatic symptoms. Most of the psychiatric disorders discussed in this volume have cognitive, behavioral, somatic, and emotional/affective symptoms. The symptoms converge in the individual, each of whom manifests the disorder differently.

This model draws and integrates knowledge from the biological, psychological, and social sciences and applies them in keeping with social work values. The particular areas of knowledge and theories that the clinician uses are selected because of their relevance to the particular case and on the basis of research evidence supporting their primacy. In trying to understand and work with a client with respect to social work values, a "strengths perspective" (Weick, Rapp, Sullivan, & Kisthardt, 1989, p. 350) is taken, that is:

> All people possess a wide range of talents, abilities, capacities, skills, resources, and aspirations. No matter how little or how much may be expressed at one time, a belief in hu-

man potential is tied to the notion that people have untapped, undetermined reservoirs of mental, physical, emotional, social, and spiritual abilities that can be expressed. (p. 352)

Above all, the client is viewed as *an individual with a disorder,* not a category. Knowledge about a particular psychiatric disorder and modes of treatment is applied with the idea that the client is a person with dignity and that even the disorder is uniquely manifested in the individual. Futhermore, the client is viewed as an active participant rather than a passive recipient of services. The client has legal and ethical rights (e.g., least restrictive environment, self-determination) that should be protected (see chapter 5) as well as the right to competent, informed, effective service. The social worker assures that the client participates in the development of the treatment plan and goal setting and that the client makes his or her own decisions to the extent possible. The clinical social worker recognizes that the client has the capacity for growth or self-transformation based on a perceived inner sense of his or her own needs (Weick, 1987). In no way does the clinician give up hope for the client. The social worker helps clients who are oppressed by forces of sexism, racism, handicapism, homophobia, ageism, or classism in their struggles, promoting their empowerment (cf. Solomon, 1976).

This perspective also assumes that clients actively engage in a process of meaning-making. As humans, they have some awareness of their place in the cosmos and their relationship to themselves, others, and the material environment. Existence has a purpose that is to be discovered and realized. Individuals seek wholeness, connectedness, actualization, and growth as they and their respective cultures define these qualities. Meaning-making can be viewed as a process that has a developmental course (Kegan, 1982), a spiritual quest, as well as a perceptual-cognitive activity (Sands, 1986). The dimension of meaning is a primary concern of existential psychologists (e.g., Frankl, 1984). As an integral part of the conceptual framework used here, it is related to biological, psychological, and social perspectives.

The following sections will discuss a number of biological, psychological, and social perspectives that contribute to a holistic understanding of the person. In each section exemplars of these perspectives are presented and explained. Although they are discussed separately, it is expected that the clinical social worker integrate them in practice. Figure 3.2 illustrates how these bodies of knowledge are organized in this chapter. A study case at the end of the chapter will help the reader gain practice in combining areas of knowledge and theory.

BIOLOGICAL PERSPECTIVES

During the second half of the twentieth century, research on the medical basis for psychiatric disorders has abounded. Findings of "revolutionary" proportions have contributed to understanding abnormalities of the brain, the establishment of diagnoses, and treatment (Andreasen, 1984). Although Freud always believed that psychiatric disorders are biologically based, it has been later scientists who have performed experimental work in line with this perspective.

In this section three areas of biological research will be reviewed—genetics, neurophysiology, and psychopharmacology. These are prominent, but not the only areas in

FIGURE 3.2
A biopsychosocial framework.

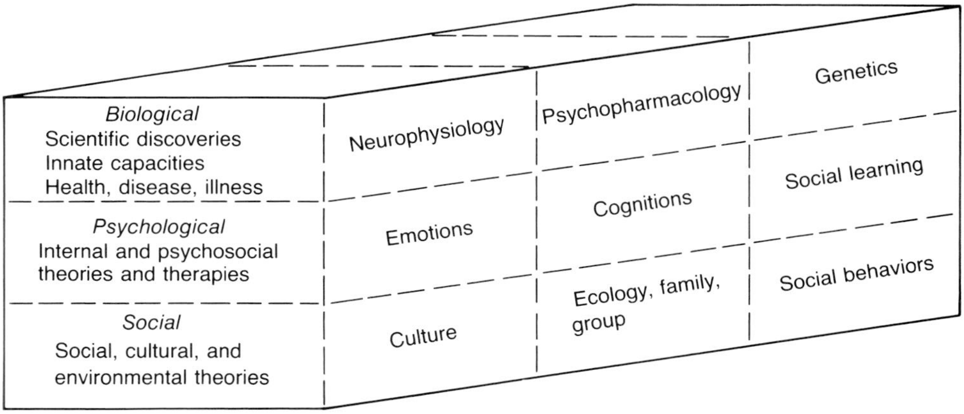

which significant research on the biology of mental disorders is making headway. Other areas include research on viruses, nutrition, endocrinology, and the prenatal environment. A fourth topic that will be discussed in this section is the maintenance of physical health.

Genetics

Inherited potential is believed to be involved in the etiology (cause) of a number of mental disorders. A large body of research examines genetic patterns associated with schizophrenia and mood disorders. Some studies have explored genetic components of alcoholism, anxiety disorders, and personality disorders. Strategies employed include family risk, twin, and adoption studies.

Family Risk. One means of looking at genetic influences is to study the prevalence of a particular disease in families with the disease and compare rates in genetically linked groups with the rate in the general population. Such research requires intensive investigation of the families of persons with an identified mental disorder through a standardized interview of relatives or from records. This research begins with an identified client ("proband" or "index case") and proceeds to "first-degree relatives" (parents, siblings) and more distant family members (Rainer, 1985). A genetic hypothesis is supported when the prevalence of a psychiatric disorder is higher among first-degree than more distant relatives, and when the rate among relatives is higher than that of the general population. First-degree relatives of persons with bipolar disorder, for example, have a 15 to 21 percent risk of getting unipolar (major depression) or bipolar disease, whereas the risk for the general population is about 1 percent (Rainer, 1985).

Twin Studies. Another approach is to study *monozygotic* (identical) and *dizygotic* (fraternal) twins. Clinical cases identified as afflicted twins are the basis for investigating whether the cotwin or other family members have had a similar mental illness. A significant genetic relationship can be inferred if the relationship between monozygotic twins is higher than that between dizygotic twins; and if the rate between dizygotic twins is similar to that among siblings (Rainer, 1985). The rate of cooccurrence is called the *concordance rate*. Research studies of schizophrenia in twins have revealed a higher rate among monozygotic than dizygotic twins (Gottesman & Shields, 1972; Kendler, 1988). The rate for dizygotic twins and siblings is similar. Furthermore, research has found that the closer the biological relationship, the higher the rate.

Twin studies have been undertaken for mood and anxiety disorders, too. With respect to bipolar psychotic mood disorders, the concordance rate for same-sex dizygotic twins is 23 percent whereas the rate for monozygotic twins is 68 percent (Klerman, 1988). For anxiety disorder, the rate for dizygotic twins is 5 to 10 percent; for monozygotic it is 30 to 40 percent (Andreasen, 1984). These rates indicate that genetics is a factor in anxiety and bipolar disorders and that its role in bipolar disorder is stronger than it is in anxiety disorders.

However illuminating these findings may be, they also raise questions about the social environment. If genetic factors were the only influence, the concordance rates between monozygotic twins would be 100 percent. Clearly other factors are involved. Twins share a similar prenatal environment; within the family, however, one of a pair of twins may be treated differently from the other (Rainer, 1985). Because it is difficult to separate the contributions of social, environmental, and genetic factors in the etiology of the disease, another approach has been used—adoption studies.

Adoption Studies.   Adoption studies are of a variety of forms. Some compare adopted children whose biological mothers are afflicted with a mental disorder with a control group of adopted children with normal parents; others compare children with and without a family history of a mental disorder with children raised by afflicted foster parents. The incidence of mental disorders among the children raised in different homes and the characteristics of parents are compared.

Studies of adoptees have been undertaken largely to determine the differential roles of genetics and environment in schizophrenia. Results indicate a higher prevalence of schizophrenia and of schizophrenic spectrum disorders (related disorders such as the schizotypal personality disorder) among children of schizophrenics than among controls (Rainer, 1985). Studies using the reverse strategy, that is, first identifying adopted adults with schizophrenic spectrum disorders and then interviewing relatives, have found an excess of schizophrenia and spectrum disorders among relatives (Kendler, 1988). Furthermore, paternal half-siblings of adoptees with schizophrenia have an unusually high rate of schizophrenia diagnoses, challenging the contributions of interuterine environment and early mother–child relationship (Rainer, 1985).

Overall, the twin and adoption studies suggest that genetics and the environment affect persons with schizophrenia, with genetics exercising a stronger effect. Kendler (1988) estimates that inheritance contributes between 60 and 70 percent to the variance in liability of schizophrenia, whereas environment contributes less than 20 percent. Nevertheless, these studies have their limitations. Controlled adoption studies require random assignment of children to adoptive homes. Ethically this cannot be done. Many of the adoption studies include different disorders under schizophrenic spectrum disorders, thus affecting the comparability between studies (Rainer, 1985). Moreover, family association does not affirm that there are genetic markers for schizophrenia and related disorders. Genetic information can be more clearly acquired through molecular genetic studies.

Molecular Genetic Studies.   With the development of DNA (deoxyribonucleic acid, which constitutes chromosomes) technology, molecular genetic studies promise to identify abnormal proteins and genetic markers (Kaplan & Sadock, 1988). These studies, however, suggest questions about what exactly is inherited. The association between schizophrenic spectrum disorders and schizophrenia suggests that the genetic factor is not specific for schizophrenia. Negative cases revealed in twin and family studies (i.e., the cotwins who do not become schizophrenic) suggest that some individuals who have a biological potential for the disease do not get it. It is hypothesized that reduced *penetrance* (manifestation of the disease) is associated with environmental factors, such as social supports, that mediate between genetic potential or vulnerability and a disease outcome. Genetic potential and vulnerability, however, are vague qualities that are difficult to trace to genes (Kety & Matthysse, 1988).

One possibility is that traits other than schizophrenic ones are genetically significant. Recent research on hospitalized persons with schizophrenia found that 50 to 85 percent of the experimental group but only 8 percent of the controls had deviant eye tracking. This trait has also been found more extensively in monozygotic than in dizygotic twins and in parents. Curiously, the trait has been found in parents of patients who do not have abnormal eye tracking. This research suggests that a single, dominant gene controls both eye tracking and schizophrenia (Goldin, 1988; Kety & Matthysse, 1988).

One obstacle to molecular genetic research is the heterogeneity of some disorders. It is more feasible to study one gene in a specific location than diverse genes in different locations. If the latter, *polygenetic inheritance,* proves to be the mechanism of transmission, techniques of molecular biology may not provide hoped-for findings (Matthysse & Kety, 1986).

Molecular genetic techniques have been used to identify genetic markers for Huntington's disease and depressive disorders. Huntington's disease is an inherited neurological disease that produces symptoms of dementia (cognitive impairment) and jerky movements in middle-age adults. Intensive genetic studies of families in Venezuela and the United States led to the identification of a specific gene for the disease on chromosome 4 (Gusella et al., 1983). This discovery led to the development of testing of at-risk individuals for the presence of the designated gene before they have children themselves. Research on siblings in families in which several members have depressive disorders found a gene on chromosome 6 that seems to be related to susceptibility to depression (Weitkamp et al., 1981).

Molecular genetic research on schizophrenia has produced contradictory results. One study of seven British and Icelandic families with numerous members afflicted with schizophrenia and related disorders located a gene locus for susceptibility to schizophrenia on chromosome 5 (Sherrington et al., 1988). Another study of relatives in northern Sweden produced evidence against linkage of schizophrenia to chromosome 5 (Kennedy et al., 1988). Researchers of the Swedish study remarked that there appear to be different locations for chromosomes associated with schizophrenia; thus, schizophrenia appears to be heterogeneous with respect to genetic etiology.

Family History.   Another means of assessing genetic factors is to look at the relationship between family history of the disease and responsiveness to medication. An example is found among persons with bipolar disorder. Lithium responders are more likely than nonresponders to have family members with bipolar disorder (Mendlewicz, Fieve, & Stallone, 1973). Family history of mood disorders, alcoholism, and the development of side effects to drugs can be helpful in the diagnosis and treatment of persons with mental disorders (Rainer, 1985).

Neurophysiology of the Brain

In recent years, attention has been given to neurophysiological aspects of mental disorders. With the help of new laboratory techniques, scientists have been able to obtain pictures of brain functioning and to locate structural damage and dysfunctions that might exist.

One such tool that has facilitated this process is the CAT (computerized axial tomography), or CT (computerized tomographic), scan, which creates a computerized image of the brain. Four other techniques provide more refined images of the brain and its functioning—PET scans (positron emission tomography), NMR (nuclear magnetic resonance) imaging, rCBF techniques (regional cerebral blood flow), and BEAM (brain electrical activity mapping).

PET scans provide high-resolution images of the brain and at the same time make it possible to observe how the brain responds to stimuli. "The ultimate high-technology brain-imaging technique," it lends itself to research (Andreasen, 1984, p. 179). PET scans, however, have drawbacks—they are expensive, complicated, and put participants at risk of pain and exposure to radiation (Andreasen, 1984).

Like the PET scan, the rCBF has the advantage of permitting investigators to observe the brain activity (function as opposed to structure). With this technique, the response of the blood in the brain to radioactive tracers can be observed. BEAM converts signals emitted in the EEG (electroencephalograph) into a map of brain activity (Andreasen, 1984; Taylor, 1987). The NMR technique produces images with a high resolution, with less risk than the PET scan. Instead of using radiation, it employs magnetism. Substances in the brain that are attracted to magnetism move, making it possible for pictures to be constructed (Andreasen, 1984).

Through these technological developments, evidence of structural abnormalities (lesions) among persons with schizophrenia has been accumulating. Enlargement of the lateral and third ventricles, malfunctioning of the frontal and temporal lobes of the brain and the limbic system, as well as atrophy have been associated with schizophrenia. The regions affected facilitate the reception, understanding, and organization of information from the world (Taylor, 1987). Nevertheless, these findings are not common to all persons with this disorder (Andreasen, 1984; Cohen, 1989). Furthermore, they are also found among individuals with mania and dementia (Andreasen, 1984).

Psychopharmacological Findings

Major changes in the understanding and treating of persons with psychiatric problems have arisen through the discovery of pharmacological agents that reduce disturbing symptoms. In the last 50 years, numerous drugs have been tested and then introduced. Advances in the development of pharmacotherapy have produced symptomatic relief for numerous psychiatric conditions and have enabled many individuals who would have been hospitalized for life to live in the community.

The discovery in the middle of the twentieth century of the effectiveness of chlorpromazine (Thorazine) in tranquilizing and reducing psychotic symptoms of schizophrenia was a major scientific breakthrough. This was followed by the development of other *neuroleptic* (antipsychotic) drugs and an increased understanding of brain functioning. The effects produced by neuroleptic drugs stimulated thought about the role of neurotransmitters in schizophrenia. It has been hypothesized that persons with schizophrenia have overactive dopamine systems which are blocked by antipsychotic medication (the dopamine hypothesis) (Johnson, 1984). Postmortem research on human brains has revealed that persons with schizophrenia have an excessive number of dopamine receptors. This finding was revealed in individuals who were treated as well as in those who were never treated with medication (Andreasen, 1984).

Another major scientific discovery was that lithium carbonate could control manic symptoms in manic-depressive (bipolar) disease. Although Cade discovered this relationship in Australia in the late 1940s, the drug was not tested in the United States until the late 1950s and 1960s (Fieve, 1975). Today lithium is the major drug prescribed for bipolar disorder. It is a "miracle drug" for persons who respond to this treatment.

Additional pharmacological agents that treat depression, anxiety, insomnia, and attention deficit disorder have also been utilized with success. Tricyclics such as imipramine (Tofranil) and amitriptyline (Elavil) are used to treat endogenous (biologically based) depression, as are MAO (monoamine oxidose) inhibitors. These drugs are also used to treat anxiety and sleep disorders. Medication used to treat schizophrenia, dementia, and bipolar disorder will be discussed in chapter 10, depression in chapter 12, and anxiety in chapter 13.

Although medication can treat symptoms, it does not eliminate the psychosocial problems of individuals who take the medication, clients' feelings about being dependent on drugs, or the side effects of the drugs. Medications such as neuroleptics do not cure the disease and only partially eliminate symptoms. Some prescribed drugs, especially those that treat anxiety and sleep disorders, are addictive. Withdrawal from an antianxiety agent is a painful, frightening experience (Gordon, 1979). Some of the neuroleptics inhibit sexual potency, a phenomenon that may motivate some clients to take themselves off medication.

Many psychotropic (psychiatric) drugs have side effects that should be monitored. Lithium, for example, has toxic effects, which can be prevented or regulated through blood testing. Antipsychotic drugs produce symptoms such as tardive dyskinesia, akathisia, akinesia, and parkinsonism (Cohen, 1988; Kaplan & Sadock, 1988). These effects will be described in chapter 10.

Another potential problem is the overprescription of drugs. One study in which the appropriateness of drugs was judged on the basis of specific criteria (Holloway, 1988) found that psychiatrists commonly prescribed more sedative-hypnotic and antipsychotic medication and anticholinergic agents (which treat side effects of antipsychotics) than needed. The author was also impressed with the extensiveness of the practice of polypharmacy (using more than one psychotropic drug).

Although social workers do not prescribe drugs, they are aware of their positive and negative effects on clients. Gerhart and Brooks (1983) advise social workers to be knowledgeable about medication, their side effects, and related legal issues (e.g., right to refuse medication) and to advocate for and against medication on the basis of the observed effects on individual clients. Social workers should understand the major categories of medication, know how long it takes for some drugs to be effective, and recognize harmful drug interactions (Levine & Dang, 1977). They should learn to distinguish between side effects of drugs and symptoms of psychopathology, where possible. Normally clients take a lower dosage of drugs in the community than they did in the hospital. Clients may, however, be given more medication than they need. On the basis of their observations, social workers may recommend changes to psychiatrists (Gerhart & Brooks, 1983; Matorin & De Chillo, 1984).

Physical Health Maintenance

The biopsychosocial perspective recognizes that the human body needs protection, care, and nurturance throughout the life cycle. Protection is provided in part by a safe, sanitary, living environment that is heated during cold weather. Persons without safe homes are subject to the vicissitudes of street life, where they may be physically beaten, raped, and robbed. Poor sanitary conditions in some homes are a seedbed for the development of physical disease. Homes in which physical or psychological abuse prevails are dangerous to one's physical safety and mental health.

Physical nurturance is fostered by eating a well-balanced diet. Eating healthy foods in moderation and regularly keeps the body going. Furthermore, eating can be a social activity that connects people with one another. Deficiencies and excesses in one's diet can lead to physical and psychiatric disorders. Persons with particular health problems, such as diabetes, must restrict their diets in certain ways. Clients on some psychotropic medications also must make changes in their diet.

Drinking is an activity that some people are able to do in moderation. Others, however, abstain because of their personal or cultural values or because they are alcoholics who cannot control their drinking. Except for persons who are on prescribed medications or are addicted to chemical substances, people do not need alcohol or drugs. (See chapter 11 for further discussion on chemical addiction.)

Physical health maintenance is a lifelong activity that begins in infancy when parents are responsible for maintaining their offspring's health. In adulthood one is expected to be responsible for one's own physical well-being by eating properly, getting sufficient sleep, exercising, and monitoring one's own physical health. Adults prevent health problems by consulting physicians and dentists on a regular basis for checkups and when they feel sick. Persons who take care of their bodies in this way are exercising control over their physical health.

During times of stress, the body can break down. Conditions such as poverty, widowhood, and job loss are associated with diminished resistance to disease (Weiner & Fawzy, 1989). When multiple stressors converge on the same person around the same time, a person's coping resources are pushed to the limits. At such times concurrent physical and psychological symptoms may develop. Similarly, when one is physically ill one may develop psychological symptoms that are a reaction to the illness. Here, too, the biological and psychological components are connected.

PSYCHOLOGICAL PERSPECTIVES

Psychological theories provide explanations for the inner workings of the mind. In this section two types of psychological approaches will be discussed—ego psychology and cognitive theory. These theories may be regarded as both "theories of understanding," which provide an explanatory framework for normal and pathological psychological functioning, and "theories of intervention," which provide guidelines for practice (Fischer, 1978). Although empirical findings on the effectiveness of ego psychological treatment are limited (Goldstein, 1986), its theory of understanding rests on research on infants (Spitz, 1965) and parent–child dyads (Mahler, Pine, & Bergman, 1975). Ego psychological theory was chosen also because of the richness it provides to understanding many mental disorders and its popularity among clinical social workers. Cognitive theory was selected because of its strong record of practice effectiveness and its coming to the fore as a significant theory for social work intervention. Although some behavioral theories have a psychological (inner) dimension, behavioral theory will be considered in the Social Environmental Perspectives section.

Today there are so many theories, practice modalities, and techniques that the practitioner is in a quandary about which ones to use and under what conditions. The psychological theories that were chosen for discussion are fundamental ones, but they do not in any way exhaust the theories that are used. These and many alternative theories are developed in other texts (e.g., Dorfman, 1988; Turner, 1986). Additional concepts (e.g., "stimulus window"), theories (e.g., attachment theory), practice approaches (e.g., rehabilitation), and techniques (e.g., thought stopping) will be introduced in chapters on intervention in Part II.

Ego Psychology

Ego psychology is a reconstruction of Freud's psychoanalytic theory, particularly his structural theory. Initially developed by Hartmann (1958) and his colleagues (Kris and Loewenstein), it has been enriched by the writings of Anna Freud (1946), Erikson (1950, 1959), and White (1959), as well as object relations theorists. Its departures from classical, doctrinaire psychoanalysis (especially the drive theory and psychic determinism) and its emphasis on the reciprocal relationship between the person and the environment make ego psychology particularly compatible with social work.

In psychoanalysis and ego psychology, three hypothetical structures—the ego, id, and superego—comprise the psychic system. The id represents impulses, desires, and wishes that know no boundaries; the superego encompasses the conscience and ego ideal; and the ego is responsible for perception, reality testing, and mediation. In ego psychology the ego is vested with more independence than it had in classical psychoanalysis. In psychoanalysis, the ego derives from the id and attempts to achieve the aims of the id in realistic ways. In ego psychology, both ego and id arise from an "undifferentiated matrix" that is present at birth; ego and id become differentiated from this matrix and develop separately and in concert with each other. The ego develops "apparatuses of primary autonomy," inborn capacities for perception, intelligence, thinking, motility, and the like, which can develop outside psychic conflict. In addition, the ego develops "apparatuses of secondary autonomy," defenses that are associated with conflict early in life but which are later transformed through a process "change of function" to interests, goals, and preferences. With the expansion and increased autonomy of ego functions in ego psychology, the ego became more than a mediator among the three parts of the psychic system and between the psyche and the external reality. The ego in ego psychology organizes, forms object relations, and promotes adaptation (Blanck & Blanck, 1974, 1979; Dixon, 1981; Hartmann, 1958).

Adaptation refers to the capacity to achieve a state of equilibrium with the environment. It includes the ability to survive, respond, make one's needs known to others, and solve problems. An active process, it depends partially on the possession of biological equipment and partially on the capacity of the environment to respond. According to Hartmann (1958), people are born with a capacity to adapt to an "average expectable environment," that is, an environment that is safe, provides food and warmth, and is reasonably nurturant. A child cannot be expected to cope with an abusive environment. Hartmann also posits that there is a reciprocal relationship between the person and the environment. Strengths and deficits in the person and the environment affect each other.

Ego psychology builds upon, reinterprets, and makes modifications of Freud's drive theory. Freud postulated that there are two primary drives that motivate human behavior—libido and aggression. Blanck and Blanck (1979) assert that these drives should be distinguished from affects, that is, libido and love are not equivalent; nor are aggression and hostility. On the basis of Freud's later work, Blanck and Blanck conclude that libido refers to the drive to unite or bond with others and that aggression refers to undoing connections (and consequently destroying them). This interpretation permits aggression to include the separation–individuation process, which was described by Mahler et al. (1975). The two drives, as revised, are complementary, rather than polar opposites. Like the ego and id, they are innate capacities latent in the undifferentiated matrix. In early life, the libido is dominant, fostering the development of object relations. Soon the drive to be separate and individuated becomes dominant. But both drives coexist and function in concert with each other (Blanck & Blanck, 1979).

Building on the ideas of Hartmann and other ego psychologists, White (1959) postulated that there is a source of motivation for human behavior that does not emanate from the two drives. This source does not seem to have as its goal the one Freud proposed, the reduction of tension. White identified a motivation for competence that is exemplified in exploration, manipulating objects, and mastery—activities that are pursued for their own sake. He stated further that participation in activities such as these may, in fact, increase tension rather than reduce it. Competence motivation, which is associated with the ego, engages the person with the environment.

White came up with a new term, *effectance,* to capture the feeling of efficacy (having an impact on the environment), which comes from the exercise of competence. He suggested that independent ego energies provide fuel for effectance. The emphasis on mastery of the environment through effective activity (that is, coping) is an important contribution to ego theory.

Ego psychology also includes a developmental perspective. The stage theory outlined by Erikson (1950, 1959) indicates that human growth is a continuous activity that occurs throughout the life span. Although deficiencies can lead to fixations at early stages, one has the potential to move back and forth among developmental issues and to resolve early issues in their adult form. The writings of Erikson and other adult developmentalists provide an alternative to psychic determinism, which maintained psychoanalytic theory fixated on early childhood experiences.

Ego psychology has also been enriched by the contributions of neoanalytic and object relations theorists in the United States and England who are interested in childhood development. Although there is considerable diversity among individual thinkers, they share an emphasis on the development of object relations. Objects are persons, the self and others, who take on a life of their own as structures that are introjected within the psyche. The infant develops into a social human being in the context of social interactions with significant others. Through an emotionally charged interpersonal relational process, the ego incorporates representations of the self and significant others into the self. At first infants fuse with their principal caregivers. In time and with some ambivalence, they become aware of differences and they become more independent. As they develop, they form mental images (internalized representations) of themselves and others, which allow them to carry significant others and others' images of themselves with them as they become separate. Successful negotiation of early developmental stages promotes the formation of permanent, stable personality structures (Blanck & Blanck, 1986).

Mahler, Pine, and Bergman (1975) describe a sequence of stages in which object relations develop, principally during the first 3 years of life. During these stages the child achieves increased autonomy and separateness at the same time as he or she forms a constant internalized representation of the image of the caretaker. This developmental scheme provides clues to understanding psychopathology that developed during the first 3 years of life. The psychiatric disorder that is most reflective of deficient development of object constancy is the borderline personality disorder. With this disorder, the adult continues to form "split" images of the self and others, experiences ambivalence, and develops dependent, "sticky" interpersonal relationships. The narcissistic personality, too, has unrealistic perceptions of the self and others, which are rooted in deficient self object formation.

The cumulative contributions of ego psychologists and object relations theorists make it possible to obtain a more expansive view of the role of the ego in adaptive functioning. The ego promotes personality organization and object relations (Blanck & Blanck, 1979, 1986). It regulates internal processes, links the person with the environment, and promotes mastery. The ego helps the individual distinguish between internal and external demands, control impulses, and develop interpersonal relationships. It fosters growth throughout the life cycle through a process of bonding (libido) and separation–individuation. The defense mechanisms described by Anna Freud (1946) and others are also associated with the ego.

Ego Psychological Treatment.   Ego psychology is implemented in the context of a therapeutic relationship in which the social worker conveys empathy, acceptance, and support. The therapist serves as an auxiliary ego to the client. Goldstein (1984) describes two types of ego psychological treatment: ego-supportive and ego-modifying. The ego-supportive approach aims to help the client adapt or achieve mastery over an immediate problem, crisis, or stressful situation. Intervention focuses on a current situation and engages the client's conscious thoughts and feelings. Change is directed at the person, the environment, and/or the interaction between the person and the environment. The therapist works with the existing and latent strengths of the client's ego and builds upon these. Through understanding, reflecting upon, and utilizing these capacities, the client comes to resolve an immediate problem and attain a sense of satisfaction in utilizing internal capacities and external supports. Ego-supportive treatment may be brief or long term.

Therapeutic techniques that implement ego support include, but are not limited to, sustenance/support, direct influence, ventilation, and person–situation reflection (Goldstein, 1984; Hollis & Woods, 1981). In sustenance or support, the social worker communicates empathy, acceptance, and reassurance. The client is told verbally, nonverbally, and through actions that the social worker understands what the client is going through, cares about the client, and is willing to be there for the client. Techniques of direct influence go beyond support in recommending certain courses of action. These include reinforcing an idea introduced by the client, offering suggestions, persuasion, and giving advice. (Because some of these techniques may compromise the client's right to self-determination, they should be used sparingly.) Another technique is ventilation. Here the client is encouraged to share experiences and express feelings that are associated with the experiences. The feelings may generate pain, embarrassment, anger, or anxiety. This technique can provide relief and release to a client who is experiencing a great deal of stress. Finally, person–situation reflection is recommended. When this is used in ego-supportive treatment, clients are encouraged to understand the circumstances and interpersonal relationships connected with the troubling situation, their own reactions and attitudes, and how the situation can be resolved.

The ego-modifying strategy emphasizes the development of insight and the resolution of intrapsychic conflict. Accordingly, past historical material is utilized and the transference that arises in the therapeutic relationship is interpreted. The client is engaged in a process of self-disclosure, uncovering, and working through recurrent maladaptive patterns. Generally ego-modifying treatment is long term and appropriate only for certain clients. Goldstein (1984) recommends this strategy primarily for clients with good ego strengths but some maladaptive patterns, but says that it can be used selectively with clients with more severe pathology. For the client who has developmental deficits that interfere with object constancy, the social worker becomes an object for the client and facilitates the development of object constancy. This kind of intervention takes a great deal of skill.

Techniques in keeping with the ego-modifying approach include reflection and interpretation. Goldstein (1984) recommends three kinds of reflection, which are described by Hollis and Woods (1981)—person–situation reflection, pattern-dynamic reflection, and developmental reflection. Person–situation reflection has already been described under ego-supportive techniques. With pattern-dynamic reflection, the client, in concert with the social worker, examines sets of behaviors or situations or defenses that occur repeatedly in a person's life, for example, getting into battering relationships. The purpose is to understand what is happening and what needs it fulfills, so as to set the stage for making changes in these patterns. With developmental reflection, the client looks at events of the present in relation to the past as a means to gain awareness of their connection and to promote progressive changes.

Ego-supportive and ego-modifying techniques may be used together or sequentially with the same client. During crises, ego support may be called for, whereas ego modification is used to promote personality change. Microcounseling skills such as active listening, reflection of feelings, paraphrasing, and summarizing can be incorporated in both approaches.

Ego-supportive treatment is beneficial to persons with severe mental disorders, such as schizophrenia, who need ongoing support yet cannot tolerate intrusive therapy. Ego-modifying treatment can be helpful to persons with borderline and narcissistic personality disorders as well as other characterological and neurotic difficulties. In this volume, however, therapeutic work with persons with personality disorders is not emphasized. Table 3.2 lists the applications of the two types of ego-psychological treatment that have been described to target populations and the associated techniques.

TABLE 3.2
Application of Ego-Psychological Treatment

Type	Target Populations	Techniques
Ego supportive	Severely mentally disabled Persons in crisis	Sustenance/support Direct influence Ventilation Person–situation reflection
Ego modifying	Borderline personality disorder Narcissistic personality disorder Other characterological and neurotic problems	Person–situation reflection Pattern–dynamics reflection Developmental reflection Interpretation

Source: Based on Hollis and Woods (1981) and Goldstein (1984).

Cognitive Theory

Cognitive theory focuses on thinking, beliefs, interpretations, and images. Associated with diverse theorists, most hold that emotional reactions and maladaptive behavior are mediated by thoughts. Cognitive theory has been intellectually traced to the Greek stoic philosophers (Beck, 1985). It was introduced to psychological thought by Adler and Kelly (Chatterjee, 1984). Today a cognitive perspective is shared by social scientists and therapists concerned with information processing, stress theory, interactional processes, self-efficacy, and irrational belief systems. Many have combined cognitive theory and therapeutic procedures with behavioral approaches in cognitive-behavioral therapy (e.g., Meichenbaum, 1977).

Cognitive theories have introduced a number of concepts that provide anchors for understanding. One is the *scheme* or *schema.* Piaget (1936/1974), a cognitive developmental theorist, proposed that in the course of acting in relation to the environment, the infant develops schemes or structural units that correspond with and organize experience. As the child grows, the schemes widen, become more complex, and become encoded in symbolic forms. Cognitive theorists have used the term *scheme* to refer to the individual's units of thought or information. Accordingly, one may have a scheme for one's parents ("they care about me"), one's friends ("they do not care enough about me"), and so on. Kelly (1963) came up with a related term, *personal construct,* to describe an individual's mode of interpreting experiences and anticipating consequences.

Another term used in cognitive theory is *automatic thoughts* (Beck, 1976). These are messages one gives oneself, often in a telegraphic form, which precede an experience of emotional arousal. The messages may be instructional, interpretive, self-praising, or self-critical. Persons experiencing depression, for example, may have thoughts about their own worthlessness; those with anxiety may think about unrealistic dangers that lurk in the environment. Automatic thoughts are evident in verbal self-statements and mental images. According to Beck (1976), automatic thoughts influence subsequent emotions and behavior.

Appraisal is a kind of automatic thought in which a judgment is made about the nature of an event and its meaning. Lazarus and Folkman (1984) view appraisal as a cognitive process that intervenes between the presentation of a stimulus and the development of stress. They describe three kinds of stressful appraisals—harm/loss, threat, and challenge. In harm/loss, a loss in physical functioning, property, or personal relationship is recognized. With threat, loss or harm is anticipated, usually on the basis of something that has already happened. Challenge is associated with possible learning or growth that may occur. Appraisals such as these, together with a person's reservoir of coping mechanisms, play a part in determining whether a person will go into a crisis or effectively manage a stressful life event.

Attributions, a term from social psychology, are causal explanations of an event (Sarasan & Sarasan, 1989). Associated with one's cognitive schemes, attributions blame, assign responsibility, or give credit to oneself, other persons, nature, or other phenomena. Usually a distinction is made between internal and external attributions, that is, whether one holds oneself or outside forces responsible for one's situation

(Rotter, 1966). Depressed persons tend to blame themselves for their troubles, regardless of whether or not they are responsible for the situation. In cognitive therapy, efforts are made to correct inappropriate attributions.

Two contemporary cognitive theorists are Albert Ellis and Aaron Beck. Ellis developed a therapy known as *rational emotive therapy* (RET). He holds that irrational beliefs (B), aroused by activating events (A), are responsible for the development of neurotic symptoms or dysfunctional behaviors (C). Beliefs that engender these consequences are generally grandiose, narcissistic, and unrealistic, such as the ideas that one must be loved by all people one considers significant; that one must be thoroughly competent; and that when one gets frustrated, the situation in which one finds oneself is awful (Ellis & Harper, 1975). These beliefs have an exaggerated quality and often use the words *should* and *must*. Irrational beliefs represent logical fallacies in which one misconstrues oneself, others, and situations.

Ellis recognizes that behaviors, beliefs, and emotions are related. By changing irrational beliefs through a course of therapy, dysfunctional emotions and behaviors dissipate and are replaced by constructive ones. Therapy consists of identifying irrational ideas, refuting them through logical argument, and replacing irrational with rational "self-talk." RET is didactic and experiential. It utilizes homework assignments, role play, practice exercises, and imagery. Generally it is short term and concerned with conscious, current experiences (Ellis, 1979).

Aaron Beck's cognitive theory and therapy is similar to Ellis's. Beck (1976, 1985) believes that "automatic thoughts" trigger affects (anxiety, sadness, anger, affection) and behavior (flight, withdrawal, attack, approach). Characteristic of normal and psychopathological reactions, automatic thoughts can become so distorted that they result in dysfunctional responses. These thoughts are endowed with meaning that is idiosyncratic to the individual and specific to the psychopathological syndrome.

Beck (1985) identified several cognitive errors made by depressed and anxious people. One, called *selective abstraction,* is a generalization that accounts for only one aspect of a situation, while at the same time other components of the situation are ignored (e.g., "I am a bad mother because my child got a C"). This is similar to another error, *overgeneralization,* in which an inference resting on one experience is applied to all like situations ("I can't do anything right"). Another logical error is *arbitrary inference.* Here an inaccurate conclusion is drawn from a neutral experience (e.g., "Jack is avoiding me" when Jack, in fact, did not see anyone). With *personalization* one endows events with meaning related to oneself. In this case others' statements or affective responses ("mother looks perturbed") are viewed as causally related to one's own behavior ("I hurt her feelings"). Another cognitive error is *dichotomous* (or *polarized*) *thinking.* Here the individual perceives only two contrasting and extreme alternatives—a phenomenon that is often described as "tunnel vision." With *magnification or minimization* one exaggerates the difficulty of a task or underestimates one's ability to accomplish it.

Depressed persons make cognitive errors to support negative pictures of themselves, their experiences, and the outlook for the future—three dimensions that Beck (1985) describes as the *cognitive triad.* They may, for example, generalize from a single experience (e.g., "I was turned down for a job") to prospects in the distant future ("no one will ever hire me"). They see themselves as totally worthless and attribute neutral actions on the part of others to themselves. Anxious persons err in their interpretation of signals of danger. Accordingly, they become apprehensive in situations that are objectively safe. Thoughts focus on an anticipated "catastrophe," such as death, losing control, or failure.

Beck's treatment appears to give more attention to the therapeutic relationship than Ellis'. Therapist and client are viewed as partners working together to bring about cognitive restructuring. The therapist conveys warmth, acceptance, and understanding. Like the RET therapist, Beck's therapist is an intellectual guide, who leads the client in understanding the belief system that is related to the problem and in making changes in thinking and behavior.

Cognitive treatment begins with helping the client identify automatic thoughts (Beck, 1985). The client may be asked to describe a stressful situation in order to recognize the thought that precipitated it; or to keep a diary of fleeting thoughts. After the thoughts are identified, the cognitive errors embedded in the thoughts are discussed. Distortions in thinking are identified and alternative explanations are proposed. This process, *reattribution training,* opens up alternative ways of thinking (schemes) to the client. Next cognitive distortions, such as overgeneralizations, are subjected to an empirical test in the outside world (Beck, 1985). The client is given the task of testing false expectations (e.g., "no one wants to talk to me") by initiating new activities (e.g., talking to a number of people and documenting their responses). These exercises may be rehearsed in advance and are discussed after they are performed. Afterward the client's distortions are reexamined in the light of empirical findings. The client's level of stress is monitored during the course of treatment (Beck, 1985).

Cognitive therapy is said to help individuals understand and modify thoughts associated with anxiety, depression, phobias, obsessions, compulsions, mania, delusions, and other conditions (Beck, 1976, 1985) (see Table 3.3). Usually therapy is brief and focused on an immediate problem. In this volume special attention will be given to Beck's method of treating depression (see chapter 12). Empirical findings on Beck's

TABLE 3.3
Application of Cognitive Therapies

Concepts	Targeted Symptoms	Techniques
Schemes	Depression	Identify irrational ideas or automatic
Automatic thoughts	Anxiety	thoughts
Appraisal	Phobias	Refutation
Attributions	Obsessions	Reattribution training
Cognitive errors	Compulsions	Empirical testing
	Mania	
	Delusions	

Sources: Based on Bandura (1982), Beck (1976, 1985), Ellis (1979), and Lazarus and Folkman (1984).

model of treatment of depression indicate that not only is cognitive therapy effective, it is sometimes superior to treatment with antidepressant drugs used alone (Beck, 1985).

Social work practice theory contains its own adaptation of cognitive theory. Goldstein (1982) views cognitive theory as "educational rather than therapeutic" (p. 540), that is, it is "concerned with the patterned ways in which clients construct and give meaning to their individual versions of reality" (p. 541). Berlin (1980) sees potential in social work's adopting a cognitive-learning perspective that incorporates cognitive and social learning theories. Social learning and other behavioral theories will be discussed in the next section.

SOCIAL ENVIRONMENTAL PERSPECTIVES

Social work is unique in its orientation toward the environment, the context, the culture, and social interactions. The person-in-situation perspective has been a unifying theme throughout the history of social work. Knowledge of the social environment has been created by social workers as well as colleagues in related disciplines. A few of the theoretical perspectives that attend to the social environment will be discussed here.

Behavioral Theories

Behavioral theories are concerned with environmental events or conditions that surround behaviors. These theories assume that regardless of whether behaviors are adaptive or maladaptive, they are learned. Through an understanding of scientific principles of learning, one can implement procedures that extinguish, maintain, or modify existing behaviors and foster the development of new ones.

Behavioral theories are empirically grounded. Originally based on animal research, they have been carefully applied to and researched in relation to human individuals and groups. Behavioral therapies employ rigorous scientific procedures in the assessment process, during implementation, and in evaluation. In each case, specific, observed, problematic behaviors are identified, and changes are implemented, monitored, and measured. Behavioral therapies have a strong record of practice effectiveness (Thomlison, 1986).

Within the behavioral school, there are three major approaches, each of which has contributed to an understanding of the person in relation to the environment and to therapeutic approaches. These are respondent (classical) conditioning, operant (instrumental) conditioning, and social learning theory. Although these schools emerged sequentially, in practice their boundaries have come to be blurred. As indicated, some behavioral therapies are informed by and integrated with the cognitive perspective.

Respondent Conditioning. *Respondent conditioning* was the earliest of the behavioral theories to appear. Also called classical conditioning and stimulus–response (S-R) theory, it was discovered by the Russian physiologist, Pavlov, who, in the course of his work with dogs, noticed that the dogs produced saliva automatically when they were given meat, a reaction he called an *unconditioned reflex.* But salivation also occurred in response to a bell that had been previously presented together with the meat but was later presented alone. Pavlov concluded that the bell, a neutral stimulus, acquired the capacity of the meat, a natural stimulus, to evoke the response after the two were paired together a few times. Pavlov called the meat an *unconditioned stimulus* (US) and the salivation an *unconditioned response* (UR) and determined that these were connected through a biological, reflexive process. He described the bell as a *conditioned stimulus* (CS) and the saliva produced by the bell alone a *conditioned response* (CR) and concluded that these became connected through a process of pairing or association (Chance, 1979).

Pavlov also noticed that dogs would salivate when something similar to the conditioned stimulus was presented, for example, a bell with a different tone. He called this tendency to respond to related stimuli *stimulus generalization* (Chance, 1979). Nevertheless, dogs could be taught to discriminate between similar stimuli when they were reinforced (or rewarded) for responding to some but not to other objects. Pavlov called differential conditioning *stimulus discrimination* (Chance, 1979).

In the process of experimentation, Pavlov induced dysfunctional behavior in the laboratory. Dogs that had learned to discriminate between similar stimuli (e.g., a circle and an ellipse) were asked to make finer and finer distinctions between two closely related pictures. When the dogs reached the limits of their capacity to discriminate, they became aggressive. Pavlov used the term *experimental neurosis* to characterize the dogs' behavior. It demonstrated that dysfunctional behavior is a product of frustrating environmental conditions (Chance, 1979).

Two therapeutic procedures are based on respondent conditioning. One, *extinction,* is based on Pavlov's discovery that a conditioned response could be eliminated. If the conditioned stimulus is presented repeatedly without the unconditioned stimulus, the association between conditioned and unconditioned stimuli weakens. The result is *extinction.* The principle of extinction is used to eliminate undesirable behaviors.

Another therapeutic technique that is based on principles of respondent conditioning is *systematic desensitization.* Developed by Wolpe (1982), systematic desensitization pairs an unconditioned stimulus, such as relaxation exercises, with a conditioned stimulus (e.g., a mental image of a situation about which one is phobic). A client who begins the session with relaxation exercises is presented with a hierarchy of situations, from the least anxiety provoking to the most, to imagine. The client participates in this exercise up to the point of experiencing anxiety. In subsequent sessions, the client proceeds through the hierarchy of situations, increasing tolerance along the way.

Systematic desensitization is based on the principle of *reciprocal inhibition* (Wolpe, 1982). Relaxation, an inhibiting stimulus, produces an effect that is the opposite of anxiety. By pairing relaxation with mental images of situations producing a phobia, the bond between the phobic situation and the anxiety loosens. The result is the elimination of an undesired (phobic) response. Systematic desensitization does, however, work with cognitions (mental imagery), placing it in the borderland between a behavioral and a cognitive technique (Wolpe, 1982).

Operant Conditioning.   *Operant conditioning* is a more widely held current behavioral theory. It differs from respondent conditioning in its emphasis on the *consequences* (or what follows) behavior, that is, the *reinforcement*. Also called *instrumental conditioning*, it is associated with B. F. Skinner. Skinner's theory is considered radical behaviorism because its attention to environmental contingencies minimizes the role of cognitive processes (Maddi, 1980).

According to operant conditioning, a behavior is strengthened (that is, it is likely to recur) when it is followed by a reinforcement (Salkind, 1985). The reinforcement may be a reward or some action, consequence, or occurrence that increases the likelihood that the previous behavior will recur. *Positive reinforcements* are actions, stimuli, or consequences that follow the occurrence of a behavior, and which usually result in increased satisfaction. These may be primary (of biological importance, such as food) or secondary (of acquired value, such as a gold star). *Negative reinforcements* are consequences that allow one to escape or avoid an unpleasant situation (e.g., eliminating critical behavior following the performance of desired behavior) (Salkind, 1985). Regardless of whether the reinforcements are positive or negative, they promote the continuance of the preceding behavior.

Punishment is also used in operant conditioning (Crain, 1985). Punishment is an unpleasant or aversive consequence that results in decreasing a behavior. Punishments may be positive (add an unpleasant experience) or negative (something desired is taken away). Spanking, losing privileges, and having to pay fines are examples of punishments. Punishments (as well as reinforcements) should be tailored to the individual. Sometimes what appears to be a punishment (e.g., yelling at someone) becomes a reinforcement (increased attention).

Behavior modification based on principles of operant conditioning can be implemented successfully when several principles are observed. For one, the reinforcement should occur immediately after the behavior. Second, reinforcers that are meaningful to clients and relevant to their level of maturity should be chosen. Third, a schedule of reinforcement should be adopted. Initially a continuous schedule, in which reinforcement occurs following every desired behavior, might be adopted. This requires constant attention, but it does maintain the behavior. Later an intermittent schedule in which reinforcements are dispensed according to a fixed ratio (e.g., every sixth time), a fixed interval (e.g., every 10 seconds), or on a variable or random schedule may be desirable (Salkind, 1985). Intermittent reinforcement more closely parallels the operation of the real world.

A variety of behavior modification techniques can be used to create desirable behaviors as well as extinguish undesirable ones. *Shaping* consists of progressively reinforcing behaviors as they come closer and closer to what is desired (Crain, 1985). At first behaviors that are "in the ballpark" of the desired behavior are reinforced (e.g., a child's sound "mm"). Later behaviors that more closely resemble what is desired (e.g., "mum") are reinforced until the desired outcome is achieved (e.g., "mama"). Persons with phobias can eliminate fears by gradually approaching the object feared. Close approximations are reinforced.

Another technique that is used is *time-out*. A kind of negative punishment, it is implemented by removing an individual from a pleasant situation to an unpleasant one. An example of this was the removal of a client who had an annoying cough that was not medically caused from the day treatment program room to a "coughing room" in which there was no furniture or other attractive stimuli. The client's deprivation of positive reinforcement from the group through this punishment resulted in a reduction in the frequency of his coughing behavior.

A third approach is the *token economy*. Tokens are items such as chips that can be traded in for products or privileges. Many residential institutions and some community programs utilize this mechanism. Clients in programs using this procedure earn tokens for desirable behaviors but can lose them when they violate rules. This way, clients can work toward goals that they choose and learn the consequences of not abiding by rules of the program. A problem encountered by clients who have lived in residential settings utilizing a token economy arises when they move into the community. It is easier to manipulate rewards and punishments in a controlled than in a natural environment.

Behavior modification therapy is implemented after careful study. Initially extensive information about problematic behaviors is sought. Specific data about the *antecedents* (what precedes the behavior), the *behavior* itself, and the *consequences* are gathered. This includes what happens, when, where, who is involved, and how often. The client, parents, or caregiver may be asked to document the specific observable events and frequency of the behavior prior to intervention to gather *baseline data* on the initial problem. Very often charts or inventories are used to record this information. On the basis of this information, problematic behaviors are prioritized and one or more target behaviors are selected for modification. Next an individualized program is set up. The client and the worker together select and create a contract, spelling out the *contingencies* (conditions under which reinforcements and/or punishments will occur) and the reinforcements. Accordingly, the individual is able to receive reinforcements after performing certain behaviors (e.g., listen to music after maintaining a diet for a day). If the individual does not live up to the terms of the contract, punishments may be instituted (e.g., must give money to opposing political party). Homework assignments are given in response to issues raised in therapy sessions. Data and charts are kept throughout the process and for a short time following achievement of the goal (Thomlison, 1986).

Behavior modification is widely used in community mental health. It has been used successfully to treat individuals with addictive, fearful, sexual, and obsessive-compulsive behaviors, as well as physiological problems (Walen, Hauserman, & Lavin, 1977). It is used with groups and families, with children and older adults. Its application with individuals who are anxious will be described in chapter 13.

Social Learning Theory.   *Social learning theory* is a behavioral theory in which observational learning is emphasized. Associated with Rotter (1954) and Bandura (1977), it also uses principles of classical and operant conditioning. In recent years social learning theory has been giving increased attention to cognition. Because of its recognition of mental processes that mediate between behaviors that are observed and those that are performed, social learning theory may be considered a cognitive-behavioral theory.

According to social learning theory, behavior is acquired by observing other persons or events. One need not perform the behavior oneself to learn about it. Observers can learn or acquire new behaviors by watching, listening to, or reading about models.

Observation encompasses the process (what models do, how they perform) and the consequences (rewards or punishments provided to the model or observer) that are perceived to occur. Inferences are made about what can be anticipated (*expectancy*) and rules that guide the model's behavior (*abstract modeling*) (Bandura, 1977). Observers develop inner symbolic representations of what they have seen and match their own behaviors with these. This way they can reproduce behaviors they have observed.

Social learning theory is guided by the principle of *reciprocal determinism* (Bandura, 1978). Accordingly there is a three-way interaction among the behavior, the external environment, and internal events (including cognition). The environment affects the individual's behavior through the mediation of cognition; the individual's behavior and cognition in turn affect the environment.

Four interrelated subprocesses promote observational learning—attention, retention, motoric reproduction, and reinforcement and motivational processes (Bandura, 1977). First of all, the model must be able to attract the *attention* of the observer. Qualities such as beauty, status, power, and emotionality seem to promote attention. Second, the observer must be able to remember and store what was observed. *Retention* is aided by two representational systems that encode what is observed. One system, imaginal, consists of pictorial representations of what is observed. The other, verbal, is comprised of words that describe what was seen. The third subprocess is *motoric reproduction,* the transformation of recalled symbolic representations into behavior. Here one matches one's performance with a mental image or verbal representation of what is to occur. Motoric reproduction requires practice, integration, and performance. In the process of performance, the individual corrects errors and makes adjustments. The fourth process is called *reinforcement and motivational processes* and encompasses incentives to reproduce observed behavior. When one recognizes that the model is rewarded rather than punished, or that the reproduction of observed behavior is rewarded, there is reason to replicate the behavior.

Behavioral change, maintenance, or control can occur through the use of reinforcements, punishment, and self-regulation. Reinforcements and punishments can be applied to the participant or observer or to oneself. Individuals can regulate their own behaviors by observing and assessing their own behaviors and cognitions and by responding and correcting their own behaviors. Through self-regulation, the self (through its cognitive faculties) takes on the function of the environment of providing rewards and punishments (Lundin, 1983). The self develops a feeling of *self-efficacy,* or competence (Bandura, 1982).

Clinical social workers can use principles of social learning theory in their practice with clients by modeling prosocial behaviors for clients with asocial or antisocial tendencies. In working with clients with phobias, social workers can convey confidence in the face of situations that clients fear. Social workers can model the desired behavior first and then have clients practice and perform what was observed. Similarly social workers can demonstrate the performance of social skills, assume the client's role in role plays, and otherwise model desirable behaviors for clients with severe mental disabilities. Social skills training with this population will be described in chapter 10. Table 3.4 illustrates how the various behavioral therapies are applied.

TABLE 3.4
Application of Behavioral Therapies

Types*	Target Symptoms	Techniques and Procedures
Respondent	Maladaptive behaviors of the severely	Extinction
Operant	mentally disabled	Systematic desensitization
Social learning	Dysfunctional family patterns	Reinforcement (positive and negative)
	Anxiety	Punishment
	Depression	Shaping
	Addictions	Token economy
	Obsessive-compulsive behavior	Role modeling
		Role rehearsal
		Role playing

*Although the types listed were once discrete, today techniques and concepts from the various schools overlap.

Ecological Systems Theory

The ecological systems approach is another social perspective. A hybrid between general systems theory and the ecological perspective, ecological systems is concerned with the relation between parts and wholes, their interactions, and the promotion of an adaptive fit between person and environment. A unifying perspective encompassing a holistic view of practice (Meyer, 1983), the ecological systems approach can encompass many of the theories discussed earlier at the same time as the linkage between the person and the environment is emphasized.

The systems perspective has been an important framework guiding social work practice for some 20 years. Concepts from general systems theory are utilized to describe the organizational, structural, and homeostatic functions of social systems. Individuals, families, groups, communities, and cultures are viewed as systems that mutually influence and interact with each other (Anderson & Carter, 1984). Individual problems are viewed in a social context that has a dynamic of its own. Social workers assess the diverse influences and act in collaboration with identified action systems to promote change (Pincus & Minahan, 1973).

The ecological perspective and its practice model (the "life model") were developed by Germain (1973) and Gitterman (Germain & Gitterman, 1980, 1987). Although they utilize systems concepts, they prefer the "living" language of ecology to the mechanistic systems terminology. Their emphasis on health, potentiality, and competence highlights human adaptability and problems in living rather than psychopathology (Germain & Gitterman, 1987). Furthermore, they look at the physical as well as the social environment.

Ecological systems perspective is social in its focus on human relatedness, attachment, and person–environment transactions. Germain & Gitterman (1987), for example, view human relationships as the outcomes of interactions and regard the need for relatedness, support, and affiliation as essential to human functioning. Individual problems may be rooted in maladaptive relationships with other persons or institutions—

problems that may be remedied through social environmental interventions as well as an individual approach.

More than the other perspectives, this one provides a framework for the practitioner to identify forces within and outside a client system as well as the transactions between systems that contribute to a problem and can assist in the development of a solution. Attention is drawn to the function the problem serves within each system and those forces in the person and environment that contribute to the maintenance of the problem. Furthermore, resources that can improve the fit between person and environment by fostering growth, development, and affiliation are identified. The social environment presents obstacles and provides resources for change.

Ecological theory is applicable to all clients, but is particularly germane to understanding and intervening with clients who are severely mentally disabled, many of whom are poor, socially isolated, and underserved by the human service system. In working with this population, the clinical social worker can bridge the gap between the person and the environment to create a better fit. With its emphasis on competence, mastery, and coping in the context of the natural environment, ecological theory provides a lens that can be helpful in understanding the situation of these clients and mobilizing resources and supports that are needed (Libassi, 1988).

Family Theories

Social workers have also contributed to the development of another social perspective, family therapy theory (e.g., Satir, 1967; Scherz, 1954). Although family therapy is informed by a number of theories (e.g., experiential, psychoanalytic, structural, behavioral, strategic), most share a systems perspective. Accordingly, the family unit is viewed as a whole composed of interacting parts that exist in space and time in an environmental context. Family members affect and are affected by each other and external systems. Although the system tends to maintain an equilibrium, developmental as well as other changes can precipitate an imbalance. Maladaptive responses to such changes bring some families to mental health agencies for help.

Therapeutic intervention with a family aims to change structure, communication patterns, organization, and behaviors. Roles and responsibilities may be reallocated; boundaries between members and between the family and others may be redefined; feelings may be expressed, shared, and understood; and dysfunctional behaviors may be identified and changed.

Family therapists tend to focus on interactions between individuals within the family rather than intrapersonal dynamics. Depending on the theoretical perspective used, problematic interactions are viewed as patterns acquired from the preceding generations, learned behaviors that are reinforced, and the like. Clinicians work with the nuclear family as a whole, subunits (parents, children), and multiple generations of family members to move the family away from dysfunctional patterns to more constructive modes of interacting.

Hartman and Laird (1983) have developed a version of family therapy—family-centered practice—that is particularly amenable to social work. They view the family as the client and mobilize family resources to promote adaptation. Their definition of family recognizes the existence of nontraditional primary associations, such as gay and lesbian couples, heterosexuals who are cohabiting, and residents of group homes:

> We are adopting a phenomenological stance in saying that a family becomes a family when two or more individuals have decided they are a family, that in the intimate, here-and-now environment in which they gather, there is a sharing of emotional needs for closeness, of living space which is deemed "home," and of those roles and tasks necessary for meeting the biological, social, and psychological requirements of the individuals involved. (Hartman & Laird, 1983, p. 30).

According to this definition, whomever the client identifies as significant others should be regarded as the family. Hartman and Laird's (1983) "ecological" family perspective also looks at the environment to assess the family's external resources and produce changes that benefit the client.

Family therapists use a number of assessment tools to guide them in their work. Hartman (1978) has developed the ecomap to assist social workers in their assessments of families. This visual representation of the family identifies the social systems that comprise the context of life of the family and its members. Another tool, the genogram, is also used to assess intergenerational family patterns. This is a family tree of three or four generations of the family in which family members are identified and characterized by the family. The ecomap and the genogram are constructed collaboratively with the family.

In community mental health practice, the individual is usually identified as the "case." Nevertheless, the family may be contributing to or reinforcing maladaptive individual patterns. In such instances, the family should have some involvement in treatment. Often the problem can be appropriately defined as familial, in which case the family should be the locus of treatment. In work with families with severe mental disorders, the family needs to be educated about the nature of the family member's disorder and how to respond. In such cases a family psychoeducational approach is used (see chapter 10).

Group Theory

Groups are used widely in community mental health. Some provide psychotherapy to individuals with problems or symptoms that interfere with their adaptation. Others are programs or residences in which clients with mental health problems participate together. Group theory is applicable to both types of groups.

Like family therapy theory, group theory has a variety of schools, each with its own perspective. Some of the therapeutic groups incorporate behavioral, psychoanalytic, and existential theories into practice. Other groups use concepts from group dynamics theory. As with the case with family theory, systems theory is common to these diverse theories. With groups the focus is largely on interactions among participants.

Groups provide a place in which clients can express their feelings, identify problematic behaviors, gain insight into their problems, and make changes. With the support of a peer group and clinical social workers, clients can talk about or nonverbally act out problems that they ordinarily would keep to themselves. The group serves as a point of reference and support for the client to achieve autonomy, self-determination, and a feeling of competence and worth. The acceptance the group provides enables the client to achieve self-acceptance.

Group theory is concerned with a number of aspects of individual behavior in groups and the group process. One dimension is the roles participants assume in groups. Some members tend to assume instrumental roles to keep the group on task, while others concerned with the emotional climate assume maintenance roles. Some members of some groups disrupt the group by clowning, aggressive behavior, and the like.

Another aspect of the group is its own process or stages. In the beginning of a group's life, participants are tentative and noncommittal. Their own needs predominate over the group's. Over time they form an emotional bond with each other and feel a commitment to coming and a feeling of belonging to the group. Eventually their commitment to the group transcends their personal needs. As the group completes its work, group members terminate their membership. This is a difficult process for persons who have invested a great deal of emotion in the group.

In the course of a group's development, conflict is bound to occur. Although pressures to conform to norms prevail in groups, the group will feel a need to address the conflict. Conflict threatens the harmony of the group temporarily. Resolution of the conflict, however, can create a stronger, more intimate group.

Group intervention techniques vary according to the goals and purpose of the group and the theory that drives it. Theories and methods of group work are described in a number of social work textbooks (Garvin, 1981; Hartford, 1971; Toseland & Rivas, 1984). The group approach to social skills training is described in chapter 10.

Cultural Theory

Another social environmental theory looks at the cultural dimension of human behavior. Cultures are communities that embody shared history, knowledge, language, values, and behavior. Their shared ways of viewing experience enter into their daily interactions among themselves and with outsiders and are transmitted through socialization processes from one generation to the next. Patterns of perceiving, experiencing, evaluating, and knowing provide persons who are socialized in a particular culture with unique ways of viewing the world. Culture is expressed in verbal and nonverbal behavior, artifacts, rituals, stories, and social organization.

Although mental health is the dominant mode of describing and addressing individual and social problems in mainstream American culture of today, many clients do not share this perspective. Cultures vary in their definitions of emotional problems and where they place responsibility (the individual, a curse engendered in a previous generation, the gods, etc.). Moreover, cultures provide their own ways of treating emotional troubles or their equivalents and specialized personnel, such as folk healers.

Social work practitioners work with members of diverse ethnic groups whose family interaction patterns, style of communication, and behavior may be different from that of the social worker. Culture is an important dimension of understanding that should be brought into the assessment and treatment of clients. The impact of culture on the delivery of mental health services will be discussed at length in chapter 7.

Feminist Theory

Another perspective that recognizes the impact of the social environment on social functioning is feminism. As chapter 6 will explain, feminists have found many of the traditional psychological theories (especially psychoanalysis and some of the cognitive developmental theories) biased because they either consider women defective men or they generalize from men to women. Women need to be viewed as full persons in their own right and to be helped to achieve their goals. Frequently they are impeded from accomplishing life goals because of the pervasiveness of patriarchal attitudes in women's personal and economic lives.

Feminist therapies on the individual, family, and group levels promote women's self-realization and feelings of empowerment. Women are helped to become aware of the connection between the personal and the political and to remedy these problems through assertiveness and social change. Feminist theory and therapy will be described more fully in chapter 6.

SUMMARY

Clinical practice in community mental health is informed by an integrative biopsychosocial perspective. Accordingly neither biological, nor psychological, nor social dimensions determine mental health. Instead, knowledge and theories arising from these perspectives infuse each other and are interrelated. The integrative model proposed here is nonlinear and multifaceted. It is predicated on a view of the person as an active agent who strives for empowerment and meaning. Health and mental health are viewed as positive goals. Clients' strengths and uniqueness are recognized and respected.

Biological knowledge about mental illness has been increasing. Research findings support the argument that genetic factors are related to mental disorders such as schizophrenias, bipolar disorder, and major depression. Other research shows that the neurophysiology of the brain is associated with some disorders. Breakthroughs in psychopharmacology have led to treatments for many persons with psychiatric difficulties.

The psychological perspective, as presented in this chapter, refers to intrapsychic experiences. Two theories that focus on the psyche are ego psychology and cognitive theory. Although ego psychology accepts the existence of intrapsychic structures (the ego, id, and superego), it also recognizes the reciprocal relationship between the person and the environment. Its emphasis on ego strengths, competence, and mastery provides a constructive approach for practice. Cognitive theory focuses on thoughts and beliefs that are related to distressful symptoms. In cognitive theory dysfunctional thoughts are identified, challenged, and changed. The social environmental perspective is represented by a number of theoretical approaches. Behavioral theories view maladaptive behavior as learned responses that can be changed by changing environmental contingencies. Respondent conditioning, operant conditioning, and social learning theory are representative of the behavioral school. Five other approaches that look at social and environmental factors are the ecological systems approach, family therapy theory, group therapy, feminist theory, and cultural theory. These contribute to the understanding of transactions between individuals and the environment.

CASE STUDY

Mrs. Marilyn Holden is a well-groomed Caucasian 40-year-old woman of average height who came to the outpatient mental health center at the suggestion of the admissions director at a nursing home where her husband was recently placed following a stay in the state psychiatric hospital. Mrs. Holden had told the director that ever since she had her husband committed to the state hospital, she has felt depressed.

Mrs. Holden told the clinical social worker at the mental health center that she had her husband committed because he was "acting up" at home. He was drinking a keg of beer every three or four days, cursing loudly, and hitting her and the children (a boy and a girl who are 12 and 14, respectively). In the past, he has choked her, pulled out her hair, and doused her with beer, and has threatened to hurt the children. When he raised a knife at their son recently, she called the police, who brought him to the state hospital. Mrs. Holden explained that her husband was given the diagnosis of Huntington's disease several years ago, but he refused to take the medication that was prescribed after he was told that he could not drink while taking the medicine. He has not worked for 5 years because of difficulties he had holding a job. He has been receiving Social Security and Medicare. She has been working part time.

Mrs. Holden said that she and her husband have been married 22 years. They met in high school and married after they were graduated. Mrs. Holden said that during the first 2 years of their marriage they lived with her parents, who supported them until the couple were able to obtain stable jobs and save money for housing. During that period, her parents were critical of her for marrying when she was young. Later the couple were able to buy a home, where Mrs. Holden and the children live now. Mrs. Holden expressed affection for her husband "the way he used to be" but said that he has changed. During the last few years, he has followed her around the house and has made her account for her every move. Although his sexual demands have increased, she has felt increasingly repelled. Mrs. Holden expressed feelings of guilt about "dumping him" in the state hospital and a nursing home, at the same time she admitted feeling relieved.

Mrs. Holden said that during the past few years, the children have taken "breaks" from the family by staying with her mother and friends. They have spoken of "hating" their father and fearing that they would inherit the same disease. Mrs. Holden said that she had no idea when she married him that this disease ran in his family; she learned about it only after her husband was diagnosed and she began to ask questions. Since then she learned that his mother and uncle died of the disease and that cousins have the disease today. His family does not like to talk about it.

Mrs. Holden said that when Mr. Holden was living at home, she thought about killing him with a billy club. Since he has been out of the home, however, she has thought about killing herself. She said that she felt confused about "what she owed her husband and what she owed the children" and believes that over the years she has been a "bad mother" and now she is a "bad wife." She said that she had been ignoring his abusive behavior and drinking in the past, even though these behaviors affected her and the children. She reported feeling like a failure and wished that she could feel better about herself.

Mrs. Holden said that her mother continues to provide support to her family. Her mother believes that Mrs. Holden did "the right thing" in placing him in a nursing home but did "the wrong thing" over the years in ignoring the feelings of the children. Mrs. Holden has frequent contact with her mother, a widow in poor health, whom Mrs. Holden helps with household chores and shopping. Other supports include friends and the Huntington's disease support group. There are relatives on her husband's side who are critical of her for placing him in the nursing home. Nevertheless, none of them was willing to have him stay with them. Mrs. Holden requested support from the social worker in sticking with her decision to leave her husband in the nursing home and asked for help dealing with the children. She also expressed bewilderment at how she would live her life without her husband at home.

Discussion Questions

1. Identify biological, psychological, and social issues in this case. How are they connected?
2. Identify the theories discussed in this chapter that are most applicable to this case.
3. Why is Mrs. Holden depressed?
4. What irrational ideas are affecting Mrs. Holden's feelings?
5. How has Mr. Holden's disease affected the family as a system? (Include the extended family.)
6. How is Mrs. Holden oppressed as a woman?
7. How might Mrs. Holden become empowered?
8. What meaning did Mr. Holden have to Mrs. Holden? Why was it so difficult for her to let go?
9. What issues remain to be resolved for Mrs. Holden, for the children, and for the family? How does Mr. Holden fit into the picture?

REFERENCES

Anderson, R. E., & Carter, I. (1984). *Human behavior in the social environment: A social systems approach* (3rd ed.). New York: Aldine de Gruyter.

Andreasen, N.C. (1984). *The broken brain: The biological revolution in psychiatry.* New York: Harper & Row.

Bandura, A. (1977). *Social learning theory.* Englewood Cliffs, NJ: Prentice-Hall.

Bandura, A. (1978). The self system in reciprocal determinism. *American Psychologist, 33,* 344–358.

Bandura, A. (1982). Self-efficacy mechanism in human agency. *American Psychologist, 37,* 122–147.

Beck, A. (1976). *Cognitive therapy and the emotional disorders.* Madison, CT: International Universities Press.

Beck, A. (1985). Cognitive therapy. In H. I. Kaplan & B. J. Sadock (Eds.), *Comprehensive textbook of psychiatry/IV* (pp. 1432–1438). Baltimore, MD: Williams & Wilkins.

Berlin, S. (1980). A cognitive-learning perspective for social work. *Social Service Review, 54,* 537–555.

Blanck, G., & Blanck, R. (1974). *Ego psychology: Theory and practice.* New York: Columbia University Press.

Blanck, G., & Blanck, R. (1979). *Ego psychology II: Psychoanalytic developmental psychology.* New York: Columbia University Press.

Blanck, R., & Blanck, G. (1986). *Beyond ego psychology: Developmental object relations theory.* New York: Columbia University Press.

Chance, P. (1979). *Learning and behavior.* Belmont, CA: Wadsworth.

Chatterjee, P. (1984). Cognitive theories and social work practice. *Social Service Review, 58,* 64–80.

Cohen, D. (1988). Social work and psychotropic drug treatments. *Social Service Review, 62,* 576–599.

Cohen, D. (1989). Biological basis of schizophrenia: The evidence reconsidered. *Social Work, 24,* 255–257.

Crain, W. C. (1985). *Theories of development: Concepts and applications* (2nd ed.). Englewood Cliffs, NJ: Prentice-Hall.

Dixon, S. L. (1981). *An introduction to ego psychology and the dynamics of human behavior.* Lexington, MA: Ginn.

Dorfman, R. A. (Ed.). (1988). *Paradigms of clinical social work.* New York: Brunner/Mazel.

Ellis, A. (1979). Rational-emotive therapy as a new theory of personality and therapy. In A. Ellis & J. M. Whiteley (Eds.), *Theoretical and empirical foundations of rational emotive therapy* (pp. 1–60). Monterey, CA: Brooks/Cole.

Ellis, A. & Harper, R. A. (1975). *A new guide to rational living.* North Hollywood, CA: Wilshire Book.

Erikson, E. (1950). *Childhood and society.* New York: Norton.

Erikson, E. (1959). Identity and the life cycle. *Psychological Issues, 1,* 50–100.

Fieve, R. (1975). *Moodswing: The third revolution in psychiatry.* New York: William Morrow.

Fischer, J. (1978). *Effective casework practice: An eclectic approach.* New York: McGraw-Hill.

Frankl, V. E. (1984). *Man's search for meaning* (rev. & updated ed.). New York: Washington Square Press.

Freud, A. (1946). *The ego and mechanisms of defense.* New York: International Universities Press.

Garvin, C. D. (1981). *Contemporary group work.* Englewood Cliffs, NJ: Prentice-Hall.

Gerhart, U. C., & Brooks, A. D. (1983). The social work practitioner and antipsychotic medications. *Social Work, 28,* 454–460.

Germain, C. B. (1973). An ecological perspective in casework practice. *Social Casework, 54,* 323–330.

Germain, C. B. (1987). Human development in contemporary environments. *Social Service Review, 61,* 565–580.

Germain, C., & Gitterman, A. (1980). *The life model of social work practice.* New York: Columbia University Press.

Germain, C., & Gitterman, A. (1987). Ecological perspective. In A. Minahan et al. (Eds.), *Encyclopedia of social work* (18th ed., Vol. 1, pp. 488–499). Silver Spring, MD: National Association of Social Workers.

Goldin, L. R. (1988). Biological variables as predictors in relatives at risk. In D. L. Dunner, E. S. Gerson, & J. E. Barrett (Eds.), *Relatives at risk* (pp. 1–8). New York: Raven Press.

Goldstein, E. (1984). *Ego psychology and social work practice.* New York: Free Press.

Goldstein, E. (1986). Ego psychology. In F. J. Turner (Ed.), *Social work treatment: Interlocking theoretical approaches* (pp. 375–405). New York: Free Press.

Goldstein, H. (1982). Cognitive approaches to direct practice. *Social Service Review, 56,* 539–555.

Gordon, B. (1979). *I'm dancing as fast as I can.* New York: Harper & Row.

Gottesman, I. I., & Shields, J. (1972). *Schizophrenia and genetics: A twin study vantage point.* New York: Academic Press.

Green, J. W. (1982). *Cultural awareness in the human services.* Englewood Cliffs, NJ: Prentice-Hall.

Gusella, J. F., Wexler, N. S., Conneally, P. M., Nayer, S. L., Anderson, M. A., et al. (1983). A polymorphic DNA marker genetically linked to Huntington's disease. *Nature, 306,* 234–238.

Hartford, M. (1971). *Groups in social work: Applications of small group theory and research to social work practice.* New York: Columbia University Press.

Hartman, A. (1978). Diagrammatic assessment of family relationships. *Social Casework, 59,* 465–476.

Hartman, A., & Laird, J. (1983). *Family-centered social work practice.* New York: Free Press.

Hartmann, H. (1958). *Ego psychology and the problem of adaptation.* New York: International Universities Press.

Hollis, F., & Woods, M. E. (1981). *Casework: A psychosocial therapy* (3rd ed.). New York: Random House.

Holloway, F. (1988). Prescribing for the long-term mentally ill: A study of treatment practices. *British Journal of Psychiatry, 152,* 511–515.

Johnson, H. C. (1984). The biological bases of psychopathology. In F. J. Turner (Ed.), *Adult psychopathology* (pp. 6–72). New York: Free Press.

Kaplan, H. I. & Sadock, B. J. (1988). *Synopsis of psychiatry: Behavioral sciences/clinical psychiatry* (5th ed.). Baltimore, MD: Williams & Wilkins.

Kegan, R. (1982). *The evolving self: Problems and process in human development.* Cambridge, MA: Harvard University Press.

Kelly, G. A. (1963). *A theory of personality.* New York: Norton.

Kendler, K. S. (1988). The genetics of schizophrenia and related disorders. In D. L. Dunner, E. S. Gershon, & J. E. Barrett (Eds.), *Relatives at risk for mental disorder* (pp. 247–263). New York: Raven Press.

Kennedy, J. L., Giuffra, L. A., Moises, H. W., Cavalli-Sforza, L. L., et al. (1988). Evidence against linkage of schizophrenia to markers on chromosome 5 in a northern Swedish pedigree. *Nature, 336,* 167–170.

Kety, S. S., & Matthysse, S. (1988). Genetic and biochemical aspects of schizophrenia. In A. M. Nicholi, Jr. (Ed.), *The new Harvard guide to psychiatry* (pp. 139–151). Cambridge, MA: Belknap Press of Harvard University Press.

Klerman, G. (1988). Depression and related disorders of mood (affective disorders). In A. M. Nicholi, Jr. (Ed.), *The new Harvard guide to psychiatry* (pp. 309–336). Cambridge, MA: Belknap Press of Harvard University Press.

Lazarus, R. S., & Folkman, S. (1984). *Stress, appraisal, and coping.* New York: Springer.

Levine, C., & Dang, J. C. (1977). Psychopharmacology and social work skills. *Social Casework, 58,* 153–158.

Libassi, M. F. (1988). The chronically mentally ill: A practice approach. *Social Casework, 69,* 88–96.

Lundin, R. W. (1983). Learning theories: Operant reinforcement theories and social learning theories of B. F. Skinner and Albert Bandura. In R. J. Corsini & A. J. Marsella (Eds.), *Personality theories, research and assessment* (pp. 287–330). Itasca, IL: Peacock Press.

Maddi, S. (1980). *Personality theories: A comparative analysis* (4th ed.). Homewood, IL: Dorsey Press.

Mahler, M., Pine, F., & Bergman, A. (1975). *The psychological birth of the human infant.* New York: Basic Books.

Matorin, S., & De Chillo, N. (1984). Psychopharmacology: Guidelines for social workers. *Social Casework, 65,* 579–589.

Matthysse, S., & Kety, S. S. (1986). The genetics of psychiatric disorders. In S. Arieti (Ed.), *American handbook of psychiatry,* (2nd ed.): *Vol. 8. Biological psychiatry* (pp. 160–169). New York: Basic Books.

Meichenbaum, D. H. (1977). *Cognitive behavior modification: An integrative approach.* New York: Plenum Press.

Mendlewicz, J., Fieve, R. R., & Stallone, F. (1973). Relationship between the effectiveness of lithium therapy and family history. *American Journal of Psychiatry, 130,* 1011–1013.

Meyer, C. H. (Ed.). (1983). *Clinical social work in the eco-systems perspective.* New York: Columbia University Press.

Piaget, J. (1936/1974). *The origins of intelligence in children.* Trans. by M. Cook. New York: International Universities Press.

Pincus, A., & Minahan, A. (1973). *Social work practice: Methods and models.* Itasca, IL: Peacock Press.

Rainer, J. D. (1985). Genetics and psychiatry. In H. I. Kaplan & B. J. Sadock (Eds.), *Comprehensive textbook of psychiatry/IV,* (4th ed. pp. 25–42). Baltimore, MD: Williams & Wilkins.

Rotter, J. (1954). *Social learning and clinical psychology.* Englewood Cliffs, NJ: Prentice-Hall.

Rotter, J. B. (1966). Generalized expectancies for internal versus external control of reinforcement. *Psychological Monographs, 80.*

Salkind, N. J. (1985). *Theories of human development* (2nd ed.) New York: Wiley.

Sands, R. G. (1986). The encounter with meaninglessness in crisis intervention. *The International Forum for Logotherapy, 9,* 102–108.

Sarasan, I. G., & Sarasan, B. R. (1989). *Abnormal psychology.* Englewood Cliffs, NJ: Prentice-Hall.

Satir, V. (1967). *Conjoint family therapy: A guide to theory and technique* (rev. ed.). Palo Alto, CA: Science & Behavior Books.

Scherz, F. (1954). What is family centered casework? *Social Casework, 34,* 343–348.

Sherrington, R., Brynjolfsson, J., Petursson, H., Potter, M., et al. (1988). Localization of a susceptibility for schizophrenia on chromosome 5. *Nature, 336,* 164–167.

Solomon, B. (1976). *Black empowerment: Social work in minority communities.* New York: Columbia University Press.

Spitz, R. (1965). *The first year of life: A psychoanalytic study of normal and deviant development of object relations.* New York: International Universities Press.

Taylor, E. H. (1987). The biological basis of schizophrenia. *Social Work, 32,* 115–121.

Thomlison, R. J. (1986). Behavior therapy in social work practice. In F. J. Turner (Ed.), *Social work treatment: Interlocking theoretical approaches* (pp. 131–153). New York: Free Press.

Toseland, R., & Rivas, R. (1984). *An introduction to group work practice.* New York: Macmillan.

Turner, F. J. (Ed.). (1986). *Social work treatment: Interlocking theoretical approaches.* New York: Free Press.

Walen, S. R., Hauserman, N. M., & Lavin, P. J. (1977). *Clinical guide to behavior therapy.* Baltimore, MD: Williams & Wilkins.

Weick, A. (1987). Reconceptualizing the philosophical perspective of social work. *Social Service Review, 61,* 218–230.

Weick, A., Rapp, C., Sullivan, W. P., & Kisthardt, W. (1989). A strength perspective for social work practice. *Social Work, 34,* 350–354.

Weiner, H. (1984). An integrative model of health, illness, and disease. *Health and Social Work, 9,* 253–260.

Weiner H., & Fawzy, F. I. (1989). An integrative model of health, disease, and illness. In S. Cheron (Ed.), *Psychosomatic medicine: Theory, physiology, and practice* (Vol. 1, pp. 9–44). Madison, CT: International Universities Press.

Weitkamp, L. R., Stancer, H. C., Persad, E., Flood, C., & Guttormsen, S. (1981). Depressive disorders and HLA: A gene on chromosome 6 that can affect behavior. *The New England Journal of Medicine, 305,* 1301–1306.

White, R. F. (1959). Motivation reconsidered: The concept of competence. *Psychological Review, 66,* 297–333.

Wolpe, J. (1982). *The practice of behavior therapy* (3rd ed.). New York: Pergamon.

Zimmerman, J. H. (1989). Determinism, science, and social work. *Social Service Review, 63,* 52–62.

4 | The Biopsychosocial Assessment

Assessment is an evaluative process and product through which the clinical social worker develops an understanding of clients in relation to their situations. A professional judgment that draws from theoretical knowledge, clinical observations, and analytic skills, assessment is ongoing, open-ended, and always subject to revision. An assessment evolves from the interaction between the social worker and the client; as such, it is reflective of that specific relationship. The social worker's thinking, however, should encompass dimensions of the client's life that extend beyond the client–worker relationship.

For many years, social workers viewed the assessment from a linear perspective. As such, assessment was the second of three discrete stages of intervention. During the first stage, *study,* the practitioner gathered facts from the client, significant others, and agencies the client may have used. This process included listening to the client's life history, as well as obtaining information about the client's significant relationships, occupation, and social environment. After sufficient data were gathered, the social worker could proceed to the second, *diagnostic,* stage. At this point the clinician would arrive at an understanding of the client's personality and factors in the past and present that seemed to cause current difficulties. A diagnostic formulation that emphasized psychodynamics was made. The final stage, *treatment,* followed from the diagnosis. Specific diagnoses suggested specific treatment approaches.

In this volume, assessment is viewed as a continuous process that develops from the client–social worker relationship and is fed back and forth between worker and client. The term *assessment* is preferred to *diagnosis*. The latter is a medical term that suggests the saliency of a particular category of disease, such as those described in the *DSM-III-R*. A clinical social work assessment of a client served at a community mental health agency includes a diagnosis as one of many components of the process. A biopsychosocial assessment, however, is wholistic, inclusive, comprehensive. Any diagnostic terms that are used are viewed in relation to the multiple facets of the client's life.

Furthermore, assessment is viewed as an attempt at *understanding* rather than as a scientific *explanation*. Despite the breakthroughs in biological medicine, it is not possible to draw valid inferences about specific biological factors that cause mental health problems. The etiology of many mental disorders is unknown, nonspecific, or debatable. Furthermore, the reliability of the diagnostic categories used in the *DSM-III-R* is questionable (Kutchins & Kirk, 1986).

This is not to say that scientific thinking should be dispensed with altogether. Assessments should be related to data. Issues or conditions that seem to be contributing to distress should be identified. Efforts should be made to distinguish between facts and opinions. Many observations of the same client, multiple sources of data, and the experiences of other mental health team members with the same client can provide confirmation of one's assessment. The process of coming to an assessment of a client is akin to doing human science research of the naturalistic type (Rodwell, 1987).

Assessment is useful to social workers, clients, and agencies. Social workers benefit from the process of thinking analytically about the client and reflecting on their own practice. In doing so, clinicians gain distance from the individual client and their own involvement. Clinical social workers try to make sense of the case as a whole by looking at how the specifics are related to each other. Moreover, assessment provides an opportunity for workers to see how theory is related to practice. Because treatment is related to an understanding of the case, clinicians' enhanced awareness should result in appropriate treatment. Furthermore, assessment is valuable as a means to demonstrate accountability to clients and agencies.

This chapter will focus on the development of a preliminary written biopsychosocial assessment of the client by the social worker and on related processes of the interdisciplinary team. The written assessment, usually drawn up after a few sessions, is necessarily provisional, because new information may be revealed and changes can occur any time during the treatment process. Nevertheless, the initial assessment should represent the social worker's best thinking on the basis of the information at hand at the time of the writing. Although the emphasis here will be on written documents, the conclusions are not meant to be private or for professionals only. It is expected that clinical social workers will share the essence of their findings with clients during the course of treatment.

The assessment described here will focus on the individual. Although family and group modes of treatment are prevalent in community mental health practice today, case records are predominantly on individuals. This is not to say that an individual's family and social milieu are excluded. In the assessment described here, the multiple contexts of an individual's life will be described.

This chapter includes the following topics: (a) components of a comprehensive interdisciplinary assessment; (b) understanding the person in context; (c) the use of psychological theories; (d) the mental status examination and diagnosis; (e) writing a biopsychosocial summary and treatment plan; (f) case review with an interdisciplinary treatment planning team.

COMPONENTS OF A COMPREHENSIVE INTERDISCIPLINARY ASSESSMENT

Ideally an assessment of a client should be performed by a team of professionals. Such a team might include a psychiatrist, a social worker, a community mental health nurse, a physician, a psychologist, a recreation therapist, and a vocational rehabilitation specialist. A team has the resources of diverse specialties, each of which has a unique lens through which to perceive the client. The team uses the expertise of different professionals to gather and make sense of data, which are pooled and integrated. The inclusion of multiple professionals promotes a more comprehensive understanding of the client and client system.

The major components of an interdisciplinary assessment are as follows:

1. Medical assessment
2. Psychological examination
3. Rapid assessment instruments
4. Psychosocial history
5. Psychiatric evaluation, mental status examination, and diagnosis
6. Functional assessment

Medical Assessment

Many psychiatric symptoms are the consequence of physical conditions. In order to determine whether the symptoms are medically based, organic findings should be ruled out (determined to be nonexistent or irrelevant) first. A client should routinely have a medical examination, regardless of whether or not the physician is a member of the team. Kutchins and Kirk (1987) state that "there is a great risk of erroneous or overlooked diagnoses of physical disorders" that can occur "when psychotherapists who are not physicians are asked to use DSM-III, a medical handbook" (p. 205). Social workers have a professional obligation to obtain information on a client's medical condition. Furthermore, Axis III (physical conditions and disorders) of the *DSM-III-R*'s multiaxial diagnosis, is based on medical findings. Social workers "should limit their entries on Axis III to conditions that have already been diagnosed, and they should state who made the diagnosis" (Williams, 1981, p. 103).

A further medical evaluation is the neurological examination. Through a clinical examination and specific tests, such as the electroencephalograph (EEG), neurologists can determine whether there is organic brain damage (organicity) that is producing psychiatric symptoms. Furthermore, the EEG and other tests can assess sleep disorders.

Some laboratory tests used by physicians and psychiatrists can assist in the diagnosis of psychiatric disorders. Urine tests can identify alcohol and drugs ingested by clients. The DST test (dexamethasone suppression) is sometimes used to assess biological signs of depression (Andreasen, 1984). Neurophysiological tests, such as the CAT scan, can identify brain lesions (see chapter 3).

Table 4.1 provides examples of medical conditions with symptoms that resemble psychiatric symptoms. The social worker should become familiar with these and other medical conditions that produce similar affective, behavioral, and cognitive signs. Huntington's disease, for example, resembles psychotic disorders such as schizophrenia (Sands, 1984). If medical diseases are determined to be present, medical treatment for these illnesses should be pursued.

TABLE 4.1

Examples of Physical Disorders in Which Psychiatric Symptoms Are Presented

Huntington's disease
Alzheimer's disease
Multiple sclerosis
Cardiovascular disease
Hypoglycemia
Parkinson's disease
Nutritional deficiency diseases
Substance abuse disorders
Systemic lupus erythematosus
Amyotrophic lateral sclerosis
Acquired immune deficiency syndrome (AIDS)

Source: Adapted from Kaplan & Sadock (1988).

Psychological Testing

Psychological testing may be called for under some circumstances. Such examinations help clarify the diagnosis, assess intellectual ability, and uncover unconscious material. Some psychological tests are capable of diagnosing organic brain damage. A social worker who is the first professional who sees a client should refer the client to a psychologist if clarification seems to be needed.

Psychologists have a wide repertoire of tests, which can be administered as a package. Such batteries of tests require interpretation as a whole. Among the personality tests, the one that is most commonly used in community mental health settings is the *Minnesota Multiphasic Personality Inventory,* which is usually referred to by its acronym, MMPI. This test contains over 500 questions describing emotional states, attitudes, and behaviors, such as "I have trouble making friends." Persons who take the test indicate for each statement whether it applies to them. Certain questions tap specific mental health conditions such as hypochondriasis, depression, and paranoia. Responses to some questions suggest that the respondent was lying or defensive. Results are put on a graph, in which the peaks and valleys are evident. Findings should be interpreted by a psychologist. The MMPI can be helpful in arriving at a diagnosis (Graham & Lilly, 1984).

Projective tests encourage subjects to reveal indirectly what they may find difficult to state directly. For these tests, clients are presented with ambiguous stimuli about which they are asked to talk. One well-established projective test is the *Rorschach Test,* which has subjects respond to a set of inkblots. Another is the *Thematic Apperception Test* (TAT), which contains a set of pictures about which clients are asked to develop a story. A third type of projective test is the *Sentence Completion Test* (SCT), which consists of a series of statements with blanks for the subject to complete, for example, "I am afraid of . . . ." These tests reveal areas of conflict or anxiety.

Another test is the *Bender Gestalt* visual motor test. This test is used for adults and children primarily to detect organic dysfunction (Kaplan & Sadock, 1988) but also as a projective tool (Graham & Lilly, 1984). Here subjects are asked to reproduce certain designs, such as a circle and a square that touch.

Psychologists also administer intelligence tests to some clients who receive mental health services. Testing may be required for a vocational or rehabilitation program the client wishes to enter, or to clarify the client's potential. The best known of these tests is the *Wechsler Adult Intelligence Scale* (WAIS). There are other versions of this test for children.

Psychological testing has certain advantages. For one, the findings are empirically based. Many of the instruments used are reliable and valid. Tests provide measured scores on specific dimensions. Many psychological tests are sensitive to personality dimensions that are not revealed in face-to-face conversations and in behavior.

As valuable as psychological tests may be, they do not replace understanding the person in his or her natural life space. Testing is usually performed in a clinical environment, the demands of which differ from those of the everyday life of the client. Questions are presented in a standardized way and do not account for the diverse social, cultural, and handicapping conditions of individual clients. Tests may be biased toward the prevailing white majority. Results that are distorted or reflect a transient state can become reified in a diagnosis.

Rapid Assessment Instruments

In addition to the diagnostic tests performed by psychologists, there are rapid assessment instruments that can be administered by social workers. These tools have functions that go beyond the gathering of diagnostic information. They can be used to gather baseline data prior to implementing a treatment plan to compare with data gathered during and after intervention. Clinicians use the results of these tests to monitor and assess the client's progress and to assess their own effectiveness as clinicians. Corcoran and Fischer (1987) have compiled many of these in their sourcebook, *Measures for Clinical Practice*.

Although there are some instruments that assess global functioning, most are adapted to particular problems (e.g., poor assertiveness) or clinical states (e.g., depression). On the basis of information gathered during early sessions, the social worker determines which areas to assess and monitor during treatment. Usually it is the client who completes the instrument, but there are some that can be filled in by family members, care givers, and the clinician. Instruments in the Corcoran and Fischer (1987) collection that pertain to populations and problems covered in this book are as follows:

Alcoholism	Michigan Alcohol Screening Test
Assertiveness	Rathers Assertiveness Schedule
Depression	Beck Depression Inventory
	Self-Rating Depression Scale
Hostility/anger	State-Trait Anger Scale
	Argumentativeness Scale
Obsessive compulsivity	Compulsivity Index
	Obsessive-Compulsive Scale

Phobias	Fear Questionnaire
	Mobility Inventory for Agoraphobia
Schizophrenia spectrum disorders	Cognitive Slippage Scale
	Magical Ideation Scale
Self-concept, self-esteem, self-efficacy	Index of Self-Esteem
	Ego Identity Scale
	Self-Efficacy Scale
Social Support	Provision of Social Support

Other instruments can be found in the Corcoran and Fischer book and elsewhere. Specific additional tools relevant to the topics that will be addressed in Part II will be mentioned where relevant.

Psychosocial History

The psychosocial history is a comprehensive report on the client's current problem and symptoms, life history, and situation. It is gleaned from a number of sources—the client, significant others (family, gay/lesbian partner, friends), reports from other agencies, the case record, and so forth—provided that the client consents to the participation of others. Although the production of a written psychosocial history is frequently assigned to the clinical social worker, in some settings professionals and students of any of the mental health disciplines develop the written document.

In this volume the psychosocial history will be referred to as a *biopsychosocial assessment*. The written report will include a summary of medical findings obtained from the physician, as well as psychological and social findings. This is consistent with the biopsychosocial conceptual framework described in chapter 3. The components of this assessment include a description of the client, the presenting problem, the client's life circumstances, medical history, psychiatric history, financial/occupational information, and family/relationships. It will also include the mental status examination and diagnosis. A recommended outline for this assessment will be presented later on in this chapter.

Psychiatric Evaluation, Mental Status Examination, and Diagnosis

The evaluation performed by the psychiatrist can include the client's history as described. The process resembles the history taking of the social worker but reflects the medical training of the psychiatrist. The psychiatrist may explore the client's psychiatric history more closely than the social worker, but ignore social environmental factors. The name used by psychiatrists for the psychiatric history is *anamnesis*.

In the process of explaining his or her current difficulties and history, the client reveals the symptoms. The client's reported complaints, as well as the verbal and nonverbal behavior accompanying the report, provide clues to the client's diagnosis. Further clarification of the nature of the client's psychiatric problem can be obtained by performing a *mental status examination* along with the history gathering. The mental status examination is to the psychiatrist what the physical examination is to the physician. Each is a clinical means to assess the presence of pathology in the client and to come to an accurate diagnosis. Although psychiatrists are frequently the professionals who perform these evaluations, social workers and psychologists are also capable of conducting them. An outline for this examination will be presented later in this chapter.

The psychiatric examination also includes an evaluation of the need for further medical testing and current medical needs. The psychiatrist may recommend a neurological examination, laboratory tests, or a referral for additional medical procedures. The psychiatrist has particular expertise about psychotropic medication. Many clients can benefit from psychotherapy without medication. Others require medication along with psychosocial treatment. The psychiatrist explores the client's medication history and any indications of an inclination to abuse drugs. The medication that is prescribed is related to the client's symptoms and diagnosis.

Functional Assessment

A further area for assessment is the extent of the client's ability to conduct his or her life independently in the community. An assessment of functioning is of particular import for chronically mentally ill who live in the community, but is also relevant for persons with mental retardation or developmental disabilities; individuals with physical impairments or handicaps; and the frail elderly. In many community mental health agencies, the nurse is responsible for performing a functional assessment; but the social worker may be the one who assumes this responsibility.

Among the areas that may be addressed in a functional assessment are the following:

1. Ability to communicate his or her needs to others. What language(s) does the client use (English, Spanish, sign language, gestures, none)?
2. Ability to use public transportation.
3. Ability to drive a car.
4. Ability to take care of physical needs independently—eating, bathing, grooming, dressing, use toilet unaided.
5. Ability to handle and manage money; budgeting, counting change, shopping.
6. Literacy: ability to read, reading level.
7. Physical mobility: walking, climbing stairs, transfer from wheelchair to bed.
8. Social skills: ability to interact with others, ability to initiate, develop, and maintain relationships.
9. Ability to manage a household independently—cooking, cleaning, laundry, dishes, making bed.
10. Occupational/employment skills and experience: work skills, ability to follow directions and accept supervision, ability to get to work on time.
11. Ability to assume responsibility for taking own medication consistently.
12. Sensory functions: sight, hearing, and so on.
13. Ability to protect self and others from fire.
14. Ability to protect oneself from involuntary sex, assault, and other kinds of exploitation.
15. Use of leisure time.

Scales that assess adaptive behavior skills such as the Independent Living Skills Survey (Wallace, 1986) can be used.

The functional assessment contributes to identifying the client's strengths and needs. The client's strengths and the client's, agency's, and community's resources are used to address the client's needs.

UNDERSTANDING THE PERSON IN CONTEXT

A biopsychosocial assessment of an individual must encompass the various situational contexts of the person's life. The biological context includes current and past physical conditions, genetic factors, and health. The psychological context encompasses inner conflicts, cognitions, behaviors, emotions, and the dimension of meaning. The social dimension is extensive. It accounts for interpersonal relationships with the family and/or significant others and the employment/financial/educational situation. A further contextual element is environmental and includes the neighborhood, housing, density of the living situation, and the like. Any alleged psychopathology should be seen in relation to these coexistent areas of a person's life. These multiple contexts should be evaluated carefully before any conclusions are reached about the client.

In this section, the biological, social, and environmental contexts will be discussed separately. In actuality, however, these are not discrete categories; rather they interrelate and interpenetrate a person's life. Furthermore, psychological factors, or personality, contribute to the context. Psychological factors will be discussed in the section on the use of psychological theories.

The Biological Context

Physical functioning depends on the state of health of the organism. The presence of illnesses, injuries, disabilities, and genetic abnormalities can produce stress on the body. The organism responds to these threats by mobilizing its defenses and resisting their impact (Selye, 1976). The individual's life style can offset the debilitating effects of physical dysfunction or intensify the stress.

Physical functioning is assessed by the physician, who identifies the patient's chief complaints, conducts a physical examination, runs specific laboratory tests, and takes a medical history. The medical history reveals the history of the presenting complaints, the client's past illnesses and injuries, allergies, hospitalizations, medication usage and reactions, nutrition, and substance use. In order to assess possible genetic factors, a history of illnesses among relatives is taken. Specific genetic tests may also be ordered.

The mental health worker is particularly interested in determining whether there are physical diseases or conditions that are producing psychiatric symptoms. Accordingly it is desirable that the physical evaluation determine whether a specific organic disorder such as Alzheimer's disease or hypoglycemia is present, or whether the client is having an adverse reaction to medication.

The physical evaluation should also explore the use and abuse of chemical substances. Although alcohol use is part and parcel of social and business life for many, excessive use and dependence cause physical problems. Similarly the use of street drugs such as heroin and cocaine creates personality problems as well as addiction. Physicians may take blood and urine tests to assess drug and alcohol use.

The state of the individual's health is partially under her or his own control. Eating well-balanced meals in moderate amounts contributes to good health. Overeating, binging and purging, starving oneself, or emphasizing some foods and excluding others can have a debilitating effect on the organism. Regular exercise and sufficient sleep have a salutory effect on the individual. Taking prescribed medication and following prescribed diets are ways in which individuals can promote their own health.

The biological assessment should be based on medical findings. Nevertheless, the clinical social worker may ask the client and significant others about significant medical problems, current physical conditions, illnesses in the family, substance use, and eating and sleeping patterns. If the social worker sees the client prior to the appointment with the physician, the social worker should identify particular areas of concern that the physician should explore.

Social Context

The social assessment encompasses an understanding of interpersonal relationships that are part of a person's life. This includes the family and other significant relationships. The cultures that permeate the client's life affect individual and social functioning.

In order to understand the social dimension of a person's life, several interrelated topics should be addressed in the assessment. Although these are discussed separately for the sake of clarity, it should be recognized that they are coexistent in the person's life. The topics to be discussed are (a) the family or household; (b) the culture or cultural group; (c) other social supports; and (d) social environmental stressors and resources.

The Family or Household.   The persons with whom a person lives are intimately connected with the client. These individuals may represent the family of origin (parents, siblings), the family of procreation (spouse, children), extended family (relatives such as grandparents, aunts, cousins), or nonrelatives (gay/lesbian or heterosexual partner, friends, residents of a group home).

In making an assessment of the family or household, one is interested in determining who is in the household, the quality of the relationships (emotionally supportive, conflictual, competitive) of the household as a whole and of component parts, the nature of the interactions (domineering, reciprocal), the strength of the bonds, and sensitive family issues. This can best be done by meeting with the group, particularly in their home.

The problems of the identified client should be looked at in relation to his or her household or family. It should be determined what functions these problems serve for the family, how the family responds to the client, and how the client feels about the family. The family's concern about the client, the members' willingness to be involved in treatment, and their resourcefulness should be assessed. Many of the dimensions described in family systems theory—boundaries (openness, permeability); communication patterns; organizational structure (roles, rules, subsystems); linkage with other systems (extended family, community); and power relations—should be assessed.

The family or household may or may not provide support to the client. The social worker should determine who is supportive in what ways; and the obstacles presented by those who are not supportive. If there are obstacles, their nature and purpose should be explored so that a strategy to overcome them can be developed.

The Culture(s). The individual and family may be part of an ethnic community that influences the client's identity, values, feelings of belonging, as well as individual behavior and family patterns of interaction. Cultures provide structure and meaning. For some people, however, association with a cultural group that is not valued by the larger society may be a source of conflict or ambivalence.

The clinical social worker has a responsibility to understand the client in relation to the client's respective culture(s). Workers who are not familiar with the client's particular ethnic group (e.g., the Amish), should ask questions of the client so as to encourage the client to explain the meaning system of the cultural group. Suggestions for engaging in culturally sensitive interviewing are given in chapter 7.

The assessment should identify significant ethnic groups and describe the nature of the client's ties and identification. Cultural patterns, such as ideas about sharing private feelings, modes of decision making, valued goals, and the role of kin in their lives, should be assessed. The cultural group, with its sense of community, shared life-cycle events, and holidays should be viewed as a potential resource for the client. Furthermore, the client's mental health problems should be viewed in terms of normative values and behaviors of the cultural group; what is psychopathological in one culture may be normal in another.

Other Social Supports. Clients may have additional interpersonal relationships that provide them with emotional support. These persons and groups provide friendship, personal help in time of need, concrete services (e.g., baby-sitting, transportation), or the like. The "supporters" may be personal friends, work associates, or neighbors. Doctors, lawyers, and ministers also provide social support, as do church or synagogue members. Barbers and beauticians, bartenders, and grocers may also be part of a client's interpersonal network.

The client may have a peer group that provides friendship at the same time it fosters a problematic behavior. Such a peer group may be "drinking buddies," collaborators in antisocial activity, and the like. If these groups are significant to the individual and comprise a large proportion of the client's social relationships, they may present an obstacle to treatment.

Some individuals are estranged from their families and have few friends. For whatever reason, it may be difficult for them to make or keep friends. In these cases human service workers from a number of agencies may constitute the client's social support network.

Social supports may also be in the form of organized community groups and activities. Self-help groups that focus on particular issues (e.g., alcoholism, rape, child abuse, loss of a child) provide a network of individuals who can support each other. Settlement houses, YMCAs, and Jewish Community Centers offer social programs, recreational activities, cultural events, and classes that can contribute to the well-being of clients.

Social Environmental Stressors and Resources.   Clients live in environmental contexts that may provide protection from or promote stress. Financial resources and employment can provide a buffer against distress, whereas poverty and inadequate housing can be psychologically wearing on the individual and family.

Conflict between the individual or family and "the system" is threatening. Legal problems over child support, debts, and driving while intoxicated involve individuals with lawyers and courts, the rules and practices of which are mystifying to those who are not familiar with the system. Defending oneself under such circumstances is costly and takes time away from employment. Trouble with the law and other difficulties with "the system" are taxing, making one vulnerable to physical and mental disorders.

Discrimination based on race, sex, class, sexual orientation, and handicap is also stressful. Furthermore, holding more than one job, being a single parent, or caring for a mentally disabled person make extra demands on a person.

Changes in one's circumstances or roles can also create stress. Accordingly, graduating, getting married, changing jobs, getting promoted, and retiring are transitions that can be anxiety provoking. Even though the client may not complain of these changes, it is expected that he or she will be making adjustments in adapting to the new circumstances.

A biopsychosocial assessment should identify the social environmental buffers and stressors in a person's life and describe the impact of these conditions on the individual. Often what looks like symptoms of psychopathology is the result of carrying a heavy burden of responsibility.

THE USE OF PSYCHOLOGICAL THEORIES

Assessment of the psychological dimension is a function of the theory used by the practitioner. At the present time, social workers are informed by a multitude of psychological theories, many of which are borrowed from other disciplines and adapted to social work practice (Turner, 1986; Dorfman, 1988). These theories contain concepts that serve as lenses through which clients can be understood.

The psychological theories discussed in chapter 3 look at intrapsychic dynamics (ego psychology), thinking (cognitive theory), and behavior (learning theories). Assessments that draw on these theories should analyze the client in terms of the constructs developed by the respective theory. Ways in which these theoretical perspectives guide assessment will be described in the following.

Ego Psychology

Ego psychology provides a framework through which intrapsychic dynamics can be assessed. Such an assessment looks at the ego functioning of the individual and draws inferences about the other intrapsychic structures (id, superego) and their dynamics.

This is determined by observing how the client interacts with the social worker, reported interactions with others, decision-making processes that are observed and revealed, as well as the client's affect, thinking, and behavior.

An ego assessment is made by evaluating the client's ego functions, developmental issues, and environmental conditions and the relationship among these dimensions. Particular emphasis is given to ego strengths that can be utilized in the solution of problems (Goldstein, 1984, 1986). Goldstein (1984, 1986) identifies a number of ego functions that aid the individual's adaptation to the world. These include object relations, reality testing, sense of reality, control of impulses, judgment, thought processes, adaptive regression, stimulus barrier, defensive functioning, autonomous functioning, synthetic integrative functions, and mastery competence. Functions such as reality testing, judgment, and thought processes are evaluated in the mental status examination that will be described later.

An assessment utilizing ego psychology as a frame of reference addresses the following components:

1. Identification of symptoms (e.g., anxiety, depression) and degree of debilitation.
2. Determination of the nature of the client's situation. This includes the presenting problem, social roles, significant others, supports, and stressors.
3. Effectiveness of ego functioning. Each of the functions is evaluated.
4. Developmental issues: how current developmental issues (e.g., parenthood, mid-life transition) are being managed; how unresolved issues from the past may be intruding on present life.
5. Identification of specific ego strengths (capacities that promote social functioning), such as intelligence, ability to handle stress, effective functioning in certain roles, motivation.
6. Environmental factors: identification of social, physical, organizational, cultural, and economic conditions that affect the client; determination of whether these are supportive or deleterious.

On the basis of this information, the clinical social worker determines the extent to which the client's difficulties are related to impairments in ego functioning, situational stress, social roles, developmental issues, environmental insufficiencies, or an interaction among any of these; and which ego strengths and environmental resources can be mobilized to help the client ameliorate the problems (Goldstein, 1984).

Cognitive Theory

Cognitive theory draws attention to the thinking processes that are related to the client's symptoms and behaviors. Accordingly, the assessment should highlight the specific cognitions, feelings, and behaviors and their connection.

An assessment based on cognitive theory will identify thinking patterns that are associated with the client's difficulties. Although many thoughts are the product of socialization in the past, the focus is on current thoughts and how they guide behavior and future goals. Because thoughts such as anticipations may be in visual form, the thoughts may be represented through visual images or fantasies (Beck, 1976).

Clients' perceptions of themselves, others, and the environment should be identified. Clients may, for example, think of themselves as fat, stupid, and inept, while at the same time they think of others as perfect; or they have an inflated opinion of themselves and think others are deficient. Some clients believe that others are responsible for their problems, that others are excessively judgmental, or that others' opinions are more valid than their own. Other clients have distorted perceptions of the impact of the environment on their lives.

In addition, thoughts about the future should be elicited. It should be determined whether clients believe that their prospects of feeling better are possible; that they have the power (with help) to change themselves or life circumstances; that the future holds promises of opportunities.

According to cognitive theory, positive or "promotive" thoughts are related to "core life values" that give meaning to people's lives (McMullin, 1986). Accordingly, it is helpful to determine what these values are. McMullin suggests that clients be asked the following three questions:

What do you want from life?

How would you like to spend the next 5 years?

If I knew now that I would be struck dead by lightning 6 months from today, how would I live until then? (p. 308)

Furthermore, the social worker should determine whether there are irrational beliefs (Ellis, 1979) and, if so, what they are. Individuals who have negative cognitions ("everything is hopeless") and a negative self-concept ("I'm a worthless human being") can be helped after these irrational ideas are identified, challenged, and replaced with more realistic ideas.

During early interviews, specific irrational ideas may be identified. In these specific instances, the assessment should include the "activating experience" (A) around which the complaint is centered; the beliefs associated with the experience (B); and the resulting consequences (C)—symptoms and/or dysfunctional behavior (Ellis, 1979). The identified irrational beliefs can then be targeted for change efforts.

Wright (1988) recommends the use of specific psychological tests to help in the identification of distorted cognitions. One is the Dysfunctional Attitude Scale (DAS) developed by Weissman (1979). Because negative cognitions are often associated with depression, the Beck Depression Inventory (BDI) (Beck et al., 1979) is also advised.

Behavioral Theories

Behavioral theories focus on the circumstances surrounding client actions. A behavioral assessment identifies the problematic behaviors, when they occur, who is present, what happens prior to their display (antecedents), and the consequences following the behaviors. Practitioners using behavioral techniques ask clients to provide specific information about behaviors. Often this involves the collection of baseline data (information prior to intervention) on the frequency and circumstances related to the behavior. Tables, charts, and diaries are frequently used to record this information.

Because behavioral theory looks to social environmental factors that affect problematic behaviors, the behavioral assessment is dependent on the social. Key persons in the client's environment may be inadvertently contributing to a client's problem by reinforcing undesirable behavior, by ignoring positive behavior, or by the modeling they are providing. The behavioral assessment should identify the persons (e.g., parents, caregivers at foster homes) or groups (e.g., peers) that are closely connected with the client. These persons may become important players in a plan to change the client's behavior.

THE MENTAL STATUS EXAMINATION AND DIAGNOSIS

The mental status examination explores the client's complaints, symptoms, and demeanor in order to determine the nature of the psychological difficulty and arrive at a diagnosis. The client is assessed in many areas. A consistent pattern of dysfunctions across specific areas of psychosocial functioning points to a specific diagnosis.

Traditionally diagnosis has been a responsibility of the psychiatrist. With the shortage of psychiatrists and increasing responsibility of clinical social workers for assessment and treatment, social workers today often make diagnoses—or provide a preliminary diagnosis that is reviewed by a psychiatrist, a psychologist, or an interdisciplinary team. In order to arrive at an accurate diagnosis, the mental status examination is performed.

Spitzer et al. (1989) have developed the Structured Clinical Interview for *DSM-III-R*, an instrument that is also known as SCID. This provides a series of questions that help the clinician arrive at a diagnosis. The following are some questions utilized to assess a current major depressive syndrome:

During this time . . . did you lose or gain any weight? (How much?) (Were you trying to lose weight?)

IF NO: How was your appetite? (What about compared to your usual appetite?) (Did you have to force yourself to eat?) (Eat [less/more] than usual?) (Was that nearly every day?)

. . . how were you sleeping? (Trouble falling asleep, waking frequently, trouble staying asleep, waking too early, OR sleeping too much? How many hours a night compared to usual? Was that nearly every night?) . . . . (Spitzer et al., 1989)

Although some fixed formats for interviewing clients can be helpful, many practitioners gain their impressions through the history-gathering interview (psychosocial interview or anamnesis). At the same time the client is describing the presenting problems or complaints, the examiner is able to observe the client's affect, interpersonal behavior, mood, and so on. As the troubling symptoms become visible, the therapist can ask questions that elicit more specific information. As the interview draws to an end, the examiner probes further into dimensions of psychosocial functioning that were either glossed over or were not revealed by the client.

There are many formats for reporting the results of the mental status examination. Many mental health agencies provide examiners with check sheets or forms in which the dimensions that are to be explored are assessed. Whether one completes a form or writes a narrative report, at least seven areas should be addressed.

1. *General Appearance and Attitude:* Describe the client's physical characteristics (height, weight), mannerisms, facial expression, clothing, and grooming. How does the client relate to the therapist (cooperative, compliant, evasive, aggressive)? How does the client come across (angry, sad)?

2. *Behavior and Motor Activity:* Observe motor activities, such as pacing, gesturing, tremors, jerky movements, and tics. Describe posture and gait. Assess the quantity of the activity (overactive, lethargic) as well as the quality.

3. *Speech and Language:* Assess the client's knowledge and fluency in own primary language (e.g., Spanish, sign language) as well as English. If the client speaks, determine whether loudness and speed (accelerated, slow) are congruent with norms of his/her own cultural group. Note any unusual speech patterns—slurring, stammering, puns, slang expressions, rhyming, perseveration. How talkative is the client?

4. *Feeling, Affect, and Mood:* Identify the feelings that the client expresses (e.g., sadness, anger, fear), the affect (e.g., flat, blunted, animated), and the mood (dysphoric, euphoric) that are observed. Does the client shift from one feeling state to another (i.e., lability)? Determine the congruence between what is the client's own description of his or her feelings and what is observed, that is, whether the affect is appropriate or inappropriate.

5. *Thinking (Thought Processes, Intelligence, and Cognition):* Identify the content of the client's thought (themes, preoccupations, e.g., suicide, specific symptoms); the quality of the thinking (unrealistic beliefs such as delusions, obsessions, phobias), and any peculiar ideas (ideas of reference, thought broadcasting). Assess the nature of the thinking processes as manifested by speech (loose associations, flight of ideas, thought blocking, accelerated thinking). Determine the general level of intelligence and intellectual functioning. Assess whether client has an impairment in the ability to think abstractly that is not related to intelligence, education, or cultural group norms. Evaluate the functioning of the client's memory (immediate, recent, and remote). Is the client oriented to time, place, and person (does the client know where he/she is, with whom he/she is talking, and where)? Is there any impairment in consciousness (in a stupor or fugue state, inalert, clouded consciousness)?

6. *Perception/Sensory Experiences:* Does the client accurately perceive environmental stimuli? Does he/she have sensory experiences (visual, auditory, tactual, gustatory) that do not emanate from external stimuli? Describe any illusions or hallucinations the client reveals. Does the client have marked feelings of detachment from his or her self (depersonalization) or the environment (derealization)?

7. *Judgment and Insight:* Is the client capable of distinguishing between thoughts, feelings, and actions? Does the client have the ability to assess alternatives and arrive at a reasonable course of action? Does he/she appear capable of being responsible for him/herself? Does the client understand the consequences of his/her own behavior? Is the client dangerous (suicidal, homicidal)? Does the client acknowledge the presence of problems and his/her own role in their development? (Adapted from Kaplan & Sadock, 1988 with modifications.)

Clinical social workers can refer to instruments such as the SCID to help them formulate questions that tap each of these dimensions; or they can develop questions of their own. There are some questions psychiatrists frequently use to assess the presence of gross psychopathology; for example, they often ask clients to interpret a saying such as "a rolling stone gathers no moss." Responses to questions such as this provide indicators of the client's ability to think abstractly (but also may be misleading because persons of some cultural backgrounds and socioeconomic groups are unfamiliar with sayings of this sort). Other questions tap orientation, such as "What is today's date? Where are you? Who am I?" Examples of questions that investigate hallucinations are, "Do you ever see (or hear) things that other people do not see (or hear)? What do they look like (or sound like)? When you hear voices, where do they come from?"

On the basis of the information that is incorporated in the mental status report, one should be able to arrive at one or more diagnoses described in the *DSM-III-R*. Nevertheless, this is not always possible. Despite the specificity of diagnostic categories in the manual, the same symptoms characterize a number of disorders. Rather than affix a definite category, one may defer the diagnosis, pending further evaluation (including physical examinations, laboratory tests, psychological tests, interviews with significant others), or designate a provisional diagnosis and alternative categories to consider.

WRITING A BIOPSYCHOSOCIAL SUMMARY

The preliminary biopsychosocial report summarizes the findings of the initial interviews with the client and significant others, medical findings, reports from other agencies and professionals (if available), and results of psychological and rapid assessment tests (if performed). The report should be comprehensive and provide a view of the person and problem in the context of his or her life. Care should be given to present the client as an individual who is experiencing a difficulty—rather than as a diagnostic category.

Recommended Format

Many community mental health agencies have a preferred format for presenting the summary. Often these formats reflect the purpose of the agency and its philosophy of treatment. The one presented here is necessarily broad but may not apply to the specific function of every agency. Furthermore, particular theoretical perspectives result in the emphasis of some information over others.

    I. Identifying Information
      A. Demographic information: age, sex, ethnic group, current student/employment/household roles, marital status, etc.
      B. Referral information: referral source (self or another), reason for referral.
      C. Data sources used in writing this report: interviews with identified persons (list dates and persons), examinations and tests performed, other data used.

II. Presenting Problem
   A. Detailed description of the problem, situation, and symptoms for which help is sought *as presented by the client*. Use the client's words, if possible. What precipitated the current difficulty? What feelings and thoughts have been aroused? How has the client coped so far?
   B. Who else is involved in the problem? How are they involved? How do they view the problem? How have they reacted? How have they contributed to the problem or solution?
   C. Past experiences related to current difficulty. Has something like this ever happened before? If so, how was it handled then? What were the consequences then?
   D. Other recent problems. Identify stressful life events or circumstances that have occurred in the last year, how they were managed, and what they have meant to the client.

III. Current Situation
   A. Description of family or household: who is in the household (names, ages) and relationship (natural child, stepparent, friend), quality of relationships, distribution of roles.
   B. Social network: extended family, friends, peer groups, community affiliations.
   C. Guardianship information (if applicable).
   D. Economic situation: who is working; nature of employment; receiving public assistance, social security, SSI, or retirement income; adequacy of income; state of indebtedness. Identify economic needs, if applicable, and money management practices.
   E. Physical environment/housing: nature of living circumstances (apartment, group home or other shared living arrangement, crowded conditions, homeless); neighborhood.
   F. Significant issues, roles, or activities: student, retired, military, health problems, handicapped, substance abuse, legal problems.

IV. Background History
   A. Developmental history: from early life to the present (if obtainable).
   B. Family background: description of family of origin and family of procreation (if applicable).
   C. Marital/intimate relationship history.
   D. Education and/or vocational training.
   E. Employment history.
   F. Military history (if applicable).
   G. Use and abuse of alcohol or drugs, self and family.
   H. Health issues: accidents, allergies, disabilities, diseases; health problems in family; nutrition; sleep; exercise.
   I. Previous mental health problems and treatment: nature of difficulties and treatment, kind of treatment (outpatient, hospitalization), outcome of treatment, mental health problems in family.
   J. Cultural background: ethnic group(s), identification and association with ethnic group.

V. Analysis

    A. What is the key issue or problem from your perspective? How does your perspective compare with the client's? How serious is the problem?

    B. How effectively is the client functioning?

    C. What factors (thoughts, behaviors, personality issues, circumstances) seem to be contributing to the problems? Are these factors within the client, in the client system, from the social environment, or from social interactions?

    D. Identify the strengths, sources of meaning, coping ability, and resources that can be mobilized to help the client.

    E. Identify stressors, obstacles, vulnerabilities, and needs.

    F. Assess client's motivation and potential to benefit from intervention.

    G. Present major findings of the mental status examination and the diagnosis (five axes).

VI. Recommendations/Treatment Plan

    A. What course of action do you recommend? Specify:

        1. Type(s) of intervention (case management; individual, family, or group therapy; environmental intervention).

        2. Referral to psychiatrist for assessment for pharmacotherapy.

        3. Referral for special program within agency (day treatment services, lithium group).

        4. Referral to other agencies for services.

        5. Advocacy on a particular issue.

        6. Further testing.

    B. What are the goals of intervention? (See treatment plan.)

    C. How long do you think it will take to achieve the goals?

                                 Name of social worker and degree

                                 Title

The treatment plan that is described in a preliminary form in section VI of the outline is negotiated between the client and the social worker (or other mental health professional). Clinical social workers should offer their own perception of the client's problem and needs, but should also give the client the opportunity to do the same. In keeping with the values of self-determination (as well as client empowerment), the client's needs and priorities should be reflected in the treatment plan.

Many agencies have a form that staff members complete collaboratively with clients, in which the problems, needs, goals, and objectives are outlined, usually in behaviorally specific language. Usually the items that are included are designed to conform with the requirements of the Joint Commission on the Accreditation of Health Organizations and medical assistance programs. The following is a list of the kinds of items that are generally included in the treatment plan:

Description of problem areas and needs

Problem list (in priority order)

Strengths/assets

Obstacles

Goals

Objectives: list and for each indicate:

- Method of intervention
- Staff member(s) responsible for implementation
- Target date for achieving objective
- Criteria for assessing accomplishment of goal

Review date

Goals are usually global (Jack will improve his social skills), whereas objectives are more concrete and specific (Jack will join a bowling league in the next month). Some agencies use a method of recording called *problem-oriented record keeping;* for such agencies progress notes will reflect the problems that are listed. Other agencies use a goal-oriented system, in which they record accomplishments achieving goals or objectives.

CASE REVIEW WITH AN INTERDISCIPLINARY TREATMENT PLANNING TEAM

Although agencies vary in their interdisciplinary practices, it is valuable to have the team participate in the assessment and treatment planning of clients. To the mental health professional, group meetings provide an opportunity to obtain perspectives of colleagues of other disciplines; to learn from group discussion and deliberation; to obtain consultation and advice from others. Furthermore, clients benefit from gaining the additional professional expertise of a team.

Some agencies follow a procedure in which all cases that have gone through an intake procedure (preliminary screening and development of the written psychosocial assessment) are discussed in an open meeting of a team of professionals. The team listens to a description of the case, deliberates over the diagnosis, and develops an initial treatment plan collaboratively. Some agencies invite the client, significant others, the case manager, and others to the meeting. At this time, cases may be assigned to another worker, to a special program, or referred to the psychiatrist or psychologist.

Many agencies also have the team conduct periodic reviews of the client's progress. The primary therapist may, for example, present a report on the client's progress in psychotherapy and in obtaining resources at periodic intervals—for example, after 60 days, 90 days, 6 months. In this way the diagnosis and the treatment plan can be reviewed and modified as more information is obtained and circumstances change. Moreover, the professional staff is monitoring cases corporately—thus fulfilling their responsibility to clients, the agency, and the funding sources.

Other teams meet on a daily basis to report on new developments and to come to a consensus about consistent strategies of intervention to be used in relation to particular clients. Such teams are continually revising their assessment and treatment plan to address the immediate needs of clients.

The participation of the client and significant others in the periodic reviews of the client's progress is a valuable component of this process. Treatment is not a regimen one imposes on someone. The client should be working on problems that are of personal relevance and import. Goals and objectives should reflect the client's wishes and priorities. More than paperwork required by "the system," the review provides a means to evaluate and revise the plan so that it reflects the client's voice.

SUMMARY

The psychosocial assessment is an open-ended, ongoing activity in clinical work with clients. It is a product of the client–worker relationship as well as the social worker's thinking about the client's biopsychosocial functioning in multiple contexts. Often the assessment is put into writing in the form of a written summary.

The assessment process, however, is interdisciplinary. The client should be evaluated by a physician to determine whether there is underlying medical pathology or whether there are medical problems that need attention. Laboratory tests can also be helpful in understanding the nature of the client's problem. Similarly, psychological testing can clarify the diagnosis. Rapid assessment instruments help workers gather preliminary assessment data and monitor the client's progress. The social worker takes a psychosocial history, gathering information and asking questions that encompass multiple areas of psychological and social functioning.

Although the psychiatrist has been traditionally charged with the responsibility of performing a mental status examination, social workers are also capable of conducting these. Often the dimensions addressed evolve naturally in the initial (intake) interview. Questions that explore specific diagnostic possibilities or areas that were not addressed in the interview are added (e.g., cognitive functioning).

The deinstitutionalization of persons with severe mental disabilities has made it desirable to perform an assessment of the client's ability to function autonomously in the community. Areas that should be included are vocational skills, ability to drive or use public transportation, literacy, and physical mobility.

This chapter provided recommended formats for the biopsychosocial summary, the mental status examination, and the functional assessments. These are developed in interaction with the client and significant others by the social worker and colleagues on the interdisciplinary team. Team members can help in the development of assessments by providing alternative perspectives, consultation, testing, and validation to each other.

DISCUSSION QUESTIONS

1. Review cases in your agency, considering the following:
   a. Did the client have a physical examination or laboratory tests that facilitated the ruling out of medical conditions?
   b. Was the client's psychiatric disorder viewed in relation to the expectations of his or her cultural group?
   c. How was the diagnosis reached?
   d. Have the diagnosis and the treatment plan been reviewed periodically by a treatment-planning team?
   e. Did the client participate in the treatment-planning process? To what extent?
2. How are psychological tests used in your agency?
3. Are functional assessments performed in your agency? If not, how is information on client functioning obtained?
4. Using the suggested format, write a psychosocial summary on a case with which you are working currently. Identify the psychosocial theory or theories you are using and apply

them to this case. Assess the supports and stressors that affect the client.

5. Consider the case presented for discussion at the conclusion of chapter 3. Using sections V and VI of the format for a psychosocial summary suggested in the present chapter, analyze and develop a treatment plan for this case.

REFERENCES

Andreasen, N. C. (1984). *The broken brain: The biological revolution in psychiatry.* New York: Harper & Row.

Beck, A. T. (1976). *Cognitive therapy and the emotional disorders.* Madison, CT: International Universities Press.

Beck, A. T., Rush, A. J., Shaw, B. F., & Emery, G. (1979). *Cognitive therapy of depression.* New York: Guilford Press.

Corcoran, K., & Fischer, J. (1987). *Measures for clinical practice: A sourcebook.* New York: Free Press.

Dorfman, R. A. (Ed.). (1988). *Paradigms of clinical social work.* New York: Brunner/Mazel.

Ellis, A. (1979). Rational-emotive therapy as a new theory of personality and therapy. In A. Ellis & J. M. Whitely, (Eds.), *Theoretical and empirical foundations of rational emotive therapy (pp. 1–60).* Monterey, CA: Brooks/Cole.

Goldstein, E. (1984). *Ego psychology and social work practice.* New York: Free Press.

Goldstein, E. (1986). Ego psychology. In F. J. Turner (Ed.), *Social work treatment: Interlocking theoretical approaches (pp. 375–406).* New York: Free Press.

Graham, J. R., & Lilly, R. S. (1984). *Psychological testing.* Englewood Cliffs, NJ: Prentice-Hall.

Kaplan, H. I., & Sadock, B. J. (1988). *Synopsis of psychiatry,* (5th ed.). Baltimore, MD: Williams & Wilkins.

Kutchins, H., & Kirk, S. A. (1986). The reliability of DSM-III: A critical review. *Social Work Research and Abstracts, 22,* 3–12.

Kutchins, H., & Kirk, S. A. (1987). DSM-III and social work malpractice. *Social Work, 32,* 205–211.

McMullin, R. E. (1986). *Handbook of cognitive therapy techniques.* New York: Norton.

Rodwell, M. K. (1987). Naturalistic inquiry: An alternative model for social work assessment. *Social Service Review, 61,* 231–246.

Sands, R. G. (1984). Social work practice with victims of Huntington's disease. *Social Work in Health Care, 9,* 63–71.

Selye, H. (1976). *The stress of life.* New York: McGraw-Hill.

Spitzer, R. L., Williams, J. B. W., Gibbon, M., & First, M. B. (1989). *Structured clinical interview for DSM-III-R SCID.* New York: New York State Psychiatric Institute.

Turner, F. J. (Ed.). (1986). *Social work treatment: Interlocking theoretical approaches* (3rd ed.). New York: Free Press.

Wallace, C. J. (1986). Functional assessment in rehabilitation. *Schizophrenia Bulletin, 12,* 625–629.

Weissman, A. W. (1979). The Dysfunctional Attitude Scale: A validation study (Doctoral dissertation, University of Pennsylvania). *Dissertation Abstracts International, 40,* 1389–1390B.

Williams, J. B. (1981). DSM-III: A comprehensive approach to diagnosis. *Social Work, 26,* 101–106.

Wright, F. D. (1988). Cognitive therapy. In R. A. Dorfman (Ed.), *Paradigms of clinical social work* (pp. 179–195). New York: Brunner/Mazel.

5 | Legal and Ethical Issues

Values and ethics are integral to social work practice. The profession is driven by such values as the dignity of the individual, social justice, self-actualization, and self-determination. These preferred ideas about human nature, human rights, and how social workers should intervene guide professional practice (Gordon, 1965; Levy, 1973, 1979). Ethics has to do with right and wrong behaviors that affect others (Levy, 1979). Because social workers are obligated to act on the basis of professional values, "as far as *professional* values are concerned, values and ethics tend to converge" (Levy, 1979, p. 2). The ethics and values of the social work profession are outlined in the Code of Ethics of the National Association of Social Workers (1980).

Social work practice in community mental health is also guided by state and federal court decisions, laws, regulations, and public policies. These may or may not coincide with social work values and ethics. Professional beliefs about what is in clients' best interests are not necessarily congruent with clients' rights to liberty and freedom of choice. Professional values such as confidentiality at times diverge from statutory requirements to disclose information to protect others. Social workers must be knowledgeable about legal requirements and rights and reconcile these with social work values and ethical principles.

This chapter will provide an overview of several legal and ethical issues that affect clinical social work practice in community mental health. The convergence and divergence between legal and ethical requirements and social work values will be identified and discussed. Case examples will be introduced where appropriate.

The court cases that are cited here may or may not apply to the state in which the reader lives. Case law, which derives from decisions of state and federal courts in one's own state and from Supreme Court decisions, affects practitioners directly. Judicial decisions that are made in higher courts of other states are often used as examples of appropriate decisions by those advocates who are arguing in state and federal courts on cases involving similar issues. Such precedents are not, however, binding on other states. States do at times enact laws that are consistent with decisions made in other states or with model laws created by special-interest groups. But states and localities also enact legislation of their own, which applies to their own constituencies (i.e., statutory law).

INVOLUNTARY CIVIL COMMITMENT

Clients may be involuntarily committed to psychiatric hospitals through civil procedures. The state has assumed the authority to do so through its historical role as parent (*parens patriae*) and through the *police power* to protect the public from danger. As "parent," the state takes a benevolent interest in the welfare of helpless and impaired citizens, whom it tries to protect. The state was acting as parent when it built state hospitals that provided custodial care to indigent mentally ill individuals. When the state assumes the parental role, it acts in what it perceives to be the best interest of the client. In contrast, when the state assumes police power, its focus is on the interests of the community (Brakel, Parry, & Weiner, 1985).

In the course of acting on these powers, certain abuses have occurred. In hospitalizing individuals against their will without due process of law, the state has deprived people of due process and their civil rights. Court cases during the 1970s had the effect of limiting the state's authority to commit the mentally ill without procedural safeguards.

Although states vary in their statutory criteria for involuntary civil commitment, most recognize three criteria that apply to the client. First of all, mental illness must be present. In order to demonstrate illness, a diagnosis of a psychiatric disorder is necessary. Second, individuals must be considered dangerous to themselves or others. This requirement suggests suicidal or homicidal threats or acts, but some states include destructiveness toward property. Regardless of the behavior, the "dangerousness" must be related to the mental illness. The third criterion is the client's inability to provide for his or her basic needs; that is, the client is "gravely disabled." Where this is a criterion, it is usually not the sole requirement that must be met (Brakel, Parry, & Weiner, 1985).

The standard of dangerousness is rooted in several court cases. In the Wisconsin case of Lessard v. Schmidt (1972, 1974, 1975, 1976), it was ruled that commitment was justified only if it is likely that a person would do "immediate harm to himself or others." In Donaldson v. O'Connor (1975), a man who was institutionalized for close to 15 years was said to be wrongfully confined because he was *not* dangerous. In this case the Supreme Court supported a lower court's order to award Donaldson compensatory damages for being confined for no legitimate reason (American Bar Association, 1984/1988).

Other cases have set case law precedents for the protection of clients' rights during and after commitment procedures. The case of Addington v. Texas (1979) held that the state's criteria must be based on "clear and convincing evidence" (American Bar Association, 1984/1988), thus requiring that the basis for dangerousness be documented. Some states have differing statutory limitations on the length of time for emergency and regular commitments. Furthermore, periodic case reviews are often required (American Bar Association, 1984/1988).

Clinical social workers employed in emergency or community mental health services participate in the involuntary commitment of individuals to psychiatric hospitals.

These social workers perform a screening interview of clients, making the initial determination that a client meets criteria for hospitalization. Even though the psychiatrist may make the decision about commitment, the social worker influences the psychiatrist and may be the one who facilitates the process. Moreover, during the assessment process, the social worker may join other staff members in the physical restraint of aggressive clients—a process that not only violates client self-determination but also is an affront to the client's dignity and worth.

Involuntary hospitalization is a coercive procedure that runs counter to the social work value of self-determination. Presumably it is justified by the client's mental illness, which can interfere with judgment. Nevertheless, many clients who are committed are aware of themselves and their situations. Involuntary hospitalization is not equivalent to being legally "incompetent," which requires additional evidence and a separate procedure. A stronger reason for involuntary commitment is to protect clients from harming themselves or others. In such cases, the social worker is acting "paternalistically"—"interfering with an individual's freedom for his or her own good" (Reamer, 1983, p. 254). Still, social workers who participate in these procedures should be aware that they are assuming a parental role in relation to a client who may strongly object to what is transpiring.

However paternalistic and coercive involuntary hospitalization may be, established criteria allow many persons with serious mental health needs to fall through the cracks. Decompensated, homeless, mentally ill persons, for example, may not be dangerous enough to be involuntarily committed; nevertheless, they do not get the physical or mental health care that they need. Commitment policies emphasize "rights" over "needs" (Belcher, 1988), making it illegal for mental health professionals to impose treatment. An example of a homeless woman, Billy Boggs, who was not getting care, was reported in *The New York Times*:

> Lawyers and psychiatrists clashed in a courtroom at the Bellevue Hospital Center yesterday over whether New York City had the right to take a homeless woman from the streets and treat her against her will in a psychiatric ward.
>
> The arguments came in what city officials say is a key challenge to a new Koch administration campaign to forcibly hospitalize mentally ill homeless people.
>
> During five hours of testimony yesterday city psychiatrists depicted the woman as severely mentally ill, saying she ran in front of cars, lived in her own feces and was so sick that she was completely unaware of her illness.
>
> But the woman's lawyers sharply challenged case records showing that she had pelted city workers with fruit and a container of milk and depicting her as an "eccentric" who wanted to live on the streets and be left alone . . . .
>
> "The patient needs to be hospitalized in a psychiatric hospital for her own good," said one city psychiatrist, who warned that the woman could either be assaulted by others or kill herself by running into traffic.
>
> But her lawyer, Robert Levy, said Miss Boggs had been taken to another city hospital, Metropolitan, five times in the last year against her will. Each time, he said, doctors refused to admit her because they had determined that she was not a danger to herself.
>
> At least once, the attorney said, the doctors had clearly concluded that Miss Boggs was not psychotic . . . ("Hospitalization of Homeless Challenged," 1987, November 3, p. B2).

Boggs' civil rights were sustained by a lower court, but an intermediate-level appeals court reversed the decision on the basis of evidence that Boggs' behavior appeared to be provoking an assault (American Bar Association, 1984/1988).

The case of Billy Boggs highlights the ethical and legal issues facing social workers engaged in community practice with the homeless mentally ill. Client self-determination is expressed in the choice some people make to live in the streets and not accept help. These individuals are not necessarily suicidal or homicidal; yet they do not appear to be taking care of themselves and are vulnerable to the dangers of street life. Some homeless, mentally ill individuals have a history of psychiatric hospitalization. Either they did not comply with discharge plans for housing and aftercare, or no discharge plans were made, or the plans that were made did not work out. These clients continue to need mental health services, as well as economic and social resources; yet their transiency, mental disorders, and unwillingness to comply interfere with follow-up. Social workers, who have a commitment to human rights and human welfare, as well as an obligation to live within the law, must decide on the direction of their advocacy. Whichever course of action they decide to pursue, they face a formidable and frustrating situation.

An emerging practice in community mental health is involuntary outpatient commitment (IOU), in which clients are involuntarily committed to a community treatment center rather than a hospital (American Bar Association, 1984/1988). Under regulations, community tenure may be tied to compliance with the treatment plan, such as taking medication. A variation of IOU is preventive commitment, which has been instituted by some states to protect persons who look as if they might deteriorate. These options may make it easier to treat the homeless mentally ill and other individuals who fall through the cracks. The civil rights implications of involuntary outpatient commitment are yet to be determined. Conceivably, they can put the social worker in the role of a "parole officer" who is enforcing a treatment plan.

CLIENTS' CIVIL RIGHTS

Consumers of community mental health services have the same rights as other citizens, unless they are declared incompetent. But even persons who are adjudged incompetent and have legal guardians or conservators who look out for their interests do not surrender all their rights. These guardians may have limited areas (e.g., money management) in which they make decisions on behalf of the client, leaving the client with civil rights in other areas (e.g., the right to refuse medication, the right to vote or marry, etc.).

Many of the patients' rights that have been affirmed in court cases pertain specifically to the hospitalized client. Among these are the right to treatment, the right to refuse treatment (including medication), the right to informed consent, due process, and such citizens' rights as the vote, the right to use the telephone, and the right to legal representation. The Wyatt v. Stickney (1971, 1972) Alabama case, for example, ruled that the purpose of hospitalization is treatment; persons who are hospitalized but are not being treated are simply residents and should be discharged to an appropriate setting (American Bar Association, 1984).

In a recent Supreme Court case, Washington v. Harper (1990), the court affirmed the right of prison authorities to treat inmates with severe mental illness with psychotropic medication without their consent. The implications of this decision for persons who are not prisoners are yet to be determined. Many states make a distinction between clients' rights in emergency as opposed to nonemergency situations, denying clients their rights in the former instances. Similarly, involuntary clients who are determined through proper procedures to be incompetent can be given a treatment (such as medication) that they do not want. In Rennie v. Klein (1983), the court ruled that involuntary clients whose refusal to take antipsychotic medicine did not put themselves or others in danger could refuse. If, however, medication was needed to prevent the client from becoming dangerous, the staff could administer medication. In New York, Rivers v. Katz (1986) required a judicial determination of the capacity to exercise the right to refuse treatment (American Bar Association, 1984/1988). Interestingly, Billy Boggs (also known as Joyce Brown), the homeless woman described earlier, was successful in a later court battle involving her objections to involuntary medication (Cournos, 1989).

The refusal to take antipsychotic medication may be based on rational considerations. Antipsychotic drugs have side effects that not only are disturbing to the client, but also make visible the individual's status as a psychiatric patient. Among these are lethargy, jitters, tremors, facial grimacing, restlessness, impotence, and gait disturbances. Estroff (1981), a researcher who took antipsychotic medication herself in order to gain an understanding of the life-style of participants in a community treatment program, reported experiencing stiffness, the shakes, and flat affect.

Clients receiving services have a number of rights that should be respected. For one, they have the right to be informed about the nature of the treatment offered. The potential therapeutic and side effects of medication should be explained. Furthermore, clients have a right to confidentiality. Information about the client's condition and treatment cannot be shared with anyone, including significant others, without the client's permission. The limitations of confidentiality should be carefully explained. The client's consent should be requested for tape recording interviews and participation in research studies. Clients should participate in the development of their own treatment plans and should be consulted about recommended changes.

Many states have adopted a "bill of rights" for persons with mental and physical disabilities. An example of such a bill is presented in Table 5.1.

LEAST RESTRICTIVE ALTERNATIVE

Several court cases have affirmed that clients have a right to treatment in the "least restrictive alternative" (Lake v. Cameron, 1966; Covington v. Harris, 1969; Wyatt v. Stickney, 1971, 1972, 1974; Dixon v. Weinberger, 1975). The Wyatt case, for example, ruled that clients in Alabama institutions for the mentally ill and mentally retarded have a right to humane treatment in conditions that introduce the least restrictions necessary to achieve the goals of treatment. In addition, there were to be individualized treatment plans and sufficient numbers of qualified staff to implement treatment (Rinas & Clyne-Jackson, 1988). These cases established a standard that has been written into many state laws.

TABLE 5.1
Bill of Rights for People Receiving Mental Health Services

A person admitted to a program or facility for the purpose of receiving mental health services shall be accorded:

A. **The right to appropriate treatment** and related services in a setting supportive of personal liberty.

B. **The right to an individualized, written, treatment or service plan,** the right to treatment based on this plan, the right to periodic review and necessary revisions, and to a plan for discharge.

C. **The right to ongoing participation in service planning** and information about treatment goals and possible harmful effects of treatment.

D. **The right to refuse treatment.** You must give informed, voluntary, written consent to treatment, except in an emergency or if you are specifically court ordered to participate in certain types of treatment.

E. **The right to refuse to participate in experimentation.** If you choose to participate you may revoke consent at any time.

F. **The right to freedom from restraint or seclusion** other than as a mode of treatment or during an emergency.

G. **The right to a humane treatment environment** that affords privacy and reasonable protection from harm.

H. **The right to confidentiality of records.**

I. **The right to see your records.** The only exceptions are:
   □ Information provided by someone who has been assured this information will remain confidential; and
   □ Specific material that has previously been determined, in writing, to be potentially harmful. However, such information may be made available to a health professional you choose. This person can provide you with any or all parts of this material.

J. **The right to talk privately, and to have access to telephone, mail and visitors.** The only exception is if a mental health professional treating you denies access to a particular person for a specific, limited and reasonable time. This must be in writing and part of the treatment plan.

K. **The right to be informed** promptly of these rights.

L. **The right to file a grievance** if your rights are not respected. Your grievance must be impartially considered within a reasonable period of time.

M. **You have a right to access** for the purpose of receiving assistance to understand, exercise and protect your rights to:
   □ The rights protection service within the program or facility,
   □ The client advocate in the mental health system,
   □ The system established under Title I to protect and advocate the rights of mentally ill individuals.
   □ Another qualified advocate.

N. **The right to exercise these rights without reprisal,** including reprisal in the form of denial of appropriate, available treatment.

O. **The right to referral** to other mental health services upon discharge.

Source: P.L. 99–319 Protection and Advocacy for Mentally Ill Individuals Act of 1986 as abridged by Ohio Legal Rights Service and author.

The "least restrictive" criterion was defined in the *Report to the President* by the President's Commission on Mental Health (1978) as:

> . . . maintaining the greatest degree of freedom, self determination, autonomy, dignity, and integrity of body, mind, and spirit for the individual while he or she participates in treatment or receives services. (p. 44)

It is widely accepted that treatment should only minimally compromise a person's freedom.

The criterion of "least restrictive environment" is closely associated with the deinstitutionalization movement, which grew out of concerns about the way in which public hospitals had been run. During the 1960s, many of the abuses of hospitalization were described in the social science literature. In his book, *Asylums,* Goffman (1961) described the process of dehumanization and degradation that occurs in "total institutions." The impersonal treatment of masses of people in a psychiatric institution strips a person of any sense of identity or dignity. Barton (1966) described a psychiatric syndrome, "institutional neurosis," that is a by-product of hospitalization.

> Institutional neurosis is a disease characterized by apathy, lack of initiative, loss of interest more marked in things and events not immediately personal or present, submissiveness, and sometimes no expression of feelings of resentment at harsh or unfair orders. (p. 14)
>
> Schizophrenia, depression, mental subnormality, or organic dementia may predispose to withdrawal and apathy, but isolating a patient and forcing him to lead a dependent regimented life will produce apathy and dependence in its own right. (p. 5)

Wing's (1962) research provided further support for the argument that hospitals promoted dependence. He found that long-term hospitalization was associated with a negative attitude toward discharge.

The least restrictive alternative applies to the treatment environment and the modes of intervention that are used. Both are evaluated in relation to the treatment objectives for the individual client (Brakel, Parry, & Weiner, 1985). The *most* restrictive environment is the most confining and intrusive (Rinas & Clyne-Jackson, 1988); for example, an institution that keeps the client behind locked doors. The *least* is a community setting in which the client has freedom of movement. At the point of screening for admission, the client's treatment needs should be assessed in relation to alternative settings in which these needs can be met. For example, if an individual can be treated effectively in a community mental health center and partial hospitalization program while living at home, hospitalization should be avoided. Similarly clients who are hospitalized should not be placed in constricting units, such as maximum-security wards, if this degree of restriction is not therapeutic. Clients who are moved to more confining units or treatment facilities are entitled to a hearing (Brakel, Parry, & Weiner, 1985).

The kinds of interventions used are also encompassed under least restrictive alternative. Those therapies that affect physical functioning (e.g., medication, shock treatment) are more intrusive than "talk" therapies; aversive treatment is more coercive than systematic desensitization; physical restraints are more confining than calm coaxing. Mental health practitioners are encouraged to use the lesser alternative that promises to help the client (Rinas & Clyne-Jackson, 1988).

The client's medication also falls under the rubric of least restrictive alternative (Brooks, 1988). Clients who object to a medication for a particular reason, such as its side effects, can be offered alternative medication that does not have these effects or a treatment strategy other than medication that is therapeutic. Social workers have a responsibility to be knowledgeable about medication and at times to consult with psychiatrists on behalf of clients, advocating for alternative medications (Gerhart & Brooks, 1983; Matorin & De Chillo, 1984). Information about medication is provided in chapters 10, 12, and 13.

The least restrictive alternative standard poses a challenge to local communities to provide a range of alternatives to institutionalization. Yet one city may have several innovative programs while another may have few options between the outpatient facility and the hospital. The court cases and statutes are ambiguous about the community's responsibility to provide alternatives (Brakel, Parry, & Weiner, 1985).

Bachrach (1980) finds the term *least restrictive environment* imprecise, semantically confusing, and difficult to operationalize. She remarks that living environments are not, by definition, restrictive or nonrestrictive; they vary according to the personality of administrators or caretakers, size, locations, rules, and other variables. For example, a family care home in the community may be more restrictive than a hospital if the family care home is managed by a caretaker who confines the residents to the house. Bachrach suggests that the characteristics of the client and the facility be evaluated along multiple dimensions; that, most important, is the client's need for "the most therapeutic environment" (p. 102).

Social workers are in positions in which they put the least restrictive alternative standard into practice. Whether they work in emergency services, in community mental health centers, on admissions units, or in community hospitals, they are faced with the task of identifying and exploring placements in the community that have the potential to provide mental health services that meet the objectives for a client's care. The social worker has a responsibility to be familiar with the particular settings, what they have to offer, the climate within each alternative, the personality of the administrators, and whether there are openings at a particular time.

Social workers employed in the community have the opportunity to *foster* the principle of least restrictive alternative by helping clients progress from a more restrictive to a less restrictive living situation. Accordingly, a client may live in a cloistered family care home upon discharge, but after a few months, move to a halfway house that has a more aggressive treatment program. Upon completion of a period of treatment and vocational rehabilitation, the client may share an apartment with a friend.

Although Brooks (1988) asserts that social workers' obligation is to make "a good faith effort" to explore less restrictive alternatives, many social workers will want to actively assist clients in their movement toward increasing autonomy. These workers, however, may encounter resistance from clients, family members of clients, and coworkers. Clients and their families may be fearful of a move from a secure but restrictive facility to a more open one; they may have doubts about a client's capacity to handle freedom and worry that the client will fail. Coworkers may be less committed to libertarian values and more protective of clients than the social worker. Or there may be a combination of resistances, including political interference, which is illustrated in the following case.

Ella Frank, a 58-year-old widow, was discharged from a state hospital to a family care home in a small town in the Midwest. Ella had been hospitalized for major depression, which developed after the death of her husband. The client, who was judged unable to care for herself at the time she was admitted to the hospital, remained in the hospital for 4 months. She was put on antidepressant medication and, upon discharge, was assigned to a young clinical social worker (Claire) in the community outpatient department of the hospital. After a year of working with this client, the social worker was convinced that Ella could live successfully in her own apartment. Ella had financial resources managed by her brother (he became her guardian at the time of her hospitalization), as well as social security income. The social worker worked with Ella to increase her social and financial management skills. The client wanted to live independently but had some fears about being on her own.

Objections to this plan came from Ted, the housing specialist for the outpatient department. He complained to Claire's supervisor that she was too inexperienced to assess the client's needs; that Ella was comfortable in the family care home and would not even have aspired to move had not the social worker suggested this. Some time later, it was learned that Ella's brother, a local politician, had been putting pressure on Ted to oppose Ella's move. The brother wanted to remain her guardian and argued that Ella was "safe" in the family care home.

In this case, interference came from a colleague who held a specialized work role. Ted was asked by Ella's brother, a politician, to stop the social worker from promoting changes in Ella's situation. This politician had the power to influence the city's zoning regulations of future group homes. The social worker felt that her actions were in the best interest of the client and consistent with the requirement that treatment take place in the least restrictive environment. Fortunately for Claire and Ella, Claire was supported by her supervisor, who filed an internal complaint about Ted's interference.

Certainly the client's attitude about moving toward a less restrictive environment should be considered. Sometimes clients are comfortable in settings, such as boarding homes, that appear to the social worker to be restrictive. Clients' feelings about relocating from a familiar place and increasing their responsibility for self-care should be explored thoroughly. The right to self-determination should always be respected.

CONFIDENTIALITY AND THE DUTY TO WARN

Confidentiality

Confidentiality is a value and an ethical principle, and in some states it is also a legal principle. Social workers are bound to maintain the privacy of communications shared by clients by not disclosing that the individual is a client or the particular information shared by the client without the client's consent; and by taking precautions to assure the security of case records. According to the Code of Ethics of the National Association of Social Workers (1980), "the social worker should respect the privacy of clients and hold in confidence all information obtained in the course of professional service" (p. 5).

Confidentiality should be distinguished from a closely related concept, privileged communication. Information shared in confidence with mental health professionals, lawyers, clergy, and physicians is usually protected from inquiry by the court; that is, it is "privileged." (State laws should indicate which professions are included.) Accordingly, the client has the right to have this information withheld in legal proceedings. There are, however, instances in which privileged communication is disregarded. The client may sign a waiver and give consent to have the information revealed in court. Other possible occasions include child abuse, involuntary commitment, and dangerous behavior (Rinas & Clyde-Jackson, 1988).

In mental health practice, confidentiality protects a client from the prejudicial community attitudes toward the mentally ill. Although social workers may regard help seeking as a strength, many uninformed people have negative attitudes toward recipients of mental health services. Some view seeking help as a moral weakness. Others assume that if one is receiving help, one is "sick" and potentially violent. A stigma is still attached to the status of being a mental health client (Ziegenfuss, 1983).

Confidentiality is a critical feature of a therapeutic relationship. It is a way in which clients are able to feel that it is safe to share their feelings. In promising confidentiality, the social worker conveys a willingness to protect the interests of the client. Thus confidentiality contributes to the strength of the therapeutic alliance.

Nevertheless, confidentiality is rarely "absolute" (Wilson, 1978, p. 3). Usually some information in some form is communicated inside an agency. Social workers share information about clients with supervisors. "Difficult" clients may be well known by the entire staff of a community mental health agency. Case records are reviewed by internal and external auditors. In some agencies, anyone working there has access to case records.

There are circumstances in which the social worker will be obliged to violate confidentiality. The National Association of Social Workers (1980) recognizes the limits on confidentiality in the Code of Ethics: "The social worker should share with others confidences revealed by clients without their consent, only for compelling professional reasons" (pp. 5–6). The social worker must make a judgment regarding whether the reasons are "compelling" and with which "others" the confidences should be shared.

The Obligation to Warn

Two Tarasoff rulings and subsequent court decisions lay out the obligations of psychotherapists to warn others of possible harm. The initial case arose under the following circumstances. Prosenjit Poddar, a graduate student who was receiving psychotherapy at the University of California Student Health Service in Berkeley, told his therapist that he intended to kill Tatiana Tarasoff, a female student who had indicated that she was not romantically interested in him. The therapist responded by (a) getting Poddar to promise that he would not act on his desires and (b) informing the campus police in order to initiate an involuntary commitment. The police investigated the matter and were assured by Poddar that nothing would happen. After Tarasoff returned from a vacation, however, Poddar killed her (Brakel, Parry, & Weiner, 1985).

On the basis of information revealed at Poddar's trial, Tarasoff's family sued two of Poddar's therapists, the University of California, and the campus police, stating that Tarasoff should have been warned that she was in danger. The state Supreme Court said that the therapist and police could be liable for failing to warn Tatiana. The case was later reargued before the court (in a case heard in 1976 that is referred to as Tarasoff II). This time the court said that the therapist could be culpable if he did not "exercise reasonable care" to protect the victim. Such steps as warning the victim or others who could warn the victim; notifying the police; or other reasonable steps were recommended (Tarasoff v. Regents of the University of California, 1976). The court did not have the opportunity to determine whether the therapists in this case were negligent, as an out-of-court settlement was reached. Since Tarasoff, rulings on a number of other cases have stipulated that the victim should be a specific and identifiable person or group of persons (Brakel, Parry, & Weiner, 1985).

Although Tarasoff II provided options besides warning the victim, the Tarasoff decisions pose a dilemma to clinical social workers. The Code of Ethics of the National Association of Social Workers provides little guidance with respect to warning victims (Weil & Sanchez, 1983). The code does specify that confidentiality can be violated only for "compelling reasons." Although clients' statements about violent intentions toward others appear to be compelling reasons, intentions are not necessarily communicated directly. A client may talk vaguely about a fear or fantasy that may or may not be acted upon. Many clients have aggressive fantasies, but most do not act on them. The social worker, however, must make a judgment about how serious the client is about carrying out such an act, whether there is a specific victim, and whether the intended victim is in danger. If the act seems likely to occur, the social worker (or other mental health professional) is obligated to warn the victim or take some other reasonable step.

The Tarasoff rulings put pressure on mental health workers not only to make assessments about a client's "dangerousness," but to *predict* whether an individual poses a threat to another. A task force of the American Psychiatric Association reported serious reservations about the ability of therapists to foresee violent behavior; mistakes can be made. Moreover, warning a victim or other appropriate parties can jeopardize the therapeutic relationship (Brakel, Parry, & Weiner, 1985). In warning another, a therapist is violating the client's trust. The resulting sense of betrayal may make it virtually impossible for the therapeutic relationship to continue.

Several channels are open to the social worker faced with such a case. First, one should get legal information about how the Tarasoff rulings are interpreted in one's own state. In the state of Ohio, for example, an amendment to a mental health reorganization act provides immunity to mental health workers:

> No person shall be liable for any harm that results to any other person as a result of failing to disclose any confidential information about a mental health client or failing to otherwise attempt to protect such other person from harm by such client. (Ohio S.B. 156, 1989, p. 143)

In states that do not provide immunity (and even those that do), one should consider a range of options regarding whom one should warn (the intended victim, the police, or others), as well as initiating involuntary hospitalization for the client. Consultation with another staff member, especially a psychiatrist, is desirable (Brooks, 1988). Similarly, the agency's attorney might be contacted.

LABELING

A label is a name or category assigned to an entity that provides information about the entity. A shorthand way of describing something or someone, on the surface, this appears to be a neutral process. Some labels, however, have negative connotations. More than simply providing information, they arouse feelings of fear, horror, or distaste. When a negatively valued label is assigned to a person, the individual may be rejected by employers, friends, and landlords.

Diagnostic Labels

Diagnoses are labels used by mental health professionals to determine the category of mental disorder that is applicable to the case. Ordinarily they correspond to the categories described in the *DSM-III-R*. Because treatment is based on diagnosis (as well as other dimensions of the assessment), it is helpful to make these determinations. Diagnoses are also needed to obtain third-party payments.

Diagnostic categories, like other labels, sometimes harm clients. In such instances, a client is equated with the diagnosis—"a schizophrenic," or "a borderline"—rather than as a *person with* a particular disorder or diagnosis. Clinical social workers should recognize that the diagnostic categories describe disorders, not people, and that regardless of the label, individuals have feelings, hopes, dreams, needs, talents, and beliefs that should be appreciated. It is possible to use diagnostic categories to guide treatment without losing sight of the individuality of the client.

A number of research studies have demonstrated the inadequacy of diagnostic practices. Rosenhan (1973) described a study in which eight pseudopatients presented themselves for admission at 12 different hospitals across the country. The participants provided biographical information that closely resembled their actual experiences, but complained of having auditory hallucinations. Surprisingly, all eight were admitted, seven with the diagnosis of schizophrenia. Once they were hospitalized, they ceased presenting symptoms other than a short-lived expression of anxiety. While hospitalized, other patients, rather than staff, suspected the pseudopatients' sanity. Behaviors of pseudo and actual patients that were context-related (e.g., pacing in response to boredom) were interpreted as pathological. The author commented about the minimal contacts between patients and staff and the overwhelming feelings of powerlessness and depersonalization that the pseudopatients experienced. He concluded that "we cannot distinguish the sane from the insane in psychiatric hospitals" (p. 257).

Temerlin (1970) conducted research that had similar goals. In his study, groups of mental health professionals and nonprofessional subjects assessed the mental status of an actor posing as a mentally healthy man. The part that was portrayed was a man who had a high social status, was happily married, was effective in his work, appeared self-confident without being arrogant, and enjoyed warm social relationships. Experimental subjects (psychiatrists, clinical psychologists, clinical psychology graduate students, law students, and undergraduates) were led by a prestigious professional to believe that the man was psychotic; the controls, nonprofessionals, were not given any biasing information. In response to questions about the man's diagnosis, none of the controls considered him psychotic and most considered him healthy. The diagnoses made by the experimental group were largely psychosis and neurosis or character disorder. Among the mental health professionals, psychiatrists were most likely to give a diagnosis of psychosis. The author noted the negative impact of biasing information by prestigious colleagues on the perception of mentally healthy behavior. He recommended that mental health professionals use a definition of mental health that encompasses social functioning.

In the field of mental health, diagnostic labels can follow individuals as they move through the system. Initial diagnoses may have been made hastily, without complete information. A diagnosis of schizophrenia may be applied to a "socially and vocationally disabled person with a severe personality disorder intensified by drug and alcohol use or abuse" (Pepper, 1988; p. 7). Such a diagnosis is retained in case records and referral summaries. Even though diagnoses are not very reliable (Kutchins & Kirk, 1986) and can change over time, often enough they are not revised.

Labeling refers to more than the diagnosis. Sometimes clinical social workers use pejorative language to describe clients in case records. Clients characterized as hostile-dependent, manipulative, defensive, and controlling are being labeled as undesirable clients. The negative evaluations, which remain in case records, follow persons throughout their careers as clients. Similarly, the use of disparaging language in informal conversations with coworkers can have a negative impact on their perception of clients.

In developing diagnoses, clinical social workers should beware of their own ethnocentrism. Some behaviors and statements made by individuals of diverse cultural groups make sense within their own reference group but appear odd and peculiar to outsiders. The social worker who is not familiar with the meaning system of a client's cultural group cannot make an accurate diagnosis of a client's condition.

Social work values can be used as a guide for clinical social workers in their work with clients who have been given diagnoses. The clinician should perceive the client as a complex individual rather than in terms of his or her status ("chronically mentally ill") or diagnosis. This can be done as one social work student described:

> I *never* say that a person *is* "X," rather that they are suffering from the symptoms of "X." I try to talk about strengths that I see can be built upon; I talk about ways in which adverse effects of an illness can be minimized. I try to utilize the pain and fear associated with an illness like schizophrenia as a *motivating* force for taking some action — rather than as an excuse for social withdrawal. When I'm speaking with the family, rather than using labels, I talk about the behavioral implications of the illness.
>
> —Christopher Russell, a student

The client should not be discriminated against on either of these bases, nor described in negative terms to colleagues or in case records. In addition, social workers should be sensitive to behaviors that, although they may seem unusual to the clinician, are meaningful in the context of the client's ethnic or cultural group.

Inaccurate Diagnoses

Increasingly, clinical social workers are responsible for the psychiatric diagnosis of clients with whom they work. Specifically, they are asked to utilize the *DSM-III-R* (American Psychiatric Association, 1987).

According to a survey of a national sample of clinical social workers (Kutchins & Kirk, 1988), 80 percent of the respondents said that they used the manual several times a month or more. Their reasons for using it, however, raise questions about their belief in the value of the document. The primary motivation for using the manual is administrative—for insurance purposes, to complete paperwork for Medicaid or Supplemental Security Income, and because their agencies require it. Furthermore, many of the respondents did not find the manual useful for treatment planning. Although diagnosis is supposed to provide guidelines for treatment, respondents did not use it that way. The authors conclude that diagnosis has "business functions."

The same authors raise more serious questions in other writings (Kirk & Kutchins, 1988; Kutchins & Kirk, 1987). The same survey revealed that social workers make milder diagnoses when more serious ones are called for (i.e., they underdiagnose) and more serious diagnoses when milder ones are in order (i.e, they overdiagnose). Social workers underdiagnose disorders to protect clients from possible damaging effects of labeling. Accordingly, they might use "adjustment disorder with depressed mood" rather than "major depression," for example. In contrast, overdiagnosis occurs in order to assure that a client will qualify for reimbursement by third-party payees. Some diagnoses (such as V-codes describing family systems problems) do not denote individual disorders. The *DSM-III-R* is primarily concerned with mental disorders that reside in the individual.

Social workers who underdiagnose or overdiagnose may sincerely believe that they are doing this for the client's own good. Social workers understand how damaging labeling can be, how labels can interfere with a person's opportunities. Moreover, it is in the tradition of the profession to help clients work through the system in order to get services for clients. Nevertheless, it is not ethical to lie about a client's diagnosis. Furthermore, overdiagnosis produces a label that can be damaging to a client.

At issue is the need to provide an accurate diagnosis. Poor reliability, however, suggests that even honestly obtained diagnoses are not altogether scientific (Kutchins & Kirk, 1986). At best, clinicians agree on the overall category (e.g., anxiety disorder) but not the subtype (e.g., generalized anxiety disorder). Still, one does have a responsibility to be knowledgeable about the *DSM-III-R* categories and how to use them. As Kutchins and Kirk say, one should recognize its hierarchical orientation; that is, one needs to rule out medical disorders first and then the more serious psychotic disorders. Only then can one consider less severe mental disorders (Kutchins & Kirk, 1987).

Social workers are not the only professionals who are experiencing conflict over diagnosis. In the course of his participant and nonparticipant observation research study of psychiatrists and students of psychiatry who were making diagnoses in a community mental health center, Brown (1987) discovered that these professionals were affected by many external influences. Demands from third-party payors, the prison prerelease program, the paper bureaucracy, and government cost-containment policies constrained the psychiatrists in his study. In order to cope with conflicting demands, clinicians developed such strategies as minimizing the client's problems, evading a formal diagnosis, and criticizing diagnostic models. Joking was a common response. "Pressure to refine diagnostic procedures in this clinic is less directed to patient care than to other goals" (p. 49).

The Right to Know One's Diagnosis

Clients have a right to be provided information about their treatment. In fact, the NASW Code of Ethics asserts that clients should have "reasonable access to any official social work records concerning them" (p. 6). Learning one's psychiatric diagnosis, however, might generate in the client negative self-evaluations as well as hopelessness and acting out.

In a survey of social workers, psychiatrists, and psychologists at a voluntary psychiatric hospital, different patterns appeared for the different professions and different diagnoses with respect to telling families and patients the diagnosis (Gantt & Green, 1985/86). All three professions were more in favor of revealing diagnoses of manic-depressive disorder, unipolar depression, and obsessive-compulsive disorder than they were of schizophrenia, borderline personality, and organic brain disorder. The psychiatrists were most in favor of revealing diagnoses; psychologists least. The social workers' scores on telling clients were higher than those on informing families. All professions were predominantly supportive of having another professional reveal the diagnosis to the client or family, but there was some reluctance that a professional of another discipline inform individuals and families of the diagnoses of borderline personality and schizophrenia. These findings conflict with a major approach to family management of schizophrenia—psychoeducation—in which the provision of diagnostic information to the family is essential (see chapter 10).

Clinical social workers have an ethical responsibility to provide clients with competent care. They are expected to be honest and forthright with clients, respecting the client's "right to know." Reluctance to share information may be based on the assessment of the client—for example, that the client cannot handle the information—but, more likely, it is a reflection of the social worker's fears rather than the client's best interests. Clients have difficulty making their own decisions if they do not have information on the nature of their psychiatric condition.

Telling or not telling the diagnosis is also related to the culture of the treatment center. The perspective of a medical director, an administrator, a single profession, or the group as a whole may have a strong influence on practices of mental health professionals who function as a team in the setting. In cases in which telling is opposed, the clinical social worker who holds a different opinion does, however, have options. These include raising the issue for team discussion, bringing in speakers from a consumers' group, or risking the team's disapproval in the best interest of the client.

A POSTMODERN DILEMMA

Clinical social workers practicing in community mental health today are experiencing cross-currents of ideas and values that come from the field of mental health, the profession, and the law, as well as the realities of the contemporary life. The early court cases that supported deinstitutionalization and clients' rights to liberty and autonomy set the tone for social work practice with clients with severe psychiatric problems. In the 1980s, however, homelessness became a serious social problem, drawing attention to those homeless who are also mentally ill. Many of these individuals are not taking prescribed medication and appear to be unable to take care of themselves. As caring people who are members of a human service profession, social workers have concern for and want to help persons who seem to be suffering on the streets.

Social workers value civil rights and client self-determination. At times, however, they become paternalistic and act as wise parent to clients who do not seem to be capable of making their own decisions. Two sets of contradictory values—freedom and care—seem to be operating simultaneously, arousing feelings of inner contradiction and turmoil in practitioners.

Postmodern feminism has encountered similar difficulties (Hutcheon, 1988; Sawicki, 1988). This new development in feminist theory is critical of dichotomous categories, such as justice/caring, man/woman, emotions/reason, and the like. These categories emphasize polarities; yet the boundaries between the categories are fluid and the categories overlap. Rather than accept these categories as fixed, postmodern feminists "deconstruct" the poles to get to their various meanings. Meanings are multiple and related to the situation. Although public issues tend to be expressed in extremes, in practice both sides present important characteristics.

Similarly, social workers working in community mental health find themselves believing in "both/and" rather than "either/or." Client self-determination, social justice, and civil rights are germane to the social work profession. At the same time, clients' well-being and the safety of the community are important. The legal and ethical issues described in this chapter may be resolved in this way.

DISCUSSION QUESTIONS

1. Consider the rights and needs of persons with severe mental disabilities who are homeless. Are they capable of taking care of themselves? Do they recognize their need for mental health treatment? Do they have the right to live as they wish on the streets?
2. What are the obligations of the social worker with respect to a client who refuses to take prescribed medication?
3. How do you feel about sharing a client's diagnosis with the client? With the client's family?
4. Discuss how the rights of clients may be jeopardized by involuntary community treatment.

5. Identify several agencies in your community that provide mental health treatment. Evaluate these agencies according to their "restrictiveness."
6. What are the laws, rules, and procedures used in your state with respect to involuntary commitment?
7. How is the "duty to warn" interpreted in your state?
8. What are the obligations of social workers with respect to the diagnostic process? How can one diagnose without labeling?

REFERENCES

Addington v. Texas, 441 U.S. 418, 3MDLR 164 (1979).

American Bar Association. (1984/1988). *Mental disability law primer* (3rd ed.). Chicago: Author.

American Psychiatric Association. (1987). *Diagnostic and statistical manual of mental disorders (DSM-III-R)* (3rd ed., rev.). Washington, DC: Author.

Bachrach, L. L. (1980). Is the least restrictive environment always the best? Sociological and semantic implications. *Hospital and Community Psychiatry, 31,* 97–103.

Barbanel, J. (1987, November 3). Hospitalization of homeless challenged. *The New York Times,* p. B–2. (Copyright 1985 by The New York Times Company. Reprinted by permission.)

Barton, R. (1966). *Institutional neurosis.* Bristol, UK: John Wright.

Belcher, J. R. (1988). Rights versus needs of homeless mentally ill persons. *Social Work, 33,* 398–402.

Brakel, S. J., Parry, J., & Weiner, B. (1985). *The mentally disabled and the law* (3rd ed.). Chicago: American Bar Foundation.

Brooks, A. D. (1988). Law and the chronically mentally ill. In A. D. Brooks, K. S. Brown, L. F. Davis, P. Fellin, U. C. Gerhart, & A. B. Hatfield (Eds.), *Services for the chronically mentally ill: New approaches for mental health professionals* (Vol. 1, pp. 62–75). Washington, DC: Council on Social Work Education.

Brown, P. (1987). Diagnostic conflict and contradiction in psychiatry. *Journal of Health and Social Behavior, 28,* 37–50.

Cournos, F. (1989). Involuntary medication and the case of Joyce Brown. *Hospital and Community Psychiatry, 40,* 736–740.

Covington v. Harris, 419 F.2d 617 (D.C. Cir. 1969).

Dixon v. Weinberger, 405 F. Supp. (D.D.C. 1975).

Donaldson v. O'Connor, 422 U.S. 563 (1975).

Estroff, S. E. (1981). *Making it crazy: An ethnography of psychiatric clients in an American community.* Berkeley, CA: University of California Press.

Gantt, A. B., & Green, R. S. (1985/86). Telling the diagnosis: Implications for social work practice. *Social Work in Health Care, 11*(2), 101–110.

Gerhart, U. C., & Brooks, A. D. (1983). The social work practitioner and antipsychotic medications. *Social Work, 28,* 454–460.

Goffman, E. (1961). *Asylums: Essays on the social situation of mental patients and other inmates.* Garden City, NY: Doubleday/Anchor.

Gordon, W. E. (1965). Knowledge and value: Their distinction and relationship in clarifying social work practice. *Social Work, 10*(3), 32–39.

Hospitalization of homeless challenged. (1987, November 3). *The New York Times,* p. B2.

Hutcheon, L. (1988). *A poetics of postmodernism: History, theory, fiction.* New York: Routledge.

Kirk, S. A., & Kutchins, H. (1988). Deliberate misdiagnosis in mental health practice. *Social Service Review, 62,* 225–237.

Kutchins, H., & Kirk, S. A. (1986). The reliability of DSM-III: A critical review. *Social Work Research and Abstracts, 22,* 3–12.

Kutchins, H., & Kirk, S. A. (1987). DSM-III and social work malpractice. *Social Work, 32,* 205–211.

Kutchins, H., & Kirk, S. A. (1988). The business of diagnosis: DSM-III and clinical social work. *Social Work, 33,* 215–220.

Lake v. Cameron, 364 F.2d 657 (D.C. Cir. 1966).

Lessard v. Schmidt, 349 F. Supp. 1078 (E.D. Wis. 1972), vacated and remanded on other grounds, 414 U.S. 473 (1974), redecided, 379 F. Supp. 1376 (E.D. Wis. 1974), vacated and remanded on other grounds, 421 U.S. 957 (1975), redecided, 413 F. Supp. 1318 (E.D. Wis. 1976), LMDLR 32.

Levy, C. S. (1973). The value base of social work. *Journal of Education for Social Work, 9*(1), 34–42.

Levy, C. S. (1979). *Values and ethics for social work practice*. Washington, DC: National Association of Social Workers.

Matorin, S., & De Chillo, N. (1984). Psychopharmacology: Guidelines for social workers. *Social Casework, 65,* 579–589.

National Association of Social Workers. (1980). *Code of ethics*. NASW policy statements: 1. Silver Spring, MD: Author.

Ohio Department of Mental Health Reorganization Bill, S.B. 156 (1989).

Pepper, B. (1988). What's in a diagnosis—and what isn't? *Hospital and Community Psychiatry, 39,* 7.

President's Commission on Mental Health. (1978). *Report to the President*. Washington, DC: U.S. Government Printing Office.

Reamer, F. G. (1983). The concept of paternalism in social work. *Social Service Review, 57,* 254–271.

Rennie v. Klein, 720 F.2d 266 (3d Cir. 1983), 8 MPDLR 18.

Rinas, J., & Clyne-Jackson, S. (1988). *Professional conduct and legal concerns in mental health practice*. Norwalk, CT: Appleton & Lange.

Rivers v. Katz, 67 NY 2d 485 (1986).

Rosenhan, D. L. (1973). On being sane in insane places. *Science, 179,* 250–258.

Sawicki, J. (1988). Identity politics and sexual freedom: Foucault and feminism. In I. Diamond and L. Quinby (Eds.), *Feminism and Foucault: Reflections on resistance*. Boston, MA: Northeastern University Press.

Tarasoff v. Regents of the University of California, 551, P.2d 334 (Cal. Sup. Ct.) (Tarasoff II) (1976).

Temerlin, M. K. (1970). Diagnostic bias in community mental health. *Community Mental Health Journal, 6,* 110–117.

Washington v. Harper, 110 S. Ct. 1028 (1990).

Weil, M., & Sanchez, E. (1983). The impact of the *Tarasoff* decision on clinical social work practice. *Social Service Review, 57,* 112–124.

Wilson, S. (1978). *Confidentiality in social work: Issues and principles*. New York: Free Press.

Wing, J. K. (1962). Institutionalism in mental hospitals. *British Journal of Social Clinical Psychology, 1,* 38–51.

Wyatt v. Stickney, 325 F. Supp. 781, aff'd, 344 F. Supp. 1341 (M.D. Ala. 1971), and 344 F. Supp. 373 (M.D. Ala. 1972), aff'd sub nom, *Wyatt v. Aderholt*, 503 F.2d 1305 (5th Cir. 1974).

Ziegenfuss, J. T. (1983). *Patients' rights and professional practice*. New York: Van Nostrand Reinhold.

6 | Women's Issues and Mental Health Practice

As the twentieth century draws to an end, the status of women in American society remains problematic. Despite the changes fostered by the women's liberation movement, women continue to have primary responsibility for managing households and taking care of family members, while at the same time most women are employed. Women's labor is concentrated in lower level jobs and is rewarded with less than 70 percent of the salary of men (U.S. Bureau of the Census, 1988). At home or in the workplace, women's lives are regulated by a normative structure that supports the interests of men and impedes the economic, social, and psychological well-being of women.

Sociological studies of help-seeking behavior in the past have consistently found that women use mental health services more than men (Gove, 1984; Kessler, Brown, & Broman, 1981). Women are thought to feel more comfortable in the sick role than men. A more recent study of the usage of community facilities for mental health problems, however, revealed that women were more likely than men to consult with a physician in the general medical sector (family doctor or other physician) about a mental health problem, but that there were no gender differences in usage in the mental health specialty sector (mental health and substance abuse clinics, private practitioners) (Leaf & Bruce, 1987). A National Institute of Mental Health (1986) survey of patterns in diverse community mental settings found that slightly more men than women are consumers (see Table 6.1).

Women's mental health status is complicated by poverty, which makes extra demands on them to struggle to survive. Disproportionate numbers of women and children are poor (Sands and Nuccio, 1989). Women of color have the added stress of dealing with racism.

This chapter will discuss problematic issues in theory and practice with and for women. It begins with a discussion of feminist perspectives and criticisms of traditional theories about individuals and families. Next feminist theory is applied to selected populations that present problems to social work clinicians in community mental health settings. Then kinds of psychopathology that are frequently attributed to women

TABLE 6.1

Distribution of Men and Women Clients in Outpatient Mental Health Facilities

Type of Organization	Percent Men	Percent Women
State and county mental hospitals	50.7	49.3
Private psychiatric hospitals	48.9	51.1
VA psychiatric organizations	95.7	4.3
Freestanding psychiatric outpatient clinics	46.1	53.9
Multiservice mental health organizations	48.1	52.0
General hospital psychiatric units	45.4	54.6
TOTAL	51.9	48.1

Source: Table 21A_OP. National Institute of Mental Health (1986).

will be interpreted from a feminist perspective. Finally alternative approaches to treatment in which women are valued and encouraged to develop as full human beings will be discussed. Case examples will be included where applicable.

THEORETICAL CONCERNS

Clinical social work practice in community mental health takes place in a historical context in which theories that guided practice during the second and third quarters of the twentieth century (e.g., psychoanalysis, psychosocial theory, cognitive developmental theory) have been challenged during the last quarter. Feminist revisions of these theories and alternative conceptions of women are in an early stage of development.

Feminist Theory

During the third quarter of the twentieth century, feminist theory developed along with a multiplicity of women's movements affirming the rights of women to political participation, employment opportunities, reproductive freedom, and personal independence. Stereotypical ideas about femininity (passive, dependent, emotional), women's bodies (ideally thin), and woman's "place" (in the home) were challenged as products of patriarchy. Men's control over economic resources, their advantaged political positions, and their status as "heads" of households, together with a lack of opportunities for women to improve their economic status, were viewed as structural constraints on the ability of women to achieve the freedom and opportunities they needed. Women who became aware of their subordinate position within the social structure and the forces and sources that contributed to their maintenance in this position began to view themselves as a population that was oppressed. Some of these women became social activists who worked toward making changes in the legal system and political processes. Others examined assumptions, biases, and omissions in the theories that guided their respective professions.

Contemporary feminist theories are influenced by the writings of the French philosopher de Beauvoir (1968), who characterized women in patriarchal society as "other." Accordingly, male experiences, positions, and perspectives are viewed as normative and determine what is considered as legitimate knowledge. In contrast, the experiences of women (the "other") are discounted or are valued negatively. De Beauvoir considered gender a fundamental definitional category that results in the devaluation of women.

The "otherness" of women is actualized in the historical assignment of men and women to two separate spheres–public and private (Benn & Gaus, 1983). Women have been relegated to the domestic (private) sphere, where they are responsible for child care and home management, whereas men's place is in the public sphere of work, politics, and commerce. The appropriation of women to a separate (and unequal) place has resulted in discrimination against women, especially those who need and want to participate in public life. American history reveals formidable obstacles women have encountered in becoming educated, attaining the vote, and obtaining well-paying jobs.

The devaluation of women in the public sphere has made a mark on women's psyches (Fraser, 1987). Many women internalize negative stereotypes, a process that leads them to accept subordinate positions in the family and workplace. Others respond to abuse or exploitation passively. Many women need to find a way to value themselves as significant individuals who are strong and competent and have personal, political, and economic rights. Feminist theory provides a lens through which women are viewed as strong, but oppressed by structural restraints that maintain them in weak positions. Personal problems are linked with the social structure, that is, "the personal is political."

Actually feminism is not a single, monolithic theory or perspective; there are a number of feminist philosophical positions and theories. Nes and Iadicola (1989) describe three orientations—liberal, socialist, and radical. Liberal feminists seek equal opportunities and rights for women within the existing political system, whereas socialist feminists wish to change the interacting effects of sexism, racism, and class divisions in society, and radical feminists focus on patriarchy, which they wish to see overturned. Tong (1989) describes additional traditions—Marxist, psychoanalytic, existentialist, and postmodern feminisms. Thus there are multiple ways in which one can identify with feminist thought and a variety of ways to look at issues surrounding women and mental health. In this chapter, an attempt is made to address certain baseline issues. It is likely, however, that the same issues are viewed differently by feminists of different persuasions.

Indeed women themselves are diversely constituted; they represent a wide range of racial/ethnic groups, social classes, sexual orientations, occupations, and the like. What they share is discrimination based on their gender status. In keeping with the heterogeneity among women, as well as the conceptual framework of this book (see chapter 3), when the terms feminism, feminist theory, or women are used here, multiplicity is implied.

A number of social work writers familiar with feminist theory have made attempts to explain it and adapt it to social work practice. Collins (1986) affirms that sexism is part and parcel of the social structure; that feminism includes ideas, values, and beliefs about societal change. American feminism is imbued with a desire to transform society from one that is hierarchical and misogynous to one that is emancipatory or empowering. Wetzel (1986) adds that feminism values unity, wholeness, and context over linear, positivist thinking. Both writers find much compatibility between a feminist world view and social work.

Since the 1970s, feminist thinkers and practitioners in mental health professions have acknowledged the extent to which patriarchal attitudes have infused the theories and practices of their fields. Chesler (1972), a psychologist, illuminated the patriarchal character of the therapeutic relationship, the overrepresentation of women in treatment populations, and the social factors that seemed to contribute to "madness." She pointed out how sexual exploitation might occur in the context of a "therapeutic" relationship. Weisstein (1970) took on Freud, Erikson, and other theorists who, she said, "constructed" woman from their own imaginations. As Weisstein summarizes:

> . . . the first reason for psychology's failure to understand what people are and how they act, is that clinicians and psychiatrists, who are generally the theoreticians on these matters, have essentially made up myths without any evidence to support these myths; the second reason for psychology's failure is that personality theory has looked for inner traits when it should have been looking at social context. (p. 209)

Research studies have come up with challenging findings. Using the Thematic Apperception Test (TAT), Horner's (1973) research revealed that women were apprehensive about being successful. Women experienced a conflict between being feminine and achieving. Research on mental health practicners' concepts of adult functioning found that both mentally healthy men and the (ungendered) person were described as active, assertive, and independent, whereas the mentally healthy woman was described as passive and dependent (Broverman et al., 1970). Bem's (1975; Kelly, 1983) research on androgyny, in which gender-associated qualities are shared by both sexes, provides an alternative model of mental health for men as well as women.

Feminist research, theory, and practice are critical of traditional views about sex roles, women's development, and perceptions of the problems of women. The critique of older views has led to new thinking about women's development.

Feminist Critique of Traditional Human Behavior Theories

Freud.   Much of the early feminist criticism of human behavior theories was directed at Freud. According to his psychoanalytic theory, women are "anatomically inferior" because they lack a penis. This suggests that men represent the normal way of being and women are deficient (cf. "other"). Similarly, Freud posed that women experience penis envy—when what they really envy is man's freedom, not his penis (Chodorow, 1978). In addition, Freud believed that women were masochistic and had underdeveloped superegos.

Freud's theory focused on sexual repression. He believed that infants and children were sexual; that unresolved psychosexual issues stemming from childhood contribute to adult psychopathology—particularly neuroses. Nevertheless, trauma suffered during the early years of life could be overcome through a corrective, psychoanalytic, therapeutic relationship.

Among the women Freud theorized about was one he referred to as Anna O. This educated, intelligent woman, a patient of his friend, Josef Breuer, was later identified as Bertha Pappenheim, one of the world's first social workers (Stewart, 1985). Freud initially believed that her hysterical symptoms and the defenses associated with them were a means of protecting her from an awareness of sexually traumatic experiences that occurred during her childhood. Subsequently Freud reinterpreted phenomena observed in this case and others, concluding that the sexual content represented fantasies about a parental figure, and not actual events. Recent scholarship suggests that the "fantasies" were actual experiences of childhood sexual abuse (Masson, 1984). The attribution of real events to the imagination is a way of invalidating women's lived experiences.

Freud's genetic theory posed that there are developmental stages, which begin with infancy, that lay the foundation for later life. Of these (oral, anal, phallic, latency, genital), the phallic or oedipal stage was particularly important. During this period, boys are enamored of their mothers and develop a rivalry with their fathers, fearing that their fathers will castrate them. Boys resolve the oedipal complex by relinquishing their amorous feelings toward their mothers and identifying with their fathers. Freud hypothesized that women undergo a similar conflict in the opposite way. During the phallic stage, the female child becomes aware that she does not have a penis, blames her mother, and shifts her affection to her father (desiring to possess his penis or have his baby). She resolves the conflict by recognizing that it is hopeless to possess her father and identifies with her mother.

In recent years, feminist scholars have raised questions about Freud's interpretation of the preoedipal experiences of girls. Chodorow (1978) argues that girls' attachment to their mothers is continuous during and beyond the preoedipal and oedipal stages; that although girls form an attachment to their fathers, they do not break off from their mothers. Furthermore, girls' attachment to their mothers emphasizes relational qualities and is more prolonged and less differentiated than the mother–son relationship. Consequently the boundaries between mothers and daughters may become blurred.

Chodorow is representative of a number of contemporary feminist psychoanalytic thinkers in the United States and abroad who continue to find value in psychoanalytic ideas but wish to correct the misinterpretation of women in the theory. Many of these theorists identify with object relations theory, which in itself is a development of psychoanalysis. Object relations theory emphasizes the relationship between the self and others and the formation of personality patterns from the relational field (Hockmeyer, 1988). This is in contrast with classical psychoanalysis, which gives primacy to drives. Nevertheless, feminist revisionist psychoanalysis uses biological arguments to explain sex role differences and blames mothers for problems of their daughters while it deemphasizes sociocultural contributions (Hockmeyer, 1988).

Erikson.   Erikson expanded Freud's developmental theory to encompass the entire life course. Erikson's well-known psychosocial theory poses that there are eight life stages—trust vs. mistrust, initiative vs. guilt, autonomy vs. shame and doubt, industry vs. inferiority, identity vs. role diffusion, intimacy vs. isolation, generativity vs. stagnation, and integrity vs. despair. The stages unfold in sequence according to a ground plan that Erikson called the *epigenetic principle*. In this theory, Erikson recognized the interplay of biological, psychological, social, cultural, and historical factors in the unfolding of individual lives. Erikson saw this pattern as universal.

Some of Erikson's writings present several difficulties for feminists. On the basis of his work with children at play, Erikson concluded that boys are oriented toward performance in "outer space" whereas girls concentrate on interiority, or "inner space" (Erikson, 1968). These descriptors mirror men's and women's anatomy as well as their respective activity and passivity. This interpretation of men's and women's essences, based on observed stereotypical behavior of children, seems to contradict the sociocultural, contextual tenets of his theory. Feminists have argued with Erikson about the inner space/outer space dichotomy, which he has defended (Erikson, 1974).

A further difficulty inherent in Erikson's theory has to do with the sequencing of his life stages for women. Erikson places the stage of identity vs. role diffusion before intimacy vs. isolation. Research by Douvan and Adelson (1966) found that girls address intimacy before identity issues. Furthermore, Gilligan (1982) argues that the issues of intimacy and identity are intertwined for women. Erikson's "universal" stages seem to be based on men's life cycle.

Kohlberg.   Kohlberg was a cognitive developmental psychologist in the tradition of Piaget who developed stages of moral development. He studied children and adolescents, predominantly boys, of a range of social classes. Kohlberg came up with a sequence of developmental stages encompassing three levels—preconventional (self-serving), conventional (respecting societal norms), and postconventional (emphasizing values and principles). In his early work, there were six stages (two per level); later he relinquished the sixth stage (Crain, 1985).

Kohlberg proposed that his stages were universal, hierarchical, and sequential. One moves from the lowest level of moral development to higher stages, from the simple to the complex. Few people reach the highest stage. Each stage represents a significantly different way of thinking.

Kohlberg's stage theory has been challenged by Gilligan (1982), who noticed that most of Kohlberg's subjects were boys and that when girls took the same moral development tests boys were given, girls achieved lower scores. Rather than accept the conclusion that women were morally inferior or deficient, Gilligan explained that girls do not perform as well as boys because women make moral judgments based on relational considerations rather than abstract ideas about justice. She posed that there was an ethic of caring and responsibility that contrasted with the ethic of justice reflected in Kohlberg's work. Criticizing Freud, Erikson, Kohlberg, and Piaget, Gilligan cited the work of several women theorists (Loevinger, Horner, Chodorow) to support her position. Gilligan pointed out that because of their fear of fusion, men have difficulty with intimacy; and conversely, because of their fear of separation, women have difficulty with autonomy.

Gilligan's work has stimulated feminist writers to develop theory and practice which are in keeping with women's voices. One research team (Belenky et al., 1986) observed that finding one's own authentic voice is an outcome of a developmental process. Kaplan and Surrey (1984) describe a "self-in-relation"—"the way in which being a relational being evolves as a core component of women's psychological development" (p. 79). They outline three aspects of the mother–daughter relationship (primary identification, mutual identification, mutual reciprocity and empowerment) that foster the development of the relational self. Similarly Berzoff (1989) emphasizes connectedness, rather than separateness, as a hallmark of women's development. Kaplan and Surrey, as well as Berzoff, criticize several additional developmental theorists (Levinson, Gould, Mahler, Sullivan, Vaillant), who emphasize individuation and autonomy over connectedness.

The emphasis on women's relational qualities over autonomy suggests that there is a distinct category, "woman," and an essential "womanness." Postmodern feminist theory is critical of categories such as man/woman, justice/care, interpersonal/autonomous that create oppositional polarities. Both autonomy and connectedness, for example, are dimensions of human development that characterize some women and men in some contexts, historical periods, and cultures. Men and women develop in both (and other) directions simultaneously and in diverse ways. These categories are not mutually exclusive; nor are they opposites. Postmodern feminism calls attention to diversity among women and their multiple identities.

Feminist Concerns About Family Therapy

Family therapy theory and practice is another area of concern to feminist practitioners. The politics of families in which men are dominant and women are subordinate are played out in the course of family therapy. The clinical social worker functioning as a family therapist is in the position of either reinforcing stereotypical patterns or providing alternative models of family interaction.

One concern about family therapy lies in the definition of the family. Much of family therapy theory assumes a two-parent nuclear family. The fact that 24 percent of children are raised in single-parent families (U.S. Bureau of the Census, 1989) attests to the prevalence of this alternative family form. Mother-headed single-parent families tend to be viewed as deficient; those that are headed by Black women have been denigrated for being "matriarchal" (Moynihan, 1967; Sands & Nuccio, 1989). Nevertheless, single-parent families have strengths (Miller, 1987) that are rarely acknowledged.

Many clients of social workers live in other alternative family forms. Some are gay men or lesbians, whose households and friendship networks constitute their families. Many heterosexual clients cohabit with persons of the other sex, although they are not legally married. Other family arrangements, such as grandparents raising grandchildren, brothers and sisters living together, blended families, multigenerational families, and diverse roommate and group home arrangements, are abundant.

With the increased employment of women, including mothers, the balance of power between men and women in some families has changed. The roles of men as breadwinners and women as homemakers, which characterized many middle-class white families, can no longer be justified as gender linked. Today working women can reasonably expect men to assume child and home care responsibilities. With this change, men are challenged to give up the power that came to them as sole wage earners. In many families, women continue to assume most of the responsibilities for the home and children while at the same time they participate in the labor force (O'Neil, 1985). Other couples share household and child care responsibilities more equitably.

While these social changes have been taking place, some families have sought help from family therapists so that they could adapt to changes in sex roles and resolve other family relationship problems. They may have found a family therapist (perhaps a social worker) who viewed the sex role changes as an opportunity for growth. On the other hand, they may have encountered a clinician who made patriarchal assumptions about the family, for example, that the family as a system depends on polarized roles to maintain a balance (Walters, Carter, Papp, & Silverstein, 1988).

The values of the clinician are an important factor in determining whether or not the therapy is supportive of women's development. The traditional expectation that the therapist be neutral is not possible when prejudicial attitudes toward women are explored in therapy (Ault-Riche, 1986). The profeminist clinician is aware of the way in which social stereotypes, economic dependence, and internalized devaluation of women affect women's functioning in the family and intervenes to redress inequities.

Some of the family therapy models have concepts and ideals that are inconsistent with feminist theory. Structural family therapy (Minuchin, 1974), for example, emphasizes the hierarchical structure of the family. With feminist theory and practice, hierarchy is minimized or eliminated. Other theories (e.g., Anon., 1972; Bowen, 1978) stress differentiation from the family of origin and criticize intergenerational enmeshment. These concepts, like autonomy and individuation in theories of individual development, are associated with male development in western societies. Recent feminist scholarship suggests that women's development seems to be along a relational path that is consistent with sustained, intense bonding (Ault-Riche, 1986; Libow, 1986). The emphasis on differentiation in family therapy theory conflicts with this view of women's development, as well as social expectations that women be married, have children, and be good wives and mothers.

In order to counter prejudice toward women inherent in family therapy theories and/or their interpretation, a number of recommendations have been offered. Among these are:

1. Avoid viewing symptoms as psychopathology; instead view them in their social and situational contexts (e.g., pleas for more power).
2. Encourage women to develop mutually supportive relationships with other women.
3. Avoid sexist language.
4. Be knowledgeable about the economic issues that adversely affect women (employment discrimination, low wages, lack of child care, sexual harassment on the job, difficulties collecting child support). Be prepared to advocate for women whose rights are violated.
5. Develop negotiated contracts with families as a means to make rules and power issues more visible.
6. Validate women's communication.
7. Women therapists should model competence, strength, security, and self-acceptance (Ault-Riche, 1986; Hare-Mustin, 1984; Libow, 1986).

SELECTED PRESENTING PROBLEMS

Many of the problems presented by women in community mental health are associated with their gender status. Although some men ask for help for similar problems, women are particularly vulnerable with respect to these issues. Those problems that will be discussed here are physical violation and identity issues.

Physical Violation

Women are physically violated at home, at work, and in the streets. As women, they are seen as objects of prey by those men who assert their power by physically overcoming women. Women are victims of physical violence such as rape and assault. Moreover, they are recipients of sexual harassment at work, where job security or advancement are threatened unless women are willing to provide sexual favors. An additional locale in which they are violated is the therapist's office.

The physical violation of women is expressive of sexism on the societal level. Rather than being valued and having their integrity respected, women have their physical boundaries intruded upon—as if they were someone else's property. The physical violation has its psychological counterpart. Women victims of physical abuse have reported feeling like "damaged goods."

One of the most distressing forms of physical violation is rape. In the past, attention has been focused on aggressive acts of rape that occur in alleys, cars, parks, and corridors, usually by strangers. Forced intercourse by one's conjugal partner—marital rape—continues to be legal in many states (Hanneke & Shields, 1985). "Date rape" has only recently been acknowledged as a crime rather than an act of seduction to which women acquiesce (O'Keefe et al., 1986).

Rape is a shocking experience, which arouses terror, insecurity, anger, and depression in survivors. Initially, it precipitates a crisis that raises questions for the woman about the integrity of her body, her safety, and her value as a person. To a woman who has previously been violated psychologically the rape revives feelings of inadequacy she thought she had set aside. Furthermore, the rape precipitates new fears and heightens feelings of vulnerability and powerlessness. Such was the case with Carol:

Carol is a 28-year-old single woman who held a night job at a convenience supermarket to support herself and 5-year-old Scott. As she was leaving work one night, she was accosted and raped in her own car several blocks from the supermarket. She was allowed to drive herself home.

That night Carol reported the event to the police and went to the hospital. Subsequently she learned that she had acquired a venereal disease, for which she was treated. Unable to face returning to work and suffering from "nerves," she applied for AFDC and sought psychological help at a community mental health center.

Carol told the social worker at the mental health agency that she could not sleep, was sensitive to noises day and night, and had recurring "flashbacks" about the events. At times she thought she saw the rapist on the street, after which she would experience heart palpitations. In response, she avoided going out unless it was absolutely necessary. She protected herself at home with new locks and bars she put on the windows.

Although Carol had several brothers and sisters who lived nearby, she was ashamed to tell them what had happened. Unwed when she had Scott, she felt that the family would again blame her as she blamed herself. Only after some encouragement from the social worker, who assured her that, as a victim, she was not responsible for the rape, did Carol share the experience with her sister. Carol was also referred to a rape survivors' support group run by the local task force on rape.

Carol continued to feel fearful for a few months, although the symptoms abated. She used individual sessions with the social worker to process family issues that accentuated the low self-esteem she was experiencing. During the three months of intervention, Carol attended to her health care needs, negotiated with the welfare system, and became closer to her family. Gradually she got out of the house more often and developed friends in the support group. At the time of termination, she learned that the probable perpetrator was in jail (on another charge) and she was looking for a new daytime job.

Although this case had a positive resolution, the rape and its aftermath were devastating to Carol. For a long time she lost confidence in herself and her environment. She was unable to work, contracted a venereal disease, and felt alienated from her family. A single parent who was managing to support herself and her child, she applied for welfare to help her manage until she felt better. Even though she was blameless for the attack, she felt guilty. She felt inadequate, vulnerable, and afraid.

Family violence has similar effects on the self-esteem of women. Locked in a position of powerlessness, women victims of spouse abuse are in danger of being seriously injured or killed. They live in terror for their children and themselves. Those who survived child abuse or incest that occurred during childhood are psychologically vulnerable and subject to repeated violations during adulthood.

For some time, violence in the family was a hidden, private problem. Some people believed that male heads of families had the right to beat their wives and children. Incidents of domestic violence were underreported or not reported at all. In the 1970s, research studies revealed that the problem was pervasive (Strauss, Gelles, & Steinmetz, 1979). Spousal and child abuse occurred among all social classes, all levels of education and income, in cities and rural areas, among all ethnic groups.

Family violence can take many forms. Usually it is the husband who abuses his wife. Some women, however, abuse their children. There are cases of children who abuse each other or their parents and adults who abuse their elderly parents (see, e.g., Bookin & Dunkle, 1985; Harbin & Madden, 1979). Partner abuse can occur in gay and lesbian relationships as well as between unmarried heterosexuals who cohabit.

Because women are frequently the victims of the abuse, family violence has been considered a women's issue. Groups of women around the country have organized to change laws that were protecting abusers and to develop resources to protect victims. As a result, many communities have established shelters where battered women can go to decompress from a crisis and centers where they can receive support, legal advice, and counseling.

Social work practice with women who have been battered is demanding and frustrating. Despite the "working through" that seems to occur at shelters and in counseling, victims frequently return to their abusive partners. Fear, emotional bondage, low self-esteem, and economic dependence seem to tie the victim to the perpetrator.

Like spouse abuse, sexual harassment on the job is a power play that also threatens women's body integrity. In such cases, women are subjected to verbal as well as physical gestures that are responsive to their sex—gestures that are peripheral to the job demands. When the perpetrator is the woman's employer or in an otherwise powerful position, the woman is vulnerable to losing her job or the opportunity to advance—unless she submits to the request for sexual favors. Women who are dependent on their jobs and have others dependent on them find themselves in an untenable position.

Sometimes women who are victimized in these ways do not immediately inform the clinical social worker that they have been violated. For one, they may not perceive the incidents negatively. They may hold themselves responsible for what has happened, believing that they deserved to be punished, were not careful enough, led the man on, and the like. It is incumbent on the clinical social worker to define these events as problems for which the client is not to blame.

Identity Issues

According to traditional human behavior therapists, one of the hallmarks of development is the possession of a secure sense of identity. This development of the self that is described in the works of Erikson (1951, 1968, 1980, 1982) does not have a clear line of evolution for women. If women's sense of self is relational rather than autonomous (Kaplan & Surrey, 1984), then they are vulnerable to situations of loss or threatened loss. For during a crisis, women fear losing themselves as well as the person or situation that precipitated the crisis (Dixon & Sands, 1983).

According to Erikson (1968), identity is an interactional

> . . . process taking place on all levels of mental functioning by which the individual judges himself in the light of what he perceives to be the way in which others judge him in comparison to themselves and to a typology significant to them; while he judges their way of judging him in the light of how he perceives himself in comparison to them and to types that have become relevant to him. (pp. 22–23)

According to this statement, identity is not a fixed, immutable state but is subject to change over time and across situations (Dixon & Sands, 1983). Insofar as a person's interpersonal relationships and personal circumstances change, identity is subject to alterations.

Some life circumstances or conditions affect the person so markedly that the identity becomes "spoiled" (Goffman, 1974). Knowledge that one has had prior hospitalization in a mental hospital or prison, for example, can interfere with an accurate assessment of such an individual, causing psychological damage to the individual and lack of access to employment opportunities. Goffman's discussion of "stigma" in relation to these examples, as well as the physically handicapped and persons of color, did not include women—whose socially constructed identity is also "spoiled."

Women seen in clinical practice frequently have difficulties projecting and living out an identity that is consistent with their own inner needs. Socialized to conform to stereotypical women's roles and accustomed to accommodating others, they may have difficulty identifying their own voice and vision. Significant others in their lives, such as parents, husbands, and children, may not be sympathetic with the woman's individual search; on the contrary, they may perceive her as selfish and disloyal.

One of the reasons women seem to be having such a difficult time finding themselves is that they may be looking for a fixed, essential quality when identities are multiple and situation driven. The complexity of women's lives and the roles they play do not necessarily cohere in the integrated way suggested by human behavior theories. As the case of Sylvia will demonstrate, women sometimes feel split because the demands are disparate. Their own wants and the expectations of others may be inconsistent.

> Sylvia was 30, married, and the mother of two preschool children when she presented herself at a mental health agency. She reported feeling "stressed out" and depressed. In the last year she had returned to work as an English teacher in an inner-city school. Recently she was staying late after school with students in one of her classes to help them put on a dramatic performance of *Raisin in the Sun*. Sylvia shared the enthusiasm of the students, who wanted to develop their talents as well as use the performance to raise money for the school. Although Sylvia's children were well cared for in a day care center that was open several hours after school, Sylvia's husband complained that she was coming home late and dinner was not ready for him. Yet he refused to pick up the children at the day care center and to start dinner himself.

Like many women, Sylvia was trying to balance a job with a family and wanted to do the best job she could in both areas. During her first year back to work after a break, she increased her responsibilities and experienced increasing demands. In the school she found meaning in helping the children put on a play. While in her mind she could be a committed teacher and a devoted wife and mother, her husband did not agree. In complaining that she was not available when he wanted, he was provoking her feelings of guilt and inadequacy and stimulating negative feelings about a job she loved. He wished to retain his privileges as "head" of the household, with her picking up the children at day care and then serving him dinner when he came home. Sylvia responded to these unrealistic demands by developing symptoms.

There are some women, however, whose difficulties go beyond managing their various identities in the context of a hierarchical marital relationship. "Women who love too much" (Norwood, 1985) love men while they do not value themselves. These women appear to have a high level of tolerance for mistreatment by their partners. Like Bonnie in the movie "Bonnie and Clyde," they overlook the moral violations of their lovers. Confusing their mutual need with love, they accept physical abuse and neglect. Although they do not appear to be getting anything out of the relationship, they feel affirmed in being in a love relationship. However fragile, the relationship supports their feelings of self-worth and gives them an identity that is associated with their partner.

Some women who are intimately involved with alcoholics fall in this category. In their quest to help their lover, they assume responsibility for his problem. Women enmeshed in the partner's addiction are frequently treated as "codependents," who share symptoms such as denial, rationalization, and isolation with the alcoholic. These women experience pain that extends beyond that which is associated with the identified alcoholic (Schaef, 1986) and can be helped by groups that address the dynamics of codependence and addictive relationships. Before referring a woman to such a group, the social worker should investigate whether the group blames women for their codependence. If the group "blames the victim," it is oppressing women.

PSYCHOPATHOLOGY ATTRIBUTED TO WOMEN

Although the *DSM-III-R* (American Psychiatric Association, 1987) purports to be objective, many diagnoses are not assigned to men and women on an equal basis. Men, for example, have high rates of substance abuse and specific personality disorders (paranoid and antisocial), whereas other categories (e.g., agoraphobia, dependent personality disorder, depression) are more frequently assigned to women (American Psychiatric Association, 1987; Kaplan, 1983). Although some arguments have been put forth supporting biological factors that contribute to some of these differences (e.g., depression in women; Scarf, 1980), it appears that gender is a significant variable in the social distribution of diagnoses (Kaplan, 1983; Mowbray, Lanir, & Hulce, 1984).

Table 6.2 provides an illustration of the ranking of the four most frequent psychiatric disorders of men and women as determined by 6-month prevalence rates in epidemiological studies conducted in St. Louis, New Haven, and Baltimore combined. Although depression and phobias appear to be common for men and women, their rankings differ. Furthermore, substance abuse is more prevalent for men, obsessive-compulsive disorder for women.

Several of the diagnoses frequently assigned to women seem to be associated with social factors that foster the development of some traits at the expense of others. The symptoms that constitute criteria for the various diagnoses may be expressions of role conflict (e.g., Sylvia), powerlessness (e.g., Carol), or unsuccessful attempts to live up to societal expectations of women. A few such diagnoses are dependent personality disorder, eating disorders, histrionic personality disorder, depression, and agoraphobia.

TABLE 6.2

The Four Most Prevalent Psychiatric Disorders of Men and Women

Rank	Men	Women
1	Alcohol abuse/dependence	Phobia
2	Phobia	Major depressive episode without grief
3	Drug abuse/dependence	Dysthymia
4	Dysthymia	Obsessive-compulsive disorder

Source: U.S. Department of Health and Human Services. (1986), p. 5.

Dependent Personality Disorder

Personality disorders are persistent clusters of traits that constitute a style of interacting or avoiding interaction with others. Persons with the dependent type of personality disorder have difficulty making their own decisions and initiating projects. They will comply even when they disagree, lean on others for advice, and do unpleasant things for others in order to win their approval. Other characteristics include sensitivity to criticism, feelings of being hurt, discomfort with being alone, and devastation when close relationships terminate (American Psychiatric Association, 1987).

This description of the dependent personality so closely matches the stereotype of woman, it is a surprise that it is a diagnostic category at all. Women are not supposed to be assertive, independent, self-actualizing. They are expected to rely on others and to be helpless when they are not in a relationship. Nevertheless, it is to the credit of the formulators of the *DSM-III-R* that dependence is seen as a problem. Sexist attitudes foster women's dependence rather than encouraging their independence. Thus, it is potentially emancipating to view women's conformity to the expectation that they be dependent as a problem that needs to be addressed.

Nevertheless, the description of this personality disorder in the *DSM-III-R* and its predecessors promotes the diagnosis of women in this category. Women's expression of dependence is judged problematic, whereas men's is not (Kaplan, 1983). Some men are dependent on women to take care of them, their children, and homes. Unmarried men have a higher rate of mental health problems than women. Yet "men's dependency is not labeled as such, and men's dependency is not considered sick, whereas women's dependency is" (Kaplan, 1983, p. 790).

Eating Disorders

A preponderance of women are given diagnoses of eating disorders such as anorexia nervosa or bulimia. Persons with anorexia strive to be thin by not eating, taking laxatives, and purging. Bulimia is a way of maintaining one's weight through binges, purges, and related methods. Both are attempts to match one's image of one's own body with a fantasy of how women's bodies should be.

Women are valued for their physical appearance. In the United States, a lean, thin look is idealized. Many models and movie stars are teenagers, who have little if any fat. Still women are encouraged to provide food for others. The expectation that a woman prepare food for others but not partake of it herself because it will make her fat has prompted one author (Orbach, 1978) to say that "fat is a feminist issue."

Anorexia and bulimia are strategies some women adopt to cope with societal messages. Bulimia seems to be a way of resolving the double bind Orbach has described; through binging and purging one can eat and not suffer the consequences. Anorexia seems to be a means of living up to the thin ideal. A more radical interpretation of anorexia is that it is an act of civil disobedience against a sexist society. In protest, the woman goes on a hunger strike.

Whatever the motivation is, bulimia and anorexia are life-threatening conditions. A person can die of starvation (anorexia). Purging causes damage to the heart and diges-

FIGURE 6.1

Diagnostic Criteria for 308.10 Musclemaxia Nervosa

1. Refusal to allow biceps to be under 22 inches.
   Muscle mass must resemble the Atlas Man.
2. Intense fear of a skinny body.
3. Consumes steroids like candy.

tive system. Because of the secret behaviors that accompany these disorders, close interpersonal relationships are affected.

According to the literature, anorexia is associated with puberty, stress, and dysfunctional family relationships; depression is concomitant with anorexia and bulimia (Kaplan & Sadock, 1988). Nevertheless, these serious problems are reinforced in everyday interactions, where women are complimented when they look thin. Furthermore, thinness gets daily publicity in the media.

Curiously, the strategies that men employ to gain, lose, and maintain their weight and build muscles are not diagnosed as psychopathological. Figure 6.1 represents a possible diagnosis that could be attributed to male body builders.

Depression .

Women are disproportionately represented among depressed clients. Although some depressions (endogenous) appear to be biologically based (Scarf, 1980), others seem to be related to women's life circumstances. The repression of women in the home and in the larger society seems to foster the constriction of the expression of anger, a phenomenon that is associated with depression. But women's depression may also be linked to being constrained by poverty, sex discrimination in employment, a house full of children, and abuse. Some research has linked depression with interpersonal factors, such as marital dynamics (Weissman & Paykel, 1974; Gotlib & Whiffen, 1989).

Because depression is painful, many women are motivated to get help. It is important to determine whether the depression is reactive (exogenous, such as an adjustment disorder) or biologically based. A further distinction can be made between endogenous and exogenous on the one hand and noetic depression (Frankl, 1985) on the other. A noetic or existential depression is an expression of meaninglessness in the person's life. If the depression is exogenous or noetic, issues relating to the individual's sense of herself as a woman, interpersonal and social oppression, and opportunities should be explored.

One condition that often has a component of depression is suicide. Women frequently threaten but less often actually commit suicide. Suicidal gestures are traditionally regarded as strategies for asking for help. It is significant that many women reach the point of desperation that impels them to try to kill themselves. Pressures from significant others, unmet needs, and barriers in the social system that invalidate them seem to contribute to this state.

Agoraphobia

Agoraphobia is an anxiety disorder frequently applied to women. It refers to patterns of avoidance (phobias) and symptoms associated with approaching open areas from which there is no escape. There are two varieties—agoraphobia with and without a history of panic attacks.

Like the other disorders discussed, agoraphobia is consistent with societal expectations of women. Fearful of participating in the greater society, the agoraphobic seeks safety at home. When she goes out with someone else, she is able to avoid the onset of symptoms. Overall, this disorder protects her from expressing her individuality, asserting herself, and being independent.

In recent years, a number of cognitive-behavioral treatment strategies have been developed to help persons with this problem overcome their fears of the outside world. Drug therapy has been used with some success, although many drugs used to treat anxiety disorders are addictive. Dependence on prescribed drugs is a further issue of concern to women (Fidell, 1981).

Histrionic Personality Disorder

This personality disorder is the successor of the hysterical neurosis that was described by Freud. The dynamics of the two remain similar. The person with the histrionic personality plays up to an audience, demands attention, and is emotionally effusive. Other characteristics include seductiveness, superficial expression of emotion, self-centeredness, and concern with physical attractiveness (American Psychiatric Association, 1987). Like the disorders described previously, the histrionic personality type is an exaggerated stereotype of women. This category captures characteristics deemed desirable in a woman—flirtatiousness, concern with appearance, emotionality—but its classification as psychopathology indicates that being too feminine is sick. Clearly it is confusing for women to be expected to live up to norms about being a woman—but to a limited degree.

ALTERNATIVE FORMS OF TREATMENT

Clinical social work practice with women requires enlightenment about the status and vulnerabilities of women in contemporary American society. Some problems (e.g., poverty, underemployment, abuse) originate in the social context of women's lives and the patriarchy that characterizes society as a whole. These problems foster the development of feelings of depression, a dependent posture, a desire to be attractive, and fears of participating. This leaves women with difficulties with identity, separation, asserting themselves, and managing stress.

The traditional approaches of individual, family, and group therapy need to be altered so that the empowerment and the self-determination of women are encouraged. Furthermore, clinical social workers should be aware of their own biases and work on overcoming them. Women seeking mental health treatment should not have to contend with oppressive social workers.

Several alternative approaches to treatment are recommended. One is that women form their own self-help groups, such as the consciousness-raising groups that developed during the 1960s and 1970s. These groups encourage women to share deep, personal feelings and experiences that are related to their being women (e.g., first menstruation, friendship with other women, etc.). These groups, as well as some professionally led women's groups are designed not to be hierarchical. Therapy groups should encourage women to value other women (and therefore themselves), to be assertive, and to be androgynous. Differences among themselves are celebrated.

Feminist therapy with individual women is also nonhierarchical. Therapists demystify their role by sharing their own experiences and values (Israel, 1984; Ballou & Gabalac, 1985). As clients reveal their difficulties, clinicians can help them identify problems that are of their own making, those that are related to the status of women, and those which are interactional. The goal is to help women feel competent, self-aware, and confident. The clinician can help clients locate strengths within themselves to face oppressive forces and persons, achieve personal goals, express emotions, and assert themselves. Other dimensions that can be explored are intimacy (are the women asking for and receiving enough from others?) and self-actualization.

SUMMARY

Women represent a significant segment of the population of consumers of community mental health services. Their multiple roles as mothers, wives, and care givers of elderly parents at the same time as they are employed in the workforce make multiple demands on them. Devalued and viewed as deficient by patriarchal society, they are misconstrued.

The theories of individual development that have guided clinical practice during the second and third quarters of the twentieth century share a sexist bias. The ideas of Freud, Erikson, and Kohlberg have been challenged from a feminist perspective. The writings of Chodorow and Gilligan provide a new lens through which to examine these ideas. Alternative theories emphasizing women's relational qualities, caring, and responsibility have been proposed.

Family therapy has also been looked at through a "gender lens" (Abramowitz, 1988). Like the individual theories, these promote separation and differentiation over attachment and fusion. Family therapy may, however, be practiced with sensitivity toward women's social and political status. A number of means to prevent sexist practices and promote women's functioning in the family have been suggested.

Sexism fosters the development of some presenting problems that predominantly affect women. Among these are physical violation and identity problems. Women are victims of rape on the streets, in their own homes, and on dates. Physically weaker, they are viewed as prey. Similarly women are abused by spouses or lovers. Another form of violation is sexual harassment on the job. A further problem faced by women revolves around their identity. Because they

form strong attachments to others and because of the multiple demands on their lives, many women have difficulty seeing themselves as integrated individuals. Sometimes the loss of a significant person or object arouses a loss of self. Often women "love too much," to their own detriment. Clinical treatment with women may be directed at helping them uncover and discover their multiple identities.

Sexism is also reflected in the distribution of *DSM-III-R* diagnoses. Certain categories seem to be applied largely to women. The dependent personality, eating disorders, depression, agoraphobia, and the histrionic personalities represent exaggerated stereotypes or conflicts revolving about conforming to such stereotypes (Chesler, 1972; Kaplan, 1983).

Work with women in community mental health demands sensitivity to gender issues, knowledge of theory, and familiarity with alternative approaches to psychotherapy. Application of these strategies can promote the enhancement of women's capacities to make decisions, assert themselves, and make a creative contribution to society.

CASE STUDY

Ruth Manger is a 35-year-old, divorced Caucasian woman who sought help from an employee assistance program for "financial problems." She explained that she held two jobs, was paying off a mortgage and several loans, and had high legal expenses. Although some of her debts were related to home repairs and car payments, Mrs. Manger attributed her financial state to her commitment to her former husband, Leo, who is in jail for murdering his girlfriend, Linda. The client believes that he was unjustifiably incarcerated, that he killed Linda in self-defense after she threatened to turn him in to the police for dealing with drugs. Mrs. Manger said that she and her husband broke up because of his relationship

with Linda, but since Leo has been imprisoned, Leo has apologized for leaving her and has proclaimed his love for Ruth. Mrs. Manger has responded by visiting him daily and trying to help him receive fair treatment by the legal system.

In the process of assisting Leo in his negotiations with lawyers, Mrs. Manger became convinced that the court-appointed lawyer was neglecting him. With Leo's concurrence, they hired a private attorney. Mrs. Manger took a second mortgage of $5000 on her house in order to pay this lawyer. When the case went to trial, Leo lost. An appeal is currently underway. In order to pay for the appeal, Mrs. Manger has borrowed money through her bank card.

Mrs. Manger reported feeling "nervous," having frequent headaches, and losing weight. She has less energy but more on her mind than she ever had. She feels overwhelmed with her financial responsibilities and, with two jobs, she has little time to spend with Patricia, her 16-year-old daughter. Patricia is a good student, who keeps busy with her school activities and babysitting. At times, however, Patricia complains that her mother does not seem interested in her. Mrs. Manger said that her daughter has been loyal to her, as have a few of her friends. On the other hand, her brother and sister have told her that she is "crazy" to pursue the relationship with Leo and have urged her to give him up. Mrs. Manger thinks that since the murder was publicized in the newspaper, some of her coworkers have gossiped about her. Having two jobs gives her an "escape" from the criticism of others. Nevertheless, both are low-paying jobs that provide few intrinsic rewards.

Mrs. Manger is the middle of three children. Her brother and sister have stable marriages and "no problems"; she has had two divorces. When she was a child, she was picked on by her older sister and beaten by her father, who described her as "a wild card." Mrs. Manger suspected that her father was not her real father. Her parents died soon after her first marriage 15 years ago. Mrs. Manger and her first husband were divorced after 5 years of marriage, when Patricia was four, following an episode in which her husband molested their daughter. The client said that her "ex" still paid a small amount of child support but he is not allowed to visit. Mrs. Manger met Leo 8 years after her first divorce, after she had bought her house. She said that she was happy with Leo until he began to run around. She said that neither of them used drugs when they were together, but Leo may have sold drugs occasionally. Over the years he worked as an auto mechanic at several different garages. Sometimes he would come up with extra money about which she would not ask questions. She described Leo as a smooth-talking man who was able to charm his way through life. Mrs. Manger said that she loved Leo, but wondered if, as her brother and sister said, she was "crazy."

Discussion Questions

1. Explain why Mrs. Manger is a "woman who loves too much."
2. Why do you think she has remained in this relationship? What are the costs Mrs. Manger is accruing for loving Leo? What are the benefits?
3. In what ways is Mrs. Manger oppressed as a woman?
4. In what ways are Mrs. Manger's depression and anxiety related to her situation as a woman?
5. What issues is this client refusing to face? Why?
6. How would you assess this case?
7. If you were assigned this case, how would you proceed?

REFERENCES

Abramowitz, M. (1988). *Regulating the lives of women.* Boston, MA: Southend Press.

American Psychiatric Association. (1987). *Diagnostic and statistical manual of mental disorders (DSM-III-R)* (3rd ed., rev.). Washington, DC: Author.

Anon. (1972). Toward a differentiation of a self from one's own family. In J. L. Framo (Ed.),

Family interaction (pp. 113–173). New York: Springer.

Ault-Riche, M. (1986). A feminist critique of five schools of family therapy. In M. Ault-Riche (Ed.), *Women and family therapy* (pp. 1–24). Rockville, MD: Aspen.

Ballou, M., & Gabalac. (1985). *A feminist position on mental health.* Springfield, IL: Charles C. Thomas.

de Beauvoir, S. (1968). *The second sex.* New York: Modern Library.

Belenky, M. F., Clinchy, B. M., Goldberger, N. R., & Tarule, J. M. (1986). *Women's ways of knowing: The development of self, voice, and mind.* New York: Basic Books.

Bem, S. L. (1975). Sex role adaptability: One consequence of psychological adaptability. *Journal of Personality and Social Psychology, 31,* 634–643.

Benn, S. I., & Gaus, G. F. (1983). The public and the private: Concepts and action. In S. I. Benn & G. F. Baus (Eds.), *Public and private in social life* (pp. 3–27). New York: St. Martin's Press.

Berzoff, J. (1989). From separation to connection: Shifts in understanding women's development. *Affilia, 4,*(1), 45–58.

Bookin, D., & Dunkle, R. E. (1985). Elder abuse: Issues for the practitioner. *Social Casework, 66,* 3–12.

Bowen, M. (1978). *Family therapy in clinical practice.* New York: Jason Aronsen.

Broverman, I. K., Broverman, D. M., Clarkson, D. E., Rosenkrantz, P. S., & Vogel, S. R. (1970). Sex role stereotypes and clinical judgments of mental health. *Journal of Consulting and Clinical Psychology, 34,* 1–7.

Chesler, P. (1972). *Women and madness.* Garden City, NY: Doubleday.

Chodorow, N. (1978). *The reproduction of mothering: Psychoanalysis and the sociology of gender.* Berkeley, CA: University of California Press.

Collins, B. G. (1986). Defining feminist social work. *Social Work, 31*(3), 214–219.

Crain, W. C. (1985). *Theories of development: Concepts and application* (2nd ed.). Englewood Cliffs, NJ: Prentice-Hall.

Dixon, S. L., & Sands, R. G. (1983). Identity and the experience of crisis. *Social Casework, 64,* 223–230.

Douvan, E., & Adelson, J. (1966). *The adolescent experience.* New York: Wiley.

Erikson, E. H. (1951). *Childhood and society.* New York: Norton.

Erikson, E. H. (1968). *Identity: Youth and crisis.* New York: Norton.

Erikson, E. H. (1974). One more time the inner space: Letter to a former student. In J. Strouse (Ed.), *Women and analysis* (pp. 320–340). New York: Grossman.

Erikson, E. H. (1980). *Identity and the life cycle.* New York: Norton.

Erikson, E. H. (1982). *The life cycle completed.* New York: Norton.

Fidell, L. S. (1981). Sex differences in psychotropic drug use. *Professional Psychology, 12*(1), 156–162.

Frankl, V. E. (1985). *Man's search for meaning: An introduction to logotherapy.* New York: Pocket Books.

Fraser, N. (1987). What's critical about critical theory? In S. Benhabib & D. Cornell (Eds.), *Feminism as critique* (pp. 31–56). Minneapolis, MN: University of Minnesota Press.

Gilligan, C. (1982). *In a different voice.* Cambridge, MA: Harvard University Press.

Goffman, E. (1974). *Stigma: Notes on the management of spoiled identity.* New York: Jason Aronsen.

Gotlib, I. H., & Whiffen, V. E. (1989). Depression and marital functioning: An examination of specificity and gender differences. *Journal of Abnormal Psychology, 98,* 23–30.

Gove, W. R. (1984). Gender differences in mental and physical illness: The effects of fixed roles and nurturant roles. *Social Science and Medicine, 19,* 77–91.

Hanneke, C. R., & Shields, N. A. (1985). Marital rape: Implications for the helping professions. *Social Casework, 66,* 451–458.

Harbin, H. T., & Madden, D. J. (1979). Battered parents: A new syndrome. *American Journal of Psychiatry, 136,* 1288–1291.

Hare-Mustin, R. T. (1984). A feminist approach to family therapy. In P. P. Rieker & E. H. Carmen (Eds.), *The gender gap in psychotherapy: Social realities and psychological processes.* New York: Plenum Press.

Hockmeyer, A. (1988). Object relations theory and feminism: Strange bedfellows. *Frontiers, 10,* 20–28.

Horner, M. (1973). *Success avoidant motivation and behavior: Its developmental correlates and situational determinants.* Cambridge, MA: Harvard University Press.

Israel, J. (1984). Feminist therapy. In C. T. Mowbray, S. Lanir, & M. Hulce (Eds.), *Women and mental health: New direction for change* (pp. 157–161). New York: Haworth Press.

Kaplan, A. G., & Surrey, J. L. (1984). The relational self in women: Developmental theory and public policy. In L. E. Walker (Ed.), *Women and mental health.* Beverly Hills, CA: Sage Publications.

Kaplan, H. I., & Sadock, B. J. (1988). *Synopsis of psychiatry: Behavioral sciences/clinical psychiatry* (5th ed.). Baltimore, MD: Williams & Wilkins.

Kaplan, M. (1983). A woman's view of the *DSM-III. American Psychologist, 38,* 786–792.

Kelly, J. A. (1983). Sex-role stereotypes and mental health: Conceptual models in the 1970s and issues for the 1980s. In V. Franks & E. D. Rothblum (Eds.), *The stereotyping of women: Its effects on mental health* (pp. 11–29). New York: Springer.

Kessler, R. C., Brown, R. L., & Broman, C. L. (1981). Sex differences in psychiatric help-seeking: Evidence from four large scale surveys. *Journal of Health and Social Behavior, 22,* 49–64.

Leaf, P. J., & Bruce, M. L. (1987). Gender differences in the use of mental health-related services: A reexamination. *Journal of Health and Social Behavior, 28,* 171–183.

Libow, J. (1986). Training family therapists as feminists. In M. Ault-Riche (Ed.), *Women and family therapy.* Rockville, MD: Aspen.

Masson, P. (1984, February). Freud and the seduction theory. *The Atlantic Monthly,* 33–60.

Miller, D. (1987). *Helping the strong: An exploration of the needs of families headed by women.* Silver Spring, MD: National Association of Social Workers.

Minuchin, S. (1974). *Families and family therapy.* Cambridge, MA: Harvard University Press.

Mowbray, C. T., Lanir, S., & Hulce, M. (Eds.). (1984). *Women and mental health: New directions for change.* New York: Haworth Press.

Moynihan, D. P. (1967). The Negro family: The case for national action. Reprinted in L. Rainwater & W. Yancy (Eds.), *The Moynihan report and the politics of controversy* (pp. 39–124). Cambridge, MA: MIT Press.

National Institute of Mental Health (1986). Table 21A – OP. Percent distribution for end of year census by patient characteristics, outpatient care, by type of organization: United States, 1986. Mimeo.

Nes, J. A., & Iadicola, P. (1989). Toward a definition of feminist social work: A comparison of liberal, radical, and socialist models. *Social Work, 34,* 12–21.

Norwood, R. (1985). *Women who love too much.* New York: Pocket Books.

O'Keefe, N. K., Brockopp, K., & Chew, E. (1986). Teen dating violence. *Social Work, 31,* 465–68.

O'Neil, J. (1985). Role differentiation and the gender gap in wage rates. In L. Larwood, A. H. Stromberg, & B. A. Gutek (Eds.), *Women and work: Annual review* (Vol. 1, pp. 50–75). Beverly Hills, CA: Sage Publications.

Orbach, S. (1978). *Fat is a feminist issue.* New York: Paddington.

Sands, R. G., & Nuccio, K. (1989). Mother-headed single parent families: A feminist perspective. *Affilia, 4,* 25–41.

Scarf, M. (1980). *Unfinished business: Pressure points in the lives of women.* Garden City, NY: Doubleday.

Schaef, A. W. (1986). *Co-dependence: Misunderstood–mistreated.* San Francisco: Harper & Row.

Stewart, R. L. (1985). Psychoanalysis and psychoanalytic psychotherapy. In H. I. Kaplan & B. J. Sadock (Eds.), *Comprehensive textbook of psychiatry/IV* (4th ed., pp. 1331–1365). Baltimore, MD: Williams & Wilkins.

Strauss, M. A., Gelles, R. J., & Steinmetz, S. K. (1979). *Violence in the American family.* New York: Doubleday/Anchor.

Tong, R. (1989). *Feminist thought: A comprehensive introduction.* Boulder, CO: Westview Press.

U.S. Bureau of the Census. (1988). *Money income and poverty status in the United States: 1987.* Advance Data from the March 1988 Current Population Survey. (Current Population Reports, Series P-60, No. 161). Washington, DC: U.S. Government Printing Office.

U.S. Bureau of the Census. (1989). *Marital status and living arrangements: March 1988.* (Current Population Reports, Series P-20, No. 433). Washington, DC: U.S. Government Printing Office.

U.S. Department of Health and Human Services. (1986). *Mental Health, United States 1985.* C. A. Taube & S. A. Barrett (Eds.). (DHHS Publication No. ADM 86-1378). Washington, DC: U.S. Government Printing Office.

Walters, M., Carter, B., Papp, P., & Silverstein, O. (1988). *The invisible web: Gender patterns in family relationships.* New York: Guilford Press.

Weissman, M. M., & Paykel, E. S. (1974). *The depressed woman: A study of social relationships.* Chicago: University of Chicago Press.

Weisstein, N. (1970). "Kinder, Küche, Kirche" as scientific law: Psychology constructs the female. In R. Morgan (Ed.), *Sisterhood is powerful* (pp. 205–220). New York: Vintage Books.

Wetzel, J. W. (1986). A feminist world view conceptual framework. *Social Casework, 67*(3), 166–173.

7 | Cultural Issues and Mental Health Practice

"These ethnic heritages are priceless resources. That most Americans have been uninterested in them and have, perhaps without realizing it, pressured those who possess such heritage to forget them is an unconscionable waste."

—(Greeley, 1976, p. 12)

Although America is a multicultural society in which the freedoms of speech, association, and religious expression are fundamental, clinical social work theories and practices have been adapted primarily to the needs and values of Caucasians of European origins. From the time of Mary Richmond, social workers have espoused such western European values as individualism, self-reliance, and rationalism, while they have paid little attention to alternative beliefs such as community responsibility, filial piety, and spiritualism. Until the last decade or so, social work textbooks and journals have included little content on ethnic minorities (Lum, 1986). The assumption was that being "color blind" was evidence of nondiscrimination (Hopps, 1987). In social work practice, however, diversity within and across ethnic groups is ubiquitous (Cafferty & Chestang, 1976), necessitating ethnic-sensitive social work practice (Devore & Schlesinger, 1987).

DEFINITIONS

Social scientists have used a number of concepts to describe group differences. The term *race* refers to a population in which inherent biological traits are passed on from one generation to the next (Goldsby, 1977). Skin color is one of many traits that are genetically transmitted. The term race, however, has limited applicability. Because of migrations and sexual contact across groups, few traits are distinctive to a particular race; for example, the same blood-group types prevail across populations. As for skin

147

color, many Asians, Hispanics, and Native Americans look white, and some Hispanics are black.

An alternative category is *ethnicity,* which refers to the history, culture, and experience that provide a basis for group identity, beliefs, and political organization. Ethnic groups are bound by a common heritage, language, beliefs, and interactional patterns that infuse their intragroup contacts. Behavioral patterns of ethnic groups change over time in relation to the changing environment.

Culture refers to a common body of knowledge, values, symbols, ways of perceiving, and behaviors that are learned and passed on to others. A particular way of knowing, evaluating, and perceiving may be referred to as a particular (e.g., Navaho) culture. Although much of cultural knowledge is out of awareness, it is transmitted through a number of communication systems (Hall, 1959). Ethnicity is related to culture, but ethnicity is also the basis for identity and political action. Some ethnics view themselves in relation to their group's history, religion, folkways, and values. Others, however, find meaning in joining with their people to pursue political goals. Accordingly ethnicity may be behavioral (cultural) or ideological (political) (Harwood, 1981a).

Another related concept is *minority,* a term that once suggested small numbers but now is used to indicate that the group has little power and is a target for discrimination. Certain ethnic minority groups—African Americans, Hispanics, American Indians, and Asian Americans—have been subjected to racism, which has impeded their ability to survive and succeed in the larger society. These groups have histories of subjugation and exploitation, resulting in high vulnerability to poverty, infant mortality, malnutrition, and unemployment. Because of their color, they have been branded as outsiders and systematically excluded from the mainstream. The obstacles they have faced in meeting the demands of living produce stress and tax their coping resources. As a result, minorities of color continue to be oppressed.

As Table 7.1 illustrates, race and low economic status converge. In a 1988 survey of poverty in 1987, African Americans and Hispanics were disproportionately represented among the poor. According to a 1980 report on other minorities, the poverty rate among American Indian and Alaska Native families was 23.7 percent. Among the Asian and Pacific Islanders surveyed for the 1980 census, 35.1 percent of the Vietnamese and

TABLE 7.1
Poverty Status Among Populations

Group	Total (thousands)	Number Poor (thousands)	Percent Poor
African American	29,263	9,683	33.1
Hispanic*	19,404	5,470	28.2
White	203,689	21,409	10.5
All	240,890	32,546	13.5

*May be of any race.

Source: U.S. Bureau of the Census (1989b), Table 1.

27.5 percent of Samoan families had incomes below the poverty level (U.S. Bureau of the Census, 1980).

Although race (or color) is a salient category in the United States, it does not have the same meaning in other societies. During a trip to Cuba in the 1960s, Alice Walker (1983) found differences between Black Americans and Black Cubans in their perceptions of themselves:

> Watching young black Cubans is exhilarating but, frankly, I also felt bereft. Unlike black Americans, who have never felt at ease with being Americans, black Cubans raised in the revolution take no special pride in being black. They take pride in being Cuban. Nor do they appear able to feel, viscerally, what racism is. The more we insisted on calling ourselves *black* Americans and spoke of *black* culture, the more confused and distant they grew. (pp. 210–211)

Just as race and class interact in ways that exacerbate oppression in the United States, so does gender interact with race and class. As a consequence, women of color "are in multiple jeopardy, facing as they do the combined forces of racism, sexism, and, in many cases, poverty" (Hopps, 1982, p. 4). The "feminization of poverty" among single women and their children is especially pronounced among Black and Hispanic mother-headed families (Sands & Nuccio, 1989).

This chapter is concerned with cultural issues that affect the practice of clinical social work in community mental health. Here the terms *cultural* and *ethnic* groups, as well as *ethnic minority*, will be used interchangeably to refer to racial minorities. Minorities of color are emphasized because of the salience of race in American society. There are, however, other populations besides those discussed here that are oppressed. Moreover, there are other ethnic groups about which the social worker should be informed. Many useful suggestions for clinical practice with white ethnics (e.g., Irish, Italian) can be found in other sources (e.g., McGoldrick, Pearce, & Giordano, 1982). Approaches to additional oppressed groups, such as gays and lesbians and the handicapped, are described elsewhere (e.g., Hidalgo, Peterson, & Woodman, 1985; Oliver, 1983). Women were discussed in chapter 6. It is hoped that the material chosen about minorities of color will be used to prevent social workers from reproducing societal oppression in their relationships with clients. (Most helping professionals are white; Davis & Proctor, 1989). In order to place the oppression of the selected minority groups in context, a brief history is provided.

HISTORY OF OPPRESSION

America was founded and developed through a series of acts of aggression that were directed at minorities of color. The first settlers, the Native Americans (American Indians and Alaska Natives), are thought to have emigrated from Asia by crossing the Alaskan land bridge some 20,000 years ago (Kitano, 1985). At the time Columbus came to America, some 1,000 tribes and millions of people were scattered across the continent (Blanchard, 1987). Others lived throughout Central and South America. These indigenous populations presented a formidable barrier to European conquerors, who thought that they had "discovered" a new land. The Europeans dealt with the Native Americans by engaging in warfare with them, trading goods, entering into treaties with them, and depriving them of sources of their livelihood. In the process, a large proportion of American Indians were killed while others fell prey to deception and diseases and were introduced to alcohol.

After the American nation was founded, public policies that undermined American Indian cultures were implemented. These included the displacement of Native Americans from their land, the creation of reservations, sending Native American children away to American-style boarding schools, and land redistribution (Kitano, 1985). Today there are some 300 tribes (Blanchard, 1987) and 1.5 million persons (U.S. Bureau of the Census, 1980). The status of American Indian tribes as nations within a nation has created jurisdictional confusion over land, civil rights, and child placement for a number of generations (Johnson, 1982). The loss of land, tribal unity, and cultural identity has had a long-range impact on those American Indians who have survived.

The European conquerors began settlements in the New World in the sixteenth century. The French, English, Dutch, and Swedish settled in the eastern and northern sections of what is now the United States. The Spanish conquered Mexico and subsequently penetrated the natives' land, culture, and language, and married indigenous Indian women. In keeping with the pattern of expansion that was normative among Europeans at that time, the Spaniards moved into what is now the southwestern part of the United States. Later the new American nationals perpetuated this practice in the doctrine of "Manifest Destiny."

The European settlers imported Africans to serve as slaves to the colonists. Considered property, the Africans were sold for use as plantation laborers and "bred" for their progeny. Plantation owners further subjugated the African women by raping them. The forced immigration, exploitation, and separation of Africans from the same African societies resulted in the destruction of indigenous African cultures. Restrictions against marriage and the sale of African American family members undermined the establishment of stable African American families.

Although the Civil War was fought primarily to preserve the Union, conflict over the spread of slavery into newly acquired territories was one of the issues that divided the North and the South before the Civil War. The war did, nevertheless, result in the abolition of slavery and the granting of the rights of citizenship and the right to vote to African Americans. In the years that followed the Civil War, public policies, such as poll taxes and grandfather clauses, as well as illegal and malevolent activities, such as lynchings, impeded African Americans from participation in American life. The Supreme Court case Plessy v. Ferguson of 1896 endorsed segregation in establishing the principle of "separate but equal" education for African Americans and whites. Even after this decision was overturned in Brown v. the Board of Education of Topeka, Kansas in 1954 and subsequent legislation outlawed segregated housing and employment discrimination, racism and poverty have kept African Americans oppressed (Kitano, 1985).

During the mid-nineteenth century Asian immigrants (primarily single Chinese men) entered the country on the West Coast for reasons similar to those of the white immigrants from Europe who were arriving—to improve their economic lot (Kitano, 1987). They worked as miners, railroad workers, domestic servants, and as laborers in manufacturing industries. Few started families here, because of the shortage of Chinese women and the enactment of antimiscegenation laws. Because they accepted low wages, their presence aroused the rancor of whites (the "yellow peril") who were competing for the same jobs (Kitano, 1985). Discrimination against the Chinese was expressed in the passage of Chinese Exclusion Acts in 1882 and 1902 and the later Immigration Act of 1924.

From 1890 to 1924, however, Japanese were allowed to immigrate to Hawaii and the United States with their families (Kitano, 1985). Although they and their children became acculturated, they, too, suffered from discrimination. During World War II, racism directed at the Japanese reached hysterical proportions, culminating in the placement of Japanese Americans in internment camps. Other Asian populations that have come to America are the Filipinos, Koreans, Pacific Islanders, and Southeast Asians, whose immigration was facilitated by the Immigration Act of 1965 and subsequent public policies. The Southeast Asians were refugees from Vietnam, Laos, and Cambodia who sought asylum during the wars and political changes that ravaged their lands (Kitano, 1987).

America acquired Texas and the southwestern territories from Mexico during the Mexican American War, which ended in 1848, and through the Gadsden Purchase of 1853. (Mexico gained its independence from Spain in 1821.) At the time, the land was occupied by a diverse population of persons of Spanish or Mexican descent, Native Americans, and mestizos (mixed people of Indian and Spanish origins). Although the Mexicans had been granted rights of citizenship through the treaty that had been signed, in the ensuing years, Anglo Americans took over the land and secured dominance by controlling the economic, political, and educational institutions (Gibson, 1987). Nevertheless, immigrants from Mexico continued to flow into the Southwest and other parts of the United States where they were able to work. In addition, undocumented (illegal) aliens penetrated the Mexican-American borders and worked as cheap farm laborers. Other Hispanic groups, such as Puerto Ricans and Cubans, migrated in search of economic opportunities and political asylum.

Throughout American history, African Americans, American Indians and Alaska Natives, Asians, Pacific Islanders, and Hispanics have faced economic exploitation and poverty. African Americans were required to work as slaves; other minority groups were used as cheap labor. Ethnic minorities of color continue to be overrepresented among the poor. Their life expectancy is lower and infant mortality rates are higher than whites'. Segregated from the mainstream, their children have had an inferior or culturally insensitive education, in which the values of the dominant culture have been imposed as normative. Inadequate education perpetuates their exclusion from vocational and educational avenues of advancement. Minorities of color continue to have unmet basic needs for economic support, housing, and health care. These conditions produce stress, which, in turn, affects their mental health.

MULTIPLE CONTEXTS

Social work practice with oppressed minorities recognizes the multiple contexts that characterize the lives of these populations. Chestang (1976) identified two systems—the "nurturing" system and the "sustaining" system—that provide emotional support and economic livelihood to African Americans. The nurturing system consists of family and friends in the ethnic community who provide warmth and support and facilitate expressiveness; the sustaining system represents the material, political, and social provisions of the external society. The ethnic minority group member lives within, negotiates with, and needs both systems. Nevertheless, the perceptions, demands, and attitudes of the two systems may conflict. Although ethnic minorities tend to want to adapt to life amidst the dominant culture, they are asked to identify with the larger culture's racism (Norton, 1978). In order to function effectively in both worlds, ethnic minorities develop strategies that permit them to cope with conflicting environments. Social work educators have recommended that students and practitioners recognize and understand the "dual perspectives" of ethnic minority clients (Norton, 1978) and foster group pride and empowerment (Solomon, 1976).

Social scientists of the past obfuscated the position of oppressed minorities in relation to the "American dream." The idea that America was a "melting pot" into which all ethnic groups can mix was relevant and appealing to poor, white ethnic European immigrants, who were better able to accommodate to the similar American culture than racial minorities with very different cultures (de Anda, 1984). White immigrants were more likely to be served by mainstream social welfare agencies than minorities of color (Lum, 1986), whereas minorities of color faced structural barriers, such as Jim Crow laws and employment discrimination, that stood in the way of their assimilation.

During the 1960s, the melting pot theory lost credibility. This was a period in which ethnic minority groups became a significant political force that forged the civil rights movement. Their political activities, as well as increasing evidence that people of color remained poor, were misconstrued, leading to the development of the "cultural deficit model," which described poor, ethnic minorities as culturally deprived (de Anda, 1984). During this period of the War on Poverty, educational and social programs to address these "deficits" were developed. The cultural deficit model was later discredited because it evaluated diverse cultures from the perspective of middle-class norms (de Anda, 1984).

Another model that was introduced emphasized cultural differences among diverse populations (de Anda, 1984). This model, however, went overboard in emphasizing the separateness of each cultural group. Instead de Anda (1984) recommends the "bicultural socialization model," which, like the dual perspective, recognizes that there are differences as well as areas of overlap between cultures. Ethnic minority clients may need help maintaining their own identity while functioning in mainstream society. Social workers can assist them by finding or acting as mediators, translators, and role models; helping them develop their problem-solving skills; and advocating for changes in the majority culture (de Anda, 1984).

Although theories of ethnicity describe two contexts, ethnic minority clients function in a multiplicity of situations that may or may not be congruent with the majority/minority polarity. Ethnic minorities may, for example, have contact with other ethnic groups. In cities with large ethnic populations, Puerto Ricans, African Americans, Chinese, and other ethnic groups have cross-cultural contact in the local community. Regardless of clients' own ethnic group, they encounter professionals such as doctors, teachers, and social workers who represent a range of cultural backgrounds. Everyday life experiences may entail a series of encounters with individuals, groups, and institutions that are diversely constituted.

ETHNICITY AND MENTAL HEALTH HELP SEEKING

The public sponsorship of most mental health services makes it possible for consumers to represent a spectrum of ethnic groups. Clients of diverse cultural groups perceive and interpret their problems through a lens that is refracted according to the belief systems of their respective cultures. Cultural definitions and categories influence the labeling of behaviors or emotional states as problematic and the kinds of responses that are considered appropriate. Accordingly, the individual will seek help within his or her own primary culture and/or in the institutionalized system of mental health care.

Medical sociologists use a number of terms that are helpful in understanding help seeking among ethnic minority groups. Among these are *sick role, health behavior,* and *illness behavior.* The sick role was described by Parsons (1964) as a legitimized social status in which sick persons have the right to be free of blame and to abdicate their usual responsibilities at the same time they have the obligation to desire to get well and to cooperate with treatment. Health behavior refers to activities of presumably healthy persons to prevent disease or detect it prior to the development of symptoms, whereas illness behavior refers to activities of persons who feel ill to determine the state of their health and find an appropriate remedy (Kasl & Cobb, 1966). A semiannual dental checkup is an example of health behavior; a medical appointment for a cold is illustrative of illness behavior.

Sociocultural variables influence the assumption of the sick role and the practice of health and illness behaviors. In order to legitimately engage in sick role behavior, one's culture must recognize that the person is sick and sanction appropriate rights and obligations. This requires the perception of the symptoms as meaningful and the view that release from social obligations is appropriate. If the culture does not have a category that corresponds to the symptoms, it is unlikely that the person will be considered sick. Similarly health behavior is culturally relative. Although preventive dentistry and regular pediatric care may be normative among middle-class Americans, these practices are not congruent with ideas of other cultures. Illness behaviors are activities that follow from the perception that one is ill. These responses, however, may be dictated by one's culture. Accordingly, one may seek a shaman, ingest herbs, or go to the doctor.

In medical anthropology a distinction is made between *disease* and *illness.* "*Disease* refers to a malfunctioning of biological and/or psychological processes, while the term *illness* refers to the psychosocial experience and meaning of perceived illness" (Kleinman, 1980, p. 72). With illness the social and cultural patterns of perceiving, thinking, responding, and coping come into play. Most medical practitioners in the United States adhere to a disease (biomedical) model. The model is realized through an impersonal technological system in which the person is viewed as an object that houses the disease. Frequently this results in the treatment of the disease and the neglect of the person, and a divergence between the technological "voice of medicine" and the psychosocial "voice of the lifeworld" (cf. Mishler, 1984). For example, an American medical practitioner may define an *ataque* as a psychogenic seizure, whereas a Puerto Rican layperson may define the same event as a spell that was instigated by spirits. The distinction between illness and disease that is described here is incorporated in the conceptual framework of this book (see chapter 3).

Illness Behavior

With respect to mental health, illness behavior is expressed in the usage of mainstream mental health services. An analysis of data from the Yale Epidemiologic Catchment Area Project on the use of mental health services in a 6-month period found that Caucasians, as well as women, the more educated, persons between the ages of 25 and 64, and the unmarried were most likely to use services; household income, however, was not related (Leaf et al., 1985). A report from a similar study in the Baltimore area that looked at unmet need for mental health services came up with different results (Shapiro et al., 1985). In this study need was assessed by responses to the Diagnostic Interview Schedule (DIS), which lends itself to transformation into *DSM-III* diagnoses, as well as responses to other instruments; those with unmet needs reported no mental health service use in the last 6 months. The Baltimore study found that nonwhites, women, and persons living alone had higher proportions of unmet needs than whites, men, and persons living with others. These two studies together suggest that *Caucasians are receiving services whereas people of color have unmet needs.*

Some studies have looked at patterns of professional help seeking among African Americans. Broman (1987) found that Blacks were more likely than whites to seek help from mental health professionals (psychiatrists, psychologists, mental health centers) and other sources (teachers, lawyers, social workers in agencies, emergency rooms), and that whites were more likely to seek assistance from members of the clergy and medical professionals. Furthermore, African Americans were more likely than Caucasians to seek mental health professional help for economic and physical health problems. A later study by the same research group on data on African Americans found that many users of social service agencies received help from social workers and that they were satisfied with the help they got (Taylor, Neighbors, & Broman, 1989). Of the respondents, 26 percent indicated a preference for a Black practitioner. In another study of a national sample of African Americans, low-income Blacks were more likely to experience their problem at a nervous breakdown level than higher income Blacks. Of those experiencing a problem at this level, 55 percent sought professional help (Neighbors, 1984). Physical health problems were reported most frequently. This suggests that African Americans may present mental health problems in terms of somatic complaints.

A study of the utilization of state psychiatric hospitalizations in Ohio by ethnic group found that Blacks were overrepresented (29.6 percent) among inpatients in relation to their prevalence in the general population of Ohio (9.9 percent) (Ohio Department of Mental Health, 1988). In the eight largest urban areas in Ohio, a higher percentage of Blacks were hospitalized than treated in community mental health centers. This report suggests an overutilization of the hospital and an underutilization of community mental health centers by African Americans living in Ohio. Although it may be that African Americans rely on the informal helping system in their own community until there is a mental health emergency, the data suggest that there are barriers to the utilization of community mental health facilities before mental health problems become severe. The authors of the report recommend that mental health practitioners adopt culturally specific methods of service delivery.

One way to evaluate utilization practices by ethnic group is to compare the percentages of clients in treatment with their representation in the general population. Table 7.2 illustrates that nationally African Americans represent a higher percentage of the outpatient and inpatient population than their prevalence in the total population, whereas the reverse holds true for whites. Asian and Pacific Island Americans seem to be underrepresented among those in treatment, whereas Native Americans and Alaskan Natives have comparable proportions of the general population and persons in treatment. Hispanics are more likely to be treated on an outpatient basis than in the hospital; the outpatient population is close to the national percentage of Hispanics. The excessive percentage of blacks among the treatment population can be interpreted in a number of ways. It may be that African Americans experience extraordinary stress, resulting in their high utilization of mental health services. Another explanation is that the utilization figures from which the percentages were derived represent public treatment facilities, which are the only facilities African Americans who are poor can afford. Misdiagnosis and misappropriation of a social problem as a psychiatric illness are other possible interpretations. Cultural barriers may be impeding utilization by some of the other populations. Bureaucratic procedures, linguistic differences, and culturally insensitive service delivery deter clients of diverse cultures from using services. Meinhardt and Vega (1987) suggest that mental health planners consider the levels of need for each ethnic group rather than aiming to achieve parity with the group's representation in the population. In their community survey, they found that Southeast Asian refugees,

TABLE 7.2

Percentage of Population Groups in the General Population, Outpatient Mental Health Treatment Population, and Inpatient Mental Health Treatment Population*

Group	Percent General Population	Percent Outpatient Population	Percent Inpatient Population
African American	12.2	18.6	20.1
Asian/Pacific Islander	1.6	0.7	0.6
Hispanic	8.1	9.0	5.2
Native American/Alaska Native	0.7	0.6	0.5
White (non-Hispanic)	77.6	71.1	73.6

*Percentages of Asian Americans/Pacific Islanders and Native Americans/Alaska Natives are based on 1980 reports; percentages of other groups are based on 1988 statistics. Percentage of whites is an estimate based on statistics from 1980 and 1988.

Sources: National Institute of Mental Health (1986a); U.S. Bureau of the Census (1980, 1988a, 1988b).

Mexican Americans, African Americans, and Native Americans were in greater need of mental health services than whites and nonrefugee Chinese.

Underutilization of traditional mental health services does not, however, mean that ethnic minorities are not engaging in illness behavior. They may prefer to use resources within their ethnic community for support. Accordingly, they may be receiving help from close kin or individuals in their culture who are designated as healers. Moreover, communities may have special resources, such as herbs or special foods, that are remedies for psychological distress.

Misdiagnosis

As suggested earlier, cultural differences between ethnic minority clients and largely white mental health practitioners can affect diagnosis. Without knowledge of other cultures, the practitioner is likely to rely on stereotypical ideas, which can result in misdiagnosis. Clients of diverse cultures may present symptoms in ways that are consistent with their cultures but incongruent with the categories of mental illness that are described in the *DSM-III-R*. Because of differences in world views and behaviors, the client and the clinician may interpret the same symptoms differently.

Over the years, African Americans have been subject to misinterpretation of their symptoms, resulting in overdiagnosis of schizophrenia and underdiagnosis of mood disorders. Cross-cultural studies have shown a widespread practice in American psychiatry of assigning the diagnosis of schizophrenia when affective (mood) disorders, especially bipolar disorder, were appropriate (World Health Organization, 1975). Although both schizophrenia and affective disorders have associated psychotic symptoms, American psychiatrists have interpreted these symptoms as manifestations of schizophrenia, especially when clients were African American (Jones & Gray, 1986). Because schizophrenia is more debilitating than affective disorders, misdiagnosis has serious implications. Schizophrenia is a chronic disease that can be only partially treated with medication. Indeed most of the drugs used to treat schizophrenia have harmful side effects. Although the drugs prescribed to treat major depression and bipolar disorder also have side effects, the effects of drugs that treat schizophrenia are more overt and pervasive. In addition, the prognosis for mood disorders is better than that for schizophrenia.

Misdiagnosis is partially attributable to a misinterpretation of African Americans' presentations of themselves in clinical settings. Some symptoms, such as paranoia and flat affect, are adaptive strategies adopted by Black Americans to survive in an alien culture. Grier and Cobbs (1968) speak of a " 'healthy' cultural paranoia" that is essential for adaptive functioning:

> For a black man survival in America depends in large measure on the development of a "healthy" cultural paranoia. He must maintain a high degree of suspicion toward the motives of every white man and at the same time never allow this suspicion to impair his grasp of reality. (p. 135)

However adaptive paranoia may be, it is often regarded as a symptom of paranoid schizophrenia or paranoid personality disorder—which are overdiagnosed among African Americans (Steinberg et al., 1977). Similarly, control over emotional expression in response to a white therapist who is not trusted may be misinterpreted as blunted or flat affect, which are symptoms of schizophrenia (Jones & Gray, 1986).

Misdiagnosis of African Americans may result in overlooking mood and related disorders. Allen (1986) reports a high incidence of posttraumatic stress disorder (PTSD) among Black veterans of the Vietnam War. In the process of talking about the trauma of war in psychotherapy, African American veterans have revealed that they are haunted by memories of genocide against a Third World people, racism in the military, and postwar racism. Allen believes that depression underlies PTSD. Furthermore, symptoms of PTSD may be masked by substance abuse, psychophysiological complaints, and disorganized behavior.

Epidemiological studies of the prevalence of mental illness among African Americans have found that when one controls for socioeconomic status, the rates among Blacks are comparable to those of whites (Williams, 1986). Poverty and lack of education contribute to high rates of psychiatric impairment among persons of low socioeconomic status, regardless of race. Some studies Williams described found high rates of phobia and depression among African American women and substance abuse among poor Black urban men. These disorders, however, are prevalent among women and men, respectively, regardless of their ethnicity (National Institute of Mental Health, 1986b).

With the development of the *DSM-III*, with its specific criteria, it was hoped that misdiagnosis could be averted. In fact, the requirements for schizophrenia and affective disorders have been modified so that they are closer to those utilized in England and elsewhere, where the criteria for schizophrenia have been stricter. In order to test the objectivity of the new system, Loring and Powell (1988) conducted a research study in which they had Black and white male and female psychiatrists diagnose two cases along Axis I and Axis II. Although all subjects were asked to assess the same cases, the sex and race of the cases varied. Some subjects received cases in which neither sex nor race was specified. The expected diagnoses were schizophrenia, undifferentiated type on Axis I and dependent personality disorder for Axis II for both cases. When the race and sex were unspecified, responses were consistent with the expected diagnoses. When the client was described as a Black male, however, all the psychiatrists except Black males were most likely to choose paranoid schizophrenia for Axis I. Nevertheless, Black male and female psychiatrists were more likely to give white males less serious diagnoses (brief reactive psychosis or recurrent depressive disorder). As for Axis II, dependent personality tended to be assigned when the client's race and sex were the same as the psychiatrist's. When the case was a Black male, however, paranoid personality disorder was the respondents' first choice. This study suggests that, despite the alleged objectivity of the *DSM-III*, psychiatric racial stereotypes persist.

Diagnostic problems have been reported for other ethnic minority groups. Escobar (1987) discusses the prevalent presentation of somatic complaints by Hispanics. These symptoms accompany depressive and schizophrenic disorders, but rarely are of sufficient scope to indicate a *DSM-III* diagnosis of somatization disorder. Somatic symptoms are also present to a large extent among Hispanic subjects of community studies. The author challenges the validity of most of the somatoform disorders, which focus on narrow criteria, and proposes a new "somatization trait."

Other reports on mental disorders among Hispanics have come up with diverse findings. Although previous research had found less psychiatric distress among Mexican Americans, Roberts (1981) found the distribution of depressive symptoms comparable or higher for Mexican Americans. In an epidemiologic study of psychiatric symptoms and dysfunctions among Mexican Americans and Anglos in California, Warheit et al. (1985) found that Mexican Americans, especially those who were Spanish speaking, had significantly higher rates of depression, anxiety, and psychosocial dysfunctioning than Anglos. A number of demographic variables, however, contributed to these symptoms (especially being separated, female, and a low level of education). Mukherjee and others (1983) found that like African Americans, Hispanics were at risk of being misdiagnosed as schizophrenic.

Lawson (1986) identifies a need for culture-free diagnostic tools. Because the MMPI was not standardized on an African American population, Blacks tend to score higher than whites on paranoia and schizophrenia scales. Biological tests, such as the dexamethasone test (DST) for depression, seem more promising for Blacks and Hispanics than for whites. Lawson (1986) recommends that such tools be used in the diagnosis of ethnic groups for whom mood disorders are frequently overlooked.

Culture-Specific Syndromes

Medical anthropologists have described a number of syndromes that are unusually prevalent among certain cultures. Just as bulimia seems to be a North American Euroamerican phenomenon (Westermeyer, 1985), certain disorders are particular to other cultures. With the continuous migration of refugees from around the world, such syndromes appear in American mental health practice. Examples of culture-specific syndromes are described in the sections on individual cultural groups that follow.

Culturally Sanctioned Healers

Just as cultures have specific syndromes, there are also certain persons among them who are sanctioned to treat identified conditions. Although mainstream American society has assigned this role to psychiatrists, psychologists, and social workers, some ethnic groups have indigenous healers who treat ailments in ways that are congruent with the beliefs and norms of the culture. Folk healers, or *shamen,* are the equivalents of therapists. They are described by Mexican Americans as *curanderos* and by Puerto Ricans as *espiritismos* or spiritists. Native Americans, Asians, and Haitians are also known to have their own healers. Shamen may prescribe herbs, a special diet, exercise, or a healing ritual. Some of the beliefs, values, and healing practices that are associated with specific ethnic groups will be described in the next section.

CLINICAL SOCIAL PRACTICE WITH SPECIFIC ETHNIC GROUPS

Social work practice with persons of diverse ethnic minority groups is guided by knowledge of the specific culture, the degree of clients' identification with their culture of origin, and their assimilation into the dominant American culture. The specific group is influenced by its history of oppression, its social constitution, the local ecology, and economic factors. Those ethnic minority clients who live principally among their own people in isolated villages have less contact (and possibly less conflict) than those who are thrust into a competitive urban environment. Those who live in ethnic communities within larger multicultural communities experience the push and pull of different world views on a regular basis. New immigrants, such as the Vietnamese, deal with the loss of their homeland as well as adaptation to a new culture.

This section will provide descriptive information and suggested strategies for social work practice with individuals of African American, Asian American and Pacific Island, Hispanic, and Native American ethnicity. The danger in presenting this material is that it will create or affirm stereotypes. In reading this section, the reader is advised to keep in mind that there is as much diversity within cultures as between cultures; and to recognize that although persons who are socialized in a particular culture generally have knowledge of the beliefs and practices of their group, individuals do not uniformly accept these beliefs or engage in these practices. In no way are the values and behaviors that are described here to be viewed as inherent, universal characteristics of everyone associated with the group.

Furthermore, cultural ways are viewed as resources which can aid clients in their resolution of mental health problems. Accordingly, indigenous definitions and categories (what is called the *emic* perspective), which ethnic minority clients bring to the social worker–client relationships, are the ways in which the clients and their cultures view their problems. Indigenous categories encompass the "illness" rather than the "disease." As such they are an important source of meaning to the particular culture. Concepts of mental health and constructs of illness that are specific to a culture are as valid as Western "disease" constructs. The clinical social worker starts from the client's perspective, helping the client work through the problem in culturally congruent terms.

Social workers who identify with the dominant culture may have certain biases that interfere with their work with ethnic minority clients. For example, the European American values of individualism, independence, competitiveness, and achievement are different from the values of sharing, modesty, and intergenerational connectedness that are held by some ethnic minority groups. Similarly certain interpersonal behaviors that are valued by the dominant culture (e.g., assertiveness, eye contact, informality) are considered improper among persons of other cultures, whereas other behaviors (e.g., silence, deference) may be preferred by some minority groups. Expectations that clients verbalize their feelings, admit their weaknesses, and confront persons who arouse their anger are based on European American therapeutic models. In order to work with ethnically different clients, social workers must control their biases and accept clients on their own terms.

In addition, the clinical social worker should become aware of and be sensitive to language preferences of clients of diverse cultures. Many ethnic minority clients do not speak English at all. Among those who are bilingual, English may be a secondary rather than their primary language and one with which the client is not completely comfortable or competent. Persons who are bilingual tend to maintain two representational systems of meaning, only one of which can be invoked if the clinician speaks only one of the languages (Javier, 1989). Furthermore, some bilingual clients shift from one language to another in their thinking and speech (Javier, 1989). Accordingly, it is desirable that the clinician be bilingual. The bilingual therapist makes it possible for the different sets of meanings to be expressed, understood, and utilized in treatment. In the absence of a bilingual practitioner, interpreters should be used. The choice of an interpreter should, however, be culturally congruent and consistent with the client's preferences. Because of the personal nature of therapeutic conversations, interpreters who are young or of a different sex may not be appropriate. Clients may want to bring family members of their own choosing to act as interpreters.

African Americans

With over 29 million persons, representing 12.2 percent of the general population, African Americans are the largest of the ethnic minority groups in the United States (U.S. Bureau of the Census, 1988c). Although some came voluntarily as immigrants from the Caribbean, Spanish America, and Africa, most are the descendants of Africans who were forcibly captured and brought to North America, where they were sold as slaves. The Africans came from a number of west African ethnic communities. Even though their dispersion throughout the southern colonies interfered with the perpetuation of their native cultures, remnants of African cultures still remain (Pinderhughes, 1982).

Black experience of American life has been marked by domination, exploitation, and economic hardship. From the time the Africans came here, they were regarded as chattel, whose value came from their usefulness in the white-dominated American economy. The master–subject relationship that was established early in this nation's history relegated African Americans to a subhuman status in which their worth, rights, and dignity were denied (Bosmajian, 1974). Even after laws were changed to include African Americans as citizens with rights, inequality has been maintained through institutional racism.

Institutional racism directed at African Americans is reflected in census data. In 1987, the median income for Black families was $18,098, whereas for whites it was $32,274. The poverty rate the same year for Blacks was 33.1 percent, more than three times the 10.5 percent for whites (U.S. Bureau of the Census, 1988b). Among African American families headed by women with no husband present, the poverty rate was a startling 54.8 percent (U.S. Bureau of the Census, 1989b). With over half of African American families with children maintained by mothers (U.S. Bureau of the Census, 1989a), the "feminization of poverty" is especially pronounced.

Despite the overrepresentation of African Americans among the poor, many African Americans are educated and employed as professionals and skilled laborers. Although a majority live in the South (U.S. Bureau of the Census, 1988c), many have migrated to the North and to the West Coast and live primarily in urban centers (Hines & Boyd-Franklin, 1982). As a whole, African Americans are a heterogeneous population whose social problems are a function of the interaction of class, gender, and race. Their family styles, values, and behaviors are diverse (Pinderhughes, 1982).

Cultural Values and Norms. African American cultural values and norms derive from three sources—residues of African culture, values of mainstream America, and responses and adaptations to the "victim system" that arose from oppression, poverty, and racism (Pinderhughes, 1982). Variation among individuals reflects these diverse sources of identification, as well as differences in social class, education, urban/rural environment, region of the country, and individual differences.

Nobles (1976) describes the African world view as one that values cooperation, collective responsibility, and interdependence and is expressed psychobehaviorally in sameness, groupness, and commonality. African values and behaviors stand in sharp contrast with European values of competition and individual rights and psychobehavioral modalities of uniqueness, individuality, and difference. African values are expressed in strong kinship bonds (Hill, 1971; Leigh & Green, 1982) and an emphasis on religion and spirituality (Boyd-Franklin, 1989).

Although Boyd-Franklin (1989) affirms that "there is no such thing as *the* Black family" (p. 6), she and others (e.g., Leigh & Green, 1982) describe several patterns that characterize many African American families. For one, families extend beyond nuclear arrangements to include informally adopted children, friends ("aunts" and "uncles"), and distant and closely related biological kin. Children may be raised by grandparents or in multigenerational households. The paternal relatives of a child in a mother-headed single-parent family may be an important component of the family kinship system. Kinship networks are cooperative and interdependent. In her ethnographic study of poor African American families on welfare in a midwestern city, Stack (1974) was impressed with the complex system of reciprocity and exchange that existed.

Some writers describe the flexible family roles that are apparent in many African American families (Boyd-Franklin, 1989; Hill, 1971). The employment of both Black women and Black men has resulted in sex roles that tend to be egalitarian and family organization that is cooperative (Leigh & Green, 1982). During times of crisis, the extended kinship system can be mobilized to assume absentee roles (Hines & Boyd-Franklin, 1982). Children are socialized to be assertive and independent and are valued for themselves rather than for their ability to manipulate the physical world (Leigh & Green, 1982).

Religion or spirituality is frequently cited as a source of strength among African Americans (Boyd-Franklin, 1989; Hines & Boyd-Franklin, 1982; Hill, 1971; Leigh & Green, 1982; McAdoo, 1987). Rooted in the African experience and oppression during slavery, religion and religious institutions provide structures for meaning, emotional expression, affiliation, and political organization. The church is a place in which African

Americans can feel at home, reach out for spiritual support, and receive acceptance. A source of meaning beyond the material world, religion is a counterforce that provides hope for change. Although most of the churches with which African Americans are affiliated are Christian (mostly Protestant), some are Moslem and other religions. Despite the importance of the Black church in Black history and Black life, however, some African Americans are not religious (Solomon, 1976).

African American culture is also influenced by the "victim system" that has developed around them. Pinderhughes (1982) describes this as "a circular feedback process" in which negative feedback "threatens self-esteem" and "reinforces problematic responses in communities, families, and individuals" (p. 109). Barriers to achievement by African Americans lead to poverty, which in turn has an adverse effect on family relationships. Strain in the family adversely affects the ability of the family to foster individual development and work cooperatively with others to improve the community. Limited in resources, communities deteriorate and become a negative influence. This results in increased powerlessness (Pinderhughes, 1982; Solomon, 1976).

Indigenous Concepts of Health, Mental Health, and Mental Illness.   The African world view that was described in the preceding section provides a basis for a Black American mental health norm that is different from that of Americans of European extraction. In American mental health practice, however, European norms dominate and African American cultural differences are not taken into consideration. The application of an inappropriate model, together with racism, results in misappropriation of African Americans as mentally ill (Mays, 1985). This was seen earlier in this chapter in the discussion of misdiagnosis.

African American concepts of mental health and mental illness are influenced by those of the dominant white culture and by religious beliefs. As Americans, African Americans have been socialized to accept mainstream biomedical concepts (Jackson, 1981) and to use mainstream health and mental health services. For some, however, religion provides a primary system of meaning for human experiences. Others may embrace ideas that are residues of the African folk or colonial American folk culture, such as the belief in occult forces ("root work") (Jackson, 1981).

Culture-Specific Syndromes.   One of the culture-specific syndromes that is seen in Black Americans and persons of Caribbean background is called *falling out*. It is characterized by sudden collapse, paralysis, and inability to speak or see. Hearing remains unimpaired and eyes are open during these episodes (Jackson, 1981).

Illness Behavior.   African Americans use supports within the nurturing and sustaining systems to assist them with mental health problems (Chestang, 1976). Historical and ongoing oppression create distrust of mainstream services; thus, during times of crisis, they are likely to turn to friends, family, neighbors, and religious resources for help (Hines & Boyd-Franklin, 1982). African Americans who do use mainstream mental health services may hesitate to be open with clinicians. Past experience with the public assistance, child welfare, and court systems has taught Blacks to be wary (Boyd-Franklin, 1989). Accordingly, their "resistance" may be viewed as a strength (Boyd-

Franklin, 1989; Grier & Cobbs, 1968). It is not realistic or prudent to trust members of the ruling class of oppressors unless they prove themselves to be trustworthy.

Table 7.1, presented earlier, showed that relatively large proportions of African Americans utilize inpatient and outpatient mental health facilities. Nevertheless, some research indicates that African Americans have fewer sessions of psychotherapy than whites and that they leave treatment prematurely (Cole & Pilisuk, 1976; Sue, 1977). Thus, quality as well as quantity of contact needs to be improved.

In a more recent survey of the attitudes of African American adults toward community mental health centers in a northeastern city, Gary (1987) found that about 20 percent of those who were polled had negative attitudes, 33 percent had positive attitudes, and 47 percent had neutral attitudes toward the centers. Gary asserts that these findings suggest that African Americans are more receptive toward mental health services than they have been in the past.

Implications for Treatment.   Mental health problems experienced by African Americans must be seen in the context of their socioeconomic status and the suffering they have endured as people of color in a predominantly white society. Although the cultural values and adaptations to the macro system that African Americans have made are sources of strength, they vary from patterns of white Americans of European extraction who usually have dominant roles in mental health institutions. Unless clinicians of other ethnicities come to understand and appreciate the differences and strengths of African Americans, they are likely to rely on inappropriate values and stereotypes in their treatment of Blacks.

The heterogeneity among African Americans and the complex families and modes of mutual assistance and self-help within Black communities call for a systems approach to assessment and treatment. The family system and the diverse sources of support within the nurturing and sustaining systems should be identified. Clients should be helped to build supports and to eliminate obstacles to their individual and collective betterment. In order to counteract the effects of discrimination, clinical practice with African Americans should be "empowering" (Solomon, 1976). Clients should be helped to use their own inner resources as well as community resources to attain goals of their own choosing that are consistent with their values. They should be assisted to be instrumental in developing and effecting solutions to identified problems. Furthermore, African Americans should be encouraged to organize politically to attain solutions to problems in the social system.

American Indians and Alaska Natives

American Indians and Alaska Natives were the indigenous people occupying the land that the European explorers thought they had discovered. They represent diverse tribes, each of which has developed in its own way. Among their reported population of 1.5 million persons, approximately a quarter retain their own language (Red Horse, 1988; U.S. Bureau of the Census, 1980). Close to 50 percent are concentrated in California, Arizona, New Mexico, and Oklahoma, and a majority live in or near urban centers (Red Horse, 1988). In 1980 only 37 percent lived on reservations, in historic areas, in Alaska

Native villages, and on tribal trust lands (Blanchard, 1987). The Eskimos and Aleuts of Alaska are more likely to live in their native homelands than in urban centers (Red Horse, 1988).

Regardless of where they live, Native Americans have contact with nonnatives to varying degrees. Some have been educated in white-dominated boarding schools, whereas others have been educated in multicultural schools that are closer to home. Those who live in cities and participate in the labor force have many opportunities for cross-cultural contact.

Differing patterns of assimilation have resulted in diverse Indian family styles. Red Horse (1988) describes the *traditional* type as one in which the native language is preferred, the extended kinship system organizes community life, the land is revered, and the native religion is practiced. *Neotraditional* families are similar to the traditional ones, except that they may have adopted another religion, such as Christianity, and some prefer Spanish. *Transitional* families retain native values, language, and extended kinship ties in their intimate lives but adopt the customs and language of outsiders in their contacts with the wider community. If they live in an urban area, they try to bridge the gap by making frequent trips to their homeland. The fourth type that Red Horse describes is *bicultural.* These families prefer English, live in nuclear units, and convert to other religions. Nevertheless, the adults may know their native language and religion and have an awareness of the sacredness of the land. The *acculturated* families are assimilated with the dominant culture; they associate primarily with nonnatives and retain few Indian values. A revival of traditional values, traditions, and language and criticism of the American institutional system characterize the *panrenaissance* families.

Disproportionate numbers of American Indians have low incomes and suffer from poverty. In 1979 the median family income among American Indians and Alaska Natives was $13,724, whereas the national median income was $19,917. At that time the poverty rate for Indians was 23.7 percent, while it was 9.6 percent for the total population (U.S. Bureau of the Census, 1980). Similarly, life expectancy and education of Indians are relatively low and unemployment is high. Conditions associated with poverty—deficient housing, malnutrition, disease, and infant mortality—are prevalent. Accidents and alcoholism are leading causes of death (Carpenter, 1980; Kunitz & Levy, 1981).

Cultural Values and Norms.   Although the diversity among American Indian tribes makes it difficult to arrive at a set of values that applies to all groups, efforts that have been made reveal consistencies. Among these are *holism, harmony,* and *community.* In contrast with nonnative Caucasian Americans who perceive person and environment as separate entities, Indians enculturated in their own traditions find unity and continuity among natural, supernatural, and human phenomena (Anderson & Ellis, 1988; Kunitz & Levy, 1981; Lewis, 1985; Nofz, 1988). Indians feel connected to their families, peers, and forebears and the land, which is held sacred (Nofz, 1988; Red Horse, 1988). Their sense of attuneness or harmony with the natural world affects their sense of time. The Pueblos Indians schedule events when the time feels right; Navajos are oriented to the here and now; and the Hopi conceive of time in terms of the growth patterns of animals and food (Hall, 1959). Apparently American Indians do not focus on the future in the same way that other Americans do.

American Indians tend to value the welfare of the group over individual achievement. They are obligated to share their resources with their families and clans (Nofz, 1988). Because of these values, Indian children are in the untenable position in public schools that emphasize individuality and competition (Anderson & Ellis, 1988). Native Americans avoid conflict or confrontation in their interpersonal relationships. They value privacy and do not like it when outsiders interfere with their lives (Lewis & Keung Ho, 1975; Trimble et al., 1984). Unfortunately, behavior that is in keeping with their culture is frequently perceived by outsiders as passivity, shyness, and lack of ambition (Anderson & Ellis, 1988). On the other hand, they view the efforts of therapists to elicit personal experiences, thoughts, and feelings as intrusive or inappropriate (Lewis & Keung Ho, 1975; Trimble et al., 1984).

American Indians have extended families of biological and nonkin relatives who socialize the young into the culture (Red Horse, 1980b). With the movement of the Indian population to cities, many families are separated from each other geographically. Yet they do form communities within cities and return to their childhood homes for special ceremonies (Red Horse, 1980b). Although the American Indian population tends to be young, the elders occupy a position of respect in the community (Red Horse, 1980a).

Indigenous Concepts of Health, Mental Health, and Mental Illness. Native Americans do not distinguish between health and mental health. Consistent with their holistic view of the person and the environment, Indians view disturbances in their mental health in relation to other aspects of their lives as well as the cosmos (Trimble et al., 1984). The Navajo Indians see physical and mental illness as manifestations of disharmony in nature that may represent the intrusion of supernatural forces or some other external cause. The disharmony could be caused by a breach of a taboo, an intrusion of spirits, witchcraft, or an etiological agent, such as an animal or the wind (Kunitz & Levy, 1981). Ghosts, spirits of the dead, and witchcraft are capable of interfering with the living.

Culture-Specific Syndromes. Trimble et al. (1984) describe a number of psychiatric syndromes specific to American Indians. One of these, *pibloktoq,* or arctic hysteria, is a psychogenic seizure disorder something like a conversion disorder (American Psychiatric Association, 1987). This syndrome is common among female Alaskan Eskimos. Another, characterized by fainting and preoccupation with death, is called *soul loss.* Here the soul, which enters the body at birth and leaves at death, appears to be departing the body (Kunitz & Levy, 1981). On the other hand, *spirit intrusion* is a form of possession by ghosts, evil spirits, or demons that is manifested by symptoms of agitated depression, somatization, and hallucinations. American Indians may experience a range of behavioral and somatic symptoms as a result of *taboo breaking.* When they violate taboos against forms of sexual expression (e.g., incest), murder, and other forbidden behaviors, they may become afflicted with what outsiders consider mental illness (Trimble et al., 1984). An additional syndrome, *Hi-Wa itch,* is characterized by insomnia, anorexia, depression, and suicide. It is experienced by Mohave American Indians in response to an undesired separation from someone who is loved (Kaplan & Sadock, 1988).

Illness Behavior.   Illness behavior is consistent with the degree of assimilation of the Indian family. Accordingly, one would expect individuals from traditional and neotraditional families to make use of herbal remedies and participate in ritual healing ceremonies; transitional families to utilize indigenous and mainstream methods; but bicultural and acculturated families to rely principally on American institutional care (Red Horse, 1988).

Among the American Indians there are persons and groups who serve as healers. They may be shamen, medicine persons, traditional healers, or clergy (for converts to Christianity), who provide culturally congruent forms of help. Some healers provide herbal remedies; others engage afflicted persons in healing ceremonies. At times a Caucasian American clinician will make a referral to a native healer. In the following case, an Indian doctor diagnosed and successfully treated a young woman with "soul loss sickness" by calling upon his own gifts to find and retrieve her lost soul:

> . . . he also stated that his spirit power had advised that the patient should become a spirit dancer for her own future protection, or else ancestral spirits would again take hold of her soul and cause her serious ills. Drumming started and while the patient appeared to re-enter the trance state in which she had been put initially under the effect of continuous rhythmic chanting and drumming, the *Indian Doctor* made gestures as if capturing the lost soul from the air, holding it in his closed hands. He then transferred the soul back to its owner by rubbing it on the patient's chest and sides. (Jilek & Jilek-Aall, 1981, p. 22)

Implications for Treatment.   Mental health treatment of American Indians within the mainstream mental health system should be consistent with the values and behaviors of the Indian's particular tribe and his or her degree of assimilation with mainstream American culture. Some writers believe that American Indians view family therapy as interference, whereas group treatment that is focused and task-centered is in keeping with the peer group orientation of American Indians (Lewis & Keung Ho, 1975; Nofz, 1988). Nevertheless, other writers have been able to implement culturally sensitive family treatment with middle-class American Indians (Attneave, 1982).

In treating American Indians who have problems with alcohol, special attention should be given to the cultural component of drinking. For American Indians drinking tends to be a peer group phenomenon that is associated with comradeship and solidarity, rather than an individual means of escape (Anderson & Ellis, 1988). For some, drinking may be a way of overcoming shyness or their "marginal" social status (Anderson & Ellis, 1988; Nofz, 1988). Alcohol treatment in groups can use the peer group to promote cohesion without use of alcohol as a catalyst. Similarly, the cultural context of another social problem, suicide, should also be recognized (Davenport & Davenport, 1987).

Asian Americans and Pacific Islanders

Asian and Pacific Island Americans are a growing population that consists of persons who have cultural roots in four areas. These are (a) East Asia—Japan, China, Korea; (b) South Asia—Pakistan, India, Sri Lanka; (c) Southeast Asia—Indonesia, Vietnam, Cambodia, Laos, Thailand, the Philippines, Burma; and (d) the Pacific Islands—Guam, Samoa, Hawaii, and Tonga (Kuramoto et al., 1983). Although large numbers live on the West Coast and Hawaii (Kitano, 1987), many are dispersed throughout the country.

Asian American populations have immigrated to the United States in waves at different historical moments. Elderly Asian Americans who came here from the old country and newer immigrants tend to adhere to traditional values and folkways, whereas those whose families have lived in the United States for a few generations tend to be more acculturated (Ishisaka & Takagi, 1982). In delivering ethnic sensitive mental health services, clinicians should consider generational as well as cultural differences.

Asian Americans have been given the dubious compliment of being described as a "model minority" (Kim, 1973). Behaviors such as diligence and the willingness to make sacrifices, as well as demographic findings of relatively high educational levels and median incomes and low utilization of mental health resources have been viewed as indicators of successful adaptation (Crystal, 1989; Sue, Sue, & Sue, 1981). Yet these findings belie problems with racism, the struggle for survival, and the stress that characterize the lives of these Americans, and obstacles to mental health resource utilization. Furthermore, the image of success has aroused the animosity of other minorities and has rendered Asian Americans ineligible for some affirmative action programs (Crystal, 1989).

Reports of relatively high incomes of Asian Americans obscure a number of factors that contribute to the appearance of success (Crystal, 1989). For one, they are under-employed in relation to their education. Many Asian American immigrants who have been professionally trained and certified in their countries of origin have not been able to acquire licenses in the United States. Instead they take jobs that are not commensurate with their skills. Second, their incomes appear high because of the prevalence of two wage earners in the same family. Third, aging Asian Americans and Pacific Islanders have an unusually high rate of poverty (Crystal, 1989). According to the 1980 census, the Chinese, Koreans, Vietnamese, Hawaiians, Guamians, and Samoans had poverty rates that were higher than that of the general population (U.S. Bureau of the Census, 1980). Finally the statistics on the overall success of Asian Americans and Pacific Islanders diverts attention from the fact that some of the new refugee populations hold low-level, low-wage jobs (Hirayama & Cetingok, 1988).

Cultural Values and Norms.   Although there is much diversity among Asian American and Pacific Island American cultures of origin, several values and cultural norms are common. Some of these are derived from the eastern religions of Confucianism, Buddhism, and Taoism. The interrelated values that will be emphasized here are family continuity, filial piety, avoidance of shame, and self-control.

The family is a pivotal source of values for Asian and Pacific Island Americans. Among those of East Asian origin, the family links individuals with their ancient forebears on the paternal side and insures the perpetuation of the family's good name (Shon & Ja, 1982). In keeping with these goals, families tend to be hierarchical, male dominated, and highly structured (Shon & Ja, 1982; Sue & Sue, 1988). Children are obligated to exhibit filial piety, that is, they are to be deferential, obedient, and loyal to their families (Ho, 1981). Grandparents and parents are afforded a great deal of respect and authority. Above all, family members must avoid shaming the family, the welfare of which supersedes the pursuit of individual goals (Ishisaka & Takagi, 1982). Asian Americans and Pacific Islanders are sensitive to appearances; if personal problems or behaviors that are discrepant with family and community expectations come to be known to others, the Asian American feels shame and loses face (Ho, 1981). Perpetrators of such behaviors not only disgrace themselves; they dishonor the family.

Among Asian Americans from Laos or Thailand, sex roles are more egalitarian. In Thailand there was greater sex role differentiation among the urban upper class than the rural people (Moore, 1974). Among the Laotians, traditional sex roles are observed in the family, yet women exert a great deal of influence in financial decisions and elicit deference (LeBarr & Suddard, 1960).

Asian Americans value self-control and emotional restraint (Ho, 1981; Sue & Sue, 1988). Families expect members to control their emotions and avoid antisocial behavior. Asians who subscribe to these values regard them as a sign of maturity (Ishisaka & Takagi, 1982). Indeed restraint may be viewed as a resource, in that it promotes qualities of self-discipline, patience, and diligence, which are instrumental in achieving success in American society. It is not, however, consonant with prevailing models of mental health treatment that require emotional expression.

Indigenous Concepts of Health, Mental Health, and Mental Illness.   Traditional Asian medicine embraces a holistic concept of health, mental health, and treatment (Marsella & Higginbotham, 1984). Mind, body, and spirit are thought to be a unity rather than separate systems. Health is equated with harmony or balance (Gould-Martin & Ngin, 1981). Traditional Chinese conceive of illness (mental or physical) as a dysharmony between two life forces, *yin* and *yang* (Kleinman, 1980). Life forces, such as the wind, can disrupt the balance by entering the body during periods of vulnerability (Gould-Martin & Ngin, 1981). Indigenous healing methods aim to restore internal harmony as well as the unity between the person and the environment, which is as extensive as the cosmos.

Cultures of Asia and the Pacific have developed three explanations of the origins of behavioral dysfunction (Ishisaka & Takagi, 1982). The *social explanation* places responsibility on untoward circumstances, such as a death, marital conflict, or job loss. The position of victimization rather than individual responsibility is highlighted—evoking sympathetic responses, advice, and release from ordinary responsibilities from others. The second explanation, *moral,* arises when a person has violated values that the community regards as sacred. For the most part, these involve forsaking family obligations and prescribed modes of conduct. Community elders, priests, and family members intervene in response to these transgressions. The third explanation is *organic.* Asian cultures accept physical or somatic explanations and symptoms as part of life. Asian Americans have an easier time accepting somatic explanations than Western theories that blame the individual or family for dysfunctional behaviors (Ishisaka & Takagi, 1982).

Asians attach a great deal of stigma to mental illness, which invokes thoughts about family curses, witchcraft, and other supernatural forces (Marsella & Higginbotham, 1984). In order to avoid shame, Asians limit their concept of mental illness to the most severe psychotic problems (Kleinman, 1980). Symptoms that would be considered expressions of nonpsychotic mental health problems in Western cultures tend to be treated by health professionals or indigenous healers (Kleinman, 1980).

Culture-Specific Syndromes. A number of syndromes of dysfunction that are prevalent among groups of Asian origins have been described in the literature. Among these are the following.

Amok is an outburst of aggression that is particularly prevalent among Southeast Asian (especially Malaysian) men. It begins with a period of brooding and can eventuate in an act of homicide. Later the amoker experiences exhaustion and amnesia and may kill himself. The expression, "running amok," derives from this syndrome (Favazza, 1985; Kaplan & Sadock, 1988; Westermeyer, 1985).

Koro is an attack of anxiety associated with sexual organs. Men develop an intense fear that their penis is shrinking and receding into the stomach and that the result will be death. Women have similar fears centering on their breasts and labia. Koro is seen primarily in Asia, but has been reported in the West (Favazza, 1985; Westermeyer, 1985).

Latah is a startle response that is precipitated by a mild but sudden stimulus. The individual obeys and imitates the speech of others, regardless of the consequences. A syndrome of women of Southeast Asia, it has also been identified among the Bantu of Africa, the Ainu of Japan, and Malaysians (Favazza, 1985; Kaplan & Sadock, 1988; Westermeyer, 1985).

Illness Behavior. Although low rates of utilization of mental health services have been reported in the literature, such findings should not be interpreted to mean that mental health problems are not prevalent or that Asian Americans do not need help (Crystal, 1989). Illness behavior is partially a function of the historical segregation and exclusion of Asian Americans from the mainstream, which made it necessary for ethnic communities to rely on each other and on indigenous resources to manage mental health problems. Moreover, cultural attitudes emphasize the primacy of families and extended networks as care givers of members with mental health problems. The cultural values of "saving face" and avoiding shame promote the maintenance of secrecy over problems to which stigma is attached (Crystal, 1989).

Asian American communities have their own healers, herbalists, physicians, and fortune tellers who provide culturally relevant help. Some Asian Americans treat themselves at home with herbs, which can be purchased in ethnic neighborhood herb shops (Gould-Martin & Ngin, 1981). Other home treatments include special foods, tonics, and patent medicines (Kleinman, 1980). Asian Americans may contact indigenous or Western-style physicians, as well as sacred healers, before they are willing to see a psychiatrist (Kleinman, 1980).

Implications for Treatment. Mental health treatment of Asian Americans and Pacific Islanders should be in keeping with their cultural values and concepts of mental illness. The clinician should be an authority figure who respects the roles and relationships in the client's family. Demands that the client express emotions and direct anger at family members are inappropriate. On the other hand, therapy that emphasizes self-control, will power, and avoidance of disturbing thoughts may be helpful (Lee, 1982). The clinician should be aware that psychological problems are a source of stigma and may be expressed somatically. Furthermore, clinicians should recognize that Asian Americans may interact with others in ways that are in accord with cultural norms of proper behavior when, for example, they avoid eye contact (Toupin, 1981). Asian Americans have responsibilities to their families that continue throughout their lives. Rather than viewing intergenerational dependence as a problem, it should be viewed as a culturally congruent obligation (Lee, 1982) and as a strength.

Many Asian American communities have developed their own mutual assistance organizations that address the social, economic, and cultural needs of the community. These self-help organizations have arisen from needs that are not met by the larger community. Social work clinicians who work with Asian Americans should become familiar with the particular organizations that are available in the communities in which their Asian American and Pacific Islander clients live and link clients with these organizations when the client needs are consistent with the services offered by these organizations.

Political refugees from Southeast Asia have needs that are consistent with their circumstances and which should be acknowledged. At first their needs for financial aid, housing, employment, and medical care should be addressed. Moreover, they need help learning English and transferring their job skills to the American system. In addition, Southeast Asians need to come to terms with traumatic experiences and losses associated with leaving their countries and cultures of origin and to develop a sense of community in the United States.

Hispanics

Hispanic is one of numerous descriptors for Americans of Spanish New World origins. Several other terms are also used for persons of Mexican background, such as Mexicans, Mexican Americans, Chicanos, as well as Latinos. These Americans have New World roots in Mexico, the Southwest, Central America, the Caribbean, and South America and Old World roots in Spain. Although many speak Spanish as their primary language, substantial numbers are bilingual or predominantly English speaking. Historically Hispanics represent a mixture of diverse ethnic groups and races. They include persons who appear black, brown, red, yellow, white, and combinations of these categories. They are heterogeneous in their life-styles, cultural identification, politics, social class, education, and occupations. Among the Hispanic civilian population, persons of Mexican origin are the most prevalent in the United States today. They are 12.1 million in number and represent 62.3 percent of the Hispanic population. The other Hispanics are of Puerto Rican (2.5 million, 12.7 percent), Cuban (1.0 million, 5.3 percent), Central and South American (2.2 million, 11.5 percent), and other Hispanic (1.6 million, 8.1 percent) origins (U.S. Bureau of the Census, 1988a).

Hispanics are the second most populous and the fastest growing ethnic minority group in the United States. According to the March 1988 Current Population Survey, they number over 19,000,000 (U.S. Bureau of the Census, 1988a)—approximately 8 percent of the general population. These figures are probably an underestimate because of an unknown number of undocumented immigrants who enter the United States illegally. The population of Hispanics increased 34.4 percent from 1980 to 1988, while the population of persons not of Hispanic origin increased 6.6 percent (U.S. Bureau of the Census, 1988a). Their younger age structure and relatively high fertility rate make it likely that Hispanics will be the largest racial/ethnic group in the future (Estrada, 1987).

Although Hispanics live throughout the country, subgroups are concentrated in particular sections. The largest, Mexican Americans, lives predominantly in the southwestern states (especially California, Texas, New Mexico, Colorado, and Arizona); Puerto Ricans live in New York and New Jersey; and Cubans live in Florida. There are pockets of Hispanics in the metropolitan areas of Los Angeles, New York, Miami, and Chicago (Estrada, 1987).

Cultural Values and Norms.   Hispanic families and communities hold certain values that permeate the cultures. Primary among these is *respeto* (respect), which is accorded to one's parents, grandparents, elders, oneself, and others (Galan, 1985). Individuals are accorded respect on the basis of their inner qualities rather than their possessions—a form of individualism called *personalism* (Bernal, 1982; Garcia-Preto, 1982). Nevertheless, Hispanics do value hierarchy, especially within the family. Families tend to be patriarchal, with traditional sex role expectations. Men are expected to be strong, hardworking, and dominant; women, passive, virtuous, and self-sacrificing (Garcia-Preto, 1982; Galan, 1985). Still, financial pressures have made it necessary for women to participate in the labor market. When married women work or are the sole breadwinners, the role relationships between couples is altered, a phenomenon that can result in marital conflict (Bernal, 1982).

Hispanic families include biological and unrelated persons, who provide companionship and support to each other. Children have unrelated godparents who function as substitute parents and advisers to the family. Families tend to be large, cohesive, and interdependent. The strong emotional bonds within the family and three-generational families (Falicov, 1982) suggest that intergenerational enmeshment is normative.

Indigenous Concepts of Health, Mental Health, and Mental Illness and their Causation.
Most of the Hispanic cultural groups do not distinguish between health and mental health (Delgado, 1977; Schreiber & Homiak, 1981). Like the American Indians and Alaska Natives, they have a holistic view of the mind and body. When disorders that would be viewed as "psychiatric" in mainstream American culture are viewed as folk illnesses, they are treated by folk healers or with folk remedies and/or by physicians or mental health professionals. Whichever sources are used, attention to the person as a whole, rather than a specific system, is in order (de la Rosa, 1988).

Mexican Americans have a concept of illness and disease that is sometimes called the *hot/cold theory* (Schreiber & Homiac, 1981). Rooted in the early Greek "balance of humors" theory, it views illness (mental or physical) as a state of disequilibrium caused by excessive exposure to heat or cold. Various internal and external objects, as well as emotional experiences, are classified as either hot or cold. For example, water and certain foods are considered cold; the sun and herbal teas are classified as hot. Treatment consists of neutralizing the excessive condition by drawing it off or consuming its opposite.

Among Puerto Ricans, *spiritism* is a prevalent belief. This is based partially on the Roman Catholic idea of a duality between material and spiritual worlds. One form of spiritism, *santeria,* is Nigerian in origin (Berthold, 1989). Adherents of spiritism believe that disembodied spirits of divine or deceased beings attach themselves to individuals at the time they are born and continue to influence their lives (Berthold, 1989; de la Rosa, 1988; Harwood, 1981b). "Good" spirits, such as one's guardian angel, help and protect individuals and influence their reaching higher goals. On the other hand, "bad" spirits can instigate problems either on their own or at the request of a living person who recruits them to engage in sorcery. The workings of malevolent spirits can result in physical or mental ailments (Harwood, 1981b).

Culture-Specific Syndromes.   Some syndromes are reported with excess among Hispanics. Puerto Ricans are susceptible to *ataques,* sometimes referred to as the "Puerto Rican syndrome." These are seizures that usually occur following emotionally disturbing events, but they may be unpredictable and idiosyncratic (Harwood, 1981b). *Ataques* are more common among persons of lower socioeconomic classes and among women and are culturally sanctioned under trying circumstances, such as at a death (Harwood, 1981b). Another syndrome that occurs with frequency among Hispanics is *susto,* or fright. Similar to anxiety disorders, it is characterized by such symptoms as diarrhea, loss of appetite, weight loss, restlessness, and vertigo. Like *ataques, susto* develops at times of stress (Schreiber & Homiac, 1981).

Illness Behavior.   Hispanics have a number of natural support systems available to them to help with health and mental health problems—the family system, the church, merchants' and social clubs, and folk healers (Delgado & Humm-Delgado, 1982). The family system provides emotional support, baby-sitting services, and home remedies (over-the-counter drugs, herbs, etc.) to persons with health or mental health problems. Another supportive system is the church, the Roman Catholic church being the most prominent. Although the historical link of the Roman Catholic church with the external power structure has created ambivalence toward religion among Hispanics, for some the church provides a source of meaning, consolation, and support (Gibson, 1985). Merchants' and social clubs are organizations that provide information, supplies, and social contacts that are culturally congruent. One type is a botanical shop (*botanica*), which sells herbs and objects needed in healing ceremonies, gives advice about illnesses, and makes referrals to folk healers. Another establishment is the *bodega* (grocery store), which not only sells native food but also makes referrals (Delgado & Humm-Delgado, 1982).

The fourth system consists of folk healers, which have different names and functions for different Hispanic groups. Puerto Rican Americans go to spiritists for help with anxiety or somatic symptoms that have no organic cause (Delgado, 1978). Spiritists may recommend that clients participate in a healing ceremony that is attended by family members, mediums (persons who have the power to communicate with spirits), and others with infirmities. During the ceremony, candles are lit, prayers are read, the cause is discovered, and a spiritual cleansing is enacted. Spiritism, however, is not the only form of folk healing. Those Puerto Ricans and Cubans who practice *santeria* engage in its healing ceremony. Another type of folk healer is the herbalist, who recommends herbs in keeping with the hot/cold theory. A third type of healer found in Hispanic communities is the *curandero,* who views illness as the result of alienation from the Roman Catholic church. The *curandero's* treatment aims to bring the individual closer to the church and its teachings (Delgado & Humm-Delgado, 1982).

Implications for Treatment. Hispanic clients make their own decisions, in consultation with significant others, with respect to the use of indigenous and/or mainstream mental health services. Because of a tendency to focus on somatic complaints, some Hispanics may use the health care system when the mental health care system may seem to be more appropriate. Those who do use the mental health care system should be provided with culturally congruent treatment. Delgado (1988) finds commonalities between folk healing and psychodrama that make it feasible to incorporate aspects of spiritism into group work treatment. He recommends that group leaders be authoritative, that the membership be diverse, and that activities rather than only verbal expression be emphasized. Similarly, Berthold (1989) sees parallels between spiritist healing and psychoanalytic treatment. The invocation of invisible spirits and causes in spiritism is not unlike the mobilization of unconscious forces and the ego in psychoanalysis. Both systems "work the cause" and restore individual functioning.

SUMMARY

In this multicultural society, clinical social workers employed in community mental health settings are likely to work with clients who are ethnically different. Of special concern are ethnic minorities of color, who have been victims of slavery, poverty, and discrimination. The histories of oppression of African Americans, American Indians and Alaska Natives, Asians and Pacific Islanders, and Hispanics demonstrate how public policies have limited the opportunities of persons of color in the United States.

In order to understand mental health issues among minority groups, several terms from medical sociology and medical anthropology have been used. The concepts of sick role, health behavior, and illness behavior describe ways of perceiving the rights and obligations of persons defined as sick, preventive and health-preserving behavior, and behaviors directed at remedying sickness, respectively. These concepts are interpreted differently across cultures. Illness behavior is reflected in the usage of mainstream and indigenous mental health services.

A lack of knowledge of diverse cultures makes it possible for practitioners to misdiagnose clients. For example, African Americans and Hispanics have been overdiagnosed with schizophrenia and underdiagnosed with mood disorders. Blacks sometimes appear to white clinicians to have symptoms of paranoia or flat affect when their presentation of self in a clinical interview is self-protective. One study indicated that for African Americans, hospitalization is more likely than treatment in the community (Ohio Department of Mental Health, 1988).

This chapter identified and described cultural values and norms; concepts of health, mental health, and mental illness; culture-specific syndromes; and illness behavior among African Americans, American Indians and Alaska Natives, Asian and Pacific Island Americans, and Hispanics. Each of these cultures has values and norms that distinguish it from the other groups. Yet there is as much diversity within groups as between groups. All of the ethnic minority groups that were described have culture-based concepts of mental health and illness behaviors that differ from the European American based norms on which clinical practice is based. Many of these cultures have a holistic concept of health and mental health, view themselves as a community rather than as autonomous individuals, and have indigenous helping systems of their own that are culturally congruent. It is hoped that clinicians who work with clients from cultures that are different from their own consider the cultural contexts of clients' lives and work in collaboration with the rich resources of ethnic communities.

DISCUSSION QUESTIONS

1. Define and differentiate race, ethnicity, minority group, and culture.
2. Discuss whether the following groups are cultures: gay men, lesbians, the physically disabled (persons who are blind, deaf, in wheelchairs, etc.), persons with chronic mental illness, battered women, and recovering alcoholics.
3. Explain the impact of historical oppression on minorities of color.
4. Why do you think it is common among some ethnic minority groups to present psychological problems in terms of somatic complaints?
5. What is the responsibility of the clinical social worker whose ethnicity is different from that of a client with respect to relationship building, assessment, and treatment?
6. Consider the cultural issues in the following cases:
   a. A Native American man referred to Alcoholics Anonymous refuses to discuss his problems with the heterogeneously constituted group.
   b. An African American woman informed a white intake worker that she comes from a "Black middle-class family." A white American does not ordinarily say, "I come from a white middle-class family," although he or she might report a "middle-class" background. Why do you suppose the African American woman described her family background in the way she did?
   c. A woman of Puerto Rican ethnicity came to the mental health clinic with her mother. When the social worker indicated that only the daughter was to be interviewed, the daughter and mother were visibly shaken.
   d. An older Chinese American man who appeared to be socially withdrawn said very little about his problem to the white, youthful female clinician, even though a Chinese (female) interpreter was provided.
7. In what ways do European American values conflict with the values of other cultural groups?
8. Explain how race, gender, and social class interact with one another with respect to mental health.
9. What is meant by bicultural socialization? What are the implications of this phenomenon for clinical practice?
10. What are culture-specific syndromes? Explain their implications for assessment and treatment.
11. In what ways might clinical social workers and indigenous healers work together?
12. How do you explain the low utilization of community mental health services by some groups and the higher use by other groups?

Suggested Activity

Ethnographic interviewing is a means of getting to know persons of diverse cultural backgrounds which is used by anthropologists and researchers of other disciplines who have a cultural perspective. Such an approach facilitates understanding of the "emic" (indigenous) perspective. After reading about ethnographic interviewing in the following sources, conduct an ethnographic interview with a client of a culture that is different from your own.

1. Green, J. W. (1982). Language and cross-cultural social work. In J. W. Green (Ed.), *Cultural awareness in the human services* (pp. 67–83). Englewood Cliffs, NJ: Prentice-Hall.
2. Spradley, J. P. (1979). *The ethnographic interview.* New York: Holt, Rinehart and Winston.

REFERENCES

Allen, I. M. (1986). Posttraumatic stress disorder among Black Vietnam veterans. *Hospital and Community Psychiatry, 37,* 55–61.

de Anda, D. (1984). Bicultural socialization: Factors affecting the minority experience. *Social Work, 29,* 101–107.

American Psychiatric Association. (1987). *Diagnostic and statistical manual of mental disorders (DSM-III-R)* (3rd ed., rev.). Washington, DC: Author.

Anderson, M. J., & Ellis, R. (1988). On the reservation. In N. A. Vacc, J. Wittmer, & S. B. DeVaney, (Eds.), *Experiencing and counseling multicultural and diverse populations* (2nd ed., pp. 107–126). Muncie, IN: Accelerated Development.

Attneave, C. (1982). American Indians and Alaska Native families: Emigrants in their own homeland. In M. McGoldrick, J. K. Pearce, & J. Giordano (Eds.), *Ethnicity and family therapy* (pp. 55–83). New York: Guilford Press.

Bernal, G. (1982). Cuban families. In M. McGoldrick, J. K. Pearce, & J. Giordano (Eds.), *Ethnicity and family therapy* (pp. 187–207). New York: Guilford Press.

Berthold, S. M. (1989). Spiritism as a form of psychotherapy: Implications for social work practice. *Social Casework, 70,* 502–509.

Blanchard, E. L. (1987). American Indians and Alaskan Natives. In A. Minahan (Ed.), *Encyclopedia of social work,* (Vol. 1, pp. 141–150). Silver Spring, MD: National Association of Social Workers.

Bosmajian, H. (1974). *The language of oppression.* Washington, DC: Public Affairs Press.

Boyd-Franklin, N. (1989). *Black families in therapy: A multisystems approach.* New York: The Guilford Press.

Broman, C. L. (1987). Race differences in professional help seeking. *American Journal of Community Psychology, 15,* 473–489.

Brown v. Board of Education of Topeka, Kansas, 348 US 8861 (1954).

Cafferty, P. S. J., & Chestang, L. (Eds.). (1976). *The diverse society: Implications for social policy.* Washington, DC: National Association of Social Workers.

Carpenter, E. M. (1980). Social services, policies, and issues. *Social Casework, 61,* 455–461.

Chestang, L. (1976). Environmental influences on social functioning: The Black experience. In P. S. J. Cafferty, & L. Chestang, (Eds.), *The diverse society: Implications for social policy.* (pp. 59–74). Washington, DC: National Association of Social Workers.

Cole, J., & Pilisuk, M. (1976). Differences in the provision of mental health services by race. *American Journal of Orthopsychiatry, 46,* 510–525.

Crystal, D. (1989). Asian Americans and the myth of the model minority. *Social Casework, 70,* 405–413.

Davenport, J. A., & Davenport, J., III. (1987). Native American suicide: A Durkheimian analysis. *Social Casework, 68,* 533–539.

Davis, L. E., & Proctor, E. K. (1989). *Race, gender and class.* Englewood Cliffs, NJ: Prentice-Hall.

Delgado, M. (1977). Puerto Rican spiritualism and the social work profession. *Social Casework, 8,* 451–458.

Delgado, M. (1978). Folk medicine in Puerto Rican culture. *International Social Work, 21,* 46–54.

Delgado, M. (1988). Groups in Puerto Rican spiritism: Implications for clinicians. In C. Jacobs & D. D. Bowles (Eds.), *Ethnicity and race: Critical concepts in social work* (pp. 34–47). Silver Spring, MD: National Association of Social Workers.

Delgado, M., & Humm-Delgado, D. (1982). Natural support systems: Source of strength in Hispanic communities. *Social Work, 27,* 83–89.

Devore, W., & Schlesinger, E. G. (1987). *Ethnic-sensitive social work practice* (2nd ed.). Columbus, OH: Merrill.

Escobar, J. I. (1987). Cross-cultural aspects of the somatization trait. *Hospital and Community Psychiatry, 38,* 174–180.

Estrada, L. F. (1987). Hispanics. In A. Minahan (Ed.), *Encyclopedia of social work* (Vol. 1, pp. 732–739). Silver Spring, MD: National Association of Social Workers.

Falicov, C. J. (1982). Mexican families. In M. McGoldrick, J. K. Pearce, & J. Giordano (Eds.), *Ethnicity and family therapy,* (pp. 134–163). New York: Guilford Press.

Favazza, A. R. (1985). Contributions of the sociocultural sciences: Anthropology and psychiatry. In H. I. Kaplan & B. J. Sadock (Eds.), *Comprehensive textbook of psychiatry* (4th ed., pp. 247–265). Baltimore, MD: Williams & Wilkins.

Galan, F. J. (1985). Traditional values about family behavior: The case of the Chicano client. *Social Thought, 11*(3), 14–22.

Garcia-Preto, N. (1982). Puerto Rican families. In M. McGoldrick, J. K. Pearce, & J. Giordano (Eds.), *Ethnicity and family therapy,* (pp. 164–186). New York: Guilford Press.

Gary, L. E. (1987). Attitudes of Black adults toward community mental health centers. *Hospitals and Community Psychiatry, 38,* 1100–1105.

Gibson, G. (1985). Chicanos and their support systems in interaction with social institutions. In M. Bloom (Ed.), *Life span development* (2nd ed., pp. 464–479). New York: Macmillan.

Gibson, G. (1987). Mexican Americans. In A. Minahan (Ed.), *Encyclopedia of social work* (Vol. 2, pp. 135–148). Silver Spring, MD: National Association of Social Workers.

Goldsby, R. A. (1977). *Race and races* (2nd ed.). New York: Macmillan.

Gould-Martin, K., & Ngin, C. (1981). Chinese Americans. In A. Harwood (Ed.), *Ethnicity and medical care* (pp. 130–171). Cambridge, MA: Harvard University Press.

Greeley, A. M. (1976). Why study ethnicity? In P. S. J. Cafferty & L. Chestang (Eds.), *The diverse society: Implications for social policy* (pp. 3–12). Washington, DC: National Association of Social Workers.

Grier, W. H., & Cobbs, P. M. (1968). *Black rage.* New York: Bantam Books.

Hall, E. T. (1959). *The silent language.* New York: Anchor Books.

Harwood, A. (Ed.). (1981a). *Ethnicity and medical care.* Cambridge, MA: Harvard University Press.

Harwood, A. (1981b). Mainland Puerto Ricans. In A. Harwood (Ed.), *Ethnicity and medical care* (pp. 397–481). Cambridge, MA: Harvard University Press.

Hidalgo, H., Peterson, T., & Woodman, N. (Eds.). (1985). *Lesbian and gay issues: A resource manual for social workers.* Silver Spring, MD: National Association of Social Workers.

Hill, R. B. (1971). *The strengths of Black families.* New York: National Urban League.

Hines, P. M., & Boyd-Franklin, N. (1982). Black families. In M. McGoldrick, J. K. Pearce, & J. Giordano (Eds.), *Ethnicity and family therapy* (pp. 84–107). New York: Guilford Press.

Hirayama, H., & Cetingok, M. (1988). Empowerment: A social work approach for Asian immigrants. *Social Casework, 69,* 41–47.

Ho, M. K. (1981). Social work with Asian Americans. In R. H. Dana (Ed.), *Human services for cultural minorities* (pp. 307–316). Baltimore, MD: University Park Press. Originally published in *Social Casework, 57,* 195–201.

Hopps, J. (1982). Oppression based on color. *Social Work, 27,* 3–5.

Ishisaka, H. A., & Takagi, C. Y. (1982). Social work with Asian- and Pacific-Americans. In J. W. Green (Ed.), *Cultural awareness in the human services* (pp. 122–156). Englewood Cliffs, NJ: Prentice-Hall.

Jackson, J. J. (1981). Urban Black Americans. In A. Harwood (Ed.), *Ethnicity and medical care* (pp. 37–129). Cambridge, MA: Harvard University Press.

Javier, R. A. (1989). Linguistic considerations in the treatment of bilinguals. *Psychoanalytic Psychology, 6,* 87–96.

Jilek, W., & Jilek-Aall, L. (1981). The psychiatrist and shaman colleague: Cross-cultural collaboration with traditional Amerindian therapists. In R. H. Dana (Ed.), *Human services for cultural minorities* (pp. 15–26). Baltimore, MD: University Park Press. Originally published in *Journal of Operational Psychiatry* (1978), *9*(2), 32–39.

Johnson, B. B. (1982). American Indian jurisdiction as a policy issue. *Social Work, 27,* 31–37.

Jones, B. E., & Gray, B. A. (1986). Problems in diagnosing schizophrenia and affective disorders among Blacks. *Hospital and Community Psychiatry, 37,* 61–65.

Kaplan, H. I., & Sadock, B. J. (1988). *Synopsis of psychiatry* (5th ed., chap. 5.6). Baltimore, MD: Williams & Wilkins.

Kasl, S. V., & Cobb, S. (1966). Health behavior, illness behavior, and sick role. *Archives of Environmental Health, 12,* 246–266.

Kim, B-L. C. (1973). Asian Americans: No model minority. *Social Work, 18,* 44–53.

Kitano, H. H. L. (1985). *Race relations* (3rd ed.). Englewood Cliffs, NJ: Prentice-Hall.

Kitano, H. H. L. (1987). Asian Americans. In A. Minahan (Ed.), *Encyclopedia of social work* (Vol. 1, pp. 156–171). Silver Spring, MD: National Association of Social Workers.

Kleinman, A. (1980). *Patients and healers in the context of culture.* Berkeley, CA: University of California Press.

Kunitz, S. J., & Levy, J. E. (1981). Navajos. In A. Harwood (Ed.), *Ethnicity and medical care* (pp. 337–396). Cambridge, MA: Harvard University Press.

Kuramoto, F. H., Morales, R. F., Munoz, F. U., & Murase, K. (1983). Education for social work practice in Asian and Pacific American communities. In J. C. Chunn II, P. J. Dunston, & F. Ross-Sheriff (Eds.), *Mental health and people of color* (pp. 127–155). Washington, DC: Howard University Press.

Lawson, W. B. (1986). Racial and ethnic factors in psychiatric research. *Hospital and Community Psychiatry, 37,* 50–54.

Leaf, P. J., et al. (1985). Contact with health professionals for the treatment of psychiatric and emotional problems. *Medical Care, 23,* 1322–1337.

LeBar, F. M., & Suddard, A. (1960). *Laos: Its people, its society, its culture.* New Haven, CT: HRAF Press.

Lee, E. (1982). A social systems approach to assessment and treatment for Chinese American families. In M. McGoldrick, J. K. Pearce, & J. Giordano (Eds.), *Ethnicity and family therapy* (pp. 527–551). New York: Guilford Press.

Leigh, J. W., & Green, J. W. (1982). The structure of the Black community: The knowledge base for social services. In J. W. Green (Ed.), *Cultural awareness in the human services* (pp. 94–121). Englewood Cliffs, NJ: Prentice-Hall.

Lewis, R. (1985). Cultural perspectives on treatment modalities with Native Americans. In M. Bloom (Ed.), *Life span development* (2nd ed., pp. 458–464). New York: Macmillan.

Lewis, R. G., & Keung Ho, M. (1975). Social work with Native Americans. *Social Work, 20,* 375–382.

Loring, M., & Powell, B. (1988). Gender, race, and DSM-III: A study of the objectivity of psychiatric diagnostic behavior. *Journal of Health and Social Behavior, 29,* 1–22.

Lum, D. (1986). *Social work practice and people of color: A process-stage approach.* Monterey, CA: Brooks/Cole.

Marsella, A. J., & Higginbotham, H. N. (1984). Traditional Asian medicine: Applications to psychiatric services in developing nations. In P. B. Pedersen, N. Sartorius, & A. J. Marsella (Eds.), *Mental health services: The cross-cultural context* (pp. 175–197). Beverly Hills, CA: Sage Publications.

Mays, V. M. (1985). The Black American and psychotherapy: The dilemma. *Psychotherapy, 22,* 379–388.

McAdoo, H. P. (1987). Blacks. In A. Minahan (Ed.), *Encyclopedia of social work* (18th ed., Vol. 1, pp. 194–206). Silver Spring, MD: National Association of Social Workers.

McGoldrick, M., Pearce, J. K., & Giordano, J. (Eds.), (1982). *Ethnicity and family therapy.* New York: Guilford Press.

Meinhardt, K., & Vega, W. (1987). A method for estimating underutilization of mental health services by ethnic groups. *Hospital and Community Psychiatry, 38,* 1186–1190.

Mishler, E. G. (1984). *The discourse of medicine: Dialectics of medical interviews.* Norwood, NJ: Ablex.

Moore, F. J. (1974). *Thailand: Its people, its society, its culture.* New Haven, CT: HRAF Press.

Mukherjee, S., et al. (1983). Misdiagnosis of schizophrenia in bipolar patients: A multiethnic comparison. *American Journal of Psychiatry, 140,* 1571–1574.

National Institute of Mental Health. (1986a). End of year census by patient characteristics. Tables 21A–IP and 21A–0P, unpublished data.

National Institute of Mental Health. (1986b). *Mental health, United States, 1985.* C. A. Taube & S. A. Barrett (Eds.). (DHHS Publication No. ADM 86-1378). Washington, DC: U.S. Government Printing Office.

Neighbors, H. W. (1984). Professional help use among Black Americans: Implications for unmet need. *American Journal of Community Psychology, 12,* 551–566.

Nobles, W. W. (1976). Black people in white insanity: An issue for Black community mental health. *The Journal of Afro-American Issues, 4,* 21–27.

Nofz, M. P. (1988). Alcohol abuse and culturally marginal American Indians. *Social Casework, 69,* 67–73.

Norton, D. G. (Ed.). (1978). *The dual perspective: Inclusion of ethnic minority content in the social work curriculum.* New York: Council on Social Work Education.

Ohio Department of Mental Health. (1988). *Report of the minority concerns committee.* Columbus, OH: Author.

Oliver, M. (1983). *Social work with disabled people.* London: Macmillan.

Parsons, T. (1964). *The social system.* New York: Free Press.

Pinderhughes, E. (1982). Afro-American families and the victim system. In M. McGoldrick, J. K. Pearce, & J. Giordano (Eds.), *Ethnicity and family therapy* (pp. 108–122). New York: Guilford Press.

Plessy v. Ferguson, 163 US, 537 (1896).

Red Horse, J. G. (1980a). American Indian elders: Unifiers of Indian families. *Social Casework, 61,* 490–493.

Red Horse, J. G. (1980b). Family structure and value orientation in American Indians. *Social Casework, 61,* 462–467.

Red Horse, J. G. (1988). Cultural evolution of American Indian families. In C. Jacobs & D. D. Bowles (Eds.), *Ethnicity and race: Critical concepts in social work* (pp. 86–102). Silver Spring, MD: National Association of Social Workers.

Roberts, R. E. (1981). Prevalence of depressive symptoms among Mexican Americans. *Journal of Nervous and Mental Disease, 169,* 213–219.

de la Rosa, M. (1988). Puerto Rican spiritualism: A key dimension for effective social casework practice with Puerto Ricans. *International Social Work, 31,* 273–283.

Sands, R. G., & Nuccio, K. (1989). Mother-headed single parent families: A feminist perspective. *Affilia, 4,* 25–41.

Schreiber, J. M., & Homiak, J. P. (1981). Mexican Americans. In A. Harwood (Ed.), *Ethnicity and medical care* (pp. 264–336). Cambridge, MA: Harvard University Press.

Shapiro, S., et al. (1985). Measuring need for mental health services in a general population. *Medical Care, 23,* 1033–1043.

Shon, S. P., & Ja, D. Y. (1982). Asian families. In M. McGoldrick, J. K. Pearce, & J. Giordano (Eds.), *Ethnicity and family therapy* (pp. 208–228). New York: Guilford Press.

Solomon, B. (1976). *Black empowerment: Social work in oppressed communities.* New York: Columbia University Press.

Stack, C. (1974). *All our kin: Strategies for survival in a black community.* New York: Harper & Row.

Steinberg, M. D., Pardes, H., Bjork, D., & Sporty, D. (1977). Demographic and clinical characteristics of Black psychiatric patients in a private general hospital. *Hospital and Community Psychiatry, 28,* 128–132.

Sue, D. M., & Sue, D. (1988). Asian-Americans. In N. A. Vacc, J. Wittmer, & S. B. DeVaney (Eds.), *Experiencing and counseling multicultural and diverse populations* (2nd ed., pp. 239–262). Muncie, IN: Accelerated Development.

Sue, S. (1977). Community mental health services to minority groups. *American Psychologist, 32,* 616–624.

Sue, S., Sue, D. W., & Sue, D. W. (1981). Asian Americans as a minority group. In R. H. Dana (Ed.), *Human services for cultural minorities* (pp. 287–294). Baltimore, MD: University Park Press. Originally published in *American Psychologist* (1975), *30,* 906–910.

Taylor, R. J., Neighbors, H. W., & Broman, C. L. (1989). Evaluation by Black Americans of the social service encounter during a serious personal problem. *Social Work, 34,* 205–211.

Toupin, E. S. W. A. (1981). Counseling Asians: Psychotherapy in the context of racism and Asian-American history. In R. H. Dana (Ed.), *Human services for cultural minorities* (pp. 295–306). Baltimore, MD: University Park Press. Originally published in *The American Journal of Orthopsychiatry* (1980), *50,* 76–86.

Trimble, J. E., Manson, S. M., Dinges, N. G., & Medicine, B. (1984). American Indian concepts of mental health: Reflections and directions. In P. B. Pedersen, N. Sartorius, & A. J. Marsella (Eds.), *Mental health services: The cross-cultural context* (pp. 199–220). Beverly Hills, CA: Sage Publications.

U.S. Bureau of the Census. (1980). *1980 census of population: General social and economic characteristics.* (U.S. Summary PC 80-1-C1 and P80-2-1E).

U.S. Bureau of the Census. (1988a). *The Hispanic population in the United States: March 1988. Advance report.* (Current Population Reports, Series P-20, No. 431). Washington, DC: U.S. Government Printing Office.

U.S. Bureau of the Census. (1988b). *Money income and poverty status in the United States: 1987.* Advance data from the March 1988 current population survey. (Current Population Reports, Series P-60, No. 161). Washington, DC: U.S. Government Printing Office.

U.S. Bureau of the Census. (1988c). *The Black population in the United States: March 1988.* (Current Population Reports, Series P-20, No. 442). Washington, DC: U.S. Government Printing Office.

U.S. Bureau of the Census. (1989a). *Household and family characteristics: March 1986.* (Current Population Reports, Series P-20, No. 419, Table F). Washington, DC: U.S. Government Printing Office.

U.S. Bureau of the Census. (1989b). *Poverty in the United States: 1987.* (Current Population Reports, Series P-60, No. 163, Table 1). Washington, DC: U.S. Government Printing Office.

Walker, A. (1983). My father's country is the poor. *In search of our mother's gardens* (pp. 199–222). New York: Harcourt Brace Janovich.

Warheit, G. J., Vega, W. A., Auth, J. B., & Meinhardt, K. (1985). Psychiatric symptoms and dysfunctions among Anglos and Mexican Americans: An epidemiologic study. In J. R. Greenley (Ed.), *Research in community and mental health: A research annual* (pp. 3–32). Greenwich, CT: JAI Press.

Westermeyer, J. (1985). Psychiatric diagnosis across cultural boundaries. *American Journal of Psychiatry, 142,* 798–805.

Williams, D. H. (1986). The epidemiology of mental illness in Afro-Americans. *Hospital and Community Psychiatry, 37,* 42–49.

World Health Organization. (1975). *Schizophrenia: A multinational study.* Geneva, Switzerland: World Health Organization Press.

II Intervention

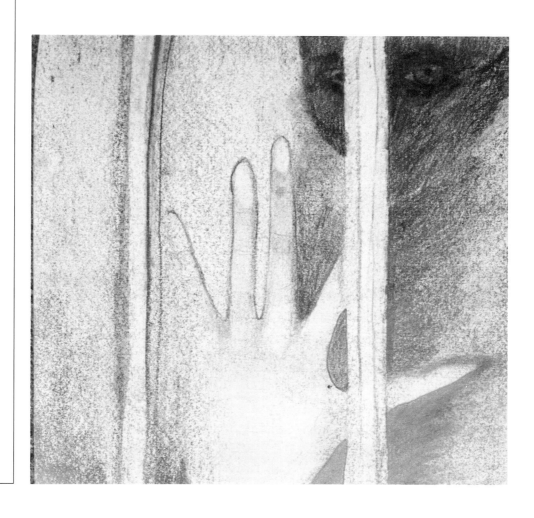

8 Intervention with the Chronically Mentally Ill: Theories, Research, and Concepts

"There are some words in the English language that carry a negative connotation, even though by definition there is no justification for such a connotation. Chronic is one of those words. You will seldom hear a long lasting, happy marriage described as chronic, nor will you hear about a person who is chronically happy. More often you'll associate chronic with chronic illness, chronic drinker, chronic complainer, or just 'a chronic.' 'A chronic' is most often used in the field of mental health to signify a client who has been in the system for a long time, who continually returns to the hospital, and for whom many professionals feel there is little hope. Chronics are often met with hostility or indifference from their primary service providers—the mental health workers."

—Nella Garrett, a student

The term *chronic mental illness* describes the expected course of mental illness of those individuals who have not responded, or who have responded only partially, to treatment. In contrast with *acute mental illness,* in which the illness flares up but has a limited trajectory, chronic mental illness is prolonged, persistent, and severe. Chronic mental illness connotes incurability and a deteriorating progression. Furthermore, it suggests disability (Bachrach, 1988).

The term *chronic* is problematic because it is a pejorative label (Bachrach, 1988; Jimenez, 1988). The perception that a psychiatric condition is permanent and persistent, despite remedial help, arouses feelings of hopelessness and creates a stigma. Some authors have come up with alternative descriptors such as "severely" or "seriously" (Bachrach, 1988) mentally disabled. Because labels affect perceptions and behaviors, many mental health practitioners choose to speak of "a person with schizophrenia," "an adult with a severe and persistent psychiatric disorder," or the like (Estroff, 1987).

183

Before deinstitutionalization, the chronically mentally ill were easily identifiable. They were the long-term, often lifelong denizens of the "back wards" of state psychiatric hospitals (Bachrach, 1988; Liberman, 1988a). Acting in a parental mode, the state provided custodial care and protection to the mentally impaired who appeared to be hopelessly sick and unable to take care of themselves. With the community as the dominant locus for treatment and the introduction of programs designed specifically for the chronically mentally ill, a need for a clearer definition has been evident.

Three criteria that establish parameters for a definition are diagnosis, disability, and duration (Bachrach, 1988; Goldman, 1984). The *diagnoses* that are usually described as chronic are psychotic disorders such as schizophrenia, delusional disorders, and some organic disorders such as dementias; mood disorders such as major depression and bipolar disorder; and schizoaffective disorder. Multiple diagnoses (both on Axis I or distributed on Axes I and II) are also possible. Moreover, other conditions, such as mental retardation and substance abuse disorders, may coexist with and complicate severe psychiatric disorders (Goldman, 1984).

The inclusion of personality disorders and other nonpsychotic disorders under the rubric of chronic disorders is controversial. Most research studies on the chronically mentally ill exclude persons with personality disorders unless they have a coexisting psychotic disorder. Nevertheless, many mental health programs that serve the severely mentally disabled are open to clients with nonpsychotic disorders (especially borderline personality disorders) when these disorders coexist with psychotic disorders, when the nonpsychotic disorder is severe, and if the client is functionally disabled. Practitioners should be guided by the diagnoses that are used to determine chronicity in their own state, as well as the criteria of disability and duration, which will be described shortly. In this chapter, as well as in chapters 9 and 10, the focus will be on treating persons with severe and persistent psychotic and mood disorders. Some of these persons may have coexisting personality disorders and/or substance abuse disorders. It should be noted that persons with borderline personality disorder can benefit from long-term ego-oriented psychotherapies that are not emphasized here. Treatment of persons with major mental disorders and substance abuse disorders (dual diagnoses) will be described in chapter 11.

Some of the diagnostic categories that are associated with chronicity are listed in Table 8.1. In keeping with the requirement in the *DSM-III-R* (American Psychiatric Association, 1987) that organic disorders be considered before the others, organic disorder is listed first. A fuller description of the major categories and specific criteria is contained in the *DSM-III-R*.

Diagnosis alone is not a satisfactory criterion, as some of the disorders that were mentioned have benign outcomes. The second criterion, *disability*, refers to impairment in emotional and behavioral functioning. Individuals whose psychiatric condition renders them unable to perform such activities as employment, housework, home maintenance, mobility, child care, and self-care (personal hygiene, grooming) are said to be mentally disabled. Psychiatric disability also interferes with the ability to engage in recreational and other activities that contribute to the quality of life (Gruenberg, 1982). Receipt of Supplemental Security Income (SSI) is one way of operationalizing disability (Goldman, 1984). Functional assessments of abilities look at basic living skills, social

TABLE 8.1

Psychiatric Disorders Associated with Chronicity

Diagnostic Category	Description	Subtypes
Organic disorder	Disturbance of the brain or brain functioning that is caused by a physical disorder, aging, or intake of a psychoactive substance	Delirium Dementia Amnestic disorder Organic delusional disorder Organic hallucinosis Organic mood disorder Organic anxiety disorder Organic personality disorder Organic disorder not otherwise specified (NOS)
Schizophrenia	Disturbance in thinking, sense of self, volition, activity, and affect that is characterized by out of ordinary experiences such as hallucinations, delusions, loose associations, and incoherence	Catatonic Disorganized type Paranoid type Undifferentiated type Residual type
Delusional (paranoid) disorder	Disorder of thinking, characterized by delusions that are not bizarre (i.e., have some grounding in ordinary experience) and behavior that ordinarily is not odd	Grandiose type Erotomanic type Jealous type Persecutory type Somatic type Unspecified type
Schizoaffective disorder	Combination of psychotic symptoms and disturbance of mood	Bipolar type Depressive type
Bipolar disorder	Disturbance of mood in which there is a history of manic (euphoric) symptoms, such as grandiosity, flight of ideas, and pressured speech; the manic episodes usually alternate with or are accompanied by depressive episodes	Mixed Manic Depressed NOS
Major depression	Disturbance of mood characterized by marked dysphoria, fatigue, loss of interest in life, lack of pleasure, and the like	Single episode Recurrent

Source: Adapted from American Psychiatric Association (1987).

activity, and adaptive behavior (see chapter 4). Psychiatric disabilities are remedied in programs of rehabilitation (Bachrach, 1986).

The third criterion is *duration*. This refers to the length of time that the individual has had the diagnosis or has been functionally impaired. Although some would determine duration by looking at the length of hospitalization, such a measure is not adequate (Bachrach, 1988). The chronic population consists of two cohorts—those who were formerly institutionalized, often for many years, and a younger group that became ill after the deinstitutionalization policy was put into place. The younger cohort (sometimes called *young chronics*) has grown into adulthood in an era in which short-term hospitalization and diversion from treatment in the hospital to the community are preferred strategies of intervention. Many of the younger group have avoided mental health facilities altogether. Another reason why long-term hospitalization is an inadequate criterion is that some psychiatric conditions are characterized by recurrent episodes of acute illness rather than a continuous course (Goldman, 1984). A history of hospitalizations regardless of the length of stay (e.g., two hospitalizations in the last year), a single hospitalization of a prescribed time period (e.g., 90 days long), an accumulation of days over years (e.g., 40 days in the last 3 years), and long-term treatment in an outpatient facility (e.g., 2 years) are other ways of addressing duration.

However useful it is to have specific criteria, they are, nonetheless, problematic. Diagnosis, disability, and duration are components of a multidimensional phenomenon. Disease and disability are not equivalent and may not be simultaneous. It is not clear which of the three dimensions is most important and how they interact (Bachrach, 1988). The following examples of clients who meet some but not all the criteria raise questions about the boundaries of the category "chronically mentally ill".

Jake is a 33-year-old man who has had bipolar disorder for 10 years. He had five hospitalizations before he was 30, but has been stable on lithium in the past 3 years. Jake is a college graduate and married. He is employed as a teller in a bank. Occasionally he has felt "highs" coming on, but he was able to prevent psychiatric episodes by having his medication adjusted. He attends a lithium compliance group.

Margaret is a 24-year-old single woman who has difficulty maintaining steady employment and social relationships. She describes her relationship with her parents as love–hate and has many ups and downs in relationships with male and female friends. Occasionally she suffers from depression, which she treats herself with alcohol and street drugs. Her parents are currently paying her rent but told her that this is the "last time" they will do so. Although she has been given the diagnosis of borderline personality disorder, she is not eligible for income maintenance or vocational rehabilitation and the treating psychiatrist refuses to prescribe medication for her. She has been in therapy with a clinical social worker for 3 months.

Roger is 45 and a veteran of the war in Vietnam. Since he was discharged, he has worked erratically in construction, a pattern that has contributed to marital problems. Roger reports having flashbacks of his war experiences, difficulty sleeping, and angry outbursts against others. Occasionally he has gotten into fist fights with men at work and on a few occasions he has beaten his wife. He has been going to the VA clinic on and off for 10 years, has been on medication, but has never been hospitalized. The mental health staff at the VA clinic suspect that he has minimal brain dysfunction, an organic condition, which is not war related, as well as post-traumatic stress disorder, which is war related. He has been turned down for disability.

These cases challenge the definitional parameters that have been described. Jake has a recurrent mood disorder that is effectively managed but not cured. He has had multiple hospitalizations, but not in the last 3 years. Jake is not disabled, but has a disease of long duration. Margaret is functionally disabled but does not have a psychotic or pervasive mood disorder. Her "disability" is complicated by substance abuse and a borderline personality disorder characterized by occasional depression. She has not been hospitalized and has been receiving outpatient treatment for only a few months. Roger has a possible organic disorder and another psychiatric disorder that is not usually considered a chronic mental illness. He has not been hospitalized and has had irregular outpatient treatment. Yet his nonpsychotic psychiatric disorders have interfered with his functioning (disability).

The *DSM-III-R* has attempted to define chronicity specifically in its description of the course of schizophrenia. If signs of the disturbance are present from 6 months to 2 years, the disorder is considered subchronic; if they are present more than 2 years, it is chronic. Two years is also used as a criterion for chronicity for other persistent mental disorders described in the diagnostic manual. Other descriptors used in the *DSM-III-R* for chronicity are the residual symptoms of schizophrenia that outlive signs of psychosis. These include marked social isolation, impaired role functioning, blunted affect, and apathy.

Nevertheless, a chronic course does not mean that the disorder persists indefinitely. Longitudinal studies of chronically mentally ill adults discharged to the community indicate that severe mental disabilities do not have a lifelong course. A follow-up study of backward patients released from Vermont State Hospital in the 1950s, for example, found that half to two-thirds of the subjects had significantly improved or recovered (Harding, Zubin, & Strauss, 1987). These results were consistent with findings of three studies conducted in Europe and one in the United States. On the basis of the five studies, the authors remark:

> Together, the data give evidence that, contrary to the expected downward and deteriorating course for schizophrenia or for other severe and chronic psychiatric disorders, symptoms can be ameliorated over time and functioning can be restored. (Harding et al., 1987, p. 724)

Styles of adaptation to community life varied among the study population. Some socialized, whereas others were isolated. There was also variability in medication compliance.

In view of the range of diverse life patterns among the population, the authors of the Vermont Study conclude that rather than a chronic course, "heterogeneity of patients' outcome" (p. 724) is to be expected. Because clinicians see a biased sample of persistent cases of schizophrenia and because of sampling deficiencies in past research, mental health professionals have a false impression that chronicity in schizophrenia is a fact (Harding, Zubin, & Strauss, 1987).

Young Adults with Severe and Persistent Psychiatric Disabilities.   Among the population with chronic difficulties, substantial numbers are between the ages of 18 and 35. This subpopulation of young adult chronic patients (YACPs) has provided a major challenge to the community mental health delivery system, which has been geared to provide "aftercare" to passive, compliant older clients. This "new generation of chronic psychiatric patients" (McCreath, 1984, p. 436) was born between the years of 1946 and 1961, the postwar period that produced a baby boom (Bachrach, 1982). They share with peers of their age strivings for autonomy, identity, intimacy, and independence, and a tendency to drift from place to place (Bachrach, 1982; Lamb, 1982). They differ from older chronic clients in their appearance (age-appropriate, not bizarre), behavior (unpredictable, variable), and aspirations (high). Their interactions with community mental health providers have generated complaints that they are "help-seeking yet help-rejecting" (Pepper, Kirshner, & Ryglewicz, 1981, p. 464); they seek assistance when they are in acute crises but do not follow through with treatment.

Young adults with severe and persistent psychiatric disabilities have been described as follows (Pepper & Ryglewicz, 1982, 1985). They are men and women whose diagnoses are varied and often multiple. Not unusually, they have a major psychiatric disorder such as schizophrenia or bipolar disorder and/or a borderline personality disorder. Many use or abuse substances—which results in the appearance of florid psychotic symptoms and aggressive or self-destructive behavior. A large proportion are single and live with or are dependent on their parents. Some, however, have children of their own. A minority have had encounters with the criminal justice system. They display assaultive behavior, which becomes a management problem in community settings (Bender, 1986; Lamb, 1982), and have negative attitudes toward hospitalization, medication, and therapists (Pepper & Ryglewicz, 1985). Although many of the young adults use a wide range of mental health services (however inconsistently), some do not use any (Bachrach, 1982). They tend to overuse emergency rooms and acute care facilities (Surles & McGurrin, 1987).

This profile has been the subject of much debate. Wintersteen and Rapp (1986) argue that the YACP concept is an inappropriate, stigmatizing label that draws attention to clients and away from deficiencies in public policy. Some authors provide evidence from research studies of the variability and strengths among the population (Intagliata & Baker, 1984; Test et al., 1985). They identify substantial numbers who are well educated, live independently, work, and do not consume substances. Sheets, Prevost, and Reihman (1982) clarify the diverse perceptions of the young adult chronic population in their description of three types—the system-dependent, the high-energy/high-demand, and the high-functioning groups. The *system-dependent group* are socialized into the client role, that is, they are passive, dependent, and accepting of mental health services. In contrast, the *high-energy/high-demand group* are impulsive, insistent on having what they want when they want it, and likely to move around within the mental health system. These young adults have high aspirations, act out sexually, and get in trouble with the law. Young adults in the high-functioning group are educated, appear attractive, and are motivated to fit in with their peers. They do not identify with other clients in the mental health system, nor do they want to participate in mental health programs. Nevertheless, they have impairments and lack the supports.

Although the term *young chronic* is not entirely satisfactory, it has a certain pragmatic utility. First of all, it speaks to the demographic picture of a burgeoning population in need of mental health services. Second, it points to historical differences between the younger and older cohorts. Many of the older adults with serious mental disorders spent years of their lives in institutions, where their lives were static (Bachrach, 1982; Pepper, Ryglewicz, & Kirshner, 1982) and they were conditioned to be acquiescent. Furthermore, the term *young chronic* suggests that the developmental needs of this population are different from those of other populations. Finally, it provides a rationale for the development of intervention programs that reflect the special needs of young adults. As Bachrach (1984) explains, "the concept of the young adult chronic psychiatric patient is an *ideal construct* that enables us to understand the deficits in the psychiatric service system" (p. 576).

Regardless of the terms used and the age groups, persons with chronic mental illness represent a population of major concern to the community mental health social worker. In this volume the definition developed by the authors of the monograph *Toward a National Plan for the Chronically Mentally Ill* (U.S. Department of Health and Human Services, 1981) will be used:

> The chronically mentally ill population encompasses persons who suffer certain mental or emotional disorders (organic brain syndrome, schizophrenia, recurrent depressive and manic-depressive disorders, paranoid and other psychoses, plus other disorders that may become chronic) that erode or prevent the development of their functional capacities in relation to (three or more) such primary aspects of daily life as personal hygiene and self-care, self-direction, interpersonal relationships, social transactions, learning, and recreation, and that erode or prevent the development of their economic self-sufficiency. Most such individuals have required institutional care of extended duration, including intermediate-term hospitalization (90 days to 1 year in a single year), long-term hospitalization (1 year or longer in the preceding 5 years), or nursing home placement on account of a diagnosed mental condition or a diagnosis of senility without psychosis. Some such individuals have required repeated short-term hospitalization (less than 90 days), have received treatment from a medical or mental health professional solely on an outpatient basis, or—despite their needs—have received no treatment in the professional-care service system. Thus included in the population are persons who are or were formerly "residents" of institutions (public and private psychiatric hospitals and nursing homes), and persons who are at high risk of institutionalization because of persistent mental disability. (pp. 2–11)

The same problems that make it difficult to define chronic mental illness affect the ability of epidemiologists to assess its prevalence. Goldman and Manderscheid (1987) used such criteria as SSI/SSDI eligibility, inability to work, and episodic and prolonged hospitalization to assess the size of the chronic population. Their estimate, based on 1977 data, was that between 1.7 and 2.4 million persons are either severely (lower figure) or severely and moderately (higher figure) mentally ill. Of these, approximately 900,000 are institutionalized in mental health facilities or nursing homes. The community population should be between 800,000 and 1,500,000. Between 25 and 65 percent of hospital patients with chronic conditions return to their families (U.S. Department of Health and Human Services, 1981).

Clinical social work intervention with persons with chronic mental illness is guided by theories and research findings that have emerged in the last 20 years. Although most of the newer developments arose from research on schizophrenia, the findings are applicable to a wider range of disorders. In addition to presenting these theories and results of empirical research, this chapter will discuss the principles of intervention, with particular attention to rehabilitation, the use of community supports, and strategies relevant to young adults with severe disabilities. Chapter 9 will provide information on case management and the range of community services in which psychosocial rehabilitation and community support take place. Model programs, such as Fountain House, will be described. Chapter 10 will describe specific treatment strategies, such as psychopharmacology, social skills training, and family psychoeducation.

THEORETICAL ISSUES

Biogenetic research supports the assumption that the major chronic disorders—schizophrenia, bipolar disorder, some major depressions, and organic disorders—are brain diseases. As discussed in chapter 3, genetic studies, neurophysiological findings, and responsiveness to medication provide substantial evidence for this assumption. Genetic studies of twins, one of whom was identified as having schizophrenia, have revealed higher rates of concordance between monozygotic than between dizygotic twins (Kendler, 1988). Studies of adoptees with schizophrenic spectrum disorders found an unusually high prevalence of schizophrenia and the spectrum disorders among natural relatives (Kendler, 1988). Similar results have been realized with respect to the genetics of unipolar depression and bipolar disorder (McGuffin & Katz, 1989). Furthermore, neurophysiological studies of the brain using sophisticated new laboratory equipment have identified structural abnormalities among persons with schizophrenia, mania, and dementia (Andreasen, 1984; Taylor, 1987; Andreasen, et al. 1990). The effectiveness of neuroleptics, lithium, and antidepressants on persons with schizophrenia, organic disorders, bipolar disorder, and major depression also supports the role of biology. Research on the role of viruses and the immune system in the etiology of major mental disorders is promising but inconclusive (King & Cooper, 1989).

Recognition of a biogenetic etiology represents a marked departure from the past, when psychoanalytic and family communication theories about the development of serious psychiatric disorders predominated. With respect to schizophrenia, psychoanalysis espoused the concept of the "schizophrenogenic mother" (Fromm-Reichmann, 1948), which not only drew attention to deficient parenting but blamed the mother. Similarly, attention to dysfunctional interaction patterns in families with a schizophrenic member gave birth to such concepts as "marital skew" and "marital schism" (Lidz et al., 1957) and the "double bind" (Bateson et al., 1956). These theories promoted a view of the family as a pathogenic agent that was to be blamed or cured. The same theories depicted families of persons with bipolar disorder as using the child, who later became afflicted with what was then called manic-depressive illness, to lift the family from its marginal social status (Cohen et al., 1954). Unipolar depression was attributed to parental rejection, devaluation, and early loss of a parent (Freedman, Kaplan, & Sadock, 1972). These theories have aroused considerable anguish and guilt in parents. With families assuming a significant role as care givers today, enlightened clinicians now view families as resources and partners (Hatfield, 1984, 1987).

A model of schizophrenia that is in keeping with biogenetic findings and the biopsychosocial framework of this book is the *stress-diathesis* or *vulnerability* model (Zubin & Spring, 1977; Liberman, 1982). It has also been described as the *stress-vulnerability-coping-competence* model (Liberman, 1988b). Accordingly, schizophrenia arises in an individual with a genetic vulnerability for schizophrenia, a low threshold for tolerating stress, and inadequate coping strategies. In the face of a socioenvironmental stressor, the predisposed individual has an episode or exacerbation of schizophrenia (Falloon & Liberman, 1983; Land, 1986).

Relapse into illness seems to be related to several peripheral aspects of the stressful life experience. For one, the episode is related to the individual's perception of the dangerousness of the demand in relation to his or her ability to respond effectively (Zubin & Spring, 1977). Furthermore, the individual's capacity and efforts to cope with the demand are relevant. In the face of an overwhelming stressor, these capacities can break down. The ensuing debilitation may be temporary, but in the eventuality of a schizophrenic episode, it is more persistent (Zubin & Spring, 1977). Persons who have a history of relatively high premorbid (prior to psychosis) functioning tend to adapt better to stress than those without such a history; if there is a breakdown, they are more likely to achieve a higher level of functioning than those with a poor premorbid history (Liberman, 1982).

Socioenvironmental supports can provide a buffer against stress (Pilisuk, 1982). These consist of family, friends, neighbors, and members of a religious community, whose help can make it unnecessary for clients to seek professional help (Gottlieb, 1985). Unfortunately, many persons with severe psychiatric disabilities have small social networks comprised predominantly of kin and do not reciprocate with persons who offer support, friendship, and love to them (Sullivan & Poertner, 1989; Tolsdorf, 1976). Often professionals and social programs fill the gap in clients' natural support systems and become part of or the entire support system. Nevertheless, family members and interested friends of clients can be educated to implement strategies that can lower the level of stress experienced by clients.

Figure 8.1 is a visual representation of the stress-diathesis model. Stressors may be environmental or internal (biochemical, intrapsychic) events that are perceived negatively and arouse anxiety and challenge the coping capacities of the vulnerable individual. Social supports provide structure, strategies, and encouragement that can mitigate stress. When stressors and supports are in balance in a vulnerable individual, social functioning can be maintained.

A related concept, the *stimulus window* (Pepper & Ryglewicz; 1986, October), has to do with the level of sensory stimulation one can tolerate and the range in which one

FIGURE 8.1

The stress-diathesis model

Vulnerability	
Stressors (−)	Social Supports (+)
Events that are perceived negatively Anxiety Unable to cope	Resources Structure Problem solving Stress management

can function effectively. Although a certain amount of stimulation (and stress) is desirable, too much (overstimulation) or too little (understimulation) can result in the development of psychiatric symptoms. The size of the window (range of tolerable stimulation) is related to one's mental health. A person with a healthy personality can tolerate a wide range of stimulation and extremes in quality and quantity. Many persons with schizophrenia have difficulty managing sensory stimuli and function best within a limited range. They may confuse internal and external stimuli and overreact to intense emotions. Persons with mood disorders, organic impairments, and severe personality disorders have difficulty regulating emotions, processing information, and managing stress, respectively. Drug and alcohol constitute chemical stressors that can have a negative impact on an organism that is naturally sensitive to stimulation.

The range of stimuli that can enter an individual's stimulus window is biologically based. Individual vulnerability and the specific disorder may affect the range. Nevertheless, the upper and lower limits and flexibility to function within a range can be extended through treatment. This should be done over a long period of time and with care not to contribute to sensory overload of the client (Pepper & Ryglewicz, 1986, October).

A similar model explaining the same phenomenon with respect to schizophrenia is the *attention-arousal* model (Anderson, Reiss, & Hogarty, 1986). Accordingly, the person with schizophrenia has a "core psychological deficit" (Anderson, Hogarty, & Reiss, 1980) in the ability to select, sort, filter, and evaluate stimuli. This deficiency results in diffuse responses and hyperarousal to stimuli, regardless of their relevance to a situation. The individual is affected by both internal and external stimuli (information), which make a demand for information processing. When the demands increase, the organism becomes distracted, inattentive, and aroused. The person with schizophrenia responds to these stimuli by maintaining a narrow focus of attention, missing the full picture. This produces a state of disintegration and sensory malfunctioning. In a state of high arousal, an individual can perceive and behave in dysfunctional ways (e.g., hallucinations, aggressive behavior). Medication can modify the internal conditions associated with arousal and attention deficits, thus reducing vulnerability; intervention with families can reduce excessive external stimulation.

Like the stimulus window concept, the attention-arousal model assumes that some, but not excessive, stimulation is desirable. Accordingly social interaction that is low keyed and nonintrusive facilitates psychosocial functioning, whereas intensive and demanding interaction can be deleterious. This has implications for the kinds of social worker–client relationships that should be developed, and the kinds of social programs that can help persons with schizophrenia. The role of environmental stress in the course of severe psychiatric disorders (especially schizophrenia) is evident in the research studies that will be described next.

In this and the following two chapters, chronic mental illnesses will be viewed as brain disorders that affect psychosocial functioning and are affected by everyday social interactions. Accordingly psychoanalytic and family etiological theories are not relevant. Treatment is directed at rehabilitating the afflicted client and supporting the client's family in its efforts to help the client. The basis for this strategy can be found in research.

BIOPSYCHOSOCIAL RESEARCH FINDINGS

Biopsychosocial empirical research initially conducted in England and later replicated in the United States has produced findings that have important implications for theory and treatment. In this section, seminal research studies pertaining to family environment, stress, and intervention strategies will be reviewed. These studies were performed largely on persons with chronic schizophrenia but also on those with paranoid, schizoaffective, and depressive disorders and their families. Research on the effectiveness of various methods of intervention that follow from British findings was conducted in the United States. Findings provide a rationale for the treatment strategies that will be described in this chapter and those that follow.

In order to ease the reading of the first group of studies, which are controversial, a summary table (Table 8.2) is provided. The implications for practice will be discussed later in the chapter.

British Studies on the Family Environment

Brown and associates conducted a sequence of studies in the 1950s and 1960s on the quality of family life of discharged patients with a diagnosis of schizophrenia in the London area. A preliminary study (Brown, Carstairs, & Topping, 1958; Brown, 1959) showed that male patients who lived with their parents or wives had a higher hospital readmission rate than those who resided with other relatives or lived in community lodgings. Furthermore, those who had extensive contact with relatives at home had a worse prognosis than those with less contact. The authors' initial conclusion was that it is not always advisable for schizophrenic patients to return to close relatives. Only later did they wonder whether there were particular qualities in these home environments that were problematic.

The authors explored the emotional climate more thoroughly in a subsequent study of 128 men ages 20 to 49 who had been hospitalized at least 1 month and were discharged from eight hospitals in London (Brown, Monck, Carstairs, & Wing, 1962). All had confirmed diagnoses of schizophrenia. Those with relatives to whom they would be discharged ($N = 101$) were interviewed on three occasions—before discharge, two

TABLE 8.2

British Studies on Expressed Emotion

Authors of Study	Sample	Major Findings
Brown, Monck, Carstairs, & Wing (1962)	128 males with schizophrenia who were discharged from hospital, 101 of whom were living with relatives	1. Among total, 41% were rehospitalized, 64% deteriorated, and 52% got worse within a year. 2. Greater deterioration in homes with high emotional involvement on part of relatives. 3. Greater deterioration among those who had 35 hours or more of face-to-face contact with relatives.
Brown, Birley, & Wing (1972)	101 men and women with schizophrenia	1. 58% from high EE homes relapsed; 16% from low EE homes relapsed. 2. Relapse rate of men was twice that of women; relapse rate of married (26%) was almost half that of unmarried (42%). 3. Relapse rate of those from high EE homes who took medication was 46%; rate for those from high EE homes who did not take medication was 66%. 4. Relapse rate of those from low EE homes was 15% for those not taking medication and 14% for those taking medication. 5. 79% relapse with high contact in high EE homes; 12% relapse with high contact in low EE homes.
Vaughn & Leff (1976)	37 males and females with schizophrenia; 30 with neurotic depression; both groups previously hospitalized	1. High EE predicted relapse for schizophrenia and depression. 2. Relapse rate for schizophrenic men twice that for women; higher rate for single than married. 3. In high EE homes, not taking medication contributed to relapse; not taking medication together with high face-to-face contact contributed to higher relapse rate. In low EE homes, drugs and amount of contact did not make a significant difference. 4. Persons with depressive neuroses required fewer critical comments for relapse than those with schizophrenia.
Leff & Vaughn (1981)	Two-year follow-up study of 25 of 37 persons with schizophrenia studied previously (1976)	1. Those from low EE homes had lower relapse rate than those from high EE homes. 2. Drugs provided significant protection for high EE group at 9 months but not at 2 years. At 2 years 43% of high EE group on medication relapsed. 3. Those in low EE group and on medication had a 0% relapse rate at 2 years.

weeks after discharge, and at readmission or at the end of the year. During an at-home interview of the patient and at least a "key" relative (usually female), researchers rated the behavior of the relative toward the patient on emotion expressed, hostility, and dominant behavior that was directed toward the patient, as well as the patient's emotion expressed and hostility toward the key relative.

A substantially large percentage of the total subjects were rehospitalized (41 percent) or clinically deteriorated (64 percent) within the year; 52 percent were considered worse. The rate of decline among those who lived in lodgings was comparable with that of those who lived with parents or wives. Those who lived with siblings showed the lowest level of deterioration.

The percentages of decline of those from homes rated high on "emotional involvement" were significantly greater than of those from homes that were low on the same quality (76 versus 28 percent deteriorated; 56 versus 21 percent were rehospitalized; $p < .001$). Furthermore, those patients from homes with high emotional involvement by a key relative and whose mental state at the time of discharge was rated moderate or severe were vulnerable to intense contact with the relative with whom they resided. Among those who had high contact with relatives (operationalized as more than 35 hours per week of face-to-face interaction), 96 percent deteriorated; among those with low contact, the percent was 50 ($p < .01$).

On the basis of these results it appeared that high emotional involvement by relatives is consistent with high levels of deterioration. Among those who lived in highly emotional homes, high contact with the patient was particularly toxic. Nevertheless, those who lived in lodgings, apart from relatives, did not fare well. Apparently, some low-intensity contact is helpful; extensive, but highly emotional contact has a deleterious effect.

Brown, Birley, & Wing (1972) replicated this study 10 years later, using more sophisticated scales, which had been developed in the interim. This time the sample ($N = 101$) included women and used patients born in the United Kingdom and living in the Camberwell section of London, as well as a sample from Bexley Hospital. The new scales of family interaction patterns included the number of critical comments, hostility, dissatisfaction, warmth, emotional overinvolvement, and an overall index of expressed emotion (EE) that was derived from these variables. Two kinds of relapse were measured—change from normal or nonschizophrenic to schizophrenia; and marked exacerbation of persistent symptoms of schizophrenia.

Once again the authors found a significant relationship between high EE in the relatives and the patient's deterioration. Among the respondents from high EE homes, 58 percent relapsed; among those from low EE homes, only 16 percent relapsed. This study also found differences in the relapse rates of men and women. The relapse rate of men was twice that of women. Moreover, married subjects had a lower rate (26 percent) than unmarried (42 percent). Regardless of marital status, the relapse rate for men was higher. The women in this study, however, were older and more likely to be married than the men.

A further refinement in this study was its examination of the effects of taking antipsychotic drugs and emotional expressiveness on relapse. Although two-thirds of the subjects took medication during the study period or until relapse, drug maintenance itself was not significantly related (but was close) to outcome. Among those who took their medication and lived in high EE homes, the relapse rate was 46 percent, whereas those in high EE homes who did *not* take medication relapsed at a rate of 66 percent. Of those in low EE homes, the rate was only 15 percent for those who were not on medication and 14 percent for those who were.

These researchers also looked at the amount of time spent in face-to-face contacts between patients and relatives. The relapse rate of persons from both types of homes who had little contact with relatives was comparable. Patients in high EE homes who had more than 35 hours a week of contact with relatives, however, had a relapse rate of 79 percent, compared with a rate of 12 percent among those in low EE homes but with high contact.

This study supported and amplified the findings of the one it had replicated. It demonstrated clearly that high emotional expressiveness is related to relapse. High interpersonal contact in high EE homes also correlated with relapse. Medication did not appear to have much of an impact in low EE homes. In high EE homes, however, medication did seem to provide some protection.

Vaughn and Leff (1976) replicated the previous study using a cohort of depressed neurotic patients ($N = 30$) as well as a group with the diagnosis of schizophrenia ($N = 37$). The findings here were similar: high EE was significantly related to relapse (48 percent relapse in high group, 6 percent in low group, $p = .007$). Once again, the relapse rate for men was twice that for women and the rate for the married was less than that for the unmarried. Furthermore, the findings with relation to medication use and face-to-face interaction were similar.

Vaughn and Leff (1976) were able to combine subjects from the previous Brown, Birley, and Wing (1972) study for further analysis. The effects of high expressed emotion in the home, degree of interpersonal contact, and drug treatments turned out to be *additive* in relation to those in high EE homes. Among those in low EE homes, medication did not seem to be protective. A study of the same subjects at a 2-year follow-up, however, revealed that medication was especially protective of subjects from low EE homes over time. Regardless of the emotional climate in the home, those who remained on medication did not have any relapses (Leff & Vaughn, 1981).

Vaughn and Leff (1976) found EE to be a significant variable in the outcomes for persons with depressive neurosis, too. Whereas they had used seven or more critical comments as a measure for EE for schizophrenics, two or more were predictive of relapse for the depressed cohort. Sixty-seven subjects whose relatives made two or more critical comments relapsed, compared with 22 percent of those whose relatives made few such comments ($p = .032$). The depressed appeared to be especially sensitive to criticism, but in contrast with the schizophrenia group, the depressed patients' amount of interpersonal contact was not predictive of relapse.

As Table 8.2 reveals, the findings on EE in the family held across studies. Nevertheless, the samples studied were small and they were confined to the United Kingdom. Sex differences that emerged in the Brown, Birley, & Wing (1972) and Vaughn and Leff (1976) studies need to be clarified.

Cross-Cultural Replication Studies on the Family Environment

Vaughn et al. (1984) performed a study in Southern California that replicated Vaughn and Leff's (1976) study and its predecessors. The sample consisted of 69 Anglo-American subjects from the ages of 17 to 50 who were hospitalized within a month prior to the initial research interview and who met the diagnostic criteria for schizophrenic or paranoid psychosis. A few departures from the British procedures were made to account for differing patient populations and mental health delivery systems. The study in California included subjects with a secondary diagnosis of drug abuse, whereas the British studies excluded any drug abuse. As it turned out, the sample consisted largely of young (mean age = 25.6), never married (87 percent) males (77 percent) who were living with one or both parents (91 percent). The British research subjects were older and included more women and married persons.

A similar association between relatives' high EE score and relapse was found in the Southern California study. Overall, however, significantly fewer of the California families were low in EE than their British counterparts. In particular, the California relatives were more critical and hostile than the British. Apparently this is reflective of a cultural difference between Anglo-Americans and the British: Americans seem to be more emotionally expressive in their families.

The sex differences found in the British studies were even more pronounced in the California study: the relapse rate for men was three times that for women. The association between high EE and relapse was markedly higher for men than for women (66 versus 14 percent). Many of the men lived in homes with a great deal of parental conflict. Moreover, drug abuse, another predictor of relapse, tended to be associated with male subjects.

The findings on medication diverged somewhat from those of the British studies. Among subjects in the low EE group, those who took medication regularly had a 0 percent relapse rate; those not taking drugs regularly had a 25 percent rate. In the high EE group, those with low familial contact and who took medicine regularly had a relapse rate of 11 percent; those who had low contact and did not take their medication regularly relapsed at a rate of 69 percent. A surprising result was that among subjects in the high EE group with high familial contact, 100 percent of those taking medication regularly and 67 percent of those not taking medication relapsed. The authors note that there is an *interaction* between taking medication and having a reduced contact with relatives. This suggests that individuals need to take medication *and* have minimal face-to-face contact with relatives to achieve maximum protection against relapse. This differs from previous findings that found the variables additive.

An epidemiological study of relatives of persons with schizophrenia in Chandigarh, North India, included an assessment of emotional expressiveness in the family. Initial findings indicated that the extent and distribution of critical comments and hostility differed from those reported in the West. The mean number of critical comments was about one-third of that reported elsewhere. Moreover, there was less overinvolvement with their relative (Leff & Vaughn, 1985). Other studies have found different rates of expressed emotion among families of schizophrenics across cultures (Koenigsberg & Handley, 1986). Furthermore, studies in Hamburg, Germany (Kottgen et al., 1984), and Sydney, Australia (Parker, Johnston, & Hayward, 1988), did not find an association between EE in the family and relapse in 9-month follow-up studies.

Research on EE has been stimulating to researchers and practitioners but troubling to families of persons with schizophrenia and other serious disorders. Researchers have found in the family environment a variable (EE) that is consistent with hypotheses based on biological research that this population is vulnerable to stress and has difficulty processing complex information (cf. stress-diathesis and attention-arousal models). With the variable of EE identified, practitioners have guidance in ways that they can intervene with families. (Implications of these findings are discussed later in this section.) On the other hand, families find in this research a revival of parent blaming that emanated from psychoanalytic and family interaction theories. To many families, research on brain pathology is more relevant.

This research was described in detail so that practitioners can evaluate its worth themselves. Moreover, some of the subsequent research on intervention that will be described incorporates the criterion of EE. Clearly, the finding on the salience of EE in England and the United States has been consistent. Furthermore, medication together with a low-intensity home environment appears to provide some protection against relapse. Nevertheless, the research on EE was performed largely on Caucasians of Anglo-Saxon origin who were reared in the West. Findings for women seem to differ from those for men. The exclusion of non-Anglo minorities from the California study raises questions about the applicability of these important findings to African Americans, Hispanics, Asians, and other ethnic groups.

American Research Studies on Drug and Social Therapy

In the last two decades, American researchers have conducted research on the relative impact and interaction between drug treatment and social therapy. Samples have tended to be larger than British samples and have included men and women and small subsamples of diverse ethnic groups. Americans have incorporated British findings on the emotional climate in the family and assessed the effectiveness of various forms of intervention.

A significant program of research was performed by a social worker, Gerald Hogarty, who collaborated with associates at Western Psychiatric Clinic, University of Pittsburgh School of Medicine, and elsewhere. These researchers initially studied a sample of 374 outpatients with diagnoses of schizophrenia and schizoaffective disorder, stratified by sex, who were released from three state hospitals in Maryland to three clinics (Hogarty & Goldberg, 1973; Hogarty et al., 1974a, 1974b). After discharge, subjects were maintained on chlorpromazine for 2 months, after which time they were randomly assigned to four groups—(a) only drug treatment, (b) only placebo, (c) drug treatment and social therapy, and (d) placebo and social therapy.

The social therapy was called Major Role Therapy (MRT), which was described as social casework and vocational rehabilitation in combination. MRT was administered by experienced social workers with master's degrees in social work, most of whom were graduates of Rankian schools of social work. The therapy was aimed principally at solving personal and environmental problems that had an impact on the client's performance of social roles such as homemaker, employee, or potential employee. It also assisted clients in their interpersonal relationships, financial management, self-care, and the like. To achieve these objectives, social workers used principles of acceptance, support, clarification, and assurance. Those who were not receiving MRT were evaluated, encouraged to keep their clinic appointments, and referred to (but not assisted in following through with) other resources.

Hogarty, Goldberg, and collaborators (1973) found that after the first year of implementation the rate of relapse was much higher among those on a placebo than those on medication (67.5 versus 30.9 percent). MRT had no overall impact on the relapse rate during the first year, but seemed to contribute to a lowered rate during the last 6 months of the year. A 2-year follow-up study (Hogarty et al., 1974a), however, amplified these findings. The relapse rate of those using chlorpromazine (48 percent) was significantly lower ($p < .001$) than that of those using the placebo (80 percent). The drugs had a more favorable influence on outcome for the women (37 percent relapsed) than for the men (63 percent relapsed). Neither race, nor clinic, nor social therapy (MRT) had an impact on the outcome (length of time a client survived in the community).

In a related paper, Hogarty et al. (1974b) looked more closely at the interaction between MRT and drug therapy among participants who did not have a relapse. Using 74 measures of psychosocial functioning as dependent variables, the researchers found a significant interaction between drug treatment and MRT at 18-month and 24-month assessment periods. Surprisingly, *those who received MRT and the placebo did poorly.* This was especially so for the men who developed pronounced psychiatric symptoms at 18 months. Furthermore, men who were on the placebo alone did better than women without drug treatment.

This research has important implications for treatment. Clearly, the combination of drug treatment *and* social therapy (MRT) helps clients maintain longevity and psychosocial well-being in the community. Nevertheless, the authors indicated that *social therapy without drug treatment can be harmful,* especially for men. Like the British studies on the family environment, these studies suggest that interpersonal contact, even from trained social workers, can be toxic. On the other hand, drug therapy combined with social therapy can be helpful.

The findings on the relapse rate during the second year reported by Hogarty et al. (1974a, 1974b) raises important questions. Although 80 percent of subjects treated with placebos relapsed in the 2-year follow-up period, *20 percent survived without any medication.* Apparently there is a substantial minority of clients with diagnoses of schizophrenia or schizoaffective disorder who are able to remain stable without medication. This suggests that drugs are not universally necessary or even desirable (considering the side effects). Still, researchers are not able to identify which clients are capable of maintaining functioning without medication. In view of the better outcomes among prescribed drug users as compared with those on placebos, *medication is preventive therapy for the population as a whole, but is not required for maintenance by everyone.*

A variable that might affect the relapse rates among medicated clients in research studies is noncompliance with medication. To test this, Hogarty et al. (1979) conducted an experimental study in which subjects were randomly assigned to receive either oral fluphenazine hydrochloride or long-acting fluphenazine decanoate (given biweekly by injection). In addition, subjects were randomly assigned to either intensive social therapy or routine surveillance. By the end of the first year, there was little difference in the relapse rates of the two medication groups (oral 40 percent, injection 41 percent). Those who had the combination of social therapy and medication by injection had the lowest relapse rate over 2 years.

The relapse rates reported by Hogarty and associates during the first year in the community are comparable with the results of studies conducted elsewhere. The overall average rate among 814 patients described in seven 1-year follow-up studies is 41 percent for those treated with medication and 68 percent for those on placebos. Fourteen studies of clients who were stablized at least a year prior to follow-up research had an average drug relapse rate of 15 percent, compared with a placebo relapse rate of 65 percent (Hogarty, 1984). It has been consistently found that although medication is helpful to most, it is not completely effective; and that for some people, medication does not seem to be needed.

More recent research performed by Hogarty and his associates looks at interventions that might reduce the relapse rate among persons with schizophrenia and schizoaffective disorder. One study (Hogarty et al., 1986) assesses various combinations of maintenance chemotherapy and two forms of intervention—social skills training of clients and family psychoeducation. The family psychoeducation that the authors implemented had the objective of reducing the emotional expressiveness of family members and adapting family expectations to a reasonable level. Social skills training worked on client behaviors that provoke high family emotional expressiveness and promoted effective strategies for coping with conflict. (These modes of intervention will be described in chapter 10.) The four groups were (a) medication and family treatment; (b) medication and social skills training; (c) medication, family psychoeducation, and social skills training; and (d) medication only. All were assessed as having high emotional expressiveness. Clients were randomly assigned to one of these conditions while they were hospitalized.

The relapse rates after a year of intervention were considerably reduced for the three experimental groups in contrast with the control group (group d):

a. Family treatment + medication: 19 percent
b. Social skills training + medication: 20 percent
c. All three interventions: 0 percent
d. Only medication: 41 percent

These percentages are reduced somewhat if only the drug-compliant clients are included, but are increased slightly if those who participated in the interventions to a partial degree are included. Nevertheless, they provide substantial support to the idea that *medication together with social treatment forestalls relapse*. Furthermore, it appears that the combination of pharmacotherapy and social skills training of the client and psychoeducation for the family provides maximum protection against another episode. These interventions improve substantially upon use of medication only.

The authors of this study recommend that family psychoeducation be used for broader populations than their research population (individuals from high EE homes). They remark that the relationship between high emotional expressiveness in the family and relapse seems to be better substantiated for unmarried male schizophrenics; but that their experience has revealed a considerable population of females with schizoaffective disorder from low EE homes who are troubled with issues over loss. They

recommend family psychoeducation and other approaches for these and other populations that are tailored to the individual case.

Two additional studies are representative of a growing number of research studies
that have been taking a close look at the dosage of medication in relation to various
outcome measures. One (Kreisman et al., 1988) randomly assigned outpatients with
schizophrenia or schizoaffective disorder who were already stabilized on medication to
two groups—standardized dose and low dose intramuscular fluphenazine deconoate
(intravenous Prolixin). The low-dose group received approximately 10 percent of the
standard amount, with some flexibility allowed. The psychiatrists were not aware of the
group assignment of their patients. Various instruments were used intermittently to
measure individual and family perceptions of the client's state and the family's attitude.
The results were provocative. Although almost half (45 percent) of the subjects on the
low dose relapsed, in contrast with 9 percent of those on a standard dose, the families
of patients on the lower dose felt more positive about their family members. Furthermore, the clients on the low dose were better adjusted, more self-sufficient, and had
more romantic contacts than those in the other group. This raises some serious questions about the relative value of a standard dose of medication with its deleterious side
effects and the risks versus benefits of a lower dosage. The authors suggest that a low
dose might be particularly beneficial for individuals from low EE families.

Hogarty et al. (1988) conducted another study in which the dosage of medication
was regulated. The sample consisted of continuous hospital admissions who met the
same diagnostic criteria of their other studies. The families' EE status was assessed
during hospitalization, but participants were not entered into the study until they were
stabilized in the community, at which time they were assigned randomly to either the
standard- or the minimal-dose group. Medication was dispensed intravenously. In contrast with the Kreisman study, in this one the lower dosage was approximately 20
percent of the standard one. Although the survivorship rate was higher for those on the
standard dose at the end of the first and second years, and highest for those who
received the standard dose and had low EE families, the difference was small. Moreover,
the low-dose clients and those who lived in low EE households were better adjusted.
There were, however, a few minor episodes of schizophrenic symptoms that occurred in
both groups. The authors remarked that the best candidates for reduction may be those
who are already on a low dosage and recommended a "minimal effective dose (MED)"
(p. 803). Medication adjustment will be discussed further in chapter 10.

Other studies look at the effectiveness of modes of family intervention in relation
to medication dose. Goldstein and Kopeikin's (1981) research study looked at the short-
and long-term effects of combining crisis-oriented family therapy with drug therapy at
moderate and low dosages. The therapy focused on stressor identification, stress avoidance, coping, developing realistic expectations, and anticipatory planning. Comparison
groups were distinguished by the presence or absence of family therapy and doses of
injectable phenothiazine. At 6-week and 6-month follow-ups, the group that had a low
dose and no family therapy had the highest relapse rates (24 and 48 percent, respectively), whereas the group with both a high dose and family therapy had a 0 percent
relapse rate at both periods. The other groups occupied close intermediate positions.
The results of this study suggest that *family therapy and drug therapy are additive in*

their effects (Schooler & Hogarty, 1987) and provide strong support for crisis-oriented family intervention.

Falloon et al. (1981) developed and evaluated a behavioral intervention with high EE families, treated in their own homes for the first 9 months. Forty clients were assigned randomly to either the behavioral family therapy group or individual supportive therapy. Following a lengthy behavioral assessment of individuals and the family group, the therapist worked with the family on identified problems, provided information about schizophrenia, and gave them training in communications skills and problem solving. In addition, the therapist modeled low "expressed emotion." The relapse rate for subjects treated with family therapy was 7 percent; for those treated individually it was 57 percent. The authors attributed some of the success of family therapy to better medication compliance by clients in the experimental group.

Implications of Research Findings

The findings of the British studies and the American research studies on expressed emotion, drug therapy, and psychosocial interventions as they relate to outcome suggest a number of intervention strategies that can prevent deterioration or relapse among persons with schizophrenia. Among these are:

1. Reduce the emotional expressiveness (criticism, hostility, overinvolvement) in the family. This may be achieved by working with the family in programs such as family psychoeducation, family crisis intervention, or behavioral family therapy; or working with clients to help them modify behaviors that provoke criticism or cope with stress more effectively (e.g., social skills training).
2. To further diffuse intense interactions in the family, encourage clients to participate in social or rehabilitation programs and family members to increase their activities outside the home.
3. Promote medication maintenance, regardless of the level of emotional expressiveness in the family. In some cases, a low dose of antipsychotic medication may be adequate. Nevertheless, medication is not in itself a sufficient intervention and for a minority may not be necessary.
4. Promote some, but not intense, contact between families and clients who do not live at home.
5. Avoid using interpersonal therapies, such as Major Role Therapy, with clients who are not on medication.

This body of research also suggests that emotional intensity produced by mental health treatment programs and mental health providers is potentially harmful. Pepper and Ryglewicz (1987) propose that *interactional intensity (II)* should be regulated in the community as well as in the home. Accordingly, treatment programs and helping relationships should be supportive but not too demanding for those clients who are especially sensitive to emotional intensity. Vulnerable clients cannot tolerate programs in which the expectations to achieve goals are too high or therapeutic relationships are intrusive. The authors provide this example:

A man spoke about his relationship with his case manager, saying, "When I talk to my psychiatrist, he just wants to know the answers to certain questions; he doesn't have time to be really interested in *me*. When I talk to my mother, there are lots of things I can't tell her, because she gets upset—she's my mother, and she worries about me. But when I talk to Nora (the case manager), we just talk; she cares, but not too much." (p. 3)

As suggested earlier, constructs such as "emotional expressiveness" and "interactional intensity" can be threatening to families. Families who are told to be less critical and less emotionally involved with a schizophrenic family member may conclude that they are to blame if a client has a relapse. Even though they may have been told that schizophrenia is a brain disease of unknown etiology, they may feel responsible for the course of the disease. Surprised that so much research attention has been given to a phenomenon that is consistent with what was already known about difficulties persons with schizophrenia have in processing stimuli, Torrey (1988a) reminds readers of his family manual that "compliance with medication-taking remains by far the single most important factor determining relapse rates" (p. 309).

The research that has been cited suggests that insight-oriented psychotherapy is not appropriate for persons with chronic schizophrenia. Such therapy is emotionally intense and can arouse anxiety. Nevertheless, alternative forms of psychotherapy do not pose such threats. Ego supportive therapy (Goldstein, 1984) provides reality-based help with immediate problems and situational crises that can overwhelm persons with schizophrenia. Similarly some of the short-term approaches, such as task-centered casework (Reid & Epstein, 1972), promote mastery over specific problems. Both of these approaches can be incorporated into case management, which will be described in the next chapter. Furthermore, the research findings on schizophrenia should not be applied to all chronic mental disorders. Research on pharmacology in relation to diverse psychotherapeutic strategies to treatment of major depression (Weissman, Jarrett, & Rush, 1987) has found that medication and psychotherapies together and separately are effective; and that psychotherapy has positive long-term effects. (See chapter 12 for further discussion of the treatment of depression.)

PRINCIPLES OF INTERVENTION

Clinical social work practice in community mental health with persons with chronic mental illness is guided by social work values and legal requirements (see chapter 5), principles of community mental health and deinstitutionalization (see chapter 1), and Guiding Principles for Community Support Systems suggested by the National Institute of Mental Health (NIMH, 1982; U.S. Department of Health and Human Services, [DHHS], 1981). The philosophy that undergirds intervention with the chronically mentally ill is rehabilitation. These principles and philosophy are incorporated in the concept of a Community Support System (CSS; Turner & Ten Hoor, 1978).

Several social work values are adopted in the NIMH (1982; DHHS, 1981) principles for Community Support Systems. Among these are *personal dignity, self-determination, individualization, nondiscrimination,* and *confidentiality.* Personal dignity refers to the respect that is given to the client. Respect is communicated by providing community services in such a way that clients' privacy, rights as citizens, and self-respect are honored. Self-determination is the client's right to make informed decisions. This is fostered with policies and practices in which clients establish their own goals, participate in planning meetings, choose their own residences, and maintain the greatest possible control over their lives. Clinical social workers promote individualization by tailoring services to the unique needs and preferences of the client as these change over time. Individualized services should be available without discrimination to whoever needs them, regardless of the consumer's race or ethnic group, age, sex, sexual orientation, disability, or other characteristic. Furthermore, services should be culturally sensitive and relevant. Finally practitioners should protect client records and keep information revealed in the course of professional contacts confidential (DHHS, 1981; NIMH, 1982).

Among the legal requirements that undergird social work practice with the chronically mentally ill is the *least restrictive alternative*. As described in chapter 5, this refers to court rulings stipulating that persons with mental health problems live in settings and receive services in which their freedom and autonomy are protected to the greatest degree possible, while at the same time their safety and quality of mental health care are not compromised. Wherever feasible, treatment should be in natural settings (NIMH, 1982). Communities that offer a continuum of residential placements, rehabilitation services, and treatment facilities provide alternatives for clients who wish to move from a more restrictive residence (e.g., foster home) to a less restricted one (e.g., transitional apartment) and from a highly supervised form of vocational rehabilitation (e.g., sheltered workshop) to full employment. Transition from one level to another should be *gradual* (DHHS, 1981), taken in incremental steps that are related to the client's capacity to handle increased autonomy. Furthermore, treatment should recognize the client's freedom to make choices based on psychological, physical, and social costs in relation to benefits.

The principles of community mental health that are particularly relevant to work with the chronically mentally ill are *comprehensiveness, accessibility, continuity of care,* and *community accountability* (DHHS, 1981; NIMH, 1982). Comprehensiveness refers to the spectrum of services such as those that were just described. These services should be diverse and available to a broad range of clients. Accordingly, a community might have some residential programs for dually diagnosed persons with mental retardation and mental illness and others for persons in crisis, regardless of diagnosis. Ideally, programs should vary in treatment philosophies (behavior management, crisis intervention, rehabilitation, client empowerment) and expectations (high, medium, low). Furthermore, programs should be accessible to the physically handicapped, conveniently located, available through public transportation, and affordable. Flexible hours, transportation services, and outreach programs enhance the accessibility of a mental health service, as does emergency coverage during the evening, holidays, and weekends. Continuity of care is fostered by the provision of programming by a stable team of professionals, and by a constant person (case manager) who coordinates services from diverse sources. Community accountability is accomplished by the inclusion of local citizens, professionals, family members, and clients on agency boards and advisory committees. The agency has a responsibility to adapt programs to the changing needs of the community.

Principles associated with deinstitutionalization that are relevant to intervention with the chronically mentally ill are *normalization* and *integration.* Clients should be helped to adapt to community life such that their patient status is not apparent and their membership in the larger community is fostered. They should be encouraged to use mainstream educational and vocational resources, recreational facilities, religious centers, stores, parks, and the like; and the community should accept their participation. When a group home is located in a neighborhood of persons of diverse ages, life-styles, and social strata, rather than in a "ghetto" of psychiatric patients, both normalization and integration can occur.

A related principle that is relevant to clinical practice with the chronically mentally ill is to engage *natural support systems* in the lives of clients (DHHS, 1980; NIMH, 1982). Natural supports are families, friends, neighbors, clergy, hairdressers, storekeepers, and other community persons who have been or are connected with the client in a meaningful way. They are the client's first line of defense against stress; as such they constitute a tremendous resource that clients can be helped to utilize. Nevertheless, natural resources, such as family members, can suffer from burnout in seeing someone they love through multiple crises. Clinical social workers need to help clients make appropriate use of natural systems. At times, however, the social worker must relieve the family of this burden and support both family and client (NIMH, 1982).

Clinical social workers who practice with the chronically mentally ill recognize that intervention may be of *indefinite duration* (NIMH, 1982). Chronic mental illness is defined partly by duration. As the research by Harding et al. (1987) indicates, some clients do recover from serious mental illness. Nevertheless, a follow-up research study on a population of chronically mentally ill for whom mental health services had been provided earlier but later were withdrawn found that in the interim, the chronically mentally ill subjects had deteriorated (Davis, Dinitz, & Pasamanick, 1974). Because many clients appear to need long-term follow-up and treatment the extent of which cannot be predicted, a long-term commitment is necessary.

Inasmuch as treatment is likely to be prolonged, contacts with the client should be directed at building a relationship that is empowering for the client. Although some dependence on the social worker is to be expected, the client's participation in *mutual and self-help groups* (NIMH, 1982) can be fostered. Clients can be encouraged to use their own problem-solving skills to solve personal problems and to give to and receive support from others. Formal and informal consumer self-help groups can help clients develop natural supports and become interdependent.

REHABILITATION

The philosophy of intervention that is consistent with the needs and diverse potentials of persons with severe and persistent mental illness is rehabilitation. Historically traceable to moral therapy, psychiatric rehabilitation is conceptually based on the practice of physical medicine and rehabilitation and was stimulated by programs for the physically disabled (Anthony, Cohen, & Cohen, 1984; Anthony & Liberman, 1986). The federal government recognized that the psychiatrically disabled can be rehabilitated in its inclusion of the mentally ill in the 1943 amendments to the Vocational Rehabilitation Act (Anthony & Liberman, 1986).

Rehabilitation refers to the promotion of physical, psychiatric, and social functioning to the extent possible for the particular individual.

> The overall goal of psychiatric rehabilitation is to assure that the person with a psychiatric disability can perform those physical, emotional, social, and intellectual skills needed to live, learn, and work in the community, with the least amount of support necessary from agents of the helping professions (Anthony 1979). (Anthony & Liberman, 1986, p. 542)

Rehabilitation prepares and equips the individual for living in a community that poses obstacles, makes demands, and requires knowledge for adaptive functioning. Accordingly, the development of skills such as cooking, doing laundry, using public transportation, maintaining relationships, and securing and holding a job are promoted. By emphasizing "the least amount of support necessary from agents of the helping profession," self-sufficiency that is consistent with the person's capacities is encouraged.

Both medical and psychiatric rehabilitation arise in the context of four stages (Anthony & Liberman, 1986; Liberman, 1988b). The first, *pathology,* involves abnormalities in the biological system, such as a lesion. Pathology can produce *impairment,* an abnormality or loss of anatomical, psychological, or physiological function or structure, which is manifested in symptoms such as hallucinations. Impairment can result in *disability,* inability, or limitation in the ability to carry out activities or perform roles in the expected manner and range, such as deficient interpersonal skills. The last stage, *handicap,* results from either an impairment or a disability. A handicap is a disadvantage that interferes with the fulfillment of a role that is culturally normative for the individual. Handicaps are exacerbated by public attitudes or stigma. Unemployment and homelessness may be consequences of a handicap.

Psychiatric rehabilitation is directed at overcoming, remedying, or compensating for disabilities and handicaps. Programs of intervention target the individual, family, group, and the social environment. Individual, group, family, or milieu therapy can be utilized to teach individuals skills in activities in daily living (self-care, transportation, laundry), interpersonal behaviors, employment, and problem solving through skills training, based on social learning theory (Anthony & Liberman, 1986). Family psychoeducation, discussed earlier, promotes the social functioning of the client by addressing stress in the family (Anderson, Reiss, & Hogarty, 1986). Psychosocial rehabilitation clubs, such as Fountain House in New York, provide a group setting through which persons with persistent mental health problems gain work experiences, socialize with others, and obtain better housing. Environmental approaches mobilize and provide support from the natural helping network and the formal (agency) system. The result is a community support system that is adapted to the individual client. Case managers play a significant role in fostering the development of environmental supports.

Anthony, Cohen, and Cohen (1984) describe several principles that guide psychiatric rehabilitation. First and foremost is a focus "on improving the psychiatrically disabled person's capabilities and competence" (p. 139). The emphasis is on developing responses to the environment that promote health; symptom reduction is not sufficient. This principle is consistent with the integrated biopsychosocial conceptual framework of this book. It is accomplished by efforts to increase coping (problem-solving) skills and acquire skills in daily living, learning, and pursuing a vocation.

The second principle is that "the benefit of psychiatric rehabilitation for the clients is behavioral improvement in their environments of need" (p. 140). Efforts are to be directed at achieving a tangible, measurable outcome that can be achieved in the client's relevant environments (e.g., residential, community, employment). Simply providing services is not adequate (Farkas, Cohen, & Nemec, 1988). The idea is to improve the individual's instrumental skills (rather than to promote insight) and the person–environment fit. Although this principle seems to suggest a behavioral theoretical perspective, the third principle is that "psychiatric rehabilitation is atheoretical and eclectic in the use of a variety of therapeutic constructs" (Anthony, Cohen, & Cohen, 1984, p. 141).

Even though problem solving and social skills are included under the umbrella of rehabilitation, "a central focus is on improving vocational outcome for the psychiatrically disabled" (p. 141). Some clients will be able to secure jobs in the competitive market, while others will hold part-time, protected, or transitional employment. Some clients will work as volunteers or manage their own homes. Work is a primary value of the larger community. The ability to hold a job enhances the individual's self-esteem and independence. Furthermore, it promotes normalization and integration. Vocational rehabilitation can be enhanced through education, training, and the modeling of work skills. Associated skills such as attendance, taking directions, and handling interpersonal conflict are also developed. Vocational rehabilitation programs provide training and practice in supervised and low-stress transitional employment settings and in natural settings. Through vocational rehabilitation a client can develop skills incrementally over time.

The philosophy of rehabilitation can be implemented best when the clinical practitioner conveys an attitude of hope (Anthony, Cohen, & Cohen, 1984). Such an attitude is particularly important in work with the chronically mentally ill who, historically, have been abandoned as hopeless. As indicated previously, many persons with severe mental disabilities have recovered or improved over time. Although the media give attention to the failures of deinstitutionalization, many live successfully in the community (Sands, 1984).

Furthermore, rehabilitation requires management of dependence that is consistent with the client's needs. When a client is released from a hospital following a psychotic episode, increased dependence on family and service providers is to be expected. Dependence on others is lessened over time as the client becomes more confident and competent. "The deliberate increase in client dependency can lead to an eventual increase in the client's independent functioning" (Anthony, Cohen, & Cohen, 1984, p. 142). Accordingly, some dependence is expected and even fostered after discharge from a psychiatric hospital; but over time increasing independence is encouraged.

Client participation in the rehabilitation process (Anthony, Cohen, & Cohen, 1984) is essential to the success of the program. The client should participate in goal setting and make decisions about living arrangements, social activities, and treatment that are compatible with personal values and experiences. Rather than being an object upon whom rehabilitation is imposed, the client should be a partner of the treatment team. This way, the client will be emotionally invested in his or her own rehabilitation. Unfortunately many agencies do not recognize the importance of client participation, as reflected by the absence of this element in mission statements and in formal assessment procedures (Farkas, Cohen, & Nemec, 1988).

According to Anthony, Cohen, and Cohen (1984), two kinds of interventions are fundamental to rehabilitation. These are client skills development and environmental resource development. Often chronic illnesses such as schizophrenia and bipolar disorder first appear in adolescence or young adulthood, by which time the individual has not sufficiently developed any vocational, social, and living skills that are needed to function relatively independently in the community. Schizophrenia and organic disorders also are associated with deficits in cognitive functioning. But regardless of the mental disorder, skills that facilitate social functioning can be taught or enhanced through programmatic interventions. Environmental resources that are related to client needs can also be developed.

PRINCIPLES OF INTERVENTION WITH YOUNG ADULTS

Young adults with serious and persistent psychiatric disabilities have required additional considerations in the design and implementation of intervention programs. The major considerations are as follows (Pepper & Ryglewicz, 1986, January):

1. Separate programming for young adults
2. Use of peer groups for intervention
3. Flexible program hours and intake procedures
4. Development of innovative approaches to treatment and rehabilitation
5. Family involvement
6. Assertive treatment, focusing on the here and now

In keeping with the younger person's age and developmental stage, separate programs are desirable. Inclusion of younger and older adults in the same programs has turned out to be problematic for both groups. The older group are disturbed by the high energy and unpredictable behavior of the younger group. Younger adults feel threatened and stigmatized when they are grouped together with bizarre, "burnt out" older adults. The young adults should have programs that address their particular needs and concerns—for example, self-esteem, dating, substance abuse, sexuality, and parenting. Young adult clients should be encouraged to participate actively in mainstream community activities (vocational, sports, cultural, religious) consistent with those of their peers.

Like other adults their age, young adults with chronic disabilities are responsive to peer group expectations. At the same time, the onset of their illness during adolescence may have interfered with their development of social skills. The group can provide a needed source of support, socialization, and acceptance. Mental health services that utilize the group method can be targeted to younger clients and should include social skills training, psychoeducational groups for themselves and their families, and residential services.

Young adults also need flexible program hours and intake procedures. Sporadic users of the mental health system, they need to have access to the system 24 hours a day. Those who work or participate in prevocational programs during the day can benefit from evening mental health programs; the opposite is true for those who work at night. Like other clients, they find lengthy bureaucratic intake procedures alienating. Clinical social workers who work with this population should strive to engage clients and provide individualized attention.

Some communities have created innovative programs that address the developmental needs of this population at the same time that they promote growth and prevent stigma. Neffinger, Schiff, and Abrams (1984), for example, have developed an adjunctive form of treatment, Wilderness Challenge, in which a group of young adult clients and their clinicians go backpacking for a few days in the mountains. This program fosters the development of group cooperation and problem solving. Stich and Senior (1984) describe a similar program of Adventure Therapy, in which adults are presented with a graduated series of physical and social tasks that are performed in the wilderness. This program fosters the development of competence and tolerance for stress. The GAP (Growth Enhancement Program) in Rockland County, New York, holds weekly group meetings for young adults in which they are encouraged to create their own support system ("Gold Award," 1985). Similar programs of network development have been described by others (Harris & Bergman, 1985).

Because substantial numbers of young adults are emotionally and financially dependent on their parents—and because of parents' own interest in participation and their need for support—family involvement is recommended. Inclusion of family sessions during crises and with ongoing work with an individual client, multiple-family psychoeducational groups, and family therapy (where indicated) are recommended (Ryglewicz, 1984). Family advocacy and mutual support are facilitated through the family's involvement in self-help groups. These mechanisms allow the family to participate in meaningful ways at the same time as growth on the part of the client and family are promoted.

Intervention with young adults with serious mental disorders requires an assertive approach in which immediate problems are addressed (Pepper & Ryglewicz, 1986, January; Stein & Test, 1982). In contrast with community mental health practices geared toward wider populations, assertive intervention involves aggressive outreach, home and neighborhood visits, and follow-up in the client's natural environment. Current problems that interfere with psychosocial functioning are given priority. By providing ongoing, relevant support to a highly mobile, unpredicable group of consumers, clinical social workers enhance the likelihood that clients receive services before they decompensate. The assertive case management model, which uses a team approach, will be described in the next chapter.

COMMUNITY SUPPORT PROGRAMS

Community Support Programs (CSPs) and Community Support Systems (CSSs) refer to a concept and pilot program developed through the National Institute of Mental Health to serve the needs of adults with severe and chronic psychiatric disabilities (Turner & Ten Hoor, 1978). The program was launched in 1977 with the allocation of 3.5 million federal dollars in contracts with state mental health agencies to fund some 20 programs. The purpose was to create demonstration projects in which comprehensive services for the target population are developed and coordinated. Since then the program has been implemented in every state with an annual budget that increased to 15 million dollars 10 years later (Torrey, 1988a). According to Torrey (1988b), however, this program was a means to remedy deficiencies in the Community Mental Health Program, which had neglected the chronically mentally ill.

Community Support Programs are implemented on the state level through block grants. They include an array of housing alternatives, treatment facilities, financial resources, and advocacy services that enhance the capacities of communities to meet the needs of persons with chronic mental illness who live in the community. Components that are missing in a community are identified, planned for, and funded.

Community Support Systems are viewed as a network of caring persons who wish to help the vulnerable, severely and persistently mentally ill to develop their potentials and meet their needs without being excluded or isolated from the community (Turner & Ten Hoor, 1978). The Community Support Program guidelines stipulate that the following 10 functions be performed:

1. Identification of the target population, whether in hospitals or in the community, and outreach to offer appropriate services to those willing to participate.
2. Assistance in applying for entitlements.
3. Crisis stabilization services in the least restrictive setting possible, with hospitalization available when other options are insufficient.
4. Psychosocial rehabilitation services, including but not limited to:
   - goal-oriented rehabilitation evaluation;
   - training in community living skills, in the natural setting wherever possible;
   - opportunities to improve employability;
   - appropriate living arrangements in an atmosphere that encourages improvements in functioning;
   - opportunities to develop social skills, interests, and leisure time activities to provide a sense of participation and worth.
5. Supportive services of indefinite duration, including supportive living and working arrangements, and other such services for as long as they are needed.
6. Medical and mental health care.
7. Backup support to families, friends, and community members.
8. Involvement of concerned community members in planning and offering housing or working opportunities.
9. Protection of client rights, both in hospitals and in the community.
10. Case management, to ensure continuous availability of appropriate forms of assistance. (Turner & Ten Hoor, 1978, pp. 329–330)

In order to fulfill these functions, Community Support Programs call upon the expertise of systems experts (case managers) to mobilize community services and link clients with resources. The way in which social workers interpret and perform in this role will be discussed in the following chapter.

SUMMARY

The term *chronic mental illness* poses definitional problems. In keeping with the meanings applied to physical illnesses, it suggests a condition that is prolonged, persistent, and severe. At the same time, chronicity connotes incurability and intractability, evoking attitudes of hopelessness. Because some mental health programs are specifically directed toward the chronically mentally ill, there is a need for definitional clarity.

Three criteria that have been used are diagnosis, disability, and duration. The diagnoses of schizophrenia, paranoia, schizoaffective disorders, and organic disorders often have a chronic course. Sometimes personality disorders, such as the borderline disorder, are included, for example, when disability or another diagnosis is present. Disability refers to impairment in social role functioning in such capacities as self-care, homemaking, and employment. Duration can be applied to the length of hospitalization, the number of hospital admissions, or the equivalent supportive care provided by community mental health services. Even with these criteria, many individuals fall between the cracks. The presence of a population of young adults who have been treated (if at all) primarily in the community complicates these definitional parameters and the expectation that consumers of mental health programs who have chronic disabilities passively accept existing services.

Clinical social work practice with the chronically mentally ill is informed by a number of theories. The stress-diathesis theory describes the impact of stress and supports on a person with a biological vulnerability to schizophrenia. The concept of *stimulus window* also describes this process, but applies to persons with additional diagnoses, who may have a different tolerance for stress. The attention-arousal model explains that when persons with schizophrenia become aroused by internal and external stimuli, they become distracted and find it difficult to process the information.

Clinical practice is also informed by research studies on the relationship between the family environment, medication, and relapse of schizophrenia. A series of studies that began in England strongly associated expressed emotion (EE) in the family with a poor outcome. Expressed emotion is characterized by criticism, overinvolvement, and hostility. More than 35 hours per week of face-to-face contact also is related to a high rate of relapse. These findings have been replicated in England and the United States. They lend support to the role of the family environment, although the findings seem most applicable to Caucasians of Anglo-Saxon origin and to men.

Research has also looked at the impact of antipsychotic medication in the treatment of schizophrenia and schizoaffective disorder. For the most part, consistent use of medication is effective. Nevertheless, medication alone is not enough and some clients do not seem to need medication. Social therapy can influence outcome, although it is not in itself helpful and can be harmful if it is not used in conjunction with medication. The combination of medication, family psychoeducation, and social skills training for clients is associated with a successful outcome.

Social work intervention with the chronically mentally ill is buttressed by professional values, legal requirements, principles of community mental health, and guidelines on Community Support Systems established by the National Institute of Mental Health. The philosophy that undergirds intervention is rehabilitation.

Rehabilitation refers to the promotion of physical, psychiatric, and social functioning to the extent possible for the individual. It aims to promote functioning with the least amount of support from professionals that is necessary. At first, however, the client may be highly dependent on mental health professionals. Development of social skills, provision of environmental supports, and client involvement in his or her own treatment planning promote the competence and empowerment of clients. Social workers, functioning as case managers, are particularly instrumental in the development of environmental supports.

When the philosophy of rehabilitation is implemented in relation to young adults with chronic disorders, certain modifications are needed. Programs should recognize the developmental issues and vulnerabilities of young adults, clients' responsiveness to group support, family involvement, and unpredictable patterns of service usage. Accordingly innovative, flexible, and assertive outreach programs should be developed.

Regardless of the age group, community supports should be mobilized. Supports consist of persons, programs, and residences that promote clients' functioning and integration in community life. Not only should these supports exist; they should be utilized in ways that respect clients' rights and promote their stabilization and rehabilitation over time.

DISCUSSION QUESTIONS

1. What is meant by "chronic mental illness"? Why is the term *chronic* problematic? What alternatives might one use instead?
2. In what ways do young adults with severe and persistent psychiatric disabilities differ from older adults?
3. What are the implications of biogenetic explanations of the etiology of severe mental disorders for work with families?
4. What role do stress and support play in the course of severe mental disorders?
5. Explain:
   a. The stress-diathesis model
   b. The concept of the stimulus window
   c. The attention-arousal model
   How are these models related?
6. How has biopsychosocial research contributed to an understanding of the role of the family in relation to schizophrenia? How, if at all, do findings about the family environment in these studies differ from the way in which families have been depicted in the past in psychological theories (e.g., double bind, schizophrenogenic mother)?

7. To what extent can findings from studies on expressed emotion be generalized to women and members of diverse cultural groups?
8. What are the implications of findings about the family environment for treatment?
9. What do the American studies on drug and social therapy reveal about the relative value of medication alone, social therapy alone, and combined treatment? Which of these interventions alone can be harmful?
10. Discuss 10 principles that guide practice with persons with severe and persistent mental disabilities who live in the community.
11. What is rehabilitation? How does it apply to work with persons with severe mental disorders?
12. What additional considerations should guide intervention with young adults with serious and persistent psychiatric disabilities?
13. What are Community Support Programs? How are they implemented in your community?

REFERENCES

American Psychiatric Association. (1987). *Diagnostic and statistical manual of mental disorders (DSM-III-R)*, (3rd ed. rev.). Washington, DC: Author.

Anderson, C. M., Hogarty, G. E., & Reiss, D. J. (1980). Family treatment of adult schizophrenic patients: A psycho-educational approach. *Schizophrenia Bulletin, 6*, 490–505.

Anderson, C. M., Reiss, D. J., & Hogarty, G. E. (1986). *Schizophrenia and the family: A practitioner's guide to psychoeducation and management.* New York: Guilford Press.

Andreasen, N. C. (1984). *The broken brain: The biological revolution in psychiatry.* New York: Harper & Row.

Andreasen, N. C., Ehrhardt, I. C., Swayze, V. W. II, Alliger, R. J., et al. (1990). Magnetic resonance imaging of the brain of schizophrenia. *Archives of General Psychiatry, 47*, 35–44.

Anthony, W. A., Cohen, M. R., & Cohen, B. F. (1984). Psychiatric rehabilitation. In J. A. Talbott (Ed.), *The chronic mental patient: Five years later* (pp. 137–157). Orlando, FL: Grune & Stratton.

Anthony, W. A., & Liberman, R. P. (1986). The practice of psychiatric rehabilitation: Historical, conceptual, and research base. *Schizophrenia Bulletin, 12*, 542–559.

Bachrach, L. L. (1982). Young adult chronic patients: An analytical review of the literature. *Hospital and Community Psychiatry, 33*, 189–197.

Bachrach, L. L. (1984). The concept of young adult chronic psychiatric patients: Questions from a research perspective. *Hospital and Community Psychiatry, 35*, 573–579.

Bachrach, L. L. (1986). Dimensions of disability in the chronic mentally ill. *Hospital and Community Psychiatry, 37*, 981–982.

Bachrach, L. L. (1988). Defining chronic mental illness: A concept paper. *Hospital and Community Psychiatry, 39*, 383–388.

Bateson, G., Jackson, D., Haley, J., & Weakland, J. (1956). Toward a theory of schizophrenia. *Behavioral Science, 1*, 251–264.

Bender, M. G. (1986). Young adult chronic patients: Visibility and style of interaction in treatment. *Hospital and Community Psychiatry, 37*, 265–268.

Brown, G. W. (1959). Experiences of discharged chronic schizophrenic mental hospital patients in various types of living groups. *Milbank Memorial Fund Quarterly, 37*, 105–131.

Brown, G. W., Birley, J. L. T., & Wing, J. K. (1972). Influence of family life on the course of schizophrenic disorders: A replication. *British Journal of Psychiatry, 121*, 241–258.

Brown, G. W., Carstairs, G. M., & Topping, G. (1958). Post hospital adjustment of chronic mental patients. *Lancet, 2*, 685–689.

Brown, G. W., Monck, E. M., Carstairs, G. M., & Wing, J. K. (1962). Influence of family life on the course of schizophrenic illness. *British Journal of Preventive and Social Medicine, 16*, 55–68.

Cohen, M. B., et al. (1954). An intensive study of twelve cases of manic-depressive psychosis. *Psychiatry, 17*, 103–137.

Davis, A. S., Dinitz, S., & Pasamanick, B. (1974). *Schizophrenics in the new custodial community: Five years after the experiment.* Columbus, OH: Ohio State University Press.

Estroff, S. E. (1987). No more young adult chronic patients. *Hospital and Community Psychiatry, 38*, 5.

Falloon, I. R. H., et al. (1981). Family management training in the community care of schizophrenia. In M. J. Goldstein (Ed.), *New developments in interventions with families of schizophrenics* (pp. 61–77). San Francisco: Jossey-Bass.

Falloon, I. R. H., & Liberman, R. P. (1983). Interactions between drug and psychosocial therapy in schizophrenia. *Schizophrenia Bulletin, 9,* 543–554.

Farkas, M. D., Cohen, M. R., & Nemec, P. B. (1988). Psychiatric rehabilitation programs: Putting concepts into practice? *Community Mental Health Journal, 24,* 7–21.

Freedman, A. M., Kaplan, H. I., & Sadock, B. J. (1972). *Modern synopsis of comprehensive textbook of psychiatry.* Baltimore, MD: Williams & Wilkins.

Fromm-Reichmann, F. (1948). Notes on the development of treatment of schizophrenia by psychoanalytic psychotherapy. *Psychiatry, 11,* 263–273.

Gold award: Addressing the needs of young adult chronic patients. (1985). *Hospital and Community Psychiatry, 36,* 1210–1212.

Goldman, H. H. (1984). Epidemiology. In J. A. Talbott (Ed.), *The chronic mental patient: Five years later* (pp. 15–31). Orlando, FL: Grune & Stratton.

Goldman, H. H., & Manderscheid, R. W. (1987). Chronic mental disorder in the United States. In R. W. Manderscheid & S. A. Barrett (Eds.), *Mental health, United States, 1987* (pp. 1–13). (DHHS Publication No. ADM 87-1518). Washington, DC: U.S. Government Printing Office.

Goldstein, E. G. (1984). *Ego psychology and social work practice.* New York: Free Press.

Goldstein, M. J., & Kopeikin, H. S. (1981). Short- and long-term effects of combining drug and family therapy. In M. J. Goldstein (Ed.), *New developments in interventions with families of schizophrenics* (pp. 5–25). San Francisco: Jossey-Bass.

Gottlieb, B. H. (1985). Assessing and strengthening the impact of social support on mental health. *Social Work, 30,* 293–300.

Gruenberg, E. M. (1982). Social breakdown in young adults: Keeping crises from becoming chronic. In B. Pepper & H. Ryglewicz (Eds.), *The young adult chronic patient* (pp. 43–50). San Francisco: Jossey-Bass.

Harding, C. M., Brooks, G. W., Ashikaga, T., Strauss, J. S., & Breier, A. (1987). The Vermont longitudinal study of persons with severe mental illness, I: Methodology, study sample, and overall status 32 years later. *American Journal of Psychiatry, 144,* 718–726.

Harding, C. M., Zubin, J., & Strauss, J. S. (1987). Chronicity in schizophrenia: Fact, partial fact, or artifact. *Hospital and Community Psychiatry, 38,* 477–486.

Harris, M., & Bergman, H. C. (1985). Networking with young adult chronic patients. *Psychosocial Rehabilitation Journal, 8,* 28–35.

Hatfield, A. B. (1984). The family consumer movement: A new force in service delivery. In B. Pepper & H. Ryglewicz (Eds.), *Advances in treating the young adult chronic patient* (pp. 71–79). San Francisco: Jossey-Bass.

Hatfield, A. B. (1987). Families as caregivers: Historical perspective. In A. B. Hatfield & H. P. Lefley (Eds.), *Families of the mentally ill: Coping and adaptation* (pp. 3–29). New York: Guilford Press.

Hogarty, G. E. (1984). Depot neuroleptics: The relevance of psychosocial factors—A United States perspective. *Journal of Clinical Psychiatry, 45,* 36–42.

Hogarty, G. E., Goldberg, S. C., & Collaborative Study Group. (1973). Drug and sociotherapy in the aftercare of schizophrenic patients: One year relapse rates. *Archives of General Psychiatry, 28,* 54–64.

Hogarty, G. E., et al. (1974a). Drug and sociotherapy in the aftercare of schizophrenic patients: II. Two-year relapse rates. *Archives of General Psychiatry, 31,* 603–608.

Hogarty, G. E., et al. (1974b). Drug and sociotherapy in the aftercare of schizophrenic patients: III. Adjustment of nonrelapsed patients. *Archives of General Psychiatry, 31,* 609–618.

Hogarty, G. E., et al. (1979). Fluphenazine and social therapy in the aftercare of schizophrenic patients. *Archives of General Psychiatry, 36,* 1283–1294.

Hogarty, G. E., et al. (1986). Family psychoeducation, social skills training, and maintenance chemotherapy in the aftercare treatment of schizophrenia: I. One-year effects of a controlled study on relapse and expressed emotion. *Archives of General Psychiatry, 43,* 633–642.

Hogarty, G. E., et al. (1988). Dose of fluphenazine, family expressed emotion, and outcome in schizophrenia: Results of a two-year controlled study. *Archives of General Psychiatry, 45,* 797–805.

Intagliata, J., & Baker, F. (1984). A comparative analysis of the young adult chronic patient in New York State's Community Support System. *Hospital and Community Psychiatry, 35,* 45–51.

Kendler, K. S. (1988). The genetics of schizophrenia and related disorders. In D. L. Dunner, E. S. Gerson, & J. E. Barrett (Eds.), *Relatives at risk for mental disorder* (pp. 247–263). New York: Raven Press.

King, D. J., & Cooper, S. J. (1989). Viruses, immunity and mental disorder. *British Journal of Psychiatry, 151,* 1–7.

Koenigsberg, H. W., & Handley, R. (1986). Expressed emotion: From predictive index to clinical construct. *American Journal of Psychiatry, 143,* 1361–1373.

Kottgen, C., Sonnichsen, I., Mollenhauer, K., et al. (1984). Families' high expressed emotion and relapses in young schizophrenic patients: Results of the Hamburg–Camberwell family intervention study II. *International Journal of Family Psychiatry, 5,* 71–82.

Kreisman, D., et al. (1988). Family attitudes and patient social adjustment in a longitudinal study of outpatient schizophrenics receiving low-dose neuroleptics: The family's view. *Psychiatry, 51,* 3–13.

Jimenez, M. A. (1988). Chronicity in mental disorders: Evolution of a concept. *Social Casework, 69,* 627–633.

Lamb, H. R. (1982). Young adult chronic patients: The new drifters. *Hospital and Community Psychiatry, 33,* 465–468.

Land, H. M. (1986). Life stress and ecological status: predictors of symptoms in schizophrenic veterans. *Health and Social Work, 11,* 254–264.

Leff, J., & Vaughn, C. (1981). The role of maintenance therapy and relatives' expressed emotion in relapse of schizophrenia: A two-year follow-up. *British Journal of Psychiatry, 139,* 102–104.

Leff, J., & Vaughn, C. (1985). *Expressed emotion in families: Its significance for mental illness.* New York: Guilford Press.

Liberman, R. P. (1988a). Introduction. In R. P. Liberman (Ed.), *Psychiatric rehabilitation of chronic mental patients* (pp. xvii–xxii). Washington, DC: American Psychiatric Press.

Liberman, R. P. (1988b). Coping with chronic mental disorders: A framework for hope. In R. P. Liberman (Ed.), *Psychiatric rehabilitation of chronic mental patients* (pp. 1–28). Washington, DC: American Psychiatric Press.

Liberman, R. P. (1982). Social factors in the etiology of schizophrenic disorders. In L. Grinspoon (Ed.), *Psychiatry: 1982 Annual Review* (Vol. 1, pp. 97–112). Washington, DC: American Psychiatric Press.

Lidz, T., Cornelison, A. R., Fleck, S., & Terry, D. (1957). The intrafamilial environment of schizophrenic patients. II. Marital schism and marital skew. *American Journal of Psychiatry, 114,* 241–248.

McCreath, J. (1984). The new generation of chronic psychiatric patients. *Social Work, 29,* 463–441.

McGuffin, P., & Katz, R. (1989). The genetics of depression and manic-depression disorder. *British Journal of Psychiatry, 155,* 294–304.

National Institute of Mental Health. (1982). *A network for caring: The Community Sup-*

port Program of the National Institute of Mental Health (Proceedings of four national conferences 1978–1979). (app. A). Washington, DC: U.S. Department of Health and Human Services.

Neffinger, G. G., Schiff, J. W., & Abrams, S. (1984). The wilderness challenge: An adjunctive treatment. In B. Pepper & H. Ryglewicz (Eds.), *Advances in treating the young adult chronic patient* (pp. 99–102). San Francisco: Jossey-Bass.

Parker, G., Johnston, P., & Hayward, L. (1988). *Archives of General Psychiatry, 45,* 806–813.

Pepper, B., Kirshner, M. C., & Ryglewicz, H. (1981). The young adult chronic patient: Overview of a population. *Hospital and Community Psychiatry, 32,* 463–469.

Pepper, B., & Ryglewicz, H. (Eds.). (1982). *New directions for mental health services: The young adult chronic patient* (no. 14). San Francisco: Jossey-Bass.

Pepper, B., & Ryglewicz, H. (1985). Guidelines for treating the young adult chronic patient. *TIE Lines, 2*(4), 1–2.

Pepper, B., & Ryglewicz, H. (1986, January). Guidelines for treating the young adult chronic patient. *TIE Lines, 3*(1), 1–5.

Pepper, B., & Ryglewicz, H. (1986, October). The stimulus window: Stress and stimulation as aspects of everyday experience. *TIE Lines, 3*(3), 1–5.

Pepper, B., & Ryglewicz, H. (1987). Is there expressed emotion away from home? "Interactional intensity" ("II") in the treatment program. *TIE Lines, 4*(1), 1–3.

Pepper, B., Ryglewicz, H., & Kirshner, M. C. (1982). The uninstitutionalized generation: A new breed of psychiatric patient. In B. Pepper & H. Ryglewicz (Eds.), *New directions for mental health services: The young adult chronic patient* (no. 14, pp. 3–14). San Francisco: Jossey-Bass.

Pilisuk, M. (1982). Delivery of social support: The social inoculation. *American Journal of Orthopsychiatry, 52,* 20–31.

Reid, W. J., & Epstein, L. (1972). *Task-centered casework.* New York: Columbia University Press.

Ryglewicz, H. (1984). An agenda for family intervention: Issues, models, and practice. In B. Pepper & H. Ryglewicz (Eds.), *Advances in treating the young adult chronic patient* (pp. 81–90). San Francisco: Jossey-Bass.

Sands, R. G. (1984). Correlates of success and lack of success in deinstitutionalization. *Community Mental Health Journal, 20,* 223–235.

Schooler, N. R., & Hogarty, G. E. (1987). Medication and psychosocial strategies in the treatment of schizophrenia. In H. Y. Meltzer (Ed.), *Psychopharmacology: The third generation of progress* (pp. 1111–1119). New York: Raven Press.

Sheets, J. L., Prevost, J. A., & Reihman, J. (1982). The young adult chronic patient: Three hypothesized subgroups. In B. Pepper & H. Ryglewicz (Eds.), *The young adult chronic patient* (pp. 15–23). San Francisco: Jossey-Bass.

Stein, L. I., & Test, M. A. (1982). Community treatment of the young adult patient. In B. Pepper & H. Ryglewicz (Eds.), *The young adult chronic patient* (pp. 57–67). San Francisco: Jossey-Bass.

Stich, T. F., & Senior, N. (1984). Adventure therapy: An innovative treatment for psychiatric patients. In B. Pepper & H. Ryglewicz (Eds.), *Advances in treating the young adult chronic patient* (pp. 103–108). San Francisco: Jossey-Bass.

Sullivan, W. P., & Poertner, J. (1989). Social support and life stress: A mental health consumers' perspective. *Community Mental Health Journal, 25,* 21–32.

Surles, R. C., & McGurrin, M. C. (1987). Increased use of psychiatric emergency services by young chronic mentally ill patients. *Hospital and Community Psychiatry, 38,* 401–405.

Taylor, E. H. (1987). The biological basis of schizophrenia. *Social Work, 32,* 115–121.

Test, M. A., Knoedler, W. H., Allness, D. J., & Burke, S. S. (1985). Characteristics of young adults with schizophrenic disorders treated in the community. *Hospital and Community Psychiatry, 36,* 853–858.

Tolsdorf, C. C. (1976). Social networks, support and coping: An exploratory study. *Family Process, 15,* 407–417.

Torrey, E. F. (1988a). *Surviving schizophrenia: A family manual* (rev. ed.). New York: Harper & Row.

Torrey, E. F. (1988b). *Nowhere to go: The tragic odyssey of the homeless mentally ill.* New York: Harper & Row.

Turner, J. C. & Ten Hoor, W. J. (1978). The NIMH Community Support Program: Pilot approach to a needed social reform. *Schizophrenia Bulletin, 4,* 319–344.

U.S. Department of Health and Human Services. (1981). *Toward a national plan for the chronically mentally ill: Report to the secretary* (1980, December). Washington, DC: Author.

Vaughn, C. E., & Leff, J. P. (1976). The influence of family and social factors on the course of psychiatric illness. *British Journal of Psychiatry, 129,* 125–137.

Vaughn, C. E., Snyder, K. S., Jones, S., Freeman, W. B., & Falloon, I. R. H. (1984). Family factors in schizophrenic relapse. *Archives of General Psychiatry, 41,* 1169–1177.

Weissman, M. M., Jarrett, R. B., & Rush, J. A. (1987). Psychotherapy and its relevance to the pharmacology of major depression: A decade later (1976–1985). In H. Y. Meltzer (Ed.), *Psychopharmacology: The third generation of progress* (pp. 1059–1069). New York: Raven Press.

Wintersteen, R. T., & Rapp, C. A. (1986). The young adult chronic patient: A dissenting view of an emerging concept. *Psychosocial Rehabilitation Journal, 9,* 3–13.

Zubin, J., & Spring, B. (1977). Vulnerability—A new view of schizophrenia. *Journal of Abnormal Psychology, 86,* 103–126.

9 Intervention with the Chronically Mentally Ill: Case Management in a Community Context

Larry Leeds is a 20-year-old single man who lives with his parents in a small southern town that is 100 miles from a metropolitan area. His father owns and runs a corner grocery store; his mother works as a bank teller. Larry is the oldest of three children, all boys. The family is active in the local church.

Larry was a shy child who performed well in school until his junior year in high school, when his grades declined and he became argumentative at home. Concerned about his "attitude," his mother discussed the problem with their family doctor, who recommended that the parents take Larry to the area's community mental health center for an evaluation. The staff there concluded that Larry was struggling with adolescent autonomy issues and referred him to their adolescent therapy group. Larry attended the weekly group for 3 months, during which time his "attitude" at home did not change but his grades improved. Larry became friendly with a couple of young men in the group who introduced him to marijuana.

Early his senior year, Larry became more belligerent at home and cut classes at school. He accused his father of being the "devil" and his mother of being a "devil worshiper." He told his parents that he had special powers to ward off the devil and that they should keep out of his way. One day, while cleaning Larry's room, Mrs. Leeds discovered knives and guns hidden in a closet. She called her husband and then the family physician, who again referred her to the mental health center. Angry that the center minimized his problems the year before, Mrs. Leeds wondered if a "stronger" approach was necessary. She and her husband decided to take Larry to the nearest hospital, where he was admitted to the acute psychiatric unit with a diagnosis of schizophreniform disorder.

Larry was hospitalized for a month and discharged with medication (Haldol). The family was told that it was suspected that he was using street drugs, which were exacerbating his psychotic symptoms. Larry was advised to avoid friends who use drugs, to take his medication as prescribed, and to return to high school. He was referred to a private psychiatrist 30 miles away for follow-up. Larry complied with this plan and completed high school.

The following year Larry attended a community college and lived at home. About halfway through the first semester, he had an argument with his academic counselor in which Larry accused his counselor of having a "pact with the devil." After Larry struck the counselor, the police were called. Larry was taken to the psychiatric unit of the community hospital, where he was admitted for the second time.

This time Larry was given the diagnosis of schizophrenic disorder, paranoid type (provisional). The diagnosis was considered provisional because the extent of Larry's drug use was unknown. The psychiatrists told the parents that the drugs bring out the "paranoid symptoms." Nevertheless, the doctors said that a diagnosis of schizophrenia was probable and told the parents that this is a serious and disabling illness. Again Larry was discharged on medication, which the parents were advised to administer. This time Larry was referred to the local community mental health center for follow-up.

Larry was assigned to both a psychiatrist and a therapist at the center. He was told that the sessions would be confidential and that no one would be provided with information about him without his consent. The therapist recommended that he participate in the day treatment program that was run by the center, but Larry refused. Larry said that he wanted to return to school and live on his own. The therapist tried to work with him to help him adapt his goals to his illness. After a while Larry stopped "therapy" and refused to take medication. Within 3 months he was rehospitalized. This time the diagnosis of schizophrenia, paranoid type was confirmed.

Larry's experience is not unusual. Like many young persons with chronic mental illness and their families, neither he nor his parents were aware of the seriousness of his illness until there was a crisis. Then they responded by utilizing the personal, familial, and community resources that were available. Because the onset of his symptoms was concurrent with his passage through adolescence and his use of street drugs, it was unclear what the nature of Larry's difficulty was.

Chronic mental disorders are complex in their diagnosis, treatment, and aftercare needs. The specific illnesses and their expression are heterogeneous, requiring intervention approaches that are tailored to the individual client. Before deinstitutionalization, persons with chronic mental illness were treated in hospitals, which provided a range of services under one roof. Today diverse, multiple, yet individualized services need to be available in the community.

Some communities, like the one in which Larry lived, have few resources. Yet, within a radius of 100 miles, other services are available. Elsewhere there are so many resources that it requires a systems expert, such as a case manager, to identify the appropriate resources and link the client with them. Intervention with the chronically mentally ill entails the coordination of community mental health services, as well as vocational, housing, and entitlement programs. Furthermore, other human needs, such as health care, socialization, transportation, recreation, artistic expression, and spiritual development, are to be addressed. The needs of families that are involved with their chronically mentally ill relatives also should be met.

This chapter will describe multifaceted community treatment approaches to clients with severe and persistent mental disorders. Not all such clients are young or have the diagnosis of schizophrenia, like Larry; some have less serious diagnoses, yet are functionally disabled; others are older, were hospitalized in state institutions for many years of their adult life, and now live in the community. Some have mental disorders that have periodic peaks, such as recurrent major depression and bipolar disorder. The chapter will begin with the critical function of case management and will proceed with a discussion of the community services that are potential supports to clients. Among the variety of social and rehabilitative programs that are described, a few outstanding ones will be highlighted.

CASE MANAGEMENT

Case management is one of the 10 essential functions of Community Support Programs that were presented at the conclusion of chapter 8. Although it was listed last, it is a central function, upon which the others are dependent. Furthermore, it is a significant factor contributing to satisfaction with mental health services by family members (Grella & Grusky, 1989). A generic term that is used in related human service fields (e.g., aging, mental retardation/developmental disabilities), it is not associated with a specific discipline or profession. In fact, some case managers do not have college degrees and are not professionals (Kurtz, Bagarozzi, & Pollane, 1984). Yet social workers are particularly well equipped to fulfill this role on a more advanced level (Johnson & Rubin, 1983; O'Connor, 1988).

Case management may be defined as "a process or method for ensuring that consumers are provided with whatever services they need in a coordinated, effective, and efficient manner" (Intagliata, 1982, p. 657). Through the establishment of one pivotal relationship, the client is helped to use community resources that will facilitate adaptation. In community mental health the goals of case management are preventive (avoid decompensation, suicide, and rehospitalization) and rehabilitative (promote psychosocial functioning at the highest level possible). The case manager may be responsible only for providing case management services to clients, or he or she may combine this responsibility with other tasks associated with work in a community mental health setting. In some settings, case managers are also psychotherapists (Johnson & Rubin, 1983).

The agency auspices of case managers vary. The case manager may, for example, work out of a city or county adult protection agency that serves the vulnerable aged, the physically disabled, and the chronically mentally ill; an outpatient department of a state hospital; a community mental health center; or a rehabilitation program. One community in which representatives of local agencies serving the deinstitutionalized chronically mentally ill met regularly as a screening team (Sands, 1984) determined that the case manager for each case would be the mental health worker who had the best relationship with the client.

The functions of the case manager that are described in the literature are manifold and reflect the diverse backgrounds of the persons occupying this role. At the very least, five functions are included—assessment, planning, linkage, monitoring, and advocacy (Johnson & Rubin, 1983). *Assessment* is a comprehensive evaluation of the client's needs based on the client's history, diagnosis, strengths, resources, and disabilities. It requires the compilation of information from various sources (psychiatric hospital, mental health center, physician, psychosocial rehabilitation services previously used) as well as the client and client system. The case manager looks at where needs are already met and where there are gaps. On the basis of the assessment, the case manager develops a *service plan* that is tailored to the individual client. In keeping with the principles of the Community Support System and social work values, the client should be an active participant in the development of the plan. Where families are involved in the support of a client, and clients consent to their participation, their inclusion in the construction of the plan is valuable (Intagliata, Willer, & Egri, 1986). Ideally the plan is also developed collaboratively with representatives of the agencies that are included in the plan. The needs, services, means of implementation, and target dates should be spelled out in behaviorally specific terms. An example of a service plan for Larry Leeds is presented in Table 9.1.

As Table 9.1 indicates, the plan encompasses more than the client's psychiatric needs. It identifies a wide range of psychosocial needs, some of which can be met by the family, while others can be addressed in the community through its social, recreational, and spiritual resources and the social service delivery system. The goals are more global than the objectives, which are concrete and specific. Target dates are set so that interim progress can be assessed. The initial plan is subject to review after 10 visits, or after 90 days as a client in a mental health agency, or sooner if needed (Joint Commission, 1989).

Case managers also assure that the client is *linked* with the appropriate community support services. In order to be able to do so, case managers should be knowledgeable about the existing resources, eligibility requirements, and how to access these sources of support. In working with the chronically mentally ill, simply making a referral is not sufficient; means should be developed to facilitate the client's use of services. This may necessitate modeling for the client how to take the bus, mobilizing family members or volunteers to provide services, arranging community transportation services, or the case manager's escorting the client to the service. The fourth component is *monitoring*. The case worker oversees the case to make sure that the client is following through with the plan. If some aspect of the plan is not implemented, the case manager determines which obstacles might be interfering and tries to remedy these. If the client is carrying out the plan but the plan is not working, it may be that some aspect of the plan should be changed. Another component of case management is *advocacy*. In fulfillment of this role, case managers act on behalf of clients to assure that clients' rights are protected and that they are able to obtain service for which they are eligible. If clients are denied services or are mistreated in the community, case managers pursue informal and formal strategies to overcome obstacles to receiving services.

These basic five functions emphasize the administrative role of the case manager. They are particularly compatible with the generalist skills taught in social work bachelor's programs and in the first year of social work master's programs. When several direct service functions are added, the advanced skills of the clinical social worker become a tremendous asset.

TABLE 9.1 (pp. 222–224)

Individual Service Plan for Larry Leeds

Strengths: Supportive family, desires independence, intelligent, likes sports

Barriers: Peer group substance abuse, overly protective family, negative past experience with mental health system, family lacks knowledge about schizophrenia

Needs and Goals	Objectives	Responsible Person	Target Dates
Medication/aftercare			
Larry needs to take antipsychotic medication as prescribed and to refrain from taking street drugs. *Goal:* Control symptoms and prevent rehospitalization (ongoing).	1. Larry will see Dr. X at ABC Community Mental Health Center. Additional appointments will be arranged by Dr. X. Larry's father will take him.	Dr. X and father	First appointment 1/5/1991, others TBA
	2. Larry will take his medication himself. If he forgets, his mother will remind him.	Larry and mother	2/5/1991
	3. Larry will agree not to take street drugs. He will also agree not to associate with friends from the past who introduced him to drugs.	Larry	2/5/1991
	4. Larry will have a case manager who is a social worker employed at the CMHC. The case manager will arrange appointments.	John Martin	1/2/1991
Housing			
Larry would like to live independently but currently does not have the economic resources or skills in independent living that are required. *Goal:* Develop skills in independent living; explore alternative living arrangements.	1. Larry will continue to live at home for the immediate future.	Larry and family	Ongoing for now
	2. Larry will make his bed and clean his own room and perform one household task for the family every week.	Larry	2/31/1991
	3. Larry and family will visit New Horizons group home in Horizonville in the next 2 months.	Larry and Family	4/30/1991

Needs and Goals	Objectives	Responsible Person	Target Dates
Economic support Larry is financially dependent on his parents, who are opposed to his applying for SSI because they consider that "welfare." Larry would like to be able to support himself some day. *Goal:* Develop long-range financial plan.	1. Case manager will discuss Larry's own feelings about applying for SSI with him.	John	2/28/1991
	2. Larry will look into earning spending money through odd jobs in the neighborhood.	Larry	3/30/1991
	3. Discuss financial issues with family.	John and family	4/30/1991
Socialization, recreation, and support When he is home, Larry stays in his room listening to music a great deal. Larry has very few friends. Some friends he knew when he was in high school are drug users. He has enjoyed sports in the past. Larry receives emotional support from his parents, brother, and grandparents. Family withdraws emotional support when he becomes verbally aggressive. The family would like him to participate in family activities. *Goal:* Larry will increase social activities with family and in community.	1. Larry will enroll in one sports activity at the YMCA.	Larry	3/15/1991
	2. Larry will go to the drop-in socialization group for aftercare clients run by the local CMHC.	Larry and CMHC	2/28/1991
	3. Larry will go to church with his family twice a month.	Family	3/31/1991
Vocational/employment issues Larry would like to learn skills that will help him get a job. He is interested in getting vocational training at some time but does not feel ready. He is not sure what kind of training he would like. *Goal:* Explore vocational options.	1. Larry will meet with a Bureau of Vocational Rehabilitation counselor to get information about vocational options and vocational testing in the next 3 months.	BVR Counselor	3/31/1991

TABLE 9.1
continued

Needs and Goals	Objectives	Responsible Person	Target Dates
Health Larry is in good physical health according to family and health records. Physical and mental health services are covered under the family's health insurance. *Goal:* Maintain physical health.	1. Medical care as needed.	Dr. Y	Ongoing as needed
Family relationships The family would like to be helpful, but feel helpless. The parents and brothers express some feelings of embarrassment. They do not know much about schizophrenia and do not know any other families who have relatives with schizophrenia. *Goal:* Develop for family to express feelings, obtain information, and receive support.	1. Family will meet with Dr. X, who will provide information about schizophrenia and medication; and with the case manager/social worker, who will help them with their feelings of embarrassment.	Dr. X and John Martin	2/15/1991
	2. Family will be referred to the NAMI group in the town of XYZ for family support.	NAMI	3/1/1991

Larry Leeds   1/30/1991
Client   Date

John Martin   1/30/1991
Case Manager   Date

One of these additional functions is helping the client with *problem solving*. Living in the community, clients with serious mental disorders encounter everyday problems with which they have difficulty. The case manager works collaboratively with the client or client system by identifying the problem and breaking it down to manageable proportions, generating alternative solutions, and promoting decision making and actions that seem to represent the best choices under the circumstances. The need for problem-solving activity arises in the process of monitoring the client over time. The problems may be personal, interpersonal, environmental, or a combination.

A related direct service function is *crisis intervention* (Intagliata, Willer, & Egri, 1986). Crises are eruptions of stress in reaction to problems that cannot be managed using a person's usual coping mechanisms. Persons with chronic mental disabilities are highly vulnerable to stress, which can emanate from within or from outside. Internal stressors are related to the disorder, which may have an exacerbation on its own or be the result of a client's going off the prescribed medication. External stressors such as poverty, eviction, interpersonal difficulties, problems on the job, and "expressed emotion" in the family—singly or in combination—can also arouse stress. Clients with severe psychiatric disorders respond to stress in extreme ways; for example, they threaten suicide, engage in violent behavior, or develop delusions or hallucinations (Flax, 1982). The case manager can provide support to the individual client, mobilize support from the family, intervene with persons who may be contributing to the problem, or call upon community resources that can be used to resolve the crisis. This may require that the case manager make home visits, accompany the client to a psychiatric emergency service, or contact others in the community. In some cases, hospitalization is necessary. When a crisis occurs, the case manager may spend large blocks of time over a couple of days with a single client.

Consider the following crisis soon after Larry's third hospitalization, after which he was assigned a case manager.

April 4: John Martin, case manager, received a telephone call from Larry's mother, requesting that he meet with Larry. The case manager made a home visit, where he spent a couple of hours with Larry and additional time with Larry and his parents together.

Larry told the case manager that he would like to have spending money, but his parents "won't let me apply for financial aid." (John recalled that during his first meeting with Larry, John told Larry about SSI.) Larry said that when he asks his parents for money, he feels like a child.

John figured out how much money Larry would receive with SSI, considering that he was living at home, and told Larry about Medicaid, for which he was also entitled. They discussed his right to receive benefits, but Larry was troubled by the prospect of going against his parents' wishes. John identified the following issues for Larry to consider: (a) Larry's respect for his parents' feelings and his fear of their disapproval; (b) his parents' coverage for him under their medical insurance at least until he is 21; (c) the amount of SSI he would receive versus his ability to earn the equivalent amount by doing chores for his parents, his grandparents, and neighbors.

During the family session, the case manager gave Mr. and Mrs. Leeds the opportunity to share their feelings about "not accepting welfare" and being responsible for Larry at least until he is 21. John described the SSI program as an entitlement to which Mr. and Mrs. Leeds, as taxpayers, have contributed. Larry shared his feelings about being financially dependent on them and not having any spending money. He articulated his desire to live on his own and hold a job some day. At the conclusion of the session, the family agreed to the following:

1. Out of respect for his parents, Larry would not apply for SSI until he was almost 21.
2. Larry's parents will pay him for performing 3 hours of yardwork weekly.
3. Larry will seek out similar jobs working for his grandparents and neighbors.
4. His parents will make efforts not to treat him like a child.
5. The case manager will work with Larry to make plans for services that will help him become more self-sufficient in the future, such as living in a halfway house.

Implicit in all the functions that have been described is that the case manager provides a *supportive relationship*. As social workers know, the relationship is what makes intervention work. Case managers demonstrate support by conveying positive regard, attentiveness, and controlled emotional involvement. They convey warmth and interest in valuing the client and share the ups and downs that usually occur. Case managers are available to the client to help with minor and major problems. As one student case manager explained:

When Jane and I are together two times a week, we engage in activities of daily living; talk about her problems, decision-making, and coping strategies; go to groups like Adult Children of Alcoholics or go and have some healthy fun. I always model through my behavior and verbalizations how Jane can deal effectively with her life on a day-to-day basis. When an emergency issue arises, Jane and I work on resolving that crisis before resuming our treatment plan. For now, we concentrate primarily on those things most people take for granted. For every tiny bit of progress Jane makes, we are both happy, because among other things, it increases her self-esteem for a little while.

—Karin Gregory, a student

Another direct service function of the case manager is *working with the family* (Intagliata, Willer, & Egri, 1986; Lamb, 1980). Many seriously and severely mentally ill persons live with their parents, spouses, siblings, or equivalent significant others. Even if the client lives apart from the family, emotional ties remain. The family can be a partner in the development and implementation of the service plan. Family members are able to provide information about the client, identify signs of relapse, provide transportation, monitor the client's response to treatment, and assist with everyday problems. Moreover, the family can advocate for an individual member and for the corporate needs of clients. Despite the contributions families make, they are frequently excluded from consideration.

Lamb (1980) has suggested a convergence of the clinical and brokerage roles in his description of the *therapist–case manager*. Here the case manager is the client's primary therapist. This role calls for a trained mental health professional who has knowledge of human behavior theories and psychopathology, as well as the philosophy of rehabilitation and appropriate therapeutic approaches. It takes a skilled clinician to make an accurate assessment, recognize signs of decompensation, and know when and how to intervene. Still Lamb (1980) does not suggest that the therapist–case manager perform therapy as it is usually understood:

> This view does not mean that the therapist–case manager should be doing in-depth psychotherapy; in many instances it may be contradicted, as generally the most meaningfull psychotherapy with long-term patients is dealing with the realities and day-to-day issues of life and survival in the community. (p. 763)

In work with the severely mentally disabled, problem solving, crisis intervention, fostering independence, enhancing coping skills, and intervening with families are therapeutic. Furthermore, the coordination of services, rational planning, advocacy, and individualized service delivery helps the client develop stability and an integrated sense of self (Harris & Bergman, 1987). Clinical social workers know how to implement these strategies effectively and apply them appropriately to the individual client. Lamb (1980) suggests that the assistance of paraprofessionals in escorting clients to services can free up time for case managers to perform therapeutic activities.

Clinical social workers who are case managers call upon their generalist skills in assessment, brokerage, case planning, and advocacy and upon their clinical skills in the assessment of mental health problems and their treatment. Clinical social workers are trained to select interventions that are compatible with clients' needs, to use community resources, and to advocate for the vulnerable. Research studies on characteristics of case managers indicate that case managers are highly educated and experienced, and that social workers are well represented (Goldstrom & Manderscheid, 1983; Kurtz, Bagarozzi, & Pollane, 1984). Unfortunately many clinical social workers view case management as a low-level skill that is not compatible with their training or their aspirations to be psychotherapists (Johnson & Rubin, 1983).

Models of Case Management

Case management has been implemented in a variety of ways in different settings. Research-based practice experience across contexts has given rise to a number of different models. Among these are the rehabilitation model, the assertive community treatment model, the developmental-acquisition model, and the Rockland County model. These are described below and in Table 9.2.

The *rehabilitation model* was utilized in a program in Toronto, which was evaluated on a sample at 6-month and 2-year intervals (Goering et al., 1988). The experimental group had experienced, credentialed professionals (a social worker, a psychiatric nurse, and two occupational therapists) in the role of rehabilitation case managers. The control group did not include staff with professional qualifications, but the group was supervised by a credentialed case manager. The experimental group was provided with

TABLE 9.2
Case Management Models

Model	Philosophy	Features
Rehabilitation	Promote and enhance adaptive functioning (social, occupational, independent)	Case management is provided by professional social workers, nurses, occupational therapists under professional supervision Small caseloads (15–20) Clients are helped to develop social and personal skills Client-centered inteviewing, support, crisis management, problem solving, service coordination Functional assessments, rehabilitation plans
Assertive community treatment	Promote functioning and independence; prevent (re)hospitalization	Team responsible for cases corporately Aggressive outreach and follow-up In vivo assistance Crisis intervention, problem solving, coping Mobile treatment team focuses on hard-to-reach clients Work with families
Developmental-acquisition model	Foster client's development of potential; ensure that client acquires community resources	Individual caseloads Teaching, modeling, practicing social skills Aggressive outreach Focus on strengths
Rockland County model	Provide services that are consistent with the developmental, psychological, and social needs of clients who are young and have severe mental disorders	Specialized individual caseloads Reduced caseloads Support for case managers Modified team approach

training in service coordination, use of community resources that would enhance clients' functioning, and patient-centered interviewing. They had caseloads of between 15 and 20 clients. In implementing the role of rehabilitation case managers, the participants developed functional assessments and implemented functional rehabilitation plans. Rehabilitation case managers provided ongoing support to clients, coordinated services, and made sure that clients had support during crises, were able to cope with the social service bureaucracy, and acquired social and personal skills. After 6 months, the experimental group of clients had a significantly higher level of occupational functioning than the controls. After 2 years, the experimental group exceeded the controls in occupational status, housing status (more independent), and social isolation (less isolated). There were no differences between the two groups in rehospitalization rates at 6 months or after 2 years. The authors attributed the success of this rehabilitation case management program in improving the quality of life of the experimental group to the rehabilitation assessment and programming, service coordination, the continuous relationship with the case manager over an extended period of time, and small caseloads.

A model that has been widely acclaimed and replicated is the *assertive community treatment, or intensive case management, model.* This model of case management and community intervention emphasizes aggressive outreach, skill development, and resource brokering. The model was pioneered by Leonard Stein (professor of psychiatry) and Mary Ann Test (professor of social work) of the University of Wisconsin. It was first implemented in Dane County, Wisconsin, in the 1970s as an alternative to hospitalization. It has been called the *Training in Community Living Model* (TCL), *Program of Assertive Community Treatment* (PACT), and, more recently, the *Mobile Community Treatment* (MCT) Program (Thompson, Griffith, & Leaf, 1990). As the model has evolved, it has become modified. Over the years, this model has spread to other communities, states, and countries with varying population densities and ethnic compositions, each program adapted to unique conditions in its respective community. Evaluations of programs using this model have demonstrated remarkable success in reducing hospitalization (Stein & Test, 1985).

The assertive community treatment model has a team functioning corporately as case managers.

> There are no individual caseloads. Every worker sees every member, on an informal rotating basis. As a result, workers can be deployed with maximum efficiency when several members are in crisis simultaneously or when our numbers have been depleted by illness or vacations. (Witheridge & Dincin, 1985, p. 71)

Teams have the advantage of providing continuous care for the client by anyone on the team. Furthermore, working in a group can generate creativity and energy and prevent burnout (Test, 1979).

Case management teams meet on a frequent basis, at which times cases are discussed, intervention strategies developed, and tasks distributed among the group. Clients are seen often and regularly in the field. The Mobile Community Treatment Program in Wisconsin, designed specifically for difficult-to-treat, predominantly young clients, has two shifts of staff, who meet daily between shifts and weekly as a total staff to give status reports on clients and coordinate their efforts (Stein & Diamond, 1985; Stein & Test, 1984).

The assertive case management model recognizes that clients with chronic mental disorders have three disabling conditions that interfere with their social functioning (Stein & Test, 1985). These are strong dependence needs, a limited range of problem-solving or instrumental skills, and the capacity to develop psychiatric symptoms in the face of stress. These characteristics interfere with community living and create vulnerability to rehospitalization. On the other hand, the model recognizes that each client has strengths that are the basis for effective functioning. In order to promote a client's functioning and prevent stress, the team assertively reaches out to clients to engage them and keep them engaged in programs. Clients who do not show up for appointments are sought out so that obstacles to their participation can be overcome.

With assertive case management, clients are also helped to become more independent. For some this entails "constructive separation" from parents by living apart from them. At the same time supports are provided for the client, structured visiting with parents is arranged, and the community is prepared to receive new residents (Training in Community Living, 1983). In other cases, separation is not pursued. "Whether we separate patients from their families or not, we continue to work closely with families" (Stein & Test, 1984, p. 66).

One of the unique features of this model is its fostering the development of coping skills in familiar surroundings in the community. Accordingly, case managers reach out to clients in their homes and local communities. They may meet clients over coffee in the client's neighborhood, at a psychosocial program, or at the client's residence. The emphasis is on in vivo (real-life) assistance with ordinary activities in the same context in which they will be used. The case manager/team member models a skill (e.g., how to use a washing machine) where the skill is needed (e.g., the neighborhood laundromat) and teaches the skill to the client. This approach differs from a program-based strategy in which the client is expected to learn a skill in one setting and apply it to another. In vivo assistance is consistent with the observation that many persons with severe and persistent mental illnesses have difficulties transferring learning from one situation to another (Stein & Test, 1984).

Another case management model, the *developmental-acquisition model,* was developed by Charles Rapp of the University of Kansas School of Social Welfare and his associates (Rapp & Chamberlain, 1985; Modrcin, Rapp, & Poertner, 1988) to remedy the social problems facing the chronically mentally ill. Their developmental-acquisition model emphasizes clients' development of their potential (utilizing their strengths) and the acquisition of community resources. Mental health services are considered among the many environmental resources clients use to promote their development. Others include housing, employment, education, and recreational services.

"In the case management described here, the role of the case manager fell somewhere between the two poles of therapist and clerk/broker" (Rapp & Chamberlain, 1985, p. 418). The case manager commits a great deal of time to each client, meeting with the client in the community and teaching, modeling, and having clients practice social skills. This model is proactive, preferring aggressive outreach to reacting to clients' requests for services.

The developmental-acquisition model was evaluated using an experimental design (Modrcin, Rapp, & Poertner, 1988). The experimental group of clients had case managers using the developmental-acquisition model, whereas the control group used the reactive approach that was essentially office bound, focused on psychopathology, and did not emphasize the use of community resources. At the end of the study, the experimental group showed more improvement in socialization skills, community living skills, vocational training, tolerance for stress, inappropriate community behavior, and perceptions of leisure time usage than the control group. The case managers utilizing the developmental-acquisition model saw clients more frequently in and outside the office, were more likely to focus on strengths than on problems or pathology, and perceived the relationship as more important than the control group of case managers.

The *Rockland County model,* a case management program developed by the mental health system of Rockland County, New York, is adapted especially to the needs of the young adult chronic population (Berzon & Lowenstein, 1984). They have certain case managers who work predominantly with the highly demanding young adult clients. The qualities they look for in filling these positions are flexibility, diversity in ethnic backgrounds, a high toleration for frustration and ambiguity, creativity, and persistence. Case managers for younger clients have reduced caseloads so that the staff has time to implement plans and to respond effectively to crises. Furthermore, the program provides support to case managers through supervision, training, peer support, and an emphasis on accepting realistic goals. Like the assertive community training model, the Rockland County model utilizes teams. In their modified team approach, clients have individual case managers, but team members back each other up when the regular case manager is unavailable.

The Rockland County case managers assume many different roles in relation to clients. Among these are friend, counselor, broker, teacher, and outreach worker. They are sensitive to the developmental needs of young adults to assume responsibility for themselves. Some of the young adult case managers have special client groups whom they serve—for example, those with dual diagnoses, anorexia, or problems with the criminal justice system.

These four models, which are described in Table 9.2, stand out among those that have been used to promote adaptive community living for persons with serious and persistent mental illnesses. The assertive and Rockland County models are particularly useful with hard-to-reach clients, such as young adults with persistent and serious disabilities. With the assertive model, however, care should be taken that high emotional intensity is not created. The attention given to strengths and growth potential in the developmental-acquisition and assertive models and to community services, problem solving, and adaptive functioning in the rehabilitation model is also noteworthy. In all these models, the case manager enters into the everyday life of the client. They differ markedly from the practice adopted by those case managers who spend most of their time in their offices, conducting their field work by telephone and paper.

ASSUMPTIONS UNDERLYING CASE MANAGEMENT PRACTICE

The implementation of case management with persons with chronic mental illness is based on assumptions that derive from social work values, the philosophy of rehabilitation, research, and case management models. These are as follows:

1. Persons with severe and persistent mental illness have the capacity to live in the community with supports.
2. Such persons have strengths that can be developed and enhanced.
3. Chronic mental illness creates vulnerability to stress, dependence, and poverty that is evident in frequent crises.

4. Persons with serious mental illnesses have the capacity to grow, change, learn, and improve their psychological and social functioning.

5. For many persons with severe mental illnesses, learning is most effective when it takes place in the environment in which it is to be used; learning takes place gradually and in incremental steps.

6. Like other citizens, the chronically mentally ill have civil rights and obligations. They have the right to freedom of speech, mobility, and autonomy so long as they do not interfere with the rights of others and do not violate the law.

7. Persons with severe and persistent mental illness have the right to participate in service planning and to make informed decisions on their own behalf.

8. Families are potentially important participants in the rehabilitation and planning process, provided that clients consent to their help.

9. The community has a responsibility to integrate persons with chronic mental illnesses into the community and to develop a continuum of services to meet their needs.

10. Treatment of clients should be the least intrusive but most therapeutic and should take place in the least restrictive environment that is consistent with clients' needs.

11. The community has a responsibility to provide services to this population for a long and indefinite time period. (Suggested by Ohio Department of Mental Health, 1987.)

These assumptions recognize that chronic mental illness has an unpredictable course. Because many individuals recover or make substantial gains in their functioning, their potential for growth should be recognized and incorporated into treatment planning and implementation. In being optimistic about clients' capacity to learn and develop, the case manager recognizes and works with the client's strengths and capacities. Nevertheless, the vulnerabilities to stress and dependence also should be considered, so that when a crisis occurs, the worker is ready to engage the client in problem solving to prevent the situation and the client from deteriorating.

The responsibility for the rehabilitation of persons with chronic mental illness is shared among the client, the family, the case manager, mental health services, other social service agencies, and the community as a whole. Clients are responsible for taking care of themselves and obeying the law. The community has a responsibility to respect the clients' rights, to accept them as citizens, and to respond to their needs. The case manager is in a critical position of mediating between the client and the community, yet representing the client's interests.

In keeping with these assumptions, the following strategies are recommended:

1. Reach out assertively to clients in their natural environments on a regular and consistent basis and at times of crisis.

2. Recognize clients' dependence, yet support their drive to be more autonomous.

3. Teach skills in the environments in which they are needed incrementally, supporting clients as they master each step.

4. Help clients arrange services and living situations that are consistent with their needs for support and autonomy. Changes from one situation to another should be

a mutual decision based on the clients' wishes and their capacity to cope with the new environment.

5. Encourage clients to use community resources. Especially support their use of mainstream facilities such as libraries, movies, parks, and schools, and their participation in the competitive job market.

6. Work with community representatives to help them understand and integrate the chronically mentally ill.

7. Advocate for clients on the individual and community levels. This includes promoting the development of additional services that meet gaps in the existing mental health service delivery system, such as residential services sensitive to the developmental needs of young adults.

8. Help clients avoid hospitalization by addressing incipient problems at an early stage, intervening at times of crisis, and utilizing services that are alternatives to hospitalization.

9. Conduct the case management role in keeping with the values of the social work profession, the community mental health ideals, and community support system principles. Be especially attentive to clients' rights to individualization, dignity, self-determination, and the least restrictive alternative; the principles of normalization, integration, and continuity of care; and clients' civil rights.

10. Assist clients in the development of a natural support system within the community.

11. Develop constructive, collaborative relationships with families of persons with serious mental disorders. (Suggested by Ohio Department of Mental Health, 1987.)

COMMUNITY SUPPORT SERVICES

Persons with severe and disabling mental disorders can benefit from a variety of community services. The particular package of services that is appropriate for each client is related to the client's assessed psychosocial needs, the client's wishes, his or her financial condition, and the services available in the community in which the client lives. At times, the social worker will develop resources that are not available by modifying services that are there (e.g., developing a program for the developmentally disabled and psychiatrically impaired through cooperative programming). The kinds of community services that will be discussed here are outpatient services, housing, crisis services, psychosocial rehabilitation, health care, entitlements, support networks, and consumer groups.

Outpatient Services (Aftercare)

For a person with a disabling mental illness, outpatient mental health treatment is a necessity. The way in which community mental health centers have evolved, however, is that they have focused primarily on the "worried well" with "circumscribed, temporary disturbances" (Bellack & Mueser, 1986, p. 178), which can be handled with psychotherapy or a combination of psychotherapy and medication. Persons with severe and persistent mental disorders require a more sustained commitment that deemphasizes traditional verbal psychotherapeutic approaches, but is nonetheless therapeutic.

Clients who have been hospitalized should be linked with an outpatient mental health service prior to discharge. Joint planning before discharge between hospital social workers and the community providers is helpful (Altman, 1982). Those who have never been hospitalized may be assisted by a case manager or other mental health professional to secure these services. Outpatient services are provided in a variety of settings, depending on the community and its range of services. Community mental health centers are one source; many of them provide not only psychiatric supervision, but also outpatient therapy, partial hospitalization (day treatment), emergency services, and programs particularly targeted to the chronically mentally ill. Some communities have free-standing outpatient clinics in which medication is supervised and case management provided. Other areas have traveling outpatient teams. Still others have outpatient clinics that are associated with public hospitals, university hospitals, and private practices.

Many persons with severe mental illness are on medication. Medication requirements within the hospital and the community are different. Moreover, the need for medication changes over time. Many psychotropic drugs have disturbing and dangerous side effects that need to be monitored. Because medication is such an important dimension of treatment and the clinical social worker has a critical role in identifying medication issues (Gerhart & Brooks, 1983), psychopharmacology will be discussed in depth in chapter 10.

Although most clients can benefit from some support, intensive psychotherapy may be harmful, especially for persons with schizophrenia (see chapter 8). Accordingly psychotherapeutic treatment should be offered on a selective basis only, for those clients with chronic disorders other than schizophrenia or those with schizophrenia who seem to be able to handle some intimacy. Structured approaches such as task-centered casework (Epstein, 1988) can help clients solve immediate problems. A calm, nonjudgmental approach on the part of the clinician is desirable.

An alternative to psychotherapy is participation in social skills training, especially in groups. With such training, clients can learn how to handle interpersonal problems and master effective social and vocational skills at the same time as they receive support from their peers. Social skills training will be described in chapter 10.

For clients who are living with their families, intervention with the family is helpful. One of the most promising means of working with families is family psychoeducation. This approach will also be discussed in the next chapter.

Although aftercare is sometimes equated with treatment, intervention with the chronically mentally ill encompasses the broad domain of adaptive living in the community. The relationship with the case manager (who may be a case manager–therapist), together with appropriate housing and psychosocial rehabilitation services and natural supports, can help sustain the client in the community.

Housing

The housing arrangements of persons with severe and persistent mental disorders are diverse. The kind of housing chosen and the neighborhood in which the housing is located are important to the client's well-being. Living accommodations are more or less clean, private, warm, and conveniently located. Similarly, neighborhoods are more or less tolerant, accessible, and safe.

Many residences are rehabilitative in design or outcome. Velasquez and McCubbin (1980) found in a 6-month follow-up study of clients remaining in the Hope Transition Center, a community-based residential program incorporating milieu therapy (a therapeutic environment), that participants showed more improvement than a comparable control group in self-responsibility, social participation, employment status, self-concept, and problem-solving ability and had a lower rate of rehospitalization. This program provided structure, support, and opportunities for social interaction; and presented clients with increasingly difficult problems to solve and tasks to perform, rewarding them when a task was completed or a problem was solved. Other research has demonstrated that in contrast with patients in state hospitals, clients living in the community perceived that their quality of life was improved (Lehman, Possidente, & Hawker, 1986) and they were less irritable, depressed, and socially isolated than previously (Christenfeld et al., 1985).

Among the housing arrangements possible for clients are the following.

Living with One's Own Family.   Many clients live with their parents, grandparents, a sibling, spouse, children, or equivalent nonrelated adults. These natural arrangements have the advantage of providing continuity with a previous pattern and a potentially caring environment. Many young adults with chronic mental disorders live with their family of origin because they need supervision and are not self-sufficient.

Torrey (1988) believes that persons with schizophrenia are better off *not* living at home. He thinks that such individuals function at a higher level and are happier elsewhere. But if they do live at home, he says, solitude and structure are desirable. A private room, quiet, and a daily routine of activities are helpful.

In arranging for a client to live with his or her own family, the desires and needs of the entire family should be considered. The family will be affected by and affect the member who lives there. The family's need for education and support, as well as the client's needs, should be addressed. Consider the following case.

> When 50-year-old Molly first returned home to her husband after she was hospitalized for the sixth time, she slept all day and paced the floors at night. They shopped for food together, but her husband Ray did all the cooking and cleaning. Ray accepted his wife's condition, because he was accustomed to it. When she began to accuse him incessantly of poisoning her food and going out with other women, however, Ray became angry. He was further disturbed by her refusal to bathe. A hard-working, long-suffering man, Ray reached the limits of his tolerance. In desperation he asked the case manager/social worker what other housing alternatives were possible for Molly.

Before considering alternative placements in the community, other arrangements can be explored. Other family members or a community service might provide *respite care,* a temporary place in which the client can stay while the primary care giver rests or goes on vacation. Respite care is an underdeveloped but highly needed community resource (Zirul, Lieberman, & Rapp, 1989). Some communities provide nursing-home beds, board-and-care placements, or alternative residences for this purpose. Such programs can result in a reduction in subsequent hospital days for participating clients (Geiser, Hoche, & King, 1988). In this case, Molly was placed temporarily in a family care home, where her behavior and medication were closely monitored and a personal hygiene behavioral program was instituted. Meanwhile Ray had time to think through his needs and obligations with the help of a clinical social worker.

Family Care Homes.   Family care or foster homes are some of the oldest existing forms of community care for psychiatric clients. In the ideal home there are one to four clients who are integrated into a family setting and encouraged to develop habits of personal care and social skills. The caretaker, who is paid for services on a per-client basis, provides the client with bed and board and assures that the client receives physical and mental health care. The caretaker administers medication, takes the client to an after-care clinic for appointments, and gets the client ready for social rehabilitation programs.

Family care homes vary in size, atmosphere, and the autonomy available to clients. In some homes, the clients occupy a separate floor or wing from the family, thus comprising their own group. In other homes, the clients interact daily with children or grandchildren of the care giver and participate in family activities such as meal preparation and gardening.

Family care homes are administered by Veterans' Administration hospitals, state hospitals, mental health agencies, or the private sector. Usually they are linked to the mental health delivery system in some way. Frequently social workers, nurses, and/or other mental health workers meet with clients and caretakers at the family care homes. During such visits, changing conditions of individual clients and the household can be observed and monitored. Family care homes are subject to state licensing laws.

Boarding Homes.   Boarding, or board-and-care, homes are relatively large establishments, usually run for profit by nonprofessional proprietors. They, too, require licenses or certification, depending on the state. These facilities provide meals and shelter and administer medication. They offer less intimate contact and supervision than family care homes; ordinarily clients are free to leave the facility and wander about in the community. Generally residents share rooms with other residents.

Payment for board-and-care homes comes from public transfer programs such as Supplementary Security Income and Social Security. Most of the monthly allotment goes to the proprietor, but a small allowance is for the client. Because the margin of profit in such facilities is small, proprietors may be tempted to economize on food or deprive clients of their spending money. "Residents of these homes are highly vulnerable to being abused, neglected, and exploited" (Blake, 1987).

Many boarding homes do not provide opportunities for socialization, rehabilitation, and social skills development. They are linked with the mental health system to the extent that the mental health worker or proprietor fosters the connection. In a survey of boarding homes in Essex County, New Jersey, Blake (1987) found that medication was not adequately reviewed, and only 7 percent of the residents were participating in mental health services in the community. Large board-and-care homes have been criticized because they have come to resemble the back wards they are supposed to replace (Lamb & Goertzl, 1971). Residents may be left to vegetate, retreat, and hallucinate.

Lodges.   Lodges modeled on Fairweather Lodge provide housing, social support, and employment opportunities to this population (McLaughlin, 1988). Beginning when the clients are hospitalized, they are engaged in a group process that is used as a catalyst for support and growth. Lodges are residences, but they also are communities that require participants to assume job responsibilities and chores. Residents are encouraged to assume increasingly challenging jobs, both within the lodge and outside. There are approximately 100 lodges of this kind nationally. For some members they are a transitional facility.

Transitional Facilities.   Transitional facilities provide a "midway station" between hospitalization and independent living, in which clients can be "partly dependent" as they work toward more independence (Gottesfeld, 1977). These facilities vary in size and scope, but most provide a group living situation and social support. Halfway houses and group homes are examples of transitional facilities. Although the boundaries between the two are fuzzy, group homes tend to be more restrictive, provide closer supervision, and assume a lower level of community living skills than halfway houses (Phipps & Liberman, 1988). Halfway houses focus on social rehabilitation by promoting socialization, independent living skills development, and integration into the community (Weisman, 1985). Both types of transitional facilities are therapeutic in that they promote an improvement in the client's social functioning. Some halfway houses are modeled on the family (Budson, 1978); they are small, personal, and caring environments in which clients are encouraged to take steps toward independence.

Transitional facilities usually have a professional staff who provide supervision around the clock. Psychiatrists see clients on a regular basis and as needed. Although rules and requirements vary among facilities, most expect clients to be responsible for their personal grooming, help with household chores, attend group meetings, and refrain from using chemical substances. Frequently clients are required to enroll in vocational rehabilitation programs or work programs or to hold a job at the same time they live in these facilities. Clients work toward increasing their independent living and social and vocational skills so that they can move to a more autonomous living situation in the future.

A missing link among transitional facilities is the *developmental residence,* designed especially to meet the needs for growth of young adult chronic patients (Pepper & Ryglewicz, 1985). This would be a fully staffed community facility in which young adults could live for up to 2 years while they attended school, received training, or participated in a treatment program. The group process would be used to foster the development of independence, self-control, decision making, and relationship building.

In recent years group homes have been providing permanent rather than transitional residence. The trend is to establish a stable living situation rather than make a series of moves from one placement to another. Group homes that are permanent provide support at the same time that they promote independence.

Supervised Apartments, Cooperative Apartments, or Satellite Housing.   These may be transitional or long-term arrangements. They serve clients who are at a more advanced level than those in halfway houses but are not ready for completely independent living. Consisting of autonomous living units, they usually are operated under the sponsorship of a hospital, agency, or social rehabilitation service. Certain apartments within an existing apartment complex are designated for client use; or certain buildings or blocks of apartments are used. The agency may own the housing units or lease the apartments or homes for the clients. In other cases, the agency's role is primarily consultative.

Unlike halfway houses, cooperative apartments do not have live-in staff members, but there are professional mental health workers who work with clients and maintain relationships with landlords (Burger et al., 1978; Goldmeier, Shore, & Mannino, 1977). Rents are affordable and may be subsidized. Generally these housing arrangements come with the expectation that residents participate in community activities in addition to their responsibility for taking care of the apartments (Lamb, 1984).

Clients residing in supervised apartments usually share units with each other. Matches may be facilitated by mental health workers or preselected by clients. Because sharing an apartment brings individuals into close contact, care should be taken to ensure that apartment mates are compatible. Furthermore, clients referred to cooperative apartments should have skills in food preparation, house cleaning, cooking, and doing laundry. It is desirable that they be able to manage their own money and use public transportation.

Single-Room Occupancy Hotels.   Some clients live in single rooms in hotels, a housing situation that has been given the acronym of SRO. These rooms are occupied primarily by poor people, usually welfare recipients. The single rooms may or may not have cooking facilities. Clients may have to use hot plates for preparing meals. Bathrooms are frequently shared. Conditions in these hotels are notoriously poor: they are unclean, cold, poorly maintained, and unsafe. Prostitution and drug dealing are rampant. Nevertheless, they are an improvement over the streets. With the gentrification of major cities, however, SROs have become increasingly depleted (Baxter & Hopper, 1984).

Other Community Facilities.   The varied American communities in urban and rural areas have other kinds of facilities that are used for or adaptable to persons with severe mental illnesses. Many YMCAs and YWCAs, for example, have single rooms that are amenable to the chronically mentally ill because they are quiet and private. These rooms may be available in a crisis or on a long-term basis. Some communities may convert hotels and motels into residences for this population.

Some clients live in housing that is public or subsidized by the government. Apartments for the elderly and disabled, many of which have medical and social service personnel on the staff, can provide comfortable living quarters for the mentally disabled. It is incumbent on the social worker/case manager to identify such alternatives in the community.

Independent Living.   Some clients are able to live in the community on their own or with a roommate. These clients are sufficiently independent to assume their own leases, manage payment of the rent, keep the apartment reasonably clean, and prepare meals without a mental health professional supervising the arrangement. Persons who live independently still may be linked with the community mental health delivery system. They may be attending an aftercare clinic and/or participating in a social rehabilitation program, such as working in sheltered employment.

Shelters for the Homeless.   Homelessness is a social problem that is connected with unemployment, gentrification of urban areas, substance abuse, and family conflict, as well as deinstitutionalization. Nevertheless, substantial numbers of the homeless are persons with chronic mental illness. Homelessness among the mentally ill may be the outcome of inadequate discharge planning, noncompliance with a service plan on the part of clients, or eviction, among other factors. With little money, food, or social support—and poor coping skills—the seriously mentally ill are forced to fend for themselves. The "bag ladies" and "shopping-cart men" who are mentally ill are familiar sights in urban areas. They eat others' leftovers and collect possessions from garbage cans. It is no wonder that many of them are physically sick and that they are robbed, raped, and otherwise exploited.

Some persons with chronic mental illness are able to make their way from the streets to community shelters for the homeless. Publicly run shelters accommodate large numbers of persons in open areas that provide little privacy or protection from theft or harassment. Shelters provide beds for a limited population, making it desirable for potential users to arrive early. Although they usually are not open during the daytime, some shelters offer social services or make referrals to appropriate mental health agencies.

Some cities have alternative facilities that serve the same purpose as shelters for the homeless. Private organizations, often under religious auspices, run smaller, more personal facilities. Clients partaking of these arrangements may be allowed to stay longer than one night and may be helped to receive entitlements, obtain medication, and secure employment. Sometimes these facilities run their own programs of vocational rehabilitation (e.g., Goodwill Industries). Some alternative shelters have accommodations for families.

Jails.   Another unfortunate housing alternative is the jail. Persons with mental illnesses end up in the criminal justice system when they are charged with stealing or violent behavior. These behaviors may be strategies for survival, maneuvers to get themselves rehospitalized, or manifestations of their mental disorders. When the behaviors are perceived as crimes rather than symptoms of disease, they are managed by the criminal justice system. The consequence is the "criminalization" of the mentally ill (Abramson, 1972).

Crisis Services

Persons with serious mental disorders are sensitive to stress and subject to exacerbations of their psychiatric illnesses. In keeping with the requirement that treatment be the least restrictive, communities have developed a number of resources that are used to contain crises and avoid hospitalization. Among these are emergency services, crisis residences, day hospitalization, and hospitalization.

Emergency services are outpatient psychiatric units that are associated with general hospitals or mental health clinics. They treat persons who walk in or are brought in for treatment of acute psychiatric symptoms as well as stress-related reactions. Persons with chronic psychiatric disorders may be escorted by family members, case managers, or the police. Police respond to a variety of situations, but particularly to those in which clients are out of control or threaten violence.

Because emergency services do not operate on an appointment basis and thus may have an unpredictably full schedule, units establish means by which to determine priorities. Some adopt a triage system in which all cases are screened briefly as soon as possible to determine which cases should be seen first and which require the services of a psychiatrist. Such systems are useful, because many persons who use emergency services are not in crisis. Some users do not know of other community resources that can meet their needs more appropriately. Others' cultural styles make it more comfortable for them to ask for help for psychosocial needs from emergency services than from other community services. Persons with borderline personalities and young adults with severe psychiatric disabilities are thought to overuse emergency services.

Clients whose needs are perceived as urgent present acute psychotic symptoms, suicidal or homicidal behaviors, or aggression. Those who are brought in by the police tend to capture the immediate attention of staff. Case managers who accompany clients who are less visibly affected but in pain need to be assertive in requesting attention.

Emergency treatment varies according to the client's diagnosis and needs. Those with acute or extreme symptoms are screened to determine whether they meet the state's criteria for hospitalization. Those with acute psychotic symptoms are often given medication. Persons with anxiety, depression, confusion, and somatic symptoms that are related to stressful life events are helped through crisis intervention strategies.

Crisis intervention is a means of helping people under acute stress to restore their psychosocial functioning to the precrisis level at the very least. The emergency service worker must work very quickly to assess the seriousness of the problem and provide treatment. The worker does this by establishing rapport, asking the client about the precipitating event (the "last straw" that preceded the request for help) and hazardous conditions that created vulnerability to a crisis, and giving the client an opportunity to express painful emotions. In the course of hearing about the problem and the client's feelings, the emergency service worker makes an assessment and, in collaboration with the client, develops strategies to help the client solve the immediate problem. By connecting the client's symptoms with the causes of the problem and formulating a plan to address immediate issues, the worker helps the client restore cognitive functioning (Dixon, 1987).

Some emergency service workers intervene in ways that limit clients' mobility. Violent or excited clients may be placed in lock-up rooms or put into restraints. When these measures are used for a limited amount of time and in conjunction with other means to help the client gain control (talking quietly and calmly to the client, medication), they can be effective. Nevertheless, these emergency interventions do present ethical dilemmas for social workers, for whom client dignity and self-determination are professional values. The least restrictive intervention under the circumstances should guide practitioners.

Crisis residences provide temporary housing for persons with acute psychiatric problems. Alternatives to hospitalization, rather than shelters, they promote the remission of psychiatric symptoms, stabilization, and resolution of the problem that led to the acute state. The primary means of treatment are medication and crisis counseling. The goal is to restore the client to a previous level of functioning and to return the client to a suitable living arrangement in the community. Crisis residences have diverse admission criteria and limitations on the length of stay.

Crisis residential care may be provided in a separate facility (such as a crisis house) or in units within a community complex of residential facilities (such as purchased shelter in boarding houses or hotels). A study in which these two forms of crisis housing were compared found that although both were effective in preventing rehospitalization and promoting stabilization, there was more staff burnout associated with the crisis house and more substance abuse with purchased housing (Bond et al., 1989).

La Posada, a crisis-oriented residential treatment center in San Francisco, provides an example of the use of crisis housing as an alternative to hospitalization (Weisman, 1985). Here the social rehabilitation model adopted by some halfway houses is combined with crisis intervention to create a highly structured, task-oriented, therapeutic program. Participants are expected to behave appropriately and assume responsibility for assigned tasks such as cooking, attending group meetings, applying for entitlements, and looking for an apartment. By the time of discharge (approximately 9 days after admission), the client is engaged in rehabilitation within the community.

Day hospitalization is a kind of partial hospitalization that constitutes another community-based alternative to complete hospitalization when a client is in an acute crisis (Rosie, 1987). It may be run administratively by a hospital or an outpatient mental health center. Clients participate in a therapeutic program during the day but return to their usual living quarters at night. Research to date indicates that this is a cost-effective, satisfying alternative to hospitalization for a large number of clients (Rosie, 1987). One study found that clients find programs most helpful when they are supportive and structured, whereas staff think that the program is most effective when personal problems are discussed (Goldstein et al., 1988). The social rehabilitative dimensions of partial hospitalization will be discussed later in this chapter.

During an acute crisis, however, *hospitalization* may be the best alternative. A single or a number of forms of hospitalization may be available in a given community, for example, an acute unit within a community or general hospital, private hospitals, Veterans Administration hospitals, and state psychiatric centers. When clients are dangerous to themselves or others, out of control, and unable to care for themselves, they need external control and care. A mental status examination will reveal whether the state criteria for hospitalization have been met. Mental health personnel who have the legal authority to commit clients to the hospital must be involved.

Hospitals vary in the quality of care provided, the individual attention given to patients, and their philosophy of care. Some hospitals primarily provide medication; others have a more aggressive therapeutic program. During hospitalization, the patient can be observed and medication can be monitored. The length of stay varies according to patient needs and local practices. Patients who are discharged before they achieve stabilization and those who leave early against medical advice (AMA) need more intensive follow-up in the community.

With the community as the primary locus of treatment, linkage with the local agencies should begin at once. In some communities, case managers and other mental health workers meet with hospital staff during the patient's hospitalization to make collaborative plans for discharge. Continuity between hospital and community is an essential component of community mental health practice.

Psychosocial Rehabilitation

Programs of psychosocial rehabilitation promote effectiveness in performing activities of daily living, problem solving, interpersonal skills, employability, and employment. In keeping with the philosophy of rehabilitation that was described in chapter 8, clients are encouraged to develop, practice, and perform psychosocial skills at the highest level possible in keeping with their individualized goals and ability to tolerate stress.

Partial hospitalization or day treatment provides structure, support, and activities that are found in total hospitals, and at the same time it enables the client to live in the community. Rosie (1987) describes three types of programs: (a) day hospitals, discussed earlier, which provide diagnostic and intervention services for persons with acute symptoms; (b) day treatment programs, which are used on a limited-time, goal-directed basis for clients whose acute symptoms are remitting, such as persons who are making the transition from the hospital to the community; and (c) day care centers, which focus on the maintenance or rehabilitation of chronic psychiatric and psychogeriatric clients. Although these variations are not present or differentiated in every community, they do describe the kinds of programs that can meet the needs of persons with serious and persistent psychiatric disabilities.

Partial hospitalization programs may occupy their own buildings, or may be situated in wings of hospitals or within community mental health centers. A minimum of a large community room and an office are needed. Self-contained programs located in houses with comfortable living rooms, dining areas, kitchens, laundry facilities, showers, and group therapy rooms provide a naturalistic environment in which rehabilitation can take place. Such settings lend themselves to the teaching of skills in food preparation, laundry, housecleaning, and personal grooming. With sufficient space, clients can have some, but not constant, social interaction with others.

Daily programs are planned cooperatively among clients and staff. Some programs begin with community meetings in which the daily, weekly, or monthly activities are discussed and responsibilities are allocated. Groups make decisions about who is to do what (e.g., shop for lunch, find out about baseball tickets), when, and how. The outcome is a schedule of planned activities. An example of a day in one program is described in Table 9.3.

The therapeutic possibilities of partial hospitalization programs are manifold. Some incorporate psychodrama, poetry therapy, yoga, medication compliance groups, and social skills training, as well as formal presentations by outside experts (e.g., a nutritionist) into their program. Others conduct individual, group, and family therapy routinely or to those who can benefit from it.

TABLE 9.3

Schedule of Activities for February 1

Time	Activity
8:30 A.M.	Arrive; informal socializing over decaffeinated coffee. Card playing and checkers.
9:00 A.M.	Community meeting is convened in living room. Schedule for February is discussed, including Valentine's Day dance. Reminder about Dr. Jones' clinic later in day; revision of list of who needs to see doctor. Discussion of headlines in the day's news.
9:30 A.M.	Stretching, yoga, and relaxation exercises.
10:15 A.M.	Occupational therapy. Group discussion, organizing, and beginning making of decorations for the Valentine's Day dance.
11:30 A.M.	Lunch preparation group leaves to prepare lunch; rest clean up.
12:00 noon	Lunch and cleanup after lunch.
1:00 P.M.	Walk to library; tour by librarian on arrival.
2:00 P.M.	Ms. Nancy Smith, home economist, will talk about budgeting one's money.
3:00 P.M.	Dr. Jones will conduct medication clinic for those due for checkup. Others have free time or time to meet with social worker.
4:00 P.M.	Leave for day.
7:00 P.M.	Psychoeducational group for families (Session 3).

Training in activities required for daily living are incorporated in partial hospitalization programs. Clients' functioning levels should be assessed individually; the kinds of training developed should be consistent with the level of skill, comprehension, and disability of subgroups of clients. Furthermore, the topics should be relevant to the client's developmental stage and life-style. Some areas that can be addressed in activities training are living within a budget, using public transportation, meal preparation, shopping for clothes, housecleaning, dating, and personal grooming. Clients who are parents may benefit from sessions on child care. Clients who already have some of these skills can assist the staff in communicating and demonstrating these skills. Clients should have the opportunity to perform the skills after they are taught or modeled. For a fuller discussion of social skills training, see chapter 10.

Regardless of the specific program components, partial hospitalization provides opportunities for socialization for persons who are likely to withdraw from others when they are left on their own. They give participants a place to go and a means to broaden their activities, skills, and interests. In the course of the significant amount of time that is spent in these programs, staff are able to observe and monitor clients' adaptation to the community and prevent incipient problems.

Vocational rehabilitation is another important component of psychosocial rehabilitation. Clients can not only be helped to develop skills related to a particular line of employment; they can be helped to use transportation to get to a job, arrive at a job on time, get along with others, and take orders from supervisors. Furthermore, they can be trained in ways to look for a job, develop a résumé, and handle an interview. Once they have found a suitable job, they can be helped to keep it (Bellack & Mueser, 1986).

Vocational rehabilitation follows from an assessment of a person's work skills (Jacobs, 1988). This is based on the individual's prior education and work history, observed behavior, and reports from previous employers, the client, or the client's family. The federal Office of Vocational Rehabilitation has local affiliates that provide testing, counseling, training, and placement of persons with physical, developmental, and psychiatric disabilities who qualify. In some cases this agency will pay for a client's college education or vocational training and for medical care required for rehabilitation.

Many communities have *sheltered workshops,* which employ persons with severe and persistent psychiatric and other difficulties. These are low-pressure, noncompetitive work settings in which clients can learn vocational skills. Generally the work days are shorter than the usual 8 hours; in some cases, clients may work only a few days. These organizations develop contractual relationships with industries for tasks such as cutting, sorting, and bagging items for retail sale. Clients are assigned particular jobs and paid at a rate below the minimum wage that is related to the speed and efficiency with which the client performs the task. For example, if a client bags 20 items in an hour, whereas an "expert" (staff member) can bag 40, the client is paid half of minimum wage.

Clients are trained to perform a variety of tasks and are encouraged to improve their performance. They are able to demonstrate progress and receive monetary rewards for performing more and more complicated tasks at a faster rate. Furthermore, clients benefit from the experience of getting to work on time, handling interpersonal relationships on the job, and using their time productively. For some clients, working in a sheltered workshop is a step toward competitive employment. Others maintain their workshop jobs for years.

An alternative and more naturalistic approach to vocational rehabilitation than the sheltered workshop is the *clubhouse model,* which was developed by Fountain House in New York and replicated nationally and internationally. Predicated on the idea that work is central to rehabilitation (Propst, 1988), the model is realized in a prevocational work-oriented day program, a transitional employment program, and independent employment.

Fountain House is a club founded in 1948 by former psychiatric patients desiring social support. It has since been housed in an attractive meeting house in midtown Manhattan and has developed an amalgam of social, vocational, and housing programs. Participants are called *members,* not clients, who belong to a community that values them:

> All members are made to feel, on a daily basis, that their presence is expected, that someone actually anticipates their coming to the program each morning and that their coming makes a difference to someone, indeed to everyone, in the program. At the door each morning every member is greeted by staff and members of the house, and in all ways each member is made to feel welcome in coming to the clubhouse.
>
> All program elements are constructed in such a way as to ensure that each member feels wanted as a contributor to the program. Each program is intentionally set up so that it will not work without the cooperation of the members; indeed, the entire program

would collapse if members did not contribute. Every function of the program is shared by the members working side by side with staff; staff never ask members to carry out functions which they do not also perform themselves. (Beard, Propst, & Malamud, 1982; p. 47)

The *Prevocational Day Program* involves clients in running the clubhouse. Members, side by side with a small staff, perform tasks that need to get accomplished. These include typing, answering telephones, running the cafeteria and coffee shop, giving tours, housecleaning, operating the duplicating machine, and data entry. Because the program is voluntary and members feel wanted and needed, motivation tends to be high. In the process of participating, members become aware of their abilities, learn new skills, and gain confidence (Propst, 1988).

Through the *Transitional Employment Program* (TEP), members are able to hold regular entry-level jobs in the community on a temporary, part-time basis. Employment placements are in business firms in the New York metropolitan area that enter a contractual agreement in which Fountain House guarantees that the work will be done but retains flexibility in splitting the job between members. If a member is unable to go to work one day, the person with whom he or she shares the job can substitute. If neither is able to work, a staff member works in their place. Members are paid the going rate for that job (minimum wage or above) for the number of hours they work. They spend the part of the day in which they are not at the TEP job at Fountain House (Propst, 1988). A survey of 120 facilities operating TEPs across the country revealed that as of August 31, 1988, there were 708 employers who provided 1421 job opportunities that generated $5,533,735 in taxable income (Fountain House, 1988).

The third vocational option, *independent employment,* provides support for full-time independent employment. This most recent program is available to those who aspire to and feel capable of holding a competitive job. Fountain House has an independent employment unit that offers counseling, advice, workshops, and placement services to members looking for jobs and evening and weekend supports to those who are already employed (Propst, 1988).

In addition to the vocational programs, Fountain House has an evening and weekend social program and a housing program (Beard, Propst, and Malamud, 1982). During evenings, weekends, and holidays, when most working people have time off, members have opportunities to socialize with each other, attend dramatic performances, and celebrate holidays together. During these times members are able to maintain friendships and receive needed support. The housing program subleases low-rent apartments that are leased by Fountain House to small groups of members who live together. The combination of social, vocational, and housing programs makes it possible for many former psychiatric patients to live productively in the community. A follow-up study of members in the program found that over a 3.5-year period, over 44 percent of members' time was spent in employment. Time spent in isolation in the community was reduced. Employment seemed to be associated with longevity in the program (Malamud, n.d.). An evaluation of a similar employment program based at Thresholds in Chicago revealed that in a 30-month period between 1981 and 1983, 41 percent of the members of their club were employed in contrast with reported rates for similar populations of between 10 and 20 percent (Bond et al., 1984).

Health Care

Persons with serious mental health disabilities are also subject to physical health problems. Because of difficulties in cognitive processing, distortions in self-awareness, as well as mistrust of outsiders, many individuals are not able to identify health problems or are unwilling to discuss them with others. Furthermore, they may not eat properly and may abuse prescribed medication as well as alcohol and drugs. It is incumbent on the clinical social worker/case manager to be sensitive to physical health issues and to assure that the client receives health care.

Most persons with chronic mental illnesses are able to qualify for either Medicare or Medicaid, which should cover expenses of visits to physicians and medication. Veterans may be treated in Veterans' Administration facilities. Advocacy for those who do not qualify for medical services may be effective. Those who still are unable to receive benefits can be helped to secure a job with medical benefits, or to obtain medical care at public hospitals or clinics.

Health care management should be part of the client's individual service plan. The client should be helped to maintain a balanced diet, live in a clean environment, and identify symptoms of health problems. The client should be linked with a doctor, clinic, or hospital in which ongoing and emergency health care are available. The client's teeth, eyes, ears, and feet may need the attention of specialists.

Women clients of childbearing age can use the services of a family planning clinic or an understanding gynecologist. They should be provided with information about birth control, sexuality, and childbearing. The impact of birth control pills on their physical and mental health, as well as the interaction between psychotropic medication and pregnancy and lactation (Mogul, 1985), should be discussed. Furthermore, women should be helped to protect themselves from situations that make them vulnerable to sexual exploitation, such as homelessness.

Schwab, Drake, and Burghardt (1988) recommend that in dealing with health care providers, the case manager act as a "culture broker." As such, the case manager should gain an understanding of the client's mental functioning; of how the client perceives his or her body, symptoms, and the medical care system; and of the constellation of the client's social system, so that communication with a physician who does not understand the client's social world can be facilitated. Furthermore, barriers to receiving health care should be identified. Utilizing personal observations and knowledge obtained from the client's medical and psychiatric records, the case manager can bridge the gap between the client's culture and the medical system, interpreting one to the other.

Entitlements

Serious and persistent mental illness entitles persons to a range of public benefits for which they must apply. Each entitlement has its own set of requirements and stipulations. The case manager should be familiar with the programs for which an individual may qualify, eligibility requirements, and the application procedures. The case manager should work closely with the client in applying for benefits.

If clients are not working or if they are underemployed, they may be eligible for some form of financial assistance. One can qualify for Social Security disability insurance on the basis of one's own work history and mental or physical impairment; or because one is a widow or a disabled child of a person with a work history. Those who qualify for Social Security are also eligible for Medicare. If the Social Security allotment is not sufficient or if the applicants turn out to be ineligible, they can apply for Supplemental Security Income (SSI) and Medicaid. To qualify as "permanently and totally disabled" under Social Security or SSI, medical documentation must be provided. Other possible sources of financial assistance are Aid to Families with Dependent Children (AFDC) for parents and their children, Veterans' Administration disability pensions, and local public welfare programs. Persons who have work histories might be eligible for disability or retirement insurance that was a fringe benefit where they worked.

Another entitlement is food stamps. Those who are eligible for other forms of public assistance may also be eligible for food stamps. Some clients may qualify for food stamps only, or for stamps on an emergency basis only. Food stamps can be used instead of money at grocery stores. Certain restrictions apply; for example, they cannot be used to pay for cigarettes or alcohol.

With the burgeoning population of homeless, many soup kitchens and pantries have come into existence. Food kitchens provide one or two free meals a day; food pantries supply applicants with canned goods, cheese, and other food items. Often these establishments are housed in churches or community centers. Shelters for the homeless also provide users with free meals.

Clients in poor financial straits might also receive help from religious organizations that have funds for the poor. The case manager may have to make several telephone calls and personal visits to receive this kind of help. Emergency help may also be available from the city, from generous individuals, and from families of clients.

Support Networks

Most of the community resources that have been described comprise a formal network of supports that can be mobilized to help an individual client adapt to community life. Mental health services, programs of entitlement, and housing units are needed components of the formal system. Institutional services, they tend to be impersonal. Embedded in these services, however, are personal relationships that can emerge naturally and serve as a more intimate helping resource.

Natural supports are persons and groups that develop over time and through everyday interactions. These are made up primarily of people who care—one's family, however one defines it, friends, neighbors, people with whom one prays, and coworkers. They also might include hairdressers, storekeepers, bartenders, landlords, and others with whom one interacts informally. The persons one meets in support groups and community programs can become part of the natural system of supports.

Research on the social networks of persons with severe mental health problems has found that this population tends to have small, dense networks that are comprised primarily of kin and that the networks contain few clusters (groups of people who interact with each other) and lack reciprocity (Cutler, 1984). Considering that persons with schizophrenia and some of the other severe disorders withdraw from social relationships and are threatened by emotional intensity, their narrow social world is not surprising.

One of the responsibilities of the case manager is to help the client build and expand supportive social networks. Interpersonal relationships are important because they serve as a buffer against stress and involve the individual in meaningful participation in the community. The case manager can help the client develop social networks by increasing opportunities for relationships to develop. This can result from linking the client with social and recreational groups, encouraging the client to reconnect with persons who were meaningful to him or her in the past and to maintain those current social contacts who might become friends, promoting the client's use of psychosocial rehabilitation services, creating socialization groups, and supporting the client's participation in the world of work.

The family is an important social support for some clients. Among family, the potential to care, give, and help is great and should be engaged. Nevertheless, one should also take care to discourage the family's overinvolvement and the perpetuation of a client's dependence on them. Thus the relationship with family should be sustained but the intensity reduced. Some communities have volunteer programs, such as Compeer, in which community people provide peer support and friendship to persons with severe mental disabilities. For clients who do not have kin, or do not have relatives who live nearby or are supportive, friends and service providers become the equivalent of a family.

As the client enlarges his or her social networks, conflict may occur. Conflict may arise when the client does not reciprocate in a relationship. If this is so, the client needs to be helped to give as well as receive, learning that will affect the development of future relationships (Cutler, 1984). Furthermore, the case manager can help the client to accurately interpret vagaries in interpersonal relationships, manage their intensity, and solve problems.

Consumer Groups

Persons with severe mental disorders and their families not only deal with the unpredictable course of the illnesses, they also experience the stigma that is still attached to being mentally ill and feel isolated from normative living. No institutionalized resource can compensate for the emotional pain, suffering, and loneliness that accompany severe mental disorders.

Consumer groups have arisen to help clients and their families deal with the stigma, the disease, and the mental health service delivery system. As persons who have "been there," they know what it is like to have been mistreated or to have needs, wants, and rights that are not recognized by service providers. Client consumers (primary consumers) may be able to recall horrible experiences of being locked in psychiatric wards, where they were beaten, sexually abused, or ignored. Parent consumers (secondary consumers) know what it is like to be blamed for a child's illness but excluded from the treatment process. Groups that call themselves *consumers* see themselves as citizens who have the right to receive, evaluate, choose, and refuse services.

Client consumers have formed self-help groups through which they can help each other solve problems individually and take actions collectively. They may give advice to other consumers about particular mental health services, psychiatrists, or social workers; work for the creation of new resources; or lobby for a desired bill. Some of these groups are unique to a locality or state; others are part of a national network. Professionals may be allowed to join but not vote.

The National Alliance of Mental Patients, which holds a radical perspective, is critical of the disease model of mental illness and of the emphasis on drug therapy. It emphasizes client empowerment and self-help. The National Mental Health Consumers' Organization represents a more moderate political position. Other consumer groups provide a forum in which clients can share problems and receive help from each other. Recovery, Inc., and Emotions Anonymous, for example, hold regular meetings in which persons with diverse mental health problems can receive support. The National Depressive and Manic Depressive Association provides support and advocates for persons with mood disorders, who are sometimes overshadowed by the louder voices of advocates for schizophrenia.

One of the most influential of the secondary consumer groups is the National Alliance for the Mentally Ill (NAMI) and its local affiliates. NAMI represents the interests of families of persons with severe psychiatric problems. On the local level, they educate members and the public about mental illness, provide information about resources, promote the development of better aftercare services, and the like. NAMI members are sensitive to the historical trend of holding parents responsible for the development of mental illness in their children. In contrast with the National Alliance of Mental Patients, NAMI holds that mental illness is a disease.

Social worker/case managers have a number of responsibilities in relation to consumer groups. For one, they should become knowledgeable about the groups in their own community and inform clients and families about their existence, what they do, and the potential benefits (information, social contacts, empowerment, a source of meaning). Second, social workers should get to know members of consumer groups and listen to their grievances. Some of their complaints can be addressed through mediation, advocacy, and brokerage. Third, social workers might want to join some of these groups.

SUMMARY

Social work intervention with the chronically mentally ill utilizes case management, a means of coordination that is interpreted in different ways. Some case managers are nonprofessionals who process paperwork and make telephone contacts. Four models of case management that are more active are the rehabilitation, assertive community treatment, developmental-acquisition, and Rockland County models.

Case managers perform assessments, monitor clients' progress, develop individually tailored service plans, and link clients with resources. Clinical social workers who are case managers may also be therapists in so far as they make assessments and intervene with modalities that are appropriate for the population. Intervention methods that are used with persons with severe mental disabilities are problem solving, crisis intervention, and family intervention. An additional approach, social skills training, as well as family intervention will be discussed in the next chapter.

Case managers refer clients to a number of community resources that support and rehabilitate clients. Clients need aftercare, especially medication and support. A number of housing alternatives are possible, depending on the resources of the particular community. These vary in the closeness of supervision and the provision of a rehabilitative component. Among the varieties of housing are board-and-care homes, family care (foster) homes, transitional facilities (group homes and halfway houses), cooperative housing, and independent living. Clients who "fall through the cracks" may end up homeless or in jail.

Communities also provide a range of crisis and psychosocial rehabilitation services. Emergency services in hospitals or clinics address eruptions of psychiatric symptoms and reactions to stress. Some communities have day treatment and crisis residences that help clients "cool down" from a crisis. Psychosocial rehabilitation services include partial hospitalization and vocational rehabilitation programs. Fountain House in New York runs an exemplary program in which clients are able to develop confidence and skills to work part-time or independently in the community.

Other important resources that are part of the community support "package" are health care, entitlements, and consumer supports. Persons with severe psychiatric disabilities have physical health needs that can easily be overlooked. The case manager should link clients with medical, dental, ophthalmological, and other relevant resources. Furthermore, they may need special attention to nutritional and gynecological needs.

Many of the chronically mentally ill are poor. As disabled adults, they are likely to be eligible for entitlements. Among the sources of financial aid are Social Security, Supplemental Security Income, Medicare, Medicaid, Aid to Families with Dependent Children, food stamps, and public assistance. A work history may entitle them to disability or retirement insurance. Other financial resources can be mobilized from community organizations, such as churches. In an emergency, family and volunteer donors may be called upon.

Most of the community supports that have been described constitute a formal network of supports. Informal or natural supports arise historically and through social interactions. Because supports can provide a buffer against stress and they promote normalization and integration, they are a valuable resource to the client. The case manager helps clients expand their social networks, manage interpersonal conflicts, and learn to give as well as take from others.

Clients and their families are primary and secondary consumers of mental health services. Their first-hand experience with the system has given them insights and awareness of unmet needs. Consumers have organized groups in which they can provide mutual support to each other and organize politically. The groups have a range of perspectives that diverge from each other and from those of mental health providers. Clinical social workers should become familiar with the various groups and the benefits they can offer to clients. Clients should be apprised of these groups; social workers may want to join them, too.

CASE STUDY

Estrella and Juan Martinez, both 25 and Mexican Americans, live in a barrio in California. The couple met 5 years ago in a state psychiatric hospital, where they were both hospitalized with schizophrenia. After they were discharged, they set up housekeeping together for a while and married after Estrella became pregnant with their daughter, Lucia. Lucia is now four and

Estrella is pregnant. Although neither Estrella nor Juan works regularly, they have income from AFDC and SSI as well as food stamps and Medicaid. (Occasionally Juan is able to earn money doing odd jobs.) They have close ties with Juan's family in the barrio, but do not socialize with anyone other than kin.

The Martinezes have had a bilingual Mexican American case manager who has helped them obtain aftercare services in a culturally sensitive mental health center. Furthermore, this case manager has acted as "culture broker" in arranging Estrella's prenatal care and Lucia's entry into a Headstart program. Two months ago, this case manager was promoted and replaced by a new case manager who does not speak Spanish and knows very little about the Martinezes' culture and about the needs of persons with schizophrenia. Around the same time, Juan's parents moved away and Estrella had a miscarriage. These stressors put the Martinezes at risk of decompensating.

How should the case manager intervene in this case to promote support and buffer stress in a culturally sensitive way? What community services might be helpful?

DISCUSSION QUESTIONS

1. Identify problems in the mental health delivery system that impeded the diagnosis and treatment of Larry Leeds. How might such problems be prevented?
2. What is case management? Discuss the basic functions of the case manager.
3. What additional skills does the professional social worker offer in the performance of case management?
4. Discuss the importance of the client–worker relationship in case management with persons with severe and persistent mental disorders. How "intense" should such a relationship be?
5. Compare the four models of case management that were described in this chapter. How are they alike? How do they differ?
6. Consider the mental health delivery system in your community. What kinds of services are provided in relation to the categories described in the Community Support Services section (e.g., aftercare, types of housing, psychosocial rehabilitation, etc.)? What needs are met? Identify gaps in services in your community.
7. What opportunities are available in your community for paid employment for persons with severe psychiatric disorders?
8. Why is it important to assess the physical health needs of persons with severe mental disabilities? What are some special health needs of women?
9. How can the clinical social worker/case manager help clients develop social supports?
10. Identify primary and secondary consumer groups in your community. What are the concerns of each group? How do these groups relate to each other and to mental health providers?

REFERENCES

Abramson, M. F. (1972). The criminalization of mentally disordered behavior. *Hospital and Community Psychiatry, 23,* 101–105.

Altman, H. (1982). Collaborative discharge planning for the deinstitutionalized. *Social Work, 27,* 422–427.

Baxter, E., & Hopper, K. (1984). Trouble on the streets: The mentally disabled homeless poor. In J. A. Talbott (Ed.), *The chronic mental patient: Five years later* (pp. 49–62). Orlando, FL: Grune & Stratton.

Beard, J. H., Propst, R. N., & Malamud, T. J. (1982). The Fountain House model of psychiatric rehabilitation. *Psychosocial Rehabilitation, 5*(1), 47–53.

Bellack, A. S., & Mueser, K. T. (1986). A comprehensive treatment program for schizophrenia and chronic mental illness. *Community Mental Health Journal, 22,* 175–189.

Berzon, P., & Lowenstein, B. (1984). A flexible model of case management. In B. Pepper & H. Ryglewicz (Eds.), *Advances in treating the young adult chronic patient* (pp. 49–57). San Francisco: Jossey-Bass.

Blake, R. (1987). Boarding home residents: New underclass in the mental health system. *Health and Social Work, 12,* 85–90.

Bond, G. R., et al. (1989). A comparison of two crisis housing alternatives to psychiatric hospitalization. *Hospital and Community Psychiatry, 40,* 177–183.

Bond, G. R., Dincin, J., Setz, P. J., & Witheridge, T. F. (1984). The effectiveness of psychosocial rehabilitation: A summary of research at Thresholds. *Psychosocial Rehabilitation Journal, 7,* 6–22.

Budson, R. D. (1978). *The psychiatric halfway house.* Pittsburgh, PA: University of Pittsburgh Press.

Burger, A. S., Kimelman, L., Lurie, A., & Rabiner, C. J. (1978). Congregate living for the mentally ill: Patients as tenants. *Hospital and Community Psychiatry, 29,* 590–593.

Christenfeld, R., Toro, P. A., Brey, M., & Haveliwala, Y. A. (1985). Effects of community placement on chronic mental patients. *American Journal of Community Psychology, 13,* 125–138.

Cutler, D. (1984). Networks. In J. A. Talbott (Ed.), *The chronic mental patient: Five years later* (pp. 253–266). Orlando, FL: Grune & Stratton.

Dixon, S. L. (1987). *Working with people in crisis* (2nd ed.). Columbus, OH: Merrill.

Epstein, L. (1988). *Helping people: The task-centered approach.* Columbus, OH: Merrill.

Flax, J. W. (1982). Crisis intervention with the young adult patient. In B. Pepper & H. Ryglewicz (Eds.), *The young adult chronic patient* (pp. 69–75). San Francisco: Jossey-Bass.

Fountain House (1988). *Transitional employment.* (Survey Memorandum No. 290, pp. 718–721). New York: Fountain House.

Geiser, R., Hoche, L., & King, J. (1988). Respite care for mentally ill patients and their families. *Hospital and Community Psychiatry, 39,* 291–295.

Gerhart, U. C., & Brooks, A. D. (1983). The social work practitioner and antipsychotic medications. *Social Work, 28,* 454–460.

Goering, P. N., Wasylenki, D. A., Farkas, M., Lancee, W. J., & Ballantyne, R. (1988). What difference does case management make? *Hospital and Community Psychiatry, 39,* 272–276.

Goldmeier, J., Shore, M. F., & Mannino, F. V. (1977). Cooperative apartments: New programs in community mental health. *Health and Social Work, 2,* 119–140.

Goldstein, J. M., Cohen, P., Lewis, S. A., & Struening, E. L. (1988). Community treatment environments: Patient vs. staff evaluations. *The Journal of Nervous and Mental Disease, 176,* 227–233.

Goldstrom, I. D., & Manderscheid, R. W. (1983). A descriptive analysis of Community Support Program case managers serving the chronically mentally ill. *Community Mental Health Journal, 19,* 17–26.

Gottesfeld, H. (1977). *Alternatives to psychiatric hospitalization.* New York: Gardiner Press.

Grella, C. E., & Grusky, O. (1989). Families of the seriously mentally ill and their satisfaction with services. *Hospital and Community Psychiatry, 40,* 831–835.

Harris, M., & Bergman, H. C. (1987). Case management with the chronically mentally ill: A clinical perspective. *American Journal of Orthopsychiatry, 57,* 296–302.

Intagliata, J. (1982). Improving the quality of community care for the chronically mentally disabled: The role of case management. *Schizophrenia Bulletin, 8,* 655–673.

Intagliata, J., Willer, B., & Egri, G. (1986). Role of the family in case management of the mentally ill. *Schizophrenia Bulletin, 12,* 699–708.

Jacobs, H. E. (1988). Vocational rehabilitation. In R. P. Liberman (Ed.), *Psychiatric rehabilitation of chronic mental patients* (pp. 245–284). Washington, DC: American Psychiatric Press.

Johnson, P. J., & Rubin, A. (1983). Case management in mental health: A social work domain? *Social Work, 28,* 49–55.

Joint Commission, Mental Health, Substance Abuse, MR/DD Standards. (1989). *CSM: Consolidated Standards Manual.* Chicago, IL: Author.

Kurtz, L. F., Bagarozzi, D. A., & Pollane, L. P. (1984). Case management in mental health. *Health and Social Work, 9,* 201–211.

Lamb, H. R. (1984). Alternatives to hospitals. In J. A. Talbott (Ed.), *The chronic mental patient: Five years later* (pp. 215–232). Orlando, FL: Grune & Stratton.

Lamb, H. R. (1980). Therapist–case managers: More than brokers of services. *Hospital and Community Psychiatry, 31,* 762–764.

Lamb, H. R., & Goertzl, V. (1971). Discharged mental patients—are they really in the community? *Archives of General Psychiatry, 24,* 29–34.

Lehman, A. F., Possidente, S., & Hawker, F. (1986). The quality of life of chronic patients in a state hospital and community residences. *Hospital and Community Psychiatry, 37,* 901–907.

Malamud, T. J. (n.d.) Community adjustment: Evaluation of the clubhouse model for psychiatric rehabilitation. *Rehab Brief: Bringing Research into Effective Focus, 19*(2), 1–4.

McLaughlin, P. (1988). The Fairweather Lodge Society: Community residences combining employment, housing and a peer society. *TIE Lines, 5*(2), 3–5.

Modrcin, M., Rapp, C. A., & Poertner, J. (1988). The evaluation of case management services with the chronically mentally ill. *Evaluation and Program Planning, 11,* 307–314.

Mogul, K. M. (1985). Psychological considerations in the use of psychotropic drugs with women patients. *Hospital and Community Psychiatry, 36,* 1080–1085.

O'Connor, G. G. (1988). Case management: System and practice. *Social Casework, 69,* 97–106.

Ohio Department of Mental Health. (1987, August). *Case management training part 1: The delivery of case management in an integrated mental health system.* Columbus, OH.

Pepper, B., & Ryglewicz, H. (1985). The developmental residence: A "missing link" for young adult chronic patients. *TIE Lines, 2*(3), 1–3.

Phipps, C., & Liberman, R. P. (1988). Community support. In R. P. Liberman (Ed.), *Psychiatric rehabilitation of chronic mental patients* (pp. 285–311). Washington, DC: American Psychiatric Press.

Propst, R. N. (1988). The clubhouse model and the world of work. *TIE Lines, 5*(2), 1–2.

Rapp, C. A., & Chamberlain, R. (1985). Case management services for the chronically mentally ill. *Social Work, 30,* 417–422.

Rosie, J. S. (1987). Partial hospitalization: A review of recent literature. *Hospital and Community Psychiatry, 38,* 1291–1299.

Sands, R. G. (1984). Correlates of success and lack of success of deinstitutionalization.

Community Mental Health Journal, 20, 223–235.

Schwab, B., Drake, R. E., & Burghardt, E. M. (1988). Health care of the chronically mentally ill: The culture broker model. *Community Mental Health Journal, 24,* 174–184.

Stein, L. I., & Diamond, R. J. (1985). A program for difficult-to-treat patients. In L. I. Stein & M. A. Test (Eds.), *New directions for mental health services: The training in community living model: A decade of experience* (no. 26, pp. 29–39). San Francisco: Jossey-Bass.

Stein, L. I., & Test, M. A. (1982). Community treatment of the young adult patient. In B. Pepper & H. Ryglewicz (Eds.), *New directions for mental health services: The young adult chronic patient* (no. 14, pp. 57–67). San Francisco: Jossey-Bass.

Stein, L. I., & Test, M. A. (Eds.). (1985). *New directions for mental health services: The training in community living model: A decade of experience* (no. 26). San Francisco: Jossey-Bass.

Test, M. A. (1979). Continuity of care in community treatment. In L. I. Stein (Ed.), *New directions for mental health services: Community support systems for the long-term patient* (no. 2, pp. 15–23). San Francisco: Jossey-Bass.

Thompson, K. S., Griffith, E. E. H., & Leaf, P. J. (1990). A historical review of the Madison model of community care. *Hospital and Community Psychiatry, 41,* 625–634.

Torrey, E. F. (1988). *Surviving schizophrenia: A family manual* (rev. ed.). New York: Harper & Row.

Training in community living. (1983). *Practice Digest, 6,* 4–6.

Velasquez, J. S., & McCubbin, H. I. (1980). Towards establishing the effectiveness of community-based residential treatment: Program evaluation by experimental research. *Journal of Social Service Research, 3,* 337–359.

Weisman, G. K. (1985). Crisis-oriented residential treatment as an alternative to hospitalization. *Hospital and Community Psychiatry, 36,* 1302–1305.

Witheridge, T. F., & Dincin, J. (1985). The Bridge: An assertive outreach program in an urban setting. In L. I. Stein & M. A. Test (Eds.), *The training in community living model: A decade of Experience* (pp. 65–76). San Francisco: Jossey-Bass.

Zirul, D. W., Lieberman, A. A., & Rapp, C. A. (1989). Respite care for the chronically mentally ill: Focus for the 1990s. *Community Mental Health Journal, 25,* 171–184.

10 | Treatment Approaches with the Chronically Mentally Ill and Their Families

T reatment of persons with severe mental disabilities is facilitated through generic and specific approaches. The generic intervention approach—case management and the use of community supports—was described in chapter 9. In addition, three specific modes of intervention that are grounded in research (see chapter 8) are effective in controlling symptoms, promoting competent social functioning, and reducing environmental stress. These rehabilitative strategies—medication, social skills training, and family psychoeducation—are forms of tertiary prevention, described in chapter 1. As such, they promote and support clients' optimum psychosocial functioning and prevent decompensation and rehospitalization.

This chapter will begin with an overview on medication needs of persons with severe mental disabilities. Strategies through which social workers can promote medication compliance and advocate for changes in the medication regimen will be suggested. Next a form of treatment that can be implemented by social workers—social skills training—will be explained and illustrated through a case vignette. Then a form of family intervention—family psychoeducation—will be described. The chapter will conclude with a discussion on the selective use of psychotherapy.

MEDICATION

Psychotropic drugs are ordinarily used both to treat acute symptoms and to maintain the functioning of clients whose symptoms are less overt or in remission. Although the role of medication in treating persons in the latter situation is less clear than in the former (Bellack & Mueser, 1986), research on the community tenure of former hospital patients has consistently found a high association between noncompliance with a medication regimen and rehospitalization (Sands, 1984).

Psychiatrists are responsible for prescribing medication and supervising clients' use of medication over time. Community mental health nurses or their equivalents (e.g., psychiatric nurses) are responsible for the administration and monitoring of medication under the direction of the psychiatrist. As advocates of clients and consultants to psychiatrists and nurses, clinical social workers have a responsibility for observing clients' psychosocial functioning in the community and advocating for changes (Gerhart & Brooks, 1983). In the course of performing their work, social workers come to recognize clients' attitudes toward ingesting drugs, compliance or noncompliance with the medication regimen, side effects, and substance use.

Psychiatric assessments of the medication needs of clients take into consideration a client's physical health, individual and family health/mental health history, medication history, allergic reactions, age, sex, height, and weight, as well as findings from the mental status examination and diagnosis. Results of preliminary and intermittent physical examinations and laboratory tests guide the psychiatrist in the selection of appropriate drugs and in the monitoring of side effects. The psychiatrist should order tests that are related to the effects of particular drugs (e.g., liver function tests, complete blood count, electrocardiogram). Research findings, clinical experience, and the drug responses of the individual client also enter into decisions about which drugs to prescribe. The dosage is adjusted over time when the client's reactions to drugs can be observed not only by the psychiatrist but also by community mental health workers, the client, and others who interact with the client on a regular basis.

Medication ameliorates clients' symptoms, which are an expression of the client's subjective state, reaction to environmental stressors, and mental disorder. Specific gestalts of symptoms that persist over time suggest diagnoses, such as those described in the *DSM-III-R* (American Psychiatric Association, 1987). In turn, the symptoms and diagnosis suggest particular drugs or drug groups. Those medications that are used to treat persistent psychotic, bipolar, and depressive symptoms will be described here. (Medication for anxiety and less severe depression will be discussed in chapters 12 and 13.) The groups of medications considered are antipsychotic, antimanic, and antidepressant agents. Table 10.1 describes the medication groupings, target symptoms, and diagnoses. Note that there is considerable overlap in the use of drugs across diagnostic groups. In recent years, the use of more than one drug at a time (*polypharmacy*) has become more common (Torrey, 1988). In using a couple of drugs, the major diagnosis, major symptoms, and ancillary symptoms can be addressed simultaneously.

Antipsychotic Medication

The group of drugs that are employed to treat psychoses are known as antipsychotics, neuroleptics, or major tranquilizers (Kaplan & Sadock, 1988). Although psychotic symptoms are the primary target of these drugs, they also have a sedating effect. Antipsychotics are used to treat a variety of mental disorders with psychotic symptoms—schizophrenia (all subtypes), schizophreniform disorder, delusional disorder (with inconclusive success), organic disorders, and bipolar and major depressive mood disorders that have associated psychotic symptoms. They are used on a short-term basis to manage acute episodes and for long-term treatment of chronic mental disorders (Baldessarini & Cole, 1988). These drugs are capable of controlling (but not entirely eliminating) distracting hallucinations, cognitive disorganization, and agitation.

TABLE 10.1
Medication Groupings, Target Symptoms, and Diagnoses

Group	Symptoms	Diagnoses
Antipsychotic agents	Hallucinations Delusions Incoherence Bizarre behavior Stupor Mania Agitation	Schizophrenia Schizophreniform disorder Schizoaffective disorder Brief reactive psychosis Organic disorders with psychotic symptoms Major depression and bipolar disorder with psychotic symptoms (especially if mood incongruent)
Antimanic agents	Mania (euphoria, hyperactivity, pressured speech, grandiosity, flight of ideas, distractibility) Mood fluctuations	Bipolar disorder (all subtypes) Schizoaffective disorder with manic symptoms Cyclothymia Schizophrenia with mood component (as adjunctive medication)
Antidepressant agents	Dysphoria Sleep disturbances Weight loss or gain Appetite loss or gain Loss of pleasure or interest in life Fatigue, lethargy Morbid thoughts	Major depression Schizoaffective disorder with depression Schizophrenia (as adjunctive medication)

Sources: American Psychiatric Association (1987); Kaplan & Sadock (1988); Lukoff & Ventura (1988).

Neuroleptics are used widely to treat schizophrenia. They are most successful in the management of *positive, or florid, symptoms,* that is, overt expressions of unusual sensory experiences (hallucinations), disturbed thinking, incoherence, and/or bizarre behavior. They are less effective with *negative, or deficit, symptoms*—flat affect, poverty of speech, apathy, asociality, and/or impairment in attentionality (Andreasen, 1985). Unless medical science is able to come up with an "energizing" drug, the major treatment for negative symptoms is psychosocial (Andreasen, 1985; Strauss, 1985).

Antipsychotic drugs are classified into drug groups according to their chemical structure. The most well-known of these is the phenothiazine group, which includes the first neuroleptic that was discovered, chlorpromazine (Thorazine). The drug groups, subgroups, and respective trade names of major neuroleptics are listed in Table 10.2. If a client is not responsive to medication in one group, another group can be tried.

Antipsychotic drugs and drug groups can also be distinguished according to their potency. A high-potency drug is one in which a low dosage (e.g., 10 mg/day) is sufficient to address target symptoms. Examples of high-potency drugs are Haldol, Prolixin, and Stelazine. In contrast, Thorazine and Mellaril are low-potency drugs (the standard

TABLE 10.2
Antipsychotic (neuroleptic) Drugs

Group/Subgroup	Trade Name
Phenothiazines	
Chlorpromazine	Thorazine
Thioridazine	Mellaril
Trifluoperazine	Stelazine
Fluphenazine	Prolixin, Permitil
Thioxanthenes	
Chlorprothixenes	Taractan
Thiothixene	Navane
Dibenzoxazepines	
Loxapine	Loxitane
Butyrophenones	
Haloperidol	Haldol
Dihydroindoles	
Molindone	Moban, Lidone
Dibenzodiazepines	
Clozapine	Clozaril

Sources: Baldessarini & Cole (1988); Kaplan & Sadock (1988).

dosage for Thorazine is 400–1200 mg/day; Rifkin & Siris, 1987). A low dosage of a high-potency drug is the equivalent of a high dosage of a low-potency drug. Although these drugs are similar if prescribed in equivalent dosages, they differ in associated side effects (Kaplan & Sadock, 1988; Wittlin, 1988).

Antipsychotic drugs produce a number of effects, many of which are undesirable. *Sedation* is a calming response, produced especially by the low-potency antipsychotics. Sedation helps control agitation, aggressiveness, mania, and irritability, which may be desired effects. On the other hand, sedation induces sleep, lowers awareness, and limits responsiveness—which can interfere with the performance of everyday activities, work, and the operation of machinery. Sedative effects in the daytime can be minimized when a client takes the entire dosage at night (Kaplan & Sadock, 1988). *Extrapyramidal symptoms* (EPS) are disturbances in motor activity that are associated with the blockage of dopamine receptors (Wittlin, 1988). Among the variant symptoms are dystonias, parkinsonian symptoms, akathisia, akinesia, and tardive dyskinesia. Other side effects of antipsychotic drugs are anticholergic effects, postural hypotension, sexual and reproductive difficulties, and neuroleptic malignant syndrome (NMS). These adverse side effects are described in Table 10.3.

The prevention and treatment of side effects present a formidable challenge to psychiatrists. Prevention of tardive dyskinesia is facilitated by the use of low doses of antipsychotic drugs. Another strategy is to withdraw the neuroleptic—although this can result in a temporary worsening of symptoms (Baldessarini & Cole, 1988; Matorin & De Chillo, 1984; Reid, 1989; Wittlin, 1988). Sometimes antianxiety agents such as benzodiazepines are used to ease the effects of withdrawal (Simpson, Pi, & Sramek, 1986). Antiparkinsonian agents such as Cogentin, Akineton, Benadryl, and Artane, which are

TABLE 10.3
Disturbing Side Effects of Antipsychotic Drugs

Side Effect	Description
Dystonias	Muscular spasms of the throat, neck, eyes, jaws, tongue, back, or whole body. These are seen frequently during the first few days of treatment, especially in young men.
Parkinsonian symptoms	Characterized by rigidity, shuffling gait, muscle stiffness, stooped posture, drooling, and a regular, coarse tremor.
Akathisia	Muscular discomfort, manifested by motor restlessness. The client is unable to sit still and appears agitated.
Akinesia	Reduced motor activity, listlessness, low spontaneity, apathy.
Tardive dyskinesia	Involuntary movements, primarily of the face, tongue, mouth, and neck, but also of the extremities. These symptoms appear after prolonged use of neuroleptics.
Anticholergic symptoms	Symptoms include dry mouth, blurry vision, urine retention, and constipation. Nausea and vomiting are other possible symptoms.
Postural hypotension	A lowering of blood pressure related to changes in one's position. It is manifested by fatigue, loss of balance, fainting, and falling.
Neuroleptic malignant syndrome	A side effect of antipsychotic medication that is life threatening. Characterized by fever, akinesia, rigidity, delirium, dystonia, and abnormal behavior. On the surface, it looks like an acute form of schizophrenia.
Sexual and reproductive disturbances	These include difficulties having erections and ejaculating, low libido, breast enlargement, galactorrhea, and menstrual irregularities or amenorrhea. Together with such additional side effects as weight gain and skin disturbances, these symptoms can be especially disturbing to sexually active clients.

Sources: Baldessarini & Cole (1988); Cohen (1988); Kaplan & Sadock (1988); Rifkin & Siris (1987); Wittlin (1988).

used to manage extrapyramidal symptoms, are not effective with tardive dyskinesia and akathisia. Furthermore, antiparkinsonian agents, antipsychotics, and antidepressants contribute to the development of anticholergic symptoms. Medical management of anticholergic effects includes changing the drug or lowering the dosage. Clients are counseled to treat these symptoms by rinsing their mouths and taking laxatives (Kaplan

& Sadock, 1988). Postural hypotension is associated with the use of high dosages of low-potency antipsychotics and is especially common during the initial few days of treatment. It is managed by monitoring the blood pressure and counseling clients to rise slowly and prevent injuries (Kaplan & Sadock, 1988).

Antipsychotic drugs can also produce cardiac effects, jaundice, photosensitivity, blood disorders, visual problems, and allergic reactions (Baldessarini & Cole, 1988; Kaplan & Sadock, 1988). As a rule, the less potent drugs have fewer extrapyramidal side effects but are associated with more anticholinergic reactions and more postural hypotension, and are more sedating, whereas the more potent drugs produce more extrapyramidal symptoms but are less sedating and produce fewer anticholinergic effects (Baldessarini & Cole, 1988; Kaplan & Sadock, 1988; Wittlin, 1988). Many experts lean toward the use of high-potency drugs (Rifkin & Siris, 1987).

A new antipsychotic drug approved by the Federal Drug Administration for use under closely monitored conditions is clozapine (News and Notes, 1989). This medication promises to treat psychotic symptoms without precipitating side effects such as tardive dyskinesia (Torrey, 1988). Furthermore, it reduces negative symptoms (Kane et al., 1987). It appears to be effective with clients who have not responded to other antipsychotic drugs. Clozapine, however, poses the risks of agranulocytosis, which lowers the white blood cells, and seizures. To prevent potential problems of this drug from developing, white blood levels must be monitored weekly (Green & Salzman, 1990).

Antipsychotic drugs are administered orally or intramuscularly. Oral administration is respectful of clients' dignity, autonomy, and right to self-determination. Intramuscular "depot" preparations are long-acting solutions that are given to clients who do not comply with the prescribed medical treatment. Haloperidol (Haldol) and fluphenazine (Prolixin) can be administered intramuscularly. Depot preparations may be associated with increased side effects such as tardive dyskinesia and dystonia (Kaplan & Sadock, 1988).

A history of episodes of schizophrenia (i.e., chronicity) suggests that the client should remain on a maintenance dose of antipsychotic medication indefinitely. Many clinicians, however, lower the dosage over time for the client who is stable. When the client is under stress, an increase may be advised (Kaplan & Sadock, 1988). Because schizophrenia is a heterogeneous illness with diverse outcomes, alternative strategies have been used. Some persons with chronic schizophrenia are medicated on an intermittent basis (Kane & Lieberman, 1987). These individuals are closely monitored by clinicians and families. Upon recognition of the return of symptoms, the medication regimen is restored. This strategy allows clients to have periods in which they are not subjected to the adverse side effects described. An older strategy is to provide periodic "drug holidays" in which medication is eliminated for a weekend or so. Although research studies indicate that these are associated with increased risk of tardive dyskinesia (Simpson, Pi, and Sramek, 1986), this strategy may boost the morale of clients who have been on antipsychotic medication for long periods of time. Nevertheless, drug withdrawal may convince some clients that they do not need medication at all, leaving them at risk of the return of psychotic symptoms.

Research on the effectiveness of antipsychotic medication points to its ability to reduce acute psychotic symptoms (Rifkin & Siris, 1987) and prevent relapse and rehospitalization for clients on maintenance schedules (Kane & Lieberman, 1987). Nevertheless, many drawbacks remain. The multiple side effects and the long-term regimen that is usually recommended raise many questions about the risk–benefit ratio of medication (Gerhart & Brooks, 1983). Sedation, tardive dyskinesia, apathy, and bizarre movements interfere with normalization and integration into the community. Some clients may prefer to live with the risk of rehospitalization to the discomfort of side effects of neuroleptic medication.

Still, questions remain about the impact of antipsychotic medication on adult women. Many research studies on drugs exclude women of childbearing age, the rationale being that women's cyclic hormonal changes constitute a confounding variable (Mogul, 1985). It is important for women to know whether and how neuroleptics interact with their menstrual cycle, childbearing, and lactation. There is no evidence that antipsychotics are responsible for increased fetal malformations, but because antipsychotic agents penetrate the blood–placenta barrier and are secreted in human milk, it is recommended that these drugs be avoided during lactation and pregnancy, especially the first trimester (Baldessarini & Cole, 1988).

Other problems are associated with the use of antipsychotic medication by older adults with chronic mental illness, who also tend to be excluded from drug tests (Mogul, 1985). Because tardive dyskinesia is associated with a long-term consumption of neuroleptics, older clients are at high risk, if not already afflicted with the condition. Older women are particularly at risk of this condition (Simpson, Pi, & Sramek, 1986). A further consideration is that older clients may have other medical problems for which they are receiving medication that complicate diagnosis and the use of certain antipsychotics. Older adults are especially at risk for falling as a result of postural hypotonia. Generally older adults benefit from a lower dose of medication than younger clients.

Antimanic Agents

Other medications are used to treat bipolar disorder, its manic symptoms in particular (see Table 10.4). The most prevalent drug prescribed is lithium, a salt. Other drugs used are anticonvulsants (carbamazepine, valproic acid, and clonazepam) and calcium channel inhibitors.

Lithium is the standard treatment for the client with bipolar disorder. It is used prophylactically to prevent the recurrence of manic and depressive episodes. Lithium is also used during acute episodes, often together with an antipsychotic agent. The success

TABLE 10.4
Antimanic Agents

Lithium

Anticonvulsants
    Carbamazepine
    Valproic acid
    Clonazepam

Calcium channel inhibitor
    Verapamil

rate is reported to be between 60 and 80 percent (Kaplan & Sadock, 1988; Prien & Gelenberg, 1989). In addition, lithium has been used with some success in the treatment of schizoaffective disorder, cyclothymia, and bipolar II. With bipolar I (bipolar disorder, manic, depressed, or mixed), the *DSM-III-R* requires a history of a manic episode. Bipolar II disorder is characterized by a history of hypomania (low-grade mania) and at least one episode of major depression (Prien, 1987). Cyclothymia is an example of bipolar II. Some psychiatrists also use lithium and other manic agents as supplements to antipsychotic medications for persons whose primary symptoms are psychotic.

Lithium is prescribed initially after a physical examination and laboratory tests. It is problematic for pregnant women, persons with renal and cardiovascular disease, and individuals on low-salt diets (Dixson, 1981). Maintenance on lithium requires regular monitoring of lithium levels and periodic laboratory tests. The purpose of checking lithium blood levels is to assure that the client is receiving a therapeutic dose and is avoiding toxicity. (The margin between therapeutic and toxic doses is slim.) Persons on low-salt diets are at risk for toxicity (Baldessarini & Cole, 1988). The client who lives in the community has blood work monitored regularly and at decreasing frequencies (from every 2 weeks upon discharge to every 2 months after 6 months). The lithium level that is usually therapeutic for the client in an acute state (0.8–1.2 mEq/l) is higher than the level needed for maintenance in the community (0.6–0.8 mEq/l) (Kaplan & Sadock, 1988). Lithium carbonate is ingested at prescribed intervals on a daily basis.

Lithium produces some side effects that are mild and others which, in excess, are signs of lithium toxicity. The less serious side effects are weight gain, mild thirst, and headaches (Dixson, 1981). Among the signs of toxicity are severe episodes of diarrhea, vomiting, tremors, confusion, coma, and seizures—symptoms that can result in death (Kaplan & Sadock, 1988). Other effects include edema (fluid retention), frequent urination, and acne (Torrey, 1988). Clients should be counseled to report their side effects immediately. Social workers and other mental health professionals should observe bipolar clients' physical and mental states so that psychiatric intervention can be mobilized quickly, if needed.

As disturbing as these adverse effects may sound, they are fewer and less intrusive than those associated with antipsychotics. Most of these symptoms are not visible to others; thus, they do not interfere with normalization or integration. Clients with bipolar disorder who are treated with lithium remain alert, attentive, and in touch with their environment (Sands, 1985).

Lithium is a "miracle" drug for those individuals who respond to it. Nevertheless, there are substantial numbers who either do not respond to it, have disabling side effects, or cannot take it because of concurrent health difficulties. Lithium use during pregnancy and lactation poses risks to the mother and the unborn child (Baldessarini & Cole, 1988). Older adults who are vulnerable to renal complications are not good candidates for lithium (Prien, 1987). Among those who tend not to respond are the "rapid cyclers," who experience several episodes of mania or depression in a year's time, and persons with bipolar disorder, mixed (Prien & Gelenberg, 1989). Currently there are a few promising alternative drugs that can be used. The research trials for most of these, however, are incomplete.

Alternative Antimanic Agents.   Three anticonvulsive drugs that are possible alternatives to lithium are carbamazepine (Tegretol), valproic acid, and clonazepam. Of these, carbamazepine, a drug used to treat temporal lobe epilepsy, is the most promising and clonazepam is the least (Prien & Gelenberg, 1989). Although these drugs are still considered experimental as antimanic agents, some research indicates that carbamazepine is effective in cases that do not respond to lithium (Prien, 1987; Prien & Gelenberg, 1989). The three anticonvulsive drugs have been used alone or together with lithium. They all have side effects.

Another drug that has emerged as an alternative to lithium is verapamil, a calcium channel inhibitor. Like carbamazepine, this drug has been approved for other medical conditions (angina and hypertension), which it treats by blocking the influx of calcium to the cells. Research to date on the use of verapamil for long-term maintenance is inconclusive (Prien & Gelenberg, 1989).

Antipsychotic and antidepressant drugs are also used in the treatment of bipolar disorder. As mentioned earlier, antipsychotics are frequently used to treat acute mania. They work faster than lithium, which takes 1 week to 10 days to be effective. Neuroleptics are sometimes used on a long-term basis for individuals who have recurrent episodes of mania that are not controlled with lithium. Although antidepressants are sometimes used together with lithium to treat depression in clients with bipolar disorder (Kaplan & Sadock, 1988), research studies indicate that antidepressants can precipitate mania, hypomania, and rapid cycling (Prien, 1987).

Antidepressant Medication

Persons with serious and persistent mental disorders may suffer from major depression. This disabling condition produces dysphoria, loss of interest in pleasurable activities, and despair. Major depression is frequently endogenous (biologically based) and is accompanied by vegetative symptoms—sleep difficulties, loss of appetite, weight changes. The individual turns inward and is not responsive to others. Major depression can have associated psychotic features such as hallucinations, delusions, and stupor (Hirschfeld & Cross, 1987). Moreover, depressive episodes can recur.

Severe depression can be treated effectively with tricyclics, monoamine oxidose inhibitors (MAOIs), and some of the new alternative drugs (see Table 10.5). These remedies may be used in conjunction with antipsychotics and antimanic agents. Because the drugs that are used can become a means of suicide, a plan for medication management that is related to the risks should be developed. In cases in which the client is suicidal or psychotic, hospitalization may be necessary.

Tricyclic antidepressants (TCAs) represent a group of drugs that have a similar chemical structure and effect on the neurotransmitter amines. The first of these compounds that was developed is imipramine (Tofranil). Others include amitriptyline (Elavil), trimipramine (Surmontil), doxepin (Sinequan), desipramine (Norpramin), nortriptyline (Aventyl), and protriptyline (Vivactil) (Baldessarini & Cole, 1988).

Although there is little difference in effectiveness among the tricyclics, they have different associated effects. Amitriptyline, doxepin, and trimipramine are the most

TABLE 10.5
Antidepressant Drugs

Group/Drug	Trade Name
Tricyclics	
Imipramine	Tofranil
Amitriptyline	Elavil
Trimipramine	Surmontil
Doxepin	Sinequan
Desipramine	Norpramin
Nortriptyline	Aventyl
Protriptyline	Vivactil
Monoamine oxidase inhibitors (MAOIs)	
Isocarboxazid	Marplan
Phenelzine	Nardil
Tranylcypromine	Parnate
Tetracyclics	
Maprotiline	Ludiomil
Serotonin uptake inhibitors	
Fluoxetine	Prozac
Trazodone	Desyrel

Sources: Kaplan & Sadock (1988); Physicians Desk Reference (1990).

sedating; desipramine and protriptyline are the least (Kaplan & Sadock, 1988). The sedating effect, however, may be desirable because it improves sleep. The tricyclics vary, too, in associated anticholinergic effects, an effect of antipsychotic drugs, too. The most anticholinergic are imipramine, amitriptyline, and doxepin; the least is desipramine. Other side effects that are associated with several of the tricyclics are cardiovascular effects, seizures, rashes, weight gain, impotence, and ejaculatory difficulties (Kaplan & Sadock, 1988).

Tricyclics take 3 or 4 weeks to effect a reduction in the depression. Those drugs that are sedating produce improvement in sleeping in a week or two (Kaplan & Sadock, 1988). The dosage is raised gradually over time until a therapeutic level is reached. After recovery and a period of maintenance on the drug, a medical decision to withdraw the drug may be made. Withdrawal of tricyclics should also be done gradually (Kaplan & Sadock, 1988).

Monoamine oxidase inhibitors (MAOIs) offer an alternative drug treatment of depression. The major categories are isocarboxazid (Marplan), phenelzine (Nardil), and tranylcypromine (Parnate). Although MAOIs are considered effective, they pose risks and have side effects. Persons who take MAOIs are advised to avoid certain foods and beverages (e.g., aged cheese, smoked food, chocolate, wine, beer, fava beans) that are high in tyramine content. Consumption of these products can precipitate a hypertensive crisis (sweating, dizziness, high blood pressure) that is life threatening. Early indicators of an impending crisis are headaches, nausea, and vomiting. MAOIs have additional adverse effects—orthostatic hypotension (low blood pressure accompanying standing up), weight gain, edema, and sexual dysfunction—that need to be monitored (Kaplan & Sadock, 1988).

Alternative Antidepressants.   In recent years, a number of new antidepressant drugs have been introduced. The development of these drugs has provided hope that some of the drawbacks of the tricyclics and MAOIs could be overcome. Among those that have been approved for marketing in the United States are maprotiline, a tetracyclic, and fluoxetine and trazodone (serotonin uptake inhibitors). Research supports the effectiveness of maprotiline (Ludiomil) for treating bipolar disorder, depressed type and dysthymia, although this drug does produce seizures and anticholinergic effects (Physicians Desk Reference [PDR], 1990). Fluoxetine (Prozac) has had a positive impact on major depressive episodes, but some people experience anxiety, insomnia, and diarrhea when they take this drug (PDR, 1990). Trazodone (Deryrel) is a relatively safe and effective medication. It has a lower rate of anticholinergic effects and seizures than other drugs and is sedating. Trazodone, however, interferes with male sexual functioning (Blackwell, 1987).

Most of the antidepressants pose risks to older adults (Payne, 1987). The tricyclics have cardiac effects and anticholergic effects (especially constipation), which can interfere with the health of older adults. Prescription of too large a dosage or self-administered overdoses can be lethal. The food and beverage restrictions required for maintenance on MAOIs may be difficult for older adults to maintain—particularly if the forbidden foods are consonant with the client's culture. Some of the newer drugs may be advantageous to older adults.

Cross-cultural research on psychopharmacological drugs among ethnic groups suggests that drug dosage needs for Asians, Hispanics, and African Americans may be lower than for Caucasians. In a review of cross-national studies, Lin, Poland, and Lesser (1986) found that compared with Europeans and Americans, patients from non-Western countries responded to neuroleptics at a lower dosage than their Western counterparts. In some studies Hispanics, Blacks, and Asians responded to a lower dose of tricyclic antidepressants than Caucasians; Asians with bipolar disorder required a lower lithium blood level than Caucasians. Although this research has some methodological problems (e.g., different diagnostic criteria and interviewing instruments across cultures), preliminary studies suggest dosage variations across ethnic groups.

Implications for Social Work Practice

This review of the effects and side effects of medications that are frequently prescribed for persons with severe and persistent mental disorders provides a knowledge base for social work. Social workers should become aware of changes in the medication that have been ordered by psychiatrists, alterations in the client's behavior prior to and following medication changes, and contingencies that enter into the client's compliance with a medication regimen. Factors such as clients' attitudes toward taking medication, undesirable side effects, and street drug use should be explored.

As part of the mental health team, social workers have a role in monitoring clients' compliance with the treatment plan, including intake of prescribed drugs. As social workers with professional values of client self-determination, self-actualization, and human dignity, clinical social workers must balance their commitment to the treatment plan with a concern for clients' rights.

Taking medication is a responsibility that principally belongs to the client and secondarily to significant others such as parents, spouses, friends, and operators of community residences. The psychiatrist, community mental health nurse, psychologist, social worker, and other mental health team members intervene to identify and remove obstacles and promote compliance.

One obstacle to compliance may lie in the client's feelings about taking medication. Medication may be perceived symbolically as a crutch or a reminder that he or she has a serious disorder. This feeling may be particularly acute among persons with chronic mental disorders, whose psychiatric illness seems interminable. Dependence on medication may reinforce feelings of helplessness and hopelessness; interfere with self-esteem and autonomy; and contradict sociocultural values about independence, self-sufficiency, and competence.

Some clients may have thoughts related to their psychiatric difficulty that affect their medical compliance. For example, Mike, a young man with an obsessive compulsive personality disorder as well as schizophrenia, would not take his medication on days in which he overslept. In exploring the reasons for his noncompliance, the clinical social worker discovered that the directions on the medication bottle said, "Take twice daily at 8 A.M. and 8 P.M.," and that Mike concluded, "If I've slept late, I've blown it." In this case the social worker had the psychiatrist change the written instructions to "twice daily" and counsel the client about taking two tablets daily.

Clinical social workers can help clients by encouraging them to talk about their feelings about medication, so they can sort out the realistic and the unrealistic. Such was the case with Susan:

Susan, a 25-year-old musician, had the diagnosis of bipolar disorder for 3 years. She had her first manic episode during her senior year of college, which resulted in her taking a leave of absence. Later she returned to college and completed her degree.

Susan expressed a number of concerns about lithium. For one, she felt that it interfered with her creativity. During manic episodes, she would stay awake into the night, composing music. She felt less creative on lithium. In addition, Susan found it embarrassing to come to the clinic, where she sat with clients who talked to themselves and exhibited bizarre movements.

In talking with Susan, the social worker learned that Susan was frightened of the other clients and afraid that she would develop movements like theirs. When the side effects of schizophrenia were differentiated from those of lithium, Susan felt relieved. Only then did she admit that the music she composed when she was manic was not very good (she tape recorded it once so she could listen to it later). In subsequent discussions Susan recognized that her risk for recurrent episodes was high (three members of her family had the same disorder), and that lithium could protect her from interruptions in her career.

Clients also have subjective responses to the side effects of drugs. They may feel uncomfortable with the anticholinergic effects and self-conscious about obvious extrapyramidal symptoms. Weight gain, skin eruptions, and sexual dysfunctioning may prompt some clients to take themselves off the medication. A social worker who listens attentively and probes for feelings may be able to join with the client in an effort to effect a change in the medication. This approach recognizes the client's feelings while at the same time it offers the client alternatives to noncompliance. Options include a change in dosage, introduction of antiparkinsonian medications, a change in drugs, or the use of a new or adjunctive medication. Social workers can encourage clients to request medication changes and arrange appointments for that purpose. Not unusually, social workers sit in on appointments with psychiatrists. So long as it is acceptable to clients, the social worker can raise issues with the psychiatrist that clients may be reluctant to raise themselves. The social worker who is aware of alternative drugs, side effects, intermittent plans, and drug holidays can advocate for these options, if appropriate.

Medication management is another issue that may arise in the process of working with a client. Many clients take their own medications as prescribed. Others are given medication by a family member, boarding home operator, or community mental health nurse. Medication may be in the forms of capsules, tablets, or liquid, or it may be administered intramuscularly. Clients who are given medication by others may feel controlled, dependent, or childlike.

With respect to clients' rights, self-administration is the most desirable alternative. Clients who have a history of noncompliance or abuse of medication, however, may not be given that option. Social workers can work with clients and client systems to promote the maximum self-determination feasible with respect to medication and develop with clients goals that reflect their wish for more control. Tools such as calendars, daily checklists, and charts can be developed. Clients can be encouraged to keep medication in a place that is visible and to take the medication at the same time every day. Nevertheless, some clients do forget:

> When Sol had his own apartment, he would forget to take his medication some days. Other days he would consume alcohol concurrently with prescribed medication. One day the combination caused him to sleep for two days. Sol agreed with the mental health team that it would be better if the medication were dispensed at the day treatment center; and to go to Alcoholics Anonymous. He said that when he gets his alcohol problem under control, he would like to take his medication on his own.

Sometimes social workers obtain information about clients that indicates noncompliance with their treatment plan. The use of alcohol and street drugs, the sale of prescribed medication, hoarding of medication, and borrowing from or lending medication to others can result in aversive physical reactions and suicide. Concerns about these behaviors should be discussed directly and honestly with both the client and the psychiatrist. Mental health teams are an appropriate forum for the social worker to discuss ethical as well as treatment issues—and a common strategy for the team to pursue.

In working with a client who is on psychotropic medication, a social worker is working with a *person,* not a set of symptoms or a diagnosis. Attitudes toward taking medication and behaviors that interfere with his or her functioning represent the psychosocial component. Other approaches—social skills training, family psychoeducation, and the selected use of psychotherapy—can address these issues more fully.

SOCIAL SKILLS TRAINING

Persons with chronic mental disorders often have difficulties processing information, solving problems, and responding appropriately to external demands. Because of deficits in perceiving and interpreting environmental cues, as well as a limited repertoire of response patterns, they may interact with others in such a way that communication is not accomplished. Furthermore, they may be inhibited in the expression of their feelings, needs, and wishes. Their difficulties in social functioning are largely associated with their psychiatric illnesses, but may also be due to limited experiences in socialization and learning. Although medication can reduce symptoms, it is not in itself sufficient. Drug therapy neither remedies impairments in social functioning nor promotes effective coping (Liberman & Foy, 1983). Use of medication alone is limited in "its inability to impart new instrumental role behaviors and interpersonal skills" which can result in "improvements in patients' quality of life" (Wallace et al., 1980, p. 42).

Social skills training is a form of behavior therapy that has been used extensively with persons with serious and persistent mental health problems to help them cope more effectively with social living. Within the community, it is implemented on an individual, family, or group basis in mental health agencies, within programs such as partial hospitalization, and in clients' natural environments. Some clients who can benefit from social skills training have limited skills in self-care; for example, they are not able to dress themselves. Others are relatively self-sufficient but have difficulties conducting a conversation, finding a job, or making friends.

The conceptual basis for social skills training lies largely in social learning theory (see chapter 3), but some ideas from cognitive theory are also utilized. Principles of information processing and learning are incorporated in the theoretical model and its application. According to the theory guiding social skills training (Liberman et al., 1986), individuals develop social schemata (explanatory structures) that account for experience and enable them to interact with the social environment. The development of these schemata depends on (a) psychobiological functioning of memory, attention, affect, perception, and concept formation and (b) higher order cognitive processes such as taking the perspective of another, regulating one's own behavior, and inference making. If any of these functions is deficient—which often is the case among persons with chronic mental illnesses—interpersonal problem solving and coping will be disrupted.

The ability to solve problems is an outcome of the operation of social schemata and depends on the functioning of receiving, processing, and sending skills (Liberman et al., 1986). *Receiving skills* facilitate that the content and feelings associated with messages from others be understood and interpreted accurately. Accordingly, the individual takes in verbal and nonverbal information and makes sense of it. *Processing skills* refer to the way in which decisions are made about how to respond to a message. The individual thinks through alternative ways of reacting, possible effects of each option, and makes a selection that will achieve desired outcomes. With *sending skills* one is able to transmit information in a way that the desired goal is accomplished. This requires that the content be communicated verbally and nonverbally and that pacing and timing be modulated to the social demands of the situation. When individuals are able to cope by mobilizing interpersonal problem solving to achieve personal goals, they are attaining social competence (Liberman et al., 1986).

Social skills training of persons with serious and persistent psychiatric problems is directed at (a) improving attention span and higher order thinking; (b) enhancing receiving, processing, and sending skills; and (c) modifying the environment to support the use of improved social skills (Liberman et al., 1986). The first approach, especially the improvement of attentional skills, is usually used with clients whose psychotic symptoms severely interfere with their psychosocial functioning. Because many of these lower functioning clients are patients in psychiatric hospitals and this volume is concerned with persons living in the community, this approach to social skill training will not be addressed. Here the second and third approaches will be explained and integrated. These approaches emphasize the development of social, vocational, and independent living skills in the community.

Prior to implementing social skills training, the clinician makes a comprehensive assessment of the client's overall functioning (see chapter 4), including an evaluation of the client's social interaction skills and deficiencies. Interviews with family members, significant others, and operators of family care and boarding homes can reveal important information about the client's social performance in context (Liberman, DeRisi, & Mueser, 1989). The outline for a functional assessment that was described in chapter 4 should assist in the process of identifying strengths and areas in which training can be helpful. Standardized instruments such as the Rathus Assertiveness Schedule (RAS; Rathus, 1973), the Social Interaction Schedule (SIS; Liberman, DeRisi, & Mueser, 1989, app. E), and the Wallace Functional Assessment Scale (Wallace, 1986) are useful in their identification of specific needs and in their ability to evaluate progress over time.

During the assessment process those skills that need development should be identified. From these, specific skills are selected as goals. In keeping with the principle of self-determination, the choice of training goals should be negotiated with the client. This way, behaviors which the client is motivated to change are targeted. Other criteria for selecting goals are that they revolve around specific, high-frequency, and constructive behaviors and those which are functional, attainable, and likely to occur in the near future (Liberman, DeRisi, & Mueser, 1989).

The skills that are enhanced or developed in social skills training are diverse and depend on the needs of individual clients. They can be broken down to microcomponents (e.g., maintaining eye contact) or into larger bodies of skills (e.g., taking the bus to the sheltered workshop). Examples of the kinds of client competencies that can be promoted in social skills training are as follows:

- Explaining side effects of medication to the psychiatrist
- Suggesting to an acquaintance that they go out for coffee together
- Learning how to wash and dry clothes at a laundromat

- Negotiating with one's family about the use of the family car
- Carrying on a conversation with a person of the other sex
- Looking for a job

The specific skills that are to be developed in training sessions may derive from clients' needs identified in the assessment process; or they may be generic skills needed by many clients, such as money management and home finding, programs for which have been developed in packaged modules by the Clinical Research Center at UCLA-Camarilla, California.

Liberman, DeRisi, and Mueser (1989) state that clients who cannot pay attention or follow directions for at least 15 minutes are not appropriate for social skills training. Most likely these clients have uncontrolled, intrusive psychiatric symptoms such as incoherence, hallucinations, mania, and memory difficulties that interfere with their concentration. In order to assess a client's ability to attend and remember, the authors suggest an evaluation of clients' responses to questions about their name, birthdate, and the current date; their ability to speak in simple sentences; their ability to understand others' talk and to listen to others without interrupting them for 3 to 5 minutes; and their ability to follow a sequence of three directives (e.g., "go to the door, knock on the door, and return to your seat"). Furthermore, they recommend that candidates for skills training be able to interact with others without distracting behaviors (e.g., acting out, talking to oneself, pacing) and articulate motivation to improve their expression of emotions. The assessment of clients' ability to participate in social skills training may involve observing their interactions in social programs, such as partial hospitalization, or trying them out in a training session.

Social skills training uses a series of role playing of problematic situations to teach participants more effective interactional skills. The major techniques utilized are behavioral rehearsal, modeling, reinforcement, shaping, and prompting (Liberman, 1988). *Behavioral rehearsal* is the practice of social skills through simulations or role plays. First clients may be asked to perform the skill as they have been doing it in the past. After they come to recognize their difficulties and alternative approaches are suggested, clients practice more effective ways of accomplishing the skill. *Modeling* refers to the performance of the desired skill by role models and subsequent learning through imitation by observers of the models, that is, clients who are having difficulty with a particular skill. In group social skills training, other clients and the clinician demonstrate effective skill performance, which becomes a model for clients. When a client is able to imitate the performance of models, approval or *reinforcement* is provided by the therapist and others present (family or group members). Reinforcement is also given following clients' successively close approximations of performance of the desired skill, a process known as *shaping.* An additional technique used in social skills training is *prompting,* or coaching. Here the therapist or trainer provides cues that will remind the client of the requirements of the situation and the skills necessary to meet these demands. The therapist may, for example, advise the client to maintain eye contact and maintain a modulated voice during a role play of a social interaction.

One of the pitfalls of social skills training is the difficulties clients have in applying skills learned in training sessions to real-life situations (Liberman et al., 1986; Wallace et al., 1980). Persons with severe and persistent mental disabilities have varying abilities to generalize from one situation to another—at least with respect to complex skills. In order to promote generalization, several procedures are incorporated into the training. One is the use of *homework assignments*—exercises that the client is expected to perform outside the skills training session. These require that the client replicate the skill learned in training in the community, where prompting generally does not occur. Some writers recommend that clients be given index cards on which the week's assignment is written and that clients bring back evidence of having carried out the assignment, for example, the signature of a service provider the client was supposed to contact (Liberman, 1988). Another way to promote generalization is to carry out social skills training in the community contexts in which the skill is needed. In vivo training is incorporated in the assertive community treatment model pioneered by Stein and Test (1980) in Wisconsin (see chapter 9). An additional means to promote generalization is to have clients *overlearn* and practice the skills that are taught. To assure learning, the skill is modeled and practiced beyond clients' demonstration that they are able to perform the skill effectively. In addition to these approaches, families, significant others, and care givers are asked to provide prompts and reinforcements when clients practice skills at home or in other natural environments (Liberman et al., 1986).

The group provides a format in which social skills can be modeled by participants as well as the group leaders or trainers, who may be clinical social workers. The group offers clients in need of social skills development sustained relationships from session to session and a sense of belonging. Sharing one's deficiencies as well as skills in a group facilitates a feeling of being accepted at the same time it promotes growth in incremental steps. Although the group may engender a moderate amount of stress, such stress closely replicates the stress in participants' everyday life experiences (Liberman, DeRisi, & Mueser, 1989). The group that will provide an illustration of social skills training consists of five clients and a clinical social worker/trainer. (For larger groups two group leaders are helpful.) The group members and their goals are as follows:

Florence is a 30-year-old divorced woman with bipolar disorder, depressed type. Although she worked in the past in sales, she has not been employed since she was able to obtain Social Security disability insurance 3 years ago. Florence has been stable on lithium for 3 1/2 years. Currently she is experiencing problems with her boyfriend Jack, who she believes is taking advantage of her by living with her and not paying the rent. Her immediate goal is to tell him how she feels and get him to either contribute or leave. Her long-term goals are to work as a volunteer first and later to obtain a "real" job.

Joseph is a 28-year-old single man who lives with his brother and sister-in-law. Around the time he developed schizophrenia, paranoid type, he became active in a charismatic religious church, which continues to be an important resource for him. Nevertheless, Joseph does not confine his religious enthusiasm to himself and other members of his church. Wherever he goes (including the waiting room of the mental health center), he preaches to people around him. Joseph does recognize that his preaching interferes with his relationships with others. His short-term goal is to engage in social conversational behavior in place of preaching when talking to persons who are not members of his church. Eventually, he would like to get a job and live independently.

Sally, a 35-year-old married woman and mother of a 3-year-old child, has been given the diagnosis of schizoaffective disorder. Currently she is home taking care of her daughter most of the time and is feeling depressed. Her husband is a truck driver, who is out of town during the week. Sally would like to have more social contacts but is afraid to initiate them. Her short-term goals are to make friends with whom she can socialize at least once a week and to tell her husband how she feels about his being out of town so much. Her long-term goal is to improve her relationship with her husband.

Michael is a 22-year-old man with both organic impairment and an obsessive compulsive personality disorder. He lives with his parents in a rural area. After Michael was discharged from the hospital, he began to have conflicts with his parents over his "interminable" use of the shower. Furthermore, his parents are disturbed by his sleeping late and his playing loud music. Michael's immediate goal is "to keep my parents from hassling me." His longer term goal is to move into a group home.

Richard, 35 years old and married, is having difficulties taking instructions from his supervisor at the sheltered workshop. His wife, parents, and case manager are strongly supporting his continuing with the workshop job. Richard has the diagnosis of schizophrenia, chronic undifferentiated type, and a history of five hospitalizations. He is afraid that he cannot handle the pressure of the workshop. His goal is to stay on at the workshop for 6 months and then find a part-time job in the community. His immediate goal is to be able to listen to his supervisor better.

A group of these clients has been meeting weekly for 3 weeks in 90-minute sessions with the clinical social worker Matt Hughes. The group members have begun to feel comfortable with each other and with Matt. The setting is a drop-in program for formerly hospitalized adults who live in the community. The program is housed in a store on a side street of a city in the southwest. The social skills training group meets in a room in back of the store. In the front, other consumers play pool, socialize, and meet informally with mental health workers.

Matt began the formal group session after the clients were settled in their chairs in a circle and seemed to be finished chatting informally with each other. By this time, the social worker had greeted each of the clients individually and had gotten the impression from his conversation with Michael that the problems between Michael and his family were acute. Matt thought that Michael would need a great deal of attention today. Nevertheless, he asked all group members to give a brief report on how things went during the past week and about progress in performing their homework assignments. The clients took their turns, giving the following reports:

FLORENCE: I finally got up enough nerve to talk to Jack about paying the rent. I told him that he wasn't being fair to me and I needed his help.

MATT: Good for you, Florence!

FLORENCE: Well, it was hard. I was nervous the whole time—with good reason. Jack said that he couldn't pay the rent. He said he owed money to his sister and had to pay her back. He said that after he paid her, he would pitch in on the rent.

MATT: When will that be?

FLORENCE: He said 6 months. Meanwhile he promised to contribute to the groceries and pay the electric bill.

MATT: How do you feel about that?

FLORENCE: That will at least help some. I'm still not completely satisfied, but at least that's something.

MATT: I'm glad you talked to Jack about this. This was your goal and you accomplished that.

FLORENCE: I'm glad, too. But I wish I could have insisted that the rent comes first—before his debt to his sister.

MATT: Would you like to work on communicating this to Jack as your next goal?

FLORENCE: Yes, but I want to see if he really does pay for the groceries and electric bill first.

MATT: Okay. Joseph?

JOSEPH: When I went bowling with Tony and Marie Saturday, I didn't talk to anyone about religion.

MATT: Terrific!

JOSEPH: It was hard. There were a lot of people around that I wanted to preach to.

MATT: Good for you for holding back.

JOSEPH: But I didn't talk to anyone but Tony and Marie (brother and sister-in-law).

MATT: That can be your goal for next time—to talk to someone else and to talk about something other than religion.

JOSEPH: Maybe.

MATT: Sally?

SALLY: Florence didn't tell you, but she and I went out for lunch together last Wednesday. Mom babysat. I really enjoyed getting out of the house and doing something with a friend.

FLORENCE: We had a real nice afternoon. And Sally helped me get up the nerve to talk to Jack.

MATT: Sounds like it was good for both of you.

SALLY: We're planning to do it again next week.

MATT: Good for you! I'm very glad you were able to do that, Sally.

SALLY: It was easier than I thought. I just asked Florence after group last time and she said yes. Then I had to ask Mom when she could babysit and I called Florence on the phone.

MATT: You had to talk to Florence and your mother to do this, and you were able to arrange it.

SALLY: Yes. Next I want to talk to my husband about my feelings.

MATT: You can work on that next. Richard?

RICHARD: I've been trying not to get rattled when Mr. P (from the sheltered workshop) corrects me. I realize that that's his job, but he gets on my nerves. From the last session, I learned to listen to what he's trying to say. When I tried to listen better this week, I realized that one of the things that bothers me so much about him is his gruff voice.

MATT: What about his gruff voice bothers you, Richard?

RICHARD: I don't know. He just scares me and then I can't listen.
MATT: It sounds as if you've learned a lot in the last week. Good for you for making progress, Richard! How about you, Michael?
MICHAEL: I had a big fight with my parents yesterday.
MATT: Would you tell us about it?
MICHAEL: I was taking a shower Saturday morning and my mother knocked on the bathroom door. I ignored her, because she's always doing that. When I came out, she and my father started screaming at me. They told me I'm wasting water and they can't afford to pay for all that water. I told them that water don't cost nothing and I needed to get clean. Then my parents showed me the water bill—it was $50—and asked me to either work or leave. I started crying and ran to my room. Then they started knocking on the door to my room, which I locked. I wouldn't open the door. Then my Dad knocked the door down and made me sit down with them in the living room.
MATT: What happened next?
MICHAEL: They told me that something's gotta change or I've got to leave. They said that they can't tolerate my long showers, my sleeping late, and the radio. They said I'm a good-for-nothing bum.
JOSEPH: My brother tells me the same thing.
MICHAEL: They don't realize that I can't help it. I'd like to work. I'd like to live on my own. I'm on the waiting list for the group home and nothing's happening.
MATT: Your goal is to keep your parents from hassling you. What would you like to work on to get them to stop—at least long enough to get you into the group home?
MICHAEL: I'd be willing to cut down on my time in the shower. But I want to make sure I get clean.
MATT: Does anyone in the group have any ideas about how Michael can do this?
FLORENCE: You can bring an alarm clock into the bathroom and set the alarm.
MATT: Good suggestion. How long does it take the rest of you to shower?
JOSEPH: It takes me 10 minutes.
FLORENCE: About the same.
RICHARD: Ten minutes for me, too, when I do shower. I hate to shower.
SALLY: It takes me half an hour, but I take baths, not showers.
MATT: You might use up less water in a bath than a shower.
MICHAEL: I prefer showers. And I do lose track of the time. But I do worry about getting clean.
SALLY: You might try XXX soap—it gets you clean—and it's not expensive.
MATT: Good idea, Sally! The group's come up with some good ideas, Michael. Will any of these be helpful to you?
MICHAEL: Yes, I like the idea of using an alarm clock and using XXX soap. But I don't know how to talk to my parents about this. They're about ready to kick me out and I don't want to be out on the street.
MATT: Maybe the group can help.

At this point the group format switches from an introductory phase of reporting goal accomplishments to work on a specific issue with a particular client. By this time, all of the participants have gotten engaged and have been reinforced by the clinician. Some of the group members have given suggestions and other indicators of support to others. The following segment demonstrates how a "dry run" role play of a discussion between Michael and his parents about showering is set up and enacted.

MATT: In order to get a better idea about how you and your parents communicate about your showering, we want you (Michael) and a volunteer mother and father to have a discussion the way it usually goes. Michael, you can play yourself. I would like your opinion on who in the group do you think could best play your parents.

MICHAEL: Florence can play my mother—but you've gotta talk loud and act bossy, Florence. Joseph can play my father. My father doesn't talk about religion, but he's always telling me what's right and what's wrong the way you do, Joseph.

JOSEPH: Okay, I'll do it.

MATT: You told us what happened in your shower and then your room. Let's start this role play in the living room with the three of you sitting down to talk. (Waits for Michael, Joseph, and Florence to be seated.) Suppose you get the discussion started, Joseph, with you as Michael's father.

JOSEPH: (To Michael) I've had it with you, son. You're costing us an arm and a leg and all you do is eat, sleep, and take showers.

MICHAEL: I do more than that. I mow the grass every week—and you know that.

JOSEPH: That doesn't come close to paying for the water you use. And that loud music!

MICHAEL: At least I don't have to listen to you and Mom.

FLORENCE: I can't stand seeing you sleep to 2 o'clock in the afternoon. By the time you have showered and dressed, it's almost supper time. My day's almost over and you're just waking up. And then you start with that music.

MICHAEL: I don't have to listen to this (starts to walk away).

JOSEPH: You're going to have to—or we'll throw you out.

MICHAEL: But you don't listen to my side.

At this point, Matt stops the role play and asks Michael if this was typical of what happens at home. Michael said that it was in the sense that the "discussions" usually go nowhere and he ends up wanting to leave and they end up threatening to kick him out. Matt then asks the group if they could give Michael some positive feedback on how he acted in the role play. Group members comment on his good eye contact, his clear voice, and his willingness to listen until he got angry. Matt then asks Michael how he thinks his parents were feeling. Michael admitted that they were probably frustrated because he did not listen and talked back to them. Matt then proceeds to set up the next phase as follows:

MATT: Michael, what would you like to go better in a discussion like we just role played?

MICHAEL: I wish they wouldn't yell and call me names. When they threaten to kick me out, I get scared—even though they've never carried it out. I wish I would be able to tolerate their yelling at me more—instead of wanting to leave or escaping.

MATT: Does anyone in the group have any ideas about what Michael can do better?

RICHARD: You can tell them your good points—like you want to help and you plan to move out.

MATT: Good. Anyone else?

SALLY: Try to make a deal with them—like you will take a shorter shower if they would buy you a clock and some soap.

JOSEPH: You can agree to the shower if they would leave you alone about the other things—the radio and sleeping late.

MATT: These are very good suggestions. Now suppose we do the role play over with Richard playing you.

The group now moves in to the next phase in which the role play is reenacted with a model, Richard, playing Michael. The other actors remain the same. Matt directs Richard to begin the discussion with taking an attitude that shows Michael's parents that he would really like to work things out with them.

RICHARD: (Speaking softly) I'm sorry I spent so much time in the shower. I want to be clean but I lose track of the time.

FLORENCE: When you stay in the shower so long, we worry about the water bills.

RICHARD: I know. I wish I could stop myself. Really, I could use your help.

FLORENCE: How?

RICHARD: If you can get me better soap and an alarm clock, I think I could stop myself.

JOSEPH: I have an old wind-up alarm clock in the garage. You can have that, son.

FLORENCE: And I can pick up that soap—if that will help.

RICHARD: It would, I think it would. I really would like to work things out with you. You know, I'm on the list for the group home. But until they call me, I'd like to stay here.

JOSEPH: What about the radio?

At this point Matt cut the discussion. He said he'd rather they tackle one problem at a time. Matt asked Michael what he thought about the role play. Michael said it was very different from the way things usually go at home—that he never admits that he is wrong to his parents and never asks for their help. Michael remarked that Richard did a good job playing him and that he wished he could act like that. Matt suggested that he try acting the way Richard did in the next enactment of the role play.

MATT: When you play yourself, Michael, be sure to keep up the eye contact the way you did before. Keep your voice down, the way Richard did, and start out by telling your parents that you want to change but need their help.

MICHAEL: Okay . . . um . . . Mom and Dad, I want to apologize about using up so much water with the shower. I'm just thinking about myself and not you. I really want to work things out with you.

JOSEPH: We accept your apology. But we want you to change.

MICHAEL: I want to change, too . . . but I need your help.

FLORENCE: How can we help you, Michael? We would like to help.

MICHAEL: I think it would help if I had a timer in the bathroom. I can set the alarm for, say, 10 minutes—and you won't have to knock on the door.

JOSEPH: That's easy. I have an old alarm clock in the garage.

MICHAEL: One more thing—I would like to use XXX soap. It works better. I worry about getting clean enough. I hope it's not too expensive.

FLORENCE: We can buy that for you if you would take less time with the shower. I am very happy that you are willing to do that, Michael.

MICHAEL: I realize that there are other things that bother you about me—but could we just start with this? I'm hoping to get into the group home soon, but meanwhile I do want to get along with you.

MATT: Cut. Very good, Michael.

At this point the group gave Michael positive feedback. They pointed out that he was reasonable rather than argumentative; that he was willing to compromise; and that he showed his parents that he could understand how they feel. Michael said that it was hard for him to admit to his parents that he was wrong and even harder to ask them to help him. Joseph said that when he played the father in the last round he felt good about Michael, whereas the first time, he felt angry. This led into a group discussion about maintaining positive communication by being honest, direct, and admitting weaknesses.

After the completion of this role play, Matt gave Michael the homework assignment of conducting a conversation like this one with his parents. Michael thought it would be more difficult in real life, but he said he would try. When asked what was hard about it, Michael said he was in the habit of seeing things as either his way or his parents' way. He said that things didn't get heated in the role play the way they do at home—that he wanted to learn how to negotiate better. This led into another role play situation involving another client.

The preceding scenario featuring Michael's problems is exemplary of the kind of interactions that occur in social skills training groups. While the focus here was on one client, the group proceeds to develop role plays and homework assignments for all the group members. Through the medium of the role play, participants learn to interact with each other, appreciate others' perspectives, and respond appropriately. Although problem solving is not the primary purpose of this group, they do learn new ways to approach problems, too. Through skills training a group's members learn to give to each other—which is central to relationship building. In addition, they learn to listen to and benefit from each other's suggestions.

Michael's difficulties could also have been handled in an individual or family session. In an individual session, the clinician plays the client or others, switching between roles. The client learns through the clinician's example and through prompts. In family-centered social skills training, the participants initially enact their usual roles. The clinician then has family members discuss feelings that underlie their interactions and gives feedback on how family members come across. In reenacting the scene, the clinician can assume the role of the client or of other family members and provide coaching to whoever needs it. Role playing of family problems in the context of the family has the advantage of being closer to in vivo experience than role playing in a group.

INTERVENING WITH THE FAMILY

The policy of deinstitutionalization has resulted in increasing demands on families. Once blamed for the development of psychiatric problems in their children, today families are principal providers of physical, emotional, and financial support to their relative. When clients are discharged from hospitals, they frequently return to parents, spouses, siblings, and other family members. But even if the client is not sent home to the family, relatives are a significant source of support and a temporary haven during times of crisis (Ellwood & Bane, 1984).

Impact of Serious Mental Disorders on the Family

The assumption of responsibility for a relative with serious psychiatric disorders takes its toll on families' lives (Gubman & Tessler, 1987). The afflicted relative may act argumentative, withdrawn, unmotivated, aggressive, noisy, bizarre, demanding, threatening, or uncooperative. These and other idiosyncratic behaviors disrupt the family system, which is called upon to adapt to the client's ways. Older siblings are able to cope with this situation through emancipation, and employed fathers have large blocks of time away from the family. Women in particular experience the burden of care (Thurer, 1983). In a study of parents caring for their young adult children with serious mental disorders (Cook, 1988), mothers reported excessive symptoms of anxiety, depression, fear, and emotional drain.

Emotional reactions are a reflection of everyday stresses and strains, social isolation, and grief. Family members have daily encounters in which the needs of the family for participation, social interaction, and mutuality are ignored. Unable to interpret unusual behaviors they observe, they feel bewildered or frightened. Some families protect their family member and themselves from having to explain the situation to friends by isolating themselves from others. Families grieve for the life for which they had hoped and dreamed for their disabled member, who may have shown promise as a child (Hatfield, 1987a). Moreover, they grieve over the loss of time they may have anticipated having during middle and older adulthood when one is usually relieved of child care responsibilities. Plans to travel, enjoy being a grandparent, and pursue recreational interests are supplanted by day-to-day supervision of a family member whose actions are unpredictable.

Responses of families to caring for a mentally disabled member change over time (Terkelsen, 1987). Before the onset of a psychotic episode, the family may ignore or minimize dysfunctional behavior, viewing it as a stage or temporary condition. Then something happens or someone points out that the individual has a serious problem. At first family members are reluctant to believe that anything is wrong. But evidence accrues and eventually there is a crisis that calls for the intervention of the mental health delivery system. At this time the family faces their relative's status as a person with a serious mental disorder. A painful realization, this sets the family on a course in which they seek to understand causes and look for appropriate treatment programs and other resources. Families go through periods in which they are hopeful, but the ups and downs of the family member's treatment leave them with worry and doubt. They mourn the family member they once knew and develop strategies to help their relative at the same time they garner support for themselves.

Frequently families lack information about mental disorders, medication, behavioral management strategies, and community services. Even if they know the diagnosis, they do not know what the diagnosis means and they do not understand chronicity (Gantt, Goldstein, & Pinsky, 1989). In addition, they may experience frustration in their contacts with the mental health system. They may find themselves assuming the role of case manager in a system that lacks resources and excludes them from the treatment process (Francell, Conn, & Gray, 1988). The families' most frequent complaint about professionals is, "They don't understand us" (Hatfield, 1987b).

In response to their frustrations, some family members have organized into groups that both provide mutual support and advocate for the interests of families and their mentally disabled relatives. Local affiliates of the National Alliance for the Mentally Ill (NAMI) are one avenue through which families of persons with serious and persistent mental disorders can act politically to make their needs, wants, and recommendations heard. Such organizations sometimes meet with professionals or invite them to speak at their meetings.

The responsibility of linkage between families and mental health professionals does not, however, lie with families. Professionals have a responsibility to listen to the voices of relatives and address their concerns. Of all the mental health professions, social work should be most in tune with the family context that shapes clients' lives. Families are intrinsically involved in the care of identified clients and are a major source of support. Curiously, mental health professionals overestimate family satisfaction with their services (Spaniol et al., 1987).

Family Psychoeducation

One approach that has been successful in work with families is psychoeducation. This structured, goal-directed treatment modality provides both instruction and emotional support to clients and their families (Ryglewicz, 1989, April). It uses psychotherapeutic techniques such as cognitive mastery, affective experiencing, and behavioral regulation to promote psychosocial functioning and coping (Goldman, 1988). Psychoeducation has been used in relation to diverse populations and disorders, including substance abuse, dual diagnosis (substance abuse together with a major psychiatric disorder), depression, and physical illnesses such as epilepsy (Ryglewicz, 1989, April). The psychoeducation of hospitalized persons with schizophrenia provides patients with information about their mental disorder, medication, and community care (Goldman & Quinn, 1988; Greenberg et al., 1988). The focus here, however, is on family psychoeducation.

Psychoeducation of families arose from three sources (Ryglewicz, 1989, July). One was the body of research on expressed emotion (EE) that was described in chapter 8. This research found that high EE in families was related to relapse. The implementation of family psychoeducation, however, provided some protection against relapse, and the combination of medication and social skills training for clients and psychoeducation of families high on EE produced the maximum effect (Hogarty et al., 1986). Another source of psychoeducation was research on information processing deficits associated with schizophrenia that was the basis of the attention-arousal model also described in chapter 8. The third force, which converged with the others, was the family advocacy movement, which drew attention to the rights, needs, and competence of families.

There are several models of family psychoeducation and many variant forms of implementation. The most prominent models are those of Anderson, Reiss, and Hogarty (1986); Goldstein and Kopeikin (1981); Falloon and others (1982); Beels (1975); and McFarlane (1983). The one that will be described here is based on the work of Anderson, Reiss, and Hogarty (1986; Anderson, Hogarty, & Reiss, 1980, 1981). This model was chosen because social workers were instrumental in its creation and because it is empirically based. Although this model derived from research on families of persons with schizophrenia and schizoaffective disorder (mostly parents) who were considered high on EE, this approach can be adapted to the needs of spouses, siblings, and other persons emotionally involved with the client (however intensely) and to families of individuals with other major psychiatric disorders.

The Anderson model is both client and family centered. It fosters the adaptation of the client to community life by engaging the family in efforts to reduce stress and promote medication compliance. It attempts to assuage the family's anxiety and guilt by providing members with information and helping them to cope. Efforts are directed at fostering a family environment that is stable and predictable—one in which communication is clear, boundaries are specified, and emotional expressiveness (criticism and overinvolvement) is minimal. The Anderson model is task centered and proceeds in incremental steps that are consistent with the client's pace of recovery. Both family therapy and educational principles are used.

This psychoeducational program proceeds in four overlapping phases—connection, survival skills workshop, reentry and application, and maintenance (see Table 10.6). During Phase I, which begins during a client's hospitalization for an acute psychotic episode, the goal is to develop a working alliance with the family, decrease guilt, and reduce stress. This is accomplished by assuming a nonjudgmental and empathetic attitude, eliciting and acknowledging the family's feelings and experiences, and acting as an ombudsman for the family. Initially the clinician meets with the family, without the mentally ill relative present, once or twice a week. When the client's psychotic symptoms recede, he or she is able to join the family sessions.

Parents who are familiar with theories that hold them responsible for mental illness in their offspring are especially vulnerable to guilt feelings. In order to offset such feelings, the clinician is respectful and avoids blaming the family. In contrast with the patient-centered approach that characterizes many hospitals, here the family's experiences in caring for their relative and with previous mental health programs are discussed. The clinician keeps the family informed about their member's progress in treatment and, in working with the treatment team, acts as a representative of the family. The family's emotional involvement is mobilized and reframed as "concern"; the family's helplessness is channeled into commitment to perform tasks that will promote the rehabilitation of their relative.

TABLE 10.6

Phases of the Treatment Process in Psychoeducation

Phases	Goals	Techniques
Phase I: connection	Connect with the family and enlist cooperation with program Decrease guilt, emotionality, negative reactions to the illness Reduction of family stress	Joining Establishing treatment contract Discussion of crisis history and feelings about the patient and illness Empathy Specific practical suggestions which mobilize concerns into effective coping mechanisms
Phase II: survival skills workshop	Increased understanding of illness and patient's needs by family Continued reduction of family stress Deisolation—enhancement of social networks	Multiple families (education and discussion) Concrete data on schizophrenia Concrete management—suggestions Basic communications skills
Phase III: reentry and application	Patient maintenance in community Strengthening marital/parental coalition Increased family tolerance for low-level dysfunctional behaviors Decreased and gradual resumption of responsibility by the patient	Reinforcement of boundaries (generational and interpersonal) Task assignments Low-keyed problem solving
Phase IV: maintenance	Reintegration into normal roles in community systems (work, school) Increased effectiveness of general family processes	Infrequent maintenance sessions Traditional or exploratory family therapy techniques

Source: Anderson, Hogarty, & Reiss (1980), p. 495. Used by permission.

Phase I concludes with the development of a treatment contract and the establishment of rules for family therapy. The contract that is negotiated identifies goals that pertain to issues that have come to the surface during this phase and are relevant to the client's recovery. Goals should be specific, realistic, and attainable. Accordingly long-range goals such as independent living are discouraged initially. The rules that Anderson and others have found useful are:

1. The family will meet regularly with the clinician (every 2 or 3 weeks) for at least a year.
2. No family member may speak for another family member.
3. No one may lose physical or emotional control during family sessions.
4. Changes will take place in incremental, separate steps.

Phase II consists of a survival skills workshop in which several families participate. This is offered early in the process of treatment in a single day. The major component of the workshop is the communication of factual, up-to-date information about schizophrenia and its treatment, but the multiple-family format promotes sharing and the development of a support network among participants. The information that is provided in these workshops covers the following themes:

- What is schizophrenia
- The biological genesis of schizophrenia
- The experience of schizophrenia
- The course of schizophrenia
- Prognosis
- Treatment modalities
- Pharmacotherapy and side effects
- The impact of stress on the course of schizophrenia
- Family strategies to reduce stress
- Effective communication in the family
- Avoiding social isolation
- Community resources

Other themes consistent with evolving knowledge about schizophrenia and related disorders can also be introduced. Some programs include a developmental perspective (Ryglewicz, 1989, April), which can be especially helpful to families of young adults (the young chronics). Generally the workshop is conducted by an interdisciplinary team of professionals with expertise in the topics under discussion. The participation of families of recovering clients or representatives of family advocacy groups who are supportive of the program can enhance the credibility of the psychoeducational approach.

During the workshop, the family is introduced to strategies they can use to modulate the stress (i.e., emotional expressiveness) in the family environment. Among these are establishing realistic expectations, structuring, setting limits, distancing, and "time out." The families are told that excessive sleep and low motivation are common following a psychotic episode; that clients can be expected to be more active over time. Having a family structure with a regular routine, rules, and reasonable expectations promotes stability and predictability. Expectations should be concrete and specific (e.g., wash the dishes every night). The family should identify behaviors they will tolerate (e.g., wearing mismatched clothes) and those they will not accept (e.g., physical abuse) and communicate to the family member with schizophrenia the limits of their tolerance. To avoid intense emotional involvement, boundary making through distancing is encouraged. Accordingly, the family accepts some withdrawal on the part of the client, avoids criticism and conflict, and develops outside interests, activities, and supports of their own. The needs of all family members are acknowledged and differentially supported. Should conflict emerge in the family, the client and/or the family member involved in the conflict withdraws from the scene (taking time out) to his or her room or elsewhere.

During the workshop, special attention is given to communication with the client. Because persons with schizophrenia have difficulty processing information, family members are urged to keep their requests clear and simple. Multiple levels of communication and complicated messages are to be avoided. In the same vein, family members are encouraged to use "I messages" (e.g., "I don't like that") rather than indirect messages in which the person responsible, the feeling component, and the desired effect are camouflaged. Family are discouraged from reading each other's minds and engaging in discussions on abstract themes in the presence of the client. They are encouraged to focus on and reinforce positive behaviors on the part of their family member.

Although the survival skills workshop is one of several components of the Anderson model of family psychoeducation, on the community level, it can be developed into a program in its own right. It can be sponsored by a community mental health or aftercare center, a social rehabilitation program, a halfway house, or the like. Furthermore, it can be modified to meet the needs of families of persons with other disorders, such as bipolar disorder and major depression. The program is offered in blocks of separate topics and can be extended over a period of weeks. Outpatient psychoeducational groups for clients are another option.

Phase III, reentry, begins when the client leaves the hospital. Family sessions that include the client are arranged on a schedule that is consistent with the family's and client's needs—usually every 2 or 3 weeks. Crisis telephone calls and emergency sessions are accommodated. The sessions are structured around current issues and homework assignments that are allocated for work between sessions. A problem-solving, task-centered approach is used.

During this phase, which can last 6 months or longer, the family implements the skills that were introduced during the survival skills workshop. Accordingly, the family develops and articulates rules, sets limits, and reinforces intergenerational and interpersonal boundaries. Parents are encouraged to engage in social activities as a couple and to seek support from extended family and friends. The clinician supports the family's efforts to communicate effectively and to avoid and reduce conflict. Resolution of problems that inevitably emerge is negotiated in a calm, reasonable way.

Tasks assigned to the client increase and become more complex over time. This is in keeping with the gradual process of recovery and increasing energy level. At first the focus is on integrating the client into the family. Later participation in community activities (social rehabilitation programs, work) are supported, one step at a time. The client who is stable can work toward increasing autonomy and eventually independent living.

The kinds of issues that come up in family sessions include medication compliance, participation in household activities, and early warning signs of relapse. The family is helped to identify changes in behavior that signal the emergence of prodromal (preliminary) signs of schizophrenia. Following an exploration of possible sources of these changes—noncompliance with medication, the need for a medication change, stress—appropriate remedies are pursued.

Phase IV, continued treatment or disengagement, is oriented toward consolidating and maintaining the goals achieved and resumption of normalized living. Anderson and others present this phase to families as optional. Families may elect to terminate, to have periodic maintenance sessions, to continue to work on previous goals, and/or to develop a new contract in which other problems are addressed. Some families have the need for continued support with ongoing intrafamilial problems. Others foresee difficulties surrounding a family member's emancipation. During this phase, when the family may be dealing with latent family issues, the intervention is not unlike the family therapy that is practiced with other client populations.

Families of persons with schizophrenia and other mental disorders can also benefit from reading material that contributes to their knowledge. Books by professionals, persons with schizophrenia, family members, and journalists can provide information, an insider's view, and coping strategies that can fortify the family as they process their experience. Books by Andreasen (1984), Torrey (1988), Hatfield (1982), Sheehan (1982), and Wasow (1982) are especially recommended.

SELECTIVE USE OF PSYCHOTHERAPY

Although intensive in-depth psychotherapy is not generally recommended for persons with schizophrenia, alternative psychotherapeutic strategies can be implemented for clients with this condition. Moreover, clients with other diagnoses can benefit from a range of therapeutic approaches. Families that are enmeshed or have other intrafamilial difficulties may respond to traditional and nontraditional forms of psychotherapy.

Individuals with schizophrenia respond to a relationship characterized by acceptance, support, and an orientation toward reality. Ego supportive therapy (Goldstein, 1984), for example, promotes and restores ego functioning at the same time it does not require the sharing of intimate feelings, the exploration of developmental issues, and the development of a transference. Similarly, task-centered casework (Reid & Epstein, 1972) is a structured approach in which specific problems interfering with a client's everyday functioning can be identified and mastered. Although crisis intervention theory is based on a normative model (Dixon, 1987), crisis intervention techniques can be used to help persons with serious and persistent mental disorders to handle stress.

Because schizophrenia is heterogeneous in its expression, some clients may be able to respond to other approaches. One area in which some clients may be helped is in their perception of self. Estroff (1989) describes the loss and transformation of the self that is concomitant with becoming a schizophrenic. The person who "has" schizophrenia "becomes" the illness, losing his or her former identity. The role of patient or client comes to supersede all other roles, negating the client's subjective experiences. This can result in loneliness, alienation, and pessimism.

Lantz (1984) describes the existential vacuum (Lantz & Belcher, 1987) associated with the pain and suffering experienced by persons with schizophrenia. During an initial stage, the individual becomes disassociated from the consensually validated symbolic order and develops alternative symbols that are not shared by others. This results in isolation and emptiness—which can result in a loss of the will to find meaning in their lives. The authors recommend the use of logotherapy (Frankl, 1984) to help the clients find meaning in their suffering.

Lantz (1986) also finds use for logotherapy in work with families of persons with schizophrenia. Through the technique of *dereflection,* families learn to turn their attention away from a member with schizophrenia and toward some other activity that gives them meaning. Lantz recommends that the therapist provide the family with information about the chemistry of schizophrenia, challenge their attempts to "cure" the member, and encourage them to pursue other interests. These strategies are compatible with those of Anderson, Reiss, and Hogarty (1986) described previously.

Other therapeutic strategies may be helpful to persons with serious and persistent disorders other than schizophrenia. Some of the therapeutic approaches to treating depression that will be described in chapter 12 may also be used with persons with chronic depression. Psychotherapy with persons with borderline disorders is described in a number of books (Goldstein, 1984; Masterson, 1976) and articles (Eckrich, 1985; Freed, 1980).

However developed strategies of intervention with persons with chronic disabilities may be, a need remains to reach clients who "fall between the cracks" in the mental health delivery system. The creation and implementation of innovative programs, residences, and outreach approaches to individuals who are young, homeless, and chemically dependent are a major challenge for the 1990s.

SUMMARY

Treatment approaches for persons with severe and persistent psychiatric disorders include pharmacotherapy, social skills training, and family psychoeducation. Persons with psychotic disorders or who have psychotic symptoms accompanying other disorders are frequently prescribed neuroleptic (antipsychotic) medication. Such medication controls (but does not entirely eliminate) symptoms, facilitating community living. Antipsychotics, however, frequently produce side effects that are disturbing and potentially dangerous. Many persons with bipolar disorders are helped with lithium and some new antimanic agents. These, too, have side effects that need to be monitored. Antidepressant medications (new and old), which also have side effects, can help control symptoms of depression. All the medications have differential effects and risks for women, older adults, and ethnic minority groups.

Social workers should be knowledgeable about the various types of medications and be aware of clients' feelings, attitudes, and behavior in relation to using these drugs. Social workers can help clients work through their feelings about taking medication, encourage clients to discuss their feelings and drug reactions with psychiatrists, and advocate for changes in a client's regimen in their role as consultants to psychiatrists.

Although medication can address biological symptoms, it does not help a client with dysfunctional interpersonal relationships and coping. One method by which clients can learn these skills is social skills training. This method is based on principles from social learning theory. Clients are helped to master difficulties through the enactment of role plays that simulate stressful situations. Techniques such as modeling, behavioral rehearsal, and feedback are used. This can be on an individual, group, or family basis. A group in which such a program was implemented was portrayed.

An additional strategy that may be used is family psychoeducation. The Anderson model, which includes task-centered family counseling and a survival skills workshop, was described. During the survival skills workshop information about schizophrenia, medication, stress, and family coping strategies is presented and family groups that are present have an opportunity to network with each other. During family counseling, the therapist connects with the family during a client's hospitalization and works with the family in the ensuing months. Efforts are made to work with the family to reduce intrafamilial stress and promote connections in the community.

These are basic approaches to work with individuals and families who are dealing with severe mental disorders. Although intensive psychotherapy with persons with schizophrenia is generally not recommended, other approaches with this population (e.g., ego supportive therapy, task-centered casework) may be useful. Clients, as well as families, may also be helped with restoring meaning in their lives through the implementation of logotherapeutic approaches.

Although schizophrenia is one of the most common of the psychiatric disorders that are described as chronic, many persons with serious mental disorders have other disorders. For them intensive psychotherapy may be in order. Approaches to treatment for this diverse population are described elsewhere in this volume and in the literature. A need still exists to develop and implement strategies to meet the needs of clients who fall between the cracks of the mental health delivery system.

DISCUSSION QUESTIONS

1. How do neuroleptics affect symptoms? What symptoms do they ameliorate? Which remain unaffected?
2. What are the risks associated with antipsychotic medication?
3. How might drug dosage be regulated over time for persons taking neuroleptics?
4. Identify side effects and risks associated with the antimanic drugs.
5. What kinds of observations should a clinical social worker make with respect to clients on psychotropic medications?
6. Identify and discuss ethical issues associated with monitoring clients' psychotropic drug use.
7. What are special considerations that should be addressed in psychopharmacotherapy of women and older adults?
8. What is social skills training? What does it do that medication does not address?
9. Describe the therapeutic techniques used in social skills training.
10. Using the case descriptions that were provided in the social skills training section, conduct a social skills training session of your own in which the needs of clients other than Michael are highlighted. Evaluate how the group meeting went.

11. Develop a social skills training role play in the context of a family, rather than a group of clients. What are the advantages of social skills training with families compared with a group of clients? What are the disadvantages?
12. What are the special needs of families of persons with chronic mental illness? Why are women particularly affected?
13. What is family psychoeducation? How does it differ from family therapy?
14. Investigate the family approaches of Goldstein and Kopeikin (1981), Falloon et al. (1981), Beels (1975), and McFarlane (1983). What is distinctive about each of these approaches? What commonalities do these diverse approaches have?
15. Explain how the family psychoeducation model of Anderson helps both the client and the family.
16. Develop a mock psychoeducation program on one of the themes that were listed under Phase II. A group of students can be presenters; the rest can assume roles as family members. Invite the audience to ask questions. Incorporate a videotape available from your local Mental Health Association and set up a table on which literature is displayed.

REFERENCES

American Psychiatric Association. (1987). *Diagnostic and statistical manual of mental disorders (DSM-III-R)* (3rd ed., rev.). Washington, DC: Author.

Anderson, C. M., Hogarty, G. E., & Reiss, D. J. (1980). Family treatment of adult schizophrenic patients: A psychoeducational approach. *Schizophrenia Bulletin, 6,* 490–505.

Anderson, C. M., Hogarty, G. E., & Reiss, D. J. (1981). The psychoeducational family treatment of schizophrenia. In M. J. Goldstein (Ed.), *New developments in interventions with families of schizophrenics* (pp. 79–94). San Francisco: Jossey-Bass.

Anderson, C. M., Reiss, D. J., & Hogarty, G. (1986). *Schizophrenia and the family.* New York: Guilford Press.

Andreasen, N. C. (1984). *The broken brain: The biological revolution in psychiatry.* New York: Harper & Row.

Andreasen, N. C. (1985). Positive vs. negative schizophrenia: A critical evaluation. *Schizophrenia Bulletin, 11,* 380–389.

Baldessarini, R. J., & Cole, J. O. (1988). Chemotherapy. In A. M. Nicholi, Jr. (Ed.), *The new Harvard guide to psychiatry* (pp. 481–533). Cambridge, MA: Belknap Press of Harvard University Press.

Beels, C. C. (1975). Family and social management of schizophrenia. *Schizophrenia Bulletin, 1,* 97–118.

Bellack, A. S., & Mueser, K. T. (1986). A comprehensive treatment program for schizophrenia and chronic mental illness. *Community Mental Health Journal, 22,* 175–189.

Blackwell, B. (1987). Newer antidepressant drugs. In H. Y. Meltzer (Ed.), *Psychopharmacology: The third generation of progress* (pp. 1041–1049). New York: Raven Press.

Cohen, D. (1988). Social work and psychotropic drug treatments. *Social Service Review, 62,* 576–599.

Cook, J. A. (1988). Who "mothers" the chronically mentally ill? *Family Relations, 37,* 42–49.

Dixon, S. L. (1987). *Working with people in crisis* (2nd ed.) Columbus, OH: Merrill.

Dixson, D. L. (1981). Manic depression: An overview. *Journal of Psychiatric Nursing in Mental Health Settings, 19,* 28–31.

Eckrich, S. (1985). Identification and treatment of the borderline personality disorder. *Social Work, 30,* 166–171.

Ellwood, D., & Bane, M. J. (1984). *The impact of AFDC on family structure and living arrangements.* Cambridge, MA: Harvard University, Kennedy School of Government.

Estroff, S. E. (1989). Self, identity, and subjective experiences in schizophrenia: In search of the subject. *Schizophrenia Bulletin, 15,* 189–196.

Falloon, I. R. H., Boyd, J. L., McGill, C. W., Strang, J. S., & Moss, H. B. (1981). Family management training in the community care of schizophrenia. In M. J. Goldstein (Ed.), *New developments in intervention with families of schizophrenics* (pp. 61–77). San Francisco: Jossey-Bass.

Francell, C. G., Conn, V. S., & Gray, D. P. (1988). Families' perceptions of burden of relative care for chronic mentally ill relatives. *Hospital and Community Psychiatry, 39,* 1296–1300.

Frankl, V. E. (1984). *Man's search for meaning* (rev. ed.). New York: Washington Square Press.

Freed, A. O. (1980). The borderline personality. *Social Casework, 61,* 548–558.

Gantt, A. B., Goldstein, G., & Pinsky, S. (1989). Family understanding of psychiatric illness. *Community Mental Health Journal, 25,* 101–108.

Gerhart, U. C., & Brooks, A. D. (1983). The social work practitioner and antipsychotic medications. *Social Work, 28,* 454–460.

Goldman, C. R. (1988). Toward a definition of psychoeducation. *Hospital and Community Psychiatry, 39,* 666–669.

Goldman, C. R., & Quinn, F. L. (1988). Effects of a patient education program in the treatment of schizophrenia. *Hospital and Community Psychiatry, 39,* 282–286.

Goldstein, E. G. (1984). *Ego psychology and social work practice.* New York: Free Press.

Goldstein, M. J., & Kopeikin, H. (1981). Short and long term effects of combining drug and family therapy. In M. J. Goldstein (Ed.), *New developments in intervention with families of schizophrenics* (pp. 5–25). San Francisco: Jossey-Bass.

Green, A. I., & Salzman, C. (1990). Clozapine: Benefits and risks. *Hospital and Community Psychiatry, 41,* 379–380.

Greenberg, L., et al. (1988). An interdisciplinary psychoeducation program for schizophrenic patients and their families in an acute care setting. *Hospital and Community Psychiatry, 39,* 277–282.

Gubman, G. D., & Tessler, R. C. (1987). The impact of mental illness on families: Concepts and priorities. *Journal of Family Issues, 8,* 226–245.

Hatfield, A. B. (1982). *Coping with mental illness in the family: The family guide.* Washington, DC: National Alliance for the Mentally Ill.

Hatfield, A. B. (1987a). Coping and adaptation: A conceptual framework for understanding families. In A. B. Hatfield & H. P. Lefley (Eds.), *Families of the mentally ill: Coping and adaptation* (pp. 60–84). New York: Guilford Press.

Hatfield, A. B. (1987b). Systems resistance to effective family coping. In A. T. Meyerson (Ed.), *Barriers to treating the chronic mentally ill* (pp. 51–62). San Francisco: Jossey-Bass.

Hirschfeld, R. M. A., & Cross, C. K. (1987). Clinical psychopathology and diagnosis in relation to treatment of affective disorders. In H. Y. Meltzer (Ed.), *Psychopharmacology: The third generation of progress* (pp. 1021–1029). New York: Raven Press.

Hogarty, G. E., et al. (1986). Family psychoeducation, social skills training, and maintenance chemotherapy in the aftercare treatment of schizophrenia: I. One-year effects of a controlled study on relapse and expressed emotion. *Archives of General Psychiatry, 43,* 633–642.

Kane, J., Honigfeld, G., Singer, J., et al. (1987). Clozapine for the treatment-resistant schizophrenic. *Archives of General Psychiatry, 45,* 789–796.

Kane, J. M., & Lieberman, J. A. (1987). Maintenance pharmacology in schizophrenia. In H. Y. Meltzer (Ed.), *Psychopharmacology: The third generation of progress* (pp. 1103–1109). New York: Raven Press.

Kaplan, H. I., & Sadock, B. J. (1988). *Synopsis of psychiatry: Behavioral sciences/clinical psychiatry* (5th ed., chapt. 31). Baltimore, MD: Williams & Wilkins.

Lantz, J. E. (1984). Responsibility and meaning in treatment of schizophrenics. *The International Forum for Logotherapy, 7,* 27–28.

Lantz, J. E. (1986). Family logotherapy. *Contemporary Family Therapy, 8,* 124–135.

Lantz, J., & Belcher, J. (1987). Schizophrenia and the existential vacuum. *The International Forum for Logotherapy, 10,* 17–21.

Liberman, R. P. (1988). Social skills training. In R. P. Liberman (Ed.), *Psychiatric rehabilitation of chronic mental patients* (pp. 147–198). Washington, DC: American Psychiatric Press.

Liberman, R. P., et al. (1986). Training skills in the psychiatrically disabled: Learning coping and competence. *Schizophrenia Bulletin, 12,* 631–647.

Liberman, R. P., DeRisi, W. J., & Mueser, K. T. (1989). *Social skills training for psychiatric patients.* New York: Pergamon.

Liberman, R. P., & Foy, D. W. (1983). Psychiatric rehabilitation for chronic mental patients. *Psychiatric Annals, 13,* 539–545.

Lin, K. M., Poland, R. E., & Lesser, I. M. (1986). Ethnicity and psychopharmacology. *Culture, Medicine and Psychiatry, 10,* 151–165.

Lukoff, D., & Ventura, J. (1988). Psychiatric diagnosis. In R. P. Liberman (Ed.), *Psychiatric rehabilitation of chronic mental patients* (pp. 29–58). Washington, DC: American Psychiatric Press.

Masterson, J. (1976). *Psychotherapy of the borderline adult.* New York: Brunner/Mazel.

Matorin, S., & De Chillo, N. (1984). Psychopharmacology: Guidelines for social workers. *Social Casework, 65,* 579–589.

McFarlane, W. R. (Ed.). (1983). *Family therapy in schizophrenia.* New York: Guilford Press.

Mogul, K. M. (1985). Psychological considerations in the use of psychotropic drugs with women patients. *Hospital and Community Psychiatry, 36,* 1080–1085.

News and Notes. (1989). FDA approves clozapine for treatment of schizophrenia; careful monitoring required. *Hospital and Community Psychiatry, 40*(12), 1310.

Payne, D. L. (1987). Antidepressant therapies in the elderly. *Aging & Human Development, 7,* 31–41.

Physicians Desk Reference (PDR). (1990). (44th ed.). Oradell, NJ: Medical Economics.

Prien, R. F. (1987). Long-term treatment of affective disorders. In H. Y. Meltzer (Ed.), *Psychopharmacology: The third generation of progress* (pp. 1051–1058). New York: Raven Press.

Prien, R. F., & Gelenberg, A. J. (1989). Alternatives to lithium for preventive treatment of bipolar disorder. *American Journal of Psychiatry, 146,* 840–848.

Rathus, S. A. (1973). A 30-item schedule for assessing assertive behavior. *Behavior Therapy, 4,* 398–406.

Reid, W. H. (1989). *The treatment of psychiatric disorders.* New York: Brunner/Mazel.

Reid, W. J., & Epstein, L. (1972). *Task-centered casework.* New York: Columbia University Press.

Rifkin, A., & Siris, S. (1987). Drug treatment of acute schizophrenia. In H. Y. Meltzer (Ed.), *Psychopharmacology: The third generation of progress* (pp. 1095–1101). New York: Raven Press.

Ryglewicz, H. (1989, April). Psychoeducation: A wave of the present. *TIE-Lines, 6*(2), 1–2.

Ryglewicz, H. (1989, July). Psychoeducational work with families: Theme and variations. *TIE-Lines, 6*(3), 1–3.

Sands, R. G. (1984). Correlates of success and lack of success in deinstitutionalization. *Community Mental Health Journal, 20,* 223–235.

Sands, R. G. (1985). Bipolar disorder and social work practice. *Social Work in Health Care, 10,* 91–105.

Sheehan, S. (1982). *Is there no place on earth for me?* Boston: Houghton, Mifflin.

Simpson, G. M., Pi, E. H., & Sramek, J. J. (1986). An update on tardive dyskinesia. *Hospital and Community Psychiatry, 37,* 362–369.

Spaniol, L., Jung, H., Zipple, A. M., & Fitzgerald, S. (1987). Families as a resource in the rehabilitation of the severely psychiatrically disabled. In A. B. Hatfield & H. P. Lefley, *Families of the mentally ill: Coping and adaptation* (pp. 167–190). New York: Guilford Press.

Stein, L. I., & Test, M. A. (1980). Alternative to mental hospital treatment: I. Conceptual model, treatment program, and clinical evaluation. *Archives of General Psychiatry, 37,* 392–412.

Strauss, J. S. (1985). Negative symptoms: Future developments of the concept. *Schizophrenia Bulletin, 11,* 457–460.

Terkelsen, K. G. (1987). The evolution of family responses to mental illness through time. In A. B. Hatfield & H. P. Lefley (Eds.), *Families of the mentally ill: Coping and adaptation* (pp. 151–166). New York: Guilford Press.

Thurer, S. L. (1983). Deinstitutionalization and women: Where the buck stops. *Hospital and Community Psychiatry, 34,* 1162–1163.

Torrey, E. F. (1988). *Surviving schizophrenia: A family manual* (rev. ed.). New York: Harper & Row.

Wallace, C. J. (1986). Functional assessment in rehabilitation. *Schizophrenia Bulletin, 12,* 604–630.

Wallace, C. J., et al. (1980). A review and critique of social skills training with schizophrenic patients. *Schizophrenia Bulletin, 6,* 42–63.

Wasow, M. (1982). *Coping with schizophrenia: A survival manual for parents, relatives and friends.* Palo Alto, CA: Science & Behavior Books.

Wittlin, B. J. (1988). Practical psychopharmacology. In R. P. Liberman (Ed.), *Psychiatric rehabilitation of chronic mental patients* (pp. 117–145). Washington, DC: American Psychiatric Press.

11 Clinical Practice with Clients Having Dual Diagnoses: Mental Illness and Substance Abuse

Deborah K. Webb and Diana M. DiNitto

Individuals who use or abuse certain types of drugs, including alcohol, and have mental disorders present special challenges to clinical social workers in community mental health. Although the co-occurrence of mental health and substance abuse problems is not a new phenomenon, only in the past 20 years has it received serious and widespread attention by professionals in the mental health and substance abuse fields. During this period, self-help groups for this population have also begun to emerge.

A number of terms have been used to refer to those who abuse substances and have mental disorders. Many social workers use the term *dual diagnoses,* although this term can be confusing because it has also been used to refer to those with both mental retardation and mental illness. The Alcohol, Drug Abuse and Mental Health Administration (ADAMHA) of the Federal Department of Health and Human Services uses the term *comorbidity* to describe this combination of mental and addictive disorders (cf. Comorbidity: Mental and Addictive Disorders, 1989; Goodwin, 1989). The term *coexisting problems* (Kofoed & Keys, 1988) has also been used, as have acronyms such as MISA (mentally ill substance abuser), MICAA (mentally ill and chemical abusing or addicted; Sciacca, 1989a), and AODA/CMI (alcohol/drug abuse and chronic mental illness; Bricker, 1990). Even the term *the 3-D client* has been used to describe those who are "drinking, drugging and disturbed or 'dually diagnosed' " (Lawlor, 1987, p. 7). None of these terms seem inherently preferable; any of them may be used if it is made clear that both substance abuse and mental illness are the foci of concern. Several of these terms are used interchangeably throughout this chapter.

Of course, even the terms mental illness and substance abuse are vague. As described throughout this text, mental illness refers to diverse psychiatric disorders, some more severe than others, each heterogeneous. Likewise, substance abuse (also called drug abuse and chemical dependency) can include abuse of or dependence on alcohol and/or other drugs as well as substances that many laypersons would not call drugs.

This chapter provides information about the problems of alcohol abuse, alcohol dependency, and other psychoactive substance abuse disorders and their interactions with mental disorders. It begins with a description of abused substances and definitions of abuse and dependency. Then etiological theories of substance abuse and the problems of persons with comorbidity are described. The state of the art in the treatment of persons with both mental and substance abuse disorders is considered later.

SUBSTANCES OF ABUSE

Many substances are abused because of their psychoactive properties. These substances can be grouped into five categories: (a) central nervous system (CNS) depressants, (b) CNS stimulants, (c) opioids or narcotics, (d) hallucinogens, and (e) over-the-counter drugs. Table 11.1 describes chemicals that fall in the first four categories and which are controlled substances.

Depressants

Central nervous system (CNS) depressants, also called sedative-hypnotic drugs, include alcohol, barbiturates, methaqualone, benzodiazepines, and inhalants. *Alcohol* is the most widely used and abused drug in the United States because it can be obtained legally (by those of age) and it is relatively inexpensive. Even underage drinkers often have little difficulty obtaining alcohol, and for those of all ages with little or no funds, alcohol is frequently shared on the streets. Since beverage alcohol is so commonly used in society, it is often not referred to as a drug.

Among adults in the United States there are approximately 10.5 million alcoholics and 7 million alcohol abusers (Alcoholism, 1989; National Institute on Alcohol Abuse and Alcoholism, 1987). Youth also suffer from these problems. For example, 5 percent of high school seniors report that they are daily drinkers (Alcoholism, 1989). When beer, wine, and distilled spirits containing ethanol or ethyl alcohol are not readily available, the chronic alcoholic may misuse common products which contain alcohol, such as vanilla and other extracts and mouthwash. In addition, they may resort to other products containing various types of alcohol that are not meant for human consumption such as perfume, after-shave lotion, rubbing (isopropyl) alcohol, and "canned heat" (Sterno).

Other CNS depressants are *barbiturates*. "Clinically, the barbiturates are used as sedatives, hypnotics, anesthetics and anticonvulsants" (Woolf, 1983b, p. 40). Whether these drugs act as sedatives, hypnotics, or anesthetics usually depends on how much of the drug is taken: the larger the dose, the greater the effect. CNS depressants, including alcohol, are particularly dangerous drugs, because consumption of high doses by individuals in general, and withdrawal effects in those who are physically addicted, can result in serious medical complications, including death. One common barbiturate is secobarbital (generic name), which is marketed under the trade name of Seconal and is known on the streets as *reds* or *devils*. Barbiturates were once widely used in the treatment of insomnia, but have been replaced by other drugs considered better for addressing the causes of insomnia such as anxiety, depression, and pain (Witters & Venturelli, 1988). Another well-known barbiturate is phenobarbital, which is used to prevent seizures in those with epilepsy. It is also used to treat detoxification patients in

TABLE 11.1
Controlled Substances, Uses and Effects

Drugs	Schedule	Trade or Other Names	Method of Usual Administration	Possible Effects	Effects of Overdose	Withdrawal Syndrome
Narcotics						
Opium	II, III, V	Dover's powder, Paregoric, Parepectolin	Oral, smoked	Euphoria, drowsiness, respiratory depression, constricted pupils, nausea	Slow and shallow breathing, clammy skin, convulsions, coma, possible death	Watery eyes, runny nose, yawning, loss of appetite, irritability, tremors, panic, chills and sweating, cramps, nausea
Morphine	II, III	Morphine, pectoral syrup	Oral, smoked, injected			
Codeine	II, III, V	Tylenol with codeine, Empirin compound with codeine, Robitussan A-C	Oral, injected			
Heroin	I	Diacetylmorphine, horse, smack	Injected, sniffed, smoked			
Hydromorphone	II	Dilaudid	Oral, injected			
Meperidine (Pethidine)	II	Demerol, Mepergan	Oral, injected			
Methadone	II	Dolophine, methadone, methadose	Oral, injected			
Other narcotics	I, II, III, IV, V	LAAM, Leritine, Numorphan, Percodan, Tussionex, Fentanyl, Darvon, Talwin,* Lomotil	Oral, injected			
Depressants						
Chloral hydrate	IV	Noctec, Somnos	Oral	Slurred speech, disorientation, drunken behavior without odor of alcohol	Shallow respiration, clammy skin, dilated pupils, weak and rapid pulse, coma, possible death	Anxiety, insomnia, tremors, delirium, convulsions, possible death
Barbiturates	II, III, IV	Phenobarbital, Tuinal, Amytal, Nembutal, Seconal, Lotusate	Oral			
Benzodiazepines	IV	Ativan, Azene, Clonopin, Dalmane, Diazepam, Librium, Xanax, Serax, Tranxene, Valium, Verstran, Halcion, Paxipam, Restoril	Oral			
Methaqualone	I	Quaalude	Oral			
Glutethimide	III	Doriden	Oral			
Other depressants	III, IV	Equanil, Miltown, Noludar, Placidyl, Valmid	Oral			

TABLE 11.1 *continued*
Controlled Substances, Uses and Effects

Drugs	Schedule	Trade or Other Names	Method of Usual Administration	Possible Effects	Effects of Overdose	Withdrawal Syndrome
Stimulants						
Cocaine†	II	Coke, flake, snow	Sniffed, smoked, injected	Increased alertness, excitation, euphoria, increased pulse rate and blood pressure, insomnia, loss of appetite	Agitation, increase in body temperature, hallucinations, convulsions, possible death	Apathy, long periods of sleep, irritability, depression, disorientation
Amphetamines	II, III	Biphetamine, Delcobese, Desoxyn, Desedrine, Mediatric	Oral, injected			
Phenmetrazine	II	Preludin	Oral, injected			
Methylphenidate	II	Ritalin	Oral, injected			
Other stimulants	III, IV	Adipex, Bacarate, Cylert, Didrex, Ionamin, Plegine, Pre-Sate, Sanorex, Tenuate, Tepanil, Voranil	Oral, injected			
Hallucinogens						
LSD	I	Acid, Microdot	Oral	Illusions and hallucinations, poor perception of time and distance	Longer, more intense "trip" episodes, psychosis, possible death	Withdrawal syndrome not reported
Mescaline and Peyote	I	Mesc, buttons, cactus	Oral			
Amphetamine variants	I	2,5-DMA, PMA, STP, MDA, MDMA, TMA, DOM, DOB	Oral, injected			
Phencyclidine	II	PCP, angel dust, hog	Smoked, oral, injected			
Phencyclidine analogs	I	PCE, PCPy, TCP	Smoked, oral, injected			
Other hallucinogens	I	Bufotenine, Ibogaine, DMT, DET, Psilocybin, Psilocyn	Oral, injected, smoked, sniffed			
Cannabis						
Marijuana	I	Pot, Acapulco gold, grass, reefer, sinsemilla, Thai sticks	Smoked, oral	Euphoria, relaxed inhibitions, increased appetite, disoriented behavior	Fatigue, paranoia, possible psychosis	Insomnia, hyperactivity, and decreased appetite occasionally reported
Tetrahydrocannabinol	I	THC	Smoked, oral			
Hashish	I	Hash	Smoked, oral			
Hashish oil	I	Hash oil	Smoked, oral			

*Not designated a narcotic under the Controlled Substance Act.
†Designated a narcotic under the CSA.

Source: Drugs of Abuse. p. 9; courtesy of the Drug Enforcement Administration.

cases in which their withdrawal from other drugs (such as cocaine) may result in seizures (Witters & Venturelli, 1988).

Another well-known sedative drug bought on the streets is *methaqualone,* also known as Quaalude and Sopor (trade names) and *ludes, sopors,* and *quads* (street names) (Woolf, 1983b, p. 41). Like some other drugs, methaqualone was originally thought to have little potential for abuse. It received so much bad press, however, that its production was discontinued in the United States in 1985, although it continues to be imported illegally (Witters & Venturelli, 1988).

Another type of CNS depressant that is well known in both general medical and mental health settings is the *benzodiazepines.* There are several, but the two best known are diazepam (generic name), better known by one of its trade names, Valium; and chlordiazepoxide (generic name), better known by one of its trade names, Librium. These drugs are antianxiety agents and are also called *minor* tranquilizers. Also well-known are alprazolam (Xanax) and flurazepam (Dalmane). Large quantities of the benzodiazepines continue to be prescribed in the United States each year because of their beneficial properties, even though many people readily learn to abuse them. Medical professionals have been criticized for being too quick to prescribe these drugs rather than considering the causes of the patient's anxiety and seeking nondrug alternatives or, when necessary, prescribing nonaddictive medications such as buspiron hydrochloride (BuSpar).

In addition to overdose and withdrawal problems, the use of a combination of CNS depressants can also result in serious consequences, as one drug may potentiate another, resulting in a multiplier rather than an additive effect. Cross-tolerance (tolerance developed to one drug in this class may result in tolerance to other drugs in this class; Witters & Venturelli, 1988; Woolf, 1983a) and cross-addiction (when the drug of choice is not available, the addict may substitute another drug in the same class; see Moore, 1983) are also problems to be considered. Sometimes physicians and dentists inadvertently prescribe medications for patients without checking for the possibility of drug interactions or the potential for inducing a relapse in a patient who is in remission from addiction. Social workers can educate clients to communicate with medical personnel about their diagnoses and medications in order to prevent these problems.

Volatile substances, often called *inhalants* because they are sniffed, are also included in the category of CNS depressants. Plastic cement used in making models is the best known, but correction fluid, gasoline, nail polish remover, paint (especially in spray cans), and many other household products are also used. Nitrous oxide (laughing gas), which is found in cans of whipping cream, is another of these products. Although these products are usually not thought of as drugs, they can result in a wide range of physical problems, including kidney, liver, and bone marrow diseases, severe brain damage (Witters & Venturelli, 1988), and even death. Inhalants are most frequently used by youth because they are inexpensive and easily obtained at home.

Stimulants

The second major classification of drugs is **CNS stimulants.** Although *caffeine* and *nicotine* are stimulants, and nicotine in particular can be physically harmful, attention here is on other stimulant drugs, *amphetamines* and *cocaine*. These drugs keep people alert by preventing drowsiness and sleep. In the past amphetamines were widely prescribed as diet pills, because they suppress appetite, but they are now restricted to short-term use (Ray & Ksir, 1990).

One popular amphetamine is methamphetamine, also known as *speed* or *crystal*. Another popular stimulant, which in recent years has gained much notoriety, is cocaine. Few people would deny that cocaine use can result in psychological dependence, but there is a difference of opinion about its engendering physical dependence. Witters and Venturelli (1988) believe that "[use] of cocaine does not cause physical dependence" although there can be unpleasant withdrawal effects, primarily depression (p. 154). On the other hand, Gawin and Kleber (1988) have discussed evidence of withdrawal effects which, Ray and Ksir (1990) say, "now [makes it] clear that both tolerance and physical dependence are possible" (p. 133). Use of cocaine can also result in psychosis and other serious problems, including death. Chronic users can develop additional physical problems such as destruction of the nasal passage if cocaine is snorted. Some street names for cocaine are *nose candy* and *snow*. Cocaine can also be smoked and taken intravenously. Some people freebase cocaine by heating it in a particular fashion using chemicals before it is smoked; the drug becomes purified and thus much more potent. *Crack,* or rock cocaine, is also purified. Crack can be purchased inexpensively on the street and has a high potential for producing dependence (Ray & Ksir, 1990). The "rush," or high, from cocaine is said to be intense—like a terrific orgasm—and thus the popularity of the drug; however, the "crash," or depression, following the high, especially from crack, is reportedly serious. Antidepressants are sometimes used to mitigate the effects of the crash (Witters & Venturelli, 1988).

Narcotics

Opioids or narcotics include *heroin, codeine,* and *morphine.* Since 1924 heroin has been classified as a drug with a high potential for abuse and without medical value. Codeine, morphine, and other drugs in this class, however, continue to be prescribed for their analgesic (pain-relieving) qualities. They, too, are likely to be abused. Some individuals have become addicted after having been prescribed such drugs for pain relief. Withdrawal from these drugs is difficult because the acute withdrawal phase lasts much longer than it does for other classes of drugs (Woolf, 1983c).

Methadone, a synthetic narcotic, used as a substitute drug for those addicted to heroin, is not a cure for addiction. Methadone maintenance programs were designed to provide legal access to methadone in order to assist addicts and to curtail criminal activity, such as theft, pursued to obtain money to purchase heroin illegally. Methadone is administered orally and provides an alternative to needle use. This is important because needle sharing puts addicts at risk of exposure to the human immunodeficiency virus (HIV) and hepatitis B. Nevertheless, methadone also has potential for abuse, and some have criticized methadone maintenance programs as poor substitutes for a drug-free life.

Hallucinogens

Hallucinogens include LSD (*lysergic acid diethylamide*); PCP (*phencyclidine*), often called *angel dust; psilocybin* ("magic" mushrooms), *mescaline,* and *hash.* The use of LSD can result in adverse consequences, including panic reactions, psychosis, and flashbacks. The well-publicized negative effects of PCP include paranoid delusions, increased strength that can result in injury to others, and violent deaths. *Cannabis,* or marijuana, is sometimes considered a hallucinogen; it may be better to classify it separately since it generally does not produce hallucinatory effects, although it can at certain doses (Holbrook, 1983; Ray & Ksir, 1990). In addition, marijuana can produce a mild physical dependence while use of the other hallucinogens mentioned here does not produce physical dependence. Marijuana is a widely used drug that can be especially potent today (Pepper, 1988). Depending on the dose and the user's characteristics and state of well-being, its negative effects may include anxiety, panic, or paranoia (Witters & Venturelli, 1988; Holbrook, 1983). Amotivation (lack of motivation) may occur in chronic marijuana users, but the evidence is not totally clear (Witters & Venturelli, 1988; Ray & Ksir, 1990; Holbrook, 1983).

Over-the-Counter Drugs

In addition to the drugs that have been described, **over-the-counter drugs** (drugs that can be purchased without a prescription) can also be abused. Over-the-counter sedatives that people buy to help them sleep, cough and cold preparations containing drugs such as codeine or alcohol, and other nonprescription drugs purchased to ease pain also have potential for abuse.

It is important to note that many individuals use, abuse, or are addicted to more than one drug, which is called *polysubstance abuse* or *polysubstance dependence.* Substances used may be controlled and/or over-the-counter drugs.

Only a brief description of abused drugs was provided here. A thorough knowledge of abused drugs is needed by those in the mental health field. Two good recent sources for nonmedical professionals are by Ray and Ksir (1990) and Witters and Venturelli (1988).

DEFINITIONS OF PSYCHOACTIVE SUBSTANCE ABUSE

Discussing definitions of drug abuse is difficult because there are many definitions and models of alcohol and other forms of substance abuse. None is universally accepted, and much controversy surrounds the use of these terms. With these caveats in mind, this section discusses definitional issues that are of particular relevance in clinical treatment.

Much attention has been focused on definitions of alcohol abuse and alcoholism (the latter term is now frequently called *alcohol dependency*). Although Alcoholics Anonymous (A.A.), the world's largest self-help group, has no official definition, its literature states: "The explanation that seems to make sense to most A.A. members is that alcoholism is an illness, a *progressive* illness, which can never be cured but which, like some other illnesses, can be arrested" (Alcoholics Anonymous World Services, 1952, p. 4). A.A. obviously espouses the disease or illness model, but according to the National Institute on Alcohol Abuse and Alcoholism (1987), A.A. also recognizes that there is likely more than one type of alcoholic (Alcoholics Anonymous World Services, 1955, 1981).

In the 1950s the American Medical Association accepted the illness or disease concept. It was also in the 1950s that the World Health Organization (WHO) began to elaborate definitions of alcohol problems with the help of E. M. Jellinek, who contributed considerably to an understanding of the concept of alcoholism. Jellinek (1960) believed that the disease concept could reduce the stigma associated with alcoholism in order to promote the humane treatment of alcoholics, but he actually identified *five* types of alcoholism, only some of which he called diseases. (For an historical discussion of issues in defining alcoholism, cf. also Davies, 1976.)

In 1958 Keller referred to alcoholism as "a chronic behavioral disorder manifested by repeated drinking of alcoholic beverages in excess of the dietary and social uses of the community and to an extent that interferes with the drinker's health or his [her] social or economic functioning" (p. 2). This particular definition avoids use of the term illness or disease and in fact calls alcoholism a behavioral disorder.

Definitions of problems related to the use of alcohol and other drugs have evolved in successive editions of the American Psychiatric Association's *Diagnostic and Statistical Manual of Mental Disorders*. The current edition, the *DSM-III-R*, includes two major sets of these diagnoses. One is "Psychoactive Substance-induced Organic Mental Disorders," which includes the problems associated with intoxication, withdrawal, dementia, and so forth (i.e., "the direct acute or chronic effects of such substances on the central nervous system"; American Psychiatric Association, 1987, p. 165) for each of the types of drugs, including alcohol. The other set is "Psychoactive Substance Use Disorders," in which both abuse and dependence are defined for each type of drug. Abuse and dependence "refer to the maladaptive behavior associated with more or less regular use of the substances" (p. 165). The *general* characteristics of dependence and abuse of the psychoactive drugs found in the *DSM-III-R* are reprinted in Tables 11.2 and 11.3, respectively. (See the manual for specific information on dependence and abuse for each type of drug.) Dependence may be further classified as mild, moderate, severe, in partial remission, or in full remission. The description of alcohol-dependent syndrome found in the World Health Organization's International Classification of Diseases-9 (ICD-9) helped lay groundwork for the *DSM-III-R* definitions. (It should be noted that some think it is inappropriate to list alcoholism or other forms of drug problems as mental health problems per se, although they might agree that one of their consequences can be mental health problems.)

The *DSM-III-R* also avoids use of the terms illness and disease. This is probably done for a good reason—the cause or causes of alcoholism and other forms of chemical dependency have not been isolated. The community still manages, however, to offer treatment to those with psychoactive substance disorders, even though only a small

TABLE 11.2

Diagnostic Criteria for Psychoactive Substance Dependence

A. At least three of the following:

1. Substance often taken in larger amounts or over a longer period than the person intended
2. Persistent desire or one or more unsuccessful efforts to cut down or control substance use
3. A great deal of time spent in activities necessary to get the substance (e.g., theft), taking the substance (e.g., chain smoking), or recovering from its effects
4. Frequent intoxication or withdrawal symptoms when expected to fulfill major role obligations at work, school, or home (e.g., does not go to work because hung over, goes to school or work "high," intoxicated while taking care of his or her children), or when substance use is physically hazardous (e.g., drives when intoxicated)
5. Important social, occupational, or recreational activities given up or reduced because of substance use
6. Continued substance use despite knowledge of having a persistent or recurrent social, psychological, or physical problem that is caused or exacerbated by the use of the substance (e.g., keeps using heroin despite family arguments about it, cocaine-induced depression, or having an ulcer made worse by drinking)
7. Marked tolerance: need for markedly increased amounts of the substance (i.e., at least a 50% increase) in order to achieve intoxication or desired effect, or markedly diminished effect with continued use of the same amount

Note: The following items may not apply to cannabis, hallucinogens, or phencyclidine (PCP):

8. Characteristic withdrawal symptoms
9. Substance often taken to relieve or avoid withdrawal symptoms

B. Some symptoms of the disturbance have persisted for at least 1 month, or have occurred repeatedly over a longer period of time.

Source: From *DSM-III-R*, American Psychiatric Association (1987). Used by permission from the *Diagnostic Statistical Manual of Mental Disorders, Third Edition, Revised.* Copyright 1987 American Psychiatric Association.

percentage receive help and fewer recover. The vast majority of chemical dependency treatment programs in the United States *say* they espouse the disease model of alcoholism and other forms of drug abuse, but these programs generally rely on "talk therapies," cognitive approaches, behavioral approaches, and psychodynamic approaches, and refer clients to 12-step self-help programs. This broad range of approaches has been successful in helping many people "recover" from chemical dependency, but the treatment is not biologically based.

Sobell and Sobell (1976) proposed that *some* alcoholics can be taught to drink in a controlled fashion, a position that has aroused considerable controversy. This chapter is not a place to get into this argument, especially because the clients discussed here are vulnerable to mood or mind altering chemicals, but Pattison, Sobell, and Sobell (1977)

TABLE 11.3
Diagnostic Criteria for Psychoactive Substance Abuse

A. A maladaptive pattern of psychoactive substance use indicated by at least one of the following:
  1. Continued use despite knowledge of having a persistent or recurrent social, occupational, psychological, or physical problem that is caused or exacerbated by use of the psychoactive substance
  2. Recurrent use in situations in which use is physically hazardous (e.g., driving while intoxicated)
B. Some symptoms of the disturbance have persisted for at least 1 month, or have occurred repeatedly over a longer period of time.
C. Never met the criteria for psychoactive substance dependence for this substance.

Source: From DSM-III-R, American Psychiatric Association (1987). Used by permission.

do offer an alternative to the disease model (see also Pattison & Kaufman, 1982). They suggest that alcohol problems can be thought of as occurring on a continuum ranging from no problem to severe problems. This conceptualization can help avoid labeling individuals as "alcoholics" or "addicts," designations that can stand in the way of clients' accepting treatment, especially young people and others who have difficulty seeing themselves as stereotypical "skid row" alcoholics or addicts. Even though skid row alcoholics comprise only 3 to 5 percent of all alcoholics (Royce, 1989; Witters & Venturelli, 1988), this stereotype is still likely to be prominent, and it may interfere with abusers' entering treatment.

Pattison and others' conceptualization makes room for more individualized and multivariate treatment planning to assist abusers. Many of today's chemical dependency treatment programs (especially inpatient programs) do not allow for much individualization. For the most part, treatment is done in groups. Clients who do not "fit in" are frequently considered unmotivated, not ready for treatment, or inappropriate for the program. Among those who do not fit in are persons with dual diagnoses.

Many programs refuse or discourage admission of clients who abuse drugs *and* have severe mental disorders. Furthermore, traditional programs have not been particularly successful in helping these clients, once admitted. Nevertheless, chemical dependency treatment programs are encountering more dually diagnosed clients, and they are recognizing the need for better treatment models to help these individuals.

In ending this section, an important concern is to find a definition of the problems related to substance use and abuse that clients can understand and appreciate, one that can help them make a connection between the life problems they are experiencing and their use and abuse of psychoactive drugs. Kofoed and Keys (1988, p. 1210) suggest the following definition of substance abuse problems for use with clients based on Atkinson's (1985) work: "A loss of consistent control over substance use." Another straightforward definition is the repeated use or abuse of substances that results in serious life problems, including family, social, psychological, job-related, and legal problems. Clients do not automatically make a connection between their life problems and their use of chemicals. An important role of the social worker is to help the client understand this relationship. Although these definitions may seem simplistic, their use in a therapeutic context can be surprisingly useful.

ETIOLOGICAL THEORIES OF SUBSTANCE ABUSE

The biopsychosocial approach used throughout this book is clearly applicable to substance abuse. Although the cause or causes of alcoholism and other forms of chemical dependence have not been identified, there are a variety of biological, psychological, and sociological theories that have been suggested to explain the occurrence of these problems. To this list, moral and multivariate or multicausal models will be added.

Moral Model

The oldest explanations for substance abuse fall under the moral model. According to this perspective, alcoholism (the oldest and most common form of substance abuse) is a result of the individual's personal weaknesses or shortcomings and occurs as the result of one's failure to exercise will power to end the problem. For example, in the American colonies, drinking was a well-accepted custom, but drunkenness was not well received. Those who persisted in public drunkenness might have been flogged or placed in the stocks for all to see. Drunkenness was also considered a sin, and those susceptible to it were called upon to repent. In the last quarter of the nineteenth century, the Women's Christian Temperance Union and the Anti-Saloon League were formed to fight the excesses of alcohol use. (For more about historical perspectives on the concept of alcoholism, cf. Paredes, 1976.)

The moral model is also reflected in the perception of alcohol and other drug use as a crime. Prohibition, which became law as the Volstead Act in 1920 and amended the U.S. Constitution, made the manufacture, sale, and transportation of alcoholic beverages a crime. Drinking, of course, continued, as did the practice of treating public drunkenness as a criminal offense. Public drunkenness became the country's most pervasive crime (see Pittman, 1982). It was not until the 1950s that major medical organizations formally espoused the disease model of alcoholism and state governments began to consider treatment needs of alcoholics. In 1955, 31 states had alcoholism commissions (Lewis, 1955). During the late 1960s, concerted efforts to decriminalize public intoxication became successful and in 1970 the federal government passed the comprehensive Alcohol Abuse and Alcoholism Prevention, Treatment and Rehabilitation Act (known as the Hughes Act after its sponsor Senator Harold Hughes), which established the National Institute on Alcohol Abuse and Alcoholism (NIAAA). In 1974, the National Institute on Drug Abuse (NIDA) was established. Since then the number of alcoholism and drug abuse treatment programs across the country has increased substantially.

Despite recognition of the need for treatment, remnants of the moral model persist. The Reagan and Bush administrations have been criticized for their lax responses to the treatment needs of alcoholics and addicts and their emphasis on the "drug war," which relies heavily on interdiction and other aspects of law enforcement. The *Report of the Presidential Commission on the Human Immunodeficiency Virus Epidemic* (1988) called for "treatment on demand" for drug abusers, but there are waiting lists and an insufficient number of treatment slots in public and not-for-profit programs to meet treatment needs.

Biological Model

The most widely discussed etiological theories about alcoholism today fall under the biological model. Schuckit (1986b) believes that these theories are the easiest to test, and this is the reason why they have garnered considerable attention. Funding sources also seem to favor research in this area. Studies that have suggested a possible genetic cause of alcoholism have confirmed that alcoholism occurs more frequently in some families than in others (e.g., Cotton, 1979); alcoholism concordance rates are higher in identical twins than in fraternal twins (Kaij, 1960); and animal strains can be bred which have a preference for alcohol (Meisch, 1982).

Adoption studies have been of particular interest (NIAAA, 1987). For example, Goodwin, Schulsinger, Hermansen, Guze, and Winokur (1973) and Boham (1978) have found that adopted sons of alcoholics are considerably more likely than adopted sons of nonalcoholics to develop alcoholism. Studies published in the early 1980s continue to suggest a genetic link and have also looked at the role of the environment in the etiology of alcoholism. Among these, Boham, Sigvardsson, and Cloninger (1981), Cloninger, Boham, and Sigvardsson (1981), and Boham, Cloninger, von Knorring, and Sigvardsson (1984) studied 862 men and 913 women who had been adopted early in life by nonrelatives. One of their most widely reported findings concerns the identification of two types of alcoholism. Type I, known as milieu limited, is found in men and women and is associated with alcoholism in either biological parent, but a certain environmental factor—low occupational status on the part of the adoptive father—also had to be present for this type of alcoholism to occur in offspring. Type II, known as male limited, accounts for fewer cases and is the more severe form. It is found only in men and is transmitted from fathers to sons. It accounts for 25 percent of alcoholism cases in males and it does not appear to be affected by environmental factors. Of course, not all children of alcoholics become alcoholics, and it is important to consider why some are not affected.

Other biological theories of alcoholism related to genetics are based on research pointing to differences in neurophysiological functioning, neuropsychological differences, and biochemical differences (cf. NIAAA, 1987, for a useful summary and bibliography of recent genetic evidence). Although all these studies shed light on possible causes of alcoholism, they have yet to isolate the specific mechanisms through which alcoholism might be transmitted. Recently Blum et al. (1990), however, have identified a gene they believe may provide a link "to at least one form of alcoholism" (p. 2055).

Still other biological theories suggest that consumption of alcohol may result in the brain producing a morphinelike substance that triggers an addiction (Bloom, 1982), or that allergies to certain substances used to make alcohol may produce addiction (cf.

Mackarness, 1972), or that the potential for addiction may result from abnormalities in metabolizing sugar (Lundquist, 1971). The problem with many of these theories is that it is usually impossible to distinguish which came first, the difficulty in the body's functioning or the alcoholism (cf. Schuckit, 1986b, for a summary of these theories).

Psychological Model

Schuckit (1986b) also offers a concise description of psychological and sociological theories. Among the psychological theories is that some people become dependent on alcohol because it acts to reduce tension or provides reinforcement or some other positive function in one's life such as the elimination of psychological or physiological pain from childhood or later experiences. Researchers have also expended time and effort in trying to determine whether there are particular personality characteristics or a particular personality profile that characterizes alcoholics or other drug abusers. No definitive evidence has been found, but Nurco (1979) reviewed studies on a number of factors, including deviance and antisocial behavior, that may be predictors of drug addiction. Alan Lang's research also indicates that impulsivity, difficulty in delaying gratification, antisocial behavior, a tendency toward sensation seeking, nonconformity, social alienation, tolerance of deviance, and a high stress level may contribute to a propensity toward addiction (Nelson, 1983). But according to Keller's (1972) law: "The investigation of any trait in alcoholics will show that they have either more or less of it" (p. 1147); in other words, no psychological theory has yet provided the information needed to ascertain the cause or causes of chemical dependence.

Sociological Model

Sociocultural theories also consider a variety of factors and have been used to study differences in the levels of substance abuse problems across cultures or across various subgroups within a culture. Some suggest that the degree of stress in a culture is related to the level of substance abuse problems or that cultural norms that encourage, permit, or inhibit the use of alcohol and other drugs are related to the level of substance abuse problems (see Bales, 1946; Bacon, 1974). Such theories have been used to explain why the United States and France have much higher levels of alcoholism than Italy, why the Irish have higher rates of alcoholism than Jews, why American Indians and African Americans often encounter more alcohol-related problems than Caucasians, and why women seemingly have lower levels of alcoholism than men.

Multicausal Model

Although researchers have established that alcoholism rates vary among groups, they are still not certain why this is so. Cultural factors may play a part, but other potential explanations—biological and psychological—also appear to be implicated. For example, women may drink less as a result of social and cultural norms, but they also seem to metabolize alcohol differently than men (e.g., Frezza et al., 1990), suggesting a biological explanation. Cultural norms may limit the consumption of alcohol in Asian countries, but after drinking small amounts of alcohol, many Asians are said to have a flushing response that promotes discomfort and may also act as an aversion to drinking (Murray & Stabenau, 1982). The milieu-limited type of alcoholism described earlier suggests an interplay of genetic and environmental factors. It may be that several factors must be present for alcoholism or drug abuse to occur, such as a combination of biological, psychological, and/or sociological factors. Such a combination would constitute a multicausal, multimodal, or multivariate model of substance abuse. In addition, the causes of substance abuse may vary among abusers. Given the difficulties to date in isolating the cause or causes of substance abuse, it is likely that there is no single or simple explanation.

THE FACES OF COMORBIDITY

As discussed in earlier chapters, severe mental disorders include psychotic disorders such as schizophrenia and schizoaffective disorder as well as mood disorders such as bipolar disorder and major depression. All these are classified as Axis I disorders in the *DSM-III-R*. Psychoactive substance abuse and dependence are also Axis I diagnoses. In the case of a person who first experiences a severe mental disorder and later psychoactive substance abuse or dependence, the primary diagnosis is the mental disorder and the secondary diagnosis is substance abuse or dependence, but both diagnoses are recorded on Axis I. Some examples of how such diagnoses would be recorded are as follows:

Axis I:	295.34	Schizophrenia, paranoid type, chronic with acute exacerbation (primary)
	305.20	Cannabis abuse (secondary)
Axis II:	V71.09	No diagnosis

or

Axis I:	296.44	Bipolar disorder, manic with psychotic features (primary)
	303.90	Alcohol dependence (secondary)
Axis II:	V71.09	No diagnosis

Listing one diagnosis as primary and another as secondary does not necessarily mean that one disorder is more serious or more important to treat than the other, but that one may be identified as occurring first. Sometimes, especially with young persons, it is difficult to determine which is the primary and which is the secondary problem. (Minkoff, 1990, believes that when two Axis I disorders are of concern, it is more appropriate to classify *both* of them as primary.)

In other cases, an individual may first develop a psychoactive substance disorder and later a mental disorder. A common example of how these diagnoses might be recorded is as follows:

Axis I: 291.20   Dementia associated with alcoholism

Axis II: V71.09   No diagnosis

Because both conditions are contained in a single diagnosis, the terms "primary" and "secondary" are not used here.

There are also serious Axis II diagnoses that commonly appear in conjunction with psychoactive substance abuse disorders, including borderline, antisocial, and dependent personality disorders (e.g., Daley, Moss, & Campbell, 1987; Bricker, 1990). Depending on the individual's circumstances, the Axis II diagnosis or the substance abuse disorder may be the client's primary problem. The following is an example of how these diagnoses may be recorded:

Axis I: 305.60   Cocaine abuse (secondary)

Axis II: 301.83   Borderline personality disorder (primary)

Sciacca (1989b) has distinguished between the mentally ill and chemically abusing or addicted (MICAA) who has a serious Axis I mental disorder in addition to a substance abuse disorder and the chemically abusing person with mental illness (CAMI) who has no free-standing Axis I mental disorder but has a chronic substance abuse disorder and an Axis II mental disorder. Such distinctions may be important in determining the course of treatment for the client. For example, Sciacca (1990) believes that the substance abuse problems of CAMI clients can be treated successfully in traditional chemical dependency programs, because these individuals can better tolerate the confrontation used in these programs. On the other hand, MICAA clients need specialized programs; these clients and their treatment needs are the focus of the remainder of this chapter.

Incidence and Prevalence

Just how prevalent is comorbidity in the general population? According to the NIMH Epidemiologic Catchment Area (ECA) Study:

> Analyses of ECA lifetime prevalence data indicate that for an adult with a primary mental disorder diagnosis, the chance of having an alcohol or drug abuse disorder at some point is nearly 1 in 3; for the alcoholic, the likelihood of suffering a mental disorder or drug abuse disorder is nearly half; for the individual with a diagnosed drug disorder, lifetime probability of a mental disorder or alcohol abuse disorder is 7 in 10. (Comorbidity: Mental and Addictive Disorders, 1989)

Kofoed, Kania, Walsh, and Atkinson (1986) surveyed studies indicating that 25 to 40 percent of all psychiatric patients also have substance abuse problems. Similarly Bauer (1987) reported that "it is common to see prevalence rates of substance abuse ranging between 20–50 % of any psychiatric population" (p. 1). (Also cf. Alterman, 1985; Menicucci, Wermuth, & Sorensen, 1988; Drake & Wallach, 1989). Minkoff (1987) believes that 50 to 70 percent of mentally ill young adults have serious substance abuse problems. With respect to substance abuse patients, there is also considerable variation in the estimates of comorbidity. In a study of 285 male alcoholic veterans, Schuckit

(1983a) found that 24 percent were primary alcoholics with "severe secondary affective disturbances" while 3 percent had primary affective disorders with secondary alcoholism and 7 percent had primary antisocial personality disorders with secondary alcoholism; the remainder had diagnoses of alcoholism only (p. 712). In contrast, Ross, Glaser, and Germanson's (1988) study of 501 patients seeking substance abuse treatment in Canada revealed that 78 percent also had a lifetime psychiatric disorder and 65 percent had a current psychiatric disorder.

Some of the variance in the estimates of comorbidity may be explained by the differences in problem definition and population groups studied. For example, Minkoff (1990) believes that any use of particular drugs by those with serious mental disorders should be considered abuse, while others use more restrictive definitions. Younger mentally ill clients are more likely to have experienced substance abuse than older mentally ill clients (Bauer, 1987; Minkoff, 1987; Pepper & Ryglewicz, 1987). Consequently, those who work with young adult chronic clients are likely to report higher estimates of comorbidity. Others on the front lines of service to those with mental illness across the age spectrum note that approximately 50 percent of these clients also exhibit serious problems with substance use or abuse (Webb, 1990).

Another reason why it is difficult to obtain accurate data on the incidence and prevalence of comorbidity is that mental health professionals tend to overlook substance use and abuse problems ("everyone drinks") and substance abuse professionals tend to minimize mental health problems ("they will clear up with sobriety"). In addition, administrative rules and regulations have discouraged accurate reporting. For example, Menicucci, Wermuth, and Sorensen (1988) report that "many [psychiatric treatment] units are unable to record two primary diagnoses because of computerized systems that allow for the recording of only one major diagnosis" (p. 619). As a result, the number of dual-diagnosis patients is underreported.

Dilemmas in Service Provision

The literature has become replete with acknowledgments of the difficulties that direct treatment providers, administrators, and funders have identified and have sometimes also caused in assisting dual-diagnosis clients (e.g., Thacker & Tremaine, 1989; Drake & Wallach, 1989; McLellan, 1989). Clients with serious mental illness and substance abuse problems do not fit well into traditional treatment settings for the mentally ill or for alcoholics and addicts. In fact, many programs actively exclude such clients by using rigorous screening criteria. It is not unusual for substance abuse treatment programs to deny admission to seriously mentally ill substance abusers. Grounds for denial vary, but may include the following: they are so different that they would be ostracized by others in the program; they do not have the proper cognitive skills to benefit from treatment; they have been psychologically unstable or suicidal too recently (cf. Harrison, Martin, Tuason, & Hoffman, 1985); or they appear unmotivated to participate. Mentally ill substance abusers may be offered minimal help by admission to detoxification units for a few days, but they are often released quickly, without adequate plans for long-term treatment.

Frequently managers of substance abuse programs are skeptical about the potential of seriously mentally ill clients to benefit from their services. They have had negative experiences with such clients, such as premature termination of treatment, extreme acting-out episodes, suicide attempts (Bauer, 1987; Harrison et al., 1985), and verbal and physical aggression. Dually diagnosed clients may jeopardize not only their own treatment goals, but often those of their peers by sharing substances with them or engaging them in fights (although this can also be true of those with a single diagnosis of substance abuse). Thus in residential programs where unit managers are responsible for residents 24 hours a day, consideration of what is best for the whole group may cause the dually diagnosed client to be rejected for admission.

Likewise, traditional community mental health centers focus on the identification and treatment of severe mental illnesses. Often enough, careful patient histories are not constructed, and questions about drug and alcohol use are seldom asked. If comorbidity is identified, residential programs for persons with mental disorders, such as halfway houses and supervised apartments, are likely to screen out these clients. The client may be asked to attend an inpatient chemical dependence program by the mental health specialist, but may be denied admission by the substance abuse specialist. Another problem for clients occurs when they successfully complete a chemical dependency program, but are later denied access to residential programs for those with mental disorders because a substance abuse problem has been confirmed; or clients may be asked to attain a specified period of sobriety on their own (Harrison et al., 1985), such as a month or more (and prove it by submitting urine toxicologies), before admission to a residential program for those with mental disorders is considered. Without constant support and supervision, it is unlikely that the client will be able to achieve sobriety.

During the heyday of deinstitutionalization (the 1970s and early 1980s), older chronically mentally ill clients were discharged from state hospitals, filling programs designed for them to capacity. While confined in mental hospitals as young adults, few had access to alcohol or the street drugs available at that time. Today's young adult chronic clients (ages 18 to 35) present a different picture because of the ready availability of alcohol and drugs. Pepper, Kirshner, and Ryglewicz (1981), Bachrach (1982), Lamb (1982), and others have described these young adult clients at length (see also chapter 8 of this volume). They demand yet reject services for their problems; they have unrealistic goals and expectations for their futures, and they often have extensive histories of drug and alcohol abuse or use. Their substance abuse or use tends to exacerbate their mental illnesses and vice versa. In fact, the effects of their substance abuse may mimic mental illness symptoms and lead to misdiagnosis and inappropriate medication regimens. In view of their life-styles, behaviors, and mixed symptoms, it is often difficult to determine which of their symptoms appeared first and to formulate appropriate treatment plans.

In order to obtain services for clients with comorbidity, professionals sometimes feel pressured to make the clients' diagnoses fit the available treatment programs. In such cases, primary and secondary diagnoses may be interchanged in order to qualify clients with comorbidity for traditional services or to satisfy admission requirements of programs. For example, a halfway house for mentally ill persons may have a funding source which excludes primary alcoholics from sponsorship. In order to facilitate a referral to these programs, some professionals may list a primary diagnosis of adjustment disorder with depressed mood and call the substance abuse secondary, in remission, or not present. But when the same client needs substance abuse treatment, the primary diagnosis may be listed as psychoactive substance abuse disorder with or without a secondary mental illness diagnosis, depending on what is likely to get the client served. Professional ethics demand that clients' diagnoses be recorded accurately, but the pragmatics of securing services for clients can raise dilemmas for practitioners serving dually diagnosed clients.

Recognizing Comorbidity

Researchers such as Schuckit (1986a) have discussed the benefits of determining which of a client's problems appeared first, or is primary. Useful tools, such as Mee-Lee's (1985) decision tree, have been developed, and careful histories are encouraged. Nevertheless, as polysubstance abuse becomes increasingly prevalent with ever younger individuals, even early symptoms of mental illness can be masked by drug use. The first challenge for clinicians is to recognize and document substance abuse since it is commonly overlooked by medical doctors in the general population (Clark, 1988), just as it is often overlooked by professionals who treat individuals with mental disorders.

Substance-induced psychoses can look very similar to an acute exacerbation of a severe mental illness upon presentation for help at a psychiatric emergency screening unit. One way to establish a diagnosis is to obtain a carefully completed detailed history. Pepper (1988) laments that in many treatment settings, history taking is a lost art. Self-reports of clients are not enough, especially during emergencies. Consultation with the family and significant others, as well as close screening of previous inpatient and outpatient records and court records, can reveal information that the client may not be willing or able to provide. Social workers are particularly skilled in gathering data that can contribute to the team's formulating a treatment strategy for the individual. Identification of temporal relationships, if any, between substance abuse or use and exacerbation of mental illness symptoms is necessary to the development of reliable treatment plans. Concrete evidence, such as urine toxicologies done in times of crisis and upon hospital admissions, can reveal the extent and types of substance use and abuse.

Mee-Lee (1990) also suggests using careful histories to determine results of previous trials of medications and/or intake of abused substances. This has vital implications for treatment because, unlike an individual with schizophrenia, a person who appears to have substance-induced psychosis may be treated without medications or with different medications, while a person who has a known history of mental illness and who in the past had poor results when taken off medications, may be treated with psychotropic medications beginning immediately after admission to an inpatient unit.

Relationships Between Abused Drugs and Mental Disorders

It seems that there are associations between particular mental disorders and abused drugs of choice. Treffert (1978), for example, addresses the propensity of persons with schizophrenia, paranoid type, to use marijuana, a phenomenon Khantzian (1985) calls nonrandom, self-medication. Schneier and Siris (1987) reviewed a number of studies and found that "schizophrenic groups' use of amphetamines and cocaine, cannabis, hallucinogens, inhalants, caffeine, and tobacco was significantly greater than or equal to use by control groups consisting of other psychiatric patients or normal subjects" and that their "use of alcohol, opiates, and sedative hypnotics was significantly less than or equal to use by controls." They agree that these patterns are not random (p. 641). McLellan, Childress, and Woody (1985) report that among psychiatric patients, amphetamines or hallucinogens were preferred by persons with paranoid schizophrenia but were less likely to be used by depressed patients, whereas barbiturates were more likely to be preferred by depressed rather than schizophrenic patients. Furthermore, they found that among substance abusers, stimulant and mixed-drug users showed greater psychiatric symptomatology (especially schizophrenia, psychasthenia, and paranoia) than other drug users, whereas opiate users had less psychiatric symptomatology, except for depression and psychopathy.

McLellan et al. consider both "self-medication" and "causative" explanations for their findings. The causation view suggests that chronic drug use causes mental illness as the result of biological changes in the individual. The self-medication explanation, which has engendered considerable discussion (cf. Khantzian, 1985; Schneier & Siris, 1987) among mental health and substance abuse professionals, suggests that those with symptoms of depression are drawn to barbiturate, benzodiazepine, and sedative-hypnotic use because these drugs help alleviate distressful symptoms (although, over the long run, these drugs may exacerbate symptoms). This self-medication view is less clear with respect to users of hallucinogens and amphetamines, as these drugs may, for example, serve to increase dysphoria by exacerbating the patient's hallucinations, confusion, and suspiciousness. Some effects of amphetamines may be pleasing, such as greater awareness, energy, and feelings of power. The exact nature of the relationship between the problems of mental illness and substance abuse, however, remains unclear.

The discussion of mental illness in this chapter refers to clients whose fragile brain chemistry can easily become unbalanced; when talking about drug use or abuse, reference is to clients using psychoactive substances that directly affect brain chemistry and create chemical imbalances. In some instances, internally versus externally influenced changes in brain chemistry may be indistinguishable to the brain, the client, his or her family, and the treatment team. Many people with mental disorders are adversely affected by *abuse* of substances, but many more have such fragile brain chemistry that "social" use can also cause psychotic episodes. Take the case of a young man who had three mental hospital admissions in 1 year. All of his treatment workers assumed it was noncompliance with medications that precipitated his episodes. None had asked about or discovered that the client usually drank up to a six-pack of beer before each admission occurred. When the client independently recognized the association between his drinking and his psychotic episodes, and decided to quit drinking altogether, he was able to stay out of the hospital for 3 years to date. In another example, a caseworker who had known a female client well for 3 years was asked at a brain-storming session whether the client, who had had multiple hospitalizations, ever drank or used drugs. The caseworker gave a strong negative response and offered a long list of daily observations that did not indicate addiction or intoxication. Subsequently the client met with the mental health team and was asked what symptoms she had noticed before admissions. Much to her caseworker's surprise, the client replied that every time she drank even one beer, the next thing she knew, she was in the hospital. Such examples demonstrate the need to screen for substance use as well as abuse.

Although mental disorders and psychoactive substance abuse disorders may have separate etiologies and courses (see Alterman, 1985), evidence from the Epidemiologic Catchment Area Study "seems to support the hypothesis that mental illness and substance abuse occur together more frequently than chance would predict" (Lehman, Myers, & Corty, 1989, p. 1019). In addition, when a client has comorbidity, exacerbation of one illness can exacerbate the other and lead to rehospitalization. Bakdash (1983) has commented on the cyclical nature of the problems of dually diagnosed clients (Figure 11.1). Traditional treatments without modifications have not met the needs of these individuals. Hybrid and new approaches to treatment are currently being developed. To practice with these clients, one must attain specialized knowledge, methods, and skills concerning mental illness *and* substance abuse.

TREATING DUALLY DIAGNOSED CLIENTS

Rather than treating the problems of mental illness and substance abuse in tandem, Minkoff (1989) describes a *parallel* treatment approach to address mental illness and substance abuse concurrently. This approach consists of four stages of treatment: (a) acute stabilization; (b) engagement to participate in treatment; (c) prolonged stabilization, including abstinence from substances and control of the symptoms of mental illness; and (d) rehabilitation. Osher and Kofoed (1989) describe four similar phases of treatment: (a) engagement into treatment; (b) persuasion to stabilize over a long period

FIGURE 11.1
Cyclical process of the dual problem. From Bakdash (1983). Used by permission. *Substance Abuse; Pharmacologic, Developmental, And Clinical Perspectives.* By E. Gerald Bennett, Donna Woolf and C. Vourackas. Delmar Publishers Inc., Copyright 1983.

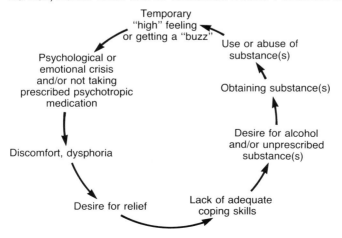

of time; (c) active treatment; and (d) relapse prevention. (For additional information on parallel or simultaneous treatment, see also Harrison et al., 1985; Ridgely, Osher, & Talbott, 1987.) In this section the continuum of care and the components of treatment that can assist dually diagnosed clients toward recovery are reviewed. The unique treatment issues that arise in assisting this group of clients are also addressed.

Educating Clients About Dual Diagnoses

Few educational materials about substance use and abuse have been integrated into the ongoing treatment of persons with psychiatric disorders. Although strong emphasis is placed on compliance with psychotropic medications and clients are educated about potential side effects of these drugs, the potential adverse effects of using alcohol and nonprescribed drugs are often ignored. Thus the first step toward successfully educating mentally ill persons about substance abuse is to educate and raise the awareness of social workers and other helping professionals so that they can educate clients and their families (cf. Sciacca, 1987).

The messages to clients should be clear and consistent: *use or abuse* of alcohol and/or other nonprescribed drugs can adversely affect mental stability. In addition, the *interactions* of nonprescribed and prescribed drugs can be harmful or lethal. Slogans such as "just say no to drugs" and "only sick people use drugs," however, can confuse some mentally ill clients. One must continually differentiate between "medications" (drugs prescribed by the psychiatrist or primary health care physician and used as prescribed) and "street drugs," over-the-counter drugs, alcohol, and improperly used prescription drugs (Bricker, 1988b, 1989).

One of the most important outcomes of substance abuse education is for clients to connect the temporal aspects of their drug use or abuse with the exacerbation of their mental health problems and vice versa (Sciacca, 1987). This can be especially difficult because clients' learning, judgment, and memory are generally impaired when they become mentally unstable. Thus a psychotic episode is likely to destroy the client's ability to see the relationship between a behavior (such as drinking or drug use) and the consequence of this behavior (such as the exacerbation of mental illness) or the precipitation of a mental health crisis. Careful history taking and attention to preceding events can assist mentally ill clients in discovering a repeated cycle of substance use before mental illness exacerbations occur (Schuckit, 1983b) or a pattern in which increases in psychiatric symptoms (such as may occur when clients take their medication differently than prescribed, do not take it at all, or run out of medication) may result in the use of nonprescribed psychoactive drugs. Kofoed and Keys (1988) describe the use of a persuasion group with psychiatric inpatients to help them to "acknowledge their drug addiction and to seek continued substance abuse treatment" (p. 1210; cf. also Osher & Kofoed, 1989, on persuasion and engaging clients into treatment).

It may also be useful to help clients recognize the parallels or similarities between their two types of problems. In both conditions, for example, denial is common, there is a loss of control over behavior and emotions, and there is a need for formal treatment (cf. Bricker, 1989; Minkoff, 1989; Carey, 1989).

Assessment: Instruments and Social Histories

The assessment process begins with the very first contact a client has with the mental health system. Accurate identification and assessment of problems provide the cornerstone for proper treatment. Symptoms of mental illness such as grandiose delusions or auditory hallucinations can be easily observed clinically. Covert drug use, however, may go unnoticed without the aid of lab work (Hall, Popkin, Stickney, & Gardner 1978). The assessment process is complicated in a number of ways. Clients who think concretely tend to offer information only in response to specific questions. Because clients tend to present themselves in the "best possible light" when attempting to gain access to services, they may not volunteer information about drug and alcohol problems. Other clients may not have insight into the deleterious effects of substance use and abuse on their precarious mental health. Asking the right questions is imperative. Fischer, Halikas, Baker, & Smith (1975) suggest asking clients how many drugs they have tried as a screening strategy.

Mental status examinations tend to be standardized, so clients who have had frequent contacts with mental health services expect to be asked such questions as "Who is the president?," "What is the date?," and "How are you sleeping?" Drug use and abuse, however, are often ignored or missed by psychiatrists, psychologists, and social workers. One way to consistently gain this valuable information is to include drug abuse screening instruments as part of all initial assessments. Several screening instruments are available. Caragonne and Emery (1987) mention 10 scales. One of the most widely researched screening instruments is Selzer's (1971) Michigan Alcoholism Screening Test (MAST). It has high reported validity ($r = .90$) and reliability ($\alpha = .95$). The MAST consists of 24 questions which can be easily answered. Moore (1972) used the MAST with 400 inpatients and concluded that it offered a cost-effective and easy way to screen for alcoholism. Selzer (1990) recommends the shortened version of the MAST (SMAST) (Pokorny et al. 1972; Selzer et al., 1974) for screening persons with serious mental disorders. Mulinski (1988) also recommends this.

Another easily administered screening or prescreening instrument is the CAGE questionnaire. Originally developed by Ewing and Rouse (1970), it consists of four simple questions (cf. Mayfield, McLeod, & Hall, 1974). Sciacca (1986) has modified this instrument slightly to include drug use. The questions are:

1. Have you ever felt that you should *cut down* on drinking?
2. Have people *annoyed* you by criticizing your drinking?
3. Have you ever felt *guilty* about your drinking?
4. Have you ever had a drink first thing in the morning to steady your nerves or get rid of a hangover (*eye opener*)? (J. A. Ewing, "Detecting alcoholism, the CAGE Questionnaire," *JAMA,* vol. 252, pp. 1905–1907, copyright 1984, American Medical Association.)

An affirmative answer to one or more questions indicates a need for follow-up by staff versed in assisting dually diagnosed clients. Sciacca cautions that even if all answers are negative, further assessment is warranted if (a) the client's mode of responding is unusual; (b) information from other sources indicates a potential substance abuse problem; or (c) the professional believes the clinical picture is unclear.

Many researchers in the field of comorbidity are making a standard practice of using McLellan, Luborsky, Woody, and O'Brien's (1980) Addiction Severity Index (ASI). The ASI is a structured clinical interview designed to determine the severity of problems in six life areas. The interview takes a minimum of about 30 minutes to complete. With information from standardized screening instruments and thorough social histories, the client's denial or lack of insight regarding substance abuse may be addressed and professionals are less likely to accept the client's judgment that substance abuse is not a problem (cf. Mulinski, 1988).

Detoxification Programs

There are two types of inpatient alcohol and drug detoxification programs for physically addicted individuals. Both are medical, but one type is hospital based and the other is found in a special community facility. In order to be "detoxed" in a hospital, the patient must be admitted by a physician. Hospitals are able to treat all forms of drug withdrawal, but many patients can be detoxified successfully in a community facility. A nurse may admit the patient to a community detoxification program. The most common community-based detoxification programs are for alcoholics. Other types of drug withdrawal may also be treated there, but if severe problems arise, such as delirium tremens (DTs), which can occur during withdrawal from alcohol and other depressant drugs, it is likely that the patient will be transferred to a hospital.

Drug abusers who are not physically addicted may also need assistance in becoming drug-free. Some programs (sometimes called *social setting programs*) offer support to those who are psychologically but not physically dependent to help them terminate drug use.

A client in a community-based detoxification program who also has a major mental disorder presents special management problems. When individuals are admitted while intoxicated or high, it is impossible to tell whether they also have a serious mental disorder, unless the patient's history is already known to the staff. After the client is admitted and withdrawal progresses, the mental health problem is likely to become evident. At this point, the client will probably be transferred to a mental health program. Many community detoxification programs prefer not to admit persons with severe mental health problems, because they are usually not equipped to treat serious mental disorders. For this reason, hospitals in which substance abuse and mental disorders are treated at the same facility are preferred for many dually diagnosed clients. Clients with multiple admissions to community detoxification programs, so-called revolving-door clients, are often accused of abusing the system. In response, these programs may adopt the controversial policy of restricting the number of admissions a client is permitted within a given period of time.

Some addicts can be detoxified on an outpatient basis. Outpatient detoxification can be a cost-effective alternative to inpatient detoxification (Hayashida et al., 1989), but it is not a viable option if the patient does not have supervision to promote compliance with the protocol and if emotional support during this difficult period is lacking. Persons with serious mental disorders who are also substance abusers frequently fall into this category, making inpatient detoxification a better alternative for them.

Missions and Shelters

Mentally ill persons, substance abusers, and clients with both these problems often spend time in missions and shelters when they have nowhere else to go. Law enforcement officers may not wish to arrest these individuals for vagrancy, loitering, or public intoxication, but may see that they find their way to a mission or shelter. The informal communication network of street people also leads clients to these facilities when shelter is needed. Their stay is often brief and is usually provided free or at minimal cost. The Salvation Army is the organization best known for providing these types of services. The "Sallie," as it is known, generally provides meals and shelter, and participants may attend its religious services. Individuals with alcohol, drug abuse, and mental disorders are generally welcomed as long as they do not prove to be serious management problems (i.e., they do not act out), but they are not usually permitted to remain at the shelter during the day. Some residents remain for longer periods of time and may receive treatment services provided by the Salvation Army or other community agencies; they may also work in the Salvation Army's thrift stores or in the community. Mission programs under other auspices operate in a similar fashion.

There are a growing number of shelters for homeless individuals around the country. Persons who have been drinking, using drugs, and/or are currently experiencing serious mental health problems are not well served in many of these programs. These individuals present management problems because of their unmet medical and mental health needs.

Intensive Inpatient Treatment

This form of treatment for substance abuse and mental disorders is available in most areas if clients have the resources to pay for it. Third-party payers, however, generally restrict the number of days this care will be covered and dually diagnosed clients may soon exhaust their benefits. For those without the financial means who are not committed involuntarily to publicly supported programs, obtaining intensive inpatient services promptly can be difficult. Public and private not-for-profit treatment programs may have waiting lists for which dually diagnosed clients generally cannot wait. Substance abusers are often referred to intensive inpatient treatment programs following detoxification, and mentally ill clients are often referred to them following treatment for acute psychiatric episodes. If inpatient treatment or other supportive living arrangements are not available, a client may be forced onto the streets, where it is difficult to maintain abstinence or control symptoms of mental illness. Caton, Gralnick, Bender, and Simon (1989) emphasize that dually diagnosed clients "cannot be managed on an outpatient or brief inpatient basis. Long-term hospital care is often required" (p. 1039).

At first it may seem that a reasonable approach to inpatient care for dually diagnosed clients lies in their attending traditional inpatient substance abuse programs and traditional inpatient psychiatric programs in tandem. Because of differences in treatment approaches between chemical dependency and psychiatric treatment staff, this strategy has not proven very successful (Osher & Kofoed, 1989; Ridgely et al., 1987; Minkoff, 1989; Menicucci et al., 1988). One difference is that in order to break down denial, chemical dependency counselors may use strong forms of confrontation which mentally ill clients may not be able to tolerate (Osher & Kofoed, 1989; also cf. Carey, 1989). Another is that mental health staff may not emphasize the need for abstinence, giving clients the erroneous impression that recreational drug use, particularly alcohol use, cannot be harmful to them. Interactions between dual- and single-diagnosis clients may also be problematic. For one, chemically dependent clients may be uncomfortable with clients who are also struggling to control symptoms of mental illness (such as hallucinations) and who may need more concrete approaches to substance abuse education and group therapy. Clients with mental illness may feel inhibited talking about their psychiatric problems in chemical dependency treatment programs and, in order to "fit in," may deny their mental illness. Second, psychiatric clients may resent treatment with drug abusers whom they see as socially deviant. Mentally ill clients are likely to view their psychiatric conditions as involuntary, while they may view substance abuse as voluntary behavior. As a consequence, dually diagnosed clients in psychiatric programs may minimize their drug abuse.

Programs which offer simultaneous treatment or parallel treatment for mental illness and substance abuse remain scarce. Some substance abuse programs do offer help for mental illness, usually by recruiting a mental health professional to provide additional services to the client. Likewise, some psychiatric programs offer help with substance abuse problems, usually by having a substance abuse counselor work with clients individually or in groups (cf. Hendrickson, 1988). Substance abuse programs are responding to the increase of dually diagnosed clients on their caseloads by hiring professional staff who are acquainted with both mental illness and substance abuse. Lawlor (1987) and Sciacca (1987), however, believe that clients with more than one diagnosis are best served in psychiatric settings where the expertise to treat mental health problems with therapeutic interventions, including psychotropic medications, is available. Staff in these programs can then be educated about substance abuse. Lawlor implores mental health professionals to stop "passing the buck" and to take responsibility for treating these individuals. Recommendations for inpatient treatment of dually diagnosed clients have been described by Minkoff (1989), Ridgely et al. (1987), Oregon Health Department (1990), Harrison et al. (1985), Allen and Manchaca (1989), and Kofoed and Keys (1988). Some of these programs present mental illness and substance abuse as similar or parallel types of problems, but treatment focuses on the *unique* problems of clients who experience both problems concurrently. For example, differentiations must be made between the use of prescribed medications and nonbeneficial substances. The cyclical nature and interplay of substance abuse and mental illness can also be addressed in these programs without concern that the time of clients with a diagnosis of substance abuse *or* mental disorder could be put to better use. The treatment *modalities* used in special programs for dually diagnosed clients are the same as those used in inpatient psychiatric and substance abuse programs and include education, group therapy, individual therapy, family education, family therapy, and an introduction to self-help programs. Individualization of treatments offered to clients is also stressed.

Supervised Living Arrangements

As Daley et al. (1987) suggest, dually diagnosed clients who lack supportive social networks may particularly benefit from residential treatment. One type of residential treatment setting is a halfway house. Clients often enter a halfway house after stabilization of acute problems related to mental illness and/or substance abuse.

Although many halfway houses serve mentally ill clients, only some accept mentally ill clients who also have substance abuse problems. Following arrival at the halfway house, independent living skills and social skills are observed and assessed. Clients typically participate in individual and group therapy, psychiatric services, educational classes, and social and recreational activities geared to promote their functioning and develop their independent living skills. Before referring clients to these programs, clinicians are wise to ensure that abstinence from alcohol and other nonprescribed drugs is part of the treatment regimen. Other halfway houses are designed for substance abusers; some will accept dually diagnosed clients whose mental illnesses are in remission. Social workers should be careful to determine whether the program admits clients taking psychotropic medications.

Clients with concurrent problems are best referred to programs that treat both disorders simultaneously. Programs in which the length of stay is based on individual need are particularly desirable, since the length of treatment required by dually diagnosed clients may exceed that *needed* by singly diagnosed clients or *permitted* by halfway houses that serve substance abusers *or* mentally ill persons. Until special programs for dually diagnosed individuals become more prevalent, social workers and other case managers are left with piecing together services for clients.

Clients with dual diagnoses often have sporadic work histories, limited job skills, and no present source of income [unless they have previously met the criteria for Supplemental Security Income (SSI), Social Security Disability Insurance (SSDI), or Social Security retirement benefits]. They may need several types of transitional services before independent living can be considered. For example, the client might leave a state psychiatric hospital and live at a board-and-care home or group home while continuing to stabilize at a partial hospitalization or day treatment program. When stable, the client will likely have a vocational assessment and attend work adjustment training, prevocational training, or work in a transitional employment program. At some point the client may move to a halfway house and seek competitive employment. After learning how to find and keep a job, the client may move to a supervised apartment program for a few months before independent living occurs.

Clients with more severe impairments and limited abilities might require foster home placement or placement in domiciliaries (such as those operated by the Veterans Administration). Other facilities of this type for debilitated alcoholic clients are often referred to as "farms" because they are located out of town or in a rural area. These facilities encourage clients to perform self-care activities, and they provide 24-hour supervision. Clients are usually readmitted to these residences following rehospitalization for acute episodes.

Day or Night Treatment

If a client has a "clean" (drugfree) environment in which to live, such as with a supportive and enlightened relative, or is a resident of a community support residential program, day treatment can be a good alternative to traditional inpatient treatment. It might actually be night treatment, because some programs are conducted in the evenings so clients can pursue daytime employment. Day treatment (also known as partial hospitalization) programs are used widely and successfully in the mental health system at substantial savings over inpatient care. Sciacca (1987) describes a model day treatment program for dually diagnosed clients that incorporates many of the principles mentioned in this chapter, such as "nonconfrontational" approaches and assistance in helping clients identify the interrelationships between their drug use and their mental illness.

Outpatient Treatment

In many communities outpatient services for mentally ill clients and services for substance abusers are administered by two separate agencies, complicating the coordination of services for dually diagnosed clients. In other communities the same agency (typically a community mental health center) is responsible for services for mentally ill clients and substance abusers, but services to these client groups are provided by separate programs or treatment teams. In these situations, one team monitors the client's psychiatric symptoms, medications and their side effects, and compliance with medications, while the other team is concerned with the client's sobriety, relapse prevention, and 12-step activity. Communication and collaboration between program staff are necessary to successfully assist dually diagnosed clients assigned to two programs. A better approach is for one team with expertise in both areas to oversee client services. Unfortunately many community mental health outpatient centers do not have such teams or are just beginning to develop them. In addition, the amount of contact and the quality of interaction with each client are often far less than desirable. Assessments are often hurried and not comprehensive; treatment plans are not as fleshed out, creative, or individualized as they could be.

The need for an integrated approach to assessment and treatment is illustrated in the following case example of how an outpatient mental health staff failed to identify a client's substance abuse problem.

Clara, a 19-year-old woman, consistently blamed her troubles on her poor relationship with her parents. She had been able to obtain jobs but could not keep them. During some outpatient visits, she dressed and acted appropriately, but at others she dressed seductively and wore bizarre makeup. Her daily cocaine habit went unnoticed until she found herself without a place to live and felt forced to enter a halfway house. Daily observations and urine tests at the halfway house confirmed her drug abuse. In counseling sessions she eventually admitted and explored her feelings about exchanging sexual favors for drugs, and learned about the consequences of this behavior, including the possibility of contracting the human immunodeficiency virus (HIV). Upon discharge from the halfway house, Clara was referred back to the outpatient mental health unit for follow-up and treatment by a social worker who specialized in substance abuse treatment. In addition, her family was referred for educational sessions, as they continued to deny their daughter's drug abuse. Without the ongoing professional observation and concrete evidence (urine toxicologies) of conjoint mental illness and substance abuse provided in the halfway house, this client's substance abuse problem may have continued to progress undetected. Following the comprehensive services she received at the halfway house, the client was able to function with periodic outpatient visits.

Services for dually diagnosed clients are still in their infancy. Grants earmarked for the development of programs and treatments for dually diagnosed individuals became available in the late 1980s through the National Institute on Mental Health (see *Community Support Network News,* 1989, for a listing of demonstration projects). Evaluations of these projects should contribute to improving inpatient and outpatient interventions with dually diagnosed clients.

Developing Social and Independent Living Skills

Persons with severe mental disorders frequently have poor social skills. They are often withdrawn and appear unfriendly, or they are overly friendly and inappropriately gregarious with total strangers. With practice in a supportive and understanding environment, appropriate social skills can be cultivated, maintained, and generalized. Social activities can spawn many pleasant opportunities to practice such skills. Educational classes such as assertiveness training are particular favorites. Role-playing assertive scripts is fun as well as constructive. More skillful clients usually encourage and support the others. Also, sports such as volleyball and baseball reinforce team goals and social interactions. At the Homestead Supervised Apartment Program in Austin, Texas, clients and staff practice social skills weekly for an hour and a half in the context of the "Lunch Bunch." Side by side, clients and staff prepare and enjoy lunch and conversation. Attention is focused on pleasantries instead of problems, crises, and "putting out fires." Alumni members and prospective referrals are also welcomed. The only restriction is that intoxicated or "high" clients are not allowed to participate. Thus, another important purpose that this activity serves is to model how to have fun without drinking or taking drugs.

Mentally ill substance abusers, especially those who have been living on the streets, also need help with independent living skills, which can be taught through social skills training and educational programs that use showing and doing rather than lecturing. (See chapter 10 for a description of social skills training.) The need to develop such skills distinguishes dually from singly diagnosed alcoholics and other drug abusers who may have been quite independent and functional in the past.

Family Involvement

The family of a client can be the most important ally a treatment team has. Experience in observing and often living with the client for decades and in various situations sensitizes families to the most subtle nuances of behavior changes. Often naive about treatment options and referral procedures, however, family members may experience considerable frustration and feelings of helplessness and guilt during the client's first psychotic episodes. Information and referral services at the local community mental health center and an ongoing educational series for family members are important services. When families recognize the signs of illness early, prompt intervention can result in less restrictive treatment. For example, the client might be stabilized by attending a partial hospitalization program daily for a short period of time, thereby avoiding a lengthy hospitalization and perhaps preventing interruption of living arrangements and employment. The toll on the client's self-esteem may also be minimized. (Families of substance-abusing clients can also be taught to recognize early warning signs of relapse; cf. Gorski & Miller, 1986.)

Family members can provide invaluable information for the construction of an accurate social history. This sort of partnership with families is particularly vital with the dually diagnosed client. Family members who help create and understand treatment goals can also share the task of reinforcing accomplishments. For instance, family members can learn the values of being consistent, practicing "tough love," giving positive reinforcement, shaping and extinguishing behaviors, and so on.

Family members often feel alone when facing the mental illness and substance abuse of a loved one. The stigma of these conditions often keeps them from sharing their feelings and fears with others. Support groups can offer tremendous relief through acceptance, understanding, and fellowship. Al-Anon is a well-known self-help group for families and friends of alcoholics. Nar-Anon is a similar group for the loved ones of addicts. More recently, self-help groups have been developed for family members of the mentally ill through the National Alliance for the Mentally Ill (NAMI). In the last decade NAMI has been growing strong by realizing that political power through numbers gets the attention of those who fund research and treatment programs. Local chapters now exist in many locations. For many patients and their families, as well as for some professionals, an active advocacy role has become a constructive alternative to passive resignation to problems in the delivery of mental health and substance abuse services. Interested parties can keep abreast of the latest developments by reading NAMI newsletters and attending its stimulating, reasonably priced state and national conferences.

One of the newest self-help formats, which is for the loved ones of dually diagnosed individuals, is called MICAA-NON (cf. Sciacca, 1989a). Developed in conjunction with NAMI chapters, it focuses on problems unique to those with mental illness and drug abuse and their families. "MICAA-NON groups presently are led by professionals, though it is hoped they will eventually be co-led by the family members" (Sciacca, 1989a, p. 7).

TIE-Lines is a useful and reasonably priced publication for professionals, clients, and families of young adults with severe mental illness. It now includes a page on dual diagnoses in every issue. Other materials on dual diagnoses are readily available through The Information Exchange (TIE). (For further information, write 151 S. Main St., Suite 212, New City, NY 19056.)

Sober Peer Groups

Twelve-step programs constitute the fastest growing self-help movement of this century. Just as alcoholics benefit from the original 12-step program, Alcoholics Anonymous (A.A.), adaptations of these steps have evolved to help those with other types of problems. Addicts feel understood at Narcotics Anonymous (N.A.) and Cocaine Anonymous (C.A.) meetings, and many mentally ill individuals benefit from Emotions Anonymous (E.A.). Family and friends of alcoholics and addicts find help in Al-Anon, Nar-Anon, Alateen, and Adult Children of Alcoholics groups. All of these groups recognize the spirituality of human beings, and they augment traditional mental health services for those with mental illness and substance abuse and their loved ones.

Bricker and his associates at dePaul Belleview Extended Care in Milwaukee, Wisconsin, have devised a support group for what they call the "doubly troubled." This group, called Support Together for Emotional and Mental Serenity and Sobriety (STEMSS; Bricker, 1988a, 1989b) was originally started by J. Thomas Erickson in 1984 for individuals with schizophrenia and chemical abuse problems. A six-step approach adapted to those with dual disorders is used. Weekly meetings of this group offer direction and social interaction for those with dual problems. Bricker has compared STEMSS and 12-step recovery programs (Table 11.4) and shown how chemical dependence and mental illness are parallel disorders (Table 11.5). Hilary Ryglewicz, editor of *TIE-Lines,* and Bert Pepper, Executive Director of The Information Exchange on Young Adult Chronic Patients (TIE, Inc.), have also discussed the need for this type of meeting for those with dual disorders (Ryglewicz, 1989).

One reason special support groups are needed is that *some* traditional A.A. and N.A. members do not understand severe mental illness. They have been known to advise mentally ill substance abusers to go off all psychotropic medications, which they lump together with all "drugs." This can lead to confusion and rehospitalization for dually diagnosed individuals. In 1984 a group of physicians who are members of A.A. published *The A.A. Member—Medications and Other Drugs.* It includes examples of people who use medications properly and improperly and clearly admonishes that "No A.A. Member Plays Doctor." Because this message will not reach all A.A. members, mental health service providers who make referrals to A.A. and N.A. can help prepare clients for well-intended but misguided advice, without alienating A.A. and N.A. members, undermining the principles of these groups, or adding to clients' denial. Special support and education groups for dually diagnosed individuals are alternatives to A.A. and N.A. In areas where self-help groups for dually diagnosed individuals are not yet available or

TABLE 11.4
STEMSS and 12-Step Recovery Programs: A Comparison*

Core Concept	STEMSS (Support Together for Emotional and Mental Serenity and Sobriety)	General 12-Step Recovery Program (e.g., Alcoholics/Narcotics Anonymous, OA, etc.)
Acceptance	1. I admit and accept that my mental illness is separate from my chemical dependency, and that I have a dual illness.	1. We admitted we were powerless over our addiction—that our lives had become unmanageable.
Surrender	2. As a result of this acceptance, I am willing to accept help for my illnesses.	3. Made a decision to turn our will and our lives over to the care of God as we understand him.
Hope	3. As a result of this willingness, I came to believe that, with help and understanding, recovery is possible.	2. Came to believe that a Power greater than ourselves could restore us to sanity.
Need for *both* medication and therapy	4. As a result of this belief, I accept the fact that medical management must play a large part in my recovery Program.	4–11. Includes all the remaining recovery steps as worked through in Therapy and AA/NA Program participation.
Abstinence	5. As part of this recovery Program, I accept the fact that I must maintain an alcohol and drug† free lifestyle.	1. We admitted we were powerless over our addiction—that our lives had become unmanageable.
Recovery as the key to the *future*	6. In following these steps throughout my life, I will reach my goals and help others to begin the recovery process.	12. Having had a spiritual awakening as the result of these Steps, we tried to carry this message to alcoholics, and to practice these principles in all our affairs.

*Note that the STEMSS and 12-Step Recovery models are complementary, and designed to be used together. By "working" both Programs simultaneously, they offer the promise of recovery from both chemical dependency and chronic mental illness. Working together, they offer experience, strength and hope for the "doubly-troubled."
†"Drug" in this context refers to recreational chemicals, not prescribed medications.
Source: 1987, 1989 Michael G. Bricker, STEMSS Coordinator, Cramer House Keystone Program, DePaul Belleview Extended Care, Milwaukee, WI 53211. Used by permission.

where these groups meet infrequently, it is beneficial for clients to learn to take advantage of 12-step programs both for chemically dependent persons and for emotionally and mentally ill persons. Participation in these groups can lead to the development of a network of sober peers. Without sober peers with whom to identify and socialize, many clients with dual disorders find it difficult to stay sober.

TABLE 11.5

The Twelve Parallels Between Chemical Dependency and Mental Illness

1. Both are physiological diseases with a strong genetic/hereditary component.
2. Both are physical/mental/spiritual diseases which result in global affliction of the person.
3. If left untreated, the course of both illnesses is progressive, chronic, incurable, and potentially fatal.
4. Denial of the disease process(es) and noncompliance with attempts to treat are cardinal symptoms of the disorder.
5. Both diseases manifest loss of control in behavior, thought, and emotions. Both are often seen by self/others as a "moral issue."
6. Both diseases afflict the whole family as well as all relational systems.
7. Growing powerlessness and unmanageability lead to feelings of guilt, shame, depression, and despair.
8. Both are diseases of vulnerability and isolation; victim is exquisitely sensitive to psychosocial stressors.
9. Both the primary symptoms of each disease *and* loss of control in behavior/thought/emotion are reversible with treatment.
10. Recovery consists of:
    □ Stabilization of the acute disease
    □ Rehabilitation of body, mind, and spirit, and
    □ Launching upon an ongoing Program of recovery.
11. The risk of relapse in either disease is always high, and will inevitably trigger a relapse in the other.
12. The only hope for lifelong recovery lies in working our Program(s) *one day at a time*.

Source: © 1989 Michael G. Bricker. Used by permission.

A MODEL RESIDENTIAL PROGRAM FOR DUALLY DIAGNOSED CLIENTS

Model programs for dually diagnosed clients are now emerging. Examples are the LINC (Living in the Community) Program in Portland, Oregon (Maynard, 1988), and the dePaul Cramer Keystone Program in Milwaukee, Wisconsin (Jacobson, 1990; cf. also Osher & Kofoed, 1989; Carey, 1989; Minkoff, 1989; Harrison et al., 1985; Sciacca, 1987). These and other programs provide a basis for the conclusion of this chapter, which offers some suggestions for developing a treatment program for those with serious mental disorders and substance abuse disorders in a community-based residential psychosocial rehabilitation unit. Major program goals would include lengthening clients' periods of sobriety, mental stability, and independent community tenure. Individual goals and objectives would be tailored to each client's strengths and needs. A halfway house setting that serves 15 residents and allows each resident a stay of 6 months to 1 year, depending on individual need, seems well suited to this client population. Entry criteria for clients would include a history of severe mental disorder and current stabilization of that disorder (including the use of medications, if prescribed); a history of substance abuse or use problems with detoxification completed; 18 years of age or older; desire to participate in the voluntary program; willingness to submit to periodic urine toxicologies; agreement to discontinue all use of alcohol, illegal, and other nonprescribed drugs; and willingness to follow all program rules.

The program would be distinguished by its integration of mental health and substance abuse treatment approaches in the psychosocial rehabilitation milieu. Education and treatment components would be designed with the cognitive problems and fragile nature of persons with serious mental disorders in mind. As in all psychosocial programs, each client's mental status would be evaluated and monitored periodically, with regular appointments with a program psychiatrist who is knowledgeable and interested in the treatment of substance abuse and mental illness. A number of program components would be similar to those commonly employed in community support programs for persons with mental illness (Stein & Test, 1980; Sandall, Hawley, & Gordon, 1975). For example, medication education and monitoring would be offered with the goal of clients' managing their own medication regimens independently. Individual sessions one or more times per week with a social worker who specializes in treating dually diagnosed clients would also be part of the treatment protocol.

Upon entry most of the client's time would be spent in structured programming. A peer, or "buddy," assigned to each client would answer questions, provide companionship, introduce the client to other residents, and help the client learn the program schedule. Passes for new clients would not be permitted until a 30-day sobriety chip is earned at A.A., N.A., or a similar self-help program. At that point, clients would be encouraged to take passes only with staff or their buddy.

The client's first task would be to meet and interact with program peers. Chores such as cooking breakfast and cleaning the living room would be assigned on a rotating basis and observed daily by staff, who would assess independent living skills (ILS). Deficits would be addressed in one-to-one sessions and in ILS classes.

The Monday through Friday schedule would be as follows:

7:00– 8:00	Wake up, shower, dress, make beds, etc.
8:00– 9:00	Fix own breakfast and cleanup
9:00–10:00	Medication class
10:00–11:00	Social skills or independent living skills class
11:00–11:45	Morning break
11:45– 1:00	Attend A.A. or N.A. meeting in community
1:00– 2:00	Lunch (cooking and cleanup assigned)
2:00– 3:00	Afternoon break
3:00– 4:30	Substance abuse education (audio and video tapes, staff lectures, group discussions, etc.)
4:30– 6:00	Group recreational activities (cards, basketball, bowling, TV, volleyball, swimming, walking, etc.)
6:00– 7:00	Supper and cleanup
7:00– 8:00	"Double Trouble" self-help group at unit
8:00–10:00	Free time, visitors, special passes
10:00	Curfew and lights out

Individual appointments with the psychiatrist, social worker, case manager, and other treatment providers would take priority over scheduled activities.

On Saturdays and Sundays, clients would attend A.A. or N.A. meetings of their choice in the community and take passes to attend religious services if they like. Transportation and escort to A.A. and N.A. dances and parties would be provided. Alcohol and other drugfree activities would be scheduled on holidays, when clients might invite guests. Clients would host at least one unit party or activity each month and would be encouraged to practice other drugfree leisure skills on weekends.

With permission from clients, family members and significant others can be invited to attend an ongoing education and support group at the residence (Maynard, 1988) where they have the opportunity to learn about various mental and substance abuse disorders while they gain empathy and support from others who understand their situation. Family members can also be advised of organizations they might want to join, such as Al-Anon, NAMI, and Family and Individual Reliance (FAIR), which has support groups for those with mental illness and their families. Families should be offered the opportunity to be viable members of the comprehensive treatment team of their loved ones.

As clients progress at the unit, they can complete ILS and social skills class modules and begin prevocational assessment and Job Club. The opportunity to begin sheltered part-time employment can be offered upon receiving a 90-day sobriety chip at A.A. or N.A. Later the client can begin a search for competitive employment. After maintaining a significant period of sobriety (at least 6 months), obtaining a job, and adjusting to work, clients may graduate from the program and move to a more independent setting, such as their own apartment. At this time, alumni can be invited to join the formal follow-up program of the unit, overseen by their case manager. For at least 1 year clients would be expected and encouraged to attend regularly one "Double Trouble" group at the unit and to have one weekly in-person contact with their case manager (Jacobson, 1990). The program should have an open-door policy so graduates may attend activities and receive help at any time, around the clock. After the 1-year follow-up, the client would maintain the right to access the program as needed.

The program should have staff coverage 24 hours per day, 7 days per week, with personnel selected on the basis of their attitudes, knowledge, and experience concerning mental and substance abuse disorders. It is important that staff share the same treatment philosophies, program goals, and hope for clients; be team-oriented; model behaviors congruent with program goals; have great patience and tolerance for inappropriate behavior; understand and practice the principles of learning theory; and be able to notice and appreciate small increments of improvement. The recommended staff complement for 15 residents plus follow-up participants is one master's or Ph.D. level program manager; two master's level clinical social workers; two case managers; one part-time psychiatrist; two therapist technicians; one secretary; one nighttime worker; and two part-time weekend shift workers.

The most obvious divergence from traditional substance abuse treatment that would characterize the model described here is the lack of heavy confrontation concerning denial of substance use or abuse (Sciacca, 1990). Instead, an assertive but supportive approach would be utilized. Clients would not automatically be discharged for using substances (called *slips* or *lapses*) but would be empowered by learning to reframe traditional all-or-none thinking about relapse typified by the saying "one drink, one drunk." Instead lapses would be treated as learning experiences (cf. Gorski & Miller, 1986; Marlatt & Gordon, 1985) so that continuing choices for sobriety are reinforced (Jacobson, 1990). Just as clients are taught to seek help as soon as symptoms of mental illness reappear, they would be taught to seek help immediately when a substance use lapse occurs. Clients who have experienced repeated failure in maintaining stability and a sense of low self-esteem are not helped by harsh reprimands. A basic belief underlying this program is that only when the helping system is realistic and accepting, rather than judgmental and perfectionistic, are clients offered the opportunity to successfully maintain mental health and sobriety.

SUMMARY

It is not only abuse of alcohol and other drugs that can pose problems for those with mental disorders. Casual use can distort judgments or cause problematic interactions with prescribed medications, resulting in exacerbations of mental health problems and increased use of nonprescribed drugs. The interaction of mental and substance abuse disorders can be thought of as a cyclical process in which increases in disturbing symptoms of mental illness may precipitate increased drug use, and increased drug use may result in exacerbations of symptoms of mental disorders.

In the last few decades there have been significant improvements in treating those with mental disorders as well as those with substance abuse disorders. These successes may have encouraged attempts at developing better methods to assist individuals who suffer from both mental and substance abuse disorders. A number of terms, including dual diagnoses and comorbidity, have been used to describe these clients. Clearly, a thorough knowledge of mental disorders and substance abuse is needed to treat them. Furthermore, drugs of abuse—depressants, stimulants, narcotics, and hallucinogens, as well as over-the-counter preparations—were described. Many clients use or abuse more than one type of drug.

One obstacle to treating dually diagnosed clients is the lack of consistency in defining the various mental and substance abuse disorders. Some think alcoholism, narcotics addiction, and other forms of drug abuse problems are unitary phenomena and fail to consider the various types of alcohol and drug users and abusers. The American Psychiatric Association uses a number of indicators, many of them behavioral, to describe both psychoactive substance abuse and psychoactive substance dependence. Of equal importance to clinical definitions are those that can be appreciated by clients who have these problems. One definition of alcohol and drug problems that can be useful with clients is the repeated use of one or more drugs that results in serious life problems such as family, social, legal, occupational, or health problems.

The major obstacle in defining substance abuse disorders is the lack of a clearly identified etiology of these problems. The earliest idea was that alcohol abuse was a moral issue, but a myriad of biological, psychological, and sociological theories have also been proposed. It is quite likely that a combination of factors may be responsible for the development of substance abuse disorders.

Although the etiologies of substance abuse disorders and many mental disorders have yet to be identified, recent studies indicate that the likelihood of developing a substance abuse disorder increases if one has a mental disorder and vice versa. Dually diagnosed clients are often described as presenting more serious life problems than clients with a mental *or* a drug disorder. Their problems have been compounded by existing treatment systems which frequently deny admission to dually diagnosed persons. Chemical dependency programs are usually not equipped to treat serious mental disorders; conversely, mental health programs are usually not equipped to treat substance disorders. Mental health professionals often fail to diagnose substance abuse because they fail to make appropriate inquiries about the use of drugs and sequelae following use, and chemical dependency professionals often dismiss symptoms of mental disorders as problems that will clear with sobriety.

Once a dually diagnosed client has been stabilized following an acute episode, long-term treatment for both the mental and the substance abuse disorder is usually needed. Treating these problems in tandem has not proved successful, because the philosophies of chemical dependency and psychiatric treatment programs are often contradictory.

Guidelines for practice with dually diagnosed clients have begun to emerge. The new model programs for these clients are hybrids which combine appropriate strategies from both types of programs in a parallel or simultaneous format. Treatment modalities in these hybrids are the same as in mental health and in chemical dependency programs, but the unique problems of the dually diagnosed individuals are the focus of treatment. A period of time in a residential facility such as a halfway house is needed by many clients because they often lack supportive environments where medication compliance *and* abstinence from nonprescribed substances are encouraged. Treatment modifications include less confrontational methods and more supportive approaches than are used in traditional chemical dependency programs, greater emphasis on education about nonprescribed drugs than is found in many mental health programs, and education about the cyclical nature of mental and substance disorders, which is usually not found in either type of program. Teams of treatment providers composed of both mental health and substance abuse professionals are one approach to treating dually diagnosed clients, but there is increasing recognition that professionals knowledgeable about both types of disorders are preferable.

DISCUSSION QUESTIONS

1. How do substance abuse and dependence interact with mental disorders?
2. What is a polysubstance user? Give examples of drugs that are used together. What are the risks of polysubstance use?
3. How does the *DSM-III-R* classify problems related to substance abuse and dependence?
4. How are the various theories explaining substance abuse that were described in this chapter reflected in the methods of treatment used in the community?
5. What is the difference between a primary and a secondary diagnosis? How can you establish which diagnosis is primary?
6. Get copies of some of the assessment tools that were mentioned in this chapter and use them to screen clients on your caseload. What did you learn about the client from using these instruments?
7. What kinds of services (if any) in your community are tailored especially for persons with dual diagnoses? If there are no specialized services, what existing resources are available to this population? What kinds of services are needed in your community to serve persons with dual diagnoses?
8. Explain the "parallel" method of treatment. What are its advantages?

9. Why are traditional mental health and substance abuse treatment programs reluctant to include persons with dual diagnoses? What do you think about their attitudes?
10. Why is comorbidity underdiagnosed?
11. How is an ideal program for the dually diagnosed different from one that is for persons with a single disorder?

12. Escort a client you are working with to a support group for persons with a single or dual diagnoses and observe the group. How sensitive was the group to participants with more than one problem?

REFERENCES

Alcoholics Anonymous World Services. (1952). *Forty-four questions and answers about the A.A. program of recovery from alcoholism.* New York: Author.

Alcoholics Anonymous World Services. (1955). *Alcoholics Anonymous.* New York: Author.

Alcoholics Anonymous World Services. (1976). *Twelve steps and twelve traditions.* New York: Author.

Alcoholics Anonymous World Services. (1984). *The A.A. member—Medications and other drugs.* New York: Author.

Alcoholism. (1989, March/April). *ADAMHA News* (15th anniversary issue), *15*(2), 2–3.

Allen, P., & Manchaca, E. (1989, December). *Workshop on Texas Young Adult Chronic Program at San Antonio State Hospital.* Austin, TX: Texas Department of Mental Health and Mental Retardation.

Alterman, A. I. (1985). Substance abuse in psychiatric patients: Etiological, developmental, and treatment considerations. In A. I. Alterman (Ed.), *Substance abuse and psychopathology* (pp. 121–136). New York: Plenum Press.

American Psychiatric Association. (1987). *Diagnostic and statistical manual of mental disorders (DSM-III-R).* (3rd ed., rev.) Washington, DC: Author.

Atkinson, R. M. (1985). Persuading alcoholic patients to seek treatment. *Comprehensive Therapy, 11,* 16–24.

Bachrach, L. (1982). Young adult chronic patients: An analytical review of the literature. *Hospital and Community Psychiatry, 33*(3), 189–197.

Bacon, M. K. (1974). The dependency-conflict hypothesis and the frequency of drunkenness. *Quarterly Journal of Studies on Alcohol, 35,* 863–876.

Bakdash, D. P. (1983). Psychiatric/mental health nursing. In G. Bennett, C. Vourakis, & D. S. Woolf (Eds.), *Substance abuse: Pharmacologic, developmental, and clinical perspectives* (pp. 223–239). New York: Wiley.

Bales, R. F. (1946). Cultural differences in rates of alcoholism. *Quarterly Journal of Studies on Alcoholism, 6,* 480–499.

Bauer, A. (1987). Dual diagnosis patients: The state of the problem. *TIE-Lines, 4*(3), 1–4, 8.

Bloom, F. E. (1982). A summary of workshop discussions. In F. Bloom et al. (Eds.), *Betacarbolines and tetrahydroisoquinolines,* pp. 401-410. New York: Alan R. Liss.

Blum, K., et al. (1990). Allelic association of human dopamine D_2 receptor gene in alcoholism. *Journal of the American Medical Association, 263*(15), 2055–2060.

Boham, M. (1978). Some genetic aspects of alcoholism and criminality: A population of adoptees. *Archives of General Psychiatry, 35,* 269–276.

Boham, M., Cloninger, C. R., von Knorring, A. L., & Sigvardsson, S. (1984). An adoption study of somatoform disorders. III. Cross-fostering analysis and genetic relationship to alcoholism and criminality. *Archives of General Psychiatry, 41,* 872–878.

Boham, M., Sigvardsson, S., & Cloninger, C. R. (1981). Maternal inheritance of alcohol abuse: Cross-fostering analysis of adopted women. *Archives of General Psychiatry, 38,* 965–969.

Bricker, M. G. (1989a). *STEMSS and 12-step recovery programs: A comparison.* Milwaukee, WI: DePaul Belleview.

Bricker, M. G. (1988). *STEMSS, support together for emotional and mental serenity and sobriety.* Milwaukee, WI: DePaul Belleview.

Bricker, M. G. (1989b). *The twelve parallels between chemical dependency and mental illness.* Milwaukee, WI: DePaul Belleview.

Bricker, M. G. (1990, January). The operation was a success but the patient died: The phenomenon of relapse on Axis II. *TIE-Lines, 7*(1), 3–4.

Caragonne, P., & Emery, B. (1987). *Mental illness and substance abuse: The dually diagnosed client.* Rockville, MD: National Council of Community Mental Health Centers.

Carey, K. B. (1989). Emerging treatment guidelines for mentally ill chemical abusers. *Hospital and Community Psychiatry, 40*(4), 341–349.

Caton, C. L. M., Gralnick, A., Bender, S., & Simon, R. (1989). Young chronic patients and substance abuse. *Hospital and Community Psychiatry, 40*(10), 1037–1040.

Clark, W. (1988). Alcoholism: Epidemiology and clinical presentation. (Pamphlet with tape *Alcoholism: Part I*). Macon, GA: Charter Medical Corp.

Cloninger, C. R., Boham, M., & Sigvardsson, S. (1981). Inheritance of alcohol abuse. *Archives of General Psychiatry, 38,* 861–868.

Comorbidity: Mental and addictive disorders. (1989, March/April). *ADAMHA News* (15th anniversary issue), *15*(2), 13.

Community Support Network News. (1989, June/July). (Available from [Boston University Center for Psychiatric Rehabilitation]).

Cotton, N. A. (1979). The familial incidence of alcoholism: A review. *Journal of Studies on Alcohol, 40*(1), 89–116.

Daley, D. C., Moss, H., & Campbell, F. (1987). *Dual disorders: Counseling clients with chemical dependency and mental illness.* Center City, MN: Hazelden Foundation.

Davies, D. L. (1976). Definitional issues in alcoholism. In R. E. Tarter & A. A. Sugerman (Eds.), *Alcoholism: Interdisciplinary approaches to an enduring problem* (pp. 53–73). Reading, MA: Addison-Wesley.

Drake, R. E., & Wallach, M. A. (1989). Substance abuse among the chronic mentally ill. *Hospital and Community Psychiatry, 40*(10), 1041–1046.

Ewing, J. A. (1984). Detecting alcoholism, the CAGE questionnaire. *Journal of the American Medical Association, 252,* pp. 1905–1907.

Ewing, J. A., & Rouse, B. A. (1970, February). *Identifying the "hidden alcoholic."* Presented at the 29th International Congress on Alcohol and Drug Dependence, Sydney, NSW, Australia. Cited in Swenson, W. M., & Morse, R. M. (1973). The use of a self-administered alcoholism screening test (SAAST) in a medical center. *Mayo Clinic Proceedings, 50,* 204–208.

Fischer, D. E., Halikas, J. A., Baker, J. W., & Smith, J. B. (1975). Frequency and patterns of drug abuse in psychiatric patients. *Diseases of the Nervous System, 36,* 550–553.

Frezza, M., di Padova, C., Pozzato, G., Terpin, M., Baraona, E., & Lieber, C. S. (1990). High blood alcohol levels in women: The role of decreased gastric alcohol dehydrogenase activity and first-pass metabolism. *New England Journal of Medicine, 322*(2), 95–99.

Gawin, F. H., & Kleber, H. D. (1988). Evolving conceptualizations of cocaine dependence.

Yale Journal of Biology and Medicine, 61, 123–136.

Goodwin, D. W., Schulsinger, F., Hermansen, L., Guze, S. B., & Winokur, G. (1973). Alcohol problems in adoptees raised apart from alcoholic biological parents. *Archives of General Psychiatry, 28,* 238–243.

Goodwin, F. K. (1989, June 23/30). From the Alcohol, Drug Abuse, and Mental Health Administration. *Journal of the American Medical Association, 261,* 3517.

Gorski, T. T., & Miller, M. (1986). *Staying sober: A guide for relapse prevention.* Independence, MO: Independence Press.

Hall, R. C., Popkin, M. K., Stickney, S. K., & Gardner, E. R. (1978). Covert outpatient drug abuse: Incidence and therapist recognition. *Journal of Nervous and Mental Disease, 166*(5), 343–348.

Harrison, P. A., Martin, J. A., Tuason, V. B., & Hoffman, N. G. (1985). Conjoint treatment of dual disorders. In A. I. Alterman (Ed.), *Substance abuse and psychopathology* (pp. 367–390). New York: Plenum Press.

Hayashida, M., et al. (1989). Comparative effectiveness and costs of inpatient and outpatient detoxification of patients with mild-to-moderate alcohol withdrawal syndrome. *New England Journal of Medicine, 320,* 358–365.

Hendrickson, E. L. (1988). Treating the dually diagnosed (mental disorder/substance use) client. *TIE-Lines, 5*(4), 1–4.

Holbrook, J. M. (1983). Hallucinogens. In G. Bennett, C. Vourakis, & D. S. Woolf (Eds.), *Substance abuse: Pharmacologic, developmental, and clinical perspectives* (pp. 86–101). New York: Wiley.

Jacobson, R. (1990). [Personal communication]. DePaul Cramer House Keystone Program.

Jellinek, E. M. (1960). *The disease concept of alcoholism.* New Haven, CT: College and University Press.

Kaij, L. (1960). *Alcoholism in twins: Studies on the etiology and sequels of abuse of alcohol.* Stockholm, Sweden: Almquist & Wiksell. Cited in Schuckit, M. A. (1986). Etiologic theories on alcoholism. In M. J. Estes & M. E. Heinemann (Eds.), *Alcoholism: Development, consequences, and interventions* (pp. 15–30). St Louis, MO: Mosby.

Keller, M. (1958). Alcoholism: Nature and extent of the problem. In S. D. Bacon (Ed.), *Understanding alcoholism: Annals of the American Academy of Political and Social Science* (pp. 1–11). Philadelphia, PA: American Academy of Political and Social Science.

Keller, M. (1972). The oddities of alcoholics. *Quarterly Journal of Studies on Alcohol, 33,* 1147–1148.

Khantzian, E. J. (1985). The self-medication hypothesis of addictive disorders: Focus on heroin and cocaine dependence. *American Journal of Psychiatry, 142*(11), 1259–1264.

Kofoed, L., Kania, J., Walsh, T., & Atkinson, R. M. (1986). Outpatient treatment of patients with substance abuse and coexisting psychiatric disorders. *American Journal of Psychiatry, 143*(7), 867–872.

Kofoed, L., & Keys, A. (1988). Using group therapy to persuade dual-diagnosis patients to seek substance abuse treatment. *Hospital and Community Psychiatry, 39*(11), 1209–1211.

Lamb, H. R. (1982). Young adult chronic patients: The new drifters. *Hospital and Community Psychiatry, 33*(6), 465–468.

Lawlor, L. (1987, July). Re: The 3-D client: Responsibility abyss. *TIE-Lines, 4*(3), 7.

Lehman, A. F., Myers, C. P., & Corty, E. (1989). Assessment and classification of patients with psychiatric and substance abuse syndromes. *Hospital and Community Psychiatry, 40*(10), 1019–1025.

Lewis, J. A. (1955). Summary of federal and state alcoholism programs in the United States. *American Journal of Public Health, 435,* 1417–1419.

Lundquist, F. (1971). Influence of ethanol on carbohydrate metabolism. *Quarterly Journal of Studies on Alcohol, 32,* 1–12.

Mackarness, R. (1972). The alergic factor in alcoholism. *International Journal of Psychiatry, 18,* 194–200.

Marlatt, G. A., & Gordon, J. R. (1985). *Relapse prevention: Maintenance strategies in the treatment of addictive behaviors.* New York: Guilford Press.

Mayfield, D., McLeod, G., & Hall, P. (1974). The CAGE Questionnaire: Validation of a new alcoholism screening instrument. *American Journal of Psychiatry, 131*(10), 1121–1123.

Maynard, G. (1988, April). Integration of substance abuse treatment in a psychosocial program [Summary]. *Proceedings of the Dually Diagnosed Young Adult Patient 8th Annual Conference of the Information Exchange on Young Adult Chronic Patients.* New City, NY: TIE-Lines.

McLellan, A. T. (1989). Issues in the evaluation of treatment interventions for the psychiatrically ill substance abuser. New City, NY: TIE-Lines.

McLellan, A. T., Childress, A. R., & Woody, G. E. (1985). Drug abuse and psychiatric disorder: Role of drug choice. In A. I. Alterman (Ed.), *Substance abuse and psychopathology* (pp. 137–172). New York: Plenum Press.

McLellan, A. T., Luborsky, L., Woody, G. E., & O'Brien, C. P. (1980). An improved diagnostic instrument for substance abuse patients: The Addiction Severity Index. *Journal of Nervous and Mental Disease, 168*(1), 26–33.

Mee-Lee, D. (1985). *Decision tree for addictions vs. other psychiatric diagnoses. Either or both?* Marblehead, MA: Parkside Medical Services Corp.

Mee-Lee, D. (1990, March). *Dual diagnosis: Dilemmas and directions workshop.* Presented at the Parkside Medical Services Corporation workshop, Austin, TX.

Meisch, R. A. (1982). Animal studies of alcohol intake. *British Journal of Psychiatry, 141,* 113–120.

Menicucci, L. D., Wermuth, L., & Sorensen, J. (1988). Treatment providers' assessment of dual-prognosis patients: Diagnosis, treatment, referral, and family involvement. *The International Journal of the Addictions, 23*(6), 617–622.

Minkoff, K. (1987). Beyond deinstitutionalization: A new ideology for postinstitutional era. *Hospital and Community Psychiatry, 38*(9), 945–950.

Minkoff, K. (1989). An integrated treatment model for dual diagnosis of psychosis and addiction. *Hospital and Community Psychiatry, 40*(10), 1031–1036.

Minkoff, K. (1990, May). *Dual Diagnosis Workshop.* Austin, TX: Texas Department of Mental Health and Mental Retardation.

Moore, D. F. (1983). Over-the-counter drugs. In G. Bennett, C. Vourakis, & D. S. Woolf (Eds.), *Substance abuse: Pharmacologic, developmental, and clinical perspectives* (pp. 102–109). New York: Wiley.

Moore, R. A. (1972). The diagnosis of alcoholism in a psychiatric hospital: A trial of the Michigan Alcoholism Screening Test (MAST). *American Journal of Psychiatry, 128*(12), 115–119.

Mulinski, P. (1988, March). Alcoholism and co-existing psychiatric disorders. *Social Casework, 69,* 141–146.

Murray, R. M., & Stabenau, J. R. (1982). Genetic factors in alcoholism predisposition. In E. M. Pattison & E. Kaufman (Eds.), *Encyclopedic handbook of alcoholism* (pp. 135–144). New York: Gardner Press.

National Institute on Alcohol Abuse and Alcoholism. (1987). *Sixth special report to the U.S. Congress on alcohol and health.* Rockville, MD: U.S. Department of Health and Human Services.

Nelson, B. (1983, January 18). The addictive personality: Common traits are found. *The New York Times,* pp. 11, 15.

Nurco, D. N. (1979). Etiological aspects of drug abuse. In R. L. Dupont, A. Goldstein, & J. O'Donnell (Eds.), *Handbook on drug abuse* (pp. 315–324). Washington, DC: National Institute on Drug Abuse.

Oregon Health Department. (1990). *Dual diagnosis demonstration project.* Marion County, OR: Author.

Osher, F. C., & Kofoed, L. L. (1989). Treatment of patients with psychiatric and psychoactive substance abuse disorders. *Hospital and Community Psychiatry, 40*(10), 1025–1030.

Paredes, A. (1976). The history of the concept of alcoholism. In R. E. Tarter and A. A. Sugerman (Eds.), *Alcoholism: Interdisciplinary approaches to an enduring problem* (pp. 9–52). Reading, MA: Addison-Wesley.

Pattison, E. M., & Kaufman, E. (1982). The alcoholism syndrome: Definitions and models. In E. M. Pattison & E. Kaufman (Eds.), *Encyclopedic handbook of alcoholism* (pp. 3–30). New York: Gardner Press.

Pattison, E. M., Sobell, M. B., & Sobell, L. C. (1977). *Emerging concepts of alcohol dependence.* New York: Springer.

Pepper, B. (1988, April). Plenary address—Personality development. mental illness and substance use: An interactive model [Summary]. *Proceedings of the Dually Diagnosed Young Adult Patient 8th Annual Conference of the Information Exchange on Young Adult Chronic Patients.* New City, NY: TIE-Lines.

Pepper, B., Kirshner, M. C., & Ryglewicz, H. (1981). The young adult chronic patient: Overview of a population. *Hospital and Community Psychiatry, 32*(7), 463–469.

Pepper, B., & Ryglewicz, H. (1987). *Schizophrenia: A constant brain disorder in a changing world.* Presented at the 140th annual meeting of the American Psychiatric Association, Chicago, IL. [Reprint]. New City, NY: TIE-Lines.

Pittman, D. J. (1982). The police court system and the public intoxication offender. In E. M. Pattison & E. Kaufman (Eds.), *Encyclopedic handbook of alcoholism* (pp. 938–945). New York: Gardner Press.

Pokorny, A. D., et al. (1972). The brief MAST: A shortened version of the Michigan Alcoholism Screening Test. *American Journal of Psychiatry, 129,* 343–345.

Ray, O., & Ksir, C. (1990). *Drugs, society and human behavior* (5th ed.). St. Louis, MO: Times Mirror/Mosby.

Report of the Presidential Commission on the Human Immunodeficiency Virus Epidemic. (1988). (Publication No. 0-214-701:QL3). Washington, DC: U.S. Government Printing Office.

Ridgely, M. S., Osher, F. C., & Talbott, J. A. (1987). *Chronic mentally ill young adults with substance abuse problems: Treatment and training issues.* Baltimore, MD: University of Maryland School of Medicine.

Ross, H. E., Glaser, F. B., & Germanson, T. (1988). The prevalence of psychiatric disorders in patients with alcohol and other drug problems. *Archives of General Psychiatry, 45,* 1023–1031.

Royce, J. E. (1989). *Alcohol problems and alcoholism: A comprehensive survey* (rev. ed.). New York: Free Press.

Ryglewicz, H. (Ed.). (1989, October). *TIE-Lines.* New City, NY: TIE-Lines.

Ryglewicz, H., & Pepper, B. (1989). Editor's note. *TIE-Lines, 6*(4), 8.

Sandall, H., Hawley, T., & Gordon, G. (1975). The St. Louis Community Homes Program: Graduated support for long-term care. *American Journal of Psychiatry, 132*(8), 617–622.

Schneier, F. R., & Siris, S. G. (1987). A review of psychoactive substance use and abuse in schizophrenia: Patterns of choice. *The Journal of Nervous and Mental Disease, 175*(11), 641–652.

Schuckit, M. (1983a). Alcoholic patients with secondary depression. *American Journal of Psychiatry, 140*(6), 711–714.

Schuckit, M. (1983b). Alcoholism and other psychiatric disorders. *Hospital and Community Psychiatry, 34*(11), 1022–1026.

Schuckit, M. (1986a). Genetic and clinical implications of alcoholism and affective disorder. *American Journal of Psychiatry, 143*(2), 140–147.

Schuckit, M. A. (1986b). Etiologic theories on alcoholism. In N. J. Estes & M. E. Heinemann (Eds.), *Alcoholism: Development, consequences, and interventions* (pp. 15–30). St. Louis, MO: Mosby.

Sciacca, K. (1986). Modification of the CAGE questionnaire.

Sciacca, K. (1987, July). New initiatives in the treatment of the chronic patient with alcohol/substance abuse problems. *TIE-Lines, 4*(5).

Sciacca, K. (1989a). MICAA-NON: Working with families, friends and advocates of mentally ill chemical abusers and addicted (MICAA). *TIE-Lines, 6*(3), 7–8.

Sciacca, K. (1989b, October). Workshop on the dually diagnosed, Big Spring, TX.

Sciacca, K. (1990, May). *Dual Diagnosis Workshop.* Austin, TX: Texas Department of Mental Health and Mental Retardation.

Selzer, M. (1971). The Michigan Alcoholism Screening Test: The quest for a new diagnostic instrument. *American Journal of Psychiatry, 127,* 1653–1658.

Selzer, M. (1990). [Personal communication].

Selzer, M. L., Vinokur, A., & Van Rooijen, L. A. (1974). Self administered Short Michigan Alcoholism Screening Test (SMAST). *Journal of Studies on Alcohol, 15,* 276–280.

Sobell, M. B., & Sobell, L. C. (1976). Second year treatment outcomes of alcoholics treated by individualized behavior therapy: Results. *Behavior and Therapy, 14,* 195–215.

Stein, L. I., & Test, M. A. (1980). Alternative to mental hospital treatment I: Conceptual model, treatment program, and clinical evaluation. *Archives of General Psychiatry, 37,* 392–397.

Thacker, W., & Tremaine, L. (1989). Systems issues in serving the mentally ill substance abuser: Virginia's experience. *Hospital and Community Psychiatry, 40*(10), 1046–1049.

Treffert, D. A. (1978). Marijuana use in schizophrenia: A clear hazard. *American Journal of Psychiatry, 135*(10), 1213–1215.

Webb, D. K. (1990). [Personal communication]. Homestead Supervised Apartment Program, Austin-Travis County MHMR.

Witters, W., & Venturelli, P. (1988). *Drugs and society* (2nd ed.). Boston, MA: Jones and Bartlett.

Woolf, D. S. (1983a). CNS depressants: Alcohol. In G. Bennett, C. Vourakis, & D. S. Woolf (Eds.), *Substance abuse: Pharmacologic, developmental, and clinical perspectives* (pp. 17–38). New York: Wiley.

Woolf, D. S. (1983b). CNS depressants: Other sedative-hypnotics. In G. Bennett, C. Vourakis, & D. S. Woolf (Eds.), *Substance abuse: Pharmacologic, developmental, and clinical perspectives* (pp. 39–56). New York: Wiley.

Woolf, D. S. (1983c). Opioids. In G. Bennett, C. Vourakis, & D. S. Woolf (Eds.), *Substance abuse: Pharmacologic, developmental, and clinical perspectives* (pp. 70–85). New York: Wiley.

12 | Clinical Practice with Depressed Clients

Depression is a heterogeneous disorder that was found among 3 to 6 percent of the population in a 6-month period (Myers et al., 1984; National Institute of Mental Health, 1986). The lifetime prevalence for women is approximately twice that for men (Boyd & Weissman, 1986; Regier et al., 1988). The higher rate for women is attributable to biological differences and social conditions (e.g., oppression of women) or it may be that men manifest depression in their higher rate of substance abuse and trouble with the law (Weissman & Klerman, 1977). Depression is particularly prevalent among young adults, with the median age of onset in the mid 20s (Boyd & Weissman, 1986). A disorder that is accompanied by physiological symptoms, depression is often presented for treatment to physicians, who may not recognize it as a psychiatric disorder.

The "blues" and "down days" are ordinary experiences, which are associated with everyday disappointments, losses, and changes that are a part of life. Usually these feelings follow an event or interaction that is inconsistent with one's expectations or hopes. Ordinarily the feelings fade on their own or are relieved when one comes to terms with the situation or takes assertive action. Depressed feelings are regarded as manifestations of a mental disorder when they are experienced with great intensity, when they have a prolonged course, when they interfere with psychosocial functioning, and when they are clustered with other symptoms.

Depression is a dysphoric mood state characterized by sadness, irritability, lack of energy or interest in life, slowed movements, pessimism, feelings of worthlessness, guilt, morbid thinking, and changes in patterns of eating and sleeping. The prevailing feeling is pain that does not seem to go away. As Table 12.1 indicates, depression is expressed in biological, cognitive, affective, and behavioral symptoms.

The diagnoses in the *DSM-III-R* (American Psychiatric Association, 1987) that include marked symptoms of depression are the mood disorders of major depression, dysthymia, depressive disorder not otherwise specified, bipolar disorder, and cyclothymia; adjustment disorders with depressed mood, mixed emotional features, and mixed disturbance of emotions and conduct; organic disorders associated with intake or

TABLE 12.1
Symptoms of Depression

Type of Symptom	Description
Biological	Decreased or increased appetite, changes in sleeping patterns (hypersomnia, insomnia, early morning wakening), decreased libido, diminished energy
Cognitive	Worthlessness, hopelessness, self-depreciation, self-blame, guilt, pessimism, incompetence, deprivation, expectation of failure or punishment
Affective (mood)	Sadness, dejection, downcast, suffering, disinterest, irritable
Behavior	Slowed or diminished activity, withdrawal from usual activities, excessive sleeping, crying, passivity, decreased interpersonal/social behavior

withdrawal of chemicals, Alzheimer's disease, and organic mood syndrome; and uncomplicated bereavement.

In this chapter approaches to the treatment of major depression without psychotic features and of dysthymia, neither of which is complicated by substance abuse or dependence, will be discussed. At first the two disorders will be described. Next terminology, biological aspects, social dimensions, and psychosocial theories will be explained. A discussion of medication issues, interpersonal therapy, and cognitive therapy will follow.

DESCRIPTION OF MAJOR DEPRESSION AND DYSTHYMIA

Major depression is a syndrome that has single or recurrent episodes. According to the *DSM-III-R,* a major depressive episode is characterized by the following symptoms:

A. At least five of the following symptoms have been present during the same two-week period and represent a change from previous functioning; at least one of the symptoms is either (1) depressed mood, or (2) loss of interest or pleasure. (Do not include symptoms that are clearly due to a physical condition, mood-incongruent delusions or hallucinations, incoherence, or marked loosening of associations.)
   1. Depressed mood (or can be irritable mood in children and adolescents) most of the day, nearly every day, as indicated by either subjective account or observation by others
   2. Markedly diminished interest or pleasure in all, or almost all, activities most of the day, nearly every day (as indicated by either subjective account or observation by others of apathy most of the time)
   3. Significant weight loss or weight gain when not dieting (e.g., more than 5 percent of body weight in a month), or decrease or increase in appetite nearly every day (in children, consider failure to make expected weight gains)
   4. Insomnia or hypersomnia nearly every day
   5. Psychomotor agitation or retardation nearly every day (observable by others, not merely subjective feelings of restlessness or being slowed down)

6. Fatigue or loss of energy nearly every day
7. Feelings of worthlessness or excessive or inappropriate guilt (which may be delusional) nearly every day (not merely self-reproach or guilt about being sick)
8. Diminished ability to think or concentrate, or indecisiveness, nearly every day (either by subjective account or as observed by others)
9. Recurrent thoughts of death (not just fear of dying), recurrent suicidal ideation without a specific plan, or a suicide attempt or a specific plan for committing suicide

B. 1. It cannot be established that an organic factor initiated and maintained the disturbance.
   2. The disturbance is not a normal reaction to the death of a loved one (Uncomplicated Bereavement).

   Note: Morbid preoccupation with worthlessness, suicidal ideation, marked functional impairment or psychomotor retardation, or prolonged duration suggest bereavement complicated by Major Depression.

C. At no time during the disturbance have there been delusions or hallucinations for as long as two weeks in the absence of prominent mood symptoms (i.e., before the mood symptoms developed or after they have remitted).

D. Not superimposed on schizophrenia, schizophreniform disorder, delusional disorder, or psychotic disorder NOS. (Reprinted by permission, American Psychiatric Association, 1987)

Before considering major depression, the clinician should consider organic conditions, bipolar syndromes, uncomplicated bereavement, and disorders with psychotic symptoms that predate the depression. Major depression can have psychotic features the content of which is mood congruent (consistent with the prevailing mood) or mood incongruent. Furthermore, major depressions vary in severity (mild, moderate, and severe), may be chronic, and may have a seasonal pattern (American Psychiatric Association, 1987).

Dysthymia is a depressive mood disorder of at least 2 years. The *DSM-III-R* requires the following criteria for this chronic disorder to be present:

A. Depressed mood (or can be irritable mood in children and adolescents) for most of the day, more days than not, as indicated by either subjective account or observation by others, for at least 2 years (1 year for children and adolescents).

B. Presence, while depressed, of at least two of the following:
   1. poor appetite or overeating
   2. insomnia or hypersomnia
   3. low energy or fatigue
   4. low self-esteem
   5. poor concentration or difficulty making decisions
   6. feelings of hopelessness

C. During a two-year period (one year for children and adolescents) of the disturbance, never without the symptoms in A for more than 2 months at a time.

D. No evidence of an unequivocal Major Depressive Episode during the first two years (one year for children and adolescents) of the disturbance.

   Note: There may have been a previous Major Depressive Episode, provided there was a full remission (no significant signs or symptoms for 6 months) before development of the Dysthymia. In addition, after these two years (one year in children or adolescents) of Dysthymia, there may be superimposed episodes of Major Depression, in which case both diagnoses are given.

F. Has never had a Manic Episode . . . or an unequivocal Hypomanic Episode . . . .

G. It cannot be established that an organic factor initiated and maintained the distur-bance, e.g., prolonged administration of an antihypertensive medication. Reprinted by permission. (American Psychiatric Association, 1987)

Accordingly, the diagnosis of dysthymia requires fewer symptoms but a longer duration than major depression. An episode of major depression, however, may be superimposed on dysthymia, a condition that is referred to as *double depression.*

Terminology

Over the years, a number of terms have been used to categorize depressions. The term *endogenous* refers to depressions that are internally or biologically aroused. These depressions are characterized by "vegetative" symptoms (e.g., early morning awaken-ing, loss of sex drive, loss of appetite), as well as psychomotor agitation, diminished reactivity to the environment, and lack of pleasure (Hirschfeld & Goodwin, 1988). In contrast, *exogenous,* or *reactive,* depressions arise in response to a precipitating event or stressor. Because the presence or absence of a stressor is unrelated to the nature of the depression, these terms are valuable primarily as descriptors (Hirschfeld & Good-win, 1988). Another term that has been utilized is *neurotic* depression, which is a consequence of personality traits or character structure. This kind of depression is now encompassed by (but not identical with) dysthymia. The neurotic depression is con-trasted with the *psychotic* type, in which hallucinations, delusions, and/or stupor is present. More recently a distinction has been made between *primary* and *secondary* depression. Primary depression is the first and predominant disorder; secondary de-pression follows another psychiatric disorder or a physical condition (Hirschfeld & Goodwin, 1988). A further distinction has been made between *unipolar* and *bipolar* disorders. Whereas bipolar-type disorders (bipolar disorder, cyclothymia, and bipolar disorder not otherwise specified) are characterized by highs and lows, unipolar disor-ders (major depression, dysthymia, and depressive disorder not otherwise specified) have primarily low moods. Nevertheless, unipolar disorders may have recurrent cycles of low and normal moods.

MULTIPLE DIMENSIONS

Biological Aspects

Increasing evidence supports consideration of depression (especially major depression and bipolar depression) as a disease. Studies of genetic factors have found a higher percentage of depression among relatives of persons with depression than in the general population (Klerman, 1988). Moreover, studies of twins have revealed that identical twins have a rate of concordance for major mood disorders that is two to five times the rate for fraternal twins (McGuffin & Katz, 1989). Although cohorts studied include twins with bipolar as well as major depression, evidence points to a genetic component in major depression. Some research has identified a gene on chromosome 6 that contributes to vulnerability to depressive illness (Weitkamp et al., 1981).

Other evidence that depression is a biological disorder comes from medical findings. The Dexamethasone Suppression Test (DST), in which a drug that normally lowers the cortisone level of the body is administered, is able to identify melancholic depression in persons whose cortisone level is not reduced (Johnson, 1984). Responses to a urine test, MHPG (methoxyhydroxyphenylglycol), can differentiate unipolar nonendogenous depression from other kinds of depression (Johnson, 1984). Studies using computerized axial tomography (CT scans) reveal enlarged cerebral ventricular-brain ratios in persons with mood disorders in a quarter of the subjects (Hirschfeld & Goodwin, 1988). Furthermore, the effects of antidepressants on symptoms have suggested hypotheses about the involvement of neurotransmitter systems (Hirschfeld & Goodwin, 1988).

Social Dimensions

Depression has been associated with the occurrence of stressful life events and the absence of supports. Using data from an epidemiological study of mental health needs in the southeastern United States, Warheit (1979) found that respondents who had high life-event scores were more depressed than those who had low or moderate scores. The results of this study also indicated that persons of low socioeconomic status experienced more losses than those of a high status; and the absence of resources was associated with depression. Other research (Hirschfeld & Cross, 1982) suggests that the absence of a social network enhances the risk of depression. These findings support the implementation of psychosocial interventions when there is an accumulation of stressful life events and few resources. Nevertheless, in a comprehensive review of research on stress, social support, and coping, other authors (Kessler, Price, and Wortman, 1985) concluded that most people who are exposed to stressful life events or chronic stress do not develop psychopathology. These authors did, however, observe that exposure to stress does stimulate a process of adaptation.

Psychological and Social Theories About Depression

Various psychosocial theories provide explanations for the development of depression. According to the *psychoanalytic school*, depression has reverberations in the oral stage of human development (Hirschfeld & Goodwin, 1988). Persons who have had conflictual experiences during this period (e.g., through the death of a parent or dysfunctional patterns of communication) may be fixated in this stage. As adults, such individuals continue to be dependent on others to meet needs that were unmet during the first couple of years of life. Later experiences of loss or perceived loss threaten their ego integrity. On the other hand, persons who have not been orally deprived may regress to the oral stage in response to a loss. Regardless of whether fixation or regression is involved, the depressed individual suffers from the loss of an introjected object (Freud, 1917). During uncomplicated bereavement ("mourning"), the depressed person grieves, reliving past experiences and letting go of the lost object "bit by bit" to free energy for the development of new relationships. If the loss is complicated ("melancholia"), the individual will have ambivalent and angry feelings toward the internalized object, and thus toward the self. If suicidal, the individual will want to obliterate the self/object. The melancholic person has a more difficult time breaking loose of the lost object than the mourner (Freud, 1917).

In more recent years, *attachment theory* has been used to explain reactions to object loss. Based on observations of mothers and infants, as well as ethological research, Bowlby (1969) posed that there is a human instinct to adapt to one's environment, which is expressed initially in attachment to maternal figures and later in relationships with others. Attachment behavior is expressed in efforts to be in close proximity to a specific object, closeness arouses feelings of security whereas separation arouses anxiety. During the developmental process, young people relinquish their attachment to parents as principal love objects and form relationships with peers (Weiss, 1982). In adulthood, love relationships based on attachment provide a source of meaning as well as security and comfort (Marris, 1982). Loss is a disruption of the attachment process that is accompanied by longing, protest, and a search for the lost object. Grief work entails the relinquishment of the lost object and the restoration of meaning (Marris, 1982).

Another contemporary theory is described as *learned helplessness*. Based on Seligman's (1975) experimental work with dogs, which became passive after experiencing exposure to shock under conditions from which there was no escape, the theory poses that helplessness (and the accompanying belief that one lacks control over one's environment) is learned. When opportunities to escape are presented to someone who has been exposed to harsh, unpredictable demands, the response is passivity. Learned helplessness explains the behavior of abused spouses who do nothing to change their situations. It is also an analogue to depression.

Beck's *cognitive theory* of depression is another contemporary theory. Depressed persons have cognitions that represent misinterpretations of their experiences and depressogenic assumptions (Beck et al., 1979). The cognitions are represented in a "cognitive triad"—a view of oneself as defective or inadequate, a tendency to interpret experiences negatively, and a dim view of the future—and in cognitive structures (schemas) that categorize experiences. The depressed person uses inappropriate schemas based on faulty assumptions to interpret life events. In cognitive therapy these distorted beliefs are examined, challenged, and replaced by more accurate ones (Beck et al., 1979). (See chapter 3, Cognitive Theory.)

According to *behavioral (learning) theory*, depression is a motivational deficit, which is associated with a lack of social skills and a low level of self-generated activities that produce positive reinforcements (Rosenhan & Seligman, 1984). Without sufficient reinforcements, individuals do not feel motivated to act. Instead they become passive and feel depressed. Behavioral therapy aims to enhance social skills, increase the activity level, increase reinforcement, and promote assertiveness.

Regardless of how depression is explained, it is a painful and debilitating experience. It interferes with a sense of well-being, satisfying interpersonal relationships, productivity, and the fulfillment of life goals. Unmonitored and untreated, it can result in suicide. Fortunately, a number of effective modes of intervention have been developed. The approaches to treatment that will be emphasized here include medication, interpersonal therapy, and cognitive therapy.

MEDICATION

Medication provides depressed persons with relief from pain and reduces associated anxiety and difficulties in sleeping. The major drugs used to treat major depression (tricyclics, MAOIs, and new alternative drugs) were described in chapter 10. (It is suggested that the reader review the section on antidepressants in chapter 10.) Research in which the effectiveness of tricyclics in the maintenance (long-term) treatment of depression was compared with placebo use for the same population has found significantly higher rates of relapse among the placebo users, with an overall relapse rate of 53 percent among those who took placebos and 27 percent among those who ingested tricyclics (Davis, 1976). These results suggest that maintenance therapy for persons with depression prevents relapse. Because depressions tend to recur in persons with major depression and recovery is often incomplete (Prien, 1987), this conclusion is particularly relevant to the treatment of persons with a history of major depression. The research also reveals that tricyclics are effective for many, but not for all. Depression is a heterogeneous disorder which cannot be treated with the same medications for everyone. Furthermore, the research points to substantial numbers of people who maintain a stable mood on placebos. For them, factors that are not biological (e.g., the relationship between doctor and patient; events and supports in their own lives) may contribute to the healing process.

Because dysthymia is a relatively new category that is heterogeneous, research on the effectiveness of medication for its treatment is scant. The little research that has been conducted reports that tricyclics can control depressive symptoms in about half of the cases (Hirschfeld & Cross, 1987; Kocsis et al., 1988a). The use of imipramine (Tofranil) to treat persons with chronic depression is also associated with improvement of social and vocational adjustment (Kocsis et al., 1988b). A newer drug, the tetracyclic maprofiline (Ludiomil), is used to treat dysthymia, although this drug does have side effects that need to be monitored (Physician's Desk Reference, 1990). As indicated earlier, dysthymia and major depression can coexist (double depression). The drugs used to treat major depression are also used to treat dysthymia.

For clients who do not respond to or have medical problems that preclude using the drugs that have been described, several alternatives are possible. Some psychiatrists suggest combining antidepressant agents such as tricyclics and MAOIs; or combining antidepressant medication with lithium (Brotman, Falk, & Gelenberg, 1987). The use of lithium in this way is thought to activate the effects of the antidepressant. Another alternative is electroconvulsive therapy (ECT), in which electricity is used to produce a seizure. ECT induces a rapid recovery from major depression, although its ability to produce a sustained remission is unclear (Kaplan & Sadock, 1988). Additional somatic treatments include the use of high-intensity light for the treatment of seasonal affective disorder and sleep deprivation (Hirschfeld & Goodwin, 1988).

Research on Medication and Psychotherapy

In the last 20 years, research on the treatment of depression in which different forms of psychotherapy were compared with each other and with psychopharmacology has abounded. In a review of studies published from 1974 to January, 1984, Conte et al. (1986) concluded that the combination of psychotherapy and drugs was more effective than were placebo conditions which entailed minimal contact. Nevertheless, the results of the 17 studies that the authors analyzed indicated that the combination of therapy and drugs was only slightly superior to psychotherapy alone, psychopharmacology alone, or either of these treatments combined with a placebo. In a study of 59 patients with recurrent unipolar depression who were treated with medication and interpersonal psychotherapy themselves and whose families attended a psychoeducational workshop, Kupfer and Frank (1987) found that the relapse rate after 8 weeks was only 8.5 percent.

Research on psychotherapeutic treatment methods looks primarily at cognitive (individual and group), behavioral, interpersonal, marital or family, and group therapies. In a meta-analysis of 31 studies of treatment that was predominantly cognitive or behavioral, in which the Beck Depression Inventory was used to measure outcome, another group of researchers found that (a) individual therapy is more effective than group therapy, (b) psychotherapy produces outcomes of moderate clinical significance that are maintained at follow-up, and (c) the kind of therapy used was not related to improvement (Nietzel et al., 1987).

Some research on combined treatments suggests that medication and psychotherapy have differential effects. Medication relieves vegetative symptoms, whereas interpersonal therapy affects psychosocial functioning (DiMascio et al., 1979) and cognitive therapy affects the self-concept (Rush, Beck, Kovacs, Weissenburger, & Hollon, 1982). Furthermore, psychotherapy alone or together with medication seems to produce more sustained long-term effects than medication alone (Weissman, Jarrett, & Rush, 1987).

During the 1980s, the National Institute of Mental Health undertook and completed the Collaborative Research Study of the Treatment of Depression (Holden, 1986). Subjects consisted of 239 outpatients who were randomly assigned to treatment with (a) the tricyclic, imipramine hydrochloride, plus clinical management, (b) cognitive therapy, (c) interpersonal therapy, or (d) a clinically managed placebo. This study was undertaken in research centers in Pittsburgh, Washington, DC, and Oklahoma City. In the 16-week period of treatment, all four treatments resulted in reduced depression and improved functioning (Elkin et al., 1989). Among the four interventions, imipramine plus clinical management was the most effective, the clinically managed placebo was the least, and the psychotherapies were in between, but closer to clinically managed imipramine. When participants were classified in terms of the severity of the depression, active medication or interpersonal therapy was favored for the severely depressed, but there was no difference in effectiveness among the four treatments for the less severely depressed (Elkin et al., 1989). Although imipramine produced rapid initial improvement, by 16 weeks cognitive and interpersonal therapies produced comparable effects (Holden, 1986).

The equivalence of psychotherapeutic and psychopharmacological treatments indicates that clients who are unable to take or who do not respond to antidepressant medication, as well as those who do not believe in using pharmaceutical products, have a safe and effective alternative. For example, group cognitive therapy has been shown to produce improvements in sleep and subjective states for older adults (Beutler et al., 1987)—a population that is sensitive to medication and may have medical problems that preclude the use of antidepressants.

In a review of recent research on the effectiveness of psychotherapy in the treatment of depression, Weissman (1989) concluded:

> There is some suggestion that psychotherapies and pharmacotherapies are approximately equivalent for the milder depressions and that the psychotherapies may even be superior. The evidence for efficacy of the combination of pharmacotherapy and psychotherapy over either treatment alone still persists although these findings are strongest in the earlier maintenance trials. There is no evidence for a negative effect of combined treatment. There is some evidence from one- and two-year follow-up studies for the long-term effects of psychotherapy. (p. 1822)

Although many kinds of psychotherapies have been found to be effective in the treatment of depression, with and without pharmacotherapy, two will be explained and illustrated in the next two sections. Interpersonal and cognitive therapies have been chosen because of the research evidence of their effectiveness. Still, it is recognized that many practitioners use psychodynamic approaches. Weissman (1989) reported that psychodynamic insight therapy was compared with other therapies in only two studies she reviewed; yet, she believes, this approach is used pervasively in clinical practice. Before considering one of these or other psychotherapies, the clinician should, of course, make a thorough assessment of the client's mental status and situation. Often depression is related to a stressful life situation that can be remedied through the mobilization of environmental supports. Furthermore, the client should be screened for substance abuse, which can complicate the treatment that is recommended (see chapter 11). Clients who are suicidal should be evaluated for hospitalization or treated with crisis intervention strategies. Later in this chapter, the use of crisis intervention therapy with persons with reactive depression and suicidal ideations will be discussed.

INTERPERSONAL THERAPY

Interpersonal therapy (IPT) was developed by practitioners and researchers associated with the New Haven–Boston Collaborative Depression Project (Weissman & Klerman, 1989). It has been tested on nonbipolar depressed persons, using comparison groups treated with medication, alternative therapies, and placebos. Its effectiveness alone or in combination with medication has been substantiated (Weissman & Klerman, 1989).

Interpersonal therapy recognizes that depression develops in an interpersonal and social context (Klerman, Weissman, Rounsaville, & Chevron, 1984). Theoretically interpersonal therapy is rooted in the psychobiological thinking of Adolf Meyer (see chapter 2) and the interpersonal theory of Harry Stack Sullivan. Meyer viewed psychiatric disorders as the outcome of attempts to adapt to the environment; Sullivan was interested in the interactions *between* people (Weissman & Klerman, 1989). The team responsible for the development of interpersonal therapy also acknowledge the contributions of other theorists (e.g., Frieda Fromm-Reichmann and Silvano Arieti) who looked at the social and interpersonal dimensions of depression.

This therapy recognizes that depression derives from many sources and has diverse forms of expression. A number of causes—genetics, environmental stress, personality characteristics, and early life experiences—"combine in complex ways to produce the etiology and pathogenesis of depression" (Klerman, Weissman, Rounsaville, & Chevron, 1984, p. 38). Similarly, depression may be manifested differently in different clients. The proponents of this therapy utilize the medical model when they define depression as an illness and allow clients to assume the "sick role" (Klerman et al., 1984). Although medication may be utilized, the focus of psychotherapy is social.

Interpersonal therapy is a brief, focused, present-oriented, time-limited form of treatment (Klerman et al., 1984). The weekly psychotherapy usually lasts 12 to 16 weeks, during which time one or two problems related to an individual's current interpersonal relationships and life situation are addressed. No attempts are made to alter the personality structure or promote insight into intrapsychic conflicts, defenses, and the transference. Primarily an individual therapy, significant others can be involved as needed. Early life experiences, dysfunctional behaviors, and distorted cognitions are viewed in relation to current interpersonal relationships rather than as problems in themselves (Klerman et al., 1984).

The Therapeutic Relationship

The relationship between the clinician and the client in interpersonal therapy is developed along the lines established by Rogerian therapy, that is, the therapist is warm and nonjudgmental and communicates unconditional positive regard (Klerman et al., 1984). A positive transference is left alone; discord between the client and the clinician is compared with problematic interpersonal relationships in the client's life. In interpersonal therapy the clinician is more active than in ego psychological treatment. Nevertheless, the client is responsible for making changes. The clinician assumes the role of client advocate and provides support, reassurance, and optimism to promote the client's efforts to change (Klerman et al., 1984).

Stages of Intervention

Interpersonal therapy is implemented over three phases, each of which encompasses specific activities. At all times work is directed at achieving the goals of interpersonal therapy—reduction of depressed symptoms and improvement of interpersonal functioning. The content of these phases that will be summarized hereafter is adapted from Klerman et al.'s *Interpersonal Psychotherapy of Depression* (1984).

During the *initial phase* of one to three sessions, the client describes the symptoms and the interpersonal context of his or her life, a diagnosis is made, and a treatment contract is developed. Before a diagnosis is made, a client is referred to a physician to discern whether a medical condition is producing the depression. Meanwhile the clinician gathers information about the client's history, symptoms, and current functioning. The team that developed interpersonal therapy recommends the use of the Hamilton Rating Scale for Depression to guide the review of symptoms with the client. This scale includes questions that probe for a depressed mood, feelings of guilt, insomnia, suicidal ideations, somatic anxiety, psychomotor retardation, sexual symptoms, weight loss, and the like. If the symptoms are consistent with a diagnosis of depression (and a medical condition is ruled out), the clinician links the symptoms with a diagnostic label and informs the client that he or she is depressed.

The clinician then proceeds to educate the client about depression. This includes the nature of depression, its course, and means of treatment. Facts about its prevalence in the general population, distribution among men and women, and the effectiveness of treatment should be explained. The clinician should convey optimism about prospects for recovery. At this point, the client is given permission to adopt the "sick role," which allows the client to be excused from some social role obligations while seeking treatment. Next the client may be referred to a psychiatrist for an evaluation for medication.

During the initial phase, information is gathered and an assessment is made of the interpersonal context of the client's life. The clinician can start by asking the client to explain what was happening in his or her life when the symptoms began. The client is asked to identify and describe relationships with significant persons (family members, friends, coworkers), recent life events (infidelity, laid off from a job), and contexts (home, work) that constitute the contours of the person's life. The clinician encourages the client to talk about conflictual interpersonal relationships and interactions and about expectations of each party in a relationship. The client is asked to identify positive and negative aspects of relationships and how these relationships might change. Although the emphasis is on current relationships and life situations, the client may also talk about important past relationships.

Discussions about the interpersonal context should facilitate the identification of major problem areas. The developers of interpersonal therapy identified four issues that predominate in clients with depression. These are grief, interpersonal disputes, role transitions, and interpersonal deficits. The clinician and the client try to arrive at a mutual decision about one or two primary issues that will become the focus of treatment. In order to do this, the clinician promotes the client's awareness of the relationship between symptoms of depression and interpersonal issues.

The initial phase concludes with the clinician providing an oral summary of the problem, an explanation of the concepts of interpersonal therapy, and the development of a treatment contract. First the clinician communicates an assessment of the major problems and how they are related to the interpersonal context of the client's life. For example, Tom Smith, a 35-year-old recently separated man was told:

You seem to be depressed about being apart from your wife and children. You are living alone now, and you seem to be feeling lonely. It is clear that you do not want to lose your family and you are hoping that your wife will change her mind. Your wife, however, is acting as if she wants a divorce. You seem to be confused about what to do—try to win her back or come to terms with a divorce.

Some clients may have difficulty grasping the relationship between their mood and the interpersonal context of their lives. Instead they may blame themselves for their problems. These clients need to be told that life is made up of people and that the way relationships go affects feelings. Similarly, the lack of significant relationships can interfere with one's happiness. As one clinician put it:

Relationships are complicated; they cause problems. On the other hand, not having relationships is also difficult.

The explanation of concepts of interpersonal therapy includes practical aspects (short-term, weekly 1-hour sessions, fees, rules about cancellation and missed appointments) and expectations. The client is given the responsibility to use the sessions to review relationships and bring up current issues and feelings, including feelings about the therapeutic relationship.

The treatment contract consists of an oral agreement on the major problems and on two or three goals to be reached during therapy. These goals should be related to the problems and should be realistic and achievable within the short time span of treatment. For example, the 35-year-old man described earlier had problems in all four areas (grief, interpersonal disputes, role transitions, interpersonal deficits). The contract, however, was to work on limited goals:

1. Understand the circumstances and disputes that led up to the separation (interpersonal dispute).
2. Determine whether the disputes between his wife and him can be repaired (interpersonal dispute).
3. If the marriage cannot be repaired, grieve over the loss of previous roles (husband, live-in father) and come to terms with and assume new roles (single man, visiting father) (role transition).

During the *intermediate phase* the problem areas and related goals are addressed, and at the same time attention is paid to the client's depressive symptoms. Efforts are made to engage the client in treatment and to prevent its disruption. During therapy, the client is encouraged to understand the relationship between symptoms and interpersonal problems. As Table 12.2 indicates, the intervention goals and strategy during the intermediate phase are related to the problem area.

If the issue is grief, the client is helped to mourn by reviewing life with the lost person up to and following the loss, exploring feelings, and establishing new relationships. When role transition is the problem, the client is encouraged to discuss the advantages and disadvantages of the previous and new roles, mourn the loss of the old role through the expression of feelings, and develop a positive attitude, supports, and skills that are consistent with the new role. As for interpersonal disputes, the history,

TABLE 12.2
Implementation of Interpersonal Therapy During the Intermediate Phase

Problem	Goals	Strategies
1. Grief (over a death)	1. Facilitate mourning process 2. Help the patient reestablish interest and relationships to substitute for what has been	1. Review depressive symptoms 2. Relate onset of symptoms to death of significant other 3. Reconstruct the patient's relationship with the deceased 4. Describe the sequence of events and consequences of events just prior to, during, and after the death 5. Explore associated feelings (negative as well as positive) 6. Consider ways of becoming involved with others
2. Role transitions (change from one situation and associated role to another)	1. Mourning and acceptance of the loss of the old role 2. Help the patient to regard the new role as more positive 3. Restore self-esteem by developing a sense of mastery regarding demands of new roles	1. Review depressive symptoms 2. Relate depressive symptoms to difficulty in coping with some recent life change 3. Review positive and negative aspects of old and new roles 4. Explore feelings about what is lost 5. Explore feelings about the change itself 6. Explore opportunities in the new role 7. Realistically evaluate what is lost 8. Encourage appropriate release of affect 9. Encourage development of a social support system and of new skills called for in a new role
3. Interpersonal disputes (conflicts)	1. Identify dispute 2. Choose plan of action 3. Modify expectations or faulty communication patterns to bring about a satisfactory resolution	1. Review depressive symptoms 2. Relate symptoms onset to overt or covert dispute with a significant other with whom patient is currently involved 3. Determine stage of the dispute (renegotiation, impasse, dissolution) 4. Understand how nonreciprocal role expectations relate to dispute (issues, different expectations and values, options, likelihood of finding alternatives, resources) 5. Are there parallels in other relationships (benefits, assumptions)? 6. How is the dispute perpetuated?
4. Interpersonal deficits	1. Reduce the patient's social isolation 2. Encourage formation of new relationships	1. Review depressive symptoms 2. Relate depressive symptoms to problems of social isolation or unfulfillment 3. Review past significant relationships including their negative and positive aspects 4. Explore repetitive patterns in relationships 5. Discuss patient's positive and negative feelings about therapist and seek parallels in other relationships

Source: From *Interpersonal Psychotherapy of Depression,* by Gerald L. Klerman, M.D., Myrna M. Weissman, Ph.D., Bruce J. Rounsaville, M.D., Eve S. Chevron, M.S. Copyright 1984. Reprinted by permission of Basic Books, Inc., Publishers, New York.

stage of dispute, and discrepant role expectations are discussed and actions are taken to reconcile or resolve the problem. If the client has interpersonal deficits, the goals are to reduce social isolation and develop new relationships through a review of past relationships, identification of repetitive interpersonal patterns, and a discussion of parallels between the interaction with the therapist and relationships in the client's personal life. For Tom Smith, the intermediate phase went as follows:

Mr. Smith explained, tearfully, that he and his wife were happy during the first 10 years of their marriage, although there had been hard times. Last year, when he became unemployed, his wife took a job at a local warehouse, her first job. Although she claimed that she loved her job, Mr. Smith thought that she "changed for the worse" since working. She went out drinking after work with her new friends (while he babysat) and lost interest in housework. Meanwhile Mr. Smith had trouble finding a new job. Finally he located a well-paying job as a truck driver. When he told his wife that she no longer had to work, she refused to quit her job. In the past few months, they were increasingly distant. Their sex life was minimal and they hardly saw each other (he worked days and she worked nights). Mr. Smith said that he wants his old Cindy back, but the new Cindy does not seem to want him. He suspected that she was having an affair.

In the course of therapy during the intermediate phase, Mr. Smith recognized that his wife had changed over the years from a dependent "girl" to a woman who wanted more independence. He, however, wanted their relationship to stay the same. He also recognized that his wife was not satisfied with his unsteady pattern of working and wanted security. He expressed willingness to change himself by changing his expectations of the relationship.

Nevertheless, Mr. Smith's efforts to meet with his wife to discuss his willingness to change were unsuccessful. Mrs. Smith blocked his calls with an answering machine and did not return his messages. When he picked up the children for visits, a relative or friend greeted him at the door. His letters were not answered, except for a brief note advising him that all communications should be handled through her attorney. Mr. Smith heard rumors that she was going out with her boss. Finally Mr. Smith was served with divorce papers.

The accumulation of circumstances led Mr. Smith and the clinician to believe that it was not possible to resolve the interpersonal dispute between Tom and Cindy Smith; that divorce was inevitable. At this point he began to grieve the loss of Cindy and his role as husband and live-in father. Mr. Smith cried during therapy sessions and reported early morning wakening, loss of appetite, and feelings of depersonalization. He was referred to a psychiatrist for an evaluation for medication, which was prescribed. Meanwhile Mr. Smith shared his feelings about not having a wife and not sharing a home with her and the children; he had a difficult time being alone. He reported having great love for his wife, even though she did not seem to love him. He said that having a wife and family to go home to gave him a purpose for living and people to work for. Further exploration of his feelings, however, led to his expression of anger and anguish. He felt that he had been a devoted husband who was "dumped" when someone more affluent came along. He felt rejected sexually (and as a man) and longed for his wife's affection.

Nevertheless, Mr. Smith continued to work as a truck driver. Toward the end of the intermediate stage, he and the clinician discussed ways he could be a visiting father. He came up with such ideas as taking the children camping, on picnics, and to the zoo. He also (working through a lawyer) negotiated a visitation plan that included dinner a couple of evenings a week and overnight visits on weekends. In addition, Mr. Smith considered other ways to fill up his empty evenings, such as visiting his father and siblings (who had been making efforts to reach out to him), becoming involved in a local church, and joining Parents without Partners. Mr. Smith said that he did not feel ready to go out with other women at this time. Although he still reported sadness over the loss of his wife and the family as he knew it, he recognized that it was possible to build a new life in the future.

Early in the *termination phase* (last three or four sessions) the client is told that therapy will be ending shortly. The client is given the opportunity to express feelings about termination and about the therapist. The clinician helps the client grieve over the impending loss while at the same time assuring the client that he or she is capable of coping independently. The remaining time is used to evaluate the gains made in treatment and to prepare for the future. At times issues of loss that were present during treatment are replayed:

Upon hearing that he had only four sessions left, Mr. Smith expressed sadness and feelings of hopelessness. At this point, the clinician reviewed with him the issues of loss that he has been facing and difficulties he has been having in being alone. Mr. Smith expressed gratitude to the therapist for being there and tried to convince her to extend the sessions beyond the 12 that had been agreed upon. The therapist noted that there were parallels in his wanting the therapy to last and his unwillingness to accept the impending divorce from his wife. Mr. Smith described himself as a "needy guy who doesn't see the handwriting on the wall." When asked how he felt about termination, the client expressed feelings of rejection. After a couple of sessions, however, he recognized that the therapy was supposed to be 12 weeks and that he had benefited from it. Mr. Smith said that although he felt bad about the divorce and about termination, he felt challenged at having a chance to rebuild his life as a single man. He reported joining a support group for single adults at a nearby church and increased contacts with his children, father, and siblings. Hopeful for a better future, he no longer was depressed.

Techniques

In interpersonal therapy, the clinician utilizes a number of techniques.

Exploratory Techniques. Eliciting information about the client's problems and symptoms through directive and nondirective questioning and responses. Nondirective techniques include open-ended questions, nonverbal or minimal communication ("uh huh"), encouraging the client to continue to talk, inviting the client to expand on ideas that are presented, and the use of silence as an encourager. Directive techniques include the use of questions related to specific symptoms and interpersonal relationships.

Encouragement of Affect.   Promotion of the expression and experience of painful emotions. The clinician elicits the client's feelings ("how did you feel about that?") and responds by accepting the client's pain. This is especially useful in work with clients who have difficulty identifying and expressing their feelings. For clients who are overwhelmed with affect, the client should be helped to control feelings.

Communication Analysis.   Analysis of communication breakdown, especially in problems involving interpersonal disputes. The clinician asks the client to describe in detail specific incidents of faulty communication. Together they identify ambiguous messages, false assumptions, and indirect methods of response. Alternative interpretations and responses are suggested.

Clarification.   Efforts by the clinician to get the client to rethink a previous statement and thus arrive at a deeper understanding of what has been said. This can be achieved by paraphrasing a client's message, asking the client to rephrase his or her own words, examining the implications of what a client has said, or drawing attention to unusual beliefs and inconsistencies between messages.

Behavior Change Techniques.   Changes that are discussed or modeled during therapy but enacted in interpersonal behavior in everyday life. These are implemented through directive techniques, such as limited setting, giving suggestions or advice, providing information or education, modeling, and provision of direct assistance; decision analysis; and role playing. Therapeutic efforts to assist the client in the resolution of problems are predicated on the client's willingness to assume responsibility for his or her own actions. Accordingly, directive techniques are used cautiously in such a way to preserve the client's autonomy. With decision analysis the client examines alternative solutions to a problem and probable consequences of each option. The clinician offers ideas about solutions and helps the client think through the alternatives, but the client makes decisions. With role playing, the clinician plays the role of a person in the client's life with whom the client is having a problematic relationship. This technique is used so that the clinician can assess the nature of the problem and the client can learn more constructive communication strategies.

Use of the Therapeutic Relationship.   Although interpersonal therapy does not emphasize the development of a transference, the client is encouraged from the beginning to share positive and negative feelings about the clinician and the therapeutic process. Moreover, if the client interacts with the clinician in distorted ways, the clinician will discuss these patterns with the client. Distortions in the client–therapist relationship are of diagnostic value; they suggest ways in which the client interacts with others. The clinician's acceptance of the clients' feelings about the clinician provides an opportunity to correct distortions and deal with sensitive issues in relationships.

In the case that was described in this chapter, several of these techniques were used. Exploratory techniques were used in the initial and intermediate phases to determine what was going on in Mr. Smith's life, who his significant others were, and whether repair of the marital dispute was possible. When Mr. Smith provided this information in a distorted way ("she's changed for the worse"), clarification techniques were used to determine what and who had changed and why. When the client realized that there was no hope of reconciliation, he began to grieve. The clinician encouraged him to express feelings, which were primarily sadness, loneliness, anger, anguish, and longing. Mr. Smith also felt the loss of his wife as a sex partner and felt that his masculinity had been challenged by a competitor. Mr. Smith was encouraged to change his behavior through a discussion of options that were available to him as he made the transition to the roles of visiting father and single adult. The therapeutic relationship was used in the end to help Mr. Smith deal with the separations in his life.

Interpersonal therapy encompasses the perspectives and strategies used by clinical social workers. First of all, interpersonal therapy gives the social field the primary focus of attention, which is consistent with the person-in-situation perspective used in social work. Task-centered casework (Reid & Epstein, 1972) utilizes a similar strategy of working on targeted problems over a brief period of time. Many social work practice texts describe intervention in terms of stages that include information gathering, assessment and planning, intervention, and termination (e.g., Compton & Galaway, 1984; Strean, 1985). The techniques that have been described are pervasive in the social work literature (e.g., Hollis, 1949; Kadushin, 1983; Shulman, 1984). Not surprising, one of the developers of interpersonal therapy (Myrna Weissman) has a master's degree in social work.

Interpersonal therapy is particularly compatible with the biopsychosocial conceptual framework of this book. For one, it recognizes that depression has a biological base. Where appropriate, clients are offered the opportunity to take medication and assume the sick role. Second, it recognizes the social environmental context in which human problems arise and psychological problems that contribute to becoming frozen in social roles. Interpersonal therapy recognizes that there are multiple forces that influence the development and creation of problems. Its emphasis on the social context differs from the emphasis on cognition that is evident in the approach that will be discussed next.

COGNITIVE THERAPY

Cognitive therapy for depression was developed by Aaron Beck and his associates (Beck, 1976; Beck, Rush, Shaw, & Emery, 1979). Working separately, Beck arrived at conceptualizations and strategies that were similar to those of Albert Ellis (Beck, 1976). Cognitive therapy is predicated on the idea that automatic thoughts and images (cognitions) precipitate depression and other symptoms of emotional disturbance. Treatment is directed at changing distorted, maladaptive, inaccurate cognitions to more adaptive ones. Sometimes called cognitive-behavioral therapy, the treatment uses behavioral as well as cognitive strategies.

Although cognitive therapy does not preclude biological or developmental explanations or the use of medication (Beck, 1976), it is concerned principally with the thought patterns or schemas that underlie depression. A life experience, such as a loss, can activate latent schemas (e.g., attitudes about loss) that developed earlier in life. A person with unipolar depression is likely to interpret later life events in ways that emphasize the negative aspects, ignore the context, and reflect poorly on the individual. Selectively attending to those elements of the situation that coincide with "depressogenic" schemas, the individual construes the situation in a partial way, without considering the whole (Beck et al., 1979). The following are examples of maladaptive explanations of a brief exchange between two coworkers at the coffee pot one morning:

Conversation:

AL: Hi Bob. How ya' doing?
BOB: Pretty good. How are you?
AL: OK. Gotta go. (Rushes off)

Bob's maladaptive explanations of Al's rushing off:

Al doesn't like me.
Al doesn't like me anymore.
I wonder what I did wrong.

An accurate assessment of this situation reveals that Al greeted Bob with warmth and friendliness. Yet Bob viewed the interaction as a reflection of Al's negative feelings toward him. Alternative explanations for Al's behavior are: (a) Al had an appointment or a meeting; (b) Al needed to prepare for a busy day of work; (c) Al went to the coffee pot for coffee, not to socialize; and (d) Al is a workaholic. Essentially Al's reasons had nothing to do with Bob. The negative interpretation was a reflection of Bob's schemas.

Persons who are depressed are prone to make inaccurate interpretations of their experiences. Automatic negative thoughts intervene between life events and emotional responses, creating a negative bias. Depressed persons view life events that would ordinarily be viewed as undesirable, disappointing, or neutral as catastrophes. Convinced that their perception of reality is the same as reality (Beck, 1976), they feel pain associated with their own interpretations. Soon they become preoccupied with themes of rejection, inadequacy, and failure and blame themselves for unfortuitous experiences. As the depression deepens, the depressive themes predominate and reality testing becomes impaired (Beck, 1985).

The Therapeutic Relationship

Beck's cognitive therapy is implemented through a collaborative relationship between the clinician and the client. The therapist fosters those conditions that facilitate the development of a relationship and which are described in Rogerian therapy—warmth, genuineness, accurate empathy (Beck et al., 1979). Much attention is given to developing rapport and building trust. Although cognitive therapy emphasizes cognitions, emotions are not ignored. The client is given the opportunity to express feelings and the clinician accepts the feelings the client shares.

Although the relationship is a partnership, the roles of clinician and client are different. The cognitive therapist may be viewed as a teacher, the client as a learner. The clinician explains cognitive theory to the client, provides structure to the sessions, asks questions of the client, and assigns homework. Before proceeding with the therapeutic work, the clinician explains that they will be working together to develop hypotheses and test them out (Hirschfeld & Shea, 1985). The clinician assumes an active role in identifying problems, in focusing on specific issues, and in the implementation of cognitive and behavioral techniques (Beck, 1985). The client is expected to describe feelings, cognitions, and behaviors, to work at revising inaccurate thoughts, and to carry out assigned activities and homework.

The Nature of Cognitive Therapy

Like interpersonal therapy, cognitive therapy is brief, present oriented, and focused. The time period varies from 10 to 25 weeks, with the usual pattern consisting of 20 sessions, of which the first eight are conducted on a twice-a-week basis and the remainder weekly (Jarrett & Rush, 1989). Some clients continue in intermittent "booster" sessions for 6 months to 1 year after the conclusion of the initial period (Jarrett & Rush, 1989). Although cognitive therapy can be implemented in couple and group formats (Jarrett & Rush, 1989), the individual approach will be described here.

Cognitive therapy employs the scientific method that is used in research. Throughout the process, information is gathered, hypotheses are tested, and logical conclusions are drawn. The clinician and the client examine thoughts and interpretations and create and evaluate experiments clients perform in their daily lives that test hypotheses. The client is encouraged to discard ideas that are illogical and do not reflect observed reality.

Hypotheses and experiments provide insight into underlying "depressogenic assumptions" and rules (Beck et al., 1979), which also can be tested. Beck (1976) identified several assumptions that are related to depression:

1. In order to be happy, I have to be successful in whatever I undertake.
2. To be happy, I must be accepted by all people at all times.
3. If I'm not on top, I'm a flop.
4. It's wonderful to be popular, famous, wealthy; it's terrible to be unpopular, mediocre.
5. If I make a mistake, it means that I am inept.
6. My value as a person depends on what others think of me.
7. I can't live without love. If my spouse (sweetheart, parent, child) doesn't love me, I'm worthless.
8. If somebody disagrees with me, it means he doesn't like me.
9. If I don't take advantage of every opportunity to advance myself, I will regret it later. (pp. 255–256)

The goals of cognitive therapy are to promote relief of depressive symptoms and to prevent a recurrence (Beck et al., 1979). Subjectively, the client should have enhanced feelings of satisfaction and well-being. These goals are achieved by teaching the client to:

(a) Learn to identify and modify his faulty thinking and dysfunctional behavior and (b) recognize and change the cognitive patterns leading to dysfunctional ideation and behavior. (Beck et al., 1979, p. 75)

The Process of Cognitive Therapy

Beck and his associates describe a process in which the strategies and techniques of cognitive therapy vary over time. Prior to admission to treatment, they perform a preliminary evaluation of potential clients. The evaluation includes a history of the current difficulty, past history, a mental status examination, and a battery of tests. Among the tests that are used are the Schedule of Affective Disorders and Schizophrenia, the Hamilton Scale for Depression, the Hopelessness Scale, the Scale for Suicide Intentionality, the Minnesota Multiphasic Personality Inventory, the Spielberger State-Trait Anxiety Scale, and the Beck Depression Inventory (Beck et al., 1979).

The First Interview.   During the first interview, attention is initially given to establishing rapport, inquiring about the client's expectations of therapy, and eliciting attitudes toward the self, the clinician, and therapy. On the basis of information that was gathered during the preliminary evaluation and observations about the client's mental status that are made in this session, the clinician identifies "complaints" ("I do not see any reason to go on") and transforms them into "target symptoms" (suicidal thoughts) or problems (difficulty completing school work) (Beck et al., 1979). When more than one symptom or problem is identified, potential targets are prioritized on the basis of the distress they arouse in the client and their amenability to treatment. The clinician and the client come to a negotiated agreement about the symptom or problem that will be focal.

The clinician devotes considerable time during the first session to educating the client about cognitive therapy. The cognitive theory of depression and intervention techniques (see next section) should be explained. Particular attention is given to the client's responsibility to perform homework assignments between sessions. Beck and associates give the client a booklet, *Coping with Depression* (Beck & Greenberg, 1974) to read. Inquiries are made about the client's activity level, and the client is assigned the task of keeping a record of the activities that are performed between this session and the next. Before this interview concludes, the client's feelings about the interview are elicited (Beck et al., 1979).

The Second Interview.   During the second interview, the client is again encouraged to share feelings about the first session, but is also invited to raise questions about the reading material or the process. The clinician answers the client's questions and responds to questions. In addition, the homework assignment on activities is reviewed. If the client appears to be having difficulty getting motivated to be active, the clinician and the client together develop a schedule of activities to be performed by the client. The client is given the homework assignment of rating each activity performed with respect to degree of mastery and pleasure (Beck et al., 1979).

Throughout therapy, sessions are structured. Sessions begin with the clinician and the client developing an agenda of what they wish to accomplish during the session (Beck et al., 1979). This usually includes the client's summary of experiences since the last session and a review of the homework assignment. Issues and concerns pertaining to the previous session can also be raised. The client and the clinician together identify problems and negotiate about which ones will be addressed in the session. The client chooses among strategies suggested by the clinician (e.g., role playing, refuting automatic thoughts, etc.) for looking at targeted problems in the session. Sessions also include an elicitation of the client's feelings, summary statements by the clinician, and a description of the next homework assignment (Beck et al., 1979).

In each session the client is asked about depressive symptoms and about events that have occurred since the previous meeting. The clinician responds to the recitation of experiences by inquiring about the client's feelings, thinking, and behavior. During these discussions the client reveals distorted thinking that is associated with life events. The clinician begins to point out the relationship between the client's negative cognitions and depression (Beck et al., 1979).

Middle Phase.   During the middle phase of intervention, attention is given to automatic thoughts that are associated with disturbing feelings (sadness, anxiety, and lack of interest in life). Clients may be asked to perform homework assignments in which they record the circumstances related to these feelings, that is, the precipitating event and cognitions. During the sessions, clients are questioned about aspects of the situations they describe (orally or in assignments) that they may have excluded. This is because persons who are depressed frequently construe their experiences narrowly, omitting dimensions that do not conform with their negative schemas. The clinician challenges the client's distorted thinking and presents alternative explanations based on a comprehensive consideration of evidence. In addition, the clinician elicits (during the sessions and in homework assignments) rational alternative explanations from clients. Other techniques are used to help clients identify dysfunctional cognitions and restructure them. Clients are given further information about the relationship between their feelings and depressogenic assumptions. At times, clients are asked to test out their assumptions in assigned activities to be performed between sessions.

Concluding Sessions.   As therapy draws to a close, the client is given more responsibility for initiation of the agenda, homework assignments, and setting goals. Cognitive and behavioral techniques are used to anticipate and practice rational strategies of interpreting experiences. During the last few sessions, the client is prepared for termination and for retaining the benefits of thinking constructively in the future. Client and clinician discuss issues the client is likely to face in the future and strategies with which to handle them.

Techniques of Cognitive Therapy

Cognitive therapy employs an array of cognitive and behavioral techniques and procedures, some of which are used throughout therapy and others that vary in relation to the severity of the depression and the stage of therapy.

Behavioral Techniques.   If the client is severely depressed, behavioral strategies are used early in the process. Clients who are so depressed that they cannot get out of bed, for example, are helped to become more active through the use of *activity schedules* and *graded task assignments* (Beck et al., 1979). At first the clinician has the client write up a schedule of daily activities. If the client does not appear to be sufficiently active, the clinician and the client develop a schedule of hourly activities that expand upon the client's usual repertoire. New and more demanding activities are added gradually over time (graded task assignments). Clients are also asked to keep a record of activities that are accomplished and to grade them on a scale from 0 to 5 according to the degree of pleasure (P) and sense of mastery (M) that are experienced (Beck, 1979, 1985).

Other behavioral techniques complement cognitive strategies (Beck, 1979). *Role playing,* with the clinician and the client taking the roles of parties described by the client, makes visible the difficulties a client is having in a social interaction. Identified problems are often related to automatic thoughts. In addition, *cognitive rehearsal* helps clients prepare mentally for the performance of tasks the client anticipates will be difficult. With this technique, the client is asked to imagine performing a task, step by step. In walking through the situation, the client identifies obstacles and thinking patterns that impede accomplishment of the task. The cognitive rehearsal is repeated until the obstacles are overcome in the imagination. Then the client is asked to perform the task in real life. In addition, *diversion* techniques are used. The client is encouraged to become distracted from painful emotions by engaging in other activities, focusing on environmental stimuli, and imagining pleasant scenes.

Cognitive Techniques.   Although cognitive techniques are implemented throughout therapy, the nature of these techniques varies over time. In the beginning, the clinician uses a didactic approach to explain what automatic thoughts are and how they affect emotions and behavior (Beck et al., 1979). Then the client is helped to *identify automatic thoughts* in his or her daily life. The client may be given a homework assignment to keep a record of events and associated negative cognitions and emotions that occur between sessions. This assignment, as well as specific examples that the client offers during sessions, can be used as a basis for a *discussion of cognitive errors*. The client and the clinician together look at the facts and the client's interpretation of the event and *generate alternative explanations*. Such a logical examination can result in *distancing* oneself from one's experience (becoming more objective) and in shifting responsibility from the client to another source (*reattribution*). The client can learn how to modify negative cognitions through a homework assignment in which automatic thoughts and alternative explanations are listed; or through a process of questioning and presenting modified interpretations during the session (Beck, 1985; Beck et al., 1979).

During the course of therapy, *hypotheses* that underlie a client's behavior are identified and *tested empirically*. For example, Mrs. Dell, who was depressed and slightly overweight, spent little time outside her home. She explained that she only shops for groceries early in the morning because later in the day, when the store is crowded, people stare at her large body. The hypothesis the clinician formulated was, "Because you are depressed, you expect other people to view you in a negative way." This woman was asked to shop at various times and keep track of the number of people who stared at her each time she shopped. She discovered that whatever time she went, very few people stared at her.

Case Example

Maxine Brown is a 45-year-old married woman who entered therapy saying that she was so far down and could not get up. She reported a loss of appetite, sleeping excessively, and a lack of energy. Mrs. Brown said that she was having difficulty getting motivated to take care of all the people who needed her and felt like a failure as a wife and stepmother. The client related that she has been married to Mr. Brown for a year and that everything was "perfect" until Mr. Brown's 16-year-old son Todd moved in with them 4 months ago. Todd leaves his dirty clothes scattered throughout the house, uses foul language, and expects Mrs. Brown to pick up after him. Mrs. Brown said that instead of feeling love for Todd, she resents him.

Mrs. Brown said that she could hardly manage her responsibilities before Todd moved in. She has a part-time job as a bookkeeper, is principal care giver for a sick uncle who lives alone in an apartment Mrs. Brown cleans, and has homemaking responsibilities. Mrs. Brown explained that Mr. Brown takes care of the lawn and home repair but considers housework "woman's work." Although the client usually keeps up with the housework, since Todd moved in with them, she has let the laundry and cleaning accumulate. She has been going to work regularly, but she does not work as quickly as she used to.

When asked how Todd came to live with them, Mrs. Brown said that his mother arranged this with Mr. Brown several months ago. Apparently Todd's mother was planning to remarry and the relationship between Todd and her gentleman friend was not good. When asked if she was involved in the decision to take Todd, she said that her husband did not ask her; he acted as if they had no choice. When asked how she felt about not being asked, Mrs. Brown said she felt slighted. She said that she would have agreed to take Todd if she were asked, because Mr. Brown had an obligation to his son, but she would have liked to have been part of the decision. Mrs. Brown said that she has a great deal of resentment built up inside because after she struggled for 15 years as a single parent, her own children are independent and she was looking forward to married life as a couple without parental responsibilities. She wondered if she was a selfish person.

During the preliminary evaluation and the first interview, the clinician established that Mrs. Brown had a diagnosis of major depression, single episode. The client reported previous times in her life when she felt depressed, but she has always been able to "snap out of it." According to the Beck Depression Inventory, Mrs. Brown was mildly to moderately depressed. She showed strengths in continued functioning at home and at work.

In the first session, the client and the clinician (a social worker) identified several problems and target symptoms. They agreed that she had problems communicating her feelings to her husband, difficulty setting limits with her stepson, and problems managing her responsibilities. Target symptoms were sadness, lack of motivation, anger, and lack of interest in eating. She had vague suicidal thoughts but no intention to kill herself. The client and the social worker agreed that Mrs. Brown's difficulty getting motivated to perform her responsibilities and the anger that Mrs. Brown felt but did not express would be the target symptoms initially. The client was asked to bring an hourly schedule of her activities to the next session.

At the beginning of the next session, the clinician and Mrs. Brown developed an agenda for this meeting. They would review the client's homework, discuss events of the past week, and explore the target symptoms they had discussed last time. When Mrs.

Brown handed the schedule to the social worker, she mentioned that she did not feel that she accomplished very much during the past week. Nevertheless, the clinician observed that Mrs. Brown's schedule was packed. The client spent most of her time cooking, cleaning, taking care of others, or at work; and she spent little time resting or engaging in recreational activities. When asked what else she thinks she should have accomplished, Mrs. Brown said that she did not clean her uncle's kitchen, did the laundry only twice a week, and did not clean her stepson's room, although it was a mess. This led into a discussion of events in her life during the last week. Mrs. Brown said that she felt better after the last interview and that since then she has become more aware of her anger. She said that she resents cleaning up after her stepson; therefore, she puts off the task of cleaning his room. She also has resentment toward her husband for agreeing to have his son come and toward Mr. Brown's former wife for sending him here. Mrs. Brown said that she feels tired as well as resentful. The social worker then asked the client to explain her expectations of herself in relation to Todd. Mrs. Brown said that she expects herself to feel love toward Todd and to care about him as she cared about her own children. She believes that she has an obligation to take on the responsibility of mothering him without resenting it. She views this as something she owes her husband, who is the principal wage earner. The social worker asked Mrs. Brown if she thought she could force herself to feel love if she did not feel this emotion. Mrs. Brown supposed that she could not, but blamed herself for not being able to love Todd. She said that she wished that she were not so angry at Todd; that maybe she could feel love if she did not feel anger. The social worker questioned Mrs. Brown's reasoning about feeling love.

SOCIAL WORKER: What makes you think you must love Todd?
MRS. BROWN: If I'm his stepmother, I should love him.
SOCIAL WORKER: You can be a stepmother to him without feeling love.
MRS. BROWN: How can I? If I didn't love him, I'd be a cruel stepmother.
SOCIAL WORKER: It sounds as if you believe that you need to love him in order to treat him well—that if you didn't love him, you'd be cruel.
MRS. BROWN: I'm not cruel and I don't hate him; but I don't especially like him either. I think I could like him better if he would cooperate.

The social worker and the client then discussed Mrs. Brown's resentment of Todd's lack of cooperation further. This led into the following discussion:

SOCIAL WORKER: Can you be more specific and tell me what you are angry at Todd about?
MRS. BROWN: He doesn't seem to be in the least concerned about me and all the work he has created for me. He doesn't make his bed or clean his room. He doesn't bring his dishes to the table. He doesn't do the laundry. My girls took care of their own rooms and they used to help me with the dishes. Todd doesn't do anything.
SOCIAL WORKER: It sounds as if you believe he has responsibilities around the house and he isn't doing his part.
MRS. BROWN: Yes.
SOCIAL WORKER: I wonder if you have communicated this to him.

MRS. BROWN: I never had to tell my girls; they just knew. I keep waiting for Todd to
                   volunteer to do something but he seems to expect to be waited on. He
                   should know he has responsibilities.
SOCIAL WORKER: It looks as if he does not know. He can't read your mind. Now that he's
                   living with you, it's up to you to tell him what the rules are.
MRS. BROWN: You mean I should tell him what I want him to do around the house?
SOCIAL WORKER: Yes, tell him what you expect of him. Regardless of how you feel about
                   him, you have the right to have expectations of him.

The homework that was assigned after this session had two parts. The first assignment was for Mrs. Brown to communicate her expectations of Todd to both her husband
and Todd. It was important for Mrs. Brown to explain to her husband that she could not
assume responsibilities that should be Todd's. In addition, Mrs. Brown was to continue
to record her activities, but was to rate them in terms of the pleasure she received.
Meanwhile she was encouraged to do more activities that she enjoyed.

Next time Mrs. Brown reported satisfaction in how the conversation with Todd
went. She told him that he was responsible for cleaning his room, setting the table, and
washing the dishes. He complained but said he would go along with what she wanted.
She said that her husband questioned her decision to have Todd set the table and wash
the dishes, but when she told her husband that Todd's lack of cooperation was contributing to her depression, he supported her. Mrs. Brown rated all her activities in the low
end of the scale in pleasure, except for an hour a day she took to watch TV, which she
rated 3.

During the next few sessions, Mrs. Brown reported feeling satisfied that Todd was
cooperating. Nevertheless, she still felt depressed. The social worker identified some of
the client's beliefs that seemed to be problematic for her. Mrs. Brown believed that she
had to be a perfect housekeeper and that she had to take care of whatever is asked of her
by family members. Her depressogenic assumption was, "in order to be happy, I have to
be successful in whatever I undertake" (Beck, 1976, p. 255). During one session, the
following conversation took place:

SOCIAL WORKER: What do you think would happen if you did not do all of the chores you
                   usually do next week?
MRS. BROWN: I would feel like a failure.
SOCIAL WORKER: What do you think would happen to the work you did not get done?
MRS. BROWN: I would probably get it done the following week.
SOCIAL WORKER: So it is possible that you can do fewer things than you usually do?
MRS. BROWN: I could do less. But whatever I do get done does not seem to be enough.
SOCIAL WORKER: How can you tell what's "enough"?
MRS. BROWN: When I'm exhausted, I know I've done enough. I usually work until I am
                   exhausted.
SOCIAL WORKER: What do you think would happen if you stopped working on chores
                   before you reached the exhaustion point?
MRS. BROWN: I don't know; I've never done that.
SOCIAL WORKER: Perhaps we can work this into your homework assignment for this week.
MRS. BROWN: I'd be willing to try that.

With this and other homework assignments, Mrs. Brown recognized that she did not have to work as hard as she was working; that she could accomplish smaller amounts of work at a given time, yet leave time for her to engage in activities that are pleasurable. With her stepson doing his share, she had more positive feelings toward him. As she approached termination, she began to think of ways in which she can obtain help from a homemaker home health aide for her uncle. During the last few sessions, she discussed her reluctance to share her feelings about Todd's coming to live with them when her husband first brought up the topic. She recognized that she had the distorted belief that she was not allowed to express her feelings when they deviated from what she thought were her husband's expectations. Mrs. Brown expressed confidence that she could improve her relationship with her husband as well as her own sense of well-being by breaking this unstated rule. In the last interview, Mrs. Brown reported that she and her husband had a discussion about chores around the house and that they agreed to distribute the household tasks more equitably and to go out to eat once a week. She said that she has learned to pace herself better and was no longer depressed.

As this case illustrates, cognitive therapy can be used to help depressed individuals who have distorted ideas to change their thinking and behavior. A short-term therapy with a record of effectiveness, it can promote relief from painful emotions and dysfunctional ways of thinking about oneself, others, and the future. A therapy that is guided by scientific reasoning, it promotes logical thinking, which can be useful in problem solving. Such an approach is appealing to clinicians who value intellectual processing and to clients who are capable of learning to examine their beliefs.

ALTERNATIVE STRATEGIES AND OTHER CONSIDERATIONS

Interpersonal and cognitive therapies are two among many strategies of treating depressed persons. They were chosen because they have been subjected to the most research, with and without medication. Other interventions include short-term insight-oriented therapy, marital therapy, family therapy, and behavior modification. Research on these alternatives is promising.

Persons with reactive (exogenous) depressions frequently ask for help in emergency services or at community mental health agencies. In response to a stressful life event, such individuals may develop the spectrum of symptoms associated with a major depression. Yet with crisis intervention that is focused on solving immediate problems and restructuring faulty cognitions, psychosocial functioning can be restored in approximately 6 weeks. Principles of crisis intervention and methods of intervention are described in several other textbooks (e.g., Dixon, 1987; Everstine & Everstine, 1983; Golan, 1978).

Regardless of the method of treatment used, attention should be given to suicidal thoughts and feelings that a client might have. Although suicide and depression do not necessarily coincide, often enough suicidal ideations accompany depressions. The clinician should attend to a client's oblique references to suicide ("I wonder if I have anything to look forward to"; "I would like to get away from all the pressures") and to behaviors suggesting suicidal intention (giving away precious gifts, writing a will). The social worker should not hesitate to inquire about the meaning of these statements and behaviors and to ask clients directly whether they are thinking about suicide.

Whether the client discusses suicide directly or obliquely, the social worker should assess the depth of the client's depression, the client's personal and interpersonal resources that can facilitate coping, and the seriousness of the client's intention. Although one cannot predict accurately who will commit suicide, one can use research findings about those who complete suicides to assess a client's risk. Factors that are commonly associated with increased risk are previous attempt, suicide in the family, recent loss, social isolation, major psychiatric disorder, psychotic symptoms, alcoholism, men, unmarried, white or American Indian, older adult (Walker, 1983). Furthermore, clients should be questioned about their intended means of suicide and whether they have that means (e.g., gun, rope, pills) in their possession. Clients who have suicidal thoughts and meet any of these criteria should be screened especially carefully.

Suicidal clients need to be protected from themselves. In some cases, this means confinement in a psychiatric hospital or unit. Crisis centers with accommodations may be able to retain clients for a period of hours or overnight until the feelings become less acute. The client who has family and other social supports may be able to go home safely with a significant other, who can protect the client during the crisis. Community resources such as crisis residences are an additional alternative.

Regardless of the alternative, the suicidal client needs to be supported during the crisis and after the crisis passes. The social worker needs to inquire about the reason the client is in crisis at this time, hazardous events, supports, and stressors in the client's life. Efforts should be made to restore the client's functioning to at least the precrisis level and to prevent the conditions that led to the crisis from resurfacing. Ongoing individual, family, and group therapy can help the client gain insight, support, and coping skills that will help solve future problems in a constructive way.

SUMMARY

Although depression is experienced by most individuals in the course of their everyday lives, ordinarily such depressions surround situational problems, have a limited course, and are of low intensity. When psychopathological, a cluster of symptoms that are difficult to eradicate appear. The two forms of psychopathological depression that have been emphasized in this chapter are major depression and dysthymia. They are characterized by symptoms of dysphoria, slowed movements, weight loss, sleep difficulties, and loss of interest in life. Major depression requires more symptoms than dysthymia; dysthymia is a chronic disorder of at least 2 years.

Depression has been attributed to biological, psychological, and social factors. Evidence of a biological component comes from genetic studies and research on the impact of antidepressants on mood. Social research points to stress as a precipitator of depression and lack of support as a contributor to vulnerability. Several psychological theories purport to explain depression. These include psychoanalytic, attachment, learned helplessness, cognitive, and behavioral theories.

Tricyclic medication has been shown to be more effective in the treatment of depression than placebos. Nevertheless, some individuals do not respond to antidepressants; others are unable to ingest these medications. Some clients recover when they are treated with placebos. Some of the alternatives available to nonresponders include combining drugs, electroconvulsive therapy, high-intensity light, and psychotherapy.

Research on medication and psychotherapy reported in this chapter focuses primarily on two forms of psychotherapy—interpersonal therapy (IPT) and cognitive therapy. Both therapies have been shown to be as effective as the tricyclic medication by 16 weeks. Some research indicates that each of these therapies affects different aspects of depression (psychosocial functioning, self-concept, vegetative symptoms). There are some indications that the combination of pharmacotherapy and psychotherapy is useful or that it does not produce harm.

Interpersonal therapy was developed by the New Haven–Boston Collaborative Research Group. It is a short-term, focused, present-oriented therapy that looks at the interpersonal context of an individual's life. The client is educated about depression, allowed to enter the sick role, and enrolled in a structured program of psychotherapy. Therapy usually focuses on one or two issues among grief, interpersonal disputes, role transitions, and interpersonal deficits. The client enters into a contract to meet goals related to the identified issues. Attention

to the context, the treatment process, and the techniques used resemble those used in clinical social work.

Similarly, cognitive therapy is short term, focused, present oriented, and structured. With cognitive therapy, however, attention is paid principally to distorted ideas that are associated with depression. The client treated with this form of therapy is helped to identify dysfunctional thoughts and to change them. The clinician helps the client alter his or her thinking by asking questions about the basis for the thoughts, suggesting alternative explanations, testing hypotheses and assumptions, and changing behaviors.

Although these two forms of therapy were discussed here, other therapies are used in clinical practice with persons with depression. In addition, persons with acute episodes of depression are frequently treated with crisis intervention. During a crisis, attention is given to direct and indirect suicidal ideations and suicidal behaviors. The client at high risk needs to be protected. Suicidal clients are treated in psychiatric hospitals, acute psychiatric units, or crisis centers. Significant others can protect the client from self-injurious behavior and provide the support needed for survival. The suicidal client should be treated in therapy during the crisis and afterward.

CASE STUDY

Katie is a 19-year-old single woman who was referred to the outpatient department of a community hospital after an examination by a physician revealed that most of her physical symptoms did not have an organic cause. The physical symptoms she complained about to the doctor were weight loss, headaches, menstrual irregularity, and low energy. The physician recommended that in addition to seeing a clinician, she should have a gynecological evaluation, because it was possible that she was a DES baby (child of a mother who took a drug that inhibits

miscarriage but affects the offspring's reproductive organs). When Katie saw the clinical social worker, she reported feeling confused and sad; she did not know what to do with her life.

At the time of her first interview, Katie was living with Max, who worked as a long-haul truck driver. She said that he was 10 years older than she and had a 7-year-old son from a previous marriage who lived with his mother. Katie met Max at the restaurant where she works as a waitress. Since moving in with Max 6 months ago, the symptoms have become more and more evident. When asked to talk further about the circumstances surrounding her moving in with Max, Katie said that "In moving in with Max, I lost my parents." When asked to explain, she said that her parents considered her "loose" and have cut off communication with her. Katie does, however, keep in close contact with her brother and sister, who live together in an apartment in town. Her siblings tell her about her parents and what her parents say about Katie.

Katie said that even though she loves Max, moving in with him has not been as wonderful as she had anticipated. For one thing, he is out of town a great deal, so she is alone in their apartment much of the time. Because she is living with him, she does not feel comfortable running around with her old crowd. Last week, however, she did go out with one of the men with whom she works. It started out as a casual invitation on Richard's part that they go out for a drink, but she ended up sleeping with him. Even though Max was out of town, she did not spend the whole night with Richard. The next morning she felt terrible qualms of guilt. Nevertheless, she has not been able to get Richard out of her mind. She sees Richard every day at work and they continue to be friends. Nevertheless, Katie feels that she is "over my head in handling life."

When asked further about her family of origin, she said that she was an "abused child." She said that her father used to "kick me around while my mother stood and watched." She said that her brother and sister were also abused, but she was the only one who used to fight back with her father, even though she was small. She said that her brother and sister have managed to forgive her parents, but she cannot. Still it bothered her that they do not want to communicate with her.

Katie said that even though she and Max have two incomes, they are struggling financially. Max has to pay child support. She does not earn very much. When asked what her goals for herself were, she said that she always wanted to make something of her life, but she feels trapped. She said that a high school diploma doesn't get you very far, but she can't afford to go to college. She would like to get married some day but she does not feel mature enough to do so in the near future. She has thoughts about getting into work involving animals, which she loves, but does not know how to start. Her immediate goal, she said, was to feel "unconfused."

Discussion Questions

1. Which of the approaches to treatment for persons with depression seems more suitable to this case—cognitive therapy or interpersonal therapy? Why?
2. Develop a plan for intervention in this case using one of these approaches. Which issues do you think should be addressed first?
3. Do you think Katie is a good candidate for pharmacotherapy? Why or why not?
4. To what extent are Katie's problems psychological? social environmental? biological?
5. Depression is particularly prevalent among women. How are women's issues involved in this case?

REFERENCES

American Psychiatric Association. (1987). *Diagnostic and statistical manual of mental disorders (DSM-III-R)* (3rd ed., rev.). Washington, DC: Author.

Beck, A. T. (1976). *Cognitive therapy and the emotional disorders.* Madison, CT: International Universities Press.

Beck, A. T. (1985). Cognitive therapy. In H. I. Kaplan & B. J. Sadock (Eds.), *Comprehensive textbook of psychiatry/IV* (pp. 1432–1443). Baltimore, MD: Williams & Wilkins.

Beck, A. T., & Greenberg, R. L. (1974). *Coping with depression.* New York: Institute for Rational Living.

Beck, A. T., Rush, A. J., Shaw, B. F., & Emery, G. (1979). *Cognitive therapy of depression.* New York: Guilford Press.

Beutler, L. E., Scogin, F., Kirkish, P., Schretlen, D., et al. (1987). Group cognitive therapy and alprazolam in the treatment of depression in older adults. *Journal of Consulting and Clinical Psychology, 55,* 550–556.

Bowlby, J. (1969). *Attachment.* New York: Basic Books.

Boyd, J. H., & Weissman, M. M. (1986). Epidemiology of major affective disorders. In G. L. Klerman, M. M. Weissman, P. S. Appelbaum, & L. H. Roth (Eds.), *Social, epidemiologic, and legal psychiatry* (pp. 153–168). New York: Basic Books.

Brotman, A. W., Falk, W. E., & Gelenberg, A. J. (1987). Pharmacologic treatment of acute depressive subtypes. In H. Y. Meltzer (Ed.), *Psychopharmacology: The third generation of progress* (pp. 1031–1039). New York: Raven Press.

Compton, B., & Galaway, B. (1984). *Social work processes.* Homewood, IL: Dorsey Press.

Conte, H. R., Plutchik, R., Wild, K. V., & Karusu, T. B. (1986). Combined psychotherapy and pharmacotherapy for depression: A systematic analysis of the evidence. *Archives of General Psychiatry, 43,* 471–479.

Davis, J. M. (1976). Overview: Maintenance therapy in psychiatry: II. Affective disorders. *American Journal of Psychiatry, 133,* 1–13.

DiMascio, A., Weissman, M. M., Prusoff, B. A., Neu, C., Zwilling, M., & Klerman, G. L. (1979). Differential symptom reduction by drugs and psychotherapy in acute depres-sion. *Archives of General Psychiatry, 36,* 1450–1456.

Dixon, S. (1987). *Working with people in crisis* (2nd ed.). Columbus, OH: Merrill.

Elkin, I., Shea, T., Watkins, J. T., Imber, S. D., et al. (1989). National Institute of Mental Health treatment of depression collaborative research program. *Archives of General Psychiatry, 46,* 971–983.

Everstine, D. S., & Everstine, L. (1983). *People in crisis: Strategic therapeutic interventions.* New York: Brunner/Mazel.

Freud, S. (1917). Mourning and melancholia. In J. Strachey (Ed.), *The standard edition of the complete psychological works of Sigmund Freud* (Vol. 14, pp. 243–258). London: Hogarth Press and Institute of Psychoanalysis.

Golan, N. (1978). *Treatment in crisis situations.* New York: Free Press.

Hirschfeld, R. M. A., & Cross, C. K. (1987). Clinical psychopathology and diagnosis in relation to treatment of affective disorders. In H. Y. Meltzer (Ed.), *Psychopharmacology: The third generation of progress* (pp. 1021–1029). New York: Raven Press.

Hirschfeld, R. M. A., & Cross, C. K. (1982). Epidemiology of affective disorders: Psychosocial risk factors. *Archives of General Psychiatry, 39,* 35–46.

Hirschfeld, R. M. A., & Goodwin, F. K. (1988). Mood disorders. In J. A. Talbott, R. E. Hales, & S. C. Yudofsky (Eds.), *Textbook of psychiatry* (pp. 403–441). Washington, DC: American Psychiatric Press.

Hirschfeld, R. M. A., & Shea, M. T. (1985). Affective disorders: Psychosocial treatment. In H. I. Kaplan & B. J. Sadock (Eds.), *Comprehensive textbook of psychiatry/IV* (pp. 811–821). Baltimore, MD: Williams & Wilkins.

Holden, C. (1986). Depression research advances, treatment lags. *Science, 233,* 723–726.

Hollis, F. (1949). Techniques of casework. *Journal of Social Casework, 30,* 235–244.

Jarrett, R. B., & Rush, A. J. (1989). Cognitive-behavioral psychotherapy for depression. In American Psychiatric Association, *Treatments of psychiatric disorders: A task force report of the American Psychiatric Association* (Vol. 3, pp. 1834–1846). Washington, DC: American Psychiatric Association.

Johnson, H. C., (1984). The biological bases of psychopathology. In F. J. Turner (Ed.), *Adult psychopathology: A social work perspective* (pp. 6–72). New York: Free Press.

Kadushin, A. (1983). *The social work interview.* New York: Columbia University Press.

Kaplan, H. I., & Sadock, B. J. (1988). *Synopsis of psychiatry* (5th ed.). Baltimore, MD: Williams & Wilkins.

Kessler, R. C., Price, R. H., & Wortman, C. B. (1985). Social factors in psychopathology: Stress, social support, and coping processes. *Annual Review of Psychology, 36,* 531–572.

Klerman, G. L., (1988). Depression and related disorders of mood (affective disorders). In A. M. Nicholi, Jr., *The new Harvard guide to psychiatry* (pp. 309–336). Cambridge, MA: Belknap Press of Harvard University Press.

Klerman, G. L., Weissman, M. M., Rounsaville, B. J., & Chevron, E. S. (1984). *Interpersonal psychotherapy of depression.* New York: Basic Books.

Kocsis, J. H., Frances, A. J., Voss, C., Mann, J. J., et al. (1988a). Imipramine treatment for chronic depression. *Archives of General Psychiatry, 45,* 253–257.

Kocsis, J. H., Frances, A. J., Voss, C., Mann, J. J., et al. (1988b). Imipramine and social-vocational adjustment in chronic depression. *American Journal of Psychiatry, 145,* 997–999.

Kupfer, D. J., & Frank, E. (1987). Relapse in recurrent unipolar depression. *American Journal of Psychiatry, 144,* 86–88.

Marris, P. (1982). Attachment and society. In C. M. Parkes & J. Stevenson-Hinde (Eds.), *The place of attachment in human behavior* (pp. 185–201). New York: Basic Books.

McGuffin, P., & Katz, R. (1989). The genetics of depression and manic-depressive disorder. *British Journal of Psychiatry, 155,* 294–304.

Myers, J. K., Weissman, M. M., Tischler, G. L., Holzer, C. E., III, et al. (1984). Six-month prevalence of psychiatric disorders in three communities. *Archives of General Psychiatry, 41,* 959–967.

National Institute of Mental Health. (1986). *Mental health, United States, 1985,* C. A. Taube & S. A. Barrett (Eds.). (DHHS Publication No. ADM 86-1378). Washington, DC: U.S. Government Printing Office.

Nietzel, M. T., Russell, R. L., Hemmings, K. A., & Gretter, M. L. (1987). Clinical significance of psychotherapy for unipolar depression: A meta-analytic approach to social comparison. *Journal of Consulting and Clinical Psychology, 55,* 156–161.

Physicians Desk Reference. (1990) (44th ed.). Oradell, NJ: Medical Economics.

Prien, R. F. (1987). Long-term treatment of affective disorders. In H. Y. Meltzer (Ed.), *Psychopharmacology: The third generation of progress* (pp. 1051–1058). New York: Raven Press.

Regier, D. A., Boyd, J. H., Burke, J. D., Rae, D. S., et al. (1988). One-month prevalence of mental disorders in the United States. *Archives of General Psychiatry, 45,* 977–986.

Reid, W., & Epstein, L. (1972). *Task-centered casework.* New York: Columbia University Press.

Rosenhan, D. L., & Seligman, M. E. P. (1984). *Abnormal psychology.* New York: Norton.

Rush, A. J., Beck, A. T., Kovacs, M., Weissenburger, J., & Hollon, S. D. (1982). Comparison of the effects of cognitive therapy and pharmacotherapy on hopelessness and self-concepts. *American Journal of Psychiatry, 139,* 862–866.

Seligman, M. (1975). *Helplessness: On depression, development, and death.* New York: W. H. Freeman.

Shulman, L. (1984). *The skills of helping individuals and groups.* Itasca, IL: Peacock.

Strean, H. S. (1985). *Therapeutic principles in practice: A manual for clinicians.* Beverly Hills, CA: Sage Publications.

Walker, J. I. (1983). *Psychiatric emergencies, intervention, and resolution.* Philadelphia, PA: Lippincott.

Warheit, G. J. (1979). Life events, coping, stress, and depressive symptomatology. *American Journal of Psychiatry, 136,* 502–507.

Weiss, R. S. (1982). Attachment in adult life. In C. M. Parkes & J. Stevenson-Hinde (Eds.), *The place of attachment in human behavior* (pp. 171–184). New York: Basic Books.

Weissman, M. M. (1989). Psychotherapy in the treatment of depression: New technologies and efficacy. In American Psychiatric Association, *Treatments of psychiatric disorders: A task force report of the American Psychiatric Association* (Vol. 3, pp. 1814–1823). Washington, DC: American Psychiatric Association.

Weissman, M. M., Jarrett, R. B., & Rush, J. A. (1987). Psychotherapy and its relevance to the pharmacology of major depression: A decade later (1976–1985). In H. Y. Meltzer (Ed.), *Psychopharmacology: The third generation of progress* (pp. 1059–1069). New York: Raven Press.

Weissman, M., & Klerman, G. L. (1977). Sex differences and the epidemiology of depression. *Archives of General Psychiatry, 34,* 98–111.

Weissman, M., & Klerman, G. L. (1989). Interpersonal psychotherapy. In American Psychiatric Association, *Treatments of psychiatric disorders: A task force report of the American Psychiatric Association* (Vol. 3, pp. 1863–1884). Washington, DC: American Psychiatric Association.

Weitkamp, L. R., Stancer, H. C., Persad, E., Flood, C., & Guttormsen, M. S. (1981). Depressive disorders and HLA: A gene on chromosome 6 that can affect behavior. *The New England Journal of Medicine, 305,* 1301–1306.

13 | Clinical Practice with Anxious Clients

Anxiety is a state of tension and apprehension that is an uncomfortable but ordinary human response to internal and external stimuli. Experienced viscerally as well as psychologically, it is a concomitant of thinking, feeling, and behavior. In the face of unknown situations, anxiety can provide a warning of danger that can help an individual mobilize resources to meet the threat. When one confronts larger questions about the meaning of the cosmos, the purpose of existence, and one's own mortality, one is likely to experience existential anxiety together with awe.

According to a report on the National Institute of Mental Health Epidemiologic Catchment Area Study (Regier et al., 1988), anxiety disorders were the most prevalent disorders found in 1-month and 6-month periods in five American communities (Baltimore, MD; New Haven, CT; Durham, NC; Los Angeles, CA; and St. Louis, MO). The 6-month rate was 8.9 percent; the 1-month rate, 7.3 percent. When lifetime prevalence was considered, substance abuse was the most prevalent (16.4 percent) and anxiety disorders were second (14.6 percent). Among the specific anxiety disorders surveyed, phobias were the most prevalent (12.5 percent lifetime prevalence), obsessive compulsive disorders were second (2.5 percent lifetime), and panic disorders were the least prevalent (1.6 percent lifetime).

The 1-month prevalence rate of anxiety disorders by sex and age is also revealing (Regier et al., 1988). For women the overall rate for anxiety disorders (9.7 percent) was over twice that for men (4.7 percent). Rates were especially high for phobias among women of 18–24 and 25–44 years of age. Among men, the overall anxiety disorder rates did not vary much by age, but men 45–64 years of age had a relatively high rate for phobias (4.8 percent); and those aged 18–24 and 25–44 years had relatively high rates of obsessive-compulsive disorder (1.7 and 1.2 percent, respectively). In an analysis of lifetime prevalence in Baltimore, New Haven, and St. Louis, agoraphobia and simple phobia were especially high among Blacks in Baltimore, and simple phobia was higher for Blacks than for non-Blacks in St. Louis (Robins et al., 1984).

Anxiety is associated with subjective pain, helplessness, and an array of distressing physiological symptoms. Like depression, it is psychopathological when it is experienced with great frequency and intensity and when it interferes with psychosocial functioning. Although persons who suffer from anxiety usually are not psychotic and can form relationships and function in social roles, many are unable to work or participate in community life without overwhelming discomfort.

The anxiety disorders that are described in the *DSM-III-R* are characterized by symptoms of anxiety or avoidance behavior (American Psychiatric Association, 1987). Anxiety is either the central feature, or it is aroused in the course of mastering other symptoms, such as confronting an object of a phobia or resisting a compulsion. Although there is some variation in symptoms among the subtypes, most of the anxiety disorders are expressed in the biological, cognitive, emotional, and behavioral symptoms that are described in Table 13.1.

SUBTYPES OF ANXIETY DISORDERS

The subtypes of anxiety disorders that are described in the *DSM-III-R* are panic disorder with agoraphobia, panic disorder without agoraphobia, agoraphobia without history of panic disorder, social phobia, simple phobia, obsessive-compulsive disorder, posttraumatic stress disorder, generalized anxiety disorder, and anxiety disorder not otherwise specified. The particular criteria necessary to diagnose each of these are described in detail in the *DSM-III-R*. For ease in distinguishing these disorders, the sequence and groupings are modified here.

Panic disorder (PD) is characterized by periods of emotional intensity in which an individual becomes overwhelmed with somatic symptoms of distress. Symptoms are experienced in clusters and appear suddenly in panic attacks. The combination of physical symptoms (especially heart palpitations and dyspnea) and the cognition of impending death lead some sufferers to believe that they are having a heart attack. Not unusually, panic disorders are presented to physicians in emergency rooms.

Although for some individuals panic disorder is a discrete experience, for others panic accompanies agoraphobia. The frequency of the convergence of these two conditions led two authorities to hypothesize that the emergence of spontaneous panic is

TABLE 13.1

Symptoms of Anxiety

Type of Symptom	Description
Biological	Physical symptoms such as perspiration, heart palpitations, dyspnea, fainting, nausea, muscular tension, shakiness, flushing, gastrointestinal disturbances, insomnia
Cognitive	Worry, apprehension, anticipation of danger or doom; thoughts about contamination, going crazy, or dying; irrational fears; preoccupied by and ruminating about repetitive themes; thoughts of embarrassment, humiliation
Emotional	Keyed up, fearful, on edge, irritable, terrified, "nervous"
Behavioral	Hypervigilant, jumpy, tremors, pacing, avoidance behavior

a conditioning event that is a precursor to the development of agoraphobia (Klein & Gorman, 1987). Subsequently the person's agoraphobia revolves around the fear of having another panic attack. In a study of the onset of panic disorder with agoraphobia, however, other authors found that in 23 percent of the cases, agoraphobic avoidance preceded the first panic attack (Lelliott, Marks, McNamee, & Tobeña, 1989). In an analysis of data on panic disorder from the Epidemiologic Catchment Area Study, other authors found panic disorder coexisting with agoraphobia in about one-third of the cases of panic disorder (Markowitz, Weissman, Ouellette, Lish, & Klerman, 1989).

Agoraphobia is a fear and avoidance reaction to being in a public place. Like other phobias, it is an irrational fear of a situation or object confrontation, which results in overwhelming anxiety. In order to prevent anticipated anxiety, persons with agoraphobia avoid the situation that is associated with the reaction. They are primarily afraid of being alone in places from which they cannot escape or get help. Those who also have panic attacks may fear having a panic attack in the designated situation. Persons with agoraphobia without a history of panic disorder may have a limited number of symptoms or no symptoms of a panic attack (American Psychiatric Association, 1987).

Individuals with agoraphobia cope with their situation in a variety of ways. Some stay home all the time, a strategy that is incapacitating and further reinforces the fear of leaving the house. Others go out, but limit their activities. These individuals may go to public places in the company of others or endure the discomforting anxiety in order to accomplish needed activities. Agoraphobics who go out alone will go out of their way to avoid the situations that disturb them; for example, a person afraid to drive on highways will use side streets. Others cope by using chemical substances.

Two other subtypes of anxiety disorders are social phobia and simple phobia. *Social phobia* is an irrational fear of being in a situation in which one might be subjected to others' scrutiny. The person with a social phobia is especially sensitive to anticipated ridicule, embarrassment, or humiliation. Examples of situations that are problematic to persons with this disorder are speaking in public, eating in a restaurant, and using public lavatories. *Simple phobias* encompass phobias unrelated to fear of having a panic attack or a social phobia. These include claustrophobia (fear of enclosed spaces), acrophobia (fear of heights), and ophidiophobia (fear of snakes).

Another anxiety disorder is called *generalized anxiety disorder* (GAD). This is a pervasive, chronic condition rather than one that occurs in spurts like panic disorder. Individuals with GAD worry excessively about situations or circumstances that are not, on the surface, threatening. Irrational thinking is accompanied by numerous symptoms of anxiety.

An additional subtype of anxiety disorder is the *obsessive-compulsive disorder* (OCD), a disabling condition that intrudes on thinking and behavior. Obsessions are persistent, irrational, ego-dystonic thoughts, impulses, or images, usually of an unpleasant nature, that take over the consciousness of a person with this disorder. They usually convey thoughts about contamination, sex, or aggression and are accompanied by self-doubt. Compulsions are irrational, stereotyped, ritualistic behaviors which are attempts to counteract the obsessions. Examples include constant handwashing, cleaning, and checking. Compulsions are time consuming and repetitive; thus they interfere with the accomplishment of more constructive activities. Acting out compulsions brings release but little pleasure, whereas resisting compulsions arouses anxiety. According to the *DSM-III-R,* either obsessions or compulsions are required for a diagnosis of obsessive-compulsive disorder. The two may, however, co-occur.

The last subtype to be considered is *posttraumatic stress disorder* (PTSD). This is an anxiety reaction to a stressor that is outside the usual realm of human experience. The experiences of survivors of concentration camps and disasters have supported the belief that certain events produce reactions that endure long after the traumatic experience. The person with posttraumatic stress disorder will relive the event (cognitively and emotionally), have nightmares or flashbacks, act as if the event were recurring, or experience distress in the face of stimuli that are reminders of the event. As a result of the experience, affect, relationships, and memory become impaired and symptoms of arousal (e.g., insomnia, hypervigilance) become prominent. Clinicians frequently see persons whose PTSD was precipitated by war, rape, incest, or homicide.

Terminology

Two terms used to describe anxiety, as well as depression, are exogenous and endogenous (Sheehan & Soto, 1987). Anxiety that is *exogenous* is precipitated by a stressful life event, such as witnessing a crime or having an accident. At such times, the autonomic nervous system is mobilized to meet the threat. Anxiety disorders that are exogenous, in which the precipitating event occurred within the past 3 months, would ordinarily be diagnosed as an adjustment disorder either with an anxious mood, with mixed emotional features, or with a mixed disturbance of emotions and conduct (American Psychiatric Association, 1987). The posttraumatic stress disorder, however, may also be considered exogenous. *Endogenous* anxiety disorders are spontaneous and biologically based. Because biological and psychosocial stimuli and responses overlap in anxiety disorders, the distinction between exogenous and endogenous is not clear.

In addition, a distinction is often made between anxiety and fear. With *fear* there is a situation that is clearly dangerous to which the person is responding, for example, being held up at gunpoint by a thief. In contrast, with *anxiety* the object of concern is either vague, nonexistent, or exaggerated in relation to how it is perceived by others, for example, anxiety about using public transportation. Accordingly, anxiety is seen as neurotic or irrational, whereas fear is adaptive and reasonable.

A further distinction is made between anxiety as a state and as a trait. A *state* is a condition of arousal that is situation related, whereas a *trait* is a more pervasive characteristic. For example, a person having a cardiogram may temporarily be in a state of anxiety, whereas a person with generalized anxiety disorder feels anxious most of the time. Spielberger's (1983) State–Trait Anxiety Inventory is often used to measure and differentiate between these two dimensions of anxiety.

EXPLANATORY THEORIES

The disorders that have been described are diverse in their etiologies, expression, and theoretical underpinnings. The integrative perspective taken in this book finds value in each of these but views none of them as monolithic. In view of the multiple dimensions of anxiety disorders, biological, social, and psychological theories will be described.

Biological Aspects

Although many of the symptoms of anxiety are common to the various subtypes of anxiety disorders, the biology of anxiety has some specificity. For example, there is strong evidence that panic and obsessive compulsive disorders have a genetic basis. Torgersen's (1983) research found a substantially higher concordance of panic disorder between monozygotic than between dizygotic twins, but no such relationship in generalized anxiety disorder. Carey and Gottesman (1981) found a concordance rate of obsessive-compulsive "features" of 88 percent among monozygotic twins, but 47 percent among dizygotic twins. These rates and the discrepancy between the two types of twins did not hold, however, for the obsessive-compulsive "disorder." In a study of first-degree relatives of persons with simple phobias and family members of a healthy control group, other researchers found that 31 percent of the relatives of the experimental group but only 11 percent of the control group relatives ever had a diagnosis of simple phobia (Fyer et al., 1990). Other psychiatric disorders among the relatives of the experimental group were rare, leading the authors to conclude that "simple phobia is a highly familial disorder that breeds true" (p. 255).

Further support for a biological perspective, as well as specificity of the subtypes, comes from psychopharmacology. Medication does seem to reduce anxiety. As it will be shown in the section on medication, certain disorders respond well to specific medications.

Some research indicates a relationship between panic disorder and a cardiological condition called mitral valve prolapse. In research on 131 patients who had spontaneous panic attacks and who were evaluated by cardiologists, results indicated that one out of three suffered from mitral valve prolapse (Sheehan & Soto, 1987). But regardless of whether a physical condition or a life stressor is involved in the etiology of anxiety, the effects are biological. Anxiety may be viewed as a state of hyperarousal, characterized by the somatic symptoms that were described earlier.

Social Dimensions

Anxiety is associated with stress, which in turn is the outcome of person–environment interactions. The impact of the negative environmental influences of sexism and racism is evident when one looks at the disproportionate numbers of women and Blacks with anxiety disorders. Women have especially high rates of agoraphobia and generalized anxiety disorder (American Psychiatric Association, 1987); Blacks have relatively high lifetime prevalence rates of simple phobia and agoraphobia (Robins et al., 1984). In reaction to oppression, women seem to adopt symptoms or life-styles that are an exaggeration of behavior stereotypical of women (Kaplan, 1983); for example, some women stay home all the time (e.g., the agoraphobic), while others act "emotionally" (e.g., women with generalized anxiety disorder or panic disorder). The anxiety among African Americans may be a protective response to racism.

According to an analysis of data from the Epidemiological Catchment Area Study of a community sample (Markowitz, Weissman, Ouellette, Lish, & Klerman, 1989), participants who met diagnostic criteria for panic disorder (of whom 70 percent were female and 75 percent were white) scored relatively poorly on several measures of quality of life. These included subjective ratings of physical and emotional health, substance abuse, suicide attempts, impaired social and marital functioning, financial dependence, and use of treatment facilities. The findings on persons with panic disorder were comparable with those on persons with major depression, but distinct from persons with neither panic nor major depression. The unusually high rate of suicidal ideations and suicide attempts among persons with panic disorder or who have made panic attempts was confirmed in another analysis of the same data (Weissman, Klerman, Markowitz, & Ouellette, 1989).

Psychological and Social Theories

A number of psychological and social theories explain the etiology and expression of anxiety. Many of these theories are specific to particular kinds of anxiety disorders (e.g., phobias, obsessive-compulsive disorder). To reduce the complexity and specificity of these theories, general statements will be made about each theory.

Psychoanalysis.   Freud viewed anxiety as both normal and a potential source of neurotic development (Brenner, 1955). Normal anxiety provides a signal to the organism so that it can protect itself from harm. Pathological anxiety is associated with id instincts that cannot be held in check by the ego defenses. Because the anxiety has nowhere to go and must be expressed, it takes the form of neurotic symptoms. Anxiety neuroses (cf. generalized anxiety disorder), phobic neuroses (cf. agoraphobia and other phobic disorders), and obsessive-compulsive neurosis (cf. obsessive-compulsive disorder) represent channels for the expression of unacceptable id impulses.

Freud and later ego psychology theorists attributed the development of neuroses to failure to resolve early developmental issues. Phobias, for example, are associated with conflict in the oedipal stage, particularly castration anxiety, whereas obsessive-compulsive neurosis is traceable to conflicts during the anal stage. Phobias and panic attacks have also been attributed to difficulty mastering the task of separation–individuation (Hollander, Liebowitz, & Gorman, 1988).

Attachment Theory.   Bowlby's attachment theory, referred to in chapter 12, also applies to the development of anxiety disorders. According to this theory, infants are genetically disposed to form attachments to caretakers. When separated from significant figures, they will feel anxious (separation anxiety) and protest. The protest often has the effect of calling the caretaker to the infant's side. Infants who do not feel confident that the caretaker is available, form *anxious attachments,* which can result in the development of phobias in childhood and adulthood (Eagle & Wolitzky, 1988).

Behavioral Theory.   According to learning theory, anxiety is a response (a behavior) that is learned in association with a painful situation. Afterward the conditioned response to this situation generalizes to other situations. This maladaptive behavior can become further reinforced by the behavior of significant others, who condone it or provide support, which then provides the person with maladaptive behavior with what is called *secondary gains,* which perpetuate the anxious response. Although this pattern appears to be insidious, it can be reversed by altering the contingencies. Behavioral methods of therapy such as systematic desensitization and in vivo exposure have been very successful in the treatment of anxiety disorders.

Cognitive Theory. Cognitive theory poses that anxiety is a normal emotion that is needed for survival. A person with an anxiety disorder feels anxious upon misperceiving a situation as dangerous. Interestingly, such a person ignores environmental cues indicating that the same situation is safe (Beck, 1985). In the face of perceived threat, the autonomic nervous system becomes activated, motoric activity ensues (fight, flight, faint, or freeze), and faulty cognitions and problematic emotions are triggered. Accordingly a situation that is inherently neutral is "catastrophied." Cognitive therapy techniques such as imagery and cognitive restructuring can be helpful in the treatment of persons with anxiety disorders.

The remainder of this chapter will address the treatment of anxiety disorders. In the next section, psychotropic drugs that are used to treat anxiety disorders will be discussed. Reference will be made to particular disorders that are treated with specific medication. Next specific attention will be given to behavioral treatment, particularly in vivo exposure. Then alternative or adjunctive treatments will be described, and a case in which integrated methods are used will be presented.

MEDICATION USED TO TREAT ANXIETY DISORDERS

Over the years a number of drugs have been tried and used to treat anxiety disorders. Although these medications do not cure the disorders, they do relieve distressing symptoms, making it possible for clinicians to treat problems with psychotherapy. The drugs that have been used have varying cost–benefit ratios, which clients need to weigh before agreeing to pharmacotherapy. Major drugs that have been reported to be effective in the treatment of anxiety disorders will be discussed in the following section. Table 13.2 lists the drugs by type and indicates their respective trade names.

Tricyclic Antidepressants

A surprising development of the past two decades has been the use of medications for anxiety that have traditionally been used to treat depression. The drug that has been tested the most is *imipramine* (Tofranil), a tricyclic. This drug has been shown to be effective in treating panic disorder and anticipatory anxiety associated with agoraphobia (Mavissakalian & Perel, 1989; Zitrin, Klein, Woerner, & Ross, 1983). Preliminary results indicate that it takes a high dose to treat agoraphobia, but a moderate dose to treat the panic disorder (Mavissakalian & Perel, 1989). Furthermore, imipramine helps reduce nightmares, flashbacks, panic attacks, and mood disturbances in persons with post-traumatic stress disorder (Horowitz, 1989). This drug has the advantage of reducing anxiety while at the same time it does not pose a threat of dependence. The disadvan-

TABLE 13.2
Medications Used to Treat
Anxiety Disorders

Group/Examples	Trade Name
Tricyclic antidepressants	
Imipramine	Tofranil
Clomipramine	Anafranil
Monoamine oxidase inhibitors (MAOIs)	
Phenelzine	Nardil
Benzodiazepines	
Chlordiazepoxide	Librium
Diazepam	Valium
Clorazepate	Tranxene
Oxazepam	Serax
Alprazolam	Xanax
Lorazepam	Ativan
Buspirone	BuSpar
Beta-receptor blocker	
Propranolol	Propranolol

tages of tricyclics, their side effects (sedation, postural hypotension, anticholinergic effects, etc.), were described in chapter 10.

Another tricyclic, *clomipramine* (Anafranil), has been available in Canada and Europe for years, but was marketed in the United States only recently. Its use has been principally in the treatment of agoraphobia and obsessive-compulsive disorder. In testing its effectiveness in treating agoraphobic women, clomipramine (in comparison with a placebo) successfully treated symptoms of agoraphobia and panic (Johnston, Troyer, & Whitsett, 1988). Findings with respect to its use in the treatment of obsessive-compulsive disorder are promising. Although clomipramine does not eliminate obsessions and compulsions entirely, it does reduce preoccupation with obsessions and ritualistic behavior (Insel & Zohar, 1987). Like other tricyclics, clomipramine takes several weeks to produce changes; when the medication is withdrawn, the disorder reasserts itself (Zohar, Foa, & Insel, 1989).

Monoamine Oxidase Inhibitors

Another antidepressant medication that is used to treat anxiety disorders is the MAOI, particularly *phenelzine* (Nardil). Like imipramine, it treats panic and phobic anxiety. Moreover, MAOIs seem to be effective in the treatment of social phobias and atypical depression with panic attacks (Liebowitz, 1989), as well as posttraumatic stress disorders with panic attacks (Horowitz, 1989). However therapeutic, MAOIs require restriction of certain foods and drink (e.g., smoked food, aged cheeses) and medications (e.g., antihistamines) (see chapter 10). In addition, certain side effects are associated with this group of drugs (e.g., hypotension, sexual difficulties). For these reasons, imipramine is often preferred for the treatment of panic and agoraphobia (Liebowitz, 1989).

Benzodiazepines

Benzodiazepines are minor tranquilizers that have historically been used to treat anxiety. Among the drugs in this group are the **anxiolytics** (antianxiety agents) *chlordiazepoxide* (Librium), *diazepam* (Valium), *clorazepate* (Tranxene), *oxazepam* (Serax), *alprazolam* (Xanax), and *lorazepam* (Ativan). Some of these drugs (e.g., Serax and Ativan) have a short half-life, that is, they are eliminated from the blood rapidly; others have an intermediate half-life (e.g., Xanax); and others have a long half-life (Valium, Tranxene, Librium) (Salzman, 1989). The two short-half-life drugs, Serax and Ativan, which do not have active metabolites, and long-acting benzodiazepines with active metabolites that are prescribed in small doses and over increased intervals, are recommended for older adults (Rickels & Schweizer, 1987).

All these drugs have a calming effect. Furthermore, they produce sedation, promote sleep, and have some muscle relaxant and anticonvulsive effects (Rickels & Schweizer, 1987). The sedative effects may or may not be desired. Sedation causes drowsiness and slows reactions, which can interfere with the operation of machinery. This effect is compounded if the client uses alcohol or takes antihistamines (Rickels & Schweizer, 1987). A serious problem with these drugs is that, over time, they are addictive. Upon withdrawal, uncomfortable and disturbing experiences occur (cf. Gordon, 1979). Persons successfully treated for panic attacks, for example, can, upon withdrawal, experience *rebound panics,* recurrences that are more intense than those that were experienced previously. For these reasons, short-term use with minimal therapeutic doses (Salzman, 1989) and slow withdrawal (Barlow, 1988) are recommended.

Because the onset of the effects of benzodiazepines is rapid (especially Valium and Tranxene), these drugs are amenable to use for symptomatic relief of acute anxiety reactions (Rickels & Schweizer, 1987), such as those seen in an emergency room. Moreover, they have been found to be effective in the treatment of generalized anxiety disorder, posttraumatic stress disorder, and panic disorder (Horowitz, 1989; Noyes, Chaudry, & Domingo, 1986; Rickels & Schweizer, 1987).

Alprazolam (Xanax) has been particularly effective in the treatment of panic disorders and associated phobic anxiety. This drug appears to be less sedating than the other benzodiazepines. In addition, it has antidepressant effects on recipients, regardless of whether or not they have a secondary depression (Lesser et al., 1988). Research emanating from the Cross-National Collaborative Panic Study on approximately 500 subjects found that those who took alprazolam had a significantly higher rate of improvement in panic attacks, phobic fears, avoidance behavior, anxiety, and social disability than the control group on placebos (Ballenger et al., 1988). Improvement was evident after one week. Nevertheless, side effects that were treatment related were identified in another report by this research group (Noyes et al., 1988). These include fatigue, sedation, ataxia, amnesia, and slurred speech. These authors reported that the dropout rate among those who received the active drug was substantially lower (16 percent) than that of those who received the placebo (50 percent), a finding that suggests high acceptance of alprazolam. In another report from the same study, the researchers looked at the effects of discontinuance of alprazolam after 8 weeks of treatment (Pecknold, Swinson, Kuch, & Lewis, 1988). During a period of 4 weeks of gradual reduction of the drug, the experimental group (but not the controls on place-bos) relapsed; some experienced a rebound of anxiety or panic attacks; 35 percent had mild to moderate, but transient withdrawal symptoms. On the basis of their findings, the authors recommend a longer period of treatment (at least 6 months) and a more extensive tapering off period (at least 8 weeks), especially if the recipient is on a relatively high dose.

Buspirone

Buspirone is a promising, new antianxiety agent that is the equivalent of diazepam while at the same time it does not share many of the drawbacks of the benzodiazepines. Buspirone does not cause sedation, engender abuse or physical dependence, or act as an anticonvulsant (Eison & Temple, 1986). Accordingly, arousal, attention, and the capac-ity to act and react are preserved. Another advantage of buspirone is that it does not interact synergistically with alcohol (Eison & Temple, 1986); thus it may be useful for persons with a history of substance abuse (Salzman, 1989). Nevertheless, buspirone does not act as quickly as diazepam. Moreover, in some cases, lack of sedation may be viewed as a drawback. At this point it appears that buspirone may be useful in the treatment of generalized anxiety disorder and in the relief of symptoms of hostility and anger (Rickels & Schweizer, 1987). The high dropout rate among subjects with panic attacks in one study raises questions about its use with that population (Rickels, Sch-weizer, Csanalosi, Case, & Chung, 1988). Further research on its role in the treatment of specific disorders and side effects is needed.

Propranolol

Propranolol is a beta-receptor blocker that has been used to treat a wide range of psychiatric conditions. Reports indicate that it reduces somatic symptoms of anxiety, such as sweaty palms, tremors, and palpitations without affecting the emotions (Rickels & Schweizer, 1987). It does seem to reduce anxiety in persons with social phobias, especially stage fright (Rickels & Schweizer, 1987), and autonomic responses in post-traumatic stress disorder (Horowitz, 1989). Potential side effects that have been re-ported are congestive heart failure, hypotension, exacerbation of asthma, interference with cardiac conduction, increased susceptibility to hypoglycemia in diabetic patients, and rebound effects if the medication is withdrawn suddenly (Salzman, 1989).

Application

The aforementioned drugs are the major medications used to treat anxiety disorders. New drugs continue to be tested and introduced all the time. Moreover, some of the antidepressant, neuroleptic, and antimanic drugs that were discussed in chapter 10 are sometimes used instead of or as adjunctive treatment with some of the medications that were reviewed here. Research on which drugs are effective for which disorders contin-

TABLE 13.3
Medication Used for Specific Anxiety Disorders

Disorder	Medications
Panic disorder	Imipramine, phenelzine, benzodiazepines (especially alprazolam), clomipramine
Agoraphobia with history of panic disorder	Same as above
Social phobia	MAOIs, beta blockers
Simple phobia	Does not appear to be responsive to drugs
Generalized anxiety disorder	Benzodiazepines, buspirone
Obsessive-compulsive disorder	Clomipramine
Postraumatic stress disorder	Tricyclic antidepressants, MAOIs, benzodiazepines, propranolol

ues. Table 13.3 lists specific anxiety disorders with drugs that have been shown to be effective in research studies.

These drugs provide symptomatic relief to those individuals who are willing to take them and who respond positively to them. Many clients who are given full information about the effects and risks associated with these medications will, however, refuse consent. The prospect of dependence on benzodiazepines, for example, is frightening, especially to persons with a history of other addictions. Tricyclic antidepressants and MAOIs have side effects that many individuals find disturbing. For these reasons, some clients will initiate but not complete treatment. Others do not believe in taking medication. Regardless of whether or not clients receive medication, they can benefit from psychotherapy. Therapy can modify thoughts, emotions, and behaviors that medication does not touch. The forms of psychotherapy that have been most successful provide help in behaving and thinking more adaptively. Other forms of treatment promote insight into the problem that underlies the anxiety and provide an opportunity for the client to release disturbing emotions.

Research on Medication and Psychotherapy

The relative effects of medication and psychotherapy in the treatment of anxiety have not been subjected to studies as extensive as those with respect to depression. Such research is complicated by competing theoretical and practice paradigms (and thus vested interests) of psychiatrists and psychologists. Psychiatrists tend to have a biological orientation; psychologists tend to favor behaviorism (Klerman, 1988).

Some research looks at the relative merits of behavioral treatment and pharmacotherapy in the treatment of panic disorder and agoraphobia. Particular attention has been given to testing Klein and Gorman's (1987) model of panic and agoraphobic development. As mentioned, these researchers posed that panic precedes and conditions the development of agoraphobia. Furthermore, they suggested that imipramine is able to treat the panic attacks, but not avoidant behavior or anticipatory anxiety. One group of psychiatrists found in a controlled study that there was significant improvement among all subjects given encouragement and instructions to practice in vivo exposure on their own, with those on imipramine rating higher clinically, depending on the dose of imipramine they had (Mavissakalian & Michelson, 1986). In another analysis, however, it was found that subjects who were not told to practice exposure benefited in relation to both phobic and panic symptoms. Here, too, a relation between medication dosage and the target symptoms was found (Mavissakalian & Perel, 1989). In another study in which behavior therapy (hierarchical desensitization) with and without imipramine was compared with supportive therapy with imipramine, no differences were found among the various treatments (Klein, Zitrin, Woerner, & Ross, 1983). On the basis of these studies it appears that *medication and exposure* (as well as support), separately or together, can effectively treat panic and anticipatory anxiety.

Barlow (1988) postulates that tricyclic medication reduces anxiety rather than being specifically a treatment for panic. With somatic effects of anxiety lessened, behavioral treatments are able to be more effective. Nevertheless, he notes that because of the side effects of tricyclics (dry mouth, constipation, agitation), the dropout rates for participants in research studies are relatively high. He remarks further that one of the side effects, agitation, resembles the anxiety symptoms that are the presenting concern.

One way to bypass problems associated with medication is to pursue a course of psychotherapy first. Fortunately there are a number of treatment approaches with a record of effectiveness. If these strategies are not effective, medication can be explored. In the next section, behavioral approaches to the treatment of anxiety disorders will be described.

BEHAVIORAL TREATMENT OF ANXIETY DISORDERS

In the past 30 years, a number of behavioral methods of treating phobias have been introduced and tested for effectiveness. These treatment modalities have clear advantages over psychoanalysis, an expensive, prolonged method of unproven effectiveness. Behavioral treatment can extinguish (or reduce the intensity of) disturbing symptoms over a brief period of time. The effects are observable and measurable. Among the particular methods that have been put into practice are systematic desensitization, flooding, implosion, and in vivo exposure. These approaches have been used to treat phobias and obsessive-compulsive disorders.

Systematic Desensitization

Systematic desensitization was developed by Joseph Wolpe and described in *Psychotherapy by Reciprocal Inhibition,* which was published in 1958. His ideas are developed further in a subsequent book (Wolpe, 1982). Wolpe applied his method of psychotherapy to adults with a spectrum of phobic conditions. His approach is predicated on the principle of *reciprocal inhibition,* that is, one can weaken neurotic anxiety by countering it with a competing stimulus. The strategy employed is to use a stronger stimulus to inhibit a weak form of the neurotic anxiety. Wolpe recommended as the stronger stimulus deep muscle relaxation, which produces a physical effect that is the opposite of anxiety. Relaxation diminishes the impact of anxiety-provoking scenes the client is later asked to imagine.

Systematic desensitization is carried out in four steps (Wolpe, 1982). First the client is introduced to the Subjective Anxiety Scale. The clinician asks the client to give his or her worst experience of anxiety a rating of 100 and the state of absolute calmness a score of 0. In addition, the client is asked to rate his or her current state somewhere in between 0 and 100. Wolpe describes these ratings as *suds* (subjective units of distress).

Next the client begins training in deep muscle relaxation. Wolpe's exercises are based on those developed by Jacobson (1938), but Wolpe's are taught to the client in a period of 6 weeks, whereas Jacobson's took 50 or more sessions. The client is taught to contract and relax specific parts of the body, from head to toe, in incremental steps over time. The client is told, for example, to contract the fists, to feel the tension in the fist, hand, and forearm, and then to release the contracted fist and relax. (An abbreviated program of progressive relaxation of this kind is described by McKay, Davis, & Fanning, 1981). In addition, the client is expected to practice relaxation 10 to 15 minutes twice a day at home (Wolpe, 1982).

During the third stage, the clinician, with the help of the client, constructs a hierarchy of anxiety-producing events (Wolpe, 1982). A tentative list of items to include derives from the social history, results of instruments administered to the client prior to treatment, and discussion between the client and the clinician. Items are grouped together by theme, (a) to determine which are relevant to treatment (e.g., items suggesting agoraphobia, acrophobia, and claustrophobia are relevant; objective fears about getting pregnant are irrelevant) and (b) to develop separate hierarchies, each related to a different theme. The client is asked to give a suds rating to each item listed under each theme and to give a rationale for these ratings. From this information the clinician constructs a hierarchy of discrete, evenly spaced items for each theme (Wolpe, 1982). The following is an example of such a series, with suds scores listed in parentheses:

1. Being home alone, watching TV (10)
2. Walking down the block with my spouse (20)
3. Walking down the block alone (30)
4. Taking the bus with my spouse (40)
5. Taking the bus alone (50)
6. Going to the grocery store early in the morning (60)
7. Going to the grocery store on Friday afternoon (70)
8. Going to a shopping mall (any time) (80)
9. Going downtown during the week (90)
10. Going to the state fair on opening day (100)

Next comes the implementation of the desensitization procedure (Wolpe, 1982). This can be initiated in the third or fourth session, following relaxation training. After the client comes to a deep state of relaxation and eyes are closed, the clinician inquires how relaxed the client is. If the client says 0, the clinician offers a "control scene," such as having the client imagine a pleasant, calm, sunny, summer day. If this does not produce anxiety, the clinician begins with the lowest ranking scene from one of the lists of hierarchies and has the client imagine it. The client signals that the scene is being contemplated by raising a finger. After 5 to 7 seconds, the clinician asks the client to stop and to provide a suds rating. Sometimes presentation of the same scene twice results in a lower rating the second time. Relaxation is implemented in between scenes, with the intervals between scenes being 10 to 30 seconds. Subsequent sessions begin with items that have low ratings, but are above 0 (Wolpe, 1982).

Flooding and Implosive Therapy

Flooding is a behavioral treatment technique that was introduced after systematic desensitization. Like its predecessor, flooding requires that the client imagine anxiety-provoking scenes. In flooding, however, the client does not get into a relaxed state prior to implementation of the procedure. Treatment consists of the clinician describing in great detail a scene that is highly anxiety provoking for the client. *Implosive therapy* is similar to flooding in its use of graphic images of disturbing scenes to extinguish anxiety. With implosive therapy the clinician adds themes based on psychoanalytic insights into the client's early experiences to the scenes described during flooding, resulting in a more intense experience than that in flooding.

In Vivo Exposure

The principle that explains the effectiveness of systematic desensitization, flooding, and implosive therapy is that it is *exposure that reduces anxiety*. The methods that have been described thus far rely on cognitive processes (imagination) to extinguish anxiety. More recently it has been recognized that in vivo (real life) exposure is more readily transferred into behaviors related to the client's life. In vivo exposure can be used to treat phobias (agoraphobia, social phobia, simple phobias) and obsessive-compulsive disorders.

In vivo exposure may be *prolonged* or *graduated* (O'Brien & Barlow, 1984). With prolonged exposure, the client faces the feared situation in an intense form (high on the hierarchy) early in treatment and for long periods of time. As such, prolonged exposure is akin to flooding. With graduated exposure, the client is exposed to situations that arouse little anxiety first. The client progresses over time to more threatening situations. Graduated exposure bears some resemblance to systematic desensitization, but is carried out in a natural context.

The distinction between prolonged and graduated exposure highlights the significance of the dimensions of duration and intensity in relation to in vivo exposure. Research comparing these dimensions is equivocal. Some suggests that sessions of 2 hours or more are more effective than shorter sessions (e.g., Stern & Marks, 1973). Nevertheless, clients who have been treated with prolonged in vivo exposure were more likely to drop out of treatment than those who were treated on a graduated basis (Barlow, 1988). Furthermore, prolonged exposure has the disadvantage of adversely affecting the interpersonal system (Barlow, 1988).

In vivo exposure can be implemented with various degrees of participation by the clinician. At one end of the continuum, the clinician directs and implements treatment from an office (e.g., exposing the client to snakelike objects and snakes in the office). Another approach is for the clinician to accompany the client to places in which the client will be exposed to disturbing stimuli (e.g., walking outside, around the clinic building). Not unusually in the treatment of agoraphobia, a clinician will accompany and provide support to small groups of clients taken to shopping malls for several hours at a time (Barlow, 1988). An alternative is for the clinician to set up a program of activities for the client to carry out independently in the community between sessions. In some cases, the clinician will promote the implementation of such a program by making home visits and involving a spouse or partner of the client (Mathews, Gelder, & Johnston, 1981). At the far end of the continuum is in vivo exposure that is carried out autonomously by clients through self-help manuals (e.g., Weakes, 1968, 1972) or client-run self-help groups.

Research studies support the participation of significant others in the implementation of in vivo exposure (Barlow, 1988). The rate of improvement and the clinical ratings are higher for clients whose spouses are included in the treatment. Clearly phobic disorders, especially agoraphobia, affect the family system (Barlow, 1988). To produce desired change, family involvement is desirable. One program of in vivo exposure that includes the partner is the home-based programmed practice method of Mathews, Gelder, and Johnston (1981). This method will be described next.

HOME-BASED PROGRAMMED PRACTICE

Mathews, Gelder, and Johnson (1981) developed a home-based treatment method for persons with agoraphobia characterized by avoidance behavior. The program is clinician facilitated (through home visits) and partner assisted. This method is consistent with research findings supporting the use of graduated exposure and family involvement. It has the added advantage of being implemented in the client's own environment, where the practice exercises have immediate applicability. A method that is client controlled, it is consistent with the social work value of client empowerment.

Assessment

Prior to acceptance into treatment, a thorough assessment is made. It is important to determine whether the diagnosis is consistent with agoraphobia and that avoidance behavior is present and has a regular pattern. (If these are not present, the client should be referred elsewhere.) The specific situations that arouse phobic anxiety should be ascertained. Furthermore, it should be determined what factors contribute to the reduction of anxiety (e.g., being accompanied by a friend) and which arouse anxiety (e.g., traveling a far distance from home). The client should describe in detail the nature, frequency, and extensiveness of anxiety (or panic) reactions. This information will help in the development of an individually tailored program.

Mathews, Gelder, and Johnston (1981) have clients complete a number of questionnaires that measure their anxiety. One is the Fear Questionnaire, an instrument that measures the extent of avoidance behavior and the situations that are eschewed; the other is a behavioral diary, which describes activities performed outside the house (time, place, with whom, method of transportation). Copies of these questionnaires are included in the appendix of the authors' book. Responses provide the clinician with baseline data on the client's phobic behavior.

Information about the client's social network is also helpful. Because this program is meant to be partner assisted, it is necessary to determine who the partner should be. Although a spouse or housemate is the obvious choice, other family members or friends may be more available. In cases of persons who are socially isolated, the client can implement this program independently.

Additional information should be gathered about previous treatment. Attitudes of both the client and the partner toward these and the current program should be elicited. The clinician should explain that with the home-based method, the client and the partner must assume a great deal of responsibility and put forth time and effort. If participants are not able to devote themselves to this for some reason (e.g., marital conflict), an alternative treatment method (e.g., marital counseling) may be more appropriate.

In addition, inquiries should be made about the client's use of medication. This home-based program does not preclude the use of antianxiety medication. Nevertheless, the client is discouraged from becoming drug dependent and is encouraged to develop other means of coping with anxiety. Those clients who are on medication are helped to integrate medication use with the program.

Prior to the first session with the clinician, the client and the partner are given and are expected to read two manuals that explain agoraphobia and the treatment program. These manuals, one for client and the other for partner, are included as appendices in the book by Mathews, Gelder, and Johnston (1981).

Initial Treatment Visit

At the beginning of the first home visit, the clinician explains how long this session should take (about 1 hour and 15 minutes) and what will be discussed. The agenda includes a discussion and responses to questions about the manuals (or any other questions the couple may have about agoraphobia and the treatment program); negotiation of a treatment contract; collection of the behavioral diary; and the choosing of targets for initial practice.

Discussion and Questions Pertaining to the Manuals.   Partners who have read the manuals undoubtedly will have questions about the content. In the event that the participants have not read the manuals, the reasons they have not done so should be explored. In cases in which the client is illiterate, an alternative method of reading (e.g., having someone else read or tape the material) is arranged. Otherwise, participants are reminded that this program requires their active engagement.

To further clarify the content of the program, the clinician emphasizes several points. First of all, the roles and responsibilities of the client, partner, and clinician are clarified. The couple are told that treatment consists primarily of the practice exercises implemented by the client and the partner between sessions with the clinician and that treatment is most effective when exercises are performed daily. Any impediments to carrying out these activities are discussed, and ways to address them are developed. The couple are told that they have a key role in the treatment. The clinician's role is explained as advisory. During home visits, the clinician will review the client's progress and discuss any problems related to carrying out the program. In the beginning the clinician will make weekly visits; after a while there will be longer intervals between visits. It is expected that with practice the client will continue to make progress over time. The partner is told to be present at all meetings with the clinician and in some of the practice sessions with the client. The partner is encouraged to be supportive without being indulgent. Special attention is given to which behaviors the partner should support. The partner is urged to provide reinforcement (interest, approval, rewards) for the client's activities and efforts in carrying out the program and not to focus on symptoms of anxiety or panic. In addition, the partner helps choose the targets for practice and helps plan future activities.

In addition, the clinician explains what is meant by graded practice and how practice exercises work to combat avoidance behavior. The clinician can review examples of increasingly more difficult graded assignments described in the manual and explain the advantages of working one step at a time. Such a discussion may elicit questions about anxiety (or panic) that may be aroused in the course of implementing the program. Clients are told that if they stay with the anxiety rather than avoiding it or retreating, the anxiety will decline, particularly if one diverts attention from frightening thoughts. At this point, the following rules for coping with anxiety, which are described in the client's manual, are reviewed:

Ten Rules for Coping with Panic
1. Remember that the feelings are nothing more than an exaggeration of the normal bodily reactions to stress.
2. They are not in the least harmful or dangerous—just unpleasant. Nothing worse will happen.
3. Stop adding to panic with frightening thoughts about what is happening and where it might lead.
4. Note what is really happening in your body right now, not what you fear *might* happen.
5. Wait and give the fear time to pass. Do not fight it or run away from it. Just accept it.
6. Notice that once you stop adding to it with frightening thoughts, the fear starts to fade by itself.
7. Remember that the whole point of practice is to learn how to cope with fear— without avoiding it. So this is an opportunity to make progress.
8. Think about the progress you have made so far, despite all the difficulties. Think how pleased you will be when you succeed this time.
9. When you begin to feel better, look around you and start to plan what to do next.
10. When you are ready to go on, start off in an easy, relaxed way. There is no need for effort or hurry. (Mathews, Gelder, & Johnston, 1981, p. 183)

Clients who are taking medication may have questions related to its use during treatment. They are told that it is hoped that eventually they will not need medication, but if they are taking it, timing intake to prior to starting a new activity can be helpful. In any case, the client should consult with a psychiatrist about medication.

Collection of Behavioral Diary.   The clinician collects and reviews the client's diary. The extent and nature of the client's behavior outside the house are noted. The client is asked to continue to maintain a diary and to record practice activities on an additional form, the target sheet (see Mathews, Gelder, & Johnston, 1981, app. 4). This form contains spaces for targeted behaviors, listed in order of difficulty, and boxes in which the client records completion of the task on a daily and weekly basis.

Selection of Targets to Be Practiced.   The first session includes a discussion of possible activities that can be practiced in the immediate future. The client and the partner are encouraged to offer suggestions and to describe how difficult the tasks seem to be. Through a discussion, the three parties arrive at a list of a few targets that are at a low level of difficulty, achievable, yet of sufficient difficulty to provide a challenge. These should include at least one activity in which both the client and the partner participate. Parameters of the behavior should be specific, for example, walking to the corner of the block with partner. The client agrees to engage in targeted activities daily until the next visit.

Developing a Treatment Contract.   During the first visit, a verbal or written contract is negotiated and decided upon by the participants. Its major components are the roles of all the parties, the timing of meetings with the clinician, the frequency of practice sessions, and the client's responsibility to keep a daily behavioral diary and a record of practice activities in relation to targeted behaviors.

Second Home Visit

The second treatment visit takes place a couple of days after the first. In this session, which lasts approximately three-quarters of an hour, attention is directed primarily at observing the couple as they practice a targeted behavior in which both partners are involved. Before the clinician observes, the parties decide how and what the clinician will observe. The clinician may, for example, accompany the couple as they conduct the activity or observe from a distance. During the practice run, the clinician may model ways to cope with panic, prompt the partner to provide reinforcement, and suggest further ways to practice. Afterward the client, partner, and clinician discuss the experience and how they handled it. The partner is given feedback from the client and the clinician on the appropriateness of his or her responses to the client's anxiety and is reminded to offer the client praise for efforts and accomplishments and to avoid giving attention to the client's expressions of anxiety or self-blame. Discussions with the client center around coping with anxiety. Clients are encouraged to carry around and use the list of rules for coping and to add other coping mechanisms that they find helpful to the list. During this session, the clinician also reviews the diaries and arranges the next appointment.

Remaining Visits

Subsequent visits last about a half-hour each. These meetings begin by jointly setting an agenda for the session. The clinician then reviews the client's diaries and target sheet. If record keeping or practicing is neglected, the reasons are explored and the couple are reminded of their responsibility for implementation of the treatment. This is followed by a group discussion about the client's progress in which the partner is strongly encouraged to participate. In addition, the client is asked to comment on the nature of the support provided by the partner. If support is insufficient, appropriate behavior is modeled. In response to difficulties accomplishing targeted behaviors, new, intermediary behaviors may be targeted for performance prior to the originally targeted behavior. For example, if riding the bus alone to a particular destination is too difficult, the client begins by taking the bus one or two stops, with the partner waiting at the designated stop.

During these visits the client may express frustration about continued experiencing of anxiety. The clinician can respond by saying that the goal is to increase the client's ability to tolerate and control anxiety; that the only way to master it is to experience it in relation to situations that are at graduated levels. Throughout treatment, the clinician praises the client for coping with anxiety.

After the regimen is firmly instituted and problems are resolved, the clinician initiates discussion about long-term targets and plans they might work on in the absence of the clinician. A list of additional, more difficult targets may be added. At this time the group may want to discuss the client's more active participation in the community, such as obtaining a job or taking a class. Additional topics that might be discussed are how to handle setbacks and how to maintain gains. The couple are encouraged to continue practicing, even after termination. They are reminded to use the manual as needed and to solve problems on their own.

Follow-up Visits

Subsequent visits are scheduled at increasingly longer intervals, for example, 2 weeks, 1 month, 3 months, and 6 months after active treatment. These sessions help the client to continue practicing with partner involvement. The format is similar to that described, that is, the couple are encouraged to discuss problems related to practice and to establish additional targets. The clinician provides support for the client's accomplishments and encourages targets that are beyond the client's usual routine, such as vacations. Continued practice is emphasized.

Case Example

Marianna Williams is a 45-year-old married African American woman who sought help at a community mental health center for her "nerves." She described attacks of "nerves" at home and in the car when she felt dizzy, her heart beat rapidly, she was out of breath, and she trembled. She and her husband Damian Williams had been to the emergency room of a nearby hospital where no medical problem was identified. It was the hospital social worker who referred her to the mental health center.

Mrs. Williams described herself as a former receptionist who has been homebound for the past few months. Her husband, a factory worker, works during the day. Although Mrs. Williams can and will drive in an emergency, she relies on her husband to do most of the driving. She cut down on her driving after being hit unexpectedly by another car 3 months ago and traces her anxiety attacks to that experience. She said that she and her husband do the groceries and go to church together. Because she has been having difficulty tolerating large groups of people, she no longer plays Bingo. She has a few friends and family members with whom she talks over the telephone, but she does not visit them as much as she did in the past. At times, however, they visit her. She reported feeling lonely and inadequate.

The clinician (Mr. Stone) told Mrs. Williams that she had agoraphobia with panic attacks and described the main symptoms as avoidance behavior and anxiety attacks. The client was asked if she and her husband would be willing to participate in home-based treatment. The client said that her husband was getting "disgusted" with her, because she does not like getting out and socializing. The clinician explained that the program he had in mind would require active involvement by both of them. Mrs. Williams remarked that her husband was sitting in the waiting room and could be asked himself if he were willing to help. At this point the clinician invited Mr. Williams to join them and explained the program. Mr. Williams said that he would do anything to get her out of the house. The couple were given the manuals and asked to read them prior to the next appointment. Mrs. Williams was asked to complete the Fear Questionnaire and to maintain a behavioral diary.

At the beginning of the first home visit, Mr. Stone explained that they would be discussing any questions they had about the manual, reviewing the procedure, and setting targets. In addition, he wanted to review the behavioral diary. The Williamses had questions concerning Mr. Williams's role in view of his job. Mr. Stone said that there are many activities Mrs. Williams can practice on her own, when her husband is at work, but they can plan others after he returns. It was learned that Mr. Williams worked from 6:00 A.M. to 3:00 P.M. and got home at 3:30 P.M. Usually he liked to take a nap and take a shower after work. The couple agreed that the best time for them to engage in activities together would be 4:30 P.M. With dinner at 5:30, they had a half-hour to practice and a half-hour to prepare dinner. Mrs. Williams had additional questions about medication. She said that she was not on any medication but wondered whether she should see a doctor. It was suggested that she try to do without the medication for a month and then they would reevaluate the need. Mr. Williams had additional questions about his role. It was suggested that he and Mrs. Williams discuss her activities every day, that he praise her for her efforts and accomplishments, and that he try to ignore her anxiety attacks. Mr. Williams said that he could not possibly ignore them because Mrs. Williams complains about them all the time. It was suggested that he not add any comments to her complaints. It was also suggested that when they practice together, he encourage her to tolerate the anxiety.

Mrs. Williams had concerns about facing the anxiety without having a way to escape. She said that when she has driven, she has had the option of parking the car and resting until she felt better. Mr. Stone told her that with this program, they will start in small steps, using her home as a safety valve. She will face anxiety gradually and will learn to cope with it. She was encouraged to tolerate whatever anxiety she felt without running home and was told that her husband and the clinician would support her efforts.

At this point Mr. and Mrs. Williams discussed possible targets. Mrs. Williams mentioned that she would like to go to the grocery store on her own and could walk there, but it was two blocks away. She was afraid that she could not walk two blocks by herself. Mr. Stone suggested the following sequence of activities:

1. Walk one-half block with Mr. Williams
2. Walk one-half block alone, with Mr. Williams watching
3. Walk one-half block alone (without Mr. Williams watching)
4. Walk one block with Mr. Williams
5. Walk one block alone, with Mr. Williams watching
6. Walk one block alone

Mr. Stone emphasized that the work Mr. and Mrs. Williams do, separately and together, was the essence of treatment; that Mr. Stone would be a consultant to them and monitor Mrs. Williams' progress. The clinician gave Mrs. Williams a supply of daily diaries and explained the target sheet.

A contract was then made. It was agreed that the couple would assume responsibility for practicing daily and Mr. Williams would be supportive and participate in exercises where appropriate. They would not seek medication for at least a month. Mr. Stone said that he would make a home visit in a few days and after that would see them weekly at home a half-hour a visit to review their progress. It was estimated that the program could be accomplished in 6 months, but that Mr. Stone would be seeing them less frequently once the couple establishes a regular pattern of practice and the client makes some advances.

Mr. Stone made a home visit 3 days later. This session was spent accompanying the couple on their half-block walk. When they reached their destination, Mrs. Williams had a panic attack and started to retreat. Mr. Williams responded by asking her how she felt and said that she need not worry because they are going back now. Mr. Stone advised Mr. Williams to let her experience the anxiety and stay where she is. Mrs. Williams returned to the half-block point and held her husband's hand. Mr. Stone told her that she did very well walking to this spot and encouraged her to tolerate the feelings without leaving. After a few minutes, Mrs. Williams reported feeling better. Then the three of them walked back to the house where they talked further about the program. Mrs. Williams was encouraged to walk the half-block on her own the next day; still the couple could walk together a half-block in the evening. They agreed to work gradually at this pace so that eventually Mrs. Williams can go to the grocery store by herself. Mrs. Williams was reminded to refer to the 10 rules for coping and to practice using them. Mr. Stone reviewed the diaries and target sheets and arranged an appointment for a week later.

During the next few weeks, Mrs. Williams made successive efforts at walking on her own to the store. Although she did experience panic attacks, she was able to handle them and proceed with her tasks. On a few occasions, she stopped to talk with neighbors on the way. Within a month she was able to walk to the grocery store by herself. Every evening Mr. Williams asked her what she had accomplished and complimented her. The two of them began to enjoy their evening walks together.

With this goal met, it was time to develop a new goal and a strategy to accomplish it. During one of the meetings with Mr. Stone, Mr. Williams said that he would like for them to play Bingo again. Mrs. Williams, however, said she was not ready for that and added that she would like to drive so that she could visit old friends, but did not feel ready for that either. Instead they concluded that visiting a friend who lived one bus stop away was a possibility. They decided that Mr. and Mrs. Williams would ride the bus together once and see how Mrs. Williams reacted. If she did not panic, she would try on her own the next day but have her friend meet her at the bus stop. This goal was accomplished in a week's time.

Treatment continued in this way with the clinician's weekly involvement for 3 months. By the end of that period, Mrs. Williams was using the bus and driving short distances. In the process, Mrs. Williams was becoming less isolated. She renewed contacts with friends and family members she had previously neglected. Her next goal was for Mr. Williams and her to go to the Bingo game at a nearby church. They decided that they would try it out with Mrs. Williams sitting next to the doorway.

Mr. Stone remained in contact with the Williamses for the next few months. When it appeared that they were not practicing regularly or that Mr. Williams was reacting to his wife in a way that reinforced her anxiety, they were reminded about the procedures and advised to review the manual. The last meeting was held in Mr. Stone's office. Mrs. Williams drove.

Evaluation

The home-based method and the preceding case example are illustrative of in vivo exposure. It is one of many programs that are useful in the treatment of agoraphobia. Alternative treatment approaches based on the same principles can be conducted in an office, on an individual basis, or in groups. Regardless of the format, several components appear to be helpful in in vivo exposure:

1. A graduated approach, moving from a situation that is low in perceived anxiety to one high in perceived anxiety
2. Client control of the pace and targets
3. Inclusion of members of the client's interpersonal system
4. Structured approach
5. Goal directed
6. Implementation of tasks in the client's life space
7. Optional use of medication
8. Remaining in the anxiety-provoking situation and learning to cope with the anxiety
9. Becoming educated about the disorder

In vivo exposure does, however, have some limitations. According to Barlow (1988), exposure therapy is effective in the treatment of agoraphobia in 60 to 70 percent of the cases that remain in treatment—statistics that raise questions about dropouts and the failure rate of 30 to 40 percent. It may be that in focusing on problematic behaviors or symptoms, exposure therapy does not attend to the reason for the symptoms and the meaning of the particular symptoms to the individual. In the case of Mrs. Williams, little attention was given to her feelings about or attitude toward leaving her job, the accident, and midlife developmental issues she was experiencing. Alternative approaches take a look at psychological factors associated with the development of anxiety.

ALTERNATIVE AND ADJUNCTIVE TREATMENT APPROACHES

In the treatment of persons with anxiety disorders, historical, situational, and psychosocial dimensions are relevant to the development and maintenance of distressful symptoms. Although behavioral methods effectively treat the symptoms, at times they leave a residue of unresolved problems (Beckfield, 1987; Biran, 1987). Because it is difficult to operationalize the process of uncovering and working through of these problems, little research supporting the effectiveness of psychodynamic approaches exists (Schacht, Henry, & Strupp, 1988). On the other hand, little research shows that psychodynamic methods, such as ego psychology, do not work.

A number of case reports discuss the combined use of insight-oriented psychotherapy and in vivo exposure. Beckfield (1987), for example, described a case of a woman with agoraphobia who was initially treated with in vivo exposure and later for global problems concerning her lack of assertiveness. Only after the disturbing anxiety symptoms dissipated was she ready to look at other issues. Similarly Biran (1987) described a two-stage course of therapy with a woman with agoraphobia. During the first stage, in vivo exposure along with cognitive restructuring was implemented. In the second stage, an exploration of deep cognitions, including a developmental analysis, was pursued and challenged in relation to current issues. Straub (1987) used an eclectic approach that included desensitization, coping skills training, cognitive restructuring, neurolinguistic methods, as well as assertiveness training in the treatment of persons with panic disorder.

Among the many cognitive and behavioral methods that have been used to treat persons with various types of anxiety disorders are response prevention, thought stopping, assertiveness training, cognitive restructuring, modeling, and stress inoculation training. In the remainder of this chapter these diverse strategies will be described and a case example of a client whose treatment integrated cognitive and behavioral methods with ego psychology will be provided.

Response Prevention

This is a method of blocking the performance of rituals by persons with obsessive-compulsive disorder. As it is described by Turner and Beidel (1988), response prevention is a means to prevent reinforcement (and thus continuation) of anxiety reduction through repeated, ritualistic behavior. Accordingly, the client is deterred from carrying out a compulsion. In doing so, professional staff do not use physical force; instead they intervene by distracting, redirecting, or coaxing a client not to perform the ritual. Furthermore, they do not block the client from culturally normative activities, such as showering once a day or washing hands after handling dirt. Turner and Beidel (1988) use a combination of flooding (exposure to the feared stimulus) and response prevention in their treatment program for persons with obsessive-compulsive disorder.

Thought Stopping

This is a means of interrupting the occurrence of intrusive or irrational thoughts. It is used to treat persons with generalized anxiety disorder and obsessive-compulsive disorder. It is implemented as follows. First the client is asked to discuss and give an example of a situation in which the unwanted thoughts are present (Mahoney, 1974). Then the clinician has the client imagine being in that situation again and having these thoughts (Rimm & Masters, 1974). After the client indicates the presence of such thoughts, the clinician shouts, "Stop!" Startled, the client stops focusing on the previous thought. Exposed to this method of conditioning repeatedly, clients learn to recognize and subvocalize "stop" to themselves, thus interrupting their own thoughts. Because this method has weak empirical support (Mahoney, 1974; Turner & Beidel, 1988), it tends to be used as an adjunctive rather than as a principal treatment method.

Assertiveness Training

Some clients with anxiety disorders are unassertive. Their anxiety may be related to a feeling of lack of control in their interpersonal relationships. Training in assertiveness (especially in groups) is one way to help clients regain control and thus inhibit the development of anxiety (Rimm & Masters, 1974). Individuals raised to be submissive and deferential learn to disregard their own needs and rights in favor of others' (Wolpe, 1982). Assertiveness training aims to reverse this process.

In assertiveness training, participants learn to distinguish between unassertive, assertive, and aggressive behavior. Assertiveness is characterized by confident expression of one's wants, needs, and rights without violating those of others. In contrast, aggressive behavior disregards the positions of others. Trainees learn to be more assertive by participating in role plays in which they can rehearse and get reinforcement for performing assertive behaviors.

Cognitive Restructuring

With cognitive restructuring anxiety-producing thoughts are identified, challenged, and replaced with more accurate thoughts. At first the client is helped to recognize irrational "automatic thoughts" that accompany anxiety. This is facilitated by the assignment of homework in which experiences of anxiety are recorded and described (what happened, what the client was thinking, how the client was feeling). During therapy, the clinician challenges the rationality of the client's thoughts. For example, a client who left a party soon after arriving, when she experienced anxiety, noted that she saw someone she had gone out with previously and whom she liked but who never asked her out again. She believed that if they were to have a face-to-face encounter at the party it would be "awful." The clinician had the client explore the many possibilities their encounter might have brought (including his asking her out again) and explained the difference between possible and probable outcomes (cf. Ellis, 1962). This client was encouraged to develop alternative ways of thinking and responding that she might have had to the occasion (e.g., people who date are bound to meet people they have dated in the past; even though she was uncomfortable seeing this man, she could still enjoy the party; one way to reduce her anxiety would have been to talk to him right away "to get it over with"; even if he does not want to talk to her, she is a worthwhile human being who has a right to be at the party and enjoy herself). Cognitive methods of treating anxiety disorders are discussed in depth by Beck, Emery, and Greenberg (1985).

Modeling

Modeling is a treatment method that derives from work of Bandura (see chapter 3). By observing the behavior of models, one can learn effective ways of coping with anxiety-provoking situations. For example, videotapes showing individuals who handle snakes with confidence exemplify coping that persons who fear snakes can imitate. Alternatively, the clinician models the behavior that is desired. Behaviors that are modeled can be presented in a graduated sequence.

Another application of this technique is called *covert modeling* (McKay, Davis, & Fanning, 1981). It requires that clients imagine models, including themselves, performing a behavior that they find anxiety provoking. This method can be combined with role playing of effective behaviors. Covert modeling has been used to treat phobias and to increase assertiveness.

Stress Inoculation Training

Stress inoculation training is a form of cognitive-behavioral therapy that helps clients develop skills in coping with stress (Meichenbaum, 1985). It engages clients as collaborators in the collection of data from their everyday experiences that arouse stress and in the selection of strategies to cope with stress. Clients learn to identify maladaptive thoughts, solve problems, regulate emotional responses, and implement coping skills. Stress inoculation can be used with a wide spectrum of populations in clinical and community settings. It incorporates many of the cognitive and behavioral techniques that were described previously (relaxation training, graded exposure, identifying automatic thoughts, modeling), as well as problem solving. Stress inoculation training can be implemented with individuals, couples, and groups.

Case Example: Integrated Methods

Harold Rogers is a 22-year-old single man who complained of "stress" when he was first seen at an outpatient service of a community hospital. He reported having difficulties sleeping, weight loss, poor appetite, and recurrent episodes of heart palpitations, chest pains, difficulty breathing, and dizziness. These experiences were occurring at least once a week in the past month in a variety of contexts—when he was alone in the car on his way to work, at work, and when he was home alone. With these disturbing symptoms, he wondered whether he was "going crazy." Upon awakening in the morning, he had thoughts of staying home from work, but he went to work anyway.

Mr. Rogers was unable to provide much information about his family background during the first interview because he experienced heart palpitations when he was asked. He did say that during the last year his parents "threw him out of the house" and "forced" him to support himself. They said he was a "bum" who sat around the house during the day, went out at night, and did not work. The client coped by at first moving in with his sister for a couple of months and getting a job and later moving in with his woman friend. He also mentioned that 2 months ago he had a benign tumor removed from his back. Several months ago, he added, two close friends died—one of cancer, the other in a car accident. Mr. Rogers said that when he developed the tumor, he thought that he might have cancer, too. The client said that he thinks about death a great deal and is afraid to be alone.

Mr. Rogers is a high school graduate who was working on a construction crew, building houses. The few "attacks" he has had at work occurred when he was on the roof. He reported feeling dissatisfied that this was a "lowly job" with no future. Some day he would like to have his own business as a photographer. He has thought about looking for another job but has not made any efforts to do so. He said that he has had little contact with his parents since they threw him out; he does see his older brother and sisters and has a number of friends. He reported having a good relationship with the woman he was living with (Margaret Tyler); nevertheless, she does occasionally put pressure on him to make a commitment and he does not want to get married. He also mentioned that Margaret has made his life comfortable: she cooks, cleans, and picks up after him.

Preliminary Assessment.   This 22-year-old employed, single man developed panic attacks during a year of many stressful life events. Not only did he experience a "forced" separation from his parents; he took a job that he perceived as "lowly," he lost two close friends, and he had a medical condition that turned out to be benign. In addition, the woman he is living with, who provides much comfort, wants more of a commitment than he is willing to give. Thrust into a world that is uncertain, demanding, and insecure, he feels anxious. He appears to desire to escape from his current situation (by not going to work or fantasizing about another job) and has anxiety about being alone, but he has not developed an overt phobia. The theme of loss and separation predominates, with unresolved issues surrounding his separation from his parents. He seems to have some dependent traits and does not seem to reciprocate in relationships. His strengths include his working, living independently, ability to maintain relationships, and the willingness to ask for help. His symptoms of anxiety are compounded with mild depression. His *DSM-III-R* diagnosis is as follows:

Axis I:	300.21	Panic disorder without agoraphobia (moderate)
Axis II:	799.90	Diagnosis deferred
Axis III:	Benign tumor removed	
Axis IV:	Psychosocial stressors: forced emancipation, changes in living situation, new job, deaths of two friends, medical problem Severity: 3—Moderate (predominantly acute circumstances)	
Axis V:	Current GAF: 60 Highest GAF in past year: 75	

Treatment Plan.   In order to treat the panic disorder, two strategies will be pursued. For one, the client will be taught deep relaxation exercises in the office and will be assigned homework to practice these daily. Second, the client will be scheduled to see the staff psychiatrist. In view of his panic and concomitant mild depression, the use of a tricyclic will be discussed with the doctor. Although the primary diagnosis is panic disorder without agoraphobia, he is at risk of developing agoraphobia or a simple phobia (fear of heights). To prevent this from occurring, the clinician will advise the client "not to give in to the urge to avoid going out." In addition, activities involving his going out with his woman friend to pursue his hobby (photography) will be assigned.

Development of the Case over Time.   Mr. Rogers was seen weekly for 3 months. Initially treatment centered on his symptoms. During his consultation with the psychiatrist, it was learned that he drank beer occasionally (but not excessively) and was not eager to take medication that precluded these activities. The client, social worker, and psychiatrist agreed that medication was not necessary at this time; that they would pursue other strategies first. The social worker strongly encouraged Mr. Rogers to continue to face his fears by going to work and getting out. He practiced the relaxation exercises at home and at work. As planned, he and Margaret took expeditions in which he took photographs.

Meanwhile, the client became better able to talk about his past and his family situation. He revealed that when he was six, his father died of a heart attack at home. Soon afterward the client refused to go to school. He said that his mother took him to a child guidance center for treatment; eventually he returned to school. Mr. Rogers said that he has always been close to his mother and feels protective of her. Three years ago, however, she married a man who seemed to resent the client, the only child at home. Mr. Rogers expressed anger toward the stepfather, who, he thought, convinced his mother to throw him out of the house. When asked whether he would like to return to them, he said no, he thought it was time that he was on his own. Mr. Rogers said, however, that he did miss his mother. When asked about his not seeing her, he said that he supposed that he was angry at her, too. The client spent a number of sessions expressing feelings toward his father who died when he was six, his stepfather, and his mother. He said that after his father died, he had a fear of losing his mother, even though he realized that she was in good health. As the youngest child, he had his mother's attention much of the time and he enjoyed that. In therapy, his belief that he was "entitled" to being taken care of indefinitely by his mother was challenged as irrational and childish, and cognitions supporting his parents' right to live as they want and his responsibility to support himself were substituted. At this point the client began to become aware of his reluctance to leave the nest and be on his own. This was followed by the expression of feelings of guilt about having been inconsiderate of his mother (as well as awareness that he may be taking advantage of Margaret). When asked what he thought he might do with his feelings, he said that he would like to reestablish a relationship with his mother as an independent adult. A couple of sessions were spent planning how he might initiate contact with her and rehearsing his visit with her. The client saw his mother alone at her home on one occasion, when he apologized for his past behavior and expressed the desire to be part of the family again. She accepted his feelings and invited him to bring Margaret with him to dinner the following week.

As these separation issues were worked through, the symptoms of anxiety and depression waned and the panic attacks disappeared. Still the client expressed dissatisfaction with his job and ambivalence toward Margaret. The client continued to pursue his hobby as a photographer and planned to sell some of his photographs to a publisher. When it was suggested that he and Margaret be seen together, he said that he did not want her to get involved in his personal problems. Termination was precipitated by his taking a job in a photography shop in a distant city. He said that the job paid less than his current job, but it was a "white-collar job."

In this case a combination of methods were used. At first attention was given to the distressful symptoms. Relaxation exercises were implemented in the office and assigned for practice at home. In addition, the client was encouraged to continue to face stressful situations (in vivo exposure) and to go out on photography excursions that were in keeping with his interests. When the client was ready, ego-modifying treatment in which he reflected on patterns that arose in the past was used. It was learned that separation anxiety was a long-standing issue with him; that he had a school phobia following his father's death when he was a child. The client was given the opportunity to express feelings about his loss of his father as a child and his loss of his mother's complete attention when she remarried. He expressed anger at his mother and stepfather; yet he had the desire to reconcile with them. Cognitive therapy was used to help him recognize that his feelings of "entitlement" were irrational and inappropriate for him at this point in his life. The client was encouraged to reconnect with his mother and stepfather and was helped to do so through behavior rehearsal of his first meeting with his mother. Soon afterward, he was able to separate from his woman friend and simultaneously pursue a job that was in tune with his life goals.

SUMMARY

Anxiety is an ordinary human response to perceived danger and to the mysteries of the cosmos. Anxiety disorders represent heightened and frequent experiences of arousal or avoidance that cause subjective pain and discomfort. Such disorders are among the most common psychiatric conditions found in the general population. They are particularly frequent among women and young adults. Disproportionate numbers of African Americans have symptoms of phobia.

The anxiety disorders are heterogeneous. Those that are described in the *DSM-III-R* are panic disorder with agoraphobia, panic disorder without agoraphobia, agoraphobia without history of panic disorder, social phobia, simple phobia, obsessive-compulsive disorder, posttraumatic stress disorder, generalized anxiety disorder, and anxiety disorder not otherwise specified. In addition, there are adjustment disorders characterized by anxiety or mixed emotional features. Like depression, anxiety is described as exogenous or endogenous, depending on whether or not there is a stressor or biological features. Moreover, distinctions are made between anxiety and fear, as well as state and trait.

A number of biological, social, and psychological explanations of anxiety have been put forth. The impact of anxiety on the human organism is evident in its characteristic somatic symptoms. There is some evidence that panic and obsessive-compulsive disorders are genetic. Moreover, many of the anxiety disorders respond to medication. The disproportionate numbers of women and Blacks suffering from anxiety raise questions about the impact of sexism and racism. Psychological theories such as psychoanalysis, attachment theory, and cognitive theory explain intrapsychic, developmental, and thinking patterns that are associated with anxiety disorders. According to behavior theory, anxiety is a learned response.

One avenue of treatment of anxiety disorders is pharmacological. Surprisingly, a number of drugs that treat depression (tricyclic antidepressants and MAOIs) also are effective in the treatment of agoraphobia and panic. One tricyclic, clomipramine, seems to be helpful in the treatment of obsessive-compulsive disorders. These medications have the advantage that they are not habit forming, but they do have side effects. The benzodiazepines act more quickly than the antidepressants; nevertheless withdrawal after prolonged use is accompanied by withdrawal symptoms. One benzodiazepine, alprazolam (Xanax), appears to be effective in the treatment of panic and phobic anxiety. Other drugs used to treat anxiety are buspirone and propranolol. Research on the relative effectiveness of medication and psychotherapy is equivocal.

Behavioral treatments of anxiety disorders have a strong record of effectiveness, particularly in the treatment of phobias. One of the first that was developed is systematic desensitization. Other treatments include flooding and implosive therapy. A finding that is consistent with all these methods is that exposure, particularly in vivo exposure, is the key factor that affects treatment. In addition, family involvement is helpful. A model program of home-based programmed practice of in vivo exposure (Mathews, Gelder, & Johnson, 1981) was described and illustrated with a case example.

However effective behavioral therapy may be, it does not work in all cases. Even where it works, residual problems remain. Many clinicians have found that when they combine and integrate a few methods, they get positive results. Additional methods that can be used include response prevention and thought stopping (used to treat persons with obsessive-compulsive disorder), assertiveness training, cognitive restructuring, modeling, and stress inoculation training. A case example illustrated how ego psychology can be used together with exposure and cognitive restructuring.

CASE STUDY

Cynthia Brown is a tall 30-year-old married woman who reported that she weighed 150 pounds. She has an attractive face and dresses in such a way that she looks lighter than her stated weight. She said that her problems are of her own making: because she is ashamed of being overweight, she isolates herself. She stays home most of the time and avoids opportunities to go out. She has difficulty getting herself mobilized to go to the grocery store, usually waiting until they are out of food and she must go. The client expressed concern that she will be seen at the grocery store. Whenever her husband suggests that they go out together or with another couple, she finds a reason for them not to go out.

Mrs. Brown said that even though it looks as if she "prefers" to be at home, she does not do much when she is home. She feels as if she spends all her time serving others—even the dog—but is not doing anything for herself. She and her husband Jason have a 3-year-old daughter Amy; her husband has a son, 12, from a previous marriage, who lives with them. Mrs. Brown believes that her husband gives more attention to his son than to their daughter. To compensate, she devotes herself to Amy. Even though Mrs. Brown has allowed Amy to go to a nearby nursery school, she worries about her the whole time Amy is in school. She is afraid that "something will happen to Amy."

Mrs. Brown said that she and Jason met at the time Jason was separated from his first wife. At that time Cynthia was thin and worked as a model. Jason told her that his first wife had a weight problem; that her weight contributed to their divorce. Mrs. Brown has some concern that her husband will reject her. She said that she knows her refusal to go out has been getting on his nerves, too. She mentioned that when they first met, her husband used to worry that other men will want her. Now she worries that her husband will be attracted to other women.

The social worker remarked that Mrs. Brown has described a number of problems—fears about leaving the house, worries about her daughter, a weight problem, and marital difficulties—and asked her what she wanted to work on. The client said that if she could get over her anxiety about leaving the house, she thinks that the other problems will resolve themselves.

Discussion Questions

1. What kind of anxiety disorder does Mrs. Brown seem to have?
2. What kinds of intervention would you use? Whom would you involve in her treatment?
3. Identify Mrs. Brown's irrational ideas. How would you help her change these?
4. Do you think medication is appropriate for this client? Why or why not?
5. How are women's issues involved in this case?

REFERENCES

American Psychiatric Association. (1987). *Diagnostic and statistical manual of mental disorders (DSM-III-R).* (3rd ed., rev.). Washington, DC: Author.

Ballenger, J. C., Burrows, G. D., DuPont, R. L., Lesser, I. M., et al. (1988). Alprazolam in panic disorder and agoraphobia: Results from a multicenter trial. I. Efficacy in short-term treatment. *Archives of General Psychiatry, 45,* 413–422.

Barlow, D. H. (1988). *Anxiety and its disorders.* New York: Guilford Press.

Beck, A. (1985). Cognitive therapy. In H. I. Kaplan & B. J. Sadock (Eds.), *Comprehensive textbook of psychiatry/IV* (pp. 1432–1438). Baltimore, MD: Williams & Wilkins.

Beck, A. T., & Emery, G., with Greenberg, R. L. (1985). *Anxiety disorders and phobias: A cognitive perspective.* New York: Basic Books.

Beckfield, D. F. (1987). Importance of altering global response style in the treatment of agoraphobia. *Psychotherapy, 24,* 752–758.

Biran, M. W. (1987). Two-stage therapy for agoraphobia. *American Journal of Psychotherapy, 41,* 127–136.

Brenner, C. (1955). *An elementary textbook of psychoanalysis.* New York: Doubleday Anchor.

Carey, G., & Gottesman, I. I. (1981). Twin and family studies of anxiety, phobic and obsessive disorders. In D. F. Klein & J. G. Rabkin (Eds.), *Anxiety: New research and changing concepts* (pp. 117–136). New York: Raven Press.

Eagle, M., & Wolitzky, D. L. (1988). Psychodynamics. In C. G. Last & M. Hersen (Eds.), *Handbook of anxiety disorders* (pp. 250–277). New York: Pergamon.

Eison, M. S., & Temple, D. L. (1986). Buspirone: Review of its pharmacology and current perspectives on its mechanism of action. *The American Journal of Medicine, 80* (suppl 3B), 1–9.

Ellis, A. (1962). *Reason and emotion in psychotherapy.* New York: Lyle Stuart.

Fyer, A. J., Mannuzza, S., Gallops, M. S., Martin, L. Y., et al. (1990). Familial transmission of simple phobias and fears. *Archives of General Psychiatry, 47,* 252–256.

Gordon, B. (1979). *I'm dancing as fast as I can.* New York: Harper & Row.

Hollander, E., Liebowitz, M. R., & Gorman, J. M. (1988). Anxiety disorders. In J. A. Talbott, R. E. Hales, & S. Yudofsky (Eds.), *Textbook of psychiatry* (pp. 391–443). Washington, DC: American Psychiatric Press.

Horowitz, M. J. (1989). Posttraumatic stress disorder. In American Psychiatric Association, *Treatments of psychiatric disorders: A task force report of the American Psychiatric Association* (Vol. 3, pp. 2065–2082). Washington, DC: American Psychiatric Association.

Insel, T. R., & Zohar, J. (1987). Psychopharmacologic approaches to obsessive-compulsive disorder. In H. Y. Meltzer (Ed.), *Psychopharmacology: The third generation* (pp. 1205–1210). New York: Raven Press.

Jacobson, E. (1938). *Progressive relaxation.* Chicago, IL: University of Chicago Press.

Johnston, D. G., Troyer, I. E., & Whitsett, S. F. (1988). Clomipramine treatment of agoraphobic women. *Archives of General Psychiatry, 45,* 453–459.

Kaplan, M. (1983). A woman's view of DSM-III. *American Psychologist, 38,* 786–792.

Klein, D. F., & Gorman, J. M. (1987). A model of panic and agoraphobic development. *Acta Psychiatrie Scandinavia, 76* (suppl. 335), 87–95.

Klein, D. F., Zitrin, C. M., Woerner, M. G., & Ross, D. C. (1983). Treatment of phobias. II. Behavior therapy and psychotherapy: Are there any specific ingredients? *Archives of General Psychiatry, 40,* 139–145.

Klerman, G. L. (1988). Overview of the cross-national collaborative panic study. *Archives of General Psychiatry, 45,* 407–412.

Lelliott, P., Marks, I., McNamee, G., & Tobeña, A. (1989). Onset of panic disorder with agoraphobia: An integrated model. *Archives of General Psychiatry, 46,* 1000–1004.

Lesser, I. M., Rubin, R. T., Pecknold, J. C., Rifkin, A., et al. (1988). Secondary depression in panic disorder and agoraphobia. I. Frequency, severity, and response to treatment. *Archives of General Psychiatry, 45,* 437–450.

Liebowitz, M. R. (1989). Antidepressants in panic disorders. *British Journal of Psychiatry, 155* (suppl. 6), 46–52.

Mahoney, M. J. (1974). *Cognition and behavior modification.* Cambridge, MA: Ballinger.

Markowitz, J. S., Weissman, M. M., Ouellette, R., Lish, J. D., & Klerman, G. L. (1989). Quality of life in panic disorder. *Archives of General Psychiatry, 46,* 984–992.

Mathews, A. M., Gelder, M. G., & Johnston, D. W. (1981). *Agoraphobia: Nature and treatment.* New York: Guilford Press.

Mavissakalian, M., & Michelson, L. (1986). Agoraphobia: Relative and combined effectiveness of therapist-assisted in vivo exposure and imipramine. *Journal of Clinical Psychiatry, 143,* 1106–1112.

Mavissakalian, M. R., & Perel, J. M. (1989). Imipramine dose–response relationship in panic disorder with agoraphobia. *Archives of General Psychiatry, 46,* 127–131.

McKay, M., Davis, M., & Fanning, P. (1981). *Thoughts and feelings: The art of cognitive stress intervention.* Richmond, CA: New Harbinger.

Meichenbaum, D. (1985). *Stress inoculation training.* New York: Pergamon.

Noyes, R., Chaudry, D. R., & Domingo, D. V. (1986). Pharmacologic treatment of phobic disorders. *The Journal of Clinical Psychiatry, 47,* 445–451.

Noyes, R., DuPont, R. L., Pecknold, J. C., Rifkin, A., et al. (1988). Alprazolam in panic disorder: Results from a multicenter trial. II. Patient acceptance, side effects, and safety. *Archives of General Psychiatry, 45,* 423–428.

O'Brien, G. T., & Barlow, D. H. (1984). Agoraphobia. In S. M. Turner (Ed.), *Behavioral theories and treatment of anxiety* (pp. 143–185). New York: Plenum Press.

Pecknold, J. C., Swinson, R. P., Kuch, K., & Lewis, C. P. (1988). Alprazolam in panic disorder: Results from a multicenter trial. III. Discontinuation effects. *Archives of General Psychiatry, 45,* 429–436.

Regier, D. A., Boyd, J. H., Burke, J. D., Rae, D. S., et al. (1988). One-month prevalence of mental disorders in the United States. *Archives of General Psychiatry, 45,* 977–986.

Rickels, K., & Schweizer, E. E. (1987). Current pharmacotherapy of anxiety and panic. In H. Y. Meltzer (Ed.), *Psychopharmacology: The third generation of progress* (pp. 1193–1203). New York: Raven Press.

Rickels, K., Schweizer, E., Csanalosi, I., Case, G., & Chung, H. (1988). Long-term treatment of anxiety and risk of withdrawal: Prospective comparison of clorazepate and buspirone. *Archives of General Psychiatry, 45,* 444–436.

Rimm, D. C., & Masters, J. C. (1974). *Behavior therapy: Techniques and empirical findings.* New York: Academic Press.

Robins, L. N., Helzer, J. E., Weissman, M. M., Orvaschel, H., et al. (1984). Lifetime prevalence of specific psychiatric disorders in three sites. *Archives of General Psychiatry, 41,* 949–958.

Salzman, C. (1989). Treatment with antianxiety agents. In American Psychiatric Association, *Treatments of psychiatric disorders: A task force report of the American Psychiatric Association* (Vol. 3, pp. 2036–2052). Washington, DC: American Psychiatric Association.

Schacht, T. E., Henry, W. P., & Strupp, H. H. (1988). Psychotherapy. In C. G. Last & M. Hersen (Eds.), *Handbook of anxiety disorders* (pp. 317–337). New York: Pergamon.

Sheehan, D. V., & Soto, S. (1987). Diagnosis and treatment of pathological anxiety. *Stress Medicine, 3,* 21–32.

Spielberger, C. D. (1983). *Manual for the state–trait anxiety inventory (STAI form Y).* Palo Alto, CA: Consulting Psychologists Press.

Stern, R., & Marks, I. (1973). Brief and prolonged flooding: A comparison in agoraphobic patients. *Archives of General Psychiatry, 28,* 270–276.

Straub, J. H. (1987). An eclectic counseling approach to the treatment of panics. *Journal of Integrative and Eclectic Psychotherapy, 6,* 434–449.

Torgersen, S. (1983). Genetic factors in anxiety disorders. *Archives of General Psychiatry, 40,* 1085–1089.

Turner, S. M., & Beidel, D. C. (1988). *Treating obsessive-compulsive disorder.* New York: Pergamon.

Weakes, C. (1968). *Hope and help for your nerves.* New York: Hawthorne.

Weakes, C. (1972). *Peace from nervous suffering*. New York: Hawthorne.

Weissman, M. M., Klerman, G. L., Markowitz, J. S., & Ouellette, R. (1989). Suicidal ideation and suicide attempts in panic disorder and attacks. *The New England Journal of Medicine, 18*(321), 1209–1214.

Wolpe, J. (1958). *Psychotherapy by reciprocal inhibition*. Stanford, CA: Stanford University Press.

Wolpe, J. (1982). *The practice of behavior therapy*. (3rd ed.). New York: Pergamon.

Zitrin, C. M., Klein, D. F., Woerner, M. G., & Ross, D. C. (1983). Treatment of phobias. I. Comparison of imipramine hydrochloride and placebo. *Archives of General Psychiatry, 40,* 125–138.

Zohar, J., Foa, E. B., & Insel, T. R. (1989). Behavior therapy and pharmacotherapy. In American Psychiatric Association, *Treatments of psychiatric disorders: A task force report of the American Psychiatric Association* (Vol. 3, pp. 2095–2111). Washington, DC: American Psychiatric Association.

Epilogue

This volume was written with the recognition that clinical social work practice in community mental health is guided by a complex body of knowledge. Multiple biopsychosocial bodies of knowledge, such as genetics, psychopharmacology, epidemiology, and law, and diverse psychosocial theories and methods of intervention, have been incorporated into the book. It is hoped that with this information, social workers will be better prepared for clinical practice in community mental health.

In the course of presenting knowledge about social work practice in community mental health, little attention has been given to the feelings of clinical social workers as they interact with consumers, colleagues of other disciplines, and community service providers. Social workers are expected to address the pressing needs of clients and meet the bureaucratic requirements of the agencies in which they work, regardless of their own feelings. These demands exist regardless of whether or not the agency is supportive of staff and regardless of whether community resources that meet client needs exist. Frequently professionals are left on their own to deal with troubling countertransferences, alienating work environments, and inadequate community services. Not surprisingly, some experience burnout.

BURNOUT

Like other human service workers, clinical social workers employed in community mental health settings are vulnerable to burnout. As described by Maslach (1976) and Freudenberger (1974), burnout is a state of exhaustion and incapacitation, resulting from work-related stress. When the demands of working closely with others become too great, previously idealistic, enthusiastic workers lose the fire that attracted them to the field and begin to function like automatons. In a study of mental health workers employed in hospitals and community residences, Pines and Maslach (1978) found that the longer the staff had been employed in the field of mental health, the larger the staff–client ratio, and the higher the percentage of persons with schizophrenia among clients, the less the staff liked interacting with clients. Instead, mental health workers became distant and cold and treated clients perfunctorily. The burnt out worker feels fatigued, enervated, and unable to cope. Not surprisingly, substance abuse, insomnia, marital conflict, and headaches become prominent (Maslach, 1982).

The risk of burnout is high in occupations in which work is accomplished through close interpersonal relationships. Unlike workers who are exposed to a physical environmental hazard, community mental health workers cannot find protection by wearing goggles or hardhats. Clients are ubiquitous; they are the subjects of clinical work. But just as social workers help clients cope with stress, they need to find ways to manage stress in their own lives. Clinical social workers need to develop ways to protect themselves without becoming cold, distant, and impersonal.

Like clients, clinical social workers need social supports. These may come from their own personal network or from the workplace. Personal relationships provide workers with understanding, nurturance, affection, and space in which to be themselves. Coworkers, who have direct knowledge of the demands of the work environment, can help each other by listening to each other's experiences working with clients and by offering positive reinforcement and suggestions about ways to handle difficult cases.

Burnout can be prevented in community mental health agencies by promoting an organizational culture in which the provision of mutual support is normative. Schein (1990) defines culture as "what a group learns over a period of time as that group solves its problems of survival in an external environment and its problems of internal integration" (p. 111). Such organizational cultures are dynamic, interactive, and adaptive. In order to respond to needs emanating from within and outside, organizational cultures need to develop means to maintain the adaptive functioning of key members, the clinicians. As Pines and Maslach (1978) stated, "One of our strongest recommendations is for institutions to try to create support systems and improve the social milieu by improving work relationships between staff members" (p. 237). Some means through which this can be accomplished on the organizational level are to use interdisciplinary teams, provide opportunities for training, and modify work assignments. Individuals may elect or be advised to have their own psychotherapy. These approaches will be discussed below.

Interdisciplinary Teams

As described in this text, interdisciplinary teams are representing diverse professions or disciplines which come together to accomplish goals. In community mental health agencies, they ordinarily consist minimally of social workers, nurses, psychiatrists, and psychologists, but may also include recreation therapists, occupational therapists, housing specialists, pharmacologists, and others. The roles of team members are largely (but not completely) determined by the professional affiliations of participants. Each brings to case discussions and decision-making information and perspectives and strategies that are specific to his or her own professional field. As team members interact with each other, however, some are able to transcend their individual disciplines in their mutual concern about clients. In the process, they listen, provide information, give advice, and offer support to each other.

Membership in a team has the potential of providing many of the benefits of other groups with which one affiliates—a sense of belonging, friendship, appreciation, and support. In being a part of a group, one can enhance one's strength as an individual and work toward collective goals. Within an organization, the group can work toward organizational change, which can empower team members. These benefits can offset the frustrations that may accompany the job.

Working in interdisciplinary teams can be particularly advantageous to social workers. Because teams provide a forum in which clients can be viewed holistically, the expertise of social workers is particularly relevant. Information on a client's situation in relation to the client system is essential to a thorough assessment and case planning—which are frequently within the province of the team. Furthermore, the commitment of social workers to client advocacy can be realized in the context of the interdisciplinary team (Mailick & Ashley, 1981). Clinical social workers can persuade and gather support from their interdisciplinary colleagues in the pursuit of a particular plan of action that will benefit clients. In making a contribution to discussions and decision making on interdisciplinary teams, social workers are able to demonstrate what they know and thus enhance their own self-esteem and visibility. In addition, interdisciplinary teams assume corporate responsibility for cases, thus easing the burden on individual members (Abramson, 1984; Kane, 1983).

A further benefit of interdisciplinary teams is the intellectual stimulation they provide. Teams that use a problem-solving model, for example, articulate key issues and their ramifications, and generate alternative strategies of resolving difficulties. In the course of participating in teams, members learn how to think about a case from a variety of perspectives and to use creative solutions. As teams discuss cases, knowledge about various psychiatric syndromes and their treatment is often introduced. Thus, teamwork is an educational experience.

Opportunities for Continuing Education

The knowledge building that is a by-product of working on teams can be enhanced further when agencies offer staff opportunities for in-service and out-service training. Educational programs within an agency give clinical staff an opportunity to convene in an atmosphere that is centered on their need to develop their knowledge and skills. In-service training programs on contemporary topics such as "working with the psychotic client," "AIDS dementia," and "meeting the emergency needs of the homeless mentally ill" can be offered. In providing continuing education on the job, agencies promote the professional development of staff.

In addition, staff can benefit from training in stress management. Staff may need to learn how to relax, manage their time, identify stressors, and cope with stress. Burnout workshops aimed at helping employees to become supportive of each other and to communicate more effectively can also be implemented (Pines & Aronson, 1988).

Another mechanism for promoting staff development is to send clinicians to workshops and conferences that are offered in the community or in other cities. Not only do these programs give staff an opportunity to gain additional knowledge; they also provide an atmosphere in which staff can network with other professionals and learn about other programs. Out-of-town conferences provide a further benefit of giving staff a respite from clinical work. "Time out" from their usual routine makes it possible for them to feel refreshed when they return (Freudenberger, 1974; Pines & Aronson, 1988).

Modification of Work Assignments

Continuing education is one of many ways of diversifying the activities of clinicians. Varying work activities prevents work from becoming routine and tedious. Moreover, it makes it possible for staff to work with different colleagues and clients in different ways. Including activities other than face-to-face interaction with clients removes workers from the primary source of burnout. Institutional means of detachment through work assignments can make it unnecessary for clinicians to withdraw from clients.

A related mechanism is to reduce caseloads or staff–client ratio. Research on burnout in a variety of settings has shown that when the staff–client ratios were small, staff were more effective in their work with clients (Pines & Aronson, 1988). When clinical staff were responsible for fewer clients, they could give full attention to their cases. Although high caseloads may appear to be cost-effective, when one considers the burnout factor they are not (Pines & Aronson, 1988).

Psychotherapy

Although burnout is often viewed as an organizational problem, its impact on the individual is enormous. The symptoms of burnout resemble those presented by clients at mental health agencies on an ordinary day—anxiety, depression, depersonalization, somatic complaints, substance abuse. These symptoms intrude upon one's relationships with one's spouse, partner, or family; friends; coworkers; and clients. Providers of mental health services are responsible for their own mental health, as well as that of others. Accordingly, some clinicians arrange to have psychotherapy for themselves.

Psychotherapy offers benefits beyond stress management. It can help clinicians understand themselves better, recognize countertransferences with clients, correct distorted perceptions, and change maladaptive behaviors. Through therapy clinicians can recognize their strengths and areas that need further development. Psychotherapy can help clinicians become more assertive and communicate better with others. When one reveals one's vulnerabilities to another clinician, one learns experientially what it is like to be a client and how one can use help.

The strategies that have been discussed—interdisciplinary teams, opportunities for staff development, modification of workload, and psychotherapy—are organizational and individual means to prevent the development of burnout. They are some of many ways to mitigate an occupational hazard of working closely with persons who are experiencing mental health difficulties. In the next section, an issue that cannot be resolved so readily will be discussed—limitations of knowledge.

LIMITATIONS OF KNOWLEDGE

This book has attempted to provide the clinical social worker with up-to-date knowledge of the field of community mental health and strategies for intervention that are supported by research. In the pursuit of effectiveness as a clinical social worker in community mental health, however, one faces the limits of one's own and others' knowledge about mental disorders and their treatment. Neither this nor any book can fully account for cases such as the following:

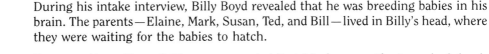

During his intake interview, Billy Boyd revealed that he was breeding babies in his brain. The parents—Elaine, Mark, Susan, Ted, and Bill—lived in Billy's head, where they were waiting for the babies to hatch.

For some time, Maxwell Thomas suspected that his former wife, June, had developed another relationship. He tried to stop her by sending her flowers and asking her to take him back. One evening Maxwell saw her return home with the new man in her life. That night Maxwell set June's house on fire.

After living in a state hospital for 50 years, Lilly Field was sent to a family care home, where she sat idly in a fetal position whenever she was not scheduled in a social program in the community. The family care giver considered her a cooperative, although seclusive, client. When Lilly died, $20,000 was found sewn in her clothes.

Cases such as these point to the limitations of human knowledge. Even if one attaches diagnoses to the behavior of these clients, one does not know how and why these individuals came to be and act the way they did. However impressive biological tests and treatments may be, they do not explain the dynamics of individual cases; however effective some psychosocial methods of therapy are, they do not work for everyone. At some point, clinicians come to ponder the mystery of life and the wonder of human variability

Clinical social workers who practice in community mental health agencies face the limitations of human knowledge as they struggle, within the confines of what is known, to help others improve their social functioning and well-being. At the same time, social work practitioners face their personal limitations as they strive to become more effective clinicians. As this book goes to press, knowledge continues to evolve; there is still much that is unknown.

REFERENCES

Abramson, M. (1984). Collective responsibility in interdisciplinary collaboration: An ethical perspective for social workers. *Social Work in Health Care, 10,* 35–43.

Freudenberger, H. J. (1974). Staff burn-out. *Journal of Social Issues, 30,* 159–165.

Kane, R. A. (1983). *Interprofessional teamwork.* (Manpower Monograph No. 8). Syracuse,

NY: Syracuse University School of Social Work.

Mailick, M. D., & Ashley, A. A. (1981). Politics of interprofessional collaboration: Challenge to advocacy. *Social Casework, 62,* 131–137.

Maslach, C. (1976). Burned-out. *Human Behavior, 5,* 16–22.

Maslach, C. (1982). *Burnout: The cost of caring.* Englewood Cliffs, NJ: Prentice-Hall.

Pines, A., & Aronson, E. (1988). *Career burnout: Causes and cures.* New York: Free Press.

Pines, A., & Maslach, C. (1978). Characteristics of staff burnout in mental health settings. *Hospital & Community Psychiatry, 29,* 233–237.

Schein, E. H. (1990). Organizational culture. *American Psychologist, 45,* 109–119.

Index

About the Author

Roberta G. Sands is a professor at the University of Pennsylvania School of Social Work, Philadelphia, where she teaches social work practice and individual and social processes. She joined the Pennsylvania faculty in 1990, after spending nine years teaching at The Ohio State University College of Social Work in Columbus, Ohio. In the course of her career, Dr. Sands has worked as a clinical social worker in community mental health programs in the South, the Midwest, and the East. She has published numerous articles in professional journals on topics related to social work practice and has conducted research on interprofessional teams, women's issues, and deinstitutionalization.